KEEPING
FAITH

KEEPING FAITH

MEMOIRS OF A PRESIDENT

JIMMY CARTER

BANTAM BOOKS
TORONTO • NEW YORK • LONDON • SYDNEY

KEEPING FAITH

A Bantam Book

PRINTING HISTORY

Bantam Hardcover edition / November 1982
Five printings through October 1983
Selected by the Book-of-the-Month Club
Excerpted in Time Magazine
Bantam Trade edition / November 1983

Library of Congress Catalog Card No.: 82-90323
ISBN 0-553-34017-4

Published simultaneously in the United States and Canada

Bantam Books are published by Bantam Books, Inc. Its trademark, consisting of
the words "Bantam Books" and the portrayal of a rooster, is Registered in the
United States Patent and Trademark Office and in other countries. Marca Registrada.
Bantam Books, Inc., 666 Fifth Avenue, New York 10103.

PRINTED IN THE UNITED STATES OF AMERICA

FG   0 9 8 7 6 5 4 3 2 1

For Jason, James, and Sarah

Contents

Chronology

1974

DEC.   12   Jimmy Carter announces candidacy for President.

1976

JULY   14   Nominated by Democratic party.

NOV.   2   Wins election.

1977

JAN.   20   Inaugurated as 39th President of the United States.

FEB.   2   Signs Emergency Natural-Gas Act.
                 First fireside chat.

MARCH   30   SALT II proposals rejected by Soviet Union.

APRIL   4   First meeting with Sadat in Washington.
              6   Signs Reorganization Act.
              18   Address to the Nation on Energy.

MAY   7–8   London Economic Summit.
              22   Foreign Affairs Address at Notre Dame.

JUNE   30   JC announces B-1 bomber production will be halted.

JULY   19   First meeting with Begin in Washington.

AUG.   4   Department of Energy established.

SEPT.   7   Panama Canal treaties signing ceremony.
              21   Bert Lance resigns.
              27   JC reaches agreement with Gromyko on framework for SALT II.

OCT.   5   Signs International Covenants on Human Rights.
              21   Sends letter to Sadat asking support for Middle East peace effort.

NOV.   15   Shah of Iran visits White House.
        19–21   Sadat visits Israel.

| DEC. | 29– | JC travels to Poland, Iran, India, Saudi Arabia, |
| | JAN. 6 | France, Belgium, and Egypt. |

1978

MARCH	16	Senate ratifies first Panama Treaty.
APRIL	7	JC defers production of enhanced radiation weapons.
	18	Senate ratifies second Panama Treaty.
JUNE	7	Foreign Policy Address at U.S. Naval Academy.
	16	JC visits Panama.
JULY	16	Bonn Economic Summit.
SEPT.	4	Camp David summit on Middle East peace begins.
	17	Camp David accords signed.
OCT.	13	JC signs Civil Service Reform Act.
	15	Congress passes energy package.
DEC.	15	JC announces normalization of relations between the United States and the People's Republic of China.

1979

JAN.	4–9	Meets in Guadeloupe with leaders of France, Great Britain, and Germany.
	16	Shah leaves Iran.
	29–31	First visit of Deng Xiaoping to Washington.
FEB.	1	Khomeini returns to Iran.
	20	Foreign Affairs Address at Georgia Tech.
MARCH	8–14	Peace mission to Egypt and Israel.
	26	Egyptian–Israeli Peace Treaty signing ceremony.
	28	Accident at Three Mile Island nuclear power plant.
APRIL	5	Address to the Nation on energy.
JUNE	12	JC proposes national health plan to Congress.
	18	Signs SALT II Treaty with Brezhnev at Vienna Summit.
	28–29	Tokyo Economic Summit.
JULY	3–12	Energy speech canceled; meetings at Camp David on the state of the administration.
	15	Address to the Nation on energy and national goals.
	17–20	Announcement of Cabinet and senior staff changes.
	26	JC signs Trade Agreements Act.
AUG.	15	Andrew Young resigns.
	31	Soviet combat troops reported in Cuba.

OCT.	17	Department of Education established.
	20	Decision to admit Shah to United States for medical treatment.
NOV.	4	U.S. Embassy in Iran overrun.
	14	Iranian property frozen by executive order.
DEC.	4	JC announces candidacy for reelection.
	12	NATO agrees to deploy theater nuclear weapons.
	27	Soviets invade Afghanistan.

1980

JAN.	4	Address to the Nation on Soviet invasion, announcing sanctions.
	21	1980 election year begins with caucuses in Iowa.
	23	State of the Union Message, including "Carter Doctrine."
FEB.	20	JC urges U.S. withdrawal from 1980 Summer Olympic Games in Moscow.
	23	UN commission arrives in Iran.
MARCH	11	UN commission leaves Iran.
	14	JC announces anti-inflation program, including a balanced budget for 1981.
APRIL	1	Bani-Sadr announces that control over American hostages will be transferred to Iranian government (not carried out).
	2	JC approves windfall-profits tax on oil.
	7	U.S. breaks diplomatic relations with Iran.
	11	Decision to proceed with hostage rescue mission.
	21	Cyrus Vance submits resignation.
	24	Hostage rescue attempt.
MAY	9	Memorial Service at Arlington.
	19	Eruption of Mount St. Helens.
JUNE	5–6	Congress overrides presidential veto, killing oil import fee.
	22–23	Venice Economic Summit.
	30	JC signs Energy Security Act.
JULY	16	Republicans nominate Ronald Reagan.
	22	JC issues statement on Billy Carter's relations with Libya.
AUG.	4	News conference on Billy Carter.
	13	Democratic Convention nominates Jimmy Carter for second term.
SEPT.	1	Campaign kick-off in Tuscumbia, Alabama.
	22	Iraq invades Iran.

OCT.	28	Carter–Reagan debate.
NOV.	4	Election.
DEC.	2	JC signs Alaska lands legislation.
	7	Warns Soviets against military intervention in Poland.
	11	Approves Superfund to control toxic wastes.

1981

JAN.	16	JC negotiates final terms for release of American hostages.
	20	Hostages released.
		JC leaves Washington.
	21	Meets hostages in Wiesbaden, Germany.

A First Word

I mmediately after returning home from the White House on January 20, 1981, I unpacked eighteen large black volumes of diary notes which I had accumulated during my four years as President. Generally, several times a day during my term, I had picked up a miniature tape recorder and dictated my impressions of the people I met and the interesting or disconcerting events that filled my life. No one but the secretary who transcribed it had access to my diary while I was in office. These highly personal papers—some 5000 pages of them—have been the primary source for this book, augmented by my own memory and the official records of my administration.

In Plains, I began to read through the diary for the first time, marking for use in this book those passages which seemed to describe most accurately my reaction to the challenges I faced, the conflicting advice I received, and the people who were involved with me in my private life and in the making of history. The quotations from my diary are as I recorded them at the time. Where my dictation was so rushed that the result was not English, I have added a word or two to make it clear.

This book is my own work, typed by me at home on my trusty word processor. There were times when I had other responsibilities or when I yielded to the temptations of my nearby woodworking shop or a convenient fishing place, but I have spent most days and nights of the past year on this project. It has been much more difficult than I had originally anticipated—both the actual research and writing and the necessity for me to reassess my own actions as President in the light of subsequent events. Although my overriding impression of the four years is one of gratitude and pleasure, a few of the memories were downright painful for me.

This is not a history of my administration but a highly personal report of my own experiences. Others who are better qualified and more objective will write comprehensive studies of my Presidency, using the private and public records that will be made available to them as soon as possible. I have emphasized those matters which meant the most to me, and particularly those events in which I played a unique part, such as the search for peace in the Middle East and the Camp David negotiations.

I have had to leave a lot unsaid. In fact, what concerns me most are the omissions—stories about many others whose contributions have not been described as deserved, who helped to shape my thoughts and actions, who deserve more credit for the successes we enjoyed, and who took too much blame for the failures and mistakes.

Nessa Rapoport, my editor, has not only made certain that I wrote this manuscript in English, but has, through her constant probing questions, forced me to face facts and to describe in adequate detail even those experiences which I would rather not have remembered so clearly. My research assistant, Steve Hochman, has joined in the editorial work, and has done his best to assure the accuracy of my words, checking documents, records, and the memory of others who were involved in the same events. Several other people have read the manuscript and have given me good advice and criticism, much of which I have used. Any remaining defects in the book are my own, and may even be helpful to the reader in giving a more accurate picture of the kind of person I am.

PLAINS, GEORGIA
JUNE 1, 1982

KEEPING
FAITH

FREEDOM

TUESDAY,
JANUARY 20, 1981

I had not been to bed since early Sunday morning, and I was discouraged and almost exhausted. Many agonizing hours without sleep had effectively removed any bright visions of the future or vivid memories of the past. I could think only of the current challenge.

It was my last day in office, and in many ways these were the most dramatic moments of my Presidency. I was now involved in a task which demanded the utmost in personal leadership and at the same time required that I exert all the influence and strength I could muster from one of the most powerful offices in the world. America's diplomatic, military, and economic forces were marshaled, ready to respond to my command. It was a challenging and, at times, tormenting experience. I needed to be constantly alert, but there were periods when I realized I was not at my best.

I was searching for new ideas, trying to understand more clearly one of the most intricate financial and political problems ever faced by any nation. At stake were the lives of 52 precious human beings who had been imprisoned in Iran for 444 days—and almost 12 billion dollars of Iranian assets.

Sometimes I was alone in the Oval Office, but most often former Chief of Staff Hamilton Jordan and Press Secretary Jody Powell were with me. Others came in and out to deliver reports or seek instruction. My wife, Rosalynn, stayed whenever she could, repeatedly urging me to get some rest. I spent most of the time at my desk, but lay down on one of the small couches before the fireplace, often with the telephones on the floor beside me, when the action was slow. I was talking to a number of people at different places in the world, and I took meticulous notes so that I would not become confused or forget what they said. No matter who was with me, we watched the big grandfather clock by the door. Time was an ever-present concern. I knew that in large measure the reputation and influence of our country were hanging in the balance—and I cannot deny that I was eager to resolve this crisis while I was still President in order to justify the decisions I had

3

made during the preceding months. I had a major responsibility to my country—and not much time left to carry it out. At noon, I would no longer be President of the United States of America.

The holding of the American hostages had cast a pall over my own life and over the American people since November 4, 1979. Although I was acting in an official capacity as President, I also had deep private feelings that were almost overwhelming. The hostages sometimes seemed like part of my own family. I knew them by name, was familiar with their careers, had read their personal letters written from within their prisons in Iran. I knew and had grown to love some of the members of their families, and had visited with them in Washington and even in their hometowns around the country. More than anything else, I wanted those American prisoners to be free.

Four days earlier my final effort for their freedom had begun, keeping us occupied throughout the weekend. On Friday, January 16, 1981, we had worked out with Iran the general terms for the release of the hostages. Since then, we had been afflicted by constant delays. Throughout this entire grim experience, it had been almost impossible to negotiate with the suspicious and irrational men who refused to communicate directly with me or any other American. We all knew quite well that the Iranians with whom we were working were under heavy attack from other, more militant officials, who vehemently opposed any plans to release the hostages.

An Algerian team, under the direction of Foreign Minister Mohammad Benyahia, were acting as intermediaries. The Iranians, who spoke Persian, would talk only with the Algerians, who spoke French. Any question or proposal of mine had to be translated twice as it went from Washington to Algiers to Tehran, and then the answers and counterproposals had to come back to me over the same slow route.

As the financial and political arrangements were highly technical, they had to be translated meticulously and in proper legal form. Ten days after the hostages were imprisoned, I had stretched my legal authority to the limit and impounded all Iranian assets held by Americans, including billions of dollars in gold and bank deposits. Provided, of course, that all the hostages were returned unharmed to freedom, I had always been willing to release the assets. Now, about two-thirds of the total amount would be transferred out of American control—those funds held by the Federal Reserve Banks and by the overseas branches of twelve American banks. (The remaining third, deposited in domestic commercial banks, would be unfrozen but subject to claims on both sides through international arbitration.) During the last fourteen months, our financial institutions had managed these huge sums as best they could under the unique circumstances, and now the twelve major banks had become an integral part of the negotiating process. They had to be certain that the transfer of these enormous sums was carried out legally and properly to avoid making costly mistakes or exposing themselves to future courtroom battles. Nor did I want to make a mistake. I had studied these financial arrangements myself for many hours.

Not only in Algiers and Tehran, but also in London, Istanbul, Paris, Bonn, and other world political and financial capitals, related negotiations had been under way for several weeks. Now we were approaching the culmination of our work. Sunday, on my last visit to Camp David, I had signed the fifteen documents necessary to initiate the financial transactions. Under the agreement we had worked out through the Algerians, enough Iranian funds would be held in escrow to pay any legitimate American claims. The Bank of England had been chosen to hold the escrow account in the name of the Algerian Central Bank. The balance would be returned to Iran. The Iranian gold we had seized had been transferred to the Bank of England on Friday, so that there would be no unnecessary delays when the final hours came. I had also directed that over the weekend we conduct a dry run in transferring the Iranian money from the Federal Reserve Banks and the private banks into the London bank. It was an intricate procedure, but the practice transfer had been completed without mishap. Secretary of the Treasury G. William Miller reported to me that this was the first time in history the Bank of England had ever been open on a weekend.

From time to time I would report to President-elect Ronald Reagan and the hostage families about our progress. Also, on occasion, I talked to British Prime Minister Margaret Thatcher, to work out details for the transfer of funds, and to German Chancellor Helmut Schmidt, to conclude arrangements for receiving the liberated Americans in his country. I had already decided that their immediate destination would be a United States military hospital in Wiesbaden, West Germany, where complete medical care would be available and where they could have a few days of rest before resuming their normal lives as free men and women.

I returned to Washington from Camp David, and on Sunday afternoon, January 18, with my key staff members, I began to coordinate our nation's efforts from the Oval Office. I stayed there nearly all the time; whenever possible Vice President Fritz Mondale,

In the Oval Office, early Tuesday morning:
(l-r) Jordan, the President, Cutler, Mondale

Presidential Counsel Lloyd Cutler, and Bill Miller joined me.
Sometimes they would have to go to their own offices, to the
State Department, or across the street to the Treasury building to
work out a particularly complicated issue with the lawyers and
accountants of one or all of the twelve banks. Most of the time
they spoke in hushed tones, as though they were in a church or
funeral parlor. At other times we all exploded into laughter at
some biting comment about the aggravating delays. The lawyers
and treasury officials seemed awestruck by the sheer size of the
sums being handled—certainly one of the largest financial transactions in history.

Ten of the banks had been cooperating, but at times during the
last few days, I had been angered because the Bank of America and
one smaller bank seemed to be trying to compensate for unwise
investment policies by claiming income from the Iranian deposits
which they had not earned. Now the twelve were in agreement,
but we had to be careful not to make a mistake that might tear
apart our fragile arrangement.

All the necessary forces of our government were focused on our common task. The communication networks of various agencies were alerted and available to me and to others on our team around the world. Secretary Ed Muskie was at his desk in the State Department, maintaining contact with Algiers, where Deputy Secretary Warren Christopher was conducting the fitful discussions with Iran through Algerian Foreign Minister Benyahia. Secretary of Defense Harold Brown was on duty in the Pentagon, monitoring security matters and arranging for services that would be needed in the Persian Gulf region and at other points along the route to freedom, which we all prayed would soon be taken by the hostages. Hundreds of other officials in our own and other governments were waiting for the final move of the cumbersome negotiating mechanism we had built. It crept slowly, haltingly, sometimes in reverse—and its progress, or lack of it, was nerve-racking.

There had already been an almost unbelievable series of crises—successive moments of exhilaration and despair. They had begun more than fourteen months ago but were now culminating in what might be our last chance for success. There could not be a drama more gripping, or a plot more involved and complicated. But until now, it had been a story without happiness or pleasure.

The moments of consternation continued to the end. At one time on Sunday, after we thought all other arrangements had been made, we were checking to be doubly sure that we were ready to transmit Iranian money from our government depository to the Bank of England. Lloyd Cutler approached me and whispered that there was no way to transfer the Iranian money—the Federal Reserve Bank of New York had no funds available! Fortunately, a shift of funds among the banks of the Federal Reserve System corrected the problem before it became generally known. We had narrowly avoided a most embarrassing oversight.

We were constantly computing the time in Tehran. Because of the war with Iraq, it was the policy of the Iranian officials to black out all lights at their airports. The Algerians had informed us that their planes carrying the liberated hostages would not take off in the dark, so that each day there had been a new deadline for the hostages' departure—when dusk came at the Tehran airport, about 9:30 A.M. Washington time. Early Monday morning, I had finally received word through Algiers that medical examinations of the hostages had been completed and all the hostages were fine; then, that the necessary airplanes were ready for their flight, and that the Americans had been moved out to the vicinity of the airport. We eventually obtained tentative agreement from the reluctant Algerians that, if absolutely necessary, their pilots would be willing to leave Iran after dark. When that message came, I felt that I could relax for a few minutes.

At my desk in a small private room near the Oval Office, I sat alone in the dark, trying to rest but troubled by an uneasy feeling that would not go away. Our signed agreements with Iran prescribed a rigid procedure for handling the funds, after which our hostages would be released. Everything seemed to be going well—except for that lingering concern in the back of my mind. I turned on the light and carefully went down my handwritten list of sequential events which would have to take place. Finally, I realized that the Bank Markazi, the central bank of Iran, had not sent in the technical instructions required for the transfer of deposits. I called Christopher, Miller, Cutler, Powell, and Muskie in that order to tell them to check. I was right—it was indeed a problem. Benyahia sent a strong message to Iran and discovered that the Iranian bank officials did not agree with the terms that had been negotiated, and were refusing to cooperate.

Everything else seemed ready; but as the hours passed, the Markazi officials would not issue the necessary papers. I began to criticize the Iranian bank executives, only to discover that they were justified in not agreeing to the terms. Many of the financial records of the Iranians had been lost or were out of date because of the revolution and our seizure of their assets, and under the current proposals, the Iranians would not have been permitted to question the deposit and interest figures in the future, even if an honest mistake were discovered.

The planes were returned to standby condition. The Americans, presumably, were back in their prison. Again I began to fear that the hostages would not be freed. The chance of their release on Monday had now passed; we would have only one more chance before my team and I left office.

That afternoon, as I bade good-bye to my Cabinet, Secretary Muskie brought me more bad news. Christopher, normally an optimist, was quite discouraged because the Algerians appeared to have lost their momentum and their commitment to the negotiating process. Their sense of urgency seemed to have vanished. We decided that Christopher should inform Benyahia that our authority would expire at noon the next day, and should order his plane to stand by for his departure from Algiers at that time. We hoped this order would impress one key fact on the Algerians and the Iranians. There *was* a deadline: noon, Tuesday, January 20.

After that, neither Christopher nor I could speak for the United States, and the entire negotiating process might have to begin anew.

We worked desperately to resolve the problem with the Bank Markazi, with some indications of success. We decided to amend the existing agreement by deleting the objectionable language and to permit the deposit records to be verified later, when they could be checked by the Iranian bankers. Drafting this change consumed several precious hours. It was shortly before midnight on Monday when the telex message from the Iranian bank began coming through—a test message, which would have to be perfected to constitute the final and official instructions to banks so that funds could be moved. I had been assured by Treasury Department officials that this kind of message would be sent almost instantaneously, using the most modern electronic technology for speed and accuracy.

Instead, the message was garbled and confused; it came through a few letters at a time. We made wry jokes about revolutionary-guard typists. The sloppy Iranians were extremely aggravating, and my friend Charles Kirbo commented, "Now I can understand why so many Iranians got shot."

There was little we could do. The American banks simply could not afford to act without legally accurate instructions. Time was running out. I received a series of reports throughout these last few hours early in the morning of Inauguration Day, and I jotted down some rough notes as they came in:

1:50 A.M., from Treasury: "The machine is burping!" The Bank Markazi was to send specific instructions to each of the twelve banks authorizing the transfer of exact amounts of principal and interest, amounting to a total of $5,500,000,000. Lawyers and officials of all twelve, the Federal Reserve System, and the U.S. Treasury Department were assembled in London, Washington, and Algiers, huddled over the teletype machines to check the accuracy of the instructions. (However, it seems the Iranian operator was only playing with the telex machine or checking out the line.)

2:23 A.M., from Bill Miller at Treasury: "The message is moving. It looks good." (In fact, the first key test number was garbled, but Bill didn't have the heart to tell me.)

2:30 A.M., from Christopher in Algiers: "We see it. Everyone is checking it. There is a problem."

2:40 A.M., from Miller: "The message is continuing but garbled. If the test number at the end is accurate, we will buy it."

2:45 A.M., from Christopher: "I am ready to go to Benyahia, but a serious difference has now developed among Americans concerning the escrow language—between Treasury and the Federal Reserve." (This involved the Iranian money that was to be held in reserve to settle legal claims.)

The Fed lawyers state that they cannot sign the necessary documents. (Treasury Department officials reported to me that the agreement was adequate. Representatives of the Federal Reserve System, an independent establishment of our government, were not convinced.)

I issue an order: "Treasury represents my position. Notify the Fed officials to comply. Let's move!"

3:05 A.M., from Miller: "The test number at the end is correct, but now we will have to correct all the errors."

I decide: "Tell the banks to move using the garbled text. They can assume that the earlier draft version from the Bank of England is correct."

3:16 A.M., from Miller: "The money is moving to London." (Cheers)

I instruct Miller: "Order all American officials to conform to my position regarding the escrow language and move accordingly."

3:40 A.M., from Robert Carswell, Deputy Secretary of the Treasury: "The U. S. Federal Reserve attorneys in Algiers still refuse to sign the agreement. Tony Solomon is the only one who can change their position."

The lawyers are claiming that without the deleted language they cannot approve the settlement terms. I call Anthony Solomon, President of the Federal Reserve Bank of New York, and ask him to instruct his attorneys to sign the agreement. He is at home. We connect him through State Department radio–telephone circuits to his lawyers in Algiers.

4:20 A.M. I listen to an unbelievable argument between New York and Algiers, with one of the irate Federal Reserve attorneys in Algeria finally saying that he is fainting and cannot discuss the subject any further! The other Fed lawyers in Algiers now claim they have never seen a copy of the agreements with Iran. Again, I tell Solomon: "Have them sign the agreement."

Solomon: "Mr. President, there are problems, but we can sign with some very minor amendments." The amendments are drafted for approval by the Algerians.

4:35 A.M., from Miller: "The money [from the private banks] is in. Will now transfer to the Fed account in London. We're checking on whether the Algerians and the Bank of England are signing the escrow agreement."

A total of $7.977 billion of Iranian money would have to be in the Bank of England and ready to be transferred from our account there to the Algerian account, the last step before the hostages can be released. I tell Bill to be sure the Bank of England is ready with its certification of deposit, so we will have no further delay after the funds are in London.

4:38 A.M., from Christopher: "There is still a problem, and it is serious. Algiers will not accept *any* amendments proposed by the lawyers for the Federal Reserve unless they are first approved specifically by Iran."

I tell Cutler: "Get Solomon, Christopher, and the lawyers on the same line. I will use all the authority I have to get this resolved. We can use the escrow agreement, the written understandings, and today's telex messages combined to cover any possible procedural problem. We can work out the remaining questions later."

We have the conference call, and I eventually convince the Fed officials and attorneys that the total package is adequate.

5:00 A.M. Finally, Solomon tells his attorneys, "Sign it!" I breathe a sigh of relief.

5:10 A.M., from Miller: "The money is now moving to the Fed account in London. The Bank of England will have to check the deposit. It will take about fifteen minutes."

5:20 A.M., from Miller: "It only took two seconds to transfer the money to London. Now all we need are three things: the signed escrow agreement, the certification of deposit from our account to the Algerian account, and for Algiers to notify Washington and Tehran that all agreements have been fulfilled."

6:05 A.M. The Operations Center reports a message from Tehran control tower: "Line up Flight 133."

From Christopher: "All parties are now signing the escrow agreement. Iran has been informed. Benyahia states that the hostages will be moved out within an hour after notice from Algeria."

6:35 A.M., from Christopher: "All escrows were signed at 6:18 EST. The Bank of England has certified that they hold $7.977 billion, the correct amount. Now the Bank must send this certification to Algiers by telex or by telephone."

6:47 A.M., from Miller: "All the money is in the escrow account. The Bank of England will now certify this fact to Algiers."

I place a call to Governor Reagan to give him the good news, and am informed that he prefers not to be disturbed, but that he may call back later. I respond that I will call him when the hostages are released.

7:15 A.M., from Christopher: "Amounts are being checked off as received. The message to Iran will be sent within fifteen minutes after the Bank of England completes its certification that the money is all there."

I reply: "Cy Vance's plane will be ready to depart Andrews Air Force Base when the hostages are airborne." I had asked Cy to meet the hostages in Germany, to welcome them on behalf of our country. He had already waited a long time at the airfield near Washington.

7:30 A.M. I tell Miller to push the Bank of England. Its delay is inexcusable. The officials there just seem to be enjoying the limelight. "The Bank of England would have been faster if they had hired the Iranian telex operator!" I exclaim.

7:35 A.M. Rosalynn comes in with my razor, followed by a barber. She says, "Jimmy, you have forgotten to shave and you need a haircut." I go into the bathroom for a quick shave, and then the barber cuts my hair while I talk on the telephone.

7:55 A.M., from our Operations Center in Washington: "The planes are getting ready to take off."

I am personally receiving reports on radio traffic almost halfway around the world—between the Tehran airport control tower and the three planes poised at the end of a runway. The airport is on the outskirts of the capital city of Iran, and only a few months ago it was one of the busiest in the world. Now it is not much used, additional evidence to us that the extremists who control this once powerful nation seem determined to commit political and economic suicide.

The long-awaited message has come to me from the Operations Center through satellite and other relay stations. I shout, "Flight 133 is ready for takeoff!" The Oval Office is filled with cheers. Now we need only the final word from Algiers to Tehran.

All of us in the Oval Office knew that Flight 133 consisted of three airplanes. Two were 727's, commercial passenger planes—one to bring out the American hostages, and the other to serve as a backup or possible decoy. The third was a smaller corporate jet that would carry home the Algerian medical team which had examined the captive Americans.

8:18 A.M., from Christopher: "The Bank certification was completed at 8:04. Algeria confirmed this at 8:06. They are now notifying Iran."

Our agreement with Algeria and Iran provides that when the

Algerian Central Bank certifies that not less than $7.955 billion has been placed in the Algerian escrow account, "Iran shall immediately bring about the safe departure of the 52 U.S. nationals detained in Iran."

I tell Operations Center: "I want a report on takeoff and also when our people have cleared Iranian airspace."

8:28 A.M., from Operations Center: "The planes are now standing at the end of the runway. One Iranian F-4 [fighter plane] is active. May be escort."

I then get a series of reports about escort planes orbiting the airport and a jeep checking the runway. I confirm the serial numbers of the two 727's to be sure they are the right ones.

(Having dealt with the Iranian officials for many months, we were not surprised when they delayed the takeoff, for no apparent rational purpose. I stayed by the telephones.)

9:45 A.M., from Christopher: "Takeoff is not imminent, but I can state for certain that it will be before noon. Iran asks Algeria not to announce departure until after the planes clear Iranian airspace."

I answer, "We will try to comply."

10:45 A.M., from Rosalynn: "Jimmy, the Reagans will be here in fifteen minutes. You will have to put on your morning clothes and greet them."

I left the Oval Office reluctantly, after making arrangements to be kept informed about every development, and walked rapidly over to my private quarters in the White House. As I put on my rented formal suit, I was able to transfer my thoughts for the first time to the Washington ceremonies now about to begin. They seemed like a dream; reality was in the Oval Office, Algiers, and Iran. I combed my hair in the President's bathroom, a convenient cubicle with rows of electrical outlets installed when Lyndon Johnson once found electrical devices plugged into all the existing ones. As I looked at myself in the mirror, I wondered if I had aged so much as President or whether I was just exhausted. As I rode to the Capitol and sat through the inaugural ceremonies, the hostages were always on my mind. I still had no assurance that all my recent efforts would be successful, and no way to know that this would soon become one of my happiest days—even happier than that day exactly four years earlier when President Gerald Ford had greeted me on the way to my own inauguration.

Less than two hours later, I was notified through the Secret Service radios that at 12:33 P.M. the first aircraft had been allowed to take off; nine minutes later the other plane had followed. I was no longer President of the United States. The American hostages were free.

It is impossible for me to put into words how much the hostages had come to mean to me, or how moved I was that morning to know they were coming home. At the same time, I was leaving the home I'd known for four years, too soon for all I had hoped to accomplish.

I was overwhelmed with happiness—but because of the hostages' freedom, not mine.

A GRADUATE
COURSE
IN AMERICA

A WALK TO THE
WHITE HOUSE

*People along the parade route, when they saw that we
were walking, began to cheer and to weep, and it was an
emotional experience for us as well.*

DIARY, JANUARY 20, 1977

The inaugural parade route stretched before us with tens of thousands of people lining the streets. I leaned forward and told the Secret Service driver to stop the automobile, then touched Rosalynn's hand and said, "Let's go!" The security men looked all around, saw only friendly faces, and opened the doors of the long black limousine. As we stepped into the street, the people seemed anxious and concerned about us. They obviously thought something was wrong with the car. Then our three sons and their wives joined us as we began to walk down the center of the broad avenue.

It seemed that a shock wave went through the crowd. There were gasps of astonishment and cries of "They're walking! They're walking!" The excitement flooded over us; we responded to the people with broad smiles and proud steps. It was bitterly cold, but we felt warm inside. Even our nine-year-old daughter Amy got the spirit, walking in front of our family group and carefully placing her small feet on the white centerline. We were surprised at the depth of feeling from our friends along the way. Some of them wept openly, and when I saw this, a few tears of joy ran down my cold cheeks. It was one of those few perfect moments in life when everything seems absolutely right.

Many people have asked why we chose to walk. A few weeks before the inauguration, Senator William Proxmire had suggested in a letter that it would set a good example for the nation's physical fitness program if a new President would walk the entire 1.2 miles from the U. S. Capitol to the White House. The idea seemed rather silly, and I discarded it immediately. Later, however, I began to realize that the symbolism of our leaving the armored car would be much more far-reaching than simply to promote exercise. I remembered the angry demonstrators who had habitually confronted recent Presidents and Vice Presidents, furious over the Vietnam war and later the revelations of Watergate. I wanted to provide a vivid demonstration of my confidence in the people as far as security was concerned, and I felt a simple walk would be a tangible indication of some reduction in the imperial status of the President and his family.

I had told few people about my decision. The leader of my Secret Service detail had been somewhat startled by the idea, but then concluded there would be no objections, provided we could keep the plan secret. I agreed with our security men that any publicity in advance could precipitate an incident or threat which might make such a walk impossible. Besides, I wanted it to be a dramatic moment.

Now I strolled hand in hand with Rosalynn, our family around us. She and I had discussed the idea of walking to the White House, just as she had worked with me on the themes of my inaugural speech. We had been married for thirty-one years and were full partners in every sense of the word. We never had any other real sweethearts when we were young, and have shared almost every experience of our adult lives. Together we raised a family of four children, organized and operated a business, and campaigned for state senator and governor. And we had planned and consummated a successful campaign for the highest office in our land. We communicated easily, and often we had the same thoughts without speaking. We had been ridiculed at times for allowing our love to be apparent to others. It was not an affectation, but was as natural as breathing.

No one could ever know how difficult our task had been or how many obstacles we had had to overcome to reach this moment. My entire family had worked together as a team, often at great sacrifice, although to my advantage. I was proud of them as we walked: our oldest son, Jack, 29, with his wife, Judy, who lived in Georgia with our grandson, Jason; Chip, 27, and Caron, obviously pregnant with their first child; Jeffrey, 24, and Annette; and our youngest, Amy. Others were with us in spirit: my mother, Lillian, whose delightful personality as a speaker and on television had done as much as anything to gain me recognition; Rosalynn's mother, Allie Smith; and thousands of volunteers who had worked on our behalf.

After completing our walk and reviewing the parade from a

pavilion in front of the White House, Rosalynn and I entered the mansion grounds, alone together for the first time since we had begun our official day. As we quietly approached our new home, I told Rosalynn with a smile that it was a nice-looking place. She said, "I believe we're going to be happy in the White House." We were silent for a moment, and then I replied, "I just hope that we never disappoint the people who made it possible for us to live here." Rosalynn's prediction proved to be correct, and I did my utmost for four solid years to make my own hope come true.

Shortly after noon, a few minutes before our walk began, I had tried to express in my inaugural address as simply and clearly as possible my ambitions for America. Over a period of several weeks I had done a great deal of work on these few words, and in the process had read the inaugural addresses of the Presidents who served before me. I was touched most of all by Woodrow Wilson's. Like him, I felt I was taking office at a time when Americans desired a return to first principles by their government. His call for national repentance also seemed appropriate, although I feared that a modern audience might not understand a similar call from me.

With Rosalynn I had discussed which of two Bible verses to cite. I had known them both since childhood, and they were an integral part of our religious beliefs. At first, I intended to use II Chronicles 7:14 ("If my people, which are called by my name, shall humble themselves, and pray, and seek my face, and turn from their wicked ways; then will I hear from heaven, and will forgive their sin, and will heal their land"), but after some second thoughts about how those who did not share my beliefs might misunderstand and react to the words "wicked" and "sin," I chose Micah 6:8.

I kept my address very brief—one of the briefest of all. Its sentiments were compatible with my announcement as a candidate in December 1974 and with my acceptance speech at the Democratic Convention. It foreshadowed the thrust of my administration, and even the farewell address to the nation which I was to give almost four years later.

I stood on the bunting-draped, ornate temporary platform at the east front of the Capitol, strangely calm as I looked out on the beautiful scene. I could pick out only a few personal friends among the upturned faces, but at that time I felt that all of them were my friends; I knew they did not want me to fail. I was eager to tell them what was in my heart, although I realized it was a time more of pageantry than sober thought for most of them. It was just the opposite for me.

I had been cautioned to speak slowly and distinctly in order to minimize the distortion of the amplifiers and loudspeakers in the tremendous outdoor arena. (Later, when I watched a television replay, I thought my words had come too slowly.) I had labored over my talk and, at least to me, it was important.

> I have just taken the oath of office on the Bible my mother gave me just a few years ago, opened to a timeless admonition from the ancient prophet Micah:
> "He hath showed thee, O man, what is good; and what doth the Lord require of thee, but to do justly, and to love mercy, and to walk humbly with thy God."

These words did not seem overly critical of our nation, but still held the reminder of the need to seek God's help and guidance as we sought to improve our commitment to justice and mercy. After Watergate, we would need a sense of remembered history, deriving our strength from our nation's diversity, its resilience, and its moral values.

> The American dream endures. We must once again have faith in our country—and in one another.... Let our recent mistakes bring a resurgent commitment to the basic principles of our nation, for we know that if we despise our own government we have no future.

I then focused on those concerns that embodied my most important values—human rights, environmental quality, nuclear arms control, and the search for justice and peace. Standing before the people that day, I could not know the complexity of these issues and how they would affect my administration and my political future.

> Our commitment to human rights must be absolute, our laws fair, our national beauty preserved; the powerful must not persecute the weak, and human dignity must be enhanced.
> ... We pledge perseverance and wisdom in our efforts to limit the world's armaments to those necessary for each nation's own domestic safety. We will move this year a step toward our ultimate goal—the elimination of all nuclear weapons from this earth.
> We urge all other people to join us, for success can mean life instead of death.

I spoke of a strong defense for a different kind of battle.

Our nation can be strong abroad only if it is strong at home,
and we know that the best way to enhance freedom in other
lands is to demonstrate here that our democratic system is
worthy of emulation. . . .
  The passion for freedom is on the rise . . . we will maintain
strength so sufficient that it need not be proven in combat—a
quiet strength based not merely on the size of an arsenal but on
the nobility of ideas . . . we will fight our wars against poverty,
ignorance, and injustice, for those are the enemies against which
our forces can be honorably marshaled.
  We are a proudly idealistic nation, but let no one confuse our
idealism with weakness.

I then broached a concept that was to prove painfully prescient
and politically unpopular: limits. We simply could not afford
everything people might want. Americans were not accustomed
to limits—on natural resources or on the power of our country to
influence others or to control international events.

We have learned that "more" is not necessarily "better," that
even our great nation has its recognized limits, and that we can
neither answer all questions nor solve all problems . . . we
must simply do our best.

Watching the sea of approving faces, I wondered how few of the
happy celebrants would agree with my words if they analyzed
them closely. At the time, it was not possible even for me to
imagine the limits we would have to face. In some ways, dealing
with limits would become the subliminal theme of the next four
years and affect the outcome of the 1980 election. My primary
thought on Inauguration Day was about the potential shortage of
energy supplies and the need for our people to stop looking to the
federal government as a bottomless cornucopia. I had pledged
during my campaign to emphasize fiscal responsibility and strive
for a balanced budget. This had not been a popular stand with
some members of my party, but it was compatible with the
beliefs of Southern Democrats and of Democratic Presidents I
admired, like Jefferson, Madison, Jackson, and Wilson.
  After reflecting on the past, I looked to the future and said
aloud what I had already been praying silently.

. . . when my time as your President has ended . . . I would hope that the nations of the world might say that we had built a lasting peace, based not on weapons of war but on international policies which reflect our own most precious values.

⟶

Even though I had been preparing to be President, I was genuinely surprised when in the benediction, the Bishop from Minnesota referred to "blessings on President Carter." Just the phrase, "President Carter," was startling to me.   DIARY, JANUARY 20, 1977

In the panhandle of Florida during the primary election campaign, I'd had my first real understanding of how much it would mean to Southerners to have one of their own elected President. Governor George Wallace had told Floridians that a vote for him would "send a message to Washington." A vote for me, I told them, would send a President there. At that time, Southerners had some messages to send to the world, and I listened to them. The most important was that we in the South were ready for reconciliation, to be accepted as equals, to rejoin the mainstream of American political life. This yearning for what might be called political redemption was a significant factor in my successful campaign.

Brandt Ayers, an Alabama newspaper editor, expressed this feeling eloquently in a piece called "The South and the Nation are Joined," published at the time of my inauguration. He wrote that Southerners had long felt themselves scorned by other Americans. "In the 1950's and 1960's during the Civil Rights Movement . . . the courage of Southern blacks made Southern whites struggle with their consciences." But the manner in which we saw ourselves portrayed on our television screens month after month, as if prejudice were unique to our region, had been extremely troubling. Ayers added, "Most Southern whites, who never committed nor considered committing any atrocities, who were trying to adjust to the new ways, got pretty fed up with the adjectives applied to them in their own living rooms."

The possibility that the nation would actually choose as a leader someone from the Deep South meant that the bitterness of the past could be overcome. As I traveled through the countryside of dogwood and magnolias, I had discovered people with hope for a full political future, and they had discovered I was one of them.

Before we arrived in Washington, some of the society-page

writers were deploring the prospective dearth of social grace in the White House and predicting four years of nothing but hillbilly music, and ignorant Bible-toting Southerners trying to reimpose Prohibition in the capital city. The local cartoonists had a field day characterizing us as barefoot country hicks with straw sticking out of our ears, clad in overalls, and unfamiliar with the proper use of indoor plumbing. I recall a full page cartoon depicting an outhouse on the White House lawn, with my mother wearing a sunbonnet and smoking a corncob pipe.

These humorous thrusts were not a complete surprise; I knew that Lyndon Johnson went to his grave convinced that he was a victim of regional prejudice. Although many Southerners were angry at the regional ridicule, our family was too exuberant to have our spirits dampened. We were able to laugh at these articles and political cartoons. I suppose that anyone moving into the White House feels a little bit "country," but we had undergone a much greater transition moving from our home in Plains to the governor's mansion in Atlanta. Interestingly, we were to find that the White House was the more relaxing place to live, with more privacy and seclusion from the large numbers of tourists and other visitors who come to see both residences. As we walked through the living quarters on my first day as President, we were properly awestruck—but comfortable, and at home.

> *I would say that they were quite similar to the quality of the quarters that we enjoyed as the governor's family in Georgia, but I have been constantly impressed—I almost said overwhelmed—at the historical nature of the White House.... And when I see a desk or a writing cabinet or a book or a sideboard or a bed that was used by Thomas Jefferson or Abraham Lincoln, ... I have a feeling of almost unreality about my being President, but also a feeling of both adequacy and determination that I might live up to the historical standards established by my predecessors.* DIARY, JANUARY 20, 1977

On that first day, I tarried in the living quarters only a few minutes, eager to get to the Oval Office. Where I would work was much more interesting to me than where we would be sleeping.

When the elevator reached the ground floor, the security men were waiting. Not certain how to find my office, I said as casually as possible, "I'm just going to the Oval Office" and followed the lead agent. We walked along the ground-floor corridor, left the mansion proper, proceeded west about forty-five paces under the south arcade, turned left, and arrived at the entrance. As soon as I entered, the security agents closed the doors and I was alone.

Only once before had I visited the Oval Office, quite briefly—about a month after the election, when Rosalynn and I came to pay a courtesy call on President and Mrs. Ford. The room was mine now, and for the first minute or two I savored my solitude. The circumstances were so different that it was difficult for me to recall how the office had looked before. The yellow oval carpet was new; I remembered that President Ford had told me one had been on order for several months. I felt a slight—very slight—sense of commiseration on realizing that he had expected to use it himself. In my uncertainty I hesitated a few seconds, wondering if it was all right for me to disturb anything. Then I boldly pulled aside the window drapes and examined the beautiful south grounds in the late afternoon sunlight.

I sat down at the President's desk and looked it over. It was a surprise to see that it was not the same one which had been photographed when John Kennedy was there, with his little son peeping out from the door underneath. My first decision: to replace this desk with the one I remembered.

As I shuffled through a few desk-top papers, I noticed that there were some scheduled appointments. The earliest one was with Max Cleland, whom I had selected to be the first Vietnam war veteran to head the Veterans Administration. Calling in my staff, I set to work.

⌣

We had the first of a very relaxed and informal series of meals with our family. Earlier, when Rosalynn was visiting the White House, some of our staff asked the chef and cooks if they thought that they could prepare the kind of meals which we enjoyed in the South, and the cook said, "Yes, Ma'am, we've been fixing that kind of food for the servants for a long time!"   DIARY, JANUARY 20, 1977

After supper we attended eleven inaugural parties, held in seven locations around the downtown area of Washington—thirty-five thousand guests in all. As many as possible of the numerous other events had been open to the public. There were free tickets to concerts, museums, tours, exhibitions, and receptions. We wanted "populist" inauguration festivities, to mirror the style of our campaign and our new administration. The diversity of entertainment was meant to reflect the heterogeneous nature of our society. Our hope was that all our friends—rich or poor—would feel wanted and at home.

A few of the society editors did not understand this goal. They chose to emphasize Rosalynn's decision to do without a new evening gown. This was a symbolic and sentimental decision of ours; her dress was the one she had worn for the governor's inaugural ball. She could not have looked more beautiful as we moved from one party to another, but later there were remarks that we did not understand the necessity for a First Lady to wear expensive designer clothes and to wear them only once in public.

We moved quickly, greeting the crowd and dancing a few steps at each place for our own enjoyment and that of the many partygoers. Amy went with us, but after some appearances which seemed very exciting to her, she would sit on the orchestra stage while we spoke to our friends and danced, looking very sleepy. Finally we said, "Amy, you can go back home." There was some momentary confusion until everyone realized that "home" now meant "White House."

Without much discussion, Rosalynn and I decided not to make major changes in the White House staffing or to remodel the mansion extensively. We liked it the way it was and valued the historic nature of the comfortable furnishings. If after living in our new home for a while we found some alterations necessary, we could make them then.

I did change a few customs. When we moved in, we discovered that the doors and stairwells connecting the first, second, and third floors were locked permanently, and that we could move vertically only by elevator. Because our family wanted more exercise and more freedom of movement, we unlocked all the doors. We opened up the living quarters between floors and to the outside, and considered the lawns and gardens part of the house itself. On my first walk to the Oval Office, I had found security men all around me, opening each door as I approached it. I told them to stay at a distance while I was in my living and working area and to let me open doors myself. I wanted to have moments of solitude as I moved around the White House and the spacious grounds, and from then on the members of the Secret Service detail always stayed at a discreet distance.

I grew to love the yards and gardens, and studied the names and origins of the various plantings. Later, I asked the horticulturists to place nameplates on them. Knowing of my interest, the White House staff gave me a color-coded map which located and identified every tree on the grounds. Some were very strange, having come from other parts of the world as gifts from foreign heads of state. I remember the drooping Camperdown elm from Scotland, the spider-leaf maple from Japan, the ginkgo from China, and a cedar of Lebanon which was supposed to have come from the same forests that had furnished the wood for King Solomon's temple. Others had been donated by previous Presidents. The oldest of all was a great American elm, planted by John Quincy Adams in 1826. Rosalynn and I planted a red maple from north Georgia, a plane tree (sycamore) and a dogwood from central Georgia, and a loblolly pine from my own farm in south Georgia.

~

In the afternoon we had the swearing-in ceremony for eight members of the Cabinet and for other officials of cabinet rank, and we established once and for all the policy of no Ruffles and Flourishes or honors being paid to me. In a nonmilitary ceremony, I believe this is appropriate.   DIARY, JANUARY 23, 1977

Although we altered little in the White House itself, I wanted to make some basic changes in how a President lived and governed. In addition to the gesture of walking down Pennsylvania Avenue, I tried in many other ways to convince the people that barriers between them and top officials in Washington were being broken down. A simpler lifestyle, more frugality, less ostentation, more accessibility to the press and public—all these suited the way I had always lived.

President Lyndon Johnson had turned off unnecessary lights in the White House. In addition to furthering a nationwide energy-conservation effort, I wanted to eliminate some of the perquisites of Washington officials, beginning with my own immediate political family. Despite some subtle but persistent objections, I issued the appropriate orders. There were a lot of news stories when senior White House staff members began to arrive for work in their own automobiles, without chauffeurs—the great publicity confirmed to me that the change was long overdue. One of the White House drivers said that, before we arrived, he had ferried the pets of staff members to veterinarians as part of his driving duties! This man, a retired Army sergeant, had been offended by the extravagance of staff "perks." He felt much closer and at ease with my White House staff—the kind of change I wanted.

I soon learned that there were other times when presidential privileges were a necessity; some special arrangements simply proved more practical than my old way of doing things. I understood this clearly on my first trip home to Plains three weeks after the inauguration. I had instructed the Secret Service that, to save money, we would go to Plains by motorcade instead of by helicopter. But I discovered that because of the tremendous amount of effort that had to go into traffic control for road intersections, it was much less expensive to go by helicopter. A good portion of the Georgia State Patrol had been marshaled to block every country crossroad for more than sixty miles! It was obvious that I was not simply one of the people anymore.

> *Our first movie in the White House was* All the President's Men. *I felt strange occupying the same living quarters and position of responsibility as Richard Nixon.*
> DIARY, JANUARY 22, 1977

As an American, I had been embarrassed by the Watergate scandal and the forced resignation of the President. I realized that my own election had been aided by a deep desire among the people for open government, based on a new and fresh commitment to changing some of the Washington habits which had made it possible for the American people to be misled. Because of President Ford's pardon of Nixon, Watergate had been a largely unspoken though ever-present campaign issue, and the bitter divisions and personal tragedies of those recent events could not quickly be forgotten. So, in spite of Ford's healing service, the ghosts of Watergate still haunted the White House. We wanted to exorcise them and welcome friendlier spirits.

However, in reducing the imperial Presidency, I overreacted at first. We began to receive many complaints that I had gone too far in cutting back the pomp and ceremony, so after a few months I authorized the band to play "Hail to the Chief" on special occasions. I found it to be impressive and enjoyed it.

During those first days we shook hands with literally thousands of people. In a series of receptions we welcomed governors, mayors, and county officials, designated Cabinet members, business executives, labor officials, Georgians, members of Congress, the diplomatic corps, military personnel, and many others. We wanted to thank some of them for their friendship and help; in other cases, we were eager to meet for the first time the political, diplomatic, and military leaders with whom I would be working in Washington.

I was particularly impressed when the officers and enlisted leaders of the armed forces visited. We noticed that, more than any other group, they were likely to make some reference to their prayers for us or to say, "God be with you." Somehow, this emphasis on their religious faith gave me a good feeling. I experienced a sense of brotherhood with them, and remembered from my own eleven years in the Navy that it was members of the military services who most wanted to maintain peace based on a strong America.

Other meetings in the receiving line resulted in embraces and kisses. This was particularly true among those several hundred guests in whose homes the members of my family had stayed overnight, because these men and women had done so much for

Playing with grandson Jason and with Amy
in her tree house on White House grounds

us when we had little money and few people either knew or cared who we were. Most of these volunteers had not been from prominent families but were simply average Americans, living proof that ours had truly been a people's campaign.

It was interesting to observe the reaction of both personal and official guests to our new surroundings. In fact, this response generated a problem which I had not anticipated. Some of our visitors were so awestruck that they found it difficult to express themselves, even if they were close friends who had spent many hours with me and my family. The usually verbose mayor of one medium-sized city in Georgia was rendered literally speechless when he entered the White House. Guests staying overnight in the Lincoln bedroom found they could not sleep a wink. During a brief appointment with me in the Oval Office, sometimes after waiting for several weeks, people would find it difficult to remember or to discuss their business. I always sought to put them at ease, but later, after leaving the office or the mansion, they often had to call back and ask a staff member to explain to me the original purpose of their visit.

There were times when some of us shared those feelings of awe and reverence. We may have been overly cautious about disturbing things. But soon we were in the yard throwing Frisbees; on the rooftop watching the night overflights of migrating Canada geese; observing the planets and constellations with Jeff's telescope; exploring the remote recesses of the basement and attic regions; and actually relaxing while we watched Amy and her friends play tag or hide-and-seek in the hallowed halls and roller-skate under the arcade and along the paths. After she and I designed a tree house and it was erected within a great sprawling silver cedar on the edge of the south lawn, we really felt like a family at home.

We led a normal life as much as any presidential family could. We had always been strong supporters of public education, and so Amy was enrolled in District of Columbia schools. She had made a few appearances with us during the campaign, but she really preferred a more private life. She had always fit in remarkably well with her classmates and friends while I was governor, but now we were afraid she would become the focal point of too much publicity. Press Secretary Jody Powell and I talked to a few of the leading reporters in the White House press room about our problem, and they seemed somewhat sympathetic but not especially concerned.

On her first day at school, Amy was distressed. As a nine-year-old child, she had left her former home and all her school friends for a strange and alien world. It was wrenching to see her on the evening news, a tiny figure with a heavy bag, struggling toward the school door through a mass of television cameras and news reporters and surrounded by a crowd of security agents and onlookers. The reporters saw it too, and afterward they agreed with us that she should be left out of the news as much as possible.

One of Amy's best and closest friends while we lived at the governor's mansion had been Mary Fitzpatrick, who had worked for us as a convict from the Georgia penitentiary near Atlanta. After I was elected President, I contacted the Georgia Pardon and Parole Board and asked if she might be allowed to come to Washington to take care of Amy. She would be paid as a regular employee, and we would be responsible for her good behavior. They agreed to these terms.

As a visitor to a small south Georgia town, Mary had been involved in a street fight in which a man she had never seen before had been killed. Without adequate legal counsel, she had been convicted of murder, and although we were convinced that she was innocent of this charge, she was serving out her life sentence. Hers was a story all too common among the poor and the black before some of the legal reforms were imposed on our nation by the Supreme Court and Congress in the 1960's.

Mary Fitzpatrick lived in a small room on the third floor of the White House and performed her duties in an exemplary manner. Very close to Amy, Mary proved to be of special help during the times when both Rosalynn and I had to be away from home. She became a valuable member of our White House family and, at the same time, worked hard to be a good citizen. There was some initial criticism and a few ugly letters because we let a "criminal" work in the White House, but we benefited as much as Mary from the arrangement. Much later, because of her good work and obviously complete rehabilitation, she was given a full pardon by the State of Georgia. One of her proudest days was when she registered to vote.

∽

I have tried to hold down drastically the ceremonial events that Presidents ordinarily attend and to let my sons and their wives and Rosalynn . . . and others substitute for me. The time pressures are so tremendous that every minute's valuable. DIARY, JANUARY 27, 1977

As is well known, the lives of our nation's First Ladies can take many directions. Some have chosen to avoid involvement in public affairs and devote their time almost exclusively to being wives and mothers. Others have relished the Washington society life that always beckons any high official. A few have decided to live a much fuller life, using the prestige of the First Family for worthwhile causes.

At the National Women's Conference, November 1977:
(l-r) Coretta King, Rosalynn, Betty Ford, Lady Bird Johnson

Rosalynn's attitude toward her White House duties was shaped by her experience as my business and political partner and her life as First Lady of Georgia. On the campaign trail, she had been as familiar with domestic and foreign issues as anyone around me, and had assumed the same basic responsibilities as I had. She had helped plan strategy, raised funds, organized volunteers, made several speeches each day, conducted news conferences and appeared on interview shows, always prepared to answer the most searching questions that were presented to all of the serious candidates. Both my staff members and the news reporters knew that she could speak for me with authority. All of us turned to her for sound advice on issues and political strategy. As the governor's wife in Atlanta, Rosalynn had served as official hostess for a broad range of visitors to the mansion, arranging events quite similar to those held in the White House. She had also been an innovative leader in alleviating the problems of the mentally afflicted, in helping the aged, and in organizing community improvement projects.

It was only natural that when we arrived in Washington she would pursue these kinds of activities, acting on many ceremonial occasions as my surrogate. She and I continued to discuss a full range of important issues and, aside from a few highly secret and sensitive security matters, she knew all that was going on. When necessary, she received detailed briefings from members of my domestic and national security staff; it was most helpful for me to be able to discuss questions of importance with her as I formed my opinions.

On some occasions, it was necessary for one of us to go to a foreign country for the inauguration of a new leader, to attend a funeral, or to commemorate an important state holiday. Usually on such visits, there was an opportunity to conduct some substantive discussions of mutual interest to the nations represented. Rosalynn was able to perform many of these duties, in addition to those normally expected of a First Lady within the White House.

ᔕ

> *The President of India died, and I called Mama to ask her to represent me there. When she answered the phone I asked her what she was doing. She said she was sitting around the house looking for something to do, and I said, "How would you like to go to India?" She said, "I'd love to go some day. Why?" I said, "How about this afternoon?" She said, "Okay, I'll be ready." ... She didn't have a long black dress, so we had one of the Washington stores meet her at Andrews Air Force Base with a selection. She picked one, and took off for India with the funeral delegation.* DIARY, FEBRUARY 11, 1977

On occasion, my mother, Lillian, was eagerly accepted as the official representative of our country and its President, especially in communities where advanced age is revered, liberal social views are appreciated, and a lively sense of humor is tolerated.

ᔕ

With Miss Lillian

Around the White House supper table and in other family councils, we discussed our individual roles and our common responsibilities. Here were my strongest supporters, but also my most severe critics. As had been the case in Georgia in earlier years, the members of my family collectively knew many things about our nation that I could never have learned myself merely through performing official duties. Rosalynn had strong opinions of her own and never gave up on one of her ideas as long as there was any hope of its being accepted. As a Democratic party worker, Chip knew the members of Congress, the governors, and many of the local officials, whom he had met during our campaign or who were now involved in campaigns of their own. A college student,

Jeffrey brought a different perspective to our discussions. Highly opinionated and also very well informed about current events, he had inherited from his mother a habit of never losing an argument. Although very open with me, Jeff and Annette struggled valiantly to stay away from the press and out of the limelight. Most of the time they succeeded. I even derived useful information from Amy as she described her experiences in the public schools. What would improve the lunch program? How could we help the children who could not speak English? Were the students being immunized against contagious diseases? What was being done to challenge the bright students in the class or to give extra help to the slow ones?

Family gathering in Plains, August 1977:
(l-r) Judy, Jason, Jack, Annette, Jeff, Rosalynn,
Amy, the President, Caron, James, Chip

Some of these were the normal questions of interest to any family, but we were in a unique position to act on the ideas generated within our small group.

There is no doubt that the members of my family helped me be a better President.

LINING UP
MY TEAM

I would like to delegate much more authority as President than I ever tried to do as governor. It's just not within the bounds of human capability to go into as much detail as I did in Georgia. Also, I believe the staff and Cabinet officers would prefer to have minimal participation by me until the final decision point is reached.
DIARY, JANUARY 24, 1977

Throughout the long primary campaign, I had been determined not to make any early commitments concerning the Vice Presidency or other major positions in the administration. I wanted to keep all my options open. In 1972, I had observed the habit of presidential candidates' insinuating to citizens in each state they visited that their governor or senator would be a good choice for Vice President. I admit that at the time I was interested in being chosen as Vice President myself, and this may have been why the practice annoyed me. Furthermore, many times during my campaign I had promised not to make a misleading statement; after I had won a few victories, the traveling press closely scrutinized every word of mine to make sure this standard was met. In any case, my campaign staff was directed to refrain from this kind of teasing, and I followed my own advice.

I had made only one early decision about the Vice President—that it was important for me to choose a member of Congress as my running mate in order to provide some balance of experience to our ticket. Without ever having served in Washington myself, I needed someone who was familiar with the federal government and particularly with the legislative branch. I did not know many of the senators or representatives on Capitol Hill and had not spent much time studying about them. Throughout the primary months, I was almost totally devoted to winning as many of the elections as possible, or at least accumulating enough delegates to gain the nomination on the first convention ballot. If I had failed in this effort and it had become necessary to consider

35

certain people among the qualified running mates in order to gain a majority of the delegates, I would not have hesitated for a moment to do so. Fortunately, before I went to the Democratic Convention, I had enough delegate votes to win, so I had a totally free hand in choosing my vice-presidential partner.

When the primary elections were over in early June, we all were exhausted. My campaign team and I took a few days off to rest, to meditate, and to plan for the future. Until that time, I had not undertaken any serious discussions about the Vice Presidency, but now it was time to begin the selection process. If an instant choice had been required at that time, it would have been Senator Frank Church of Idaho, or perhaps Senator Henry Jackson of Washington. Since both had been opponents of mine in the primaries, I was familiar with their general political philosophy, their stands on particular issues, and their campaign strengths and weaknesses. I also knew them to be ambitious and willing to face a difficult political contest.

However, it was also important to look at people with whom I was less familiar. So with Charles Kirbo, Rosalynn, and my campaign leaders, I systematically went down the roster of all the Democratic members of Congress. We sought advice from Democratic statesmen and leading citizens who were familiar with the work of those we were considering. I talked to many people by telephone, and Kirbo spent some time in Washington in private discussions about the potential nominees.

We soon reduced the list to about twenty names. Hamilton Jordan, my campaign manager, contrived a formula for weighing the qualities of these potential nominees, and we ranked them by their leadership ability, their voting record, their attractiveness to the key constituency groups among whom I needed help, their campaign effectiveness, their experience in matters where my own was limited, and their geographical strength. The overriding consideration for me was how a person might perform the duties of President.

Eventually, Senators Edmund Muskie, John Glenn, and Walter Mondale, in turn, came down to Plains to discuss in depth the advisability of our joining together. Senators Frank Church, Adlai Stevenson, Henry Jackson, and Representative Peter Rodino preferred to meet with me in New York during the days just prior to the convention. This interview procedure was highly publicized, but the discussions were very personal and very private. With each candidate I wanted to know how compatible we would be during the remaining months of the campaign and if we served together in the White House. We conferred about some of the critical issues that faced our nation and my ideas for a greatly expanded role for the Vice President. All indicated a willingness to serve except Peter Rodino, who asked that he be eliminated from consideration because of his wife's poor health.

I deliberately withheld a decision until all the interviews and investigations were completed, and I must admit that I changed my mind three or four times. Several people claimed they knew in advance whom I had chosen, and went to the news reporters with their "inside" information. There was a flood of stories by journalists, each claiming to have found the one person who knew my secret choice! But no one could have known, because I did not know myself.

Since my nomination for President was certain, my future running mate was the source of most of the speculation around the convention hotels in New York. Eventually, my choice was narrowed down to Ed Muskie and Fritz Mondale. It was a difficult decision. Both were good men, experienced legislators, knowledgeable about the nation, popular in their own states, and respected by their colleagues. I was convinced that either would be an excellent President if called upon to serve.

The night before I was to announce my preference, I settled upon Senator Mondale. When Fritz came down to Plains he had really done his homework about me and the campaign. More important, he had excellent ideas about how to make the Vice Presidency a full-time and productive job. He was from a small town, as I was, a preacher's son, and shared a lot of my concerns about our nation. We were personally compatible, and laughed a lot even as we discussed some of the more serious issues of the time.

At the convention I was told that he had installed a straight-line telephone in his hotel room and would not allow anyone to use it as he waited for my possible call. I do remember that the phone was answered immediately, before the first ring was over. When I said, "Senator, I called to ask if you will run with me," I received one of the quickest agreements of my life. I then called the others to let them know someone else had been chosen. I did not tell them who it was at the time, but did inform the Secret Service in order that security arrangements could be made before the news became public. My discussions with the candidates had been agreeable, and it was gratifying that all those who were not chosen supported the final ticket enthusiastically.

From our first meeting, Fritz Mondale had impressed me as a good and decent man, honest and intelligent, and I have always been thankful that we formed this partnership. He has sound judgment and strong beliefs and has never been timid about presenting them forcefully to me. But whenever I made a final decision, even when it was contrary to his own original recommendation, he gave me his full support. He never abused his position by overstepping the appropriate bounds of advocacy when he pursued his own ideas. Our staffs cooperated without dissension, even in the most difficult times. During our four and a half years together, I never for a moment had reason to doubt his competence, his loyalty, or his friendship.

This harmony had not existed between many of my predecessors and their Vice Presidents. Most chiefs of state had ignored their partners, did not completely trust them, or felt threatened by the obviously strong character or stature of some of them. Often, the partnership had been a "forced marriage" arranged at a national convention, where trading for delegate votes or regional influence had taken place.

Vice Presidents Hubert Humphrey and Nelson Rockefeller had been particularly helpful in giving Fritz ideas on how we might better use his ability in the White House. Immediately after we were elected, he came to me with a well-prepared book of suggestions, all of which I accepted. He did not wish to be sidetracked into heading up one or two trade councils or special study commissions just to occupy his time. Instead, we agreed that he would truly be the second in command, involved in every aspect of governing. As a result, he received the same security briefings I got, was automatically invited to participate in all my official meetings, and helped to plan strategy for domestic programs, diplomacy, and defense.

One of the most vivid illustrations of the necessity for this full involvement was demonstrated to me even before the inauguration, when I had several meetings with the Joint Chiefs of Staff and their military experts. I wanted to understand our defense organization, its capabilities and weaknesses, my proper role as Commander in Chief of the Armed Forces—and my myriad special responsibilities in the control and potential use of atomic weapons. This is a sobering duty of the chief executive of our country, and every serious candidate for this office must decide whether he is capable of using or willing to use nuclear weapons if it should become necessary in order to defend our country. Under those circumstances, I was ready to perform this duty. Later, a military aide was always with me with a black briefcase or "football," which would enable me to carry out that duty—a constant reminder of the threat of a horribly devastating war and therefore a powerful incentive for me to keep our nation strong and to maintain the peace.

The procedures for responding to a nuclear attack, originally developed when President Eisenhower was in office, are among our most carefully protected secrets. As the time for the inauguration approached, I wanted to be thoroughly familiar with these important operations, so that the military forces and I would be ready for any eventuality. After I was in office, it would be too late to start a training program for a busy and unprepared President.

I was astounded to learn that former Vice Presidents had never been involved in this process. It was obvious to me that in a nuclear exchange, the President might well be incapacitated, and the Vice President, as the *new* Commander in Chief, had to be fully qualified to assume his duties. I directed from the beginning that Fritz Mondale participate along with me and the future Secretary of Defense in closely guarded learning sessions in Blair House and at the Pentagon.

I also insisted that, for the first time, the Vice President's personal office would be located in the West Wing of the White House, adjacent to my own, and that his staff and mine be integrated as a working team. Dick Moe, Mondale's Chief of Staff, became one of my most valuable advisers. To integrate our staffs was one of the wisest decisions I made, and I quickly came to wonder why other Presidents had not utilized the services of their Vice Presidents in a similar manner. As we served together, our relationship constantly improved—a pleasant surprise to the two of us as well as to other observers of the White House scene.

When I went to Washington, I brought with me not only my personal family, but also my political family. Fritz Mondale was the first person to whom I made a public commitment, but I had made a private promise to myself to call on some of the talented Georgians who had served me as governor and as a candidate for President. My decisions about how to use them were not made casually.

I knew that my predecessors had been criticized for installing their "cronies" in the White House. Such complaints had been leveled at Presidents Roosevelt, Truman, Kennedy, and others. But when I considered the alternatives, I decided without any doubt that my predecessors had chosen wisely. The selection of loyal and well-known associates is the result of a need for maximum mutual confidence and a minimum of jealousy and backbiting within a President's inner circle.

An enormously complex screening process among political associates takes place during the evolution of a private citizen from haberdasher or schoolteacher, farmer or movie actor to President of the United States. Some of the small number chosen to work in the White House with any newly elected President have demonstrated their finer qualities during the difficult early years of campaigning, and may have served with the candidate in a lower office, such as governor or senator. They have also been able to meet the even more intense competition generated within a successful campaign for President—from the bottom echelons of the staff to the top. During the campaign we had been embarrassed by a few bad personnel selections. Though never fatal, the consequences were serious enough to arouse caution about bringing new people into our most intimate circle. Obviously, firing a member of a top political team was a very unpleasant experience in itself and something we worked hard to avoid, but on occasion it had to be done. My White House team had been tested in the political crucible and found not wanting in experience, competence, and compatibility with me and with one another.

Immediately after the inauguration ceremonies, we were all eager to put our theories and plans into action. As the members of my staff came into the Oval Office, I observed subtle changes: they were more sober, a bit more subdued, and dressed more conservatively—most in new clothes. I had a feeling that somehow we had aged, or at least matured, during the last few weeks. We had savored and celebrated our election victory; now our serious work was about to begin.

As we planned our new life, I recalled how much some of these men and women had shared with me over the years.

Hamilton Jordan had been campaign manager of my successful gubernatorial race in 1970 and then served as Executive Secretary while I was Governor. In Georgia, when the governor is out of the state, the executive secretary becomes, in effect, the acting governor. Hamilton earned my confidence by the way he performed this demanding responsibility.

Hamilton was more seriously misunderstood and underestimated by the press and public than anyone else who worked in my administration. A brilliant political analyst who had devised and managed my presidential campaign, he worked long hours under the most difficult conditions. As my chief staff aide, he would oversee personnel selections, coordinate staff activities, and represent me in routine dealings with Cabinet officers. He also served as my special emissary during the Panama Canal treaties negotiations and the efforts to free the Americans held hostage in Iran. Because of his qualities of leadership and sound judgment, Hamilton was always considered the senior man by all the other staff members in the White House, earning their affection as well as their respect. Although he and I resisted the idea for two and a half years, I eventually acquiesced to the requests of other staff members and officially designated him Chief of Staff. However, I retained direct access to my other senior advisers.

(l-r) Jody Powell, the President, Hamilton Jordan, Phil Wise

Even closer to me personally than Hamilton Jordan was Jody Powell, my Press Secretary. As a graduate student at Emory University, Jody had come to my home during the Christmas season in 1969 among a group of student volunteers. Later, when I needed to for go driving my own automobile in order to get some rest between campaign stops, I remembered Jody and the fact that he was older than the other students and seemed to know more about politics. At the time, though, I was looking for a driver—not for academic counsel or political advice.

Jody and I were together for the entire campaign. As the months went by and I began to develop political strength, it became necessary for me to spend a lot of time talking to the press. Eventually I let Jody present my views to the news reporters when the issue was not too important. After I was elected governor, I searched for a press secretary among the qualified journalists in the state, but found none completely satisfactory. I finally asked Jody if he would take the job, and he agreed.

When I began my national campaign in 1975, we repeated the pattern. Jody and I traveled together—for many months there were just the two of us. We drove rented cars, flew in borrowed single-engine airplanes, and slept on couches or in spare rooms of supporters.

There were good times and bad times. No doubt the housewives of Iowa were startled early one morning to see me in a television-studio kitchen, dressed as a chef and slicing fish filets into strips. I was demonstrating one of my favorite camping recipes, hoping that some of the voters would remember my name. I understand they still replay the tape during dull times in Iowa.

But I also remember going to Philadelphia much later, after our campaign was well under way. Jody and I had decided the time had come for a full-scale press conference. We rented an expensive meeting room in a downtown hotel and spent a lot of time on the telephone inviting the news media to send reporters to the event. This was one of the bad times. The only reporter who came was a young cub who had worked as an intern for Jody in the governor's office in Atlanta. Her friendship kept her from recording the empty room and our obvious embarrassment.

Throughout my long campaign, from beginning to end, Jody Powell was almost always at my side. We had long talks, and sometimes fierce arguments, hammering out decisions together. Hamilton Jordan and our headquarters staff in Atlanta conducted the overall campaign, but Jody and I were on the cutting edge, out in the country traveling from one community to another trying to stir up interest in me and to recruit new supporters. Jody always participated in the sessions with our local friends, relaying information and suggestions back to our national headquarters. He criticized my speeches and helped me develop answers to the growing barrage of questions we had to face. After I went to bed every night, Jody would stay on the telephone making plans for the next day. Often, he spent additional hours with local reporters, giving them information and trying to wheedle a favorable news story about our visit to the community.

When I won a few contests and became recognized as a major

candidate, my traveling staff grew substantially. Jody remained the one closest to me. The news reporters came to know that he could speak for me on almost any subject. When I was elected President, he was the natural choice for Press Secretary.

Only very rarely in the four years was Jody excluded from my discussion of even the most sensitive issues. The reporters understood this special relationship between us and learned to trust the accuracy of his statements and answers. I often grew exasperated with him when he came to work late, missed an appointment, procrastinated about a decision, or forgot to carry out my orders. In spite of this, many people—and I among them—think that Jody was one of the best White House press secretaries of all time.

Well before Inauguration Day, I could see that one of the most important staff members would be the leader of our congressional liaison group. I needed to recruit knowledgeable people to work on Capitol Hill, keep track of the voluminous legislation being considered, and provide some continuity in our efforts to put my campaign commitments into effect. I chose Frank Moore for this job. A professional management specialist, Frank had been an associate since 1966 when I hired him as executive director of a multicounty planning and development commission, where he demonstrated an ability to recruit good people and deal effectively with the competing and sometimes suspicious officials of the eight counties and twenty-two towns and cities involved.

Later, when Hamilton Jordan went to Washington to work for the Democratic National Committee, Frank replaced him in Atlanta as Executive Secretary to the Governor. Frank helped coordinate our 1976 campaign in several Southern states, and I asked him to spend a small part of his time in Washington getting to know some of the members of Congress and the national press. I was then only one of many candidates, and Frank had no staff or special budget; his overriding duty was to help with the campaign. As my successes in the primary elections began to attract increasing attention, people in Washington wanted to contact me personally, and Frank was designated as the avenue through which this might be done.

Although he worked prodigiously on his infrequent trips to Washington, Frank was unable to return all the telephone calls or answer the great volume of special requests that flooded to me through him. He had to bear the brunt of criticism from all those who were frustrated in their efforts to reach me. Characteristically, he never tried to shift any blame to others. He put together an outstanding staff and worked hard to overcome this original stigma of ineptitude.

As governor, I had been frustrated and angered by the absence of even minimal cooperation between the Nixon White House and state and local leaders around the nation. The system of federalism had almost completely broken down. It had also been extremely difficult—sometimes impossible—for us to obtain information about the federal programs that so directly affected our state and for which we were at least partially responsible. When I was elected President, I was determined to let the governors, mayors, and county officials know that they were part of my team and would always have unimpeded access to my office. When new legislation that would affect them was contemplated, I wanted them to be partners with me and Congress in drafting the laws. As old programs were phased out or modified, it was important for local administrators to be thoroughly conversant with the changes. I needed someone who was experienced in these matters, who had the ability to explain new ideas, and finally, who knew me well.

Jack Watson, an attorney from Atlanta, had served as chairman of the Georgia Human Resources Board while I was governor. This department was responsible for all welfare, health, rehabilitation, and senior-citizen services, and had to deal with the federal government and with local officials around the state in implementing the complicated and confusing laws concerning these programs. Jack had been particularly effective in explaining complex and sometimes unpopular issues to the public. I asked him to coordinate my transition from candidate to President in the fall of 1976, and then chose him for the dual role of Cabinet Secretary and Assistant for Intergovernmental Affairs. His responsibilities were to see that the various leaders of government agencies worked in harmony and that governors and other state and local officials had an effective representative in Washington. He also arranged Cabinet meetings, prepared the minutes, and insured that when new laws were passed, they were implemented properly and without delay. In June 1980 I would name Jack as my Chief of Staff when Hamilton left the White House to coordinate my reelection campaign.

During my 1970 gubernatorial campaign I was only vaguely familiar with the members of a small group of my volunteers who met each week in an Atlanta law office to discuss plans for the future of Georgia. But every now and then, I would receive a study or proposal which was brilliant in its conception, and which provided me with a clearer vision of how to improve conditions in my state. I hardly knew the leader of this group, whose name was Stuart Eizenstat.

Although quite young at that time, Stu was already experienced in issue analysis and the preparation of legislative proposals, having worked in these areas for President Lyndon Johnson, Vice President Hubert Humphrey, and the Democratic National Committee. Throughout my campaign for President, he coordinated the analysis of all national and international issues I would have to face, prepared the briefing books for the three presidential debates, and drafted position papers for presenting our views to the public. When we moved into the White House, it was logical that Stu be responsible for the preparation of our legislative proposals and for monitoring the significant bills and resolutions being considered by Congress.

Other staff members were chosen because of their demonstrated ability and knowledge of the issues we would be facing. Before we went to Washington, all the White House assignments had been carefully delineated, primarily by Fritz, Ham, and me. At first a few people struggled to expand their responsibilities, but they soon realized that their original duties were more than adequate.

I appointed as my legal counsel Robert J. Lipshutz, who had served as legal adviser and treasurer of my presidential campaign. Midge Costanza, of New York, became my Assistant for Public Liaison. The Special Assistants to the President were Joe Aragon; Peter Bourne, Health Issues; Hugh Carter, Jr., Administration; Richard Harden, Budget and Organization; Barry Jagoda, Media and Public Affairs; Tim Kraft, Appointments; Martha Mitchell, Special Projects; and Esther Peterson, Consumer Affairs. Susan Clough was my Personal Assistant/Secretary.

In a special category were Zbigniew Brzezinski, Assistant to the President for National Security Affairs; and David Aaron, Deputy Assistant. They were also, respectively, Director and Deputy Director of the National Security Council, and accorded the same rank as Cabinet secretaries and their deputies.

Originally, James Schlesinger was officially a member of the senior staff with the title Assistant to the President. However, as Secretary-designate of the proposed Department of Energy, he was generally considered to be one of the Cabinet officers.

Although some of us had worked together for several years, most of my staff and I were inexperienced in the ways of Washington. Integrating Vice President Mondale's staff with the rest of us helped to overcome this difficulty, but we still suffered from some incompatibility with Washington's leaders, particularly in the news media. Later, I brought into the White House some people with more federal service, but initially I was convinced that choosing a cabinet that was broad and diverse in its background would compensate for any lack of experience in my personal staff.

Most of these White House assistants would share with me the successes and failures of the coming years. We would go through a lot together and grow even closer as we faced the momentous events ahead. That first afternoon, Inauguration Day 1977, is still fresh in my mind. We were making the workaday plans for a President's schedule—how I would spend each day, what documents I should see, how to decide what people could visit me, how my mail would be answered. They were not earthshaking decisions and I would rarely address them again, yet the newness of each detail made those hours one of the most exciting afternoons of all.

～

As with my personal staff, I selected Cabinet members and other major officials with great care. Although I did not know these newcomers to our ranks nearly so well, I chose them from among proven leaders with reputations for competence and character. I needed people who could supplement the strengths we would bring to the White House—as well as reassure some Americans who did not yet trust a group of Southerners to manage the affairs of the country.

Part of the screening process began during the late summer of 1976, when I had to prepare for the general election and the Presidency. As the Democratic nominee, I had the counsel of people who were not particularly interested in partisan politics but were eager to help me shape our country's future. I invited a stream of these advisers down to Plains for meetings, with a structured agenda, briefing books for each session, and ample time for profitable discussions.

I learned a lot from these experts, and they learned some things from me. Many of them knew more about Washington, Wall Street, academic faculties, corporate boardrooms, and union headquarters, but I had just completed a tremendous graduate course in America, in the streets, in the factories, on the farms—and in the kitchens and livestock auction barns.

Sometimes my visitors were amused at the ways in which my Deep South Baptist ideas crept into discussions. Once when we were discussing the Far East, I remarked that the people of our country had a deep and natural affection for the people of China. When most of the group laughed, I was perplexed and a little embarrassed. It took me a few moments to realize that not everyone had looked upon Christian missionaries in China as the ultimate heroes and had not, as youngsters, contributed a penny or a nickel each week, year after year, toward schools and hospitals for the little Chinese children.

Senator Fritz Mondale was with me for all these sessions, which gave us a chance to become better acquainted and to insure that during the coming general election campaign we would be "preaching from the same text."

After my election, recommendations for personnel appointments poured in, hundreds coming through the transition office in Washington. Many of those I now considered had, in effect, auditioned for their jobs by advising me on issues during the campaign.

Hamilton Jordan began working full time on narrowing down the choices for senior positions. He, Fritz Mondale, Charles Kirbo, and Rosalynn helped me most with selections, but I personally made dozens of calls to seek advice, contacting people with experience in government as well as leaders in other walks of life.

We kept a careful record of their comments about the prospective nominees, and then cross checked them against one another. It was especially interesting for me to hear the assessments for appointments to such positions as Secretary of State from among those leaders who themselves wanted that post. Their generosity toward one another was one of the most probing measurements of character. The few generous ones tended to move nearer the top of my list. Eventually, after several weeks, the choices came down to less than half a dozen for each position.

I was determined to complete the appointments in time for us to make our plans together as a Cabinet for our first days in Washington. Early in December 1976, I went to Atlanta and borrowed from Governor George Busbee an office and a couple of rooms in the governor's mansion. From that familiar setting I conducted my final interviews with those I was considering for Cabinet posts. I had reviewed my voluminous notes about each of the prospective appointees and was well prepared with lists of questions I wanted answered.

Although I had not made any announcements about the interviews, the entrance to the mansion grounds was nevertheless thronged with reporters and television cameras, trying to identify each person who came to see me. My final choices had both geographical diversity and breadth of experience: Cyrus Vance, of New York, Secretary of State; Michael Blumenthal, of Michigan, Secretary of the Treasury; Harold Brown, of California, Secretary of Defense; Griffin Bell, of Georgia, Attorney General; Cecil Andrus, of Idaho, Secretary of the Interior; Bob Bergland, of Minnesota, Secretary of Agriculture; Juanita Kreps, of North Carolina, Secretary of Commerce; Ray Marshall, of Texas, Secretary of Labor; Joseph Califano, of the District of Columbia, Secretary of Health, Education, and Welfare; Patricia Roberts Harris, of the District of Columbia, Secretary of Housing and Urban Development; and Brock Adams, of Washington, Secretary of Transportation.

Brown, Kreps, and Marshall were drawn from the academic world; Vance, Bell, Califano, and Harris from the field of law; Bergland and Adams from Congress; Blumenthal from business; and Andrus had been Governor of Idaho. Only Kreps, Andrus, and Marshall had not served previously in the federal government, although the Labor Secretary-designate had considerable experience on federal advisory commissions.

There were a few others of cabinet rank who met with us as equals: Bert Lance, of Georgia, Director of the Office of Management and Budget; James Schlesinger, of Virginia, who would be the first Secretary of Energy; Andrew Young, of Georgia, Ambassador to the United Nations; Zbigniew Brzezinski, of New York, National Security Adviser; Charles Schultze, of Maryland, Chairman, Council of Economic Advisers; and Robert Strauss, of Texas, Special Trade Representative.

Three people not in the government who were valued advisers to me were Charles Kirbo, Atlanta lawyer and my closest friend; Gerald Rafshoon, who had handled my public relations ever since I was a gubernatorial candidate; and Patrick Caddell, a public opinion specialist. These men were an integral part of my political family. Kirbo preferred to remain in his Atlanta office, but he was a frequent visitor to Washington when his help was needed. Rafshoon joined my staff in 1978 as Assistant to the President for Communications; and Caddell continued to provide public opinion data for the Democratic National Committee and to give me advice unofficially.

These men and women—black and white, Protestants, Jews, and Catholics, from all regions of the country and with an impressive range of philosophy and experience—were to share with me, Fritz Mondale, and our staffs the experiences described in this book. Others, although not mentioned here individually, would be worthy of a chapter in any definitive history of our times.

Lunch in the President's private office

Ever since my boyhood days on the farm, I have enjoyed the solitude and beauty of the early morning hours. As President I established a routine of rising early, around six o'clock, and going to the Oval Office a half-hour later. I would begin my day with coffee, an open fire in the winter, the morning newspapers, and the overnight report from the Secretary of State, all of which were waiting for me when I arrived. I usually read the Secretary's report first, because it encapsulated in two or three pages the events or issues considered most significant by the State Department and summarized actions being contemplated in the near future.

Cyrus Vance had been Secretary of the Army under President Kennedy and later Deputy Secretary of Defense when President Johnson was in office. Cool under pressure, he had also served as special troubleshooter for more than one President when there were crises in Cyprus, Korea, and Vietnam. Cy was very knowledgeable in both military matters and foreign affairs. A natural selection for Secretary of State, Vance was almost unanimously recommended by the advisers I consulted. Even the few who had a different first choice usually listed him in second place.

During the 1976 campaign, Vance had been one of the early supporters of Sargent Shriver for President. Later that summer, I began meeting with him to discuss foreign affairs, and was particularly interested in his belief that we might be successful in alleviating the growing tension between Greece and Turkey and that, while moderate leaders were in power, it might be possible to effect a comprehensive peace settlement in the Middle East. These were ideas I was eager to explore, and I was impressed by the quiet but sound way he presented them.

Among all the members of my official Cabinet, Cy Vance and his wife, Gay, became the closest personal friends to Rosalynn and me. He and I were to spend many good times together—talking, fishing, skiing, playing tennis—as well as less enjoyable hours negotiating a Middle East settlement and working and praying for the hostages. Fortunately for all of us, Warren Christopher, a Los Angeles attorney, accepted the appointment as Deputy Secretary of State. He was to play a key role in many of the most dramatic moments of our administration.

My first scheduled meeting in the Oval Office each day was with National Security Adviser Zbigniew Brzezinski, when he brought me the Presidential Daily Briefing (known as the PDB) from the intelligence community. I would see him several times during the day at different hours, and in times of crisis he was either at my side or coordinating meetings with my Cabinet officers and other leaders in the Situation Room, the isolated and permanently secured compartment on the floor below the Oval Office.

Zbigniew Brzezinski was perhaps the most controversial member of my team. I first met him in 1973, when we were both participants in various conferences on foreign affairs. ·

Zbig was astute in his analyses, particularly knowledgeable about broad historical trends affecting the industrialized nations, and a firm believer in a strong defense for our country and in the enhancement of freedom and democratic principles both here and abroad. His proposals were innovative and often provocative, and I agreed with them—most of the time. Originally from Poland, he had made a special study of the Soviet Union and Eastern Europe. He was interested in China, the Middle East, and Africa; so was I. I was an eager student, and took full advantage of what Brzezinski had to offer. As a college professor and author, he was able to express complicated ideas simply. We got to know each other well.

As a volunteer Zbig helped me during the presidential campaign. I would study his position papers on foreign affairs in order to develop my answers to those questions all candidates had to face. He became a frequent visitor to Plains and went out to San Francisco to brief me for my second television debate with President Ford, which was devoted to defense and foreign affairs.

He received high recommendations from many sources, but a few of the people who knew him well cautioned me that Zbig was aggressive and ambitious, and that on controversial subjects he might be inclined to speak out too forcefully. When I was making the final decisions about my White House staff and considering him as National Security Adviser, an additional note of caution was expressed: Dr. Brzezinski might not be adequately deferential to a secretary of state.

Knowing Zbig, I realized that some of these assessments were accurate, but they were in accord with what I wanted: the final decisions on basic foreign policy would be made by me in the Oval Office, and not in the State Department. I listened carefully to all the comments about him, considered the factors involved, and decided that I wanted him with me in the White House. (In looking at my old notes, I find it interesting that Vance recommended Brzezinski for this job, and Zbig recommended Cy for Secretary of State. Both were good suggestions.)

With Brzezinski (center) and Vance

There were some inherent differences in the character of the White House National Security Council staff and the State Department. I attempted to tap the strongest elements in each as changing circumstances demanded.

Zbigniew Brzezinski and his relatively small group of experts were not handicapped by the inertia of a tenured bureaucracy or the responsibility for implementing policies after they were evolved. They were particularly adept at incisive analyses of strategic concepts, and were prolific in the production of new ideas, which they were always eager to present to me. I encouraged them to be unrestrained in their proposals, and consequently had to reject a lot of them. However, in the resulting discussions, we often found a better path worth following. Zbig was a first-rate thinker, very competent in his choice of staff members and able to work harmoniously with them (I do not remember any dissension at all). He was sometimes provocative in the extent and the way he expressed himself—irrepressible during hard times and exuberant during the good ones.

Comprised of highly qualified professional men and women, the State Department is a sprawling Washington and worldwide bureaucracy, with compartmentalized regional and national desks. Although I rarely received innovative ideas from its staff members about how to modify existing policy in order to meet changing conditions, the advice was generally sound, the information thoroughly researched, and the public statements mild and cautious. The inertia of the department was itself a beneficial restraint on overly rapid action or inadequately assessed plans. In many ways, Cy Vance mirrored the character of the organization he led. He was intelligent and experienced, thoroughly honorable, sound in his judgments, careful to explore all facets of a question before answering, extremely loyal to his subordinates, and protective of the State Department and its status and heritage.

At times, Cy would react to news stories about the struggle for power between the White House and State by coming to me on behalf of his bureaucracy. In most instances, the reports were inaccurate or exaggerated; they had been precipitated by an honest difference of opinion, a leak from a subordinate officer in the State Department, or a speech or interview by Zbig concerning diplomatic philosophy or a particular item of public interest. Almost without exception, Zbig had been speaking with my approval and in consonance with my established and known policy. The underlying State Department objection was that Brzezinski had spoken at all.

My own preference was that one of the roles of the Secretary of State be the education of the American public about foreign policy. Secretary Vance was not particularly inclined to assume this task on a sustained basis; it is time-consuming and not always pleasant. To adequately explain our nation's position on complex or controversial matters, it is necessary to have frequent sessions with news reporters at home or at the State Department—on and off the record—give public speeches on college campuses, and make fairly regular appearances on the Sunday television interview programs. Only a very few people in an administration can command the attention required for this task. Except on rare occasions, when another official has been designated to manage a particular controversial matter, it must be the President, the Vice President, the Secretary of State—or, if the President wishes, the National Security Adviser.

Zbigniew Brzezinski was always ready and willing to explain our position on international matters, analyze a basic strategic interrelationship, or comment on a current event. He and I recognized the problems generated within the State Department when he spoke out on an issue, and he did so much less frequently than would have been the case had he followed his natural inclinations. There were periods when we would agree that he refrain from making any public statements.

Because of his attitude and demeanor, Zbig was a natural center of public attention. This circumstance was exacerbated by his willingness to serve as a lightning rod—to take the blame for unpopular decisions made by others. Interest groups that were dissatisfied with a policy were quick to hold Zbig accountable instead of the person responsible for it—either me or the Secretary of State. During all the difficult times we faced, I never knew Zbig to try to avoid criticism by shifting blame to his boss.

To me, Zbigniew Brzezinski was interesting. He would probe constantly for new ways to accomplish a goal, sometimes wanting to pursue a path that might be ill-advised—but always thinking. We had many arguments about history, politics, international events, and foreign policy—often disagreeing strongly and fundamentally—but we still got along well. Next to members of my family, Zbig would be my favorite seatmate on a long-distance trip; we might argue, but I would never be bored.

The different strengths of Zbig and Cy matched the roles they played, and also permitted the natural competition between the two organizations to stay alive. I appreciated those differences. In making the final decisions on foreign policy, I needed to weigh as many points of view as possible. When Brzezinski and Vance were joined by Fritz Mondale and Harold Brown, plus others as required to address a particular issue, they comprised a good team.

The PDB Zbig brought to me each morning was a highly secret document, distributed to only five people: the President, the Vice President, the Secretaries of State and Defense, and the National Security Adviser. Zbig and I would discuss the report and other developments relating to defense and foreign affairs. Often, while he was still present, I would call the Secretary of State or Secretary of Defense on a secure telephone to obtain additional information or get their opinions. They, too, were early risers, always at their desks by seven o'clock.

When working on major defense issues, I was really thankful to have Harold Brown at my side. Secretary of Defense had, of course, been one of the most important posts I had to fill. I was determined to eliminate as much waste in defense spending as possible, to establish proper long-range priorities in the acquisition of highly technical new weapons systems, and to institute efficient management procedures in the Pentagon. The Pentagon needed some discipline, and I wanted both a scientist with a thorough knowledge of the most advanced technology and a competent business manager, strong-willed enough to prevail in the internecine struggles among the different military services.

After a long screening process, I had still been undecided between Harold Brown, a physicist who was serving as president of the California Institute of Technology, and Charles Duncan, former president of the Coca-Cola Company. I finally decided to try to get both men, and called Brown to tell him that I would like to have him as Secretary, provided Duncan would be his deputy. Otherwise, I said, if Brown did not agree with that arrangement, I would ask Charles Duncan to be Secretary. Harold agreed to come see me and to stop in Texas to meet Charles. They got along well, and we closed the deal as I had preferred. It was a sound decision. Most of the polls among the Washington news media ranked Harold Brown as my best Cabinet officer. I never indulged in such a ranking game, but there were certainly no others who were better than he in my administration.

Several times a week, I arranged a breakfast meeting with the leaders of Congress or other visitors, and on Friday mornings at 7:30 A.M., there was a regular foreign-affairs breakfast. At first I invited only three people—Fritz, Cy, and Zbig—but I soon added

Harold Brown to the list. Later, Hamilton and Jody and one or two others were included, depending upon which issues were of most importance at the time. For about an hour and a half, we covered the range of questions involving international and defense matters, to allow me to reach decisions and to minimize any misunderstandings among this high-level group. This became my favorite meeting of the week, even when the subjects discussed were disagreeable. (During the week, the two Secretaries and Zbig also lunched together to discuss shared responsibilities that did not require my direct involvement.)

My regular appointment schedule usually began around eight o'clock. Meetings previously approved by me were scheduled throughout the day, ranging in length from two or three minutes for a ceremonial photograph to sessions lasting for many hours, when decisions about the national budget had to be made or an international crisis assessed.

After a few weeks, Rosalynn and I came to realize how many decisions we had to make together about the mansion, correspondence, public events, official and personal visitors, and our family budget. After a full day's work at the office, I did not relish the prospect of meeting her each evening with a stack of papers between us, so every Thursday we had a working lunch during which we could resolve the questions that had accumulated. Fritz and I had a similar standing lunch engagement every Monday when we were both in town.

Jody, Zbig, and Ham were my most frequent unscheduled visitors to the Oval Office. They needed only to check with my secretary to make sure I was alone. Most other staff members or Cabinet officers would call ahead of time, to be sure it was all right to come see me.

As a general rule, I preferred to receive questions and advice in writing. I was not looking for a permanent record or more paper work—just trying to save time. Instead of holding a five- or ten-minute conversation (at least), I could read a brief memorandum and make a decision in a matter of moments; and I could do this at odd times throughout the day. One of the good things about being President was that the quality of notes coming to the Oval Office was usually very high. Most people really tried to express themselves succinctly and, when writing, succeeded. In the room with me, however, their verbal skills often deserted them, and much time would be wasted while they tried to come to the point. Jody was one of the few who resisted putting his thoughts in writing. I presumed that, like Rosalynn, he considered this procedure a little too formal. In any case, a record of all his good advice will not be available to historians—but neither will his bad advice!

Between appointments, I managed the mountains of paper work that could not be avoided. At first, sixty or seventy documents arrived on my desk each day, some of them consisting of many pages of detailed analysis. There would be proposals from Cabinet officers that I had to approve; correspondence to sign; presidential appointments to major executive posts to be considered; reports from meetings in the Situation Room on foreign, intelligence, or defense subjects; facts about legislation before Congress; or proposals we were developing to send to Capitol Hill. Throughout the day, I would also receive copies of news bulletins and diplomatic reports that Jody or Zbig thought I should see.

After working long hours at the office, I was having to carry home with me each night a briefcase of paper work. At first all of it was enjoyable, but after a few weeks I concluded that the workload would have to be reduced. With my staff I analyzed the reports, screened out the ones I did not need to see, and asked that the others be abbreviated. Then I arranged for Rosalynn, myself, and my key aides to attend weekly sessions of a speed-reading course in the Cabinet Room. After the first couple of lessons, my reading speed doubled, finally it quadrupled, and by the time the course was completed, the burden of paper work had been eased to a bearable level. Afterward, only special study of an issue would require me to work after supper, and I was usually free to read, watch a movie, or just relax with my family.

Another way I saved time was by responding to written questions by writing notes on the margins and sending a copy back to the originator. To my staff members and other top officials I sent handwritten instructions of only a few words. Most routine messages and statements were prepared by others and submitted to me for final editing or signature. On a few occasions, I wrote longer messages by hand to members of Congress or to foreign heads of state, in order to emphasize the importance of the letters and to make it clear that they came personally from me.

From the beginning, I realized that my ability to govern well would depend upon my mastery of the extremely important issues I faced. I wanted to learn as much as possible and devoted full time to it, just as I had done as a young submarine officer, a businessman, a governor, and a political candidate running against enormous odds to be elected President. There was always plenty of help available to me when I was unfamiliar with a subject.

Cabinet meeting, November 1978

∽

If you look at the Cabinet makeup, you'll see the breadth of their experience, geography and background, their knowledge of Washington, . . . of international affairs. It's very broad and very impressive. So I have not felt limited in understanding the international or the national scene excessively.

PRESS INTERVIEW, NOVEMBER 5, 1980

At the beginning, I decided to meet frequently with my entire Cabinet, and scheduled two-hour sessions every Monday morning. These meetings gave all of us a chance to know one another better and develop consistent policies—and at the same time to learn about the individual responsibilities of the men and women around the table.

It was interesting, for instance, to see the interrelationship between the Departments of State and Agriculture, whose responsibilities overlapped in dealing with foreign trade and with supply and market prices of grain and other agricultural commodities; or between Treasury and Housing and Urban Development, as financial policy affected interest rates and therefore home construction.

One persisting problem was keeping people out of the Cabinet

Room! It was not only a matter of interest, but a great symbol of prestige for any member of my staff or the directors of minor agencies to meet with us. Finally, I had to intervene personally and use my full authority to hold the group down to a reasonable size.

A lot has been written by political analysts about how Presidents should deal with top staff and executive officers. I found through experience that a collegial approach—with a group discussing the issue as equals—is good, provided the gathering includes primarily those who will be directly involved in carrying out the decision or explaining it to the public. Most often, the smaller the number of people, the more productive the discussion. A President's time is too precious to waste on many bull sessions among those who have little to contribute; but I cannot deny that, even knowing this, I sometimes permitted people to come into a discussion just so they would not be embarrassed or upset about being excluded.

A more serious problem was leaks. At the beginning of the administration, I considered opening Cabinet meetings to the press. Several of the members objected that they would be inhibited in expressing their frank opinions if these were immediately revealed to the public. I finally agreed with them, but we later found that most of our deliberations reached the press after each meeting, often in a highly distorted form. There were times when I thought that we would have been better off publishing the minutes.

We could not solve the problem of deliberate leaks. After Watergate, it seemed that every subordinate functionary in government wanted to be Deep Throat. Most major policy decisions are made after being researched and assessed in depth within the departments involved. During the early days of consideration, when a matter was not likely to have been studied thoroughly within the Oval Office, I was always careful to avoid making any public statement. Sooner or later, though, I would see news reports beginning, "Carter is considering . . ." or, "The President believes . . ." Many times I would not be at all familiar with the question, much less the possible answers. Often the reporter would make no attempt to verify the story by asking anyone in authority. When told that the source was mistaken, the reporter was likely to respond with another headline, "Administration Confused About . . ." or "Carter Reverses Policy on . . ." Some leakers were motivated by a desire to feel important, to try to shape policy through the early news reports, or to ingratiate themselves with the reporters who cover the White House, Congress, or the departments involved. Obviously, the less authority or responsibility those leakers had, the more likely it was that there would be errors in the stories they handed over. There were also a few times when I felt that stories were deliberately planted by press officers or aides in order to make their own bosses look good.

We never did find an effective way to deal with the situation. It was bothersome, but when I thought back over the experiences of Presidents Johnson and Nixon, my problems with leaks didn't seem so serious after all.

After a few months, the Cabinet meetings became less necessary. We stopped meeting as often, substituting instead smaller sessions restricted to either domestic or foreign issues or to a single subject of interest to several departments. As a result, in the first year we had thirty-six sessions with the full Cabinet; then, during the three succeeding years, twenty-three, nine, and six such meetings respectively.

Only as I got involved with foreign leaders on sensitive issues did I realize fully my own relative advantages in working with Cabinet members who serve at the pleasure of the President. In a showdown, once a decision was made, they had to be loyal to me—or resign. Within parliamentary governments, the key members of a cabinet are often leaders of opposing parties or factions; these partners can only be carefully consulted by the prime minister, not ordered to take action on an unpopular or controversial issue.

I encouraged my top advisers to be quite free in their counsel to me, and on routine matters I gave them an opportunity to appeal after they were informed about my intended decision. But once I made a final judgment, I expected them to honor it even if they had strongly advised a different course of action.

With rare exception, I was well pleased with the original members of my administration. More than thirty months passed before I replaced a Cabinet member—which made my Cabinet the most stable in modern American history.

In July 1979, I named six new department heads. Four of them were already part of the administration—Patricia Harris, Health, Education and Welfare; G. William Miller, Treasury; Benjamin Civiletti, Justice; and Charles Duncan, Energy. Moon Landrieu, Housing and Urban Development, and Neil Goldschmidt, Transportation, were new additions.

Shirley Hufstedler became the first Secretary of Education in November 1979. The next month, Philip Klutznick was confirmed as Secretary of Commerce. Ed Muskie, in April 1980, became the final addition to the Cabinet as Secretary of State.

Replacements to Cabinet-level posts included James McIntyre, Director of the Office of Management and Budget; Don McHenry, United Nations Ambassador, and Reubin Askew, Special Trade Representative.

At times it was necessary to bring people of special experience into the White House. These included Lloyd Cutler, Counsel to the President; Hedley Donovan, Senior Adviser; Alfred Kahn, Assistant on Inflation; Al McDonald, Assistant and Staff Director; Sarah Weddington, Assistant; Anne Wexler, Assistant; Phil Wise, Appointments Secretary; Stephen Aiello, Special Assistant for Ethnic Affairs; Ray Jenkins, Special Assistant; Louis Martin, Special Assistant; Al Moses, Special Adviser; Esteban Torres, Special Assistant for Hispanic Affairs; and Edward Sanders, Senior Adviser. Gene Eidenberg was promoted to Assistant for Intergovernmental Affairs and Secretary to the Cabinet.

The constant press of making lesser appointments was a real headache. Even more than for Cabinet posts, I would be inundated with recommendations from every conceivable source. Cabinet officers, members of Congress, governors and other officials, my key political supporters around the nation, my own staff, family and friends, would all rush forward with proposals and fight to the last minute for their candidates. We had to balance the lists among men and women; Hispanics, blacks, and other ethnic groups; by state, age, and background—and there were always organizations that needed to be represented on special commissions or study groups. These decisions would sometimes develop into mammoth arguments among my staff and with others. Most of the time the contention would not reach the Oval Office, but on occasion, I would be dragged into it. For instance, because so many people were involved in the process, I personally expended far more effort in choosing a chairman for the National Endowment for the Arts than I did in choosing a replacement for Cy Vance as Secretary of State or James Schlesinger as Secretary of Energy.

Although I was surrounded by people eager to help me, my most vivid impression of the Presidency remains the loneliness in which the most difficult decisions had to be made. As a matter of fact, very few easy ones came to my desk. If the answers to a question were obvious, they were provided in a city hall or a state capitol. If they involved national or international affairs and were not particularly controversial, decisions were made at some lower level in government. I delegated as much of this responsibility as possible. A President gets the tough questions, and the more difficult an issue is to resolve, the more likely his advisers are to be equally divided about it and the less eager they are to go on record with an answer that might later be criticized. I tried never to duck the more controversial issues nor to put an onerous responsibility on others when it was rightfully mine. After the laborious staff work and study were completed, I usually made decisions without delay. Option papers describing the choices I had to make rarely stayed on my desk overnight, unless it was necessary for me to consult a few more people.

And I prayed a lot—more than ever before in my life—asking God to give me a clear mind, sound judgment, and wisdom in dealing with affairs that could affect the lives of so many people in our own country and around the world. Although I cannot claim that my decisions were always the best ones, prayer was a great help to me. At least, it removed any possibility of timidity or despair as I faced my daily responsibilities.

AN OUTSIDER
IN
WASHINGTON

MY ONE-WEEK
HONEYMOON WITH
CONGRESS

Everybody has warned me not to take on too many proj-
ects so early in the administration, but it's almost impos-
sible for me to delay something that I see needs to be
done.   DIARY, JANUARY 28, 1977

From that cold morning in January 1975, when I left Plains on my first campaign trip across the United States, until the early morning hours almost two years later, when the final election returns from the state of Mississippi told me that I would be the next President, my confidence never wavered. In fact, what they called the over-confidence of an unknown candidate was the only theme I could stir up among the few news reporters who wrote about my first venture into the national political arena.

This unshakable faith in a final victory affected me in two important ways. It was of great benefit, in that it sustained me many times during weeks when I had every reason for despair. When others around me were discouraged because of our slow progress or lack of funds, their feelings had little adverse effect on me. But my freedom to act and speak during the campaign was severely restrained by the same confidence. I ran as though I would have to govern—always careful about what I promised, and determined not to betray those who gave me their support. Sometimes I irritated my opponents and the news reporters by firmly refusing to respond to questions to which I did not know the answers. And repeatedly I told supporters, "If I ever lie to you, if I ever make a misleading statement, don't vote for me. I would not deserve to be your President." Even during the earliest days I was always thinking about what would have to be done in the Oval Office after the inauguration ceremonies were over.

Of the Presidents who had served during my lifetime, I admired Harry Truman most, and had studied his career more than any other. He was direct and honest, somewhat old-fashioned in his attitudes, bound close to his small hometown roots, courageous in facing serious challenges, and willing to be unpopular if he believed his actions were best for the country. Over the years the American people had come to realize how often his most controversial decisions were, in fact, right. To a surprising degree, many of his problems were still my problems—the Middle East, China, oil and natural gas, Poland, nuclear weapons, Soviet adventurism, human rights, fights with the Democratic party's liberal wing— and I was to see ever more clearly that the judgments he made, or did not make, had a great impact on my own administration.

It was my dream not only to be elected President, but to be a good President. However, I did not wish to go down in the history books as a "great" leader of America who had finally won a war I myself had started. I wanted to maintain peace and meet successfully the challenges our nation would have to face, so the major thrust of my transition effort was toward inventorying the country's problems and determining what should be done about as many of them as possible. At least for me, it was natural to move on many fronts at once.

I took seriously the commitments I had made as a candidate. Peace, human rights, nuclear arms control, and the Middle East had been my major foreign policy concerns. I had also spoken out on issues closer to home: achieving maximum bureaucratic efficiency, reorganizing the government, creating jobs, deregulating major industries, addressing the energy problem, canceling wasteful water projects, welfare and tax reform, environmental quality, restoring the moral fiber of the government, and openness and honesty in dealing with the press and public. It was obvious that our nation would have to resolve many such serious questions, which had long been ignored or deliberately avoided because of the incompatibility of the White House and Congress, fear of special-interest lobbies, or concern about the next election.

One campaign commitment I considered essential was my promise to work well with Congress. We needed to get acquainted, and I took the initiative immediately after Election Day. I knew the Georgia House and Senate delegation in Washington, but only a few other representatives and senators. All the major candidates for President in 1972 had been to the governor's mansion in Atlanta seeking my support. Most of them had spent the night there, and I had always found an hour or two for a private discussion about their campaign plans and current events. (I later found some of them quite different as adversaries in Congress from the eager and friendly candidates who had come to Georgia on their best behavior!) A few members of Congress had run for President in 1976, and others were Democratic legislators I had studied and come to know when choosing a vice-presidential running mate. Except, perhaps, for a brief handshake at a reception, I did not know most of the other members at all, and I was eager to meet them. They were even more curious about me.

Frank Moore, my Assistant for Congressional Liaison, was already hard at work, and Fritz Mondale and his staff were also of great help in introducing me to the world of Capitol Hill. During the transition period, I was able to arrange many long and substantive discussions with congressional leaders about the relationship between the White House and Congress and about ways to work together in carrying out the campaign promises I had made. The first meeting took place on November 17, 1976, two weeks after the election, at Talmadge Farm, the home of Georgia's senior senator, Herman Talmadge. It was interesting and exciting for me to talk politics and government with these congressional leaders and to see them gamely eating a delicious Southern lunch—cheese grits and country ham. Those attending were Senators Talmadge (our host), Mike Mansfield (the retiring Majority Leader), Robert Byrd (who would later be elected Majority Leader), Hubert Humphrey, Ed Muskie, Gaylord Nelson, Alan Cranston, Floyd Haskell, and Russell Long; and Representatives Tip O'Neill (who was to be the next Speaker), James Delaney, Al Ullman, George Mahon, Brock Adams, and Andrew Young. (The latter two I would ask to join the Administration.) I had wanted to invite a few of the Republican leaders as well, which was all right with the senators, but Tip O'Neill objected strongly. He insisted that in the House, the Republicans ordinarily played the role of obstructionists, and that we would have much more productive planning sessions without them. (The Democratic majority in the House was 292 to 143 Republicans; in the Senate, 61 to 38, with one Independent.) These Democratic leaders were very supportive; I came away feeling that all of us were pleased with our mutual pledges of cooperation for the coming year.

During the transition months, I made several trips to Washington, meeting with the Foreign Relations Committees of the House and Senate, the Republican leaders of both Houses, and with the chairmen of other Senate committees. I also continued my talks with key legislators in Plains. Senator Jackson came down to consult with me on SALT (Strategic Arms Limitation Talks), and to give advice concerning national defense and energy matters. Senator John Glenn helped me devise legislative strategy to prevent proliferation of nuclear explosives among nations not yet part of this exclusive "club." The Black Caucus members discussed social legislation and possible ways to change the judicial appointment procedure in order to bring to the federal bench some judges who were black, Hispanic, or female. Ways and Means Committee Chairman Al Ullman visited in our home for an afternoon session. We had to provide him with a toothbrush, razor, and a quick home-laundering job when he stayed overnight to continue our discussions. On January 7, I had an all-day meeting at my mother's Pond House with the Democratic leadership, including the chairmen of all the financial committees of Congress, to map out our policy on jobs, the budget, and taxes.

Four days later, I went to Washington once more, for a full day's session at the Smithsonian Institution with all the members of both parties in Congress who served on any committee involved with foreign policy. Walter Mondale, my top staff members, and the newly designated Cabinet officers also attended. No President-elect had ever held such a conference. We covered the gamut of issues in international relations we would face together. These extensive discussions allowed me to learn more about the congressional committee structure, to size up the individual members, and to let my diplomatic and defense teams learn from and be known by the leaders of Congress.

Although all these and other sessions in Washington were relatively harmonious, press interviews and other statements made it obvious that the overwhelming Democratic majority in both Houses was not about to embrace me as a long-awaited ally in the Executive Branch. Several of the top leaders thought they should have been President, and the Democratic political campaigns of the last decade had engendered splits in our party between the liberals and conservatives that would prove impossible to heal. Neither group was confident that I was a member of its faction. My election victory had been a narrow one; it was generally doubted that I had a broad public mandate to carry out the programs I had espoused. But the most important reason for the conflicts between me and Congress was the extremely controversial matters we would have to address, such as energy, the Panama Canal treaties, stringent budgets, government reorganization, deregulation of major industries, civil service reform, Rhodesia–Zimbabwe, and SALT. Few of these were likely to arouse in the public the strong enthusiasm necessary for forcing unity among the contending factions in Washington—even within my own political party.

Since I had run my entire campaign on the very popular political theme that I was not part of the Washington "mess," I understood that much of the responsibility would have to be mine in developing better rapport. In the Ford Administration, the relationship of the branches had primarily been one of confrontation and a series of overridden vetoes, with little substantive consultation and few results. I was determined not to repeat this practice, but I quickly learned that it is a lot easier to hold a meeting, reach a tentative agreement, or make a speech than to get a controversial program through Congress.

I found out quickly that some of the animosities and distrust that had been prevalent during the eight years of Republican administration between the White House and Congress were still present, and I've decided to stay as close to the key members of Congress as I can.

DIARY, JANUARY 24, 1977

Some of the Democratic leaders promised me full support in implementing my general platform, but as we began to discuss the hard details, the support often evaporated. I had to seek votes wherever they could be found.

For instance, it was well known that our first major test in Congress would come on a bill authorizing the President to address the problem of the federal bureaucracy—its complexity, its remoteness when people needed help, its intrusiveness when they wanted to be left alone, and its excessive regulation of the major industries to the detriment of consumers. An important achievement of my administration when I was governor of Georgia had been to reorganize the state government, and I was eager to make similar changes in the federal government. I wanted to combine many scattered agencies into one Department of Energy; establish another department for all matters concerning education; deregulate banks, airlines, trucking, communications, and railways; hold down the number of federal employees; reduce paper work; and consolidate or eliminate as many of the small agencies and advisory groups as possible.

A key bill would authorize me to reverse the usual legislative process—to submit reorganization plans to Congress and have them become effective automatically if they were not rejected by either the House or Senate within a certain period of time. The future of this legislation would be determined in the Government Operations Committees in the two Houses of Congress, under Chairmen Jack Brooks and Abraham Ribicoff. After I was elected, Senator Ribicoff immediately offered to help me, but Representative Brooks was against the idea of reorganizing the government through a special bill. He believed it inappropriate, even though similar laws had been enacted since 1949. I had been warned—correctly—that Brooks was a tough adversary, and that it would be almost impossible to defeat him on an issue in his own committee.

On my first trip to Washington after the election, I met with both Brooks and Ribicoff to explain how important I considered this authorization. Reorganization had been a highly publicized campaign promise of mine. I knew from my experience in Georgia that it would be impossible to get a bill through Congress in the normal manner every time I wanted to make a change in the federal bureaucracy. Too many sacred cows would always be disturbed. I needed the shortcut, but I did not make any progress with Jack Brooks. Later, Bert Lance brought Representative Brooks down to see me in Plains so that I could make another effort to convert him, but he came well prepared for our argument.

He had a grin on his face and a briefcase full of records of the Kennedy and Johnson years. He said, "Governor, Lyndon Johnson was the greatest arm-twister Washington has ever seen, and he did not like to get beat on Capitol Hill. Look at this list! He was never successful in getting more than one-third of his proposed reorganization plans through Congress, even with this special procedure. If you win this argument on the legislation, you still won't have anything to show for it."

I was as stubborn as he was. I replied, "Mr. Chairman, this is something I have promised the American people. I've got to have it, and I need your help."

Again our discussion led to a stalemate. I began to envision my first White House initiative ending in a highly publicized defeat only a few days after the new Congress and I took office. Such a turn of events would be a serious blow, and an unfortunate signal of disharmony between the Democratic Congress and the first Democratic President in eight years. I decided to go all out to win this test.

On December 9, I went to Washington to meet with the newly elected leaders of the House, and later invited all the Democratic members of Congress to come to Blair House, which is used as the Washington home of Presidents-elect. The visitors were asked to come in three separate groups, to give me time to ask them individually for their help; tell them how important the reorganization bill was to to the country, to me, and to our party; and to hear their questions and listen to their advice. We tabulated their responses and began to make real progress in gaining support for our proposals. My experience in getting legislative support as a governor was beginning to pay off. However, it became obvious that depending on Democrats alone, we could not win.

I suspected that the Republicans would not be so closely wedded to the existing bureaucracy or the prerogatives of the congressional committees, and that they might even want to be the first to help a new President—and perhaps embarrass the congressional Democrats. My overtures to the House Republicans met with almost instant success, and they were eventually to provide me with the margin of victory. In fact, because of Jack Brooks's opposition, as the new Congress prepared to convene, I could not get any Democratic member to introduce my proposed reorganization legislation! The Republican leaders were eager to do it for me, and only when this became known did my Democratic supporters come forward to help.

It turned out to be a fine legislative triumph—soon forgotten. In spite of strong opposition we prevailed on March 31, 1977. I learned one lasting lesson from this hair-raising experience: it was better to have Jack Brooks on my side than against me. I found him to be an excellent legislator, and went out of my way to work closely with him in the future. We soon became good friends and allies. I consulted with him on all my subsequent reorganization plans; largely because of his support, ten of the eleven bills submitted passed Congress.

I was unsuccessful, however, in my attempts to abolish many of the small and unnecessary agencies, commissions, and boards in the federal bureaucracy. Only a positive action by Congress—rather than the special reorganization act—could have eliminated them.

Most of the Democratic members had never served with a President of their own political party, and their attitude was one of competition rather than cooperation with the White House. I had not been in office a week before the top Democratic leaders in both Houses, Speaker Tip O'Neill and Majority Leader Robert Byrd, were complaining to the press that they were not adequately consulted. It seemed that Congress had an insatiable desire for consultation, which, despite all our efforts, we were never able to meet. It was not for lack of trying. Important committee chairmen were frequent visitors to the White House; and in addition to regular working breakfasts with the elected Democratic leaders in Congress, I held frequent sessions with

Meeting with Byrd, O'Neill, and other congressional leaders

entire committees or larger groups in the Cabinet Room or at the White House. I spent many good evenings having supper and then a lively discussion of domestic and foreign affairs with groups of as many as a hundred members of Congress.

In addition to all these official sessions, I invited the two Democratic leaders as soon as possible to bring their wives to the White House for supper with Rosalynn and me—not to discuss current legislative business, but simply to get acquainted.

Since the Speaker's wife, Millie, was not then living in Washington, Senator Robert Byrd and his wife, Erma, visited us first. I was eager to know the Senator better, for my own political benefit as well as for my personal enjoyment. As the majority leader, he would play an important role in the success or failure of our legislative program, and it was imperative that we understand each other. Having met him on several occasions before the inauguration, I already knew him as a strong, able, and proud man. Completely immersed in the affairs of the Senate, he was a formidable ally or opponent. I was determined that he would be an ally, but this would not always be possible.

Senator Byrd did his homework; he was slow to make a commitment but absolutely trustworthy when he gave his word. He remembered every person who had voted for or against him in the Senate, even back in 1972, when he had mounted a quiet campaign and startled the nation by replacing Edward Kennedy as Democratic Whip. I found Byrd to be somewhat single-minded, preferring to deal with only one major issue at a time. Sometimes he refused even to discuss with me other matters of importance which he thought could be safely postponed. Sensitive about his position, he made certain I paid for my mistake whenever I inadvertently slighted him. He was also ambitious, having been an early candidate for President in 1976—but this comment should not be interpreted as criticism, coming as it does from a Southern governor who had the same ambition.

Tip O'Neill was quite different—from Bob Byrd and from me. He was a member of the old school of Boston politics, with which I was familiar only through my brief and relatively superficial Massachusetts campaign and from reading such novels as *The Last Hurrah*. When he and Millie finally scheduled a private visit, the Speaker let me know at once that he had a genuine respect for the Presidency and a great loyalty to me as the leader of our party. He had felt the same way about President John Kennedy, whose congressional district Tip now represented. Kind and considerate, Tip was always eager to help me with advice or support. Although he was much more liberal than I and flinched visibly whenever we talked about balancing the federal budget or constraining any of the Great Society programs, the Speaker did his best to be faithful to his promise to help me as the leader of our nation.

He had a nearly impossible job trying to deal with a rambunctious Democratic majority that had been reformed out of almost any semblance of discipline or loyalty to him, and on many occasions he and I were to commiserate about the almost anarchic independence of the House. But we particularly relished the times when we could jointly celebrate a legislative victory. On occasion he would call me immediately after a successful effort, to report the result of the House vote. At first, our relationship was somewhat strained because of our different backgrounds and philosophies, but eventually I grew to love this big man.

> *Had breakfast with the congressional leadership. It was fairly harmonious, with Tip pointing out how much more we had achieved than most Presidents, except Roosevelt in his first four months. We've still got a long way to go, in my opinion.* DIARY, MAY 19, 1977

Throughout the 1976 campaign, the most persistent question of the news reporters was, "Are you a liberal or a conservative?"

When forced to answer, I would say that I was a fiscal conservative but quite liberal on such issues as civil rights, environmental quality, and helping people overcome handicaps to lead fruitful lives. My reply did not satisfy them, and sometimes they accused me of being evasive, but it was the most accurate answer I could give in a few words. This was my political philosophy as Georgia's governor, as a presidential candidate, and while I served in the White House—and it has not changed.

I served in state government during the times when we were finally overcoming the regional curse of racial discrimination and when hot competition within our region for new factories and investments was threatening the natural beauty of our state. The key sentence in my inaugural address as governor covered the first issue as clearly and concisely as I knew how. "The time for racial discrimination is over."

Concerning environmental quality, I tried to be equally clear. Like most Southern governors, I spent much of my time recruiting industry, selling Georgia's products, and trying to create jobs in my state. In this effort, however, I always laid down some strict guidelines, telling potential investors, "We don't want you as a new neighbor if you come here looking for cheap labor, special tax privileges, or the right to spoil our environment."

I knew from history and from personal observation how a person, a family, or an entire region could grow and prosper when given a chance to develop and use native ability and ambition. Among the most important goals in the Southern brand of populism was to help the poor and aged, to improve education, and to provide jobs. At the same time the populists tried not to waste money, having almost an obsession about the burden of excessive debt. These same political beliefs—some of them creating inherent conflicts—were to guide me in the Oval Office.

There are few things more debilitating to a person than to be deprived of a job—a chance for self-respect, the realization that one's life is meaningful, the ability to nurture and care for loved ones. During the campaign and at the time I became President, joblessness was our most pressing economic problem. More than eight million Americans were unemployed, and the creation of jobs was a top priority for me. Tip O'Neill, Bob Byrd, and other Democratic leaders agreed that we needed a program to stimulate our lagging economy and put millions of people to work.

By the summer of 1977, we passed an emergency program for needed public works, special youth job and training programs, and an extension of CETA (Comprehensive Employment and Training Act). We pressed forward successfully on these projects throughout my term. By the end of the four years, about ten million new full-time jobs had been created, less than 10 per cent of which involved employment in government. Secretary of Labor Ray Marshall was particularly effective in making the best use of temporary work and of job-training programs, including 1,000,000 summer jobs for young people and more than 700,000 positions in job training and public service for unemployed adults. Although the budget costs of these programs were substantial, the *net* cost of this productive effort was quite small because people who worked stopped receiving welfare and unemployment-compensation payments.

Closely related to employment was improved education—a vital interest of mine throughout my public career. I had sought a seat in the Georgia senate in 1962 primarily because I was concerned about the threats to our system of education. Having served on the County Board of Education for seven years and witnessed at first hand the willingness of some Georgia leaders to destroy the public schools rather than see them become racially integrated, I wanted to help shape government policy so that black and white children would not continue to suffer from it. As a new legislator, my primary request was to be assigned to the Education Committee, where I worked during the two terms I served. As governor, my interest in education continued unabated.

Now, having been elected President, I had another opportunity to give students of all ages a better chance in school. Within the controllable part of the nondefense budget during my term, I was able to double the portion going to education. My administration emphasized the federal government's role in compensatory education—helping to remove inherent inequities among student opportunities that remained even after the best efforts of state and local authorities. In practically all states, the most effective schools were concentrated in the most affluent communities, where the property tax base was sufficient to finance better programs. The worst schools tended to be in areas where deprived families lived and where the need for special attention to many students was greatest. As we worked on this problem by extending and improving the Elementary and Secondary School Act in 1977 and 1978, we also strengthened local control of the schools and cut out many onerous regulations and much of the paper work that had been permitted to evolve over the years. One of my strongest convictions was that every academically qualified student should have the opportunity to attend college. We achieved this ambitious goal before I left office, with additional student-aid programs being phased in during each of the years I served. We were able to increase financial support for education by 25 per cent in constant dollars and to triple college-student loan programs.

When I became President, in spite of the importance of the subject, education was still sometimes treated in Washington as an afterthought or nuisance, discussed at the Cabinet level mostly when it involved lawsuits concerning equal rights for black, Hispanic, handicapped, or female students. Education programs were scattered all over the federal bureaucracy, and there was no way for a coherent policy to be considered or implemented. For those educators who came to Washington to seek help or resolve a question or dispute, it was almost impossible to locate the federal official who was supposed to be responsible.

During the 1976 campaign I had endorsed the idea of creating a cabinet-level department to correct these problems. As President, I continued to support it. Opposed by a variety of people who saw advantages in the existing situation, including HEW Secretary Joe Califano, the formation of this department was delayed until October 1979. The new department, under the clear command of our first Secretary of Education, Shirley Hufstedler, was able to give much better service, to provide a consistent policy, and to eliminate many of the legal disputes that had long plagued the system—all these benefits combined with lower administrative costs and fewer employees.

I considered the creation of jobs and the education of young people a sound investment for the future rather than a simple one-time budget expenditure. It would pay rich dividends—not only in a better life for the people served and for our country as a whole, but in actual receipts coming back into the federal treasury in the form of taxes paid by more prosperous and more productive Americans.

Combined with the progressive philosophy that motivated my initiating these programs was my real determination to reduce the federal budget deficit. I had inherited the largest deficit in history—more than $66 billion—and it was important to me to stop the constantly escalating federal expenditures that tended to drive up interest rates and were one of the root causes of inflation and unemployment. As measured in real or constant valued dollars, I forced federal spending downward, but this effort quickly brought me into a confrontation with some of the leaders in my own party, to whom the phrase "balanced budget" coming from a Democratic President was almost blasphemous. I'd had unexpected success in implementing the first programs to create jobs and stimulate a lagging economy, but after a few months the threat of rising inflation and budget deficits preyed on my mind.

> *The congressional leadership breakfast was devoted almost entirely to expressions on the part of the liberal members Tip O'Neill, Shirley Chisholm, [and] John Brademas that we were neglecting social programs in order to try to balance the budget in four years. I take very strong exception to this. . . . Because the Congress doesn't oppose what we put forward, there's been very little acknowledgment of the progress that we're trying to make. In my opinion there is no way to have available financial resources in two or three years for better health care, etc., if we don't put some tight constraints on unnecessary spending quite early.*   DIARY, MAY 3, 1977

Some of these leaders had been counting on a free-spending policy now that a Democrat was back in the White House, and would not acknowledge that one of the reasons I had been elected was to bring fiscal responsibility to the federal government. Partly because of my campaign statements, public-opinion polls now showed, for the first time, that our party was considered more fiscally responsible than the Republicans. I intended for us to live up to our new reputation.

Less than three months after my inauguration, I had to face a major fiscal and political problem—a turning point—brought about by a resurgent economy and the rapidly building pressures of inflation. In order to stimulate the stagnant economy we inherited, the congressional leaders and I had decided in January on a quick tax rebate of fifty dollars per person, and we had been working to line up the necessary votes for this proposal in Congress. The bill passed the House quite rapidly but was delayed in the Senate. To Budget Director Bert Lance, Treasury Secretary Mike Blumenthal, and me, this rebate now seemed not only unnecessary but likely to spur inflation, a growing threat we had ignored too long. My other advisers were convinced that we should go ahead with it, either because they believed it was necessary or because my reputation for consistency would be damaged if I reversed our earlier decision. In April, I decided to bite the bullet, notify the key members of Congress, and cancel my request for the quick tax reduction.

From then on, the basic course was set, but my advisers were right about the political damage. The obvious inconsistency in my policy during this rapid transition from stimulating the economy to an overall battle against inflation was to plague me for a long time. But I knew I had made the correct decision; for more than three and a half years, my major economic battle would be against inflation, and I would stay on the side of fiscal prudence, restricted budgets, and lower deficits. Discretionary domestic spending, in real dollars, increased less than 1 per cent during my term in office.

> *Had a rough meeting with about 35 members of the Congress on water projects. They are raising Cain because we took those items out of their 1978 budget, but I am determined to push this item as much as possible. A lot of these would be ill advised if they didn't cost anything, but the total estimated cost of them at this point is more than $5 billion, and my guess is that the final cost would be more than twice that amount.*   DIARY, MARCH 10, 1977

I had several serious disagreements with Congress, but the issue of water projects was the one that caused the deepest breach between me and the Democratic leadership. As governor and during my campaign, I had repeatedly emphasized the need to eliminate waste and pork-barrel projects in the federal government. Some of the people had heard and understood what I was saying. The members of Congress had not. They were amazed when I moved to cut out the worst examples of this abuse— unnecessary dams and water projects that would cost billions of dollars and often do more harm than good. The problem was that scores of these plans were in progress, from original conception to the final construction stage. Some of the more senior members had been waiting many years for their particular proposals to get to the top of the list. The projects represented major political plums for each district, tangible symbols of the representative's influence in Washington. For ten or fifteen years, in every congressional campaign, the promise of a new lake or canal was put forward to create temporary construction jobs, satisfy local pride, and win votes.

I understood the importance of these long-awaited projects to the legislators, but during the years since their initial conception, circumstances had changed, environmental considerations had increased in importance, costs and interest charges had skyrocketed, other priorities had become much more urgent, and any original justification for some of the construction had been lost forever. Still the inexorable forces toward final legislative approval moved on. Other recent Presidents, graduates of the congressional system, had looked on the procedure as inviolate. I did not, and dove in head first to reform it.

I demanded that we reassess every proposal to determine if it was still economically and environmentally justified, and insisted that the full price of the dam or canal—instead of merely the first tiny startup costs—should be covered in the budget when the project was first approved. Otherwise, I threatened, I would veto the public-works appropriation bill. There was a furor on Capitol Hill, but I stood fast and began recruiting support among the more junior members of Congress who were not committed to the system (and who had not been there long enough to get a project of their own!). None of the leaders in either House supported me, but I still made some good progress. Though I could not gain a majority, I had enough support to prevent two-thirds of the members from overriding my veto. At the end of the first year, I had won a partial victory, based on a hasty agreement I worked out with Speaker O'Neill.

I made some mistakes in dealing with Congress, and one that I still regret is weakening and compromising that first year on some of these worthless dam projects. The Speaker had called me during the heat of the congressional debate to say, "Mr. President, we have worked out a good compromise on the water projects ... with all of the Senate deletions maintained, no new projects approved, and a reduction of funds for the Clinch River breeder reactor to zero. If you can accept this without a veto, I believe we can get it through the Congress." I thought for a few seconds, considered the progress we had made in changing an outdated public-works system, decided to accommodate the Speaker, and then agreed to his proposal.

This compromise bill should have been vetoed because, despite some attractive features, it still included wasteful items which my congressional supporters and I had opposed. Signing this act was certainly not the worst mistake I ever made, but it was accurately interpreted as a sign of weakness on my part, and I regretted it as much as any budget decision I made as President.

Later, on the issue, I was not so timid. In October 1978, I vetoed the annual public-works bill because it included some of the same water projects. It was rewarding to prevail even though almost every Democratic leader lined up against me, but the battle left deep scars.

85% of the criticism of you during 1977 came from other
Democrats.   STAFF MEMORANDUM TO THE PRESIDENT

I learned the hard way that there was no party loyalty or
discipline when a complicated or controversial issue was at stake—
none. Each legislator had to be wooed and won individually. It
was every member for himself, and the devil take the hindmost!
Well-intended reforms in the organization of Congress and of the
Democratic party had undermined the power of party leaders.
This situation was completely different from the time of Lyndon
Johnson's Presidency, when he, the Speaker of the House, and the
Chairman of the House Ways and Means Committee could agree
on a tax or welfare proposal and be certain the House of Representatives would ratify their decision. The absence of discipline
or consensus within the Democratic party strengthened the influence of special-interest lobbies on the legislative process—a highly
dangerous development.

Citizens have the right to inform elected officials of their opinions on the issues of government. In fact, it can be a public duty.
Oil producers, teachers, lumber companies, veterans, and other
groups should present their perspectives and look out for their
interests. But, ultimately, public officials have to decide what
action to take for the public good.

As the Democratic party has become less able to reward or
punish its members, the rewards and punishments offered by
special interests have increased in importance. By virtue of their
wealth and freedom from regulation, some lobbies can threaten
to or actually unleash almost unlimited television and direct-mail
assaults on uncooperative legislators. At the same time, they can
legally reward those who do their bidding. The lobbies are a
growing menace to our democratic system of government.

For instance, the weapons manufacturers now play a dominant
role in this process, working with their natural allies in the
Pentagon. The resulting purchase of unnecessary military equipment is undoubtedly the most wasteful element in American
government.

The B-1 bomber issue provides a case study of the difficulty in
competing with powerful lobbyists, as well as with forces within
Congress itself. Whether or not to build a fleet of these airplanes
was a very important and controversial question, involving great
budget expenditures but also the military defense of our country.
I was required by law to address it.

For years, the bomber had been the subject of intense debate.
Should we or should we not commit ourselves to a massive

program of building and deploying another manned bomber? I soon understood why Congress and previous Presidents had been unable to make a final and binding judgment on the matter.

I was well aware that the B-1 lobby was one of the most formidable ever evolved in the military–industrial community. Four B-1 prototypes had been built, and there was tremendous pressure on Congress to go ahead with plans for an entire fleet. The members of Congress, in the election year of 1976, finally came to a conclusion: let the next President decide. They reserved for themselves the right to reverse the newly elected President's decision once it was made.

Not being thoroughly familiar with the issue when I first took office, I decided to reassess all the factors before making a final judgment. The project already had tremendous momentum, the force of which I had often felt during the 1976 campaign. Whenever I had campaigned anywhere near one of the many potential assembly plants throughout the United States or had a fund-raising reception or talked to a governor or other public official in the community, there was a reminder about the importance of the jobs associated with the building of the B-1 and its subassembly parts. At that time, jobs were a major issue, and the proponents of the bomber were effective in presenting their case to those candidates who had a chance to be elected. However, I knew that it took more than $1 million in taxpayer's money to create each job in the B-1 program, and $100 million to produce each bomber—a Pentagon cost estimate that was almost certain to soar several times over once the project was approved. Throughout the campaign, I resisted the pressure on me to make a premature commitment, but it was not easy.

Even after thorough study of the issue during the spring of 1977 with the help of the Secretary of Defense and the Joint Chiefs of Staff, deciding what to do about the B-1 bomber was still difficult for all of us—not because of the merits of the case, but because of the necessity to prevail against supporters of the B-1 once my decision was made. If I had had absolute power, the answer would have been simple: do not build it, because it would be a gross waste of money. My problem was that I would have to win the argument not merely in the Oval Office, but also in the public arena—indirectly with the American people, and then directly with a majority of Congress. As I studied the arguments, I also spent a lot of time working with key members of Congress and the news media, trying to present the facts to the public.

I was truly thankful for Secretary Harold Brown, whose technical competence, knowledge of the Defense Department, and strength of character made it possible for him to address such a difficult question in an objective manner, with the best interests of our country as the sole criterion.

> *Harold Brown has been very courageous to recommend that the B-1 not be built.*   DIARY, JUNE 24, 1977

It was not only an issue of lobbying pressures or budget waste. There were fundamental strategic considerations involving the future shape of our nation's defense system—whether or not to invest tens of billions of dollars in a manned penetrating bomber that would have as one of its prime tasks delivering short-range weapon attacks against targets within the Soviet Union. This was already a very doubtful mission for a manned bomber, and would most likely be suicidal several years in the future, when the new plane could finally be deployed. We knew that over the years the Soviet Union had invested more than a hundred billion dollars in a continental air-defense system, whose effectiveness was rapidly being improved. With satellite tracking from space and with improved air and ground radar and homing missiles, a manned bomber like the B-1 or B-52 over enemy territory would be extremely vulnerable. Furthermore, there was really not much a human pilot in a B-1 could do in such a situation that could not be done better by electronic control systems preprogrammed to provide pinpoint accuracy, using the latest technology in navigation of planes or missiles.

Was there a better alternative? Yes, there was! There were two developments, in fact, which helped confirm our judgment and which would provide our most persuasive arguments. One was well known to the public; the other was to be our most closely guarded military secret.

The cruise missile, rather than the B-1, could become our new line of attack in maintaining the airborne leg of our nuclear "triad." Along with the ICBM's (intercontinental ballistic missiles), deployed in ground silos, and our submarine-launched ballistic missiles, our nation also needed to maintain the capability of delivering an airborne attack during the follow-up phase of any nuclear exchange. This capability is a significant factor in deterring such a war and provides our country and the Soviets with the sure knowledge that some future technological breakthrough concerning antisubmarine warfare or defense against ballistic missiles will not leave the United States vulnerable to potential Soviet blackmail. The relatively inexpensive and highly accurate cruise missile meets this need. More than a hundred could be produced for the cost of each B-1 bomber, and these missiles were already being successfully tested in flight. They could be launched far from their target, from land, surface ships, submarines, or a "mother" plane. In effect, a swarm of cruise missiles, once launched, could not be intercepted short of their multiple targets. Even a fairly high attrition rate would leave a large number to conclude a successful mission. These facts were widely accepted among those responsible for our nation's defense, and well known to the Soviet leaders, who proved it by struggling so hard during the SALT negotiations to outlaw cruise missiles.

The other development, known to very few, was even more important; if successful, it could revolutionize aerial warfare. Almost all air-defense systems, including the elaborate Soviet installations, are dependent upon radar to detect flying targets, either manned aircraft or missiles. Once the attacking vehicle is detected, it can be destroyed by a short-range system using various means of tracking. In most cases, radar is the key. Our secret development would make a plane or cruise missile almost completely invisible to radar, and therefore practically invulnerable to the prevailing systems for detection and destruction. This would be a technological development of the most profound significance.

Whenever we discussed this program, we cleared the Oval Office of everyone not specifically required to be there, and ordered the room "swept" with detection devices to eliminate any possibility of electronic eavesdropping. In these tightly guarded discussions we referred to the program as the "stealth" system. When I decided not to proceed with the B-1, we did not yet know whether "stealth" would be successful, but our hopes were soon realized. The tests were increasingly encouraging, particularly with the smaller cruise missiles on which they were first conducted.

Because of the need for utmost secrecy during this developmental stage, we could not use the "stealth" information to help make our case against the supporters of the B-1. Other arguments had to suffice—and they did. Logic finally prevailed, and the right decision was made: the B-1 should not be built. I have no doubt that it was the correct decision, supported by the Secretary of Defense, key military leaders, and a majority of Congress.

But the enormous B-1 lobbying octopus was still alive and writhing. It would live to fight again after I left the White House.

Defense was not the only area where I faced formidable lobbies. Many of the controversial problems I had committed myself to solving affected powerful interests. Often I prevailed, but on several important issues I failed to gain congressional approval for my proposals. The loss of three in particular—welfare and tax reform and a national health program—were a great disappointment to me. My staff, my Cabinet, and I laboriously evolved a complete revision of the welfare system, designed to simplify the program and, through temporary public-service jobs and tax reductions for low-income workers, to move almost two million welfare-dependent people into productive employment.

I found through bitter experience, however, that *any* tax proposal—including our welfare and tax reform packages—attracted to Capitol Hill a pack of powerful and ravenous wolves, determined to secure for themselves additional benefits at the expense of other Americans. Whenever tax measures were considered, we found ourselves fortunate if we left Congress with the same hide we wore in. It was a perennial temptation for Congress to pass tax legislation that was a Christmas tree full of goodies for special interests.

In this insidious game, the number of votes available to the sponsors of a tax bill were almost exactly proportional to the number of loopholes added to the legislation. A doubtful group of representatives would say, "Well, I don't like the bill very much. It doesn't help the miners [loggers, catfish growers, homebuilders, steel industry, beekeepers, oil drillers, small businessmen], and there are a lot of them in my district." The sponsors get the word, the list of congressional supporters grows by a few names, and another little section is added to the bill. The only obstacles in the way of such legislation are the integrity of some staunch and responsible members of Congress (who can quickly become a minority) and the threat of a presidential veto, which may serve to focus the public spotlight on a giveaway bill. Only repeated threats of my veto prevented the greedy lobbyists from reaching their goals.

The tax issues were extremely complicated and difficult to explain to the public, and with the pressure of so many other simultaneous tasks, we were never successful in focusing sufficient attention on them to implement this important reform. I simply failed to marshal enough support from the American public to counter the other pressures on Congress. We had proposed to Congress substantial improvements in the income-tax laws that would have reduced taxes further and eliminated some of the gross inequities, but throughout my term it was all we could do to hold our own and prevent the tax relief avalanche that was always ready to descend and wipe out, with even more loopholes, any chance for responsible budgeting. In the end, we considered ourselves fortunate that a massive tax giveaway program was not passed over my veto. (As soon as I left office, the special interests were successful in implementing proposals far worse than those which had been considered by Congress while I was President.)

On national health insurance, our failure derived both from lobbyists and from Democratic party politics. Although American medical skill is among the best in the world, we have an abominable system in this country for the delivery of health care, with gross inequities toward the poor—particularly the working poor—and profiteering by many hospitals and some medical doctors, who prey on the vulnerability of the ill. The buffer between expensive medical care and patients' ability to pay at the time of illness is provided by insurers, who collect premiums large enough to finance such a system and still retain an adequate profit for themselves. After paying insurance premiums for a time, many people have no hesitation about unnecessarily entering a hospital, receiving expensive diagnoses while they are there, staying an extra day or two, and accepting the most elaborate service and treatment. Some even see it as a way to get back their investment in the insurance premiums. At that point, both doctors and hospital owners benefit, while the patient is an unwitting contributor to higher medical costs and inequitable distribution of medical care. From the enormous profits, unnecessary hospital facilities can be built; the cost of the empty beds and underutilized equipment is financed by the public through higher taxes to pay for Medicaid and Medicare, plus bigger hospital bills and insurance premiums for private care. Normal competitive restraints on excessive costs are almost nonexistent.

Few Americans realize how much we are paying each year for this inefficiency. Major studies conducted in 1978 revealed that per-capita cost of health care was almost $1000 per year, and these costs were doubling every six years! In some industries employing skilled workers, health-care payments for each employee were more than $3000 per year, further stimulating inflation by adding greatly to the price of whatever goods these workers were producing. Every year, the average working American spends more than a full month's wages on health care; the total amounts to almost 10 per cent of our gross national product.

Of course, many families cannot afford insurance coverage, and a serious illness can be devastating to them. Medicaid and Medicare are of great help, but with the exception of the aged and those who are disabled or poor enough to be on welfare, Americans are not eligible for public assistance that could provide for adequate medicines, hospital care, or treatment by a physician.

One of my goals as President was to correct some of these

deficiencies. My advisers and I struggled for months to provide a comprehensive health-care system for our country. Ironically, one of the major obstacles—which we were never able to overcome— was the opposition to our proposals by Senator Edward Kennedy, one of the most outspoken proponents of national health insurance and, because of his key committee assignments, able to block almost any health legislation of which he does not approve. In effect, he insisted on his own plan or nothing at all.

What the Massachusetts Senator had proposed was an enormously complicated program run entirely by the federal government, with an annual price tag estimated even then as at least $100 billion—and perhaps twice as much. Some of these federal expenditures would replace what was already being spent by private sources. Kennedy had the long-standing support of some labor leaders and senior-citizens organizations, but even after ten years or so, he had never been able to put his ideas into acceptable legislation that could be moved out of his own Senate committee.

I needed the united support of these same organized groups, and sought to convince them and the Senator that the best approach was a comprehensive system passed into law and then phased into operation as the federal budget could accommodate the costs. I wanted to emphasize the prevention of disease, outpatient care, priority attention to a complete health program for infants and young children, restraints on hospital charges, and "catastrophic" insurance to cover extraordinary medical expenses within any family in the land. Instead of the federal government's taking over all the responsibility, I advocated preserving the existing employer–employee relationships and setting basic standards that would permit private insurers to continue providing health coverage. Each family would pay some reasonable portion of the bills, depending on its ability, in order to hold down the overall cost and prevent abuse by those who might be tempted to demand unnecessary treatment. These proposals were acceptable to key legislators in both Houses of Congress; with united backing among the supporters of a comprehensive health program, there would have been a good chance to succeed.

I was prepared to announce this set of principles in July 1978, with a commitment that later in the year, after the congressional elections, legislation would be submitted to Congress. After public hearings, a vote on the proposal could come early in 1979. Stu Eizenstat and HEW Secretary Califano had many meetings with Senator Kennedy in order to explain our position and ask for his help. I met with him myself several times, including a final morning session designed to win his support and inform him that the HEW Secretary would make our announcement the next day. He asked that we delay any public statement about our plan long enough for him to study the proposal more thoroughly, and I agreed. We shook hands and parted in fairly good spirits.

Within a few hours, any hope of cooperation was gone. Kennedy held a press conference at three o'clock that afternoon to condemn our plan and to announce that he and his associates would oppose it. There was no prospect of congressional support for his own program, which was announced the following year. It was a tragedy that his unwillingness to cooperate helped spell the doom of any far-reaching reforms of the health-care system.

For most of my term, in a separate but related effort, I fought the hospital and medical lobbyists, trying to initiate hospital-cost containment measures designed to insure adequate health care at a reasonable expense. This was not an unproven idea. Several states had already implemented such a system, with notable results: much lower costs to the patients and adequately sustained profits for the hospitals and doctors.

I was never able to succeed in this effort, which would have saved the American people more than $50 billion (!) in the first five years—after leaving the hospitals free to raise their prices 50 per cent faster than the prevailing inflation rate. In the final showdown, Congress was flooded with money, in the form of campaign contributions from the health industry. As reported by Secretary Califano, the American Medical Association alone (although not affected directly by the hospital-cost containment proposals), contributed an average of more than $8000 to each of the 202 members of the House of Representatives who voted against the bill! Of the 50 members who accepted more than twice this average amount, 48 voted with the health industry. They prevailed, and the American people lost. The fight for equitable health care was one of my major efforts and one of my great disappointments.

There is no doubt that I could have done some things better. With the advantages of hindsight, it now seems that it would have been advisable to have introduced our legislation in much more careful phases—not in such a rush. We would not have accomplished any more, and perhaps less, but my relations with Congress would have been smoother and the image of undue haste and confusion could have been avoided.

Now I can also see more clearly the problems we created for

the legislators. In looking over the list of our proposals that were approved, it was hard to find many goodies for the members to take home. They showed great courage in voting for government reorganization, civil-service reform, ethics reforms, our energy bills, strip-mining controls, deregulation of airlines, trucking, railroads, financial institutions and communications, reduction of international trade barriers, Panama Canal legislation, the new China policy, foreign aid proposals, and—eventually—a sharp reduction in water projects. There was really little in the list to attract constituents, but much to alienate some of the special-interest groups that play such a strong role in financing election campaigns. Senate Minority Leader Howard Baker exclaimed to me on one occasion, "Mr. President, if I vote right many more times I'm going to lose the next election!"

Nevertheless, I did reasonably well in my overall relationship with Congress. In spite of my having to face with them some extremely controversial subjects, *Congressional Quarterly* magazine found that during my four years in office I won approximately three out of four roll-call votes on issues on which I had taken a clear position, and that this support did not vary much from year to year. It was 75 per cent in 1977, 78 per cent in 1978, 77 per cent in 1979, and 75 per cent in 1980. President Lyndon Johnson, the masterful congressional manipulator, had a support score that was only a little higher—82 per cent.

In balance, my feelings toward Congress are mixed. On most issues, the lawmakers treated me well, sometimes under politically difficult circumstances. However, when the interests of powerful lobbyists were at stake, a majority of the members often yielded to a combination of political threats and the blandishments of heavy campaign contributions.

Members of Congress, buffeted from all sides, are much more vulnerable to these groups than is the President. One branch of government must stand fast on a particular issue to prevent the triumph of self-interest at the expense of the public. Even when the system of checks and balances works, a price must sometimes be paid: beneficial legislation may be blocked by the threat of unacceptable amendments that cannot be stomached on both ends of Pennsylvania Avenue at the same time. When Congress and the President succumb to the same pressures and bad legislation is passed, the damage to our nation can be very serious.

Ultimately, something will have to be done to control the influence of special interests. (I refer to those that supported me as well as those that opposed me.) Strict laws on the financing of congressional campaigns and limits on contributions to legislators, such as now apply to Presidents, must be initiated. Obvious political campaigns run against an incumbent by special-interest lobbies should be charged to the candidate they are supporting and included within the limits prescribed for the election. These kinds of reforms must come; in the meantime, we will have to suffer as a nation until the abuses become so outrageous that they cannot be ignored any longer.

Shaping our nation's economy, educating our children, healing the sick, feeding the hungry, conserving our resources, administering justice, and hundreds of other responsibilities are considered by the American people to be the concern of the President. In some cases, he has a major role to play; in others, his is just one among many voices. Domestic issues are the ones that occupy most of his time and over which he has least control. Under our Constitution, the President has much more authority in foreign affairs—and therefore decisions can be made more quickly, more incisively, and usually with more immediate results. There are exceptions, of course—when Congress has to ratify a treaty or when foreign governments cannot be persuaded to agree with American policy. Stalemates can occur, and frustrations mount. However, during most crises in foreign affairs the President can depend on the full support of the public. It is almost impossible to arouse such support among a multiplicity of confusing and sometimes conflicting domestic issues. When he can concentrate his attention on one major thrust to the exclusion of other matters, the President can usually prevail, but such an opportunity seldom arises.

Knowing how confused and fragmented the system is, how intense the forces are that tend to induce ill-advised decisions, and how fallible the leaders who serve in public office, it is almost a miracle how well our nation survives and prospers. The answer lies in the bountiful blessings of our natural and financial resources, the wisdom of the forefathers who shaped our government, and the inherent strength of our people.

I came to the White House understanding some of these processes, and I continued to observe and learn while serving in the nation's highest office. For each of us there are focal points for our political faith—either the resilience of our diverse peoples, the wisdom of the Constitution and its derivative laws and customs, the national spirit of hope and confidence that has shaped our history, or the unchanging religious and moral principles that have always been there to guide America on its course. Sometimes we forget, and even deviate radically from our nation's historic path. But we soon remember the advantages of compassion for the weak, ethical standards, the beauty of our land, peace and human rights, the potential quality of our childrens' lives, and the strength we derive from one another as free people—unfettered except for self-imposed limits. Then we are able to correct our mistakes, repair what we have damaged, and move on to better days.

THE MORAL
EQUIVALENT OF WAR

The energy crisis has not yet overwhelmed us, but it will if
we do not act quickly. It is a problem we will not be able
to solve in the next few years, and it is likely to get
progressively worse through the rest of this century. . . .
Our decision about energy will test the character of the
American people and the ability of the President and the
Congress to govern this nation. This difficult effort will be
the "moral equivalent of war," except that we will be
uniting our efforts to build and not to destroy.

ADDRESS TO THE NATION, APRIL 18, 1977

When I declared the energy effort to be the moral equivalent of war—a phrase coined by William James and suggested to me by Admiral Hyman Rickover—it was impossible for me to imagine the bloody legislative battles we would have to win before the major campaign was over. Throughout my entire term, Congress and I struggled with energy legislation. Despite my frustration, there was never a moment when I did not consider the creation of a national energy policy equal in importance to any other goal we had.

What we finally achieved was vital to the country. There was no doubt in my mind that our national security was at stake. In 1973, at the time of the oil embargo—a crisis soon forgotten—we were importing about 35 per cent of our oil. When I took office almost four years later, our dependence on uncertain foreign oil supplies had grown to almost 50 per cent—about nine million barrels a day. We were the only developed nation without an energy policy, and our total energy consumption was at a record high.

The comprehensive program put into effect during my term has now reversed the movement toward disaster. I would have been proud of its enactment in 1977; in some ways, the bitter four-year struggle that proved necessary made the final victory even sweeter.

Our problems in 1977 were twofold. In the long run, available supplies of oil and natural gas would not be able to meet the growing demand for energy. We owed it to future generations to stop wasting so much energy and to find other sources for fuel —including replenishable supplies from the sun, if possible. The immediate problems were serious enough. Our excessive purchases on the world oil market were helping to force prices ever upward, and spasmodic shortages were damaging to the American economy. We were afflicted with both inflation and unemployment, and there was special suffering among the aged and poor, who could not afford the fuel necessary merely to cook food or keep warm.

The international dangers were also quite obvious. Since both we and our major allies were susceptible to potential political blackmail from the oil-producing nations, our international policy might no longer be free of pressure from foreign forces. Some of the other consumer nations who had little or no energy of their own were especially vulnerable to this threat, and were inclined to modify their foreign policies accordingly.

We desperately needed a comprehensive program that would encourage conservation, more fuel production in the United States, and the long-range development of alternate forms of energy which could begin to replace oil and natural gas in future years. These goals were complicated by the need to protect our environment, to insure equity of economic opportunity among the different regions of our country, and to balance the growing struggle between American consumers and oil producers.

At the same time, we had to consult closely with other nations whose economic interests were entwined with ours. Some were already complaining bitterly because we had not acted to match their newly established energy policies. Our artificially low oil and gas prices were still encouraging waste and preventing the development of other energy sources. Our foreign friends were having to compete with us in the world oil market for supplies that were becoming ever more costly and sometimes scarce. Almost all nations had some form of energy problem, but as one of the greatest oil producers and as the world's champion oil consumer, we affected everyone else by our actions.

Although most Americans did not want to face these unpleasant facts, ignoring them would have had grave consequences. Some of our more militant leaders were already talking about plans to seize foreign oil fields by force if our supplies were cut off again. Many others deeply resented that the greatest nation on earth was being jerked around by a few desert states.

From my earliest days in office, there were serious problems with distribution of fuel even when it was produced within our own country. We had plenty of American natural gas, but it was not going to the right places. That first winter, as we began work with congressional leaders and others on an energy program, the northeastern parts of the country were suffering from a severe shortage of gas. Many schools and factories had to be shut down—another stark reminder of the need for quick and vigorous action.

I went to the areas most damaged by the lack of fuel, both to marshal emergency aid and to arouse Congress. On February 1, less than two weeks after Inauguration Day, the law I sought was passed, giving me extraordinary powers to deal with the natural-gas shortage. Unfortunately, the almost unbelievable speed of Congress in enacting this legislation was not a harbinger of things to come.

Moving with exceeding haste myself, I announced that within ninety days a national energy plan would be made public and sent to Congress for immediate action. This was a major decision— and a controversial one. Because of the short time allowed for completing the project, creating a plan would require maximum coordination among the many agencies involved and would not permit the extensive consultation with congressional leaders that might insure swifter action once our legislation was sent to Capitol Hill. Nevertheless, I felt that the urgency of the issue required such quick action on my part. The plan needed to be completed without delay if Congress was to decide the matter during the first year.

I was more concerned about the difficulty of arousing public support for so complicated a program. First, awareness of the problem had been low; the energy question had rarely come up during the 1976 campaign. Then, on my visit to the areas of gas shortage people had asked me, "Mr. President, is there really a shortage? Aren't the gas companies just holding back supplies to squeeze more money out of us?" The skepticism about oil and gas companies was pervasive, leading many people to doubt the need for any sacrifice or new legislation. This doubt would continue to plague our efforts during the months ahead.

In order to emphasize the importance of the energy problem and to bring it home to the average American family, I devoted my first "fireside chat" to the subject. Wearing a cardigan sweater, I sat by an open fire in the White House library on the night of February 2, 1977, and outlined as clearly as possible what we needed to do together.

Our program will emphasize conservation. The amount of energy being wasted which could be saved is greater than the total energy that we are importing from foreign countries. We will also stress development of our rich coal reserves in an environmentally sound way, we will emphasize research on solar energy and other renewable energy sources, and we will maintain strict safeguards on necessary atomic energy production.

The responsibility for setting energy policy is now split among more than 50 different agencies, departments, and bureaus in the federal government. Later this month, I will ask the Congress for its help in combining many of these agencies in a new energy department to bring order out of chaos. . . . Utility companies must promote conservation and not just consumption. Oil and natural gas companies must be honest with all of us about their reserves and profits. We will find out the difference between real shortages and artificial ones. We will ask private companies to sacrifice, just as private citizens must do. . . . Simply by keeping our thermostats . . . at 65 degrees in the daytime and 55 degrees at night we could save half the current shortage of natural gas. . . . We can meet this energy challenge if the burden is borne fairly among all our people—and if we realize that in order to solve our energy problems we need not sacrifice the quality of our lives.

The problem with natural gas was that, in 1954, Congress had placed a very low ceiling on the price that could be charged when it was transported across a state line. The oil and gas companies were therefore eager to sell as much as possible within the producing states, where the ceiling did not apply, and as little as possible anywhere else. The nonproducing states were always last on the priority list for new gas deliveries. Other restrictive laws applied to domestic oil prices, based primarily on when and how the oil was first discovered. These regulations resulted in an incredibly complicated set of rules, some of them now useless but still enforced.

The proposal by the oil and gas industry for solving our energy shortage was simple: remove all laws and regulations and let the free market control the price and distribution of its products. The problem with this suggestion was that there was no free market or effective competitive forces relating to world oil supplies and prices. Through OPEC, a few oil-producing nations, mostly in the Persian Gulf region, were arbitrarily setting the price and could also greatly affect the level of production. It was a cartel—with such power that these oil kingdoms had already been able to quadruple the price in a few months in 1973, and

would later more than double the price again in 1979. To remove all price restraints would allow OPEC to control both the international market and our domestic oil prices. Except for an oil glut brought about by reduced worldwide demand, there would be no way to escape rapid price increases imposed at the whim of oil producers here and abroad.

We realized that our domestic prices would have to rise in order to stimulate American production and encourage conservation, but the increase needed to be brought about in a predictable and orderly fashion, so that consumers of petroleum products would be protected from unreasonable fuel bills issued by an uncontrolled semimonopoly. Also, the unearned profits from higher prices needed to be shared with the consuming public. Even with such protection, some sacrifice among the people would be required, making it doubly important that our proposed plan be fair.

I already had working with me as a senior White House assistant the best-qualified man we could find to develop this new program and help me sell it to Congress. Just before my first campaign debate with President Ford, Dr. James Schlesinger had called me and offered to help with defense and foreign-policy issues. He was a shrewd analyst of the international scene, and would have been qualified to serve as Secretary of State or to return to his former position as Secretary of Defense. Instead, he and I both understood that when a new Department of Energy was formed, he would be its first secretary. On March 1, I sent to Congress our proposal for the new department, deliberately separating this issue from the omnibus energy legislation that would follow, so that the organizational structure would already be in place when the new policies became law.

Jim had begun work on a national energy plan long before Inauguration Day, and I was confident from the start that he and his team would succeed. However, as the plan evolved, its controversial nature and its inevitable complexity became increasingly apparent. After reading his first draft, I sent him a somewhat critical note.

Our basic & most difficult question is how to raise the price of scarce energy with minimum disruption of our economic system and greater equity in bearing the financial burden. I am not satisfied with your approach. It is extremely complicated (I can't understand it). . . . A crucial element is *simplicity*. Even

perfect equity can't be sold if Americans can't understand it.
Their distrust is exacerbated by complexity.   J.

Jim and I were convinced that we should not present our plan
piecemeal, but reveal it as a well-balanced and complete proposal. Yet, in preparing the legislation, my advisers and I came to
realize that the subject was too complicated to express simply,
and that Congress was really not organized to address a single
subject so sweeping in scope. As the time approached for our
proposal to go to Capitol Hill, I was shocked to learn that it might
have to be considered by as many as seventeen committees and
subcommittees in the House of Representatives.

Speaker Tip O'Neill shared my concerns, and took the extraordinary step of inducing the House to let him appoint a special ad
hoc committee under the leadership of Representative Lud Ashley
of Ohio. It would consider the proposals, following which the
drafted legislation would be referred back to the five major committees, revised further, and sent to the floor for debate and a
final vote. This was the first major problem on which I had to
work closely with the Speaker, and it was gratifying to observe
his eagerness to overcome the seemingly insurmountable organizational problems he had to face. Because the rules of the Senate
precluded a similar approach by Majority Leader Robert Byrd, it
was inevitable that the Senate would be considering at least five
bills simultaneously. There, the two most important committees
would be Energy and Natural Resources, headed by Senator Henry
Jackson of Washington, and Finance, whose chairman was Senator Russell Long of Louisiana. Since both these men were strong-
willed and jealous of their own legislative prerogatives, some
personal conflict was inevitable.

In order to give individual members of Congress maximum
encouragement from the folks back home and help them resist
the onslaught of lobbyists, I needed to arouse and sustain public
interest in the energy issue. Following the fireside chat, I began a
series of public forums within the White House and around the
country to emphasize the importance of the legislation. It was
like pulling teeth to convince the people of America that we had a
serious problem in the face of apparently plentiful supplies, or
that they should be willing to make some sacrifices or change their
habits to meet a challenge which, for the moment, was not evident.

On April 18, 1977, I addressed the nation on the energy crisis.
Two days later, I presented my energy plan to a joint session of
Congress. It was my first visit to the House chamber. At the

beginning of my speech, I stated that because of the nature of the subject, I did not expect applause. This was one time Congress lived up to my expectations.

We continued to meet with the key members of both Houses of Congress, trying to gain support for our proposals. Predictably, those from oil-producing states were intensely interested in the legislation; I knew that Senator Long would be a key figure in determining whether it would pass or fail.

> *I talked to Senator Long again ... and asked him to come up and meet me later on in the day, which he did. Senator Long is one of the shrewdest legislative tacticians who has ever lived. He always takes the attitude that he's innocent, doesn't quite know what is going on, and the other senators put things over on him, but that he'll do the best he can. He's a shrewd negotiator, and I like him.*
>
> DIARY, APRIL 21, 1977

I did like him, but I soon learned that he and the other senators from oil-producing states were busy plotting strategy to short-circuit our plans and substitute legislation of their own, some of which was being drafted by the law firms representing the nation's oil companies.

As is often the case, the opposition forces were not very much in evidence at first, and the House finished its work on the omnibus bill expeditiously, with a final vote on our entire proposal on August 5. This was a remarkable exhibition of leadership by the Speaker, Chairman Ashley, and others who worked with them. Congress had not seen anything like it in many years. Both Houses of Congress also acted responsibly in approving our plan for a new Department of Energy, and accepted my nomination of Jim Schlesinger as the first secretary.

However, on our proposals for a comprehensive energy policy, we encountered far more serious difficulties in the Senate, where the energy industry lobbies chose to concentrate their attention. They launched a media campaign to convince the public that there really was no problem that could not be overcome if only the oil producers, public utility companies, and nuclear power industry were relieved of government interference and left to run their own business.

In the meantime, their spokesmen in the Senate were forming a quiet coalition with some of the liberals, who were characteristically uncompromising on any of their own demands. They did not want any deregulation of oil or gas prices; the producers wanted instant and complete decontrol. The liberals wanted all increased revenues from higher prices to go to social programs; the producers wanted all the resulting funds retained by the energy companies, to be used for increasing production. The liberals favored solar-power projects as a panacea for the world's energy woes; the oil producers wanted minimum competition from any energy sources they could not control. Some consumer groups saw expensive gasoline and restrictive legislation as essential for the elimination of the large gas-guzzling vehicles; the automobile companies wanted low fuel prices and no restraints on the size or style of cars. One group wanted to do away with all nuclear power plants; another wanted to remove the existing safety regulations, which, it claimed, were hamstringing the industry. The environmentalists wanted ever stricter air pollution standards; the coal producers, utility companies, and automobile manufacturers wanted to eliminate those we already had.

For a variety of conflicting reasons, all these powerful groups rejected the balanced legislation we introduced. Their combined strength constituted an ample majority in the Senate. The division of the United States into energy producing and consuming regions also insured an equivalent division in Congress.

Our only hope was to take our case to the public and work to produce acceptable legislative compromises that could attract a bare majority of votes and still preserve the benefits of our original proposals.

The influence of the special interest lobbies is almost unbelievable, particularly from the automobile and oil industries. DIARY, JUNE 9, 1977

The weeks dragged on. By the middle of October, the scheduled end of the congressional year had passed with the Senate work still unfinished. It looked as if the senators would produce five separate energy bills—but not in the forms I wanted. Key provisions concerning gas decontrol and taxation were altered to make them much more to the liking of the oil companies. All this new language bore little resemblance to our proposals, which had been passed virtually intact by the House. Any conference committees that might be formed would still face a formidable task in trying to get both Houses to agree on exactly the same bill. Nevertheless, the congressional leaders concurred with me that the work must be completed before final adjournment, and the legislative calendars were cleared of other important business to permit uninterrupted work on energy.

Tempers in the Senate were running high on both substantive and jurisdictional questions. Whose committee would play the lead role—Jackson's or Long's? They were unable to resolve their dispute within the Senate chambers. At the suggestion of the Democratic congressional leaders, I decided to bring the two contending committee chairmen together in the White House, hoping this maneuver would ease the strain.

It didn't work.

> *Met with the congressional leaders for breakfast, and we discussed almost exclusively the energy legislation. I particularly wanted Scoop Jackson and Russell Long there, so that we could have it out among a group of Democrats concerning their differences, which are very deep and personal. I thought Russell acted very moderately and like a gentleman, but Scoop ... was at his worst. ... At the same time, he is supporting my positions much more closely than Russell is. ... Long said he would recommit the bill to committee if the Jackson amendments pass, and Jackson said he would call for recommitment if his amendments fail. And of course, recommitting the bill to the Finance Committee would kill it.*
>
> DIARY, OCTOBER 25, 1977

The primary argument was about a natural-gas law. Both committees had produced their own separate bills on the subject. In addition to wanting his legislation approved by the Senate, Long also wanted to keep his "negotiating points"—provisions highly favorable to the energy companies—some of which he claimed to be willing to trade away in conference with the House in order to protect other parts of the Senate bills. Of course, this process would also leave him the undisputed conference spokesman on the most vital questions. Jackson wanted either his own bill or major amendments in the Finance Committee bill. After heated debate, Long finally prevailed and the Senate passed the last bill on October 31.

Now we had one good House bill and five separate Senate bills—one each to phase out natural-gas price controls, favor increased use of coal instead of oil and gas, provide tax breaks for those who would use energy more efficiently, reform electric utility rates, and encourage other means of conserving energy. The most divisive issue was decontrol of natural-gas prices, with the Senate narrowly in favor of removing the limits on the price of gas.

The conferees were ready to begin their most concentrated work. Unfortunately, in trying to be fair to both consumers and the oil companies, the leaders in both Houses formed conference committees whose members were *exactly* divided on the most controversial issues. For instance, all 18 members of the Senate Energy Committee, divided 9 to 9 on decontrol, were appointed as the conferees!

We kept plugging away without much success. By December 15, agreement had been reached on only the three bills that had come from Jackson's Energy and Natural Resources Committee—conservation, coal conversion, and electricity rates. The final versions were close enough to our original proposals to be acceptable. The Senate refused to consider the tax measures until after a decision was made on natural-gas decontrol. Because we did not want to split up the entire package and permit a crippling postponement of the more difficult and important parts, we had given our encouragement to the House when it refused to vote on just three-fifths of the total package. We felt certain that if we accepted the three relatively attractive and popular bills, we would never get the other two. No basis for further compromise could be found, so Congress adjourned without passing any of the bills. The deadlock would have to be resolved in 1978.

It was one of my few major disappointments of the year, but it was serious, because everyone realized the bills were our most important legislation. *Congressional Quarterly* wrote, "The first session of the 95th Congress could be said to have had two agendas: energy and everything else." On all other domestic issues, I had done extremely well, but on energy I still had a long way to go. At least I had confronted an issue which had been postponed too long—I could now understand why—and the energy issues had become clearly defined.

My first veto came near the end of the session, and it too involved energy. Buried in a $6 billion authorization bill for energy research was $80 million for commencing construction of a nuclear breeder reactor on the Clinch River near Oak Ridge, Tennessee. Because it was enormously expensive and unnecessary, and would open up a new and very dangerous plutonium industry in our country, I was determined to prevent construction of this prototype plant. However, like some water projects and the B-1 bomber, it had a strong life of its own.

This particular veto was not challenged, and Congress later deleted the item from the authorization bill, but by other means the Tennessee congressional delegation and some supporters of the nuclear power industry still managed to sustain a breath of life in the project throughout my term. I was determined that the prototype plant would not be built, but because of our uncertain energy future, I was willing to continue research in all kinds of nuclear technology.

In spite of the upcoming Senate debate on the Panama Canal treaties, I expected quick action on the other two energy bills in 1978, but again I underestimated the opposing forces. Both the conferees in sympathy with consumers and those favoring the energy industries were refusing to budge from their positions, and we had to work day after day to search out mutually acceptable agreements that might attract a slim majority—first in the conference committees and then on the House and Senate floors for final votes. Compromise had become difficult for some conferees because enormous sums of money were involved, philosophical issues were sharply drawn, and it was now a matter of trying to prevail in order to save face.

Our most fruitful efforts were among Southerners and members from the coal and oil producing states, who were at least willing to search for more ways to break the deadlocks. With them, we began to make some progress.

In many cases I feel more at home with the conservative Democratic and Republican members of Congress than I do with the others, although the others, the liberals, vote with me much more often.   DIARY, JANUARY 19, 1978

There were still a sizable number who preferred no legislation at all, and my administration leaders launched a massive lobbying campaign on all sides, trying to overcome the combined opposition from senators representing consuming states, who wanted no deregulation, and from those representing oil states, who wanted instant or very rapid decontrol of prices. For various reasons, strange combinations of conservative and liberal senators— such as Russell Long and Howard Metzenbaum, John Tower and Edward Kennedy, Paul Laxalt and George McGovern, Barry Goldwater and Floyd Haskell—were fighting the bills. In addition, the Washington leaders of the national Chamber of Commerce (for quick decontrol) and the AFL–CIO (against any decontrol) were each working to kill our legislation. Their efforts were concentrated in the Senate, where the main battle was still going on and where the threat of filibusters was always a factor to be considered.

With all this opposition, our only choice was to continue going directly to the public and particularly to increase our efforts to explain our policies to the major economic and political leaders outside of Washington, appealing to their patriotism and sense of public responsibility. During 1977, I had made three television addresses directly to the nation, and another to a joint session of Congress. All were about energy. Several times each week I was bringing to the White House groups of leaders from business, labor, agriculture, finance, transportation, the elderly, international trade, local and state government, the news media, consumer affairs, electric utilities, mining, and the oil and gas industries for briefings and appeals from me, Vice President Mondale, Secretary Schlesinger, Treasury Secretary Blumenthal, Secretary of State Vance, or others. Slowly we won more of them over, and they joined with us in appealing to Congress to act. Vice President Mondale and our entire administration team were working among those members of the House and Senate whose votes might be swayed.

Our efforts continued month after month, with the major unresolved issues still centering on the question of decontrol of natural-gas prices. Tens of billions of dollars were at stake, and the contending forces in the House and Senate were still equally divided, as were the members of the conference committees, who were looking for some compromises which could get a bare majority of votes while proving acceptable to me. We'd had to postpone the issue of deregulating oil prices, but everyone knew that the decision on natural gas would set an extremely significant precedent.

As the summer approached, I was scheduled to go to Germany to meet with the other Western leaders for our annual economic summit conference. This would be a very important meeting. Energy shortages and price surges were causing widespread unemployment and inflation in all our countries, as well as serious imbalances in world trade. Our nation's inability to deal with so crucial a question was becoming an international embarrassment. Again, I asked the congressional leaders to meet with me to see what could be done.

This morning was about as full and frustrating as any I've spent. I met with the energy leaders in the House and Senate to talk to them about the prospects for quick action on our energy proposals. They all said they could finish three of the items quickly, but natural gas would face a filibuster in the Senate. Scoop and Russell got in a shout-

*ing match about the crude-oil tax, which is one item
under Long's committee. . . . But the reason for the meeting was fulfilled when I got all of those who would speak
out to advise me . . . to tell our partners at the Bonn
economic summit meeting that if Congress did not act to
raise the domestic price up to the world level by 1980, then
I would act administratively.*   DIARY, JUNE 22, 1978

The next month, at the economic summit meeting, the leaders
of several countries discussed what each could do to help with the
deteriorating world economic situation. Our extremely cheap oil
prices were still encouraging waste and preventing exploration for
new supplies in the United States. The other leaders knew that
we were struggling to promote conservation and increased production of energy. I told them that we would let American oil
prices rise to the world level, as had been agreed in my meetings
with the members of Congress.

Under the law as it was written, I could decontrol oil prices—a
powerful legislative weapon in my hand to push the opposing
forces to work with us on legislation. If absolutely necessary, I
would do so without the participation of Congress, but this was
not the best way. I needed a demonstration of cooperation and
mutual purpose among all the leaders of our government, and
something would have to be done to share the excess oil profits
with the general public. Back in the United States, I called Senator Russell Long again.

*Russell and Carolyn Long came over for supper, and we
enjoyed being with them. Russell and I did a lot of talking
and sparring around. He is a master at circumlocution,
but it's easier for me to understand him now than before.
He hasn't quite made up his mind on natural gas . . . but
he subtly mentions the sugar problem in Louisiana as
being embarrassing to him and the other members of the
state's congressional delegation. He thinks that within three
or four days he could put together a crude-oil tax, which
he seems to favor—provided all the money can go to
energy production! He has a reverence for his father [Huey
Long, former populist governor of Louisiana] and I think
he has supported us on key foreign issues because he
thinks I'm a populist—and foreign affairs don't concern
him much. It's hard to get down to specific agreements
with him—in fact, impossible. But after our discussions*

in the past, he's always come through and helped us. I
think the evening was a success. DIARY, JULY 25, 1978

In August, however, the arguments were still dragging on. The conferees had reached agreement, but under great pressure from constituent groups, some of them, incredibly, refused to sign their own committee report! I had private meetings with individuals and finally convinced a few of them on each side to yield enough to approve the conference committee reports and send them to the full House and Senate for a vote. Now, finally, we had a good chance to cut the Gordian knot that had prevented action on natural-gas prices since 1954.

The man with the toughest job of all was Jim Schlesinger. He had to be on Capitol Hill every day, spending many long hours with individual members of Congress—attempting to get bare majorities in both Houses in floor votes on issue after issue. The intricate maneuvers and hard trading involved all 535 members of Congress and were difficult at best. In addition, Jim was having to put together the new department, work out a location for it, and move personnel around among the many former independent agencies. With patience and persistence, he gained a vote here and there, sometimes creating ill will in the process. He was always careful to assume full responsibility for the most unpopular proposals, and many of the members would therefore blame Jim for their dissatisfaction. There were enough ruffled feelings to keep all of us busy assuaging bruised egos.

Of course, throughout all this time I was involved in many foreign and domestic affairs. We had an extensive legislative agenda in addition to energy. The Senate had finally ratified the Panama Canal treaties after a bruising fight, but implementing legislation now had to pass both Houses. My quarrel with Congress on water projects was approaching the veto stage, and we were trying to devise a tax-reduction bill that would be fair to all Americans. We were also restructuring the civil-service system and deregulating the airline industry. Some of these controversial issues were further clouded by the impending congressional elections in November. At the same time, many foreign issues were pressing on me. I was trying to work out the most important differences with the Soviets on the SALT treaty and secretly exploring terms for normalization of diplomatic relations with the Chinese.

Late in August 1978, during a temporary lull in congressional activity, I went on a brief vacation in the Grand Tetons. While there, I studied the complicated Middle East issues for the up-coming Camp David meeting with President Sadat and Prime Minister Begin. However, I was forced to return early to Washington because of the imminent threat of losing the natural-gas bill. That crisis was first resolved in the Senate, where we prevailed because of a fine team effort and prodigious work by Senator Robert Byrd. He attached such importance to the passage of this legislation that he told each senator he considered it a direct test of his success or failure as the Senate Majority Leader.

After a few days, we had to face our final showdown—whether the full membership would accept the conference committee report on natural gas, which was the linchpin of our energy proposal. This time the trouble came from the House side, where all the members were up for reelection. After working on the natural-gas legislation for more than sixteen months, some of the more timid representatives had decided it would be best to omit it from the energy package altogether because it was so controversial. Some of its provisions were opposed by labor, consumers, oil and gas producers, the utility companies, and environmentalists! The key House vote would be on whether to consider the entire energy package or split it into several parts. After another round of frantic lobbying, we won this crucial decision by the skin of our teeth.

> *This day has been a nightmare. . . . The crucial vote on energy was 207–206, with the last-minute support of Republican Congressman Tom Evans, who just cracked up afterward when I called him on the phone. The abuse he received from the Republican leadership was excessive, to say the least. Tom had promised me in the Oval Office yesterday that he would vote with us, but it was very difficult for him to keep his promise.*
>
> DIARY, OCTOBER 13, 1978

He was an extremely courageous man—and one who kept his word.

By this time the 1978 elections were imminent, and we were finding it increasingly difficult to get Republican support. In addition to all the other reasons, this was a good opportunity for them to further weaken an already beleaguered Democratic President. Of the 207 votes that kept the bill alive, only 8 came from the Republican side.

Now that the way was cleared for final passage, we had to overcome a last-minute filibuster in the Senate. Finally, about daybreak on Sunday morning, October 15, 1978, all five pieces of the energy legislation were passed by both Houses of Congress, and they adjourned late that afternoon.

The total package was extremely complicated, but far-reaching in its beneficial effect on our nation. The production of gas-guzzling automobiles would be deterred by heavy penalties; electric utility companies could no longer encourage waste of energy with their distorted rate structures and would have to join in a common effort to better insulate buildings; higher efficiency of home appliances would be required; gasahol production and car pooling were promoted with tax incentives; coal production and use were stimulated, along with the use of pollution-control devices; and the carefully phased decontrol of natural-gas prices would bring predictability to the market, increase exploration for new supplies, and reduce waste of this clean-burning fuel. The new bills also included strong encouragement for solar-power development, and tax incentives for the installation of solar units in homes and other buildings. These and many more provisions now became the law of the land.

My administration achieved other energy victories. We had introduced legislation to protect the environmental quality of the land and seas while allowing the production of oil and coal. After many years of stalemated Congresses, new laws were passed, in August 1977 regulating strip mining and in September 1978 controlling the leasing of offshore drilling areas.

Jim Schlesinger and I met to discuss how best to implement the new legislation, of which we were very proud. At the end of our meeting, he said he would like to resign as Secretary now that the new department had been formed and most of the congressional action had been completed. He had been in the midst of the continuing legislative battle for almost two years. "Now, Mr. President, someone who does not bear my scars can do a better job." I refused to accept his resignation, and he agreed to stay on for a few more months. During the next year—1979—we would have to develop the second phase of our energy legislation, including oil price decontrol, taxation of the windfall profits of oil companies, and the development of synthetic fuels. I needed him to continue until this work was done.

It had been an excellent congressional session. All of us in the White House were more experienced in the ways of Washington, Frank Moore had strengthened his congressional liaison staff, and we had learned to bring literally thousands of people to the White House to lobby for our bills and encourage them to influence their own representatives and senators. Our system for monitoring action on Capitol Hill and our understanding of Congress were substantially improved over the previous year, and we had few disappointments.

During the final days of 1978, we deregulated the airlines, reformed the civil-service system, and raised the mandatory retirement age to seventy. Congress also passed a $20 billion tax reduction bill, which we needed but which was unbalanced in favor of the rich and did not include the basic tax reforms I had requested. My first inclination was to veto it, but I was dissuaded by unanimous opposition from my staff and Cabinet advisers. With some misgivings, I finally took their advice and signed the bill.

All the strain, frustration, and hard feelings of the year were quickly forgotten in the glow of adjournment. Senator Robert Byrd came by to see me and said, "I have been in the Congress twenty-seven years and have never seen such a tremendous legislative achievement as the ninety-fifth Congress has realized, nor such good harmony as has existed between us and the President." Democratic House members shared his good feelings. The only slightly discordant note came from Senate Minority Leader Howard Baker, who thought he was criticizing me when he said, "We've got a Democratic President singing a Republican song!" Coming from him, I took it as a kind of compliment.

Our work on energy was far from over. For many years, domestic oil prices had been held artificially low, while imported oil prices had been rising by leaps and bounds. The adverse effect of this federal constraint on free-market forces was threefold: it encouraged waste of an excessively cheap product, it discouraged exploration and production of new oil supplies within the United States, and it kept prices so low that such competing energy sources as solar power and synthetic fuels were underdeveloped. Correcting this situation was particularly difficult because oil products touched so many producers and consumers. I approached the problem with great reluctance and only after months of study.

The battles with Congress over the Panama Canal treaties and energy legislation had been long, drawn-out, and debilitating to the members and to me. Both our standings in the public-opinion polls had plummeted. Furthermore, my repeated calls for action on energy had become aggravating, and were increasingly falling on deaf ears among American citizens. In spite of the subject's crucial importance, the public lacked interest in energy except when long gas lines formed or a sudden price increase made people angry. On those occasions, the blame was focused on me.

> [As President,] you are the personification of problems, and when you address a problem even successfully you become identified with it.
>
> NEWS INTERVIEW, NOVEMBER 13, 1978

After two years of struggle, I really hated to stir up the energy pot all over again, but the phased decontrol of oil prices was too important to be avoided. Under existing law, all price controls on

In the control room at Three Mile Island, April 1, 1979

oil would expire in October 1981, but that law also gave me the authority to remove controls step by step at an earlier date. With the resulting increases in the price of domestic oil, enormous new revenues would be collected by the producers. The primary struggle would be over how much of this money should be retained by the oil companies and how much returned to American consumers.

We were getting new signals that some of America's energy supplies were in doubt. In January 1979, revolution erupted in Iran and world oil supplies were interrupted. On March 28, at Three Mile Island nuclear plant near Harrisburg, Pennsylvania, the worst nuclear-power accident in United States history occurred.

During the winter and early spring, Secretary Schlesinger, my other advisers, and I continued to study the energy question. Under the chairmanship of Stu Eizenstat, twenty representatives of the major government agencies involved met for several hours every day. We also worked with the key members of Congress. I received such varying opinions from them that, late in March, I finally brought in a fairly large group who could represent as many different viewpoints and interests as possible. I particularly wanted them to hear each other. In addition to Speaker Tip O'Neill and Majority Leaders Robert Byrd and Jim Wright, there were the chairmen of major committees—Senator Russell Long (Finance) and Scoop Jackson (Energy), Representative Al Ullman (Ways and Means), John Dingell (Energy), and Richard Bolling (Rules). Senator Wendell Ford of Kentucky spoke for the coal industry, and Senator Frank Church of Idaho for nuclear power. Others were strong advocates for the environmentalists, solar-power proponents, consumers, and the poor.

We talked over the whole situation for about two hours. There was a general sense that an oil tax should be imposed, and that we must act further to expand domestic production, shift to other forms of energy, and improve conservation. The only new theme, really, was higher prices for oil and a big tax on the resulting profits. After listening to the group, I met with my advisers and prepared to go to the nation again with another energy speech—a necessary and thankless task.

The hard fact was that Americans still had to reduce oil consumption, particularly of foreign imports. Duty demanded that I act, but political expediency cried out against it. After assessing all the different proposals and the likely reactions to them, I was certain they would never be adopted by Congress without direct action by me and strong support from the public. The House and Senate members, saturated with the long debates and arguments over the politically unattractive issue, had dug in their heels, even on modest proposals.

On April 5, 1979, I addressed the nation again, to propose a wide range of additional conservation measures. I also announced that I would direct a phased decontrol of oil prices, and asked Congress to pass a windfall-profits tax, most of the proceeds to go into an energy security fund for low-income families, public transportation, and the development of additional energy supplies. At best, there was a cool reception to these ideas. On Capitol Hill, there were moves to take away even the limited authority I already had.

The Prince and Princess of Liechtenstein came by for a photograph, and afterward I had lunch with the Vice President. We discussed ... the energy situation that's developing in the Congress, with almost everybody trying to demagogue decontrol and the windfall-profits tax, and the irresponsibility of the Congress in not giving us authority to handle gasoline rationing and impose conservation measures if necessary in an emergency. The Congress is disgusting on this particular subject.

DIARY, APRIL 30, 1979

I continued to work closely with the members, refraining as best I could from publicly condemning their inaction. Although they had not even touched the oil issue during my term as President, I realized how difficult it had been for them to go along with the decisions I had already made. More and more, I came to see how dismal were our prospects for further reducing oil imports through legislative action.

On June 23, I left for Tokyo on a two-day official visit, to be followed by my third annual economic summit conference, which was to be held there. Throughout the meeting the overriding subject was energy.

This is the first day of the economic summit, and one of the worst days of my diplomatic life. We had specific goals to reach for the conference to be significant: individual nations' commitments to reduce short-term imports; long-term goals after 1985; more coal use, along with environmental quality; nuclear power, with improved safety; individual and collective efforts toward alternative energy supplies; research and development on power projects

and fuel production; an end to the erratic high bidding on
the oil spot market; no stockpiling of oil when supplies are
short; encouragement of worldwide exploration among the
poorer nations; a firm system for fuel allocation by the
International Energy Agency if and when necessary; and
specific monitoring of each nation's performance in reach-
ing the goals it sets for itself.

    The Europeans had locked together in their EC [Euro-
pean Community] meeting at Strasbourg, and were ada-
mantly against any sort of individual national commit-
ment.   DIARY, JUNE 28, 1979

Around the conference table were twenty-two people—the seven leaders, each with their top foreign and finance officers, plus Roy Jenkins, who represented the European Community. As the other leaders spoke, their unanimous point was that price increases in oil and uncertain supplies were the greatest dangers we faced. However, it was obvious that Great Britain, France, Italy, and Germany had all decided in advance that in setting their import goals, they should be considered as a group by the United States, Canada, and Japan, and not as individual nations. Their purpose was obvious—for the Europeans to absorb the rapidly growing oil production in the North Sea and not have to count it in their own countries as imports from foreign governments.

At first the Europeans were lined up unanimously against the rest of us. I felt strongly that we needed to evolve a forceful commitment with specific goals, and to send a clear signal to OPEC and other nations that, if necessary, we were willing to make some sacrifices to achieve those goals.

It was an acrimonious meeting, with the exchange of some uncharacteristically harsh words. The atmosphere carried over into the private luncheon, where only the seven leaders were present.

We then had a luncheon that was very bitter and unpleas-
ant. [German Chancellor] Schmidt got personally abusive
toward me when I pushed the individual target position.
For instance, he alleged that American interference in the
Middle East trying to work for a peace treaty was what
had caused the problems with oil all over the world. We
stayed a long time, but [Japanese Prime Minister Masayoshi]
Ohira eventually proposed a compromise which I thought
everyone accepted—that the European Community later
this year would assign individual quotas to each nation

and would then monitor it. It seemed quite clear to me. But later Schmidt, [British Prime Minister] Thatcher, Jenkins and [Italian Prime Minister Giulio] Andreotti tried to wriggle out of it. Valéry [Giscard d'Estaing] helped hold it together, pointing out that we had reached "a superb agreement based on complete misunderstanding."

DIARY, JUNE 28, 1979

As we discussed economic and political problems over the next day or so and realized how much we had in common, most of the tension dissipated. After Giscard joined forces with me, Ohira, and Joe Clark, Prime Minister of Canada, our positions prevailed in the final communiqué. The European countries and Japan had done much more to conserve energy since the oil shocks of 1973 than had the United States and Canada, but they understood how hard we were now trying to do our part. We all had to take strong action to curb imports and stabilize world prices; our economic survival depended on it. The fact that OPEC had just raised its prices another 60 per cent helped convince everyone that the time for mutual recrimination and evading difficult issues was over.

These leaders were an interesting group. Before the conference, I had already spent two days in Japan with Ohira on my official visit. I had liked him when we first met in 1975, and after he became prime minister, we grew to be personal friends. We cooperated privately and effectively in alleviating special economic and defense problems between our two countries. Our families got along well, we discussed sensitive personal and political issues without restraint or embarrassment, and really enjoyed being together. Along with President Anwar Sadat of Egypt, Ohira was a special friend of mine among the foreign leaders I knew. In my diary I jotted down very brief impressions of the others.

Valéry is a very strong, competent man, still my favorite among the whole [European] group. Helmut is strong, somewhat unstable . . . postures, and drones on, giving economic lessons when others are well aware of what he is saying . . . very popular in his own country. Andreotti— smooth, good politician, compromiser, subtly tries to modify collective positions to get some advantage for Italy. . . . Margaret Thatcher is a tough lady, highly opinionated, strong-willed, cannot admit that she doesn't know something. However, I think she will be a good prime minister for Great Britain. Joe Clark and I got along well, partially because of compatibility between American and Canadian interests. He was clear-headed, had done his homework, protected Canada, but was willing to accommodate others when necessary. Roy Jenkins had as a major goal the boosting of status of the European Community and protecting the Strasbourg decision against any attempts to modify it. The final communiqué, I'm sure, was a disappointment to him. DIARY, JUNE 29, 1979

While I was in Japan, all the news from home was bad. Long gasoline lines were forming at many service stations, first in California and then all over the nation, and worse shortages were threatening. Fuel prices were jumping every week. A wildcat strike among the independent truckers was exacerbating the situation. I was getting most of the blame from the public for these troubles, and my long squabbles with Congress had convinced many people that the Democrats were just not capable of resolving the most difficult issues. Public-opinion polls indicated that my popularity had dropped to a new low.

Although the discussions in Tokyo were fruitful, I was still discouraged about the worldwide energy situation, and about the devastating impact of the exorbitant OPEC price increases on the international economy. Inflation was likely to skyrocket, and recessionary pressures would be very great. We had set stringent targets for ourselves and the other summit nations, which we would have to honor if we were to minimize our future problems.

Rosalynn and I had planned to stop in Hawaii for a few days of rest, but decided instead to return directly to Washington. I immediately met with my economic and energy advisers, and on July 3 went to Camp David to prepare my fifth nationwide address about energy. I carried with me a copy of a public-opinion poll from Pat Caddell dealing with basic American attitudes toward energy and other issues, and his voluminous memorandum that assessed the poll's meaning and significance.

Caddell's polls, I knew from experience, were remarkably accurate. His recent data had persuaded him that the American people had become completely inured to warnings about future energy shortages, convinced that both the government and the oil companies were either incompetent or dishonest—or both. In order for the people to support any energy proposals, the memorandum stated, their attention must somehow be focused on the facts, and the solutions must be cast in the form of a patriotic struggle to overcome a genuine threat to our country. Another recitation of my earlier themes would either put them to sleep or arouse in them a greater level of alienation and rejection.

Pat also seemed certain that the problem transcended the single issue of energy, and applied to the basic relationship between the people and their government and other major institutions; Americans were rapidly losing faith in themselves and in their country. He strongly advised me not to focus only on energy, but to think seriously about addressing this more general subject. I was interested in his analysis, and sent for a copy of the proposed energy speech on which my advisers had been working while I was in Japan.

> *After Rosalynn and I read it over, I told her I couldn't deliver it, that I had already made four speeches to the nation on energy and that they had been increasingly ignored. . . . I had to do something to get the attention of the news media and the public.*
>
> *I placed a conference call to Hamilton, Fritz, Jerry [Rafshoon], and Rex Granum [deputy news secretary] and told them to cancel the speech, that I was not going to make it. They asked what kind of explanation I should give, and I told them I would think about it and later on let Jody know what the reasons were.*
>
> *Rosalynn and I decided before I called the staff that we would stay at Camp David for a few days, and have some people come in whom we trusted to give me advice on where we should go from here. I felt a remarkable sense of relief and renewed confidence after I canceled the speech, and began to shape the thoughts that I would put into next week's work.* DIARY, JULY 4, 1979

I was aware that the public would be wondering what was going on at Camp David but was willing to accept some initial concern and criticism if I could dramatize the importance of the questions I was trying to answer—and also find some answers myself. These next few days were destined to be some of the most thought-provoking and satisfying of my Presidency.

No staff member was enthusiastic about my plans, but most came around when they realized I would not change my mind. Vice President Mondale was an exception. I grew quite concerned about him. He was distraught, and could not become reconciled to my abruptly canceling the speech and then methodically bringing in groups of advisers to help me make further plans while the nation was in a quandary about my intentions. It was an unorthodox thing to do, and he was convinced that it would result in political catastrophe. He and I walked around the perimeter fence surrounding Camp David, as I tried to calm him down and persuade him that we were doing the right thing. I had only partial success, convincing him to support my decision even though he could not agree with it.

Most of my advisers, including Fritz, told me that if I was determined to reassess my administration, then I also had to be prepared to make some major changes in my Cabinet. I did not see that this was necessary and argued against the idea. I was told that Schlesinger, Califano, and Blumenthal should be replaced—particularly the latter two, who were said to be both incompatible with the White House staff and ineffective when dealing with Congress. Reluctantly, I agreed to ask for opinions on the makeup of my Cabinet from some of the people with whom I would be meeting.

I had decided to invite to Camp David small groups of key advisers—governors, local officials, members of Congress, executives from business and labor, economists and energy experts, religious leaders, a small group of experienced political advisers, and some of the most senior and respected news reporters. I wanted them to spend some time with me, so that we could have leisurely conversations about our nation, my administration, and the serious problems we faced, including the important subject of energy.

One of the most extensive and helpful sessions was with a small group of senior political advisers: Charles Kirbo; Clark Clifford and Sol Linowitz, Washington attorneys; Lane Kirkland, AFL–CIO leader; John Gardner, President of Common Cause; Jesse Jackson, black activist leader; Barbara Newell, President of Wellesley College; and Bob Keefe, professional political organizer. With the exception of Ms. Newell, I had known these people for several years. We began our discussion in the late afternoon, continued through supper, and after the meal went to my cabin and talked until late in the night. Once they realized that I really wanted them to be completely frank, we all relaxed and exchanged views without restraint. Hamilton and Jody were with us. Most of the time, I sat on the floor, propped against a cushion, and took careful note of their advice.

First, we discussed the Cabinet, one by one. Everyone believed that Jim Schlesinger had exhausted his usefulness during the long and bitter struggles with Congress over the energy legislation. I told them that Jim agreed with their assessment and had twice asked me to let him resign. The group felt that although Mike Blumenthal had a good reputation in the business community, he had too much difficulty in working harmoniously with other leaders in my administration and with Congress. They were especially critical of Joe Califano, saying that he was not loyal to me and was almost completely ineffective in getting his legislative proposals approved on Capitol Hill. One of them defended Joe, saying that at least he was overt in pursuing his own goals instead of mine and was making no attempt to conceal his independence.

Then I asked Ham and Jody to leave, as we turned our attention to the staff. The group agreed that my White House team was competent, but thought that it was impossible for the press or public to acknowledge it because most of those around me had an air of immaturity about them. The strong advice of everyone present was that I bring in some more mature and substantive people to strengthen my personal staff.

Their criticisms of me were the most severe, questioning my ability to deal with the existing problems of the nation without bringing about some change in public perceptions. They told me that I seemed bogged down in the details of administration, and that the public was disillusioned in having to face intractable problems like energy shortages and growing inflation after their expectations had been so elevated at the time of my election. On the one hand, I was involved in too many things simultaneously, but, in some cases, I had delegated too much authority to my Cabinet members. The consensus was that the public acknowledged my intelligence and integrity, my ability to articulate problems and to devise good solutions to them, but doubted my capacity to follow through with a strong enough thrust to succeed. Most of this doubt about me had arisen from the struggle over energy, with my repeated exhortations and lack of final action by Congress. It was not pleasant for me to hear this, but I felt their analysis was sound.

They thought the relationship between the White House staff and the White House press corps was especially bad and, that in spite of Jody Powell's efforts, it was unlikely to improve. Everyone agreed that the news media were superficial in their treatment of national and international events and tended to trivialize the most serious problems with a cynical approach. However, they reminded me that I could not win a war with the press, and advised me to stop having so many news conferences. They also promised to recommend some good people to serve in the White House.

Although not typical, this was the kind of discussion I had with the other groups. The meetings with governors and religious leaders were especially worthwhile. The one with the economists was a waste of time; they all expounded their own conflicting theories, and seemed to be unwilling or unable to consider the views of others or to deal in a practical way with the economic problems I was having to face every day. My meeting with the congressional leaders was remarkably harmonious. Those who had been so obstructive for more than two years now seemed to compete with one another as to who could be more supportive in the future.

> *I spent 90 per cent of my time listening. I worked hard all week, some of the more strenuous work of my life. Also, it's not easy for me to accept criticism and to reassess my ways of doing things. And this was a week of intense reassessment.*   DIARY, JULY 9, 1979

I wrote down a few of the (sometimes conflicting) comments. Most indicated that there was a mood of despair and alienation among the people which I needed to address.

"We've been through a series of national crises, and the country hasn't recovered."

"Mr. President, we're in trouble. Talk to us about blood, sweat, and tears."

"Congress has collapsed on the oil tax."

"We don't have enough fingers for all the dike holes."

"The people are just not ready to sacrifice."

"We have a crisis of confidence."

"I feel so far from government. I feel like ordinary people are excluded from political power." (This from a young Pennsylvania woman.)

"People are saying, 'I love my country; it's the government I hate!' "

"There is a malaise of civilization. We are the first generation to realize that we may be the last."

"In the past we've controlled others' lives; now OPEC controls ours."

"The big shots are not the only ones who are important. Remember, you can't sell anything on Wall Street unless someone digs it up somewhere else first."

Some said that the country was waiting for stronger and clearer leadership from me.

"Mr. President, you're not leading this nation—you're just managing the government."

"Be bold, Mr. President. We may make mistakes, but we are ready to experiment."

"If you lead, Mr. President, we will follow."

"When we enter the moral equivalent of war, don't issue us BB guns."

"I want to say, 'I have one Lord, one faith, one baptism, one President, one policy!' "

"Be bold and mighty forces will come to your aid."

Others were sure of our common strength, and felt that if we could resolve the energy problem together, it would restore national unity and confidence.

"The real issue is freedom. We must deal with the energy problem on a war footing."

"The energy crisis can divide us—or it might unite us."

"We're still a blessed nation. No material shortage can touch the important things."

"There will be other shortages. How we Americans deal with this first one will lead the way to the future."

"Shortages should lead to sharing, caring for others."

"America is a nation with the soul of a church."

There was a lot of advice for me, and criticism of the press.

"Be more cautious with promises."

"Some of your Cabinet members don't seem loyal. There's not enough discipline among your disciples."

"There have been no Cabinet changes in thirty months. It's time."

"As often as we ourselves are misquoted, we still believe what the press says about others."

"We are overly intimidated by a cynical press."

Some of the poorest people emphasized their special plight.

"Some of us have suffered from recession all our lives." (This from a Chicano.)

"Some people have wasted energy, but others haven't had any-thing to waste."

"These meetings may not help your credibility, but it has sure helped mine to be invited here! Blacks have always suffered depression."

It was one of my most productive times. I learned a lot, and so did the people who visited with me. In the rare quiet moments, I mostly talked to Rosalynn and Kirbo, or read and worked on the texts of the two speeches I planned to deliver after these meetings were over. One would address the attitude of our country, with some general comments about energy; the second would outline the new energy proposals in more detail.

I wound up the Camp David sessions with unannounced trips to private homes near Pittsburgh, Pennsylvania, and Martinsburg, West Virginia, where I spent a few hours talking to a small group from the community. The last session of all was with a couple of dozen of our top news reporters; I was pleased with the accuracy of their subsequent stories.

That Sunday night, July 15, 1979, I tried to express to the American people what I had learned at Camp David. I spoke from the Oval Office about the need to have faith in our country—not only in the government, but in our own ability to solve great problems. There was a growing disrespect for our churches, schools, news media, and other institutions; this change had not come suddenly or without cause.

I acknowledged that we had some serious problems, but ex-pressed my confidence that we could solve them if we were willing to work together with courage and with concern for one another.

We were sure that ours was a nation of the ballot, not the bullet, until the murders of John Kennedy, Robert Kennedy, and Martin Luther King, Jr. We were taught that our armies were always invincible and our causes always just, only to suffer the agony of Vietnam. We respected the Presidency as a place of honor until the shock of Watergate. We remember when the phrase "sound as a dollar" was an expression of absolute dependability, until ten years of inflation began to shrink our dollar and our savings. We believed that our nation's resources were limitless until 1973, when we had to face a growing dependence on foreign oil. These wounds are still very deep. They have never been healed.

I pointed out that we had lost confidence in our government but that it was time for us to work together to realize the potential greatness of America and solve the energy problem as a major test. Everyone could help. I quoted one of the visitors to Camp David: "We've got to stop crying and start sweating, stop talking and start walking, stop cursing and start praying. The strength we need will not come from the White House, but from every house in America."

I closed with a brief outline of the new energy proposals, which would be described more completely the next day. It was one of my best speeches, and the response to it was overwhelmingly positive. Intrigued by the mystery of what I would say, about one hundred million people had listened—perhaps the largest American audience I ever had.

The next morning, when I flew to Kansas City to deliver the energy speech, people throughout the country were waiting to hear it. I then went to Detroit for a question-and-answer session at a labor convention. Again, the main interest was in energy! Even the congressional leaders now expressed their determination to act without delay.

The next order of business was to make a few changes in the Cabinet. I dreaded this duty, but the advice at Camp David had been almost unanimous. Upon reflection and further consultation, I met with all of the members in the Cabinet Room. After a brief discussion I decided that the entire group would offer to resign, and I would then quickly decide which resignations to accept. Attorney General Bell thought the resignations should be in writing, but others noted that everyone served at my pleasure anyway. I also explained how I planned to strengthen the White House staff.

I handled the Cabinet changes very poorly, and should have announced immediately that Treasury Secretary Mike Blumenthal and HEW Secretary Joe Califano had resigned, and that I had accepted the resignation which I had been offered many months ago by Jim Schlesinger. Instead, with all the Cabinet involved in the process, the changes were portrayed as a great governmental crisis and negated some of the progress we had made during the past two weeks in reestablishing better relations with the public. I made the changes rapidly and formed a very strong team with the new appointments, but the same decisions could have been made in a much more effective manner.

Now that the American people were deeply interested in the

process, it was time for all of us to implement the new energy proposals. Charles Duncan had agreed to move from his job as Deputy Secretary of Defense to become Secretary of Energy, and with his outstanding management capability and fresh approach, we were ready to tackle the energy problems—specifically oil— with renewed vigor.

Our plan was to impose a permanent 50 per cent tax on the unearned "windfall" profits and to permit domestic oil prices to rise slowly but steadily over a period of about two years, from $13 or less per barrel to the international market price of roughly twice that amount. Subsequently, 50 per cent of any increase in world oil prices would be captured in taxes and transferred to public use. The oil companies were to use the other portion of the windfall profits for increased investments in exploration and production of oil and gas within the United States.

After this program was adopted, the situation would be greatly simplified. Now, as we worked out the terms for this transition period, it was almost impossible to understand the complicated interrelationships involved. There were many different kinds of oil, oil wells, drilling requirements, transportation and refining costs, local and state tax policies, foreign supply entanglements, widely varying discovery dates of existing wells, conflicting histories of federal government commitments on the terms of price and distribution—and the ever-present complexities in the relationship among the companies, their customers, and Congress.

All these and many other factors had to be considered as tax legislation was passed, in order to be fair to everyone concerned and reach compromises that a majority could support. The stakes were high. We were talking about more than $220 billion in federal revenue during the decade of the 1980's—the largest tax ever levied on any industry in the history of the world.

Consumer groups were opposed to removing any federal constraints on domestic oil prices, but along with artificially cheap oil, they wanted the same things everyone else did—maximum conservation of energy, the production of more American oil and gas, and the development of alternative sources of energy, such as solar power and synthetic fuels. It was impossible to reconcile their conflicting demands. The best answer I could devise was to phase in decontrol of oil prices and provide optimum benefits to the American public from the windfall-tax revenues.

Although our energy proposals were compatible with what some of the industry executives and most of the congressional leaders had advised, Congress found it impossible to resolve those issues in 1979 because of the political forces exerted to benefit various groups that would be affected by the bill. The oil producers were successful in making some significant changes in our proposal, so that by the time the final legislation was passed in the spring of 1980, a variable rate ranging from 30 per cent to 70 per cent had been substituted for the flat 50 per cent rate; the revenues would not be earmarked for specific purposes but would go into the general treasury, to be expended as each Congress prepared the nation's budget; and the tax would not be permanent but would expire no later than October 1993, or earlier if the full amount of $227 billion in taxes had been collected.

This struggle for a national energy policy had been an exhausting fight involving almost every federal agency, all state and local governments, every member of Congress, dozens of interest groups, and hundreds of billions of dollars. It had spanned more than three full years of my administration. The total energy program did not please anyone completely, but overall it was a good compromise, and I knew that the final result was well worth all our efforts.

Congress also voted to establish a Synthetic Fuels Corporation to further the development of alternate sources of energy, but the House unexpectedly rejected the conference report creating an Energy Mobilization Board designed to expedite high-priority projects by cutting through government red tape. The Republican members had abruptly withdrawn their support, some of them saying that they did not want to give me yet another legislative victory.

Almost immediately after each major portion of our comprehensive program was passed, both energy conservation and domestic production were encouraged, and for the first time in years, oil imports began to decline. From the 1977 peak, the percentage of United States oil consumption from overseas dropped from 48 per cent to 40 per cent in 1980. During 1978, we were consuming nearly 19 million barrels of oil a day, almost 11 per cent more than in 1980. On an average day during this latter year, Americans had reduced both total consumption and oil imports by more than 1.8 million barrels. Many of the reasons for this improvement are now embedded in our new laws. As a result, the types of automobiles we use, methods of computing electricity bills, design of home appliances, home insulation, and many other things about the way we drive and live will, I hope, be permanent changes in the customs and attitudes of our people.

In looking back on the "moral equivalent of war" against energy waste and excessive vulnerability from oil imports, I see nothing exhilarating or pleasant. It was a bruising fight, and no final clear-cut victory could be photographed and hung on the wall for our grandchildren to admire. The results will have to speak for themselves; they are already doing so. Our administration left the country with petroleum inventories at record levels, a natural-gas surplus and a fair distribution system for it, more exploration under way for new petroleum than at any time in history, and an orderly plan for eliminating unnecessary federal restraints. The rate of growth of domestic coal production doubled, and oil imports and even total consumption dropped rapidly. A substantial portion of the succeeding oil glut was caused by the worldwide shift to more efficient uses of energy and emphasis on fuels other than oil and gas.

There will undoubtedly be alternating periods of shortages and oversupply in the future, but there is no doubt that now our country is better equipped to deal with either eventuality. The most important factor is that the attitude of the American people concerning energy has changed. Maybe our efforts have engendered a spirit of common purpose and sacrifice that will be adequate to meet new crises ahead—if we remember that the war is not over.

THE BERT LANCE
AFFAIR

BILL MOYERS: *What have you learned about this town?*

THE PRESIDENT: *There were two . . . unpleasant surprises. One was the inertia of Congress, the length of time it takes to get a complicated piece of legislation through . . . and the other was the irresponsibility of the press.*
TELEVISION INTERVIEW, NOVEMBER 13, 1978

As I look back on our campaign, it would be difficult to list all the factors that gave us our victory in 1976 against such great initial odds. Careful planning, hard work, and unswerving determination, a willingness to go into all states and win every available delegate, solid support from key black leaders, loyalty of the Southern voters to me as one of their own, the very underestimation of us that expanded each small early victory into a great triumph, an almost unbelievable family effort that multiplied my own presence—these and more have been identified and analyzed by political pundits many times over. To me, however, the most significant factors were the disillusionment of the American people following the national defeat suffered in Vietnam, the Watergate scandals, and my success in convincing supporters that we should keep our faith in America and that I would never permit any repetition of such embarrassments.

As a citizen and a governor, I had shared the people's feelings of anger and frustration, but as a candidate I was surprised at the intensity of the pain I found among them, which had quickly become obvious from their bitter comments and probing questions. I tried in every possible way to reassure them, to convince them that our leaders did not have to be isolated, immune from accountability to the public, and devious in their actions and statements. Perhaps more than the other major candidates, I saw the relationship between the people and its leaders as the most important issue.

When I became President, I was quite aware of the legacy of the last ten years—how much doubt and suspicion there was about

125

high public officials—but I was not concerned about my own administration. I was sure that our White House political team could deal with the news media on a different footing altogether. I did not have anything to conceal that might prove troubling, and I had complete confidence in those who served with me. I approached my new job with the certainty that we would never have to worry about investigations by Congress, any government agency, or the news media. Perhaps I should have known better. The day after my inauguration, a Washington *Post* reporter predicted, "Carter may have a honeymoon with Congress, but he's not going to have one with us." This was a less than enthusiastic welcome, but not entirely unexpected considering my background and that of my personal staff, as well as the kind of campaign I had run. Few of the nation's editors or publishers really knew us, and most of them had naturally supported other presidential candidates with whom they were better acquainted. Also, we were somewhat ostentatious about setting a high moral standard for ourselves, and so my administration was not to be given any room for error by the press.

When we moved into the White House, we had an important challenge which none of us adequately recognized—to learn about our influential Washington neighbors who did not serve in government, and to let them know us. However, having run deliberately and profitably as one who had never been part of the Washington scene, I was not particularly eager to change my attitude after becoming President. This proved to be a mistake. I would have many legislative battles to fight, and controversies were bound to arise that could adversely affect both myself and my administration. It was important that my attitudes and policies be clearly understood and explained to the public and that I communicate normally and frankly with those who were experienced and knowledgeable about the ways of our government. In times of trouble I would need all the help I could get, and when there were times of achievement they needed to be shared with the American public. I realized the potential benefit to be derived from solid relationships with the Washington leaders who helped to shape public attitudes, but I thought that doing the best job possible in the White House would be enough to gain their support.

I did not see that one of the important avenues to this support and understanding was through the seemingly informal but highly structured social life of the nation's capital. Much of it seemed frivolous to me, and my own lack of interest in the evening party circuit was shared by most of my White House staff and Cabinet members. We missed an opportunity to become better friends with some good and important people, who never felt that they were wanted or needed in helping to form the policies of our nation.

We came to Washington as outsiders and never appreciably changed this status. Nowhere within the press, Congress, or the ranks of the Washington power structure were there any long-established friends and acquaintances who would naturally come to our defense in a public debate on a controversial issue. Even to those who welcomed us, we were still strangers. Jody Powell said to me that, having never served in Washington, we did not have any outriders posted to defend us from flank attacks. "There never was a honeymoon with the press, but just a one-night stand."

After a year or so, Rosalynn and I had a long series of small dinner parties at the White House for the leaders among the news media. These were enjoyable and somewhat beneficial, but failed to compensate for our relative isolation on a more continuing basis from the "movers and shakers" among the Washington elite.

We first realized the adverse consequences of still being outsiders when we had to face the allegations raised against Bert Lance.

～

There is no single member of the Cabinet in whom I have any disappointment. . . . Bert Lance is a key to the entire process of budgeting and reorganization, and has been tremendous in his job. DIARY, FEBRUARY 18, 1977

It is impossible to overestimate the damage inflicted on my administration by the charges leveled against Bert Lance—a series of highly publicized allegations that began early in July 1977 and continued far beyond his voluntary resignation two months later, in September.

A lot of people have asked me, "What did it all mean? How did it happen?" These questions are difficult to answer. In Washington, at the time, there was still a great fascination with Watergate, and the reporters and members of Congress involved in the resignation of President Nixon were heroes. To uncover a new story, true or not, was considered by some to be a notable achievement, and denials or even proof of falseness were often smothered in an additional rash of stories coming at the same time.

I had met Bert Lance in 1966, and knew of his reputation as a competent and progressive banker. In 1970, when I was elected governor of Georgia, I wanted Bert to help me in Atlanta. I promised him hard work and "a lot of fun." At least a hundred times since then he has asked me, "When does the fun begin?" Second only to Charles Kirbo, who has been my friend and adviser since I first met him in 1962, Bert was the Georgia leader who helped me most. As Director of the Georgia Department of Transportation, he worked with me to reorganize the entire structure of the state government, and was really the linchpin of my Cabinet-level officers in planning political and budget strategy and in working with the members of the state legislature on controversial matters. I relied on him heavily, and he never let me down.

Bert was able to engender support for our programs among the political and professional leaders of the state. The business community looked on him as one of its own, but he also had good relations with labor and other special groups interested in civil rights, consumer affairs, and social progress. He took this skill in human relations to Washington. Of all the Georgians I brought to the White House, he was the best at cementing ties with key members of Congress, with Cabinet members, and with business and financial leaders.

It is difficult for me to explain how close Bert was to me or how much I depended on him. Even my closest friends in Georgia have never fully understood the extent of our relationship. Calm and mature, Bert also had an easy, boyish way about him, and used his sense of humor effectively among all kinds of people. He had a vicious tennis serve, and played and talked a good game. Surprisingly agile for so big a man, he described himself often as having "the size of an elephant and the grace of a gazelle."

After the 1976 campaign, I was preparing to go to Washington, a place unknown to me, where I would quickly have to learn a new life and a new set of rules. I knew well how crucial the preparation of the budget, dispensing of funds, supervision of the bureaucracy's organization, and management of the government itself had been in my Georgia administration. I needed someone to serve as Director of the OMB (Office of Management and Budget) who was honest and competent, had good business sense, and was fiscally conservative like myself. I did not hesitate in making Bert Lance the first person I asked to serve at the top level within my administration after the election. He was the only one of the Cabinet-level members with whom I had ever worked before, and I planned for him to be the leader on matters dealing with the budget and government organization.

Bert had to make a great financial sacrifice to take this job, but like several others in similar circumstances, he was willing to do so. We did not know it then, but his good sense of humor would be sorely tested in the months ahead. In order to meet the very stringent standards I established for serving with me, all potential appointees had to reveal their financial holdings and divest themselves of any corporate or professional obligations that might create a conflict of interest. Bert was a substantial stockholder in several Georgia banks, and voluntarily promised to dispose of all his stock by October 1977. This proved to be a mistake, because when it was revealed to the public during his Senate confirmation hearings that he would have to sell a large block of shares (in some cases more than 20 per cent of the total stock) their value was seriously depressed, working an immediate hardship on the banks and on the other shareholders. At the time of the final sale, Bert too would suffer heavy losses.

Toward the end of June 1977, he came to me with the problem. I was quite concerned and called Charles Kirbo for his advice. We both thought that any possibility of a conflict of interest could be avoided if Bert would place all his stock in a blind and uninstructed corporate trust, with the trustee providing for its sale on a flexible schedule as market conditions might warrant. I advised Bert to go to the Senate Governmental Affairs Committee, which had been responsible for his confirmation, inform its members of the facts, and ask them to relieve him of the obligation to sell all his stock by a specific date.

The Senate committee approved this proposal, but the process aroused a firestorm of questions from the press, followed by allegations of all kinds of improprieties—that Bert had borrowed money without adequate collateral, that he had made unsafe loans, and that he had violated banking and securities laws or regulations, or had at least observed them carelessly. All these repercussions were a great shock to me.

Bert Lance was a good country banker—one who knew and loved his community and who cared for his customers and neighbors. Bert's hometown friends explained to me that his custom had been to make many loans around the small city of Calhoun, Georgia, based on his intimate knowledge of the borrowers. He did not always depend on full collateral as much as would big-city bankers, who necessarily have to deal with most of their customers on a relatively impersonal basis. If a working employee in a local carpet factory, with a good family and church life, wanted to buy a small farm on credit, he could be reasonably confident that Bert would hear him favorably. Later, Bert's bank would offer to lend him, free of charge, a purebred bull or boar to improve the quality of the new farmer's small livestock herd. If the man's wife got sick, Bert would send flowers, and if she died, Bank President Bert Lance would be at the funeral. He was bold and aggressive as an entrepreneur, and the Calhoun National Bank had grown rapidly under his leadership.

The stories of improprieties—distortions of Bert's actions as a banker before he came to Washington—dominated the news. Congress and other sources demanded investigations by a number of federal agencies, several of which accepted the suggestion with alacrity. Both Houses of Congress eventually jumped into the picture. The Watergate syndrome was still very much alive in Washington.

There were never any allegations from any source that Bert Lance had behaved improperly while he was part of our administration in Washington, but I had placed such public emphasis on high standards of ethics and morality that I was very vulnerable to political damage from the charges against him. My staff and I soon recognized the seriousness of the problem, but all of us, and particularly Bert, had our hands full with the business of managing the nation's economy, preparing the budget for the coming year, and dealing with myriad responsibilities that directly involved OMB. I decided to let the investigations proceed without interference, and anticipated that the facts about Bert would quickly become known and the furor would die down.

I was advised by White House Counsel Robert Lipshutz not to discuss any of the specific issues with Bert. Whenever I was informed of a possible investigation by some government agency, I would merely authorize the officers to act in a completely routine manner. I did advise Bert to list every accusation that had been made against him, to spell out clearly his answers in writing, and to submit them all to me, to Congress, and to the public. When he gave those answers to the Senate committee late in July, there was a very positive reaction. A few days later, Treasury Secretary Mike Blumenthal came to tell me that the Comptroller of the Currency had finished his investigation and that no illegal conduct had been discovered. He would soon issue a final report.

By the middle of August, the Senate had completed two hearings, the Justice Department had found no evidence of wrongdoing, and now the Comptroller had also given Bert an official clean bill of health. On August 18 we delivered this latest report to the waiting press. As I concluded my brief remarks and turned to leave, I said, "Bert, I'm proud of you." We breathed a sigh of relief—which proved to be premature.

Walking with LaBelle and Bert Lance to news conference

In spite of the official findings, the questioning from the news media did not stop, and the matter continued to weigh heavily on us. A week later, two-thirds of my regular presidential news conference was still devoted to the Bert Lance affair.

In order to provide the answers, Jody Powell became an expert on Bert's background; Bob Lipshutz was equally preoccupied with the subject. It was never far from my own mind. Knowing Bert so well, we were convinced of his innocence, but there was no adequate forum within which he could be "tried," except for the daily news media. There, predictably, he had no chance.

The Washington Post *is conducting a vendetta against Bert and has apparently ordered two front-page stories*

about him each day. This morning, for instance, they had
nine separate stories about Lance—headline stories—
throughout the paper. In contrast, The New York Times
didn't mention him.   DIARY, SEPTEMBER 1, 1977

I can see now that this situation—someone accused of wrongdoing who was high in government and an intimate friend of the
President—was an investigative reporter's dream. It was inevitable that the Washington newspapers were going to concentrate on
it. In any case, they never failed to report every allegation or
insinuation, and any denial only provided an opportunity for the
original charge to be repeated. For weeks the Lance affair was the
number-one news story in the capital.

This constant attack was damaging the reputation of our administration and consuming an inordinate amount of our time. I
believed Bert Lance to be innocent, but listened carefully to
recommendations from my advisers that I ask him to resign.
Some of them strongly urged this "solution" to the problem, but I
could not bring myself to do it. I knew that such a move would
spare us trouble and embarrassment, but Bert would be permanently disgraced if he left office without having some chance to
defend himself. It did not seem fair to me to deprive him of a
right to be heard and, if possible, to clear his name.

By now a whole flock of new charges had been made. The Senate Governmental Affairs Committee invited Bert to testify on
September 15. After I talked to him candidly about the difficulties of trying to defend him from within the White House, we
agreed that he would take a leave of absence for a week or two in
order to spend all his time preparing his case for presentation to
the Senate committee. We were hoping that this would be a final
and conclusive public hearing.

Wild charges were flying everywhere. Senators Abe Ribicoff
and Charles Percy, the senior members of the committee, even
came to tell me that a convicted embezzler had claimed that Bert
had been an accomplice to the crime. The embezzler's report had
absolutely no basis in fact, but it was quickly leaked to the press.
Senator Percy announced that there were nineteen serious allegations against Bert. I urged the Senators to expedite the hearings,
to let all the facts be presented to the public, and to withhold
judgment until the truth could be revealed.

In the meantime, Bert had retained Clark Clifford, a distinguished Washington attorney who was Secretary of Defense under
President Lyndon Johnson, to help him prepare and present his
testimony. This provided some relief for us at the White House,

giving me time during this busy period to conduct my regular business and also to sign the Panama Canal treaties and have individual meetings with seventeen national leaders from Latin America.

Despite my growing concern that the publicity was damaging to me personally and to the Presidency itself, there was some encouraging evidence that within Washington we were getting a highly distorted impression of the degree of condemnation of Bert Lance and the criticism of me for not requiring his immediate resignation. On September 10, I spent a full day campaigning in New Jersey for the reelection of Governor Brendan Byrne, and was relieved that there was not a sign or poster or question about the Lance affair. Brendan sympathized with me. "I know how good it makes you feel if, when they wave at you, they use all five fingers!"

Nevertheless, we knew full well that the Washington press was still obsessed with the subject, and that this preoccupation was sapping our political strength and our reputation. I had nothing further to say on the matter, and decided to postpone my regular news conference until the Senate hearings were over, to give Bert a chance to answer all the questions himself.

On the morning of the first hearings, we met in my small inner office and had a brief prayer together. Bert was feeling quite sure of himself. In addition to my regular duties that day, I had an official visit with French Prime Minister Raymond Barre, and Rosalynn's Mental Health Commission was making its final report. I was very busy during the morning and could not watch any of the televised hearings, but every now and then I heard applause coming from some of the offices in the West Wing. At noon, the press reported that Bert had made an excellent opening statement. When I watched a few minutes of the live testimony late in the afternoon, I thought he was doing just fine, but was concerned about the cross-examination that would have to come.

Early the next morning—Friday—I telephoned Helmut Schmidt to offer him my support in his problem with terrorists who were holding hostages in Germany and demanding that other terrorists be released from prison. We also discussed the question of deploying neutron weapons in Europe. Then he asked me about Bert Lance—whether the situation was serious and whether Bert was being falsely accused. I replied, "Yes" to both questions. That afternoon, I went to Camp David to try to get some rest.

At Camp David I spent a good bit of the time talking to Ham and Jody. They are making arrangements for Kirbo to come up Sunday to meet with them and Lipshutz and the Vice President. During the afternoon we watched some of the Lance hearings, and thought he did very well. Rosalynn and I both decided that it might be better for Bert to stay and fight it out.   DIARY, SEPTEMBER 17, 1977

Most of the morning papers were fairly reasonable about Bert. I talked to Kirbo, Fritz, Ham, and Jody, who unanimously feel that Bert has won a great victory and now should step down.   DIARY, SEPTEMBER 18, 1977

After I returned to Washington that same Sunday afternoon, I called Bert and asked him to come by to see me at 6:15 A.M. Monday, September 19. I then had a long conversation with Senator Robert Byrd. He thought Bert had made great progress and that public support for him was at its highest point. Bickering among the senators on the committee had helped to make Bert look good. Byrd said that I should judge friendship and personal loyalty against possible damage to the Presidency. He reminded me that I had made morality a major issue, and that people therefore expected higher standards from me than from some previous Presidents. He also predicted that the press and some of the committee members would not let the matter rest. It was his opinion that none of the Democratic senators would be particularly disappointed if Bert resigned.

For one of the rare times in my life, I did not sleep much that night. The next morning I had a long talk with Bert. It was just a private discussion between two close friends, relaxed and free of constraint. I reminded him that a few days ago, he was being smeared by attacks from all sides, and White House mail had been running 2 to 1 against him. Now he had completely reversed the tide with his own superb performance and with revelation of the gross exaggeration of the charges. His critics had suffered a setback and he had regained the initiative, but it was clear that his antagonists were not satisfied. They were regrouping for another assault, emphasizing a few questions, such as his use of the National Bank of Georgia's airplane to entertain customers and some bank overdrafts by members of his wife, LaBelle's, family. Bert acknowledged these actions but pointed out that it had been the policy of the bank to use the airplane for this purpose long before he went to work there, and that the overdrafts, although large, were always much less than the undistributed earnings due LaBelle's family members. He had corrected these mistakes. I emphasized that he had finally proved that the system does work and that, given a chance, an honest man could explain his own position. We agreed that we had two or three days during which to make a final decision about what was best for him to do.

Bert told me that he wanted to discuss the situation with Clark Clifford, LaBelle, and a few other people before he and I made a final decision. I felt better than I had in a long time. When he left, I had no doubt that he would do what was right, for him and for me. Except for Rosalynn, I did not tell anyone about this conversation. She and I were now certain that he would resign.

I spent most of that day in long negotiations with Moshe Dayan, the Foreign Minister of Israel, seeking some avenue toward peace for Israel and Lebanon. At that time, we were still trying to agree on an arrangement that would get the disputing parties to Geneva for general negotiations.

Late that night, Senator Byrd came by, convinced that Bert had redeemed himself as much as could ever be possible, and that now would be the best time for him to step down. Byrd had read all the testimony from the public hearing, and had discussed the question with a number of senators before forming this opinion. He planned to share his views with Bert the following day— September 20.

I played tennis late in the afternoon with Bert, and he indicated to me that he wanted to resign. I didn't argue with him. He's going home and will talk to LaBelle.
DIARY, SEPTEMBER 20, 1977

Probably one of the worst days I've ever spent.
DIARY, SEPTEMBER 21, 1977

Again, I had arranged to meet with Bert at 6:15 A.M. He came by to see me at 7:15 A.M.—an hour late, which was not like him. He said that LaBelle objected so strongly to his resigning that he didn't know what he wanted to do. He asked what I thought, and I replied that I felt he had made the right decision on the tennis court yesterday—to resign now, when his name had been cleared. I reminded him that I had scheduled a press conference for the afternoon, and that we would need to have this question resolved before then. Bert agreed, and left to talk again to his attorney and his wife.

During that morning I had to study a broad range of possible questions that might arise at the press conference, which would be televised. Foreign Minister Ismail Fahmy of Egypt met with me to pursue our discussions about the planned Geneva conference on Middle East peace, and Senator Kennedy came for lunch and brought me a copy of a letter from President Leonid Brezhnev on SALT. It was a typical busy day, but I had Bert Lance on my mind.

After lunch, I met with Bert and LaBelle. She was adamantly opposed to his resigning, but she acknowledged that he and I had already made the decision. Clark Clifford came to see me and explained that they had decided, even before the Senate hearings, to try to clear Bert's name and then immediately to tender his resignation. They were very pleased with the success of their effort before the Senate committee. Clark left to meet with Bert, and after an hour or two, they brought me a letter of resignation. I read it over, and then sorrowfully but gratefully prepared my handwritten reply. After the exchange of letters, I prepared to go to the news conference, which had been delayed for two hours.

As I was leaving the Oval Office, LaBelle called to say that, in accepting his resignation, I had betrayed my best friend. I sympathized with her, but I was absolutely sure that Bert and I had made the right decision. When I discussed this with her much later, she reluctantly agreed.

The news conference went well. Afterward I had a flood of telephone calls and telegrams, primarily condemning the press and Congress for their relentless attacks on Bert Lance and congratulating me on the favorable outcome of such a disturbing and potentially heartbreaking episode. Had I known from the beginning that the Lances would have to suffer for two months before Bert resigned and left Washington, I would have found a way to give him more free time to answer the charges, and at the same time to relieve us of the obligation of defending him to the press. Each week, however, during that long summer that never seemed to end, we thought that surely it would soon be over and Bert would be exonerated.

We attended a reception for Bert and LaBelle. They seemed to be in good spirits. It is an unbelievable relief to all of us not to have the Bert Lance thing hanging over us. Even adverse votes in Congress are much easier for me to accept, and a lot of the tension is gone.

DIARY, SEPTEMBER 26, 1977

The news conference was devoted to the Middle East, to SALT, and to the energy package—for a change. Only one passing question about the Lance affair!

DIARY, SEPTEMBER 29, 1977

There was some criticism of me for not firing Bert when the first charges were made. Although I considered it seriously at the beginning of September, I could not bring myself to do it. I was convinced that it was right and fair to wait for some *proof* of wrongdoing before administering punishment to someone I believed to be innocent. Furthermore, I did not see any place for Bert to defend himself against the accusations leveled at him daily in the press; and at least he would have the forum of Senate hearings.

Bert and LaBelle Lance went home to Georgia as heroes, but he still had to face the rash of legal charges which had accumulated against him. It was months before all the allegations were either withdrawn or disproved. He paid an extremely high price in legal and accountants' fees, and in personal pain and suffering. As a matter of fact, I doubt that all the investigations of Watergate exceeded in complexity and expense the multiple inquiries into the affairs of Bert Lance. In 1981, the Atlanta *Constitution* reported that one agency of the federal government had a file on Bert consisting of four million pages!

The investigations continued for many months, and lawyers' fees incurred by the "defendant" exceeded $1 million. No proof of illegality was ever produced. The ordeal was terrible for us all, and I am not even sure what lessons were taught. I am just grateful that eventually it turned out all right, and that the Lances were strong enough in their faith not to be destroyed.

ON THE
SAME EARTH

SPEAKING OUT FOR
HUMAN RIGHTS

*It is a new world that calls for a new American foreign
policy—a policy based on constant decency in its values
and on optimism in our historical vision.*

ADDRESS ON FOREIGN AFFAIRS,
UNIVERSITY OF NOTRE DAME, MAY 22, 1977

I know how easy it is to overlook the persecution of others
when your own rights and freedoms are not in jeopardy.
I grew up in south Georgia within a legally segregated
society, and to the extent that I or my elders felt any
responsibility at all for the status of my black playmates, the
"separate but equal" ruling of the U.S. Supreme Court seemed
sufficient. As a child, I rode a bus to school each day with the
other white students, while the black children walked, and never
gave a thought to the lack of equality inherent in the separateness.
Neither did the adults who managed the education system, nor
the lawyers and judges in our courts, nor the governor, nor those
who led our government in Washington and were responsible for
the administration of justice in our great and free nation. It seems
almost unbelievable, but it was only after I had gone away to
serve in the Navy for eleven years, returned home to live, enrolled
my oldest son in the same school I had attended, and had begun
to serve as a member of the Sumter County Board of Education
that I finally came to acknowledge that black schoolchildren were
still walking to their separate schools.

It took many years of bitter and divisive struggles to change
this kind of broad discrimination. During the heat of those legal
contests, when some blood was spilled, it was shocking to observe
the degree of racial prejudice among people I admired and knew
to be otherwise fair and kind and compassionate. Some of them
became expert at finding Bible scriptures to prove that God wanted
them to be fair, kind, compassionate—and racist.

It was deeply moving to see the end of legal segregation in
the South and to observe the immediate benefits that came to all
of us. I was not directly involved in the early struggles to end

141

racial discrimination, but by the time my terms as state senator and governor were over, I had gained the trust and political support of some of the great civil rights leaders in my region of the country. To me, the political and social transformation of the Southland was a powerful demonstration of how moral principles should and could be applied effectively to the legal structure of our society.

The same lesson has been learned many times in our dealings with other nations. Our country has been strongest and most effective when morality and a commitment to freedom and democracy have been most clearly emphasized in our foreign policy. Under President Lyndon Johnson, quantum leaps forward were taken within the United States, effectively reducing racial discrimination and providing for the economic and social needs of our own people. But in recent history, President Harry Truman was the strongest and most effective advocate of human rights on an international scale. His encouragement of the formation of the United Nations and his steadfastness in the face of great pressure as he quickly recognized the new nation of Israel were vivid demonstrations of American influence at its finest. After the Second World War when American power was at its peak, we did not attempt to turn Japan and Germany into subject states, nor to impose so harsh a punishment that the sufferings of the war would be perpetuated. Instead, we took the lead in helping to establish democratic and peaceful constitutional governments in two previously militaristic nations. The subsequent benefits to their own people and to the maintenance of world peace have been obvious.

However, since Truman's days in the White House, persistent support of such a foreign policy has often been lacking. Much of the time we failed to exhibit as an American characteristic the idealism of Jefferson or Wilson. In the process we forfeited one of our most effective ways to meet threats from totalitarian ideologies and arouse the spirit of our own people. Because of the heavy emphasis that was placed on Soviet–American competition, a dominant factor in our dealings with foreign countries became whether they espoused an anti-communist line. There were times when right-wing monarchs and military dictators were automatically immune from any criticism of their oppressive actions. Our apparent commitment was to protect them from any internal political movement that might result in the establishment of a more liberal ruling group. Instead of promoting freedom and democratic principles, our government seemed to believe that in any struggle with evil, we could not compete effectively unless we played by the same rules or lack of rules as the evildoers.

I was deeply troubled by the lies our people had been told; our exclusion from the shaping of American political and military policy in Vietnam, Cambodia, Chile, and other countries; and other embarrassing activities of our government, such as the CIA's role in plotting murder and other crimes. When I announced my candidacy in December 1974, I expressed a dream: "That this country set a standard within the community of nations of courage, compassion, integrity, and dedication to basic human rights and freedoms."

I was familiar with the widely accepted arguments that we had to choose between idealism and realism, or between morality and the exertion of power; but I rejected those claims. To me, the demonstration of American idealism was a practical and realistic approach to foreign affairs, and moral principles were the best foundation for the exertion of American power and influence.

I could understand the justification for supporting some of the more conservative regimes. At least within those countries, it was not possible to conceal all the abuses of human rights. World condemnation and our influence could be much more effective there than in communist countries, where repression was so complete that it could not easily be observed or rooted out. I was determined to combine support for our more authoritarian allies and friends with the effective promotion of human rights within their countries. By inducing them to change their repressive policies, we would be enhancing freedom and democracy, and helping to remove the reasons for revolutions that often erupt among those who suffer from persecution. We might therefore accomplish our purposes without replacing a rightist totalitarian regime with a leftist one of the same oppressive character.

A human rights effort would also help strengthen our influence among some of the developing nations that were still in the process of forming their own governments and choosing their future friends and trading partners. And it was the right thing to do.

I knew from my experience in the South that this policy would not be painless, nor could it be based on a blind adherence to consistency. The world was too complex to respond to the application of a few simple rules. But when our own friends committed serious violations of human rights, their abuses would have to be acknowledged, and they would have to be encouraged to change their policies. There would also be cases when oppressed people could obtain freedom only by changing their own laws or leaders.

Whatever the particular circumstances, I wanted the leader of every nation on earth to face the same recurring question: "What do my own people and the outside world think about the protection of human rights in my country?"

I had pointed out in my speech accepting the Democratic nomination for President in July 1976 that "Ours was the first nation to dedicate itself clearly to basic moral and philosophical principles ... a singular act of wisdom and courage ... a revolutionary development that captured the imagination of mankind." It was time for us to capture the imagination of the world again.

As President, I hoped and believed that the expansion of human rights might be the wave of the future throughout the world, and I wanted the United States to be on the crest of this movement. I studied the record of abuses in different nations as reported by Amnesty International, the United Nations, and other organizations; reviewed recent legislation and other decisions of Congress in dealing with the question of human rights; and looked over the widely varying records of my predecessors in the White House. In spite of my own study of the past and planning for the future, I did not fully grasp all the ramifications of our new policy. It became clear in the early days (and increasingly so later on) that the promotion of human rights was to cut across our relations with the Soviet Union and other totalitarian governments, the emerging nations who were struggling to establish stable regimes, and even some of our longtime Western allies.

At first we were inclined to define human rights too narrowly. Human rights was not merely a matter of reducing the incidence of summary executions or torture of political prisoners. It also included the promotion of democratic principles such as those expressed in our Bill of Rights, the right to emigrate and reunite families, and protection against discrimination based on race, sex, religion, or ethnic origin. These were the issues on which most public attention was concentrated, but the right of people to a job, food, shelter, medical care, and education could not be ignored. At home I concentrated most of my energies on them. I also wanted to be sure that before we criticized other nations for violating internationally accepted standards, we had set our own house in order. As one of the signers of the agreement in Helsinki at the conclusion of the Conference on Security and Cooperation in Europe, the United States could not violate its human-rights provisions. I asked the Secretary of State for an assessment of our performance. He reported that we were in compliance, except that our government was still prohibiting travel by Americans to such countries as Cuba, North Korea, Vietnam, and Cambodia. On March 1, 1977, I lifted these restrictions.

After his first press conference, on January 21, 1977, Secretary of State Vance wrote to me in his nightly report that he was "struck by the degree of interest, even sharpness, on human-rights issues. Since we have announced that we will speak out on selected international human-rights issues, we will of course be asked continually why we are commenting on some and not on others."

It was very difficult to answer this question then or at any later time. In dealing with about 150 other nations on many interrelated matters, some involving our own national security, it was not possible to let any one factor be the sole or dominant one in our decisions. However, even without adequately specific and consistent definitions and policies, we made it clear to everyone that a significant element in our relationships with other governments would be their performance in providing basic freedoms to their people.

Judging from news articles and direct communications from the American people to me during the first few months of my administration, human rights had become the central theme of our foreign policy in the minds of the press and public. It seemed that a spark had been ignited, and I had no inclination to douse the growing flames. Although it was apparent that it would be difficult to translate a general theory into uniform bureaucratic action, there were no dissenting voices among my top advisers in the White House or the State Department concerning our promotion of human rights. We did, however, face continuing criticism from the press over both the strictness and the laxness in our policies, and complaints from the business community and from some diplomats who were most directly affected whenever South Africa, Argentina, Chile, the Soviet Union, or some other country objected to public exposure of its persecutions. Along with these criticisms, allegations of naiveté and inconsistency became increasingly prevalent. My old Navy boss, Hyman Rickover, observed the controversies that were being aroused, and came to the Oval Office to give me his comments and advice.

> Rickover said if I would stick to principle on things like water projects and human rights, I would come out all right. (He further commented, however, that I may not win reelection in 1980.)   DIARY, APRIL 18, 1977

While improving diplomatic relations with the Soviet Union was an important goal of mine, I had made it clear in the campaign that I was not going to ignore Soviet abuse of human rights, as I believed some previous administrations had done. In the friendly first exchange of letters between me and General Secretary Leonid Brezhnev at the time of my inauguration, he had made a passing remark about "noninterference in the internal affairs of the other side." I deliberately chose to interpret this as a general proposition all nations profess to observe. In discussing the matter with Soviet Ambassador Anatoly Dobrynin in Washington, I clearly stated that we would not interfere in the internal affairs of the Soviet Union but would expect all existing agreements to be carried out, including those relating to human rights. The United Nations Charter; the Universal Declaration of Human Rights approved by all nations in 1948; and, more recently, the Helsinki agreements were binding on us and on the Soviet Union. When the Soviets signed these documents, they had placed the subject of human rights firmly on the agenda of legitimate discussions between our two nations. Dobrynin responded, with something of a smile, that our two nations had different standards. He claimed that no one was deprived of a job in the Soviet Union, and that there was no discrimination against women.

In mid-February 1977, when Andrei Sakharov, the distinguished scientist and dissident who had been detained by Soviet officials, informed me of his plight, I sent him a personal pledge to promote human rights in the Soviet Union. A highly publicized photograph showed him facing the cameraman, holding the letter with my signature.

Brezhnev's tone changed to harshness in his second message on February 25. His primary objection was to my aggressive proposals on nuclear arms limitations—advocating much deeper cuts than had been discussed at Vladivostok in 1975—but he also expressed strong opposition to our human-rights policy. He seemed especially provoked by my corresponding with him and at the same time sending a letter to Sakharov, who was considered by the Soviet leader to be "a renegade who proclaimed himself an enemy of the Soviet state."

I was often criticized, here and abroad, for aggravating other government leaders and straining international relations. At the same time, I was never criticized by the people who were imprisoned or tortured or otherwise deprived of basic rights. When they were able to make a public statement or to smuggle out a private message, they sent compliments and encouragement, pointing out repeatedly that the worst thing for them was to be ignored or forgotten. This was particularly true among political prisoners behind the Iron Curtain.

We have completed the negotiations with the Soviets on the prisoner exchange. I think we've got an excellent deal, having Ginzburg and Vins, plus three others, released from the Soviet Union [these were Aleksandr Ginzburg, Georgiy Vins with his wife and five children, Valentin Moroz, Eduard Samuilovich Kuznetsov, and Mark Dymshits]. They've also agreed not to execute . . . one of our spies who had been condemned to die. In return for this, we commuted the sentences of two United Nations minor spies [Soviets] who were convicted last year.

DIARY, APRIL 26, 1979

The prisoner exchange was very successful and a highly emotional experience for all those who were there . . . it's one of the most significant things in a human way that we've done since I've been in office.

The five prisoners were awakened at 4:00 in the morning in their individual prison cells. All given practically no notice, but informed that their Soviet citizenship was revoked—that they would have to leave the Soviet Union. They were given minimal details about the substance of the exchange, informed that their families would not be punished and might be joining them, and then were transferred to an Aeroflot plane. They were kept in a small compartment, with two security guards on the aisle side of each prisoner. All their heads were shaved except Vins's, who has been living in so-called exile. When brought into the New York airport, the Soviet officials demanded that there be two ramps going into the plane, which caused some delay at the airport. They wanted the American prisoners walking up one ramp simultaneously when the five Russians walked down the other ramp, but would not agree to a meeting of the two and the five on the same ramp at the same time.

We treated the dissidents with great respect, gave them optimum opportunity for freedom (which they did not take), took them to a fairly luxurious hotel. We then let some Ukrainian leaders come in to see Moroz, and some Jewish leaders come in to see the three Jewish dissidents. Vins was quite remorseful that he had left the Soviet

*Union, even though his family is going to follow him. He
felt that the Baptists and other Christians there should not
have been abandoned by him. Late in the night and early
this morning when he was visited by one or two Baptist
leaders, he began to feel somewhat better.*

*. . . Kuznetsov and Dymshits will be arriving in Jerusa-
lem Monday morning. The Prime Minister [Begin] will
meet them personally and express my best wishes to them
as they take up their new life in Israel.*

DIARY, APRIL 28, 1979

Meeting with Vins

I was to teach Sunday school the next morning, and our pastor,
Reverend Charles Trentham, invited Vins to worship with us. The
lesson was about the persecution of Naboth (I Kings 21), and I
drew some parallels between the Bible story and religious persecution in our time. Afterward, in my private conversations with
the Baptist leaders who would act as his hosts, I encouraged them
not to demand too much of the Soviet dissident, but to let him
live his own life as much as possible. He would be at Middlebury
College in Vermont, a small school with a strong Russian-
language department. I told Vins not to feel guilty about being
sent from the Soviet Union, because he had already had an opportunity to send a Christian message to the ten million televi-

sion viewers who saw him raise his Bible when he arrived in the United States. He was still concerned about his family, and I informed him that President Brezhnev had promised me that there would be no delay or obstacles in having the families reunited.

> *These five were really an impressive group in their diversity and also in their commitment. I think the Soviets underestimated the impact of their release on American and world opinion. It is the first time we've swapped Soviet spies for Soviet domestic dissident prisoners, but I'm very pleased with it.* DIARY, APRIL 30, 1979

In all my discussions with these and other dissidents, and with citizens of other countries whose freedom had been curtailed, they always emphasized how important it was for us to continue reminding the world of their plight.

What would have been the fate of these same persecuted people if we had stayed mute on the subject? How many others would have been abused? There is really no way to know. One measure of improvement was in the number of Jews who were permitted to emigrate from the Soviet Union. In 1976, there were 14,261; in 1977, 16,736; in 1978, 28,864; and in 1979, 51,320. After the Afghanistan invasion, the number dropped back to 21,471 in 1980, and during 1981, after my term was over, only 9,447 were able to emigrate.

Although it was a subject of deep concern to both sides, I am not sure that our other important relationships with the Soviet Union were adversely affected by our disagreements on human rights. Throughout the SALT negotiations, in my personal meetings with President Brezhnev, Foreign Minister Andrei Gromyko, Ambassador Dobrynin, and other Soviet leaders, and during other times of serious discussion between our two countries, I cannot recall any instance when the human-rights issue was the *direct* cause of failure in working with the Soviets on matters of common interest. However, it did create tension between us and prevented a more harmonious resolution of some of our other differences.

In truth, this remains a moot question for me. Even if our human-rights policy had been a much more serious point of contention in Soviet–American relations, I would not have been inclined to accommodate Soviet objections. We have a fundamental difference in philosophy concerning human freedoms, and it does not benefit us to cover it up. The respect for human rights is one of the most significant advantages of a free and democratic nation in the peaceful struggle for influence, and we should use this good weapon as effectively as possible.

It will always be impossible to measure how much was accomplished by our nation's policy when the units of measurement are not inches or pounds or dollars. The lifting of the human spirit, the revival of hope, the absence of fear, the release from prison, the end of torture, the reunion of a family, the newfound sense of human dignity—these are difficult to quantify, but I am certain that many people were able to experience them because the United States of America let it be known that we stood for freedom and justice for all people.

I tried to speak with a clear voice, and to let our influence be felt in regions where our country had long ignored the cries for an end to racial prejudice. When I chose Andrew Young and Don McHenry to speak for us as Ambassadors to the United Nations, there was no doubt within the developing world that ours was an honest and sincere voice. We did not send a new message, but repeated for others to hear the same beliefs that had helped to form and shape our own country. Throughout Africa and the rest of the third world, there evolved a new confidence in what we had to say. We found valuable friends among peoples who had looked upon our country with suspicion and fear. They had been led to believe that their only friendship and support would come from communist leaders, who are always eager to encourage revolution and to provide weapons and ammunition to any who were ready to overthrow an unpopular regime.

Some of the hundreds of *desaparecidos* in Argentina—those who had vanished in the night—began to reappear, and the fear of death and torture was alleviated at least to some degree as the attention of the world was focused on the human wrongs of this once free and prosperous land. Thousands of political prisoners were released, from Cuba to Indonesia—sometimes secretly and at times with great fanfare.

Whenever I met with the leader of a government which had been accused of wronging its own people, the subject of human rights was near the top of my agenda. Almost always, the discussion was initiated by those who had been accused. They seemed eager to let me know what progress was being made in their homeland to end persecution and to redress grievances. I knew often that this was a ploy to mislead me, but even then it was possible that the seeds of reform had been planted. At least they were confronting a question they had not been forced to address before.

Our country paid a price for its emphasis on human rights. There were leaders of oppressive regimes who deeply resented any comment about their policies, because they had reason to fear the reaction of their own people against them when their oppression was acknowledged by the outside world. There is no doubt that a few of these could have been spared both embarrassment and the danger of being overthrown if they had strengthened themselves by eliminating the abuses. For those who did not survive, it may be that our emphasis on human rights was not wrong, but too late. Had America argued for these principles sooner, such foreign leaders might not have allowed themselves to become too isolated to correct the abuses without violence.

At home, I searched for ways to root out the vestiges of discrimination against our own citizens because of race, sex, age, or religion, and to eliminate as much as possible the results of past prejudice or deprivation. Such efforts were not always successful, but I made it clear that we were trying.

The abuse of human rights is still a serious problem in too many lands. The world cannot be improved by one dramatic act or by one nation's transient policy; the wheels of justice turn slowly—often very slowly. However, I know that the suffering of some people was eased and that others were given new hope. The world was reminded by salvaged lives that America cares about freedom and justice, a sufficient accomplishment to justify all our efforts.

"JIMMY CARTER IS GIVING AWAY OUR CANAL!"

April 1978

To Senator _____

As President, I want to express my admiration for your support of the Panama Canal treaties. Rarely is a national leader called upon to act on such an important issue fraught with so much potential political sacrifice.

On behalf of the people of the United States, I thank you for your personal demonstration of statesmanship and political courage.

Sincerely,
Jimmy Carter

HANDWRITTEN LETTER TO ALL U.S. SENATORS WHO VOTED FOR
RATIFICATION OF THE PANAMA CANAL TREATIES   APRIL 19, 1978

Twenty-one years before I was born, an event took place at the home of then Secretary of State John Hay that was later to confront me with the most difficult political battle I had ever faced, including my long campaign for President. On the night of November 18, 1903, a treaty was signed in Washington between the newly proclaimed Republic of Panama and the United States of America. No Panamanian had ever seen the treaty, the terms of which were highly favorable to the United States. Acting for Panama was a French businessman, Philippe Bunau-Varilla, whose authority was doubtful and who had not even visited Panama in eighteen years. The document was signed hastily, because an official delegation from Panama had already arrived in New York and would reach Washington in only a few hours.

Although the Panamanian government objected bitterly to the terms of the treaty, it was nevertheless ratified under Bunau-

152

Varilla's threat that the United States would withdraw its protection from the new republic and sign an alternative agreement which would effectively terminate Panama's existence. It was never clear whether Secretary of State John Hay or President Theodore Roosevelt concurred in this remarkable warning.

The result of this act was the construction of the Panama Canal across the isthmus of Central America, one of the great engineering achievements of all time and a boon to the seagoing nations of the world. The Canal was, of course, built and operated by the United States, located within a ten-mile-wide strip of land extending from the Atlantic to the Pacific Ocean. This Canal Zone cut the Republic of Panama in two; within the Zone, our country was granted in perpetuity "all the rights, power and authority . . . which the United States would possess and exercise if it were the sovereign of the territory . . . to the entire exclusion of the exercise by the Republic of Panama of any such sovereign rights, power or authority."

From the outset, Panamanians deeply resented this denial of their authority over part of their territory. That they retained ultimate sovereignty over the Canal Zone was clear from the treaty. Still, some people within the United States and even some members of Congress maintained that by granting the United States perpetual authority over the Canal Zone, Panama had given away sovereignty as well. The display within the Zone of symbols of sovereignty—either American or Panamanian—aroused strong emotion. In December 1963, in order to placate both countries, the flying of either the Panamanian or the American flag in front of Canal Zone schools was banned.

That agreement was violated on January 9, 1964, when a few patriotic American students raised the Stars and Stripes on a Canal Zone campus. The massive rioting that followed was met with force by United States troops. The government of Panama immediately broke diplomatic relations with the United States, accusing us of aggression. Our government maintained that we were simply defending our legal rights and protecting our own citizens. After three days of bloodshed, four American soldiers and twenty Panamanians were dead; dozens more had been injured. President Johnson and our military leaders were quite concerned, not only about the loss of life but also because they knew that the Canal locks and dams were extremely vulnerable to sabotage.

Johnson called the President of Panama, Roberto Chiari, to express his regret about the outbreak and to encourage joint efforts by both nations to maintain calm. Chiari responded that all existing treaties between the two countries must be completely revised in order to prevent further explosions of violence. Johnson later wrote in his memoirs that he was convinced "it was indeed time for the United States and Panama to take a new look at our treaties." After diplomatic relations were resumed, on April 3, 1964, both countries agreed to renegotiate the Panama Canal treaties.

In June 1967, President Johnson and Chiari's successor, Marco Robles, announced that agreements had been concluded on three treaties. However, opposition within the United States Congress was so intense that they were never submitted for ratification. The next year, when General Omar Torrijos came to power as the leader of Panama, he renounced the agreements. It seemed that new treaties, even when negotiated, were acceptable to neither side.

President Richard Nixon began the negotiations again in 1970. Four years later, a set of principles were agreed upon. However, they were vehemently attacked within the United States because the concept of American control over the Canal in perpetuity was eliminated. At the end of the prospective treaty's life, Panama would assume responsibility for the operation of the Canal. Both Presidents Nixon and Ford continued the negotiations in good faith but with great political caution.

Governor Ronald Reagan gave the Panama Canal issue special prominence during the 1976 presidential primaries. He accused the Ford Administration of maintaining a "mouselike silence" in the face of "blackmail" from Panama's "dictator." He repeatedly used a line guaranteed to get applause: "When it comes to the Canal, we built it, we paid for it, it's ours and we should tell Torrijos and Company that we are going to keep it!" Reagan's position appealed to many Americans, because he presented the issue, simplistically, as a test of our nation's power and greatness. Ford later believed he lost several primaries to Reagan over Panama.

Before 1974, I myself was only vaguely aware of any argument about this subject in the United States. But when I started my national campaign, I began to receive frequent questions about the Panama Canal. This was a surprise in itself, but even more impressive was the intensity of feeling among those who raised the subject on my visits to various communities around the country. After learning more about the history of our relations with Panama, I would respond to questioners that we should continue to negotiate with the Panamanians, that legal sovereignty was not at issue because Panama retained that under the original treaty, and that we could share responsibilities more equitably without giving up practical control of the Canal.

As I conferred with my foreign-policy advisers after the election, it seemed clear that if we were going to negotiate seriously with Panama, two facts would have to be faced: we would have to begin immediately; and the eventual agreement would have to include a phasing out of our absolute control of the Canal, as well as the acknowledgment of Panamanian sovereignty.

These were not easy decisions for me to make. I knew that we were sure to face a terrible political fight in Congress. During the fall of 1975, a Senate resolution had been introduced that directly contravened the terms our country would be offering at the negotiating table. It opposed any new treaty and expressed strong opposition to any termination of United States sovereignty over the Canal Zone. The resolution had been sponsored by thirty-eight senators, four more than the one-third needed to prevent ratification of a treaty! Furthermore, public-opinion polls showed that the American public strongly opposed relinquishing control of the Canal.

Nevertheless, I believed that a new treaty was absolutely necessary. I was convinced that we needed to correct an injustice. Our failure to take action after years of promises under five previous Presidents had created something of a diplomatic cancer, which was poisoning our relations with Panama.

In addition, though we could not talk about it much in public, the Canal was in serious danger from direct attack and sabotage unless a new and fair treaty arrangement could be forged. This concern was an important consideration for me and the Joint Chiefs of Staff. Our military leaders came to tell me—and also testified to Congress—that the Canal could not be defended permanently unless we were able to maintain a working partnership and good relations with Panama. Secretary of Defense Harold Brown expressed it well when he said that the Canal could best be kept in operation "by a cooperative effort with a friendly Panama," rather than by an "American garrison amid hostile surroundings." The commanding Army officer in the Canal Zone estimated that it would require a force of at least a hundred thousand armed men to mount a reasonable defense of the Canal within a hostile environment. Even then a successful defense would be doubtful, especially if other Latin American nations became antagonistic to us.

Both we and the Panamanian leaders had to be careful not to present this crucial argument in the form of a threat, because there would, understandably, be a negative reaction from Congress and the American public. In fact, opponents of a new treaty were the ones who would raise this issue often, claiming that we were negotiating only as a response to "blackmail."

Of course, the security of the Canal was also of crucial importance to Panama. More than anything else, the Panamanians wanted to guarantee its continued operation. The stability of their government and the strength of their economy depended on a successful resolution of the treaty dispute. Dissident groups, some known to be subject to strong communist influences, were using the old treaty terms to support their vituperative charges against the United States as an "imperialistic colonial power." These persistent attacks were not only damaging to us, but comprised a serious threat to the political and business leaders of Panama. It was certainly to our advantage to have a strong, stable, and prosperous Panama, and it was important that we prevent the strengthening of communists and terrorist groups by proving we could be fair.

I was additionally concerned because our failure to act on the treaty was driving a wedge between us and some of our best friends and allies among the other American nations. They were being forced to take sides between us and Panama, and they were not supporting us. In a way not of our choosing, this issue had become a litmus test throughout the world, indicating how the United States, as a superpower, would treat a small and relatively defenseless nation that had always been a close partner and supporter.

Despite the opposition of Congress and the public, I decided to plow ahead, believing that if the facts could be presented clearly, my advisers and I could complete action while my political popularity was still high and before we had to face the additional complication of the congressional election campaigns of 1978.

Even before the inauguration, I decided to name Sol Linowitz, a well-known expert on Latin America and former ambassador to the OAS (Organization of American States), as my representative on the negotiating team. This appointment was a clear signal that we meant business; in December 1976, the Linowitz Commission on U.S.–Latin American Relations had called the dispute with Panama "the most urgent issue" to be faced in the hemisphere. In order to avoid debilitating confirmation hearings, I took advantage of my authority to make Sol a Special Representative to serve for six months, his term to expire on August 10, 1977. During this time, he and Chief Negotiator Ellsworth Bunker were able to work together with gratifying effectiveness.

When a complex issue of major importance must be considered, the President sometimes orders a wide-ranging review, so that everyone concerned can understand the nation's policy and work in harmony toward the same goals. My very first Presidential Review Memorandum (PRM 1) addressed the Panama Canal problem. During the early months of 1977, our negotiators were hard at work, consulting with me and trying to protect our nation's interests while dealing in good faith with their Panamanian counterparts. This was not easy, because we found the Panamanians to be as tough as we were at the bargaining table. Feelings about the treaty were at a fever pitch in Panama, and it was very difficult for the leaders to compromise on the demands of the people for immediate and total control of the Zone.

Within two weeks after I was inaugurated, the Panamanian Foreign Minister, Aquilino Boyd, visited Washington to meet with Secretary Cyrus Vance and to review the outstanding issues. The United States and Panamanian negotiators then met on February 14 in Panama, but made little progress. For a while thereafter, it seemed that we would be spared the trouble of a Senate ratification fight and be faced instead with another confrontation with Panama and the other Latin American countries. Although the Panamanians considered our conditions an infringement on their sovereignty, there was no way I could yield on two or three important points. We had to have assured priority of access to the Canal, and we had to have the right to defend it against external threats at *all* times in the future.

On March 13, meeting with the Panamanians in Washington, our negotiators proposed two treaties. One would set forth new arrangements for the joint operation of the Canal for the rest of this century, at the end of which Panama would assume total control. The other would guarantee the permanent neutrality of the Canal, and the right of the United States to defend it.

By May 18, after much argument, the Panamanians agreed on the neutrality issue, with the understanding that our right of defense applied to external threats only, and that Panama would protect the Canal against danger from within. Secretary of Defense Harold Brown and Chairman of the Joint Chiefs of Staff George Brown both approved this language in the developing agreement (some called it the Brown–Brown language). By the last week in May, we were so encouraged that we began detailed briefings for the members of Congress, concentrating most of our effort in the Senate, where sixty-seven members would have to approve a treaty. We also began gearing up for the ratification debate.

Then, on May 30, the Panamanians dealt the negotiations an almost fatal blow. They demanded enormous payoffs from the United States—more than $1 billion in a lump sum and $300 million annually until the year 2000. This was a ridiculous request, which we never seriously considered, but it was great news to the treaty's opponents.

Although we offered to increase Panama's share of the proceeds, neither I nor Congress would agree to any payments to Panama other than those that could come out of revenues from the Canal itself. Our position was unwavering, but the Panamanians would not accept it as final.

As the weeks passed, it seemed the negotiators had reached a stalemate. On July 29, I met with the American and Panamanian negotiators, and was told that only a direct communication from me to General Torrijos could resolve the argument.

I personally wrote a letter to Torrijos for the Panama negotiators to deliver, stating in effect that we were making our last offer, and that it was "generous, fair, and appropriate." After consulting with other Latin American leaders, Torrijos announced on August 5 that Panama would accept our economic proposals. This was good news, but there were still unresolved defense issues, and we all knew that Linowitz could not serve after August 10, when his appointment would expire.

We made it clear that the presence of Ambassador Linowitz on our team was crucial to our aggressive effort to reach agreement. The knowledge of Sol's impending departure therefore had a beneficial effect on the Panamanian negotiators. They yielded on several points so that on his last day they could announce success. I was pleased with the terms of the agreement and breathed a sigh of relief.

Now we could draft the text of the two treaties that would be fair and beneficial to both countries. One treaty would return most of the Canal Zone territory to the Panamanians and permit them to join with us in the operation and maintenance of the Canal itself. As the "senior partner," we would have operating control of the Canal as well as the right to protect it with our existing Canal Zone forces until the end of the century. At that time, all our military forces would be withdrawn, but under a separate "neutrality" treaty, we would retain the permanent right to come back to defend the Canal from any external threat that might interfere with its continued neutral, or equal, service to the ships of all nations. One exception was that in a time of emergency, warships of the United States would always be guaranteed the right to expeditious passage.

This outcome was a notable achievement for Ambassadors Bunker and Linowitz. For fourteen years, our two countries had not been able to conclude an agreement that was satisfactory to both sides. Even now, our prospects for success on Capitol Hill seemed dismal indeed.

In the Senate (where support was stronger than in the House) we would have to obtain two-thirds of the total votes cast on ratification of each of the two treaties. At first it seemed impossible. Too many senators were already on record in opposition to any new treaty. They had made these commitments during their own election campaigns, or in response to pressure from fellow senators who were fervently opposed to "giving away our Canal."

It is not easy for a politician to change a public position even when the political rewards are obvious. To reverse oneself from a popular promise to one that is emotionally unpopular requires an exceedingly rare act of courage. For a new treaty to be approved, many United States senators would have to demonstrate this kind of courage.

Even if we were able to secure ratification of both treaties, we still would have to submit legislation to both Houses of Congress to implement all the provisions of the agreement, including the transfer of land, buildings, and equipment to Panamanian ownership. Over the years there had been repeated votes in the House of Representatives expressing overwhelming opposition to any such action.

At the time, polls indicated that 78 per cent of the American people did not want to "give up" the Canal, and only 8 per cent found the idea acceptable. Therefore, it was particularly important that we have bipartisan support; and we relied very heavily on some of the Republican leaders who had been involved in the negotiations before I became President.

> *Ford, Kissinger, and Baker all gave me encouraging reports on their attitude concerning the Panama Canal treaty, and unless the public pressure is too heavy on them I think they can help me a great deal in the Senate. . . . This past Saturday we sent all the senators a telegram urging them not to speak out against the treaty until they know the details of the agreement. Apparently it worked with most of them except a few nuts like Strom Thurmond and Jesse Helms.* DIARY, AUGUST 9, 1977

Unfortunately, the House of Representatives had not been willing to wait passively until after the Senate could consider the treaties. Treaty opponents had already gone to court claiming, on constitutional grounds, that since property would be transferred, both Houses of Congress would have to approve the agreement. We maintained that a treaty signed by the President and ratified by two-thirds of the Senate was adequate in itself. When the issue reached the U.S. Supreme Court in June, the decision had been in our favor. However, this outcome had not stopped the antagonistic House committees from beginning public hearings, even before the treaty negotiations were completed. That summer, a stream of witnesses, and some of the committee members, had paraded before the television cameras their arguments that the treaties were illegal, unpatriotic, a cowardly yielding to blackmail, a boon to communism, and a threat to our nation's security. It had been difficult for us to respond adequately, because at that time we could not reveal—in fact, did not know—what would be in the final agreement. Committee members had even attacked our negotiators and habitually referred to the Panamanian leader as either a "tinhorn dictator" or, on better days, just a plain "dictator."

Only in late September, after the treaties were signed, could the Senate committees begin their hearings. It would then be too late to conclude the debates and vote on ratification in 1977, so we could only wait—and be prepared for a protracted battle for votes in an election year.

The antitreaty forces would be happy about any delay. The *National Journal* reported that several of the archconservative groups saw this year of debate as a way to capture control of the Republican party. Richard Viguerie, the publicist for conservative causes, who would send out hundreds of thousands of computer-printed letters on the subject, predicted, "The conservatives will prevail on this, with well over 40 votes, maybe even 44 or something like that." He went on, "It's an issue the conservatives can't lose on. . . . Now conservatives can get excited about the Panama Canal giveaway and they can go to the polls, look for a person's name on the ballot who favored these treaties, and vote against him." This statement was an explicit threat to many members of Congress who were trying to decide how to vote on the Panama Canal treaties. Gary Jarmin of the American Conservative Union said, "It's a good issue for the future of the conservative movement. It's not just the issue itself we're fighting for. This is an excellent opportunity for conservatives to seize control of the Republican Party." This group sent out more than two million pieces of mail, trying to defeat the treaties.

Former Governor Ronald Reagan was a mainstay in this effort. He traveled the country and sent his radio and television tapes to hundreds of stations to rally opposition to the Senate ratification vote. We also had to face the John Birch Society, the Liberty Lobby, the National States Rights Party, and similar groups, which banded together in a formidable array.

I had to do something to seize the initiative, because the antitreaty forces had been active for more than three years—since the original principles had been published in 1974. Despite contrary advice from some senators that it might be construed as putting undue pressure on them for ratification, I decided to invite national leaders throughout this hemisphere to attend a signing ceremony on September 7.

We were overwhelmed with acceptances from eighteen heads of state, one vice president, and three foreign ministers. It became much more than a ceremonial occasion for me, because I had promised to have individual meetings with the leaders of all nations who attended. With each one I had to be prepared to discuss any possible issue that might arise between us, and so I labored over briefing books. But it was a rewarding task. President Ford and Lady Bird Johnson spent the night with us at the White House to attend the affair, and former Vice Presidents and several former Secretaries of State and other Republican and Democratic dignitaries added substance to the large delegation representing our country. It was a successful television extravaganza, and a vivid demonstration of the international significance of the treaties.

To me, however, the most impressive aspect of the evening was the deep emotion with which General Omar Torrijos approached the ceremony. As we waited in a small office before entering the large assembly hall, he tried to thank me for ending generations of frustration and despair among the Panamanian people. But before he could finish his statement, he broke down and sobbed as his wife held him. During the months ahead, the more my colleagues and I learned about this man, the greater the respect and affection we had for him. I was certainly convinced that night that we were doing the right thing, and that all our efforts were indeed worthwhile.

More of the American people were beginning to add their support. A few days before we signed the treaties, Gallup reported that 39 per cent were in favor of the treaties and only 46 per cent against them—remarkable progress over the past few weeks.

Still, the long road of ratification lay ahead of us. During the fall of 1977, I spent a lot of my time planning carefully how to get Senate votes. The task force set up for this purpose developed a somewhat limited objective: not to build up an absolute majority of support among all citizens, but to convince an acceptable number of key political leaders in each important state to give their senators some "running room." We worked closely with the individual senators on lists of state leaders, and we brought hundreds of editors, college presidents, political party leaders, elected officials, campaign contributors, and other influential people into the White House for personal briefings by me. Depending on the makeup of each group, I would invite State Department or Pentagon officials to join me, including the highly effective members of the Joint Chiefs of Staff. At times, the military uniforms were of great help.

We also briefed our top administrators at the State Department about the terms of the treaties and how best to present the facts. Altogether they made more than 1500 appearances throughout the nation to explain the treaties directly to the public. Labor unions, business leaders, the Jaycees, garden clubs, religious groups, senior citizens, schoolteachers, Common Cause, and other organizations joined us in our effort. Counteracting the Ronald Reagan opposition, such distinguished conservative leaders as John Wayne and William Buckley spoke out for ratification. By the end of the year, about half the nation's newspapers were in favor.

Once people really understood the terms of the agreement, most of them supported it. A CBS-*New York Times* poll and a separate NBC poll both found that, when they were told the United States could still move militarily in order to keep the Canal open, the respondents favored the treaties by a margin of more than 2 to 1.

All was not going well, however. Some Panamanian leaders, in their eagerness to prove that they had negotiated a good deal, were publicly interpreting parts of the treaty texts differently from my explanation of the same items to Congress. I knew I was right, but it was necessary to eliminate the confusion about the points of controversy—military intervention, the definition of neutrality, and priority for American ships' use of the Canal in an emergency. On October 14, I asked General Torrijos to come see me in Washington on his return from an extended trip through the Middle East and Europe. He and I had a good meeting; we drafted and issued a Statement of Understanding that resolved our differences satisfactorily. The Statement apparently suited the people of Panama, who strongly approved the treaties by a vote of 470,000 to 230,000.

After this official ratification of the treaties in the referendum, it was now very important that the U.S. Senate add no substantive amendments which would require resubmission of the new text to Panama's citizens for another vote. Predictably, the adoption of a "killer" amendment became the new goal of treaty opponents. As a substitute for the many unacceptable proposals, we encouraged the adoption of the terms of the Carter–Torrijos Statement of Understanding as amendments to the treaties. At the end of January 1978, the Senate Foreign Relations Committee voted to recommend that the treaties be considered favorably by the Senate. For the first time in fifty years, a treaty text was amended, but only to include the clarifying language I had worked out with the leader of Panama.

We did not fare as well in the Senate Armed Services Committee, where Chairman John Stennis and several other members opposed the treaties. They provided a forum for a few retired military officers who echoed the arguments put forward by the conservative or right-wing organizations. The active military leaders, with the responsibility for our nation's defense on their shoulders, countered every negative argument with effective testimony. (This was a pattern I was to observe many times while I was President—irresponsibly belligerent statements by older retired officers and carefully considered and reasonable testimony by those still in service.)

I worked closely with the leaders of Panama, exchanging reports and ideas almost daily after the full Senate debate began in February 1978. Gabriel Lewis, Panama's Ambassador to the United States, was a frequent visitor to the Oval Office, and through various means General Torrijos and I exchanged a constant stream of messages—about the concerns of the United States Senate, human rights, and the possibility of more democracy in Panama after the treaty issue was resolved.

I found that the most effective means of swaying undecided senators was to get them to see for themselves the situation in Panama. About forty-five of them made the trip. There they inspected the Canal and its fragile lock and dam systems, talked to the Zonians, and listened to Lt. General Dennis McAuliffe and our other military leaders who were responsible for the security and operation of the Canal. In effect, they learned firsthand the same facts that had been faced for fourteen years by our Presidents and negotiators in devising an acceptable solution to this problem.

The senators received good answers to their questions, but the most effective salesman of all was Torrijos. He impressed the visitors with his calm strength, his eagerness to give unadorned facts, his limitless patience in face of vituperative attacks leveled at him by some members of Congress, his promises to democratize Panama's government and to correct any violations of human rights, and his obvious determination to have Panama and the United States work in harmony during the decades ahead. I also encouraged our Ambassador to Panama, William Jorden, to arrange for the senators to meet with treaty opponents, both in the Zone and among the Panamanians. When they returned after a three- or four-day visit, those who had already made public announcements of their positions did not change their minds, but more and more of the uncommitted had been won over.

I kept a large private notebook on my desk, with a section for each senator. There I would enter every report or rumor about how the undecided ones might be inclined. If anyone on my staff knew of a question a senator had asked, we got the answer for him. If key advisers or supporters of a senator were known to oppose the treaties, we worked to convert them. I shared these responsibilities personally with my congressional liaison team, and worked on the task with all my influence and ability. At the time of the signing ceremonies, there were fewer than thirty commitments of support; by the end of November, there were forty-five; at the beginning of Senate debate in February, forty-eight. These were firm promises, and in spite of some occasional threats, we never lost one of them—except for the deaths of two supporters. Senator Lee Metcalf of Montana died on January 12, and Senator Hubert Humphrey passed away on January 13. Although Senator Muriel Humphrey, who was appointed to fill her husband's term, also supported the treaties, we especially missed the persuasive leadership Hubert Humphrey could have provided in the floor debates.

After several weeks of our working closely with Senator Robert Byrd, Democratic Majority Leader, and Senator Howard Baker, Republican Minority Leader, both endorsed the treaties in mid-January, giving us our biggest boost. They were formidable allies on the Senate floor, and their support made it much easier for other doubtful or timid senators to join our forces.

We organized a full-court press. I talked to all one hundred senators, meeting privately with every one except the few who were in the forefront of the opposition. During the last few days, all of my White House team concentrated on those dozen or so who were still undecided. My diary notes reveal a very discouraging picture.

Senator Dick Stone of Florida wanted me to have a joint television appearance with him to pledge that we would never withdraw or reduce our military forces from Guantanamo, Cuba, or other places in the Caribbean, following which he might be able to make up his mind.

Of the two Georgia Senators, Herman Talmadge told me that he "might hold my nose and vote for it," but he was not ready to decide. Sam Nunn said that he would try not to embarrass me, but that it would be important to him to know how Senator Talmadge would vote.

Robert Griffin of Michigan would only promise not to vote for any "killer amendments," and said he would not join the so-called truth squad, which was traveling around the nation working against the treaties.

Wendell Ford of Kentucky called a press conference to announce his opposition; we struggled to have his announcement postponed.

Quentin Burdick of North Dakota and John Melcher of Montana were concerned about maintenance of the Canal after it was turned over to Panama; Richard Schweiker of Pennsylvania, about the future of a possible sea-level canal that might someday replace the existing one, which now required a series of locks to raise and lower ships traveling across the isthmus.

Ted Stevens of Alaska was worried about the shipping costs of Alaskan oil.

> *President Ford said that he would call the undecided Republicans—[John] Heinz, [William] Roth, Schweiker, Dole, Goldwater, [Robert] Stevens, and [Milton] Young, and that he would also call two who were marked against the treaties—Griffin and [Richard] Lugar. He suggested that Kissinger and Rockefeller should be asked to call some of the same ones.* DIARY, FEBRUARY 2, 1978

I really appreciated his help, because I knew how difficult the effort was. He soon came to agree.

> *President Ford called at lunch time to tell me that he's had a tough job in trying to recruit Republicans to support the Panama treaties.* DIARY, FEBRUARY 9, 1978

Only one of the nine—John Heinz of Pennsylvania—finally voted with us. Other Republican leaders were obviously working just as hard as Ford—but for the other side.

I never gave up, even on those I knew to have been against the treaties in the past. For instance, I asked everyone I could think of to intercede with the two Georgia senators. I thought theirs might be the deciding votes, and my prediction proved to be right. Personal friends of theirs; executives from the state banks, the Coca-Cola Company, and the Georgia Power Company; political fund raisers—all joined me in this concerted effort.

Senator Edward Zorinsky of Nebraska just could not make up his mind. He said he wanted to vote for the treaties because he had ambitions to be a member of the Senate Foreign Relations Committee, and also because he knew it was the best thing to do for our country. His only concern was the lack of support back home. Zorinsky asked that we have another briefing for about a hundred prominent Nebraskans, which we hastily arranged. It went well. Then he said he would have to take a public-opinion poll, to see what his people wanted him to do. He put an ad in a major state newspaper, and the returns showed a majority in favor of his voting "aye." After all this, his vote was still in doubt, and eventually he voted "no."

There were some great speeches on the Senate floor. I asked Robert Byrd to let me listen to a tape of his speech, and found it particularly effective. Responding to his colleagues who were excessively swayed by the huge piles of antitreaty mail, he was right on the mark.

He said that if you went by public-opinion polls and telephone calls or the volume of mail, you could replace senators with an adding machine or set of scales!

DIARY, FEBRUARY 13, 1978

Public opinion was a formidable force in some of the most conservative states, such as New Hampshire. The governor, Meldrim Thompson, and the editor of the Manchester *Union-Leader,* William Loeb, had really fired up the treaty opponents. The two senators were inclined to support us, but were concerned about their political standing. I went in to try to help them.

I met Senators Tom McIntyre and John Durkin. Drove to Nashua, where [the community] had selected 500 top high school students, along with their teachers and parents—about 1500 in all—to meet [with me] for another televised town meeting. They had superb questions, carefully prepared ahead of time. The biggest surprise was that when they asked about the Panama Canal treaties and I said, "The Panama Canal treaties are good—" they interrupted with enthusiastic and sustained applause. Part of this, I think, was reaction against a few hecklers in the back of the gymnasium. But it was reassuring to John Durkin, who'd already endorsed the treaties, and to Senator McIntyre, who's still a little bit unsure of the political consequences.   DIARY, FEBRUARY 18, 1978

Our campaign was paying off; it was becoming more fashionable to support the treaties. A new Gallup Poll in February found 45 per cent in favor and only 42 per cent opposed. This was the first time we had a plurality on our side. Among those who were "better informed," 57 per cent favored the treaties.

But in mid-February, amazingly, an entirely new attack was mounted by Senator Robert Dole, Senator Jesse Helms, and other foes of the treaties. They charged that General Torrijos and his family were actively trafficking in drugs, that the treaties had been formulated by us under pressure from Panama's negotiators, and that high officials of the United States had been paid to arrange increases in the annual payments to be made to Panama. None of these charges was true, but they were highly publicized, and the Senate had to go into secret session to hear them and to have them refuted after a thorough investigation by the responsible members of the Senate Intelligence Committee.

After this incident, we had the first test of strength on February 22. Of the two treaties, I wanted to vote first on the one confirming the right of the United States to defend the Canal on into the twenty-first century, because it was our most politically attractive agreement, and the questions it raised had to be answered before many senators would be willing to consider turning over control from the United States to Panama at the end of this century. The opponents moved that the order of voting be reversed, so that the more unpopular question of giving up control would come first. Their motion was defeated by a vote of 67 to 30—but this was not a true indication of support. Several who voted with us made it clear that they had merely approved the order of voting and were not committed to ratifying the treaties.

We then had to face a flood of amendments, some of them superficially innocuous—such as putting a permanent limit on

the ship transit fees or requiring that in the year 2000 we renegotiate with Panama the right of our military forces to remain in
the Canal Zone. Still lacking the two-thirds vote for ratification,
at least we had the simple majority necessary to defeat the steady
stream of these amendments, any one of which would require—as
the opponents well knew—that the treaty be renegotiated and
resubmitted to the Panamanians for another referendum.

In spite of such progress, the debate continued on and on. We
began to worry about the heavy legislative agenda that was piling
up.

> *Senator Byrd came to discuss the delays in Senate work
> caused by the treaty debates which are going on, appar-
> ently ad infinitum. He doesn't think they'll be through
> even in April. . . . We also discussed the vote, still three or
> four short, and getting more difficult to obtain for ratifi-
> cation. I think Wendell Ford is coming around on the
> treaties, but we are fearful that we are going to lose both
> Montana votes. We've counted on those. It's going to be
> close.*   DIARY, MARCH 1, 1978

Meanwhile, Torrijos was finding it increasingly difficult to control the growing impatience in Panama, where the Senate debate
was being followed on radio as avidly as the citizens of our
country followed the Watergate hearings on television. The dis-
paraging remarks being made by treaty opponents about Panama, its people, and its leaders were scarcely noted here but
rubbed raw nerves among the Panamanians. I suspected that
some of the lurid rhetoric was designed to provoke a Panamanian
reaction that would give treaty opponents more ammunition in
their battle.

All of a sudden, on March 3, Senator James Allen of Alabama, a
formidable parliamentarian who led the opposition forces, announced that the pile of amendments that had been introduced to
stall action on the treaties would be withdrawn. The opponents
were ready for a quick victory, and we were in no position to ask
for the delay we needed.

We would approach the first climax near the middle of
March—the final decision by the Senate on the Neutrality
Treaty—and we did not have the votes. In spite of many other
issues crowding in on me, I considered the Panama Canal
ratification to be the most important. I put it first, despite the
fact that I was growing increasingly exasperated over the time it
was taking.

Kirbo called early this morning from Bainbridge [Georgia], wanting to know if he could come up and help with Long, Talmadge, and a few others. I told him "yes," to come on. Said he and Strauss could work as a team. In the meantime I'll be meeting with Talmadge and Long, perhaps Ed Brooke and William Roth. Later with [Sam] Nunn and [Pete] Dominici, if necessary, to get their support. We've got to get four of them to pass the treaties.

Afterward I had lunch with Russell Long. I told him how badly I needed his support on the treaties. He said that he would not let me down, that if his vote was important I would have it. . . . But he left open the possibility that he might support some amendments which would require Torrijos to have another referendum.

DIARY, MARCH 7, 1978

Frank Moore, Warren Christopher, others came in to discuss the latest developments on Panama. We now have 59 sure votes and varying degrees of success projected for Heinz, [Henry] Bellmon, Ford, Nunn, Talmadge, Long, [Jennings] Randolph, Brooke, [Dennis] DeConcini, [Paul] Hatfield, and Zorinsky. Byrd met with a few of them today, and they are wanting to have some amendments that would be very embarrassing to me or to the Panamanians. I urged him to hang tough, and said that I would rather yield on something important to the United States (like the provision requiring Panama and us to cooperate on a possible future sea-level canal) than to go back on my word of honor to the Panamanians. We've done a lot of damage to Torrijos with the irresponsible Senate testimony, and he would have trouble getting another referendum passed.

I asked Sam Nunn to come by the mansion to talk to me about the treaties—told him how serious the problem had been for me, that I needed his personal help. And he promised me that I had it!   DIARY, MARCH 8, 1978

Of the eleven senators named above, we had to have eight, and so far only Nunn was firmly committed. His vote would certainly help us with both Long and Talmadge, and Paul Hatfield of Montana (who had been named to take the late Senator Metcalf's seat) had told us several times that Nunn's opinion on military matters was very important to him. That night, I made arrangements to meet the next day with Dennis DeConcini of Arizona. I

had no idea that this meeting would create the single biggest
threat to the treaties.

> *Senator DeConcini came by, and I asked him to help me*
> *with the treaties. He's been wanting an amendment on the*
> *Neutrality Treaty itself, giving us the right to negotiate*
> *military bases after the year 2000. The problem with this*
> *is it requires an additional referendum in Panama and*
> *violates my word to the Panamanian people. We were*
> *trying to get him to offer the amendment to the resolution*
> *of ratification instead, which would not require the plebi-*
> *scite in Panama.*   DIARY, MARCH 9, 1978

This was a crucial difference. The resolution would be a unilateral expression of the sentiment of the Senate. An amendment to
the text of the treaty would require concurrence from the Panamanians, and would be a fatal blow to the agreement because
neither Torrijos nor his people would approve such a change. In
fact, they would strongly object even to the Senate resolution,
which stated that we would reserve the right to protect the Canal
after the year 2000 by using military force *in Panama* if necessary.

Continuing my efforts, I had lunch with Paul Hatfield, who
made it plain that our Ambassador to Japan, Mike Mansfield, was
the only one who could sway Montana opinion enough for Hatfield to vote with us. We convinced Mansfield to make an appropriate statement. In the meantime, Fritz, Cy, Warren, Harold, and
others, meeting with treaty supporters and the doubtful senators,
were reporting some progress.

> *Frank came in to tell me that Herman Talmadge's staff*
> *had asked us to call off the dogs—that he was willing to*
> *go with us on the Panama Canal treaties without com-*
> *ments.*   DIARY, MARCH 10, 1978

As a very conservative senator, who had been genuinely convinced
that we should keep control of the Canal, Talmadge was to cast
two very difficult votes, one for each of the treaties. Although he
never mentioned it to me, I will always believe that he did it out
of respect for me as a fellow Georgian, whom he saw to be quite
vulnerable to serious embarrassment and loss of prestige if the
treaties were rejected.

The next day, Russell Long called to tell me I would have his
support on the first treaty; at the same time, there was every
indication that I would lose Senators Ford and Zorinsky. On

Sunday, with four days to go, I could not see any way to win without picking up at least one completely unexpected vote. I spent the afternoon calling fifteen senators whom I had previously marked off as lost. My main argument was the damage to our country and to the Presidency if the treaties should now be rejected. They listened politely; it seemed to me that I made an impression on a few of them, but I didn't get any new commitments.

It was remarkable how many different things I had to work on during these last few days: a very serious nationwide coal strike, energy legislation, my upcoming trip to Latin America and Africa, a burgeoning crisis between Israel and Egypt plus an Israeli invasion of Lebanon, the United Nations Disarmament Conference, the midwinter Governors Conference, final approval of our complete urban program, a forthcoming trip by Brzezinski to China to work on normalization, war in the Horn of Africa, our proposals to prevent bankruptcy in New York City, negotiations with the British on air-transport agreements, a state visit by President Tito of Yugoslavia, final stages of the SALT negotiations, the Civil Service reform bill, the coming state visit of Prime Minister Takeo Fukuda of Japan, a decision about whether General Alexander Haig would stay on at NATO, F-15 airplane sales to Saudi Arabia, a visit by Israeli Defense Minister Ezer Weizman and preparations for an early visit by Prime Minister Begin, and a major defense speech at Wake Forest the day after the treaty vote.

It's hard to concentrate on anything except Panama.
                                        DIARY, MARCH 13, 1978

We're still short on assured votes for the treaties. I asked Cy to go and spend full time on the Hill, and also to ask Henry Kissinger to do the same thing. I then asked Harold Brown and the Joint Chiefs to join them there, and Fritz will be spending full time—all working personally with members of the Senate. . . . I had lunch with Senator Stennis to try to get his vote on the treaties, but failed. . . . President Ford promised to use his influence with Heinz, Bellmon, Brooke, and Schweiker. . . . Later on in the day Rosalynn called Mrs. Hatfield in Montana. She called Mrs. Zorinsky. . . . This has been one of the worst days. . . . knowing that we were lost, then gaining a little hope. . . . I went to bed early, about 10:00, and got up late, about 6:00 the next morning, to get some rest.
                                        DIARY, MARCH 14, 1978

Things were moving fast. Warren Christopher was busy at work drafting last-minute amendments acceptable to Senators Nunn and DeConcini that would apply to the resolution of ratification rather than to the treaty itself. Publicity about DeConcini's language was creating a furor among the Panamanians, who considered it an expression of intent to interfere in their internal affairs. Senator Paul Hatfield heard that Ambassador Mansfield might make a radio tape for Hatfield's potential opponent to use against him in the next senatorial election. When we convinced him this was not true, we won his vote. DeConcini came to tell me that he would support the treaties if his and Nunn's amendments were acceptable. Jim McIntyre from OMB called me to discuss a proposal for a desalinization plant in Oklahoma which was of interest to Senator Bellmon. He asked whether I would veto a public-works bill that included the plant if I thought the project was economically feasible. I told him no. Later, Senator Lloyd Bentsen of Texas reported that he had convinced Bellmon to vote with us. I never knew whether the desalinization plant was a factor in his decision—but I was not taking any chances at that point.

It was now the day before the Senate vote, and I had a new problem in Panama.

> *I had to call General Torrijos. He was planning to blast the Senate and reject the Panama treaties outright because of some amendment language that DeConcini insisted upon. I don't like the language either, but it doesn't change the text or the meaning of the treaties themselves. I agreed to send Warren Christopher and Hamilton Jordan down to Panama tomorrow afternoon after the votes are completed to explain the complete action of the Senate to Torrijos rather than having him overly concerned about one sentence in the resolution of ratification.*
>
> DIARY, MARCH 15, 1978

I had seriously underestimated the concern of the Panamanians. Over the next few days, they made a mountain out of this molehill. The amendment language, an attempt to strengthen the right of the United States to use military force *in Panama* if the Canal should ever be threatened, implied that we might use force to meet both external threats and also threats from within Panama—a violation of my agreement with Torrijos. Without success, we tried to induce DeConcini to delete the words "in Panama," but he adamantly refused. Two or three other senators informed me that their votes, too, were contingent on this language being adopted. We finally yielded, to save the treaty. Just before the vote on the Senate resolution, the DeConcini amendment to the resolution of ratification passed, and a motion to include it as an amendment to the treaty was rejected.

I gave up trying to assuage the Panamanians, who were following every word of the Senate debate and vote. General Torrijos called and asked that Hamilton and Chris not come down. He had decided to go off for a few days to be alone.

On March 16—the last day—DeConcini, Bellmon, and Hatfield announced for the treaty, Ford and Zorinsky against. After lunch, just before the voting began, I called Senator Howard Cannon again, and he decided to vote with us, giving us sixty-eight votes. He had been one of the fifteen apparently hopeless senators whom I had called in desperation.

The Senate had been debating the treaty for twenty-two days, and everyone—whether friend or foe—was ready for the verdict.

I listened to the final vote in my little private office, checking off each senator against the tally sheet where I had listed his or her commitment. I had never been more tense in my life as we listened to each vote shouted out on the radio. My assistants and I had not missed one in our count; there were no surprises. I thanked God when we got the sixty-seventh vote. It will always be one of my proudest moments, and one of the great achievements in the history of the United States Senate.

Many of the senators exhibited supreme political courage, particularly the twenty who were up for election later that same year and nevertheless voted for the treaties. I quickly voiced my admiration for them to the national press, and also thanked them personally. We had now agreed that the United States, even in the twenty-first century, would have the right to use its military forces to defend the Panama Canal against any external threat and to insure its neutrality and availability for use to all nations.

In the evening after supper I began to call some of the senators who had voted against us. They were not in a particularly good mood, but we will continue until we have called all of them. The vote on the second treaty is going to be even more difficult, in my opinion.

DIARY, MARCH 16, 1978

The antitreaty forces, now able to focus their pressure on just a very few of our weakest supporters, immediately predicted victory on the second vote—about turning over the Canal to Panama. Senator Paul Laxalt, a leader of the opponents, said, "The odds have very definitely tipped in our favor. I would not be a bit surprised to find our side with 38 or 39 votes before this is over. . . ." An ABC News poll revealed that only fifty-seven senators were now for the main treaty, with sixteen undecided.

For the time being, though, we could not concentrate our attention on the Senate. Our problem was in Panama because of the DeConcini amendment to the resolution. Torrijos was under heavy attack, repeatedly exclaiming in his public statements, "I ask myself the question: Have we by any chance lost a war? The United States didn't demand as much from Japan!" I pressed him to reserve judgment until after the second vote, because the outcome was hanging by a thread, but he continued an international campaign demanding that the Senate resolution be modified to prevent Panama's rejection of the treaties.

We discussed the Panama problems that have arisen because Torrijos is sending letters around indicating that he might renounce the treaties. We decided to review the options for him, which are very good ones. The fact is that the text of the treaty expresses our nonintervention commitment. This is repeated in the OAS and UN charters, which we certainly would not renounce, and ultimately, if Torrijos wants to, he can issue a reservation about his understanding of what the treaties mean on intervention in the internal affairs of Panama. We all decided that it would not be good to try to amend the second treaty in order to accommodate a problem with the first treaty.

DIARY, APRIL 7, 1978

But the problem wouldn't go away. We were beginning to lose support in the Senate even among our strongest allies, who, sympathizing with Panama, said they could not support the treaty unless a strong nonintervention provision was included. I met with Robert Byrd, Frank Church, and Paul Sarbanes to see if we could clarify our position and assuage the concerns of Panamanians and the senators at the same time. Since it had been impossible to deal with DeConcini directly from the White House or State Department, I decided that Panama's Ambassador Gabriel Lewis and Deputy Secretary of State Warren Christopher should work on the problem with the Senate leaders, letting them deal with DeConcini. After many hours, they finally evolved an acceptable proposal, which kept the original language and added a few other words to the Senate resolution, making it clear that nothing contravened the nonintervention language in the treaty texts. Both DeConcini and the Panamanians said this was satisfactory.

In the meantime, some of the supporters of the first treaty were threatening me over the second—but not because of the treaty itself.

> *Jim Abourezk says that because of the closed conference meetings on energy from which he is excluded, he's considering voting against the Panama Canal treaty. . . . Received an abusive letter from Senator [S.I.] Hayakawa saying that I was too soft on foreign affairs and defense and he was having second thoughts about his support of the treaties.*   DIARY, APRIL 13, 1978

Even my friend Senator Jim Sasser of Tennessee sent me word that he could not vote for the second treaty because of some of his home-state issues on which we disagreed. Senator Howard Cannon had been a very shaky vote on the first round, and he now announced that mail from his own supporters was running 20 to 1 against the treaties.

I met with all of them and tried to calm them down. I did my best to convince Abourezk, for instance, that I had no control over the congressional conference committees, and that House and Senate members decided how open their meetings should be. He would not, however, agree to vote for the treaty.

My most interesting meeting was with Senator Hayakawa, who was very gracious. We discussed a broad range of issues, with particular emphasis on Africa. He insisted that I needed his personal advice on defense and foreign matters and was adamantly in favor of our recognizing the Ian Smith regime in Rhodesia. I did not dissuade him by pointing out that no country on earth had done so. He even brought me a textbook he had written on semantics. It may not have been bedtime reading, but I needed his vote. I read the book that evening, and the next day called to congratulate him on its good points. Although my specific comments did convince him that I had indeed read his book, there was no commitment from him on the vote.

I eased the tension between myself and Sasser by inviting him to the White House for the twentieth-anniversary celebration of the Country Music Association. Tom T. Hall, Loretta Lynn, Conway

Twitty, Larry Gatlin, and Charlie Daniels proved to be a lot of
help to me and Panama that evening!

The Panama issue had almost everything else bogged down. It
was certainly not popular, and both the Senate and the public
were getting disgusted with what appeared to be a permanent
stalemate—a feeling I had shared for many months.

> *Caddell had prepared a very pessimistic report, based on*
> *public-opinion polling. I think their roughly 50% approval*
> *rating is an accurate measure of what we've achieved so*
> *far!*   DIARY, APRIL 15, 1978

During the final day—with less than twelve hours to go—it was
boiling down to this: we had to have two of the three undecided
Senators—Abourezk, Hayakawa, and Cannon.

> *During lunchtime I talked to Howard Cannon, who's mov-*
> *ing our way. He was concerned primarily about the atti-*
> *tude of the Church [of Jesus Christ of Latter-day Saints],*
> *and also about the newspaper attitude in Nevada. I called*
> *Salt Lake City to get a report from the Mormon Church.*
> *They told me they don't have any official position on the*
> *Panama Canal treaties. Ezra Taft Benson is the only one*
> *of the Church's twelve elders who had spoken out against*
> *them, and they pointed out that both Mormons and Bap-*
> *tists have people for and against the treaties. Cannon was*
> *particularly concerned about the Las Vegas newspaper*
> *editors who had been giving him a hard time. He asked*
> *me to call one of them, and I tried to do that.*
>   DIARY, APRIL 18, 1978

It took me several hours to ascertain the attitude of the Mor-
mon church leaders so that I could address the Senator's concern.
It was even more difficult to run down Donald Reynolds, editor of
the Las Vegas *Review-Journal*, because he was traveling across
Oklahoma in an automobile. When I finally reached him, he
stated that his editorial position was against the treaties. However, he agreed that his newspaper would acknowledge the political
courage of the Senator if he should support our position, and
promised to point out in his editorial comments that a statesman
should base his actions on his own assessment of controversial
issues and not on what was popular at the time. I was impressed

with him on the telephone, and made arrangements for him to visit the White House in the near future so that I could meet him personally. Senator Cannon, pleased with my two reports, moved closer to a commitment.

Abourezk has taken the position that the House and Senate rules are being violated when meetings are held in secret, and as a quid pro quo for his vote on the Panama Canal treaties (which he is for) he's demanding that I not let any Cabinet officers attend a meeting that's held behind closed doors. Obviously I can't police the House and Senate; I told him no. He said he hated to do what he had to do, and then hung up. DIARY, APRIL 18, 1978

Jim Abourezk was of Lebanese descent, and keenly interested in the rights of Palestinians, American Indians, and other people whom he considered to be oppressed in some way. I asked mutual friends in Saudi Arabia to help persuade him, and also called LaDonna Harris, wife of former Senator Fred Harris and a real champion of the rights of women and American Indians. Later I got private word directly from Prince Sultan of Saudi Arabia that Abourezk was going to vote for the treaties.

At the last minute, I received a call from some of the Senate leaders, who were closeted with Senator Hayakawa. I knew he was listening when they asked me if I needed to meet occasionally with the California semanticist to get his advice on African affairs. I gulped, thought for a few seconds, and replied, "Yes, I really do!" hoping God would forgive me. (As a matter of fact, the few later sessions I had with him were both interesting and helpful.)

All during the day we were anticipating massive violence in Panama if the treaties were defeated. When the vote started at 6:00, we were fairly sure that we would have all three of the doubtful senators with us, and that's the way the vote came out—exactly the same as it was on the first treaty.

It was a cliff-hanger for 24 hours. The Senate really performed well. I called the key members and congratulated them, and made a statement in English and then one for Latin America in Spanish. . . . Then called General Torrijos. DIARY, APRIL 18, 1978

I was exhausted, exhilarated, and thankful. We had finally passed this hurdle, one of the most onerous political ordeals of my life. Many times during the year when we were so discouraged, I had wondered if the results would justify the terrible political costs and the effort we had to exert. Each time, I decided that we simply could not afford to fail.

Privately Torrijos praised us highly, but later he revealed to the public that he had given orders for the National Guard to attack and blow up the Canal if the Senate had rejected our agreement. He said that if the treaty had been defeated, "we would have started our struggle for liberation, and possibly tomorrow the Canal would not be operating anymore." This statement was unfortunate, not at all helpful in our future task of passing through both Houses of Congress legislation necessary to implement the terms of the treaties. However, his revelation was not inconsistent with warnings we had been receiving from our intelligence agencies during the last few weeks, and confirmed that the concern of our military leaders had not been groundless. Now instead of enemies at war over a damaged—perhaps closed—Canal, we and Panama were to be allies, committed to a partnership of operating the crucial waterway for our common benefit.

Two months after the treaty vote I was in Panama, greeted with great joy by hundreds of thousands of people in the Cinco de Marzo Plaza. As General Torrijos and I signed the official transfer documents to conclude the treaty exchange, the Presidents of Mexico, Costa Rica, Colombia, and Venezuela and the Prime Minister of Jamaica were present. When we heads of state were alone, our conversation was primarily about two subjects: human rights and the relationship between the rich and poor nations of the world. We also talked about how to constrain Cuban and other communist intrusion in the internal affairs of Caribbean and Latin American countries, and how to encourage freedom and democracy in Nicaragua and minimize bloodshed there. There was no doubt that the new treaties would help to accomplish all these goals.

The next morning I met alone with Omar Torrijos and an interpreter. With some Spanish-speaking people, I could communicate directly, but Torrijos' Spanish was exceedingly hard to understand, and from time to time I had to ask for help. I wanted to comprehend every word he said, because I was pushing him hard to further democratize his government. He finally told me that the new constituent assembly being elected in August would have greatly expanded powers, and that it would select a president who would also manage more and more of Panama's affairs

The President and Torrijos with other
dignitaries at signing ceremony June 16, 1978

as he gained experience. These changes were essential. At the
same time I knew that no one could have handled the affairs of
Panama and its people more effectively than had this quiet and
courageous leader. He and his country had absorbed terrible
abuse from some of the more irresponsible United States senators
during the long debates, but he had responded with almost super-
human restraint, at least until the treaties had been approved.

*We took a helicopter tour of the Canal. I spoke to about
5,000 people about the responsibilities of the Zonians, and
how we respected and appreciated what they had done. I*

told the Army troops that I was in the Navy for 11 years,
and they booed. I told them that we depended on the Army
to keep the Canal open, and they cheered. Later, the news
reports said that there were boos and cheers during my
speech. I reckon that was an accurate report!

                                          DIARY, JUNE 17, 1978

   I arrived back home the next evening really tired but convinced
that the Panama treaties were worth all the effort.

Linowitz, Rosalynn, the President

   I am glad I couldn't anticipate then what still lay ahead. Although we expected some serious problems in the House of Representatives, none of us dreamed how difficult it would be to pass
the laws implementing the treaties before October 1, 1979, when
the process of transferring control was to begin. (Much of the
Canal Zone would be transferred then. The Canal would be operated by a joint commission through December 31, 1999.) At times,
the next sixteen months would seem like an extended nightmare.
The opponents of the treaties had not given up, nor slackened
their efforts to prevail in Congress, but only shifted their attention. They began to line up votes by hook or by crook against the
implementation legislation—needed to cover retirement benefits

to employees and relocation of military forces, to establish procedures for the orderly transfer of other property and responsibilities to the Panamanians, and to carry out the many provisions of
the now-ratified treaties. These laws would, of course, have to be
approved by a majority in both Houses of Congress, and signed
by me.

Some members of the House deeply opposed the treaties themselves; others on the Latin America committees were supporters
of President Anastasio Somoza in Nicaragua and saw a chance to
trade Panama treaty votes for support for his faltering regime;
one group was fearful of the right-wing political-action organizations during coming elections; some were irritated because the
House had not been given a voice in the ratification procedure;
and as always, there were timid members who were for the
treaties but hard to find when a controversial decision had to be
made. Meanwhile, most of our citizens and even the news media
simply assumed that the Panama Canal treaties were settled.

Beginning late in 1978, there was a series of legislative skirmishes
and later full-scale battles on the House floor, with the issue
always in doubt. We had to mount another massive lobbying
effort in the House and Senate simultaneously, this time with 535
combatants instead of a mere 100. First the House moved to
prohibit any transfers or changes in our Canal Zone military
forces. I had to notify Congress that such changes were "essential
to the national interests of the United States." Next, there was a
series of punitive votes against Panama, altering previous agreements by striking military credit sales and economic aid for job
training, schools, and the improvement of medical facilities in the
rural areas of the country. Then efforts were made to prohibit
specific provisions in the treaties, to require Panama to pay the
full costs of the Canal, and to force Canal toll fees up to exorbitant levels.

These actions, some backed by large majorities, were very troublesome, but it was necessary for us to persevere. We had to deal
with legislation coming from four House committees, each responsible for a different facet of congressional action. Some were
helpful; some against us. We won some votes but were losing
more. By late spring of 1979, more than a year after the second
treaty was ratified, we were in serious trouble. We reactivated
our task forces and began a nationwide appeal to the American
public and to all the House members we could reach.

*In the evening I spent an hour and a half briefing about
100 House members on the Panama implementation legis-*

lation. I'll be doing this two or three more times in order
to cover all the members who are willing to discuss it and
to learn. So far they've had a very negative attitude, many
of them swayed by completely misleading statements.

DIARY, MAY 8, 1979

The House members were being told that their vote could prevent control of the Canal being turned over to Panama, that we would have to pay Panama billions of dollars from United States tax revenues, that Torrijos was controlled by communist forces, that our military leaders had been forced by me to support the treaties against their will, and that the Panamanians would be blackmailing us for the rest of this century by threatening to destroy the Canal.

Secretaries Vance and Brown, General Dennis McAuliffe, and our Ambassador to Panama, Ambler Moss, all helped me with these sessions. We were making progress, but it was slow. I was forced to support an unsatisfactory implementation bill just to get it through the House, and even that stayed alive only by a vote of 200 to 198. Our one hope was to depend on the Senate to correct the bill's defects, and then for a conference committee to draft an acceptable version for final passage.

We pounded away at the facts. Here is how I summarized them on May 18 to a group of visiting editors at the White House:

The Panama treaties cannot be nullified or amended by any law passed by Congress. The President and three other Presidents before me negotiated the treaties. The Senate has now ratified them, and they are the law of the land. . . . The Panama Canal Zone will become Panama territory on the first day of October 1979, no matter what the Congress does this year. . . . The reason for the implementation legislation is to permit the United States to operate the Panama Canal between now and the year 2000 and also to defend the Canal Zone . . . with U.S. forces. If the implementation legislation is not passed in a timely fashion and in compliance with the treaty . . . we could not handle . . . obligations for and to American workers there. We could not transfer workers from one place to another. The citizenship status and basic rights of Americans in the Panama Canal Zone would be in doubt. We could not provide for the facilities and equipment to defend the Canal. In fact, the operation of the Canal itself might very well be interrupted.

These arguments had some effect, but still we did not have enough votes. The opponents then tried to block the treaties by claiming that Panama was giving aid to the opponents of Anastasio Somoza in Nicaragua, whom they tried to picture as agents of communist powers. To hear the "evidence," the House of Representatives held its first secret session in a hundred and fifty years, but it seemed that no new information was presented. We tried, without success, to convince the House members that the treaty did not give us any right to control the foreign policy of Panama—or vice versa! Some of these shortsighted legislators were playing right into the hands of the very communists and leftists they were denouncing on the floor. The one way these denounced groups *could* prevail in Panama was if we precipitated a break in diplomatic relations, destroying the strength and influence of the United States in the region, demonstrating that we were not a nation of our word, and risking armed conflict in the Canal Zone and a closing of the Canal. All these eventualities loomed as real possibilities if the terms of the treaties were now rejected.

Week after week, as the Speaker delayed action because we did not have the votes to win, I continued to meet with large groups of representatives.

> *Similar to previous meetings, but I think even better. The House members are sober; their main concern was not about the right or wrong of what they should do, but about the political consequences of voting in any way favorable toward Panama. Most of those who spoke out against it were shamed by the responsibility of the others.*
>
> DIARY, JUNE 11, 1979

On June 21, by temporarily overlooking some unacceptable amendments and by persistent and tedious work with individual members of the House similar to our earlier effort in the Senate, we won by 224 to 202. Still, some unacceptable parts of the bill would have to be removed in the Senate. A strong majority of senators was eager to protect the good work they had done in ratifying the treaties, and that was a powerful force in shaping the final version of the implementing law. Following several interim defeats and hairline victories, we finally prevailed, but it was not until September 27, 1979, three days before the treaty became effective, that I was able to sign an acceptable bill into law. The members of my administration and many other American leaders had risen to meet successfully one of the greatest legislative challenges of all time.

If I could have foreseen early in 1977 the terrible battle we would face in Congress, it would have been a great temptation for me to avoid the issue—at least during my first term. The struggle left deep and serious political wounds that have never healed; and, I am convinced, a large number of members of Congress were later defeated for reelection because they voted for the Panama treaties.

Twenty senators who voted in favor of ratifying the first treaty in 1978 were up for reelection later that year. Of those, six did not run, seven were defeated, and only seven returned for another term. The Panama Canal treaty vote remained a vital political issue until the elections two years later, when another one-third of the senators were up for election. Eleven more of the senators who supported the treaties were defeated in 1980—plus one President.

Were the treaties worth what we paid for them? There is no doubt that the answer is "Yes!" We are a nation that believes in equality, justice, honesty, and truth. As I and the doubtful senators and representatives studied the history and the facts concerning the Panama Canal, we became convinced that these principles were involved—so certain that we did not flinch, despite the political consequences. It is reassuring to remember that a strong majority of those Americans who were familiar with the basic terms of the treaties agreed with us. Perhaps President Carlos Andres Pérez of Venezuela was right when he called this "the most significant advance in political affairs in the Western Hemisphere in this century."

The benefits to Panama were clear, but to our country the treaties have been equally valuable. We have retained adequate control over the operation of the vital waterway, confirmed our right to defend the Canal as long as it is in operation, guaranteed our role in the development of any alternate sea-level canal to be built in the future, reestablished good relations with our Panamanian friends and partners, and stopped the advance into Central America of those subversive groups who were using the issue of so-called North American colonialism to gain a foothold in Panama. We had also proven our commitment to freedom and human rights, for us as well as for others whom we might criticize, and at the same time contributed to the further democratization of Panama by demonstrating that, in a showdown, a great democracy will practice what it preaches. Later, as revolution swept across other nations in Central America, our enhanced relations with Panama and other Latin American countries through the new treaties became very valuable in strengthening the beneficial influence of the United States.

Would we have gone to war with Panama if the treaties had been rejected? I honestly do not know. There is no doubt that, in a massive military confrontation, we could have prevailed against this tiny country, but in the bloody process all of us would have suffered, and the Canal would have been closed.

Some fine members of Congress had to pay with their political careers for their votes during these long and difficult months. Their courage represents the best of American government; I am proud of the role they and I played in this dramatic and historic event.

CHINA

The basic question still remains how to establish diplomatic relations with the People's Republic of China and preserve the guarantee of a peaceful life for the Chinese on Taiwan.   DIARY, JULY 30, 1977

My interest in China was kindled when I was a small boy during the 1930's, studying about Baptist missionaries there and reading letters from my Uncle Tom Gordy, a radioman in the U.S. Navy, for whom China was a frequent port of call. From the slide programs put on by itinerant missionaries on furlough I was taught to look upon the Chinese as friends in urgent need of hospitals, food, schools, and the knowledge of Jesus Christ as their Savior. Our fellow Baptists working in China were considered an elite group—exalted in our eyes above those "in the foreign field" in other countries.

The photographs and descriptions I received from my uncle, a sailor on liberty, were completely different—street scenes in front of the waterfront shops and taverns of Shanghai and Tsingtao that I presumed the missionaries never saw. Both perspectives fascinated me; I saved my nickels and dimes for the foreign-mission program, and carried on an eager correspondence with my favorite uncle.

As a young submarine officer, I was able to visit some of the same places I had been told about as a boy. During the early months of 1949, my ship cruised up the coast from Hong Kong to Tsingtao, spending a day or two in various seaports between our training operations with other ships of the British and American Navies. Although the ports I visited were still occupied by the Nationalist forces of Chiang Kai-shek, they were all besieged by troops of Mao Tse-tung, whose campfires I could see on the hills. Most of the shop windows were boarded up, but my buddies and I could still slip into the partially darkened stores to find bargains in raw silk, leather goods, and ivory and wood carvings. On the streets of Tsingtao we saw small boys and old men being recruited into the army at bayonet point. The end of Nationalist rule there was near.

We left China in April, to return to Pearl Harbor, and within six months, Chiang and his followers were forced off the mainland. They moved their government to the island of Taiwan; the United States continued to recognize it as the only government of China. During the Korean conflict, our military forces were stationed in Taiwan, and in December 1954, United States officials signed a mutual defense treaty with the Nationalists.

Although American loyalties were with Chiang Kai-shek's forces, as the years went by it became more and more obvious even to Taiwan's friends that Chiang was never going to "liberate" the mainland from Mao Tse-tung. The PRC (People's Republic of China) comprised about one billion people—almost one-fourth the world's population—and its permanence and strategic importance in international affairs were evident. The United States could not forever ignore reality.

At the beginning of the 1970's, mainland China became more concerned about its lack of a relationship with us. Its alliance with the Soviet Union had deteriorated. In 1969 the two communist states had engaged in armed conflict along their borders. The Chinese, interested in ending their isolation, made overtures to the United States. The eventual result was the visit of President Richard Nixon to China in 1972, when he and Premier Chou En-lai issued a joint communiqué in Shanghai, acknowledging that there was only one China. By doing so, the United States was implicitly saying it could not continue diplomatic relations with Taiwan once full relations with the mainland were established. The Shanghai communiqué also stated that American forces in Taiwan could be reduced as tensions eased, and that with a final resolution of differences among the Chinese, our military would be completely withdrawn.

This was a major diplomatic achievement, which I thought could lead to a new level of stability and peace in the Western Pacific, and at that time I looked forward to a burgeoning relationship with the Chinese mainland, culminating in full diplomatic relations between our two countries. A step toward that goal was taken in 1973, when liaison offices were established in Peking and Washington.

After the first flurry of excitement, however, progress toward full relations was put on hold. The Taiwan influence was very strong in the United States, particularly in Congress. In the absence of consistent presidential leadership, Taiwanese lobbyists seemed able to prevail in shaping United States policy on this fundamental issue in the Far East. I began to see how effective they could be after I won a few primaries in 1976. A flood of invitations came to my relatives and neighbors around Plains for expense-paid vacation trips to Taipei, the capital of Taiwan. Those who succumbed to these blandishments were wined and dined by the Taiwan leaders, offered attractive gifts, and urged to influence me to forget about fulfilling American commitments to China. I was able to prevent embarrassing favors to my closest family members, but my opposition to the trips and entertainment endangered my relationships with some of my hometown friends.

I did not need to be reminded that we had to improve our relationship with China without reneging on our commitments to the well-being of Taiwan and without further affecting our already strained relations with the Soviet Union. However, I believed that too many of our international concerns were being defined almost exclusively by the chronic United States–Soviet confrontation mentality, which seemed to me shortsighted and counterproductive. The United States was stalemated both ways: in our attempts to move forward with acknowledging that the government in Peking was the government of China, and in our efforts to complete the strategic arms limitation talks with the Soviet Union.

I wanted to reverse this state of affairs as rapidly as possible. Shortly after my election victory in 1976, I invited Secretary of State Henry Kissinger to come down to Plains, so that he could brief me on some of the issues he was having to address. I was eager to know about the Chinese, and questioned him closely about the impressions he had formed during his several visits to China.

He told me that the Chinese were tough and shrewd bargainers, very patient, who understood that the political situation in the United States still prevented any move toward normal diplomatic relations. He had enjoyed his dealings with the top leaders he had met. I asked him if they could be trusted, and he replied, "Yes, they will carry out meticulously both the letter and spirit of an agreement." He added that the Soviets, on the other hand, would honor the letter of an understanding, but that one had to be very careful because they would probe for every loophole in the language in order to gain some advantage, even if it violated the intent of the original deal.

Once in the White House, I studied carefully the detailed memoranda of conversations among Kissinger, Nixon, and the Chinese leaders, and also reviewed some of the private statements made by President Ford to the Chinese. All these discussions were lengthy but intriguing. I began to understand more clearly what had been accomplished almost five years earlier and how much still needed to be done. From the time of the earliest visits by Kissinger to Peking, United States–Taiwan relations had always been the foremost question to be resolved, although it often seemed to be skirted by the subtle language of the Chinese leaders. This extremely sensitive political issue had never been discussed frankly and directly with the American people.

Early in February 1977, in order to learn more about the current attitude of the Chinese leaders, I asked Huang Chen, Washington Liaison Chief of the People's Republic of China, to come by the Oval Office for a visit. As we talked about a broad range of subjects, he almost always emphasized the Soviet influence or role in each. When he spoke of the Soviet Union he grew antagonistic and distrustful, and contradicted any suggestion on my part that the Soviet leaders might be sincere in wanting to preserve the peace and control atomic weapons. He pointed out that Chinese policy on nuclear weapons was the same as the one I had expressed during the campaign and in my inaugural address—to reduce the arsenals without delay and to work toward the elimination of all nuclear weapons in every nation. He urged me to maintain a strong American presence in the Western Pacific, and was concerned about the possibility of any resurgence in Japanese military strength. (The latter position was to change. As our ties with the Chinese were strengthened, their concerns about a possible Japanese threat diminished, and they began to urge that Japan's defense capability be improved.)

Huang emphasized China's patience, but made it clear that his country was willing to move on normalization as soon as we were ready "to implement the agreements made several years ago." I told him that we would welcome a top-level visit from Chinese leaders, since so many American officials had made repeated visits to Peking, but he responded, "As long as there is a Taiwanese ambassador in Washington, this will not be possible."

This was a typical Chinese attitude of patience and stubbornness. Without being condescending about it, the Chinese always acted as though they still considered themselves members of the Middle Kingdom—at the center of the civilized world—prepared simply to wait until others accepted their position on "matters of principle." Still, throughout our conversation the overriding message was clear: the United States and China would soon be ready to move toward normal relations.

With the laborious translations, our scheduled meeting ran overtime. Later, from our embassies in other countries, we learned that the Chinese considered it significant that my meeting with

Huang had lasted longer than my recently concluded meeting with the Soviet ambassador. I had never thought about measuring the length of the two discussions.

Although there were other priorities during the first few months of my administration, I kept the China issue very much alive. In a major foreign policy address at Notre Dame on May 22, I stressed the importance of continuing progress toward normalization. To be the Chief of our Liaison Office in Peking I appointed Leonard Woodcock, recently retired president of the United Automobile Workers. I admired Leonard personally, and knew him to be quiet but forceful, a man whose age, experience, and demeanor would be an advantage in dealing with the Chinese leaders. Further, my choice of a person of his stature in the American community was a clear signal to the Chinese that we wanted closer relations.

Leonard Woodcock came by with Cy Vance and others to talk about potential normalizing of relationships with China. He'll be leaving in a week or so to go to Peking, and I told him that I thought normal relations were advisable, that I believed I could sell it to the American people, and that I would be willing to take on the political responsibility of doing so. The only remaining obstacle, of course, is our commitment not to abandon the peaceful existence of the Chinese who live on Taiwan.

DIARY, JULY 7, 1977

As a matter of courtesy to the Taiwanese, I asked Cy Vance to meet with the Taiwanese Ambassador in Washington to get his views about the Far East. Predictably, he insisted that the status quo should be preserved. After this meeting, Cy joined me and Zbig at Camp David on August 17 to decide what kind of proposal I should make to China. Cy was going to Peking soon after Woodcock took over the Liaison Office there. Now we sat around a tiny table and went over, word by word, a proposed draft for an agreement that Cy might discuss with the Chinese.

I understood from studying past records and from my discussions with Huang that there were three "matters of principle" which the Chinese considered *non*negotiable: termination of the United States–Taiwan defense treaty, establishment of diplomatic relations with the government in Peking instead of with Taipei, and withdrawal of United States military forces from Taiwan. I was willing to accept these principles provided we could do so in an honorable and orderly manner. To me this meant being able to continue to sell some defensive weapons to Taiwan; to maintain trade and other relations on an unofficial basis; to end the mutual defense treaty, on one year's notice, as that treaty provided; and to be able to state publicly and without contradiction from Peking that the dispute between the Chinese on the mainland and Taiwan would be resolved peacefully.

The difficulty would lie in assuring China's willingness to accommodate our requirements for unofficial relations with Taiwan and our permanent interest in its peaceful existence. The Chinese could cooperate either by silence (regarding United States–Taiwan trade), by interpreting the same language somewhat differently (concerning a peaceful settlement of China–Taiwan disputes), or by acknowledging an unresolved difference (such as our sale of defensive weapons to Taiwan). But they could not permit any of these issues to interfere with normalizing diplomatic relations.

I decided that we should proceed slowly, presenting our proposals to the Chinese incrementally and resolving each question before proceeding to the next. This was a tedious and time-consuming process, but it minimized the likelihood of a total impasse, which might have resulted from having to address the many differences simultaneously. In this manner, the negotiators would become better acquainted and more certain of each other's intentions. Furthermore, each side had some domestic political sensitivities that needed to be understood and accommodated by the other, and this might also take time.

Whenever the Chinese leaders and I were able to work out all our differences, I would be prepared to conclude the discussions and make a public announcement of the agreement, perhaps later this first year. Otherwise, I would be willing to wait until the Chinese were ready.

When Secretary Vance began his exploratory discussions in Peking on August 22, he found his hosts more cautious than I had anticipated. With the deaths of both Chou En-Lai and Mao Tse-tung in 1976, the new leaders of China had many internal political and economic questions to address. In addition, they were still not well acquainted with me or my policies, and probably needed a few more months before deciding how far to trust us on the major decisions.

Report from Cy Vance in China was mildly encouraging. He met with the Vice Chairman, Teng Hsiao-ping [later spelled Deng Xiaoping], and reported that tomorrow he'll meet with Premier Hua [Kuofeng]. Whether or not they'll

accept our proposals for normalization, leaving adequate
ties with Taiwan, remains to be seen.

DIARY, AUGUST 24, 1977

Although Secretary Vance had a congenial visit with the leaders of China, it was obvious as he left Peking that they were not ready to move forward on our terms. Because of an erroneous leak from some subordinate official that the Chinese had shown "unexpected flexibility," Deng Xiaoping's final statement to the press at the conclusion of Cy's visit was rather harsh. The last thing the Chinese wanted was for someone to accuse them of being flexible on a matter of principle.

For the time being, we put this project on the back burner in Washington. I did not want to make a public move on China until after the Panama Canal issue was resolved. At this time, Senator Barry Goldwater and a few other members of the "Taiwan lobby" were undecided about the treaties, and any move away from Taiwan would have driven them against us on the treaty votes. In Peking, Woodcock continued through indirect means to send signals to the Chinese leaders of our willingness to proceed. He did not receive any positive replies.

Although the very top leaders of China refused to visit the United States as long as there was an ambassador from Taiwan in Washington, they seemed eager for a few of their cabinet-level officials to come to discuss such matters as commercial trade and possible future access by China to United States technology. All of them took a uniformly hard line about our defense posture, accusing us of being too weak in our dealing with potential adversaries. It was obvious that they were talking about the Soviet Union.

On one occasion, at least, a portion of their standard propaganda spiel had to be changed. It was well known that, following the end of the Second World War, our nation's strategic war plans had been based on the ability to fight a war simultaneously in both the Atlantic and Pacific regions, plus a limited skirmish somewhere else. This was known as a "2½ war strategy." During the Nixon and Ford years, it had been changed to a plan for fighting one major and one minor war at the same time. The Chinese were always eager for United States defense forces to be maintained at a maximum level, and quick to criticize any sign of our reduced military capability.

Harold Brown reported a meeting with Huang Chen from
the People's Republic of China, and the high criticism by
him of our military posture. He was particularly critical

*about our having changed strategic planning from a
"2½ war" capability to a "1½ war" capability in recent
years. When Harold pointed out that the other war plan
had been designed for use against the People's Republic of
China, his criticisms were attenuated!*

DIARY, NOVEMBER 14, 1977

All the while, the Panama Canal treaties debate dragged on.
What we had hoped would be concluded early in the fall of 1977
was still hanging in the balance as the 1978 session of Congress
began. We had to pull out all the stops to get the final few votes
necessary for treaty ratification, and we were also working on
SALT II negotiations with the Soviet Union and on a comprehensive Middle East peace proposal. Along with energy legislation
and an overloaded domestic agenda, these efforts did not leave
much time for us to pursue the China question. Besides, it was
not the right moment to tackle another highly controversial issue.

However, although I did not know it then, Leonard Woodcock
was making *some* progress in Peking. He came home on regular
leave in February 1978, and after a brief and routine discussion
about the dormant situation in China, he asked to see me privately. He was so uncharacteristically excited that I was concerned he
might have some personal problem which would force him to
leave his post. After stammering around for a few moments, he
finally broke into a broad smile and told me that he had fallen in
love with the American nurse who worked with our diplomatic
staff in Peking, and that they planned to be married. He told me
that her name was Sharon Tuohy, and I sat down at my desk and
wrote a note of congratulations for Leonard to carry back to her. I
expressed my hope that he would have as much success with the
Chinese!

Leonard urged me to visit China, but I had decided not to go
until after one of the top Chinese leaders had returned the official
visits paid by Presidents Nixon and Ford. Though both Fritz and
Zbig were very eager to go to Peking, Secretary Vance was insisting
that any negotiations be carried out through him. I presumed
that the State Department professionals were still smarting over
Secretary William Rogers' having been bypassed when Henry
Kissinger, as Nixon's National Security Adviser, played such a
major role in preparing for the President's visit to China and in
negotiating the Shanghai communiqué.

Not long afterward, Governor Averell Harriman, one of our

most distinguished senior statesmen, came to report to me that the Soviet leaders were eager to move forward on SALT II but did not understand our intentions concerning those negotiations, since we had objected so strongly to Soviet involvement in the war between Ethiopia and Somalia. I was determined that the SALT negotiations not be delayed, so I decided to send Cy to Moscow, and at the same time told him that Brzezinski would go to Peking as soon as the Panama treaties were ratified. Cy did not like the arrangement, but he accepted my decision.

By May 1978, Zbig was ready to go. I told him to explore as many of the Chinese–American issues as possible, without setting any final agreement as his goal. The announcement of Brzezinski's trip was treated as a major news story in Peking, Tokyo, Seoul, Manila, and Taipei, showing that the Asian countries expected the visit to be substantive.

I had a meeting with Brzezinski, Brown, Vance, Mondale, Jordan to discuss Zbig's trip to China, and decided that we would move on normalization this year if the Chinese are forthcoming. Our preference is to take final action after the November election. We all agreed that a better relationship with the PRC would help us with SALT.

DIARY, MAY 16, 1978

Some of the senators known to be doubtful about a SALT II treaty with the Soviet Union had expressed the hope that we would develop stronger ties with China. I believed, therefore, that congressional support for better relations with both the Soviet Union and the People's Republic of China would be strengthened if the two peaceful moves could be combined—a SALT II treaty with the Soviets, and normalized relations with the Chinese.

In addition to resolving the question of United States–China relations, I had to decide how to treat the friendly overtures being made to us by the Vietnamese. During the early part of 1978, the Chinese sent word to me that they would welcome our moving toward Vietnam in order to moderate that country's policies and keep it out of the Soviet camp. The State Department favored our negotiating with both Vietnam and China at the same time, but the National Security Council staff and some of our friends in Congress thought there would be a firestorm whenever we had to face the China–Taiwan issue, and that this in itself would be a full agenda. The China move was of paramount importance, so after a few weeks of assessment I decided to postpone the Vietnam effort until after we had concluded our agreement in Peking. Later, when the government in Hanoi decided to invade Kampuchea (Cambodia) and also began to take on the trappings of a Soviet puppet, we did not want to pursue the idea.

Whether by a more positive response to Vietnam's earlier over-tures we could have prevented these last two moves is, in my opinion, very doubtful—but I will never be sure. This was a recurring question: whether or not to recognize a regime which had overthrown a government with whom we'd had good rela-tions. In order to resolve it once and for all, I was tempted on a few occasions to change the policy of the United States to one of giving automatic diplomatic recognition to any fully established government and exchanging ambassadors as soon as satisfactory arrangements could be worked out. If there were an unresolved dispute within the country between two contending governments, we would, of course, have to make a diplomatic judgment. Au-tomatic recognition of an undisputed regime would give us a toehold in the unfriendly country and an opportunity to ease tensions, increase American influence, and promote peace. Some other countries, including France, follow such a policy, and it seems to work well for them.

Brzezinski and I spent a lot of time before his departure discuss-ing all the ramifications of our future relationship with the Chi-nese, and how it might affect our other Asian friends, such as Japan, South Korea, and the Philippines. We believed all would consider the resulting enhancement of political and military sta-bility in the Western Pacific a benefit, and our cautious soundings through diplomatic channels later confirmed this belief. For in-stance, both we and South Korean President Park wanted the Chinese to help prevent any military moves by North Korea and to help reduce existing tensions in that peninsula.

One of the more interesting potential benefits of having China as a friend would be its ability to quietly sway some third-world countries with whom it was very difficult for us to communicate. Most revolutionary governments did not naturally turn to the United States, and the Soviets sometimes had a clear field in forming new ties—mostly by selling them weapons. China's cre-dentials among some of the developing nations were excellent; we saw our cooperation with China as a means to promote peace and better understanding between the United States and those countries.

Zbig's visit to Peking in late May was very successful. By this time, Deng Xiaoping and the other leaders were well established and knew more about our administration. More important, they had reasons for serious concern about such international developments as the rapid changes of governments in Afghanistan, the murder of government leaders in both North and South Yemen, the war in the Horn of Africa with major Soviet and Cuban involvement in Ethiopia, and a deterioration in China–Vietnam relations. These events undoubtedly increased Chinese interest in improving relations with us. The leaders in Peking seemed to enjoy the strategic and philosophical discussions with Zbig, and let me know through him that they were ready to take greater advantage of existing trade possibilities, and were prepared to move forward, though at a measured pace, toward complete diplomatic recognition. Although Brzezinski was not on a mission to negotiate any final agreement, he did a good job of laying the groundwork for subsequent progress. He also found the Chinese to be excellent hosts and delightful companions.

When I returned to Washington [from a trip to Illinois and West Virginia], Zbig had come back from China. He was overwhelmed with the Chinese. I told him he had been seduced.   DIARY, MAY 26, 1978

Zbig had left a list of suggestions with the Chinese for actions that might begin to improve the attitude of the American public toward China. From their response we could determine their attitude toward us. One request had been that they cease their stream of public criticisms of our nation's policies. The Chinese complied immediately. In June, their official newspaper even published the full text of my address on U.S.–Soviet relations to the Annapolis graduates and commented favorably on its sentiments. The newspaper also editorialized about the Cubans' ridiculous claim that their country was nonaligned, made some guarded public statements about resolving the Taiwan issue, announced that China would explore joint ventures with United States oil companies, and characterized Brzezinski's visit as "positive" and "useful." Although formal negotiations had still not begun, in Peking Woodcock continued to respond positively as the Chinese showed increased interest in further discussions. We developed specific negotiating instructions, and sent them to him.

Until this time, the contacts between Washington and Peking had followed the pattern of the previous six years. Now, however, we were ready to begin our substantive negotiations toward a final agreement. I decided that these should be conducted in secrecy in order not to arouse concerted opposition from Taiwan's supporters, as well as to avoid building up excessive expectations.

During such sensitive talks, it was also important to send unambiguous messages directly to Deng Xiaoping. As Woodcock prepared to begin his talks in Peking, I wanted the Chinese to know from me personally that I was ready to act without delay if an agreement could be reached. I also wanted our relations with China to be developed on the broadest possible basis, not merely on a superficial legal change in status. Woodcock was instructed first to work out details of how the normalization talks would be conducted, then to explore a full range of possible bilateral agreements between our governments, and finally to reach as complete an understanding as possible on the many complex international issues which would be affected by our new and more cooperative relationship. Only then would we try to resolve the final issues leading to diplomatic recognition.

I worked on every line of the communiqués going to Woodcock in Peking. In addition to conducting proper international diplomacy, I would have to defend my actions to the American people and Congress; I wanted to be certain that we prepared as strong a record as possible. To maintain secrecy, the Secretary of State would leave his department and come join us while we did this work, and we communicated with Woodcock on his negotiations only from within the White House.

I was getting favorable responses from Peking, but in a slow and fitful way. Late in November 1978, after several months of cautious and protracted talks, I sent Woodcock the final installments of our proposal, including the exact wording of three provisions which I knew would be difficult for the Chinese to accept: we would maintain a full defense agreement with Taiwan for another year; China would not contradict our statement that the Taiwan issue should be settled peacefully and with patience; and we would continue some military sales to the Taiwanese after the defense agreement expired. I added a tentative normalizing date of January 1, 1979.

When my message to Woodcock arrived in Peking, Deng was traveling outside the city, to be gone for more than a week. During that time, Brzezinski and Mike Oksenberg, our China specialist in the White House, reported to me some intriguing comments Deng had made to a foreign reporter. Deng had said that China concluded the Peace and Friendship Treaty with Japan "in one second," and that it would "only take two seconds" to normalize diplomatic relations with the United States. He had added that he anticipated a visit to America in his lifetime.

When he returned to the capital, I received a report that the Central Committee—an assemblage of the top Chinese leaders—had scheduled a special meeting. Woodcock and our Asia specialists interpreted this to be quite significant, but we did not know what was on the Chinese agenda. Much later, I learned that three important issues were to be resolved: the final consolidation of Deng Xiaoping's control over the party and the government, possible military action by China against Vietnam, and future relations with the United States.

After the meeting, Deng Xiaoping sent me a draft communiqué which contained unacceptable language concerning our future relations with Taiwan, but at the same time Woodcock was notified that his next negotiating session—on December 13—would be with Deng himself, whom Woodcock had never met. Vance, Brzezinski, and I decided to expedite the negotiating process without changing any facet of our terms for normalization. We rejected the Chinese draft, reiterating our own proposed language, and I had Zbig meet with the Chinese chief representative in Washington, Chai Zemin, to review with him the instructions we had sent Woodcock. I wanted the Chinese leaders to know that this draft had come straight from me, and I wanted Deng to have my proposal ahead of time, so he could prepare himself for the meeting with Woodcock. Zbig delivered to Chai an explicit invitation from me for Deng to visit the United States as soon as possible after our normalization agreement was concluded. Zbig also let Chai know that we had resolved all the major SALT II issues with the Soviet Union and would soon be deciding on a date for a summit meeting between me and Brezhnev.

When Woodcock met Deng, the message to me was quick and brief: "We will adopt the draft of the United States, and I accept the President's invitation to visit your country." I asked Mike Oksenberg why Deng had given such a startlingly prompt answer, and he said, "Mr. President, the Chinese have been waiting twenty-five years for the question!"

There was a lot of truth to that, but there were other factors involved. After all the preliminary arrangements had been concluded and we had begun negotiations in July, both sides wanted to be sure they could resolve questions that had accumulated over many years, such as those involving trade, financial claims, transportation and communications, and consular matters. After these discussions were completed, each of us had approached the final and most controversial questions involving Taiwan very gingerly. Neither nation wanted to be put in a position of having its ultimate proposal rejected by the other. At the time of the Deng–Woodcock meeting, the background work had all been completed, an adequate level of mutual trust had developed, and the timing was right for both governments to face potential political opposition. Only under these conditions could Deng's answer have come with such alacrity.

There was no more negotiating to be done. I decided to surprise Deng in return—by proposing that we reveal our agreement in only two days, as soon as Secretary Vance could return to Washington from the Middle East. I wanted to expedite the public announcement so that we could explain the decision in its totality and not risk its being leaked piecemeal to the news media, perhaps in a distorted fashion by someone who was opposed to our decision. So far we had been surprisingly successful in keeping the negotiations secret, but I did not want to push my luck any further.

Deng agreed to issue our joint communiqué simultaneously at 9:00 P.M., Washington time, on December 15. To meet this deadline, we had a lot of work to do in a hurry, briefing the members of Congress, preparing our presentations to the American press, and notifying leaders of other nations. Furthermore, in accepting our invitation to visit the United States, Deng had suggested a very early date for his arrival—within a month after normalization became official on January 1.

The excitement is building up concerning normalization with China—whether we can keep it secret or not. We've decided to notify the Soviets and Taiwan, Japan and our main European allies early tomorrow. By then, more than 100 people in our government will know about it.

DIARY, DECEMBER 14, 1978

Miraculously, the confidentiality of our agreement was preserved completely. During the day of December 15, as many people as possible were informed in proper sequence, and Cy and Zbig briefed the press. I called a few leaders, such as Prime Minister Ohira in Japan, Presidents Ford and Nixon, and some key members of Congress.

President Nixon was most pleased and briefly discussed the worldwide impact of our accomplishment. I gave him full credit for his original move toward China and thanked him for the advice he had given me. I also offered to send Oksenberg to give him a personal briefing on the details of our agreement. He expressed his confidence in Mike, but cautioned me about the difficulty of maintaining secrecy and the danger of placing too much faith in subordinates!

> *When I called Zbig to tell him about the Nixon conversation, I asked him if he had heard that the Chinese had canceled our agreement. He almost fainted before I could tell him I was joking.*   DIARY, DECEMBER 16, 1978

As was my custom, I had simply told the White House operator to get Dr. Brzezinski. Without my knowing it, he had been out for a walk with his family when he received word to go to the nearest phone and call me, so he was already prepared to believe there was an emergency of some kind. We laughed about the incident later, but at the time I regretted having caused him such acute concern.

I also had a meeting with the anchormen of the three television networks, to give them some background information as they prepared their broadcasts.

My foreign policy team and I, very proud of our accomplishments, were in a happy and expansive mood. It must have been infectious. The serious opposition we had expected throughout our country and within Congress simply did not materialize. The press treatment was also favorable, expressing chagrin only at the fact that, without leaks, the media had been caught by surprise. The worldwide reaction was remarkably positive. Although there were some demonstrations against us in Taiwan, most countries recognized this development as a historic one, which would contribute to peace and would open China further to the outside world.

We had been fair and honest with the people of Taiwan—even though at the time they did not agree with this assessment. In our agreement, as I announced on December 15, we had made special provisions to insure that our new relations with China would not jeopardize the well-being of the people of Taiwan. We would maintain our existing commercial, cultural, and trade relations with them through nongovernmental means, as Japan and many other countries were already doing. This change would require the passage of a special act of Congress to establish a private organization, the American Institute in Taiwan, that could carry out many of the routine functions of an embassy. There were immediate threats from some members of Congress that they would not approve any such legislation, but these friends of Taiwan were soon to realize that our diplomatic relations with China were a fact—it was a presidential prerogative to make the decision—and that without the special legislation, we could no longer maintain normal trade with Taiwan.

Under the circumstances, I wanted to make the transition as easy as possible for Taiwan. I sent Warren Christopher to Taipei on a goodwill mission to seek the country's counsel on what we could do to help. He was greeted by an abusive public demonstration that was obviously encouraged by President Chiang Ching-kuo. Only after receiving assurances from Chiang that such abuse would not be repeated did I permit Warren to remain for a couple of days of meetings, which proved to be unproductive. In the meantime, the Taiwan government was transferring the title of its Washington buildings to private owners in order to prevent the PRC from using them when its embassy was established.

The Soviet leaders, while publicly continuing to express their equanimity, soon began to change their tune through urgent messages to me and other world leaders.

On the 27th I got a very discouraging letter from Brezhnev, showing that they are almost paranoid about the People's Republic of China and demanding that I prevent our Western allies from selling any defensive weapons to the PRC. We'll delay for a few days before giving him an answer. . . . Had an excellent meeting with Cy Vance. He spent the night with us at Camp David, and I went over a broad gamut of foreign affairs questions with him. He and I agree that the most significant responsibility we have is to balance our new friendship with the PRC and our continued improvement of relations with the Soviet Union. . . . As we moved toward a most-favored-nation relationship with the PRC, we must face the need to do the same thing with the Soviet Union.

DIARY, DECEMBER 31, 1978

The Soviets were sending threatening letters to the leaders of any nation that might consider selling weapons to the Chinese. After a couple of weeks, I notified Brezhnev that our policy was not to sell weapons to either China or the Soviet Union, but that we would not try to influence other sovereign nations' policies on the sale of armaments to the Chinese. I knew that both the British and French were negotiating for such sales.

A more immediate problem involved commercial trade. Until a

country changed its emigration policies to permit reunification of families, we were forbidden by law from granting it "most favored nation" status. This amendment to the trade law had originally been aimed at the Soviet Union and a few other Warsaw Pact countries because of their repressive limits on the emigration of Jews and other minorities who wanted to join their families in the West. China was not guilty of a similar policy, so there was no legal impediment to granting it a beneficial trade status. However, if we now gave the Chinese these superior trade opportunities, there would be an imbalance in our relationship with the two major communist countries. Congress would have to approve any such action, and many of its members would oppose it with regard to both nations. Efforts while I was President to induce the Soviet leaders to permit Jews and others to join their families elsewhere had met with enough success that I personally preferred to grant most-favored-nation status to both countries. The Chinese were quite aware of the law, and I was certain that Deng Xiaoping would be discussing it with me on his upcoming visit, for which the plans were being made.

In preparation for my meeting with Deng, I gave a television interview to be broadcast in China, emphasizing to the Chinese people the value of the new relationship to us, to the Pacific region, and to the world. I let them know how pleased the people of the United States were with our decision, and stated that this feeling would be proven by the enthusiastic welcome that would be given to Vice Chairman Deng Xiaoping, his wife, and the members of his party. My Republican predecessors, Presidents Nixon and Ford, and the previous Chinese leaders, Mao Tse-tung and Chou En-lai, had laid the groundwork for our new agreement, I said—in itself an indication of broad support among the leaders of our two nations. (This television program played repeatedly in China, so that when I later visited the country, the people on the streets recognized me readily.)

⤳

The Deng Xiaoping visit was one of the delightful experiences of my Presidency. To me, everything went right, and the Chinese leader seemed equally pleased.

I was favorably impressed with Deng. He's small, tough, intelligent, frank, courageous, personable, self-assured, friendly, and it's a pleasure to negotiate with him. . . .
DIARY, JANUARY 29, 1979

We had planned three working sessions together, and decided to begin with an analysis of each country's attitude toward world affairs. Deng asked me to talk first. Speaking carefully from a brief outline, I paused after each point to let the interpreter relate my words to Deng and the other Chinese officials. Two matters were of particular concern to me: one was the instability in the area from Southeast Asia around the northern part of the Indian Ocean and into Africa, and the tendency of some outside powers to exploit it; the other was the rapid increase in Soviet military strength. I also mentioned the beliefs and values that guided our country's relations with others.

Admiring Chinese gift, Deng at
extreme right with interpreter

It was my responsibility, I said, to ensure that the United States maintained a strong and beneficial influence in world affairs. Our nation viewed favorably the growing desire of people throughout the world for a better quality of life, for more political participation, for liberation from persecution by their own governments, and for freedom from the domination of any outside power. We also viewed as a positive development the increasing influence of nations such as the People's Republic of China, and believed that having good relations with such nations would protect our security in the future.

Deng, his small frame almost swallowed by the large chair in the Cabinet Room, listened attentively. Smoking one cigarette after another, his bright eyes darting frequently from side to side, he would laugh or nod vigorously to the other Chinese as my comments were translated for him.

I then asked Deng for his assessment. He commented on the issues that were important to him, noting how many common interests were now shared by the United States and the People's Republic of China. Mao Tse-tung and Chou En-lai had long ago noted the danger of war, Deng said, which was likely to be started either by the Soviet Union or the United States. The Chinese leaders had always recognized that these two dominant nations would probably increase their influence. Over a period of years, the Chinese had begun to realize that the danger to them from the United States was less and less, while the Soviet Union was a greater concern. It was necessary for other nations to unite in opposing hegemony. In his opinion, the United States had not done enough to contain the Soviets, and the situation in the non-Soviet world had not really improved.

He went on to say that in the last five years, he had seen no basic improvement in the Middle East. The countries in the region that rejected peace efforts because of Israel's existence had long been close to the Soviet Union, and he thought some doubtful ones, such as Syria and Algeria, had moved closer to the Soviets. He further stated that the People's Republic of China recognized the entity of Israel; that there was no denying Israel's existence. But when I later asked him if there was a possibility of China's establishing relations with Israel, he replied, "No, at the present time this is not a possibility." He added that if Israel were to return to the 1967 borders, and solve the problems of Jordan, the West Bank, and the question of a Palestinian homeland, it would gain the support of 100 million Arabs. Otherwise, the problems of the Middle East were likely to spread to Saudi Arabia and other countries.

Deng Xiaoping characterized Vietnam as a Cuba of the East, with fifty million people and a powerful military force. He noted that both the United States and China had had long and unpleasant contacts with the Vietnamese. Vietnam and the Soviet Union had now proposed an Asian collective-security system, which would be very dangerous in that part of the world.

He said he was not opposed to the SALT II agreement; that it may be necessary. But he felt that this fourth negotiation was destined to have the same result as the

other three—that is, not to restrain Soviet strategic mili-
tary buildup. Deng pointed out that the PRC does not want
war. The Chinese need a long period of peace to realize
their full modernization. The Soviets will launch war even-
tually, but we may be able to postpone war for 22 years
[until the end of the century]. He did not think we ought
to have a formal alliance among U.S., PRC, and India,
but we should coordinate our activities to constrain the
Soviets.   DIARY, JANUARY 29, 1979

When we reconvened after lunch, I told him that I, too, was concerned about the expansion of Soviet influence—but I wanted him to recognize the adverse experience that the Soviets had had in Egypt, India, Indonesia, Yugoslavia, Poland and other countries in Eastern Europe, Nigeria, Guinea, North Korea, Japan, the ASEAN (Association of Southeast Asian Nations), Somalia, the Middle East, and particularly China. In southern Africa, I said, we would be making a serious mistake to write off the countries that were presently inclined toward the Soviet Union, like Zambia and Mozambique. Even Angola was now cautiously reaching out to the West. I described our work to bring majority rule to Namibia, and told him that the Chinese could pursue these same peaceful efforts in Africa.

I outlined what we had done to bring peace to the Middle East and emphasized our concern about the Palestinians. It was crucial that we have a comprehensive peace settlement, I said, and strategically necessary for such moderate nations as Saudi Arabia, Jordan, Sudan, Egypt, Israel, Algeria, and Morocco to help us reach these goals. As long as Egypt had its military forces lined up against Israel on the east side of the Suez, and while Syria, Jordan, Iraq, and other neighboring countries were all focusing hostile attention on Israel, we would be unlikely to restrict further Soviet intrusion into the area. Apparently this argument made quite an impression on him. He listened very closely, and asked me several questions about individual countries in the region.

As for other troubled areas, I spoke briefly of what we were doing in Iran, and told him we wanted a stable, peaceful government there, formed in accordance with the Iranian constitution. I said we believed the best way to treat Vietnam as an aggressor was to isolate it from the rest of the world; for the first time the developing countries in the United Nations had recently condemned Vietnam along with the Soviet Union and Cuba. I tried to encourage the Chinese to use their influence in North Korea to help arrange direct talks between the government authorities of North and South Korea. I was not sure I was making much progress on that point, but at least Deng understood my position.

We agreed that it would be a serious mistake for us to unite against the Soviet Union, a move that would only further isolate the Soviets. I commented that it was best to have a policy of cooperation with them when they were constructive, and competition with them when they were not. Our preference was to avoid war permanently, not just to postpone it for twenty-two years!

Deng then responded to my request that he use China's influence with North Korea to keep the peace. He said that many people had raised the question of Korea with him; there was absolutely no danger of a North Korean attack. It was not yet possible for the People's Republic of China and South Korea to have trade relations or direct communication, but he hoped South Korea would accept North Korea's proposals for talks and elections leading to a merger. The Soviet Union's relationship with North Korea had never been very strong, he said. It had waned considerably in recent years because the Soviets had tried to influence the government's policies—and if China tried to pressure North Korea, it too would lose its influence.

It was almost time to prepare for the evening banquet, but Deng requested that we leave our large group of advisers so that he could discuss a more confidential matter with me. Fritz, Cy, Zbig, and I went with Deng and the interpreters from the Cabinet Room into the Oval Office, and listened carefully as the Chinese leader outlined his tentative plans for China to make a punitive strike across its border into Vietnam. When he asked for my advice, I tried to discourage him, pointing out that the Vietnamese were increasingly isolated in the world community and were being condemned because they were aggressors, having crossed the border into Kampuchea. It might arouse sympathy for them and cause some nations to brand China as a culprit if Chinese forces moved toward Hanoi. Furthermore, I said, his potential military move would help to refute one of our best arguments for the new Sino-American relationship: that it would contribute toward more peace and stability in Asia. The Vice Premier thanked me for my comments, and added that it was highly desirable for China that its arrogant neighbors know they could not disturb it and other countries in the area with impunity.

As it was growing quite late, I suggested to him that we continue the conversation the following morning. Deng agreed, and an hour or so later we assembled for the state banquet—which was to be the beginning of a very enjoyable evening. He was a delightful dinner partner, completely unrestrained in his comments. Throughout the meal he preferred to talk about life in his own country, and how he thought it was changing for the better. We had a good-humored argument about the Christian missionary program in which I had been interested as a child, and he reluctantly admitted that some good missionaries had come to China. However, he insisted that many of them had been there only to change the Oriental lifestyle to a Western pattern. I reminded him of all the hospitals and schools that had been established, and he said that many were still in existence. He was strongly opposed to any resumption of a foreign missionary program and said that the Chinese Christians agreed with him, but he listened carefully when I suggested that he should permit the unrestricted distribution of Bibles and let people have freedom of worship. He promised to look into it. (Later, he acted favorably on both these suggestions.)

Deng seemed quite interested in better relations with Saudi Arabia, and again emphasized the religious aspect of the problem. There were perhaps as many as seven million Moslems in China, he said, and his government did not interfere in their worship. When I asked if these believers were allowed to travel to Mecca, he said no, but also said that if such travel was significant, this policy could be changed. We later sent this information on to the Saudi leaders.

Concerning human rights, Deng said the Chinese were struggling to make changes in their system of justice because there was no uniformity of punishment for serious crimes. China had few lawyers, and he was in a quandary about whether the country would be better off with more of them. He had observed the constant contention, delays, and apparent caste discrimination in the courts of other nations, and was not sure if he wanted to bring these problems into his country. He had apparently decided to permit the resolution of local civil and criminal cases within the small and intimate communities where disputes or crimes occurred, and to limit the increase in lawyers to those needed for negotiating agreements and contracts involving other nations. He said that China favored the unification of any divided families, was not censoring the press, and had recently been permitting substantial freedom of speech and expression. In the Chinese system, he added, these liberties had to be approached very cautiously.

We had invited both former American Presidents to the formal banquet, and, predictably, the Washington press was fascinated with the presence of President Nixon in the White House. Although he did not know the current leaders of China, he enjoyed talking to them at the brief reception about his own earlier visit. It was obvious from their private comments that for the Chinese he would always be a revered friend, and that they considered the charges involving Watergate frivolous.

In the official toasts and in private conversations, everyone was in a cheerful and festive mood, as though intent on breaking through the formal diplomatic shell that frequently stifles such occasions. I particularly enjoyed seeing the China experts from the State Department eagerly seeking firsthand information about the history and modern customs of the foreign country that they had devoted their lives to study.

> *At the Kennedy Center we had a delightful performance. Afterward, Deng and I, his wife, Madame Zhuolin, Rosalynn, and Amy went on the stage with the performers, and there was a genuine sense of emotion when he put his arms around the American performers, particularly little children who had sung a Chinese song. He kissed many of them, and the newspapers later said that many in the audience wept.*
>
> *Senator Laxalt, who has been a strong opponent of normalization, said after that performance that we had them beat; there was no way to vote against little children singing Chinese songs.*
>
> *Deng and his wife genuinely seemed to like people, and he was really a hit with the audience present and also the television audience.*   DIARY, JANUARY 29, 1979

Perhaps because he was so exuberant and so small, Deng was a favorite of Amy and the other children that night. The feeling seemed to be mutual.

Early the next morning, Deng and I met again in the Oval Office, with only an interpreter present. I read aloud and gave him a handwritten note that summarized my reasons for discouraging a Chinese invasion of Vietnam. He emphasized that if they did decide to move, they would withdraw Chinese troops after a short period of time—and the results of such an operation were likely to be beneficial and long-lasting. Quite different from last night, he was now a tough communist leader, determined that his nation not appear soft. He claimed to be still considering the issue, but my impression was that the decision had already been made. Vietnam would be punished.

Then Deng and I joined the larger group, and his mood changed again. His most serious business was done. This session, with our aides, was much more lighthearted and relaxed than those of the preceding day. We discussed the problems of our two nations' mutual claims (which resulted from the confiscation of each other's property at the time of the Chinese revolution in 1949), and pledged to work rapidly for a resolution of this and other remaining problems. Deng was quite knowledgeable about the specific details of these complicated issues.

I outlined the problem with the most-favored-nation legislation—that it would create an imbalance if we included his country and not the Soviet Union. Deng informed me that there was no equating China and the Soviet Union on the emigration question, and added, "If you want me to release ten million Chinese to come to the United States, I'd be glad to do so." And, of course, everyone laughed.

I raised a problem about the student exchange program. I did not like his decision that all the Americans would have to live in a fairly isolated group, and not among the Chinese students or families. He explained that there were not enough living accommodations in China meeting the minimum standards to which Americans were accustomed. I considered his explanation to be inadequate, and raised another point. "Once you agree on how many students can go to China, we don't want you to censor which ones can go." He smiled and said that China was strong enough to withstand a few students, and that the Chinese would not try to screen out students on grounds of ideology. There would be some limit on travel for American reporters in China, he said, but there would not be any censorship. I told him that since he offered me ten million Chinese, I offered him ten thousand journalists. He laughed loudly and immediately declined.

I asked him to refer [in his public statements while in the United States] to the Taiwan question and to use the words "peaceful" and "patience." He said he wanted the United States and Japan to urge Taiwan to negotiate, and that the only two circumstances under which they would not resolve the issue peacefully and be patient were if there was an extended period of no negotiation or if the Soviet Union entered Taiwan. He asked me to be prudent in the sale of any weapons to Taiwan after this year, and he let it

be known that they were not in favor of any sale of
weapons.   DIARY, JANUARY 30, 1979

I told Deng about our response to Brezhnev concerning weapon sales: that our policy was to sell no weapons to either China or the Soviet Union, but that we would not seek to influence our sovereign allies about their own policies. He responded, "Yes, I know that is your position. That is good."

We covered several more issues, a few of them highly confidential, in discussions that were both pleasant and productive. Deng also made a very good impression during his visit to the Capitol, with lively and humorous comments. The Chinese seemed to know how to exhibit calm self-assurance and pride in their country without being arrogant. During a private supper at his home, Zbig commented that the Chinese and French had one thing in common: each civilization thinks itself superior to all others. Deng thought for a moment, and then said, "Let us put it this way: in East Asia, Chinese food is best; in Europe, French food is best."

During our final meeting, when we signed agreements concerning consular offices, trade, science and technology, cultural exchange, and so forth, he was asked, "Did you have political opposition in China when we decided to normalize relations?" Everyone listened very carefully when Deng said, "Yes!" Then he paused for a moment and added, "I had serious opposition in one Chinese province—Taiwan."

The enjoyable ceremonies were over. Now we had the difficult job of getting legislation through Congress to implement the agreement. We had good support but faced a group of highly motivated right-wing political-action groups, which were still insisting that somehow the United States should help the descendants of Chiang Kai-shek retake the mainland. To them, Taiwan was China, and there was no way to convince them otherwise. They wanted a law that would reverse the action I had taken in recognizing the People's Republic of China or else include provisions that would be so unacceptable that China would reject the entire agreement. Luckily, we were in the driver's seat.

Instructed Vance to hold firm on the Taiwan legislation.
If it is modified to violate my commitments to the PRC or
if the security language with Taiwan exceeds that in the
treaty itself, I will have to veto the legislation, therefore

leaving it illegal to deal with Taiwan in any effective
way.   DIARY, MARCH 7, 1979

Although my veto was a real threat, we wanted to act responsibly toward Taiwan, and so we had to work most of the year in
shaping the final law with Congress. Some of the members had a
field day with demagoguery, grandstanding for the media and
the folks back home, but we finally prevailed, with just a few
days to spare before the Taiwan treaty was terminated and our
full agreement with China implemented.

China was one of our few foreign-policy tasks to prove much
more pleasant and gratifying than I had expected at the outset
of my term. I thought then that we were undertaking a project
that might fail because of Chinese intransigence on one or more
of our vital principles relating to Taiwan, unforeseen complica-
tions in other parts of Asia, some confrontation with China that
would have overriding significance, or insurmountable political
opposition among our people and within Congress.

Instead, everything went beautifully. Both before and after normalization, the Chinese exhibited a fine sensitivity about my
other duties, and also about our domestic political realities. They
were helpful in their statements about SALT II, the resolution of
the Taiwan issue, the stabilizing influence in the western Pacific
of our new diplomatic ties, the need for strong cooperation between us and Japan—and refrained through all of this from cast-
ing our new relationship with them in an anti-Soviet tone. In the
process, I learned why some people say the Chinese are the most
civilized people in the world.

SHADOW OVER
THE EARTH:
THE NUCLEAR THREAT

I went over the complete inventory of U.S. nuclear war-heads, which is really a sobering experience.

DIARY, DECEMBER 28, 1977

A s President, I was periodically given a total listing of all our nuclear weapons, from the smallest tactical shells to the largest bombs and missile warheads. Even more frequently I received a fairly accurate listing of the Soviet nuclear armaments. It was always obvious that both nations had far more weapons than would ever be needed to destroy every significant military installation and civilian population center in the lands of its potential enemies, and in the process kill tens of millions—perhaps a hundred million—people on each side. Europe, the most likely battleground, was covered by thousands of such explosives—tactical weapons of limited range but great destructive power. Longer-range missiles and airplanes located throughout the seas and land in the northern hemisphere could reach the American and Soviet homelands. All the glib talk about ICBM's, MIRV's, SLCM's, and GLCM's (the latter two known as *Slick-ems* and *Glick-ems*) tended to lull some people into indifference or resignation about the unbelievable destruction they represented. That horror was constantly on my mind.

Another responsibility of mine was to approve the testing of atomic explosive devices and the production schedule for additions to our nuclear arsenal, both of existing designs and of new and improved weapons. I realized that the leaders of the Soviet Union, Great Britain, France, and China were going through the same procedure, and I wondered if they too thought about future generations and were also sometimes very discouraged. Why could we not control this most ominous of all threats?

Our best hope lay in the Strategic Arms Limitation Talks, known as SALT. If these resulted in an arms control agreement, it would not only benefit the United States and the Soviet Union, but might serve as a model for other nations. Yet there were and continue to be serious obstacles to achieving agreement.

First of all, our two countries do not naturally trust one another, and there is a prevailing suspicion that the most innocent proposal might conceal some trick—such as a weapon secretly under development. One complication which follows from this distrust is that every item in a SALT treaty would have to be verifiable, each country using its independent capabilities to assure that all the terms were honored. If compliance could not be confirmed, the item could not be included.

In both countries, the military–industrial complex is extremely powerful and constantly pushing for larger defense budgets. New weapon systems are always being conceived; they pass through research, design, and testing, and then perhaps go on to deployment. This process can take as long as ten years, and once it gains momentum, it is almost impossible to stop. Throughout the protracted negotiations, ever more advanced weapons are being born and must somehow be accommodated within the convoluted language of the agreement. Each group of negotiators is, in effect, trying to put its mark on a rapidly moving animal without hogtying it first—and by the time it is finally branded, it may have changed into some new and unrecognizable form, even wilder and more uncontrollable than before.

No rational American would want to swap political systems with his or her Russian counterpart, but it is much easier to negotiate a SALT treaty in a totalitarian society with a relatively consistent policy, where the voices of news media and opposition political forces are either stilled or heard only in a closed room. The Politburo, in which military leaders play an important role, can make a decision, and the nation's propaganda apparatus can then proclaim the "unanimously agreed upon" new policy essential to self-defense.

On the other hand, the cacophony coming out of Washington indicates confusion and argument among Americans. It is almost inevitable that the voices heard most loudly are those of the opposition—and the more strident their attacks on the Soviets or on our own negotiators, the bigger the headlines.

Another serious problem in these negotiations is that it is difficult to compare our nuclear arsenal with that of the Soviet Union, because we have different needs and sharply contrasting histories of evolving these weapons. Quite early, we in the United States opted for a "triad," with three types of launchers almost equally balanced: silo-based missiles, submarine-launched missiles, and strategic bombers. The Soviets had about 30 per cent of their investment in submarines and almost all the rest in silo-based missiles.

The United States has most often been in the forefront of technological advances. We were first with atomic explosives, long-range missiles, submarine-launched missiles, multiple warheads on the same launcher, and miniaturized circuitry permitting greater destruction with smaller weapons. Also, for many years our missiles were far more accurate. However, the Soviet Union wiped out some of these advantages with a massive research and production effort, and in the process deployed some very large missiles with enormous warheads. At first, when the earlier SALT I treaty was completed, we had looked upon such missiles as wasteful and cumbersome and therefore of no great concern. We were satisfied with our own more advanced models, and were willing to permit the Soviets to have the exclusive right to retain about 300 of these enormous missiles which they had already deployed. But later some of these missiles were converted to carry many warheads, with greatly improved accuracy.

To oversimplify a very complicated comparison: we have more warheads with higher average accuracy, and the Soviets have more launchers with greater total explosive power.

There is another imbalance which American negotiators do not like to discuss. We prefer to talk only in terms of an equal ratio between the United States and the Soviet Union. From Moscow's perspective, however, there is a much more formidable array—not only from the United States and our allies, France and Great Britain, but also from a seemingly implacable Chinese adversary.

Some anti-SALT groups create other obstacles to success, such as "linkage" (basing progress on arms control to good behavior by the Soviets); the belief by some that we should burden the Soviets with enormous military expenditures in order to punish them; the willingness on the part of others to face the prospect of a "limited nuclear war"; and an erroneous belief by still others that the Soviet leaders have habitually violated earlier agreements, but that their defaults were somehow concealed by disloyal American leaders.

We have to do everything possible to stop this mad race. It is necessary to keep the threat constantly before the people, so that public opinion might be marshaled to support our total effort to control atomic explosives. Through mutual arms-control agreements, restraints on the sale of offensive arms, the alleviation of tension in such trouble spots as the Middle East, and the development of friendlier relations with such former enemies as the People's Republic of China, we can eventually hope to lower tension and the need for weapons. To make any of this possible, however, our country has to stay strong and at peace. Through our words and deeds, we must let our allies and all other people of the world know that we are in the forefront, constantly striving to prevent war in any part of the globe and to reduce the grossly excessive expenditures on armaments of all kinds.

In my inaugural address I had pledged to work toward the ultimate goal of eliminating nuclear weapons from the earth, but I knew there was no magic formula for accomplishing this task. I would follow the path that had been established by my predecessors in the White House, and pursue to the utmost the willingness of the Soviet Union to join us in the strategic arms limitation talks. Of all the issues I had to face, only the establishment of a national energy policy could rival the complexity of forging an effective arms control policy. In both cases the basic goals were clear enough, but to achieve them, we had to wrestle with technical, political, economic, and moral questions of enormous difficulty. Only if I, as President of the United States, remained deeply committed to answering these questions would there be any hope of success in reaching agreement with the Soviet leaders.

Restraints on the size, nature, and testing of existing arsenals were just one side of the coin; the other was preventing the spread of nuclear explosives to those nations which did not yet have them. This goal could be accomplished only if other world leaders were willing to cooperate in the nonproliferation effort. To make nuclear explosives, fissionable materials and high-technology plants are needed. Only a small number of countries—such as the United States, the Soviet Union, France, Germany, Japan, and Switzerland—could export the technology required for handling high-quality fuels that might be made into weapons. The sources of uranium and other fissionable raw materials were also limited to a few places in the United States, Canada, Australia, Africa, and the Soviet Union.

In 1974 India had shocked the world by carrying out a nuclear test explosion, and we knew that some of the other eager purchasers of nuclear power plants, intended ostensibly for the production of electric energy, also wanted the prestige and power of owning a few atomic weapons. Despite opposition from some of the other suppliers of advanced technology, I wanted to do everything possible to prevent this capability from spreading to any additional nations. However, my most difficult and important task was to negotiate an agreement with the Soviet leaders, to be known as the SALT II treaty.

The strategic arms limitation talks, which began in November 1969, were exclusively between the United States and the Soviet Union. They were designed to place mutual limits on the type and quantity of nuclear weapons that could be launched by one country against the other. Coming to an agreement was slow and tedious work, requiring the careful definition of extremely complicated terms and circumstances—between two distrustful countries. An interim agreement, known as SALT I, was signed in May 1972, and almost immediately the negotiations commenced on a somewhat more definitive agreement—SALT II.

When President Ford went to Vladivostok in November 1974 to meet with Leonid Brezhnev, they made some progress in developing a framework for further negotiations, spelling out the maximum number of intercontinental missiles each nation could deploy (2,400), and how many of these long-range missiles could contain more than one warhead (1,320). Of the unresolved issues, the primary one involved a Soviet bomber called the Backfire; the Soviets claimed it had only medium-range capability and was not a strategic weapon, but the Americans suspected it might be modified so that it could strike the United States. There was also disagreement on whether it was necessary to restrict American cruise missiles—small pilotless airplanes, each capable of delivering a warhead very accurately on a distant target. Unfortunately, SALT languished throughout the 1976 election year, when no appreciable effort was made to resolve the remaining issues.

As the new President, I immediately instructed my National Security Council staff and the State and Defense Departments to evolve proposals that would push the *limitation* talks into *reduction* talks. Simultaneously, we developed an alternative on which we could fall back if the Soviets were not ready for a bold move. This proposal would incorporate what was decided at Vladivostok, postponing the Backfire and cruise missile issues. We also began work on proposals for SALT III, the next step, which would bring about additional reductions in long-range missiles and for the first time apply stringent limits on the short-range weapons being deployed so heavily in Eastern and Western Europe.

On January 26, 1977, I sent my first personal letter to General Secretary Brezhnev, telling him that it was my goal to improve relations with the Soviet Union. In that message, the primary issue I addressed was the need for us to proceed with nuclear arms control. Six days later, I invited the Soviet Ambassador to the Oval Office so that we could discuss the same subject.

> *Had my first meeting with Ambassador Anatoly Dobrynin for about an hour and was favorably impressed with him. He seems to have direct communication with the Politburo, is a member of the Central Committee of the Communist Party in the Soviet Union. We decided that there would be a continuation of correspondence between myself and General Secretary Brezhnev, to be known only by the Soviet leaders, Fritz, Cy, and Zbig. I spelled out as clearly as I could my inclination to go ahead with SALT II talks, called for prior notification of any test missile launchings, a comprehensive test ban, demilitarization of the Indian Ocean, and deep cuts in total nuclear weapons with exact confirmable equality of strength for the SALT III goals.*   DIARY, FEBRUARY 1, 1977

In reviewing this diary entry in light of what I now know about the Soviet leaders, it is easier for me to understand why the boldness of these first proposals would cause them concern. They seemed to have doubted my motives, believing that I wanted to abandon the Vladivostok agreement and merely achieve some advantages over them in further negotiations. But the few points I suggested that day to Dobrynin were sound and reasonable. First, I wanted each country to notify the other well in advance when a long-range missile was going to be tested, so that there would be no chance that the other might mistake a test for an actual attack. The second point was that we were willing to forgo all further testing of nuclear explosives, provided a reliable system could be established to detect any violations of this agreement by either side. Also, as a clear signal to other nations that we could make progress together toward peace, I wanted to work with the Soviet leaders to establish strict limits on the permanent deployment of naval forces in the Indian Ocean, and to require prior notification if such forces had to be strengthened to protect the special interests of either nation (as was later the case when our hostages were taken in Iran). After completion of a SALT II treaty, I wanted to achieve much larger reductions in nuclear arsenals, with exact equality between the destructive forces of our two nations.

I was able to send the second letter to General Secretary Brezhnev, much more substantive than the first one. It's important that he understand the commitment I have to human rights first of all, and that it is not an antagonistic attitude of mine toward the Soviet Union—and that I'm very sincere about my desire to reduce nuclear armaments. If he's willing to cooperate, we'll get something done before four years go by. DIARY, FEBRUARY 14, 1977

My intention was to cooperate with the Soviets whenever possible, and I saw a successful effort in controlling nuclear weapons as the best tool for improving our relations. It was obvious that existing agreements had not significantly deterred either country from rapidly increasing its arsenal of ever more accurate and powerful weapons. In effect, we were leapfrogging each other in this frightening competition, and this in itself was a destabilizing factor in United States–Soviet relations. During previous talks, the American negotiating position had not been worked out carefully among the military, State, and White House officials; on occasion some of them and Congress had been surprised to see certain parts of the final texts. This lack of coordination was one of the causes of a deep split in the Ford Administration, ultimately leading to the resignation of James Schlesinger as Secretary of Defense, and perhaps partially the reason that, with divided support, no negotiations went on during 1976.

To prepare our proposals for presentation to the Soviet leaders, I spent many hours working with Secretary of State Vance; Defense Secretary Brown; National Security Adviser Brzezinski; Paul Warnke, director of the Arms Control and Disarmament Agency; and members of the Joint Chiefs of Staff. We also sought advice from members of Congress who had been involved in earlier SALT decisions. For the first time, our nation's position was being developed with wide consultation and without secret terms. This policy was in keeping with my general attitude of openness, but it required at least as much time negotiating within our country as with the Soviets. Another unanticipated result of this policy was Moscow's reaction. The Soviet leaders seemed to suspect that by making our positions known, we were waging a propaganda battle instead of negotiating in good faith.

On February 25, Brezhnev replied to my second letter and to the proposals I had outlined to Dobrynin. His reaction was very negative concerning our ideas about nuclear arms control. He characterized them, in fact, as "deliberately unacceptable."

I answered in very strong terms, letting him know that his

allegations about my insincerity were completely false, and repeating in more detail what we could accomplish together while we were both in office.

His reply of March 15 was milder and more businesslike, omitting much of the hard-line Soviet rhetoric, but he still did not agree to anything other than a very slow and cautious approach to the questions we had to face.

Because former Secretary of State Henry Kissinger had done most of the negotiating under Presidents Nixon and Ford, my colleagues and I briefed him on our new proposals and sought his advice.

Henry and Nancy Kissinger came by for supper. Cy Vance and Gay were here, and Dr. Brzezinski. He [Kissinger] thought that the deep cut [the second option described below] proposal we had put together on SALT had a good chance to be accepted by the Soviets if they are sincere and want to make progress on disarmament.

DIARY, MARCH 18, 1977

In March I sent Secretary Vance to Moscow with two alternatives. One option simply built on the Vladivostok talks, although with overall weapons limits about 10 per cent below the previously accepted figures. The second proposal was the one we preferred, requiring a much more substantial overall reduction in armaments and lessening the vulnerability of either nation to a first strike by the other. It also imposed stringent limits on qualitative improvements in weapons and reduced the threat from those missiles of most concern, such as the very large Soviet intercontinental missiles (which were permitted under SALT I) and the planned American cruise missiles and MX intercontinental missiles. This option offered severe mutual limits on the testing of existing missiles and a prohibition against the deployment of new ones.

When Cy Vance delivered our suggestions to the Soviet leaders, their response was almost immediate, and quite negative. They refused to submit any counteroffers, except a proposal to meet again in May to consider much more limited options and resolve some of the issues left over from Vladivostok. It was obvious that they wanted to move slowly and in small increments. I was angry over the Soviet attitude, and disappointed because we would have to set back our timetable for an agreement. The American and Soviet negotiators began their work, with our team instructed to seek maximum reductions and restraints.

During the two months before Vance and Gromyko met again, this time in Geneva, we developed a three-tier approach. The first agreement would be the SALT II treaty, effective through 1985; the second would last only three years and apply to a few controversial systems, such as cruise missiles and other new types; and the third would be a set of principles to guide future negotiations for a SALT III treaty involving deeper weapons reduction. Gromyko agreed to this general framework, but our two nations continued to disagree on numerous details.

On September 22 Gromyko was in Washington. I spent about three hours with him the next day in an extensive discussion about the contrasting interests and capabilities of our two countries, probing for ways to lessen tensions over human-rights issues—restricted trade, Soviet emigration policy, the upcoming conference in Belgrade to assess progress under the Helsinki accords, and public complaints about Soviet treatment of dissidents. Gromyko revealed a lot when he said that Anatoly Shcharansky—a Russian dissident who had attracted worldwide attention—was just "a microscopic dot who is of no consequence to anyone." I responded that the persecution and trial of dissidents like Shcharansky was assuming great symbolic importance in shaping American opinion about the Soviet system of government, and was therefore a major factor in determining the degree of friendship and trust that could be built between our two nations.

Despite this and other disputes, both of us agreed that we did not want to link SALT II to any other issue. Gromyko said the Soviets wanted to proceed but that the United States Senate should first ratify the Limited Test Ban Treaty, which had been signed many years before. He did admit that the treaty was being observed by both sides, even though the Senate had chosen not to act. We had a detailed discussion of SALT issues, with Gromyko maintaining that from the Soviet point of view, it was the same as at Stalingrad: "Beyond the Volga there is nothing"—meaning that the Soviets had gone as far as they would go. When I responded that such an adamant position on any of the major issues would block further progress, he changed the subject by stating that the Soviet Union had long ago offered to forgo the use of atomic weapons altogether if all other nations would too. This comment seemed incompatible with the Soviet refusal to join us in extensive reductions in existing arsenals.

Gromyko was very obstinate, refusing to agree to any specific proposal. I was familiar with Soviet negotiating technique, and had expected him to be very tough and negative at first, almost abusive at times, and then more cooperative toward the end of a session if the Soviet leaders wanted to reach agreement at all. The Soviets looked on a discussion from a perspective entirely different from our own, often considering negotiations as something of an end in themselves while we Americans saw such sessions as a necessary impediment to be overcome in order to reach a desired objective.

Even realizing all this, I was surprised at how uncooperative Gromyko was. When he left, we had not accomplished anything. I could only hope that his inflexibility was a temporary tactic.

A few days later, on September 27, Foreign Minister Gromyko, Ambassador Dobrynin, and Georgiy Kornyenko—a deputy foreign minister who specialized in United States–Soviet relations—came back to see me. This time, for some reason I have never understood, they seemed ready to reach agreement. Except for a couple of issues, which we decided not to address, they accepted the basic framework. It set forth overall limits of 2,250 total missile launchers, of which 1,250 could contain multiple warheads, provided no more than 820 were land-based in silos instead of in submarines and on long-range bombers.

We also progressed in determining how to verify one another's compliance with the treaty. Through various means, including electronic devices on land and in space, we each had to be able to know what kind of missiles were being tested and deployed in the other country. To conceal these activities would be forbidden.

The SALT I treaty was scheduled to expire in October, but we agreed to continue honoring its terms until SALT II could be put into effect. I told Gromyko that for SALT III, I wanted a reduction on the maximum limits for launchers and warheads to less than one-half of those we had just decided to establish. He understood my proposal but did not comment.

There was a good spirit about this session, after we all realized that we could continue with nuclear arms control negotiations in spite of our serious differences on other issues. Gromyko talked about Soviet concessions so much that I finally told him I had a dual responsibility. One was to protect the interests of the American people, and the other was to protect the Soviet people if he was too generous and inclined to betray their interests. He laughed, realizing he had made too much of Soviet accommodation.

Gromyko made it plain that Brezhnev was eager to meet me, but wanted assurance that a summit conference would be successful and lead to a major agreement. I said that although Gromyko had more experience than I in diplomatic affairs—

"maybe five hundred more months"—both of us knew from experience that the American and Soviet people wanted peace. I hoped their leaders would not disappoint them.

On the spur of the moment, I decided to give Gromyko a going-away present—a small wooden display I kept on my desk, showing all the American and Soviet missiles known to exist. He was taken aback that I would do such a thing, because the set of models showed the gigantic size and many types of their missiles, contrasted with the few and relatively compact American ICBMs.

When Rosalynn came by as he was leaving, he recognized her immediately, saying she was a famous and much admired woman in the Soviet Union because of her background and accomplishments. He added that he would look forward to an opportunity for his wife to meet her. Gromyko was much more charming to my wife than he usually was to the rest of us.

During the following weeks, the Soviets and Cubans became more and more deeply involved in Ethiopia, the Cubans aided Katangan rebels in an invasion of Zaire, Soviet spies in New York and an American businessman in Moscow were arrested, and the Soviet dissidents Anatoly Shcharansky and Aleksandr Ginzburg were put on trial. These disturbing events made the task of coming to an agreement with the Soviets more difficult, but in spite of them we pressed forward.

Shortly after Gromyko's visit, on October 6, I met with Secretary of Defense Harold Brown and the five Joint Chiefs of Staff to make certain that we were all in agreement. I knew that when the SALT II treaty was submitted to the Senate for ratification, the testimony of these men would be most important.

They came prepared with a long list of highly technical questions, and they seemed satisfied with my answers. As there was still some negotiating to do, I could understand the reluctance of the Joint Chiefs of Staff about making an endorsement before all our final positions had been defined. I needed them with me, however, and later decided to make the Chairman a member of our summit delegation.

I had good relations with them. Even before my inauguration, I had begun to receive briefings from the Joint Chiefs at Blair House and in the Pentagon. They were also of great help to me as we moved to rebuild our long-neglected military forces. When I studied the past defense-budget figures, it became clear that, measured in real dollars, during the past eight years there had been a 35 per cent reduction in commitments for defense, while the Soviets had increased their defense expenditures by about 4 per cent annually. The public and Congress would have to be convinced that we needed to strengthen our defenses. I would have to supply this persuasion without alarming our own people or our allies, and without our becoming so belligerent in our attitude that cooperation with the Soviet Union on other issues would be impossible.

It was important not to appear as a warmonger, interested only in potential military solutions to the intractable problems we faced. Such a posture would drive away some of our European allies, alienate the nonaligned countries of the world, and tend to isolate the United States within the community of nations. The Soviet Union had already reaped a great propaganda harvest by claiming falsely that it was the only world power that truly wanted peace and was eager to control the buildup of nuclear arsenals. Our policy of resolving regional disputes through negotiation and our unequivocal commitment to nuclear arms control, combined with a quiet, steady, and well-planned strengthening of our military capability, would signal that America was a peaceful and reliable country which would never let itself become vulnerable to threat or attack.

⌣

At the Cabinet meeting this morning Zbig made an interesting comment that under Lenin the Soviet Union was like a religious revival, under Stalin like a prison, under Khrushchev like a circus, and under Brezhnev like the U.S. Post Office.   DIARY, NOVEMBER 7, 1977

I thought Zbig's comment was apt. At least from my perspective, the Soviet bureaucracy seemed cumbersome and stifling. All my letters to Brezhnev were quite personal in nature—I even wrote some of them in longhand—while those from him to me were very cautious, always repeating the same Soviet line.

At least during this period, the letters had a decidedly positive tone. Apparently the "post-office department" in Moscow had decided to move forward on SALT, because we continued to make slow but steady progress. We were now working well with the Soviets on banning nuclear weapons tests of all kinds. Brezhnev was agreeing that we needed to have major reductions in existing arsenals; and he had not rejected the idea of ceasing all nuclear weapons construction—the same proposals I had put forward in my earliest correspondence with him.

Then came Anwar Sadat's visit to Jerusalem in November 1977.

The Soviet leader seemed to believe Sadat's trip had been orchestrated by the United States for the sole purpose of further removing the Soviets from involvement in the Middle East peace process.
The result of Sadat's grand gesture was as Brezhnev had feared,
but the primary initiative had come from Cairo, not from Washington. In any case, for a few months our progress on SALT was
slowed.

The most disturbing development came not from Moscow, but
from the Republican senators in our own country. Some of them
were helping me courageously with ratification of the Panama
Canal treaties, but were making it plain that they were not inclined to support me on the upcoming SALT treaty, no matter
what its terms might be. I got this message from President Ford
and Senator Baker, as well as from other Republican leaders,
with varying degrees of specificity and finality.

> *Jerry Ford came by and spent about an hour with me. He
> thought we ought to move much more strongly on Pana-
> ma. Expressed some concern about SALT. . . . My sense
> is that the Republican hierarchy has decided to go along
> with us on Panama and to fight us on SALT. We'll take
> them one at a time.*   DIARY, DECEMBER 20, 1977

> *I met early with Senator Baker, who wanted to give me a
> report on his trip to Panama, Mexico, Colombia, Brazil,
> and Venezuela. He's decided to support the Panama Canal
> treaties. . . . He also wants to work closer with me, as
> did his father-in-law, Senator Dirksen, with Presidents.
> He did indicate to me that the Republicans were going to
> make an issue of the SALT agreement, which I had heard
> previously.*   DIARY, JANUARY 16, 1978

The issue was partisan politics. It is almost impossible to imagine how difficult it was for some of the Republicans (and Democrats too, of course) to vote for the Panama treaties. To support a
Democratic President on two such difficult issues would have
been almost suicidal for those whose political future depended on
rich extremists who finance a lot of Republican campaigns. Some
who regretted hearing talk of this impasse around the Capitol
cloakrooms revealed it to me, and since the information came
from several independent sources, my presumption was that it
was true. Of course, I continued to work with those Republicans
anyway and to keep them informed about the evolution of the

treaty, trusting that later I could arouse a bipartisan spirit and enough public support to make it politically advantageous for them to endorse the treaty when I proved that its final terms had merit.

It was also clear that I would have strong opposition among some leading Democratic senators. For instance, there was no possibility of support from Scoop Jackson for any treaty which the Soviets were likely to sign; he was already doing everything possible to defeat the agreement even before its final terms could be known. I talked to John Stennis, Chairman of the Armed Services Committee, about this problem, and he promised me that the full committee would conduct any substantive hearings on SALT and that he would not yield to Senator Jackson's request that his own subcommittee on arms control take over this responsibility.

There was another reason for concern. Under the Constitution, thirty-four of the one hundred senators can block ratification of any treaty. This is an unhappy and unique feature of our democracy. Because of the effective veto power of a small group, many worthy agreements have been rejected, and many treaties are never considered for ratification after they are delivered to the Senate, but simply remain in force as interim agreements.

My problems with nuclear arms were not limited to the Senate or the Soviets. One of the most controversial and least understood issues I had to face as President was a NATO decision on whether or not to develop and deploy in Europe (ER) enhanced radiation weapons, the so-called neutron bomb. During 1977, the NATO military leaders were considering the deployment of this weapon, which would have a major advantage over the existing tactical nuclear weapons it would replace. In case of a Soviet invasion of Western Europe, it could be used for defense against Soviet tanks and troops with less danger of its affecting our own troops or civilians who might be in the area. The ER weapon's destructive force would come not from the relatively small explosion but from intense radiation, which enabled it to kill enemy troops with a minimum of damage to surrounding structures. This very characteristic of killing with radiation made the weapon seem particularly frightening to the public.

As the discussions among the military leaders continued, public opposition to the neutron bomb in Europe increased, so that by early 1978, I was concerned about the possibility that the weapon would never be deployed, even if it were developed. Lacking a commitment about deployment from the political leaders of Europe—even from the more forceful governments of Great Britain or West Germany—I decided to send Deputy National Security Adviser David Aaron to those key countries to ascertain their positions. After this trip, Brzezinski reported on February 2 that the West Germans would be willing to "support deployment of the neutron bomb *should an arms control initiative not work out*." He added, "The British surprisingly turned out to have a lot of trouble with publicly supporting a decision to produce and deploy. They said that the arms control linkage concept helped, but that the cabinet would have to face up to this issue. They implied that the Labour Party was split and [the] ministers would prefer to avoid a decision."

In other words, the Germans would agree to deploy the weapons only if arms control negotiations failed, and the British were equivocal even under those conditions. Without leadership from these two governments, others would almost certainly not accept the recommendations of the NATO military leaders.

It was becoming increasingly obvious to me that a sharp difference of opinion existed within each NATO country: the military commanders wanted the weapon to be deployed, but the political leaders did not. As had been the case with other new weapons in the past, the presumption of the NATO military officials was that the United States would agree to develop and produce the neutron weapons, and then the Europeans, for their own defense, would deploy them within their areas. In this case, such ultimate deployment was very doubtful, and I began to question the advisability of our proceeding with the highly unpopular and very expensive project if it would never be implemented. Because of their short range, these shells and missile warheads would be valuable only for the protection of Western Europe in case of a Soviet invasion and be of little, if any, use to American armed forces elsewhere in the world.

On March 8, the Dutch Parliament passed a resolution stating that production of the weapon was undesirable, and the prime minister informed our government that they could not now agree to deployment even if the Soviets were unwilling to negotiate on nuclear arms control. Vance informed me that American embassy officials in Europe would continue to work for a statement of support from our allies; but it never came.

The United States was now in an almost absurd position—willing to proceed with the project alone, while insisting fruitlessly on the deployment of neutron weapons by our NATO allies. In March 1978, I met with the Vice President, Secretaries Vance and Brown, and National Security Adviser Brzezinski to express my concern about the issue.

> *They had generated a lot of momentum, including an immediate agreement for me to produce these neutron weapons. My cautionary words to them since last summer have pretty well been ignored, and I was aggravated. After we analyzed the situation in a fairly combative fashion, I became more and more convinced that we ought not to deploy the neutron bomb. We've not gotten any firm commitments from a European nation to permit its deployment on their soil, which is the only place it would be deployed.* DIARY, MARCH 20, 1978

In this meeting, my advisers urged me to proceed with the development and production of neutron weapons. Although I had agreed to go ahead with the project if our NATO allies concurred, I was troubled over the advisability of trying to force neutron weapons on our allies. We decided to explore the question further with the government leaders of Western Europe. A few days later, when Prime Minister James Callaghan was in Washington for a visit, we discussed the issue. Because of the limited range of the proposed neutron weapons, they would not be used in Great Britain in any event, but some of the shells or missile warheads could be stored in the British Isles for use on the Continent.

> *He [Callaghan] said they were willing to support me if we decided to stop it or reduce it. It would not be deployed in Great Britain. He said it would be the greatest relief in the world if we announced that we were not going to go ahead with it; that it would be a very difficult political issue for him to handle in Great Britain.* DIARY, MARCH 23, 1978

After returning from a trip to South America and Africa, I immediately consulted the German leaders.

> *Met with Hans-Dietrich Genscher, foreign minister of Germany. It became obvious during the discussion between him, me, Cy, and Zbig that the Germans are playing footsie with us on the ER weapons. They want us to announce production; they will deploy them only if another European country agrees to deploy. We finally decided that after two or three days I would announce that we were deferring the decision, and then the options would*

*be predicated on European acceptance of deployment—a
determination that the ER weapon is the best way to
spend the money, better than ground-launched cruise missiles or laser-guided antitank missiles—and predicated on
the fact that the Soviets don't cooperate on MBFR (mutual and balanced force reductions), comprehensive test
ban, or SALT.*   DIARY, APRIL 4, 1978

My decision was to defer production while we continued to
consult with European leaders, using the issue of the neutron
weapon to induce additional restraints among the Soviets in
other arms control negotiations. We and our NATO allies would
reserve the option of producing and deploying the weapons in
the future. In the meantime, the United States would improve
existing tactical nuclear weapons, incorporating in their design
the capability of later conversion to ER use once our allies were
willing to agree to deployment. After consulting with my security
advisers on the language of our communiqué, this decision was
distributed to the NATO council on April 7.

There was then a contentious debate in the West German parliament. Cy Vance reported, "Opposition leaders struck hard during
today's Bundestag debate on the ER weapon. Helmut Kohl [Chris-
tian Democratic leader] stated that Schmidt's conditioned acceptance of eventual deployment in Germany was insufficient, and
that he had failed to control the SPD [Social Democrats, the
Chancellor's own party] left wing, and that his failure to make
public the government's position had contributed to today's cli-
mate in U.S.–German relations. A Schmidt spokesman called Kohl
to task for ignoring the arms control aspects of the situation and
asserted that your decision to delay production was consistent
with Schmidt's stance."

The Chancellor then called me about this debate.

*Chancellor Schmidt reported to me that he had gotten a
16-vote majority on the neutron bomb decision, approving
both his and my position. Although this seems like a
narrow margin to me, he was quite proud of it, and said
the debate went well—there was no harsh criticism compared to what he had anticipated, and that the whole
debate underlined the need for continued German–U.S.
friendship.*   DIARY, APRIL 13, 1978

In spite of these private assurances, Helmut subsequently complained to many listeners that the United States had unilaterally

aborted the plans to produce and deploy neutron weapons. The fact is that to this day no European government has been willing to agree to their deployment, and I believe that such a decision is highly unlikely in the foreseeable future. Although some confusion was generated within the NATO alliance, under the existing circumstances my final decision not to produce neutron weapons was the proper one. Not only was it logical on its own merits and compatible with the desires of most of our European allies, but it also conformed to our general policy of restricting nuclear weaponry.

‿

As we entered the second year of SALT talks, we continued to make tediously slow progress in our negotiations with the Soviet Union, under the direction of Secretary Vance and our chief negotiator, Paul Warnke. Problems were developing on both the American and Soviet sides with my comprehensive test ban proposals. For one, the military leaders and our Energy Department officials were insisting that some very low-level testing was necessary, just to confirm that the triggering mechanisms on existing armaments remained functional and dependable. The other problem concerned verifiability, or the placement of sensing devices in each country to detect an explosion which might be in violation of the agreement. The British later chose to join our discussions, which further complicated the latter issue. They and the Soviets could not agree on how many of the sensing devices should be in Great Britain, with the Soviet leaders insisting that all three of our nations must have exactly the same number, and the British equally adamant that in their much smaller country a smaller number of these expensive instruments would be adequate.

Vance and Gromyko discussed the remaining SALT issues in New York in May 1978, and immediately thereafter, I had another meeting with Gromyko. It was almost completely unsatisfactory because, despite the best efforts of the United States, the developing differences between our two countries in various places in the world were affecting progress on SALT. I wanted to send a message to the Soviets and to the world, and decided to spell out more clearly the overall relationship between our countries in a speech on June 7, 1978, to the graduating midshipmen at the U.S. Naval Academy.

The word "détente" can be simplistically defined as "the easing of tension between nations." ... Détente must be broadly defined and truly reciprocal. Both nations must exercise restraint in troubled areas [like Ethiopia, the Persian Gulf, Yemen, and Kampuchea] and in troubled times. . . . Neither of us should entertain the notion that military supremacy can be attained, or that transient military advantage can be politically exploited.

We want to increase our collaboration with the Soviet Union, but also with the emerging nations, with the nations of Eastern Europe, and with the People's Republic of China. [This was a signal of our intention to have normal relations with China without further disrupting Soviet–American relations.]

We remember that the United States and the Soviet Union were allies in the Second World War. . . . In the agony of that massive conflict, 20 million Soviet lives were lost. . . . I am convinced that the people of the Soviet Union want peace.

We will continue to maintain equivalent nuclear strength, because we believe that in the absence of worldwide nuclear disarmament, such equivalency is the least threatening and the most stable situation for the world. [Carefully balanced forces at the lowest mutually acceptable level was what I wanted.]

The Soviet Union can choose either confrontation or cooperation. The United States is adequately prepared to meet either choice. We would prefer cooperation. . . .

There was a very negative reaction to my Annapolis speech from Moscow, particularly to my references to Soviet involvement in some of the regional conflicts in Africa and Asia.

Nevertheless the SALT negotiations continued to make some progress during the summer months of 1978. In July, Vance and Gromyko met again in Geneva and succeeded in adjusting the terms of the agreement to accommodate special technical problems which scientists and military experts on both sides had detected. Their exchange had to be mutual and finely balanced, each point carefully outlined in the esoteric language used to describe humanity's most effective death machines.

Shortly after the Camp David negotiations with Sadat and Begin in September 1978, I prepared to resume discussions on SALT with Foreign Minister Gromyko, who would be in our country for the United Nations General Assembly session.

I had lunch with Rosalynn, Harold Hughes [former Senator from Iowa], and Doug Coe [organizer and promoter of the President's Prayer Breakfast and Senate prayer groups] to thank them for leading the worldwide prayer sessions while we were at Camp David. In the middle of the lunch period they called and told me that Gromyko

*had had a stroke while making a speech at the UN. We
said a prayer for him. It later turned out that he had only
been overcome with heat from the TV lights.*
                                        DIARY, SEPTEMBER 26, 1978

Gromyko came to see me a few days later and seemed somewhat embarrassed about his fainting spell. He was certainly in
top form when, for the first hour or so, he and I exchanged the
requisite barbs about Cuba, Israel, China, Ethiopia, and the pure
and peaceful nature of our own countries. After these preliminar-
ies, the meeting turned out to be our most productive one. We
agreed to conclude the SALT II treaty first, followed by a comprehensive test-ban agreement. I then outlined where we both
stood, beginning with a summary of all our agreements and
disagreements. I was convinced that the United States proposals
to resolve the disputes were reasonable, and I made sure he knew
that this was as far as we would go or needed to go for a final
agreement.

With several concessions on his part, we made a lot of progress,
but some issues still remained. As we argued over such apparently
simple definitions as "new missile," "improvements," "cruise
missile," and "range," we were laying the groundwork for the
future. Each of these terms was important, and our negotiators had spent month after month deciding how much change in
an existing launcher would be permitted before it became a new
type, whether cruise missiles with nonnuclear warheads would be
included within a SALT agreement, and whether range would be
measured along a straight line or along the wandering path of a
cruise missile as it sought out its target. Once these definitions
were decided, they could be applied to future agreements without
further debate. At times, questions had to be referred back to
Brezhnev and the Politburo for a decision at the highest Soviet
level. (I routinely approved such details in our negotiating positions after a quick consultation with the State Department and
military leaders.)

Now with Gromyko I raised a troublesome point again. The
United States objected strongly to the Soviet habit of transmitting encoded data from its missiles during test flights. We monitored these signals, and when they were in code, we could not
decipher the results of the Soviet tests. Although not a violation
of existing agreements, such encoding would hamper our ability
to detect Soviet development of a prohibited new missile after
SALT II was effective. Gromyko did not acknowledge the seriousness of this issue.

In closing, he and I summarized the primary tasks of our negotiators in Geneva. Under SALT II, the Soviet Union would be
required to dismantle about 10 per cent of its total launchers in
order to comply with reduced ceilings for intercontinental missiles. This limit did not affect us, because we had not relied so
heavily on a large number of ICBM's, preferring to depend almost
equally on weapons launched from airplanes and submarines.
How rapidly this dismantling would occur had to be decided. The
other important issue was the definition of "new missile."

> *Afterward I had Gromyko and Cy eat lunch with me in
> the White House and it was one of the best meetings I've
> ever had with any foreign leader. . . . Gromyko genuinely
> seemed to want my opinion on where we should go from
> here. . . . There was no excess verbiage, no posturing, and
> no polemics on his part. I recognize their problem in
> facing four potential nuclear adversaries—ourselves, Brit-
> ain, France, and China—whereas we don't face any of
> these except the Soviet Union and perhaps to a tiny degree
> China. I emphasized to him the advantage to the Soviets
> of our having good relations with China, and he didn't
> even disagree with this.*   DIARY, SEPTEMBER 30, 1978

I was pleased with our progress, and considered the SALT II
negotiations to be about over. It had been a long and arduous
task for all of us, but particularly burdensome for me. Most of the
technical advisers had been free to concentrate their attention
almost exclusively on this complicated issue, but for a President,
in spite of its extreme importance, it was one of many pressing
duties. In addition, some of the issues were extremely controversial among my own advisers, and very difficult for me to resolve.
There was no one else to make a final decision, and sometimes I
had to spend many hours learning about the more contentious
points. Now the details could be wrapped up without further
delay. A summit meeting between Brezhnev and me would take
care of any problems of great importance after our subordinates
had hammered out acceptable compromises ahead of time.

The next day I called Cy to make certain that his follow-up
meeting had gone all right, and was taken aback when he told me
he had already arranged to go to Moscow. This was a negotiating
error, because it implied that we were still open to further discussions on the positions that had just been covered with Gromyko.
It was time for all of us to take a hard line on the remaining
details. I was through being flexible. I finally relented and agreed

to his trip when he assured me that its primary purpose was to arrange for a summit meeting.

Working with Paul Warnke and his team of negotiators, the Soviets seemed quite eager to conclude an agreement on SALT II, and were also more friendly and cooperative in their attitude toward other nonrelated issues. We were having a lot of trouble in the Middle East, arguing with the Arab leaders about the Camp David agreement and trying to control another outbreak of violence in Lebanon. Late at night I sent Brezhnev a rare message on the hot line urging him to help us by using his influence with the Syrians to obtain a cease-fire in Lebanon.

The hot line is a direct telex connection between Moscow and Washington, dedicated exclusively to communication between the President of the United States and the leader of the Soviet Union. Staffed at all times by expert operators who speak fluent English and Russian, this system insures that messages can be delivered quickly and accurately in times of emergency such as the current one.

Quite early in the morning, even before I went to the office, I had Brezhnev's reply, pledging to give us maximum assistance. This was a good omen, and I thought how fine it would be if we could cooperate like this more often.

Paul Warnke had already stayed away from his law firm far longer than he or I had anticipated, and now he asked to be relieved of his duties immediately after the next Vance–Gromyko meeting. He had done a good job and at that time we expected our work on SALT II to be about over, so I agreed to his request. When Vance went to Moscow, however, nothing was accomplished. In fact, the Soviets seemed to reverse themselves, and at least for the time being would no longer agree to such major items as limiting the number of warheads to be permitted on each of the existing models of intercontinental missiles.

With any sign of irresolution from us, the Soviets would probe for additional concessions. I told Vance to continue the discussions with Ambassador Dobrynin in Washington, maintain our basic posture on the remaining issues, and not appear too eager for a final agreement or a summit meeting. It was now obvious that although the Soviets could accept our remaining proposals, they were holding back on one or two until they could agree to the time, place, and agenda for a meeting between Brezhnev and me.

I was sure that our announcement, in December, of plans to normalize diplomatic relations with China would cool the Soviets' willingness to conclude the SALT agreement, but I received a message from Brezhnev immediately afterward in which he stated that diplomatic recognition between nations was normal, that it was also natural for the Soviet Union to be concerned about the antagonistic Chinese attitude toward it, and that he shared my hope for an early resolution of the remaining SALT II issues.

Then Brezhnev reversed some of these private assurances through the Soviet news media. The Soviets soon made it clear to us that they would not consider any summit meeting until after the Chinese leader, Deng Xiaoping, had completed his planned visit to the United States in January. We arranged for Vance and Gromyko to meet "one more time" in Geneva late in December, and I reviewed our final negotiating proposals with the Joint Chiefs of Staff and my other advisers. I was still very worried about Soviet encoding of missile-test data, realizing that unless that point could be resolved, it could preclude any SALT treaty.

On December 21, the day the Geneva meeting began, we learned that the Soviets had tested another of their large missiles and encoded some of the data. The Vance–Gromyko meeting became bogged down on this crucial question and on the definition of "new missiles," which had been one of the integral parts of our more comprehensive proposal in March 1977. We were insisting that anything more than a 5 per cent change in important characteristics of a missile would be prohibited, while the Soviets wanted this limit to be about 20 per cent.

This episode was followed on December 27 by a letter from Brezhnev, implying that unless we prevented our European allies from selling weapons to China, there might be no further progress on arms control. It was obvious that the Soviet leaders were more concerned about our new relations with China than we had supposed and than Brezhnev had first indicated.

Early in January 1979, I met at Guadeloupe with President Valéry Giscard d'Estaing of France, Prime Minister Callaghan of Great Britain, and Chancellor Schmidt of West Germany for long and private discussions. Among our most important talks were those about nuclear weapons and our future relations with the Soviets.

Some of the leaders were concerned that the growing isolation of the Soviet Union might cause it to discount the restraining influence of détente and launch out on some military adventure. The Soviets were relatively withdrawn from the Western industrialized world and increasingly challenged by China and others for leadership among the socialist countries and the so-called nonaligned nations. There were now fewer revolutions each year

creating new nations as colonialism ended, and the Soviets therefore had less opportunity to export communism to such troubled
spots. What the Soviets depended on was enormous military
power and their willingness to export arms to gain a foothold
wherever an opportunity arose. They also had their surrogates—
Cuba and Vietnam—to serve them when military action was
required. Although the Soviet leaders had refrained from direct
involvement of their own troops since they had moved into Czechoslovakia in 1968, their use of force again was a growing possibility.

When I raised the issue of allied self-defense, a difficult conversation ensued. I pointed out that we must meet the Soviet threat
on intermediate-range missiles, that the SS-20's being rapidly
deployed by the Soviets were formidable weapons, but that no
European leader had been willing to accept on their soil our
neutron weapons, ground-launched cruise missiles, or the Pershing
2 medium-range missiles.

Giscard agreed that the Western powers had to be able to
defend themselves and also to evolve a weapon capability to
trade off for the SS-20's—a prerequisite to cutting down the
threat of the Soviet intermediate-range missile systems to Europe. Helmut was very contentious, insisting that he would permit the deployment of additional missiles on his soil only when
other European nations agreed to similar arrangements. I replied
that Helmut had initiated this entire discussion of a European
nuclear imbalance, and that we must have German willingness to
deploy these missiles in order to negotiate successfully with the
Soviets. Callaghan said it was necessary to include the European
medium-range systems in SALT III. I told him this was clearly
understood by Brezhnev and me.

This conversation was obviously inconclusive, but typical of the
problem the United States had faced for a long time in shaping a
response to Soviet threats against Europe. I was prepared to
negotiate with Brezhnev about an overall reduction in these armaments; but, pending an agreement, Europe had to be willing
to maintain the strength of our joint forces so that they would at
least be competitive with those of the Soviet Union. The European leaders would let the United States design, develop, and
produce the new weapons, but none of them was willing to agree
in advance to deploy them.

The only reasonable solution I could come up with was to move
forward with design and to develop some production capability;
go all-out to implement very restrictive SALT agreements; seek
unanimity within NATO to improve our defenses; convince the
world that, in spite of meeting the Soviet threat, the United

States was attempting to reduce existing arsenals and prevent the further proliferation of nuclear arms; and therefore drive all of us toward the drastic nuclear-arsenal reductions the United States wanted. We finally agreed that I would send someone to Europe to meet with them after they had consulted more thoroughly with their military leaders.

The big event in Washington at the beginning of 1979 was the visit to the United States by Vice Premier Deng Xiaoping. Shortly thereafter, Cyrus Vance and Anatoly Dobrynin began a series of discussions to iron out the remaining differences—another verse of the same old song.

It was amazing how different the Soviets were from the Chinese and others in their treatment of distinguished visitors. I never knew of any of our top leaders who did not return from China completely enchanted and grateful. I had learned from experience that the Panamanians also knew how to welcome and entertain their guests; General Torrijos and his people were instrumental in convincing many visiting senators to vote for treaty ratification. With the SALT II treaty vote approaching, I had been hoping that some senatorial visits to Moscow would be helpful, but they were a public-relations catastrophe. The Soviet leaders were just the opposite of the Chinese and Panamanians—heavy-handed, abrupt, rude, and argumentative. In January, I met with a group of senators who had visited the Soviet Union during the Christmas recess. Most of them had been inclined to support a nuclear arms agreement. After listening to their comments, I tried to repair the damage caused in Moscow.

> I was really taken aback by their vituperative animosity toward the Soviet Union, the ones who had been there. Ribicoff said that the Soviets don't understand the Senate. . . . Bellmon said they were two-faced. . . . [Jacob] Javits said they're not willing to give up anything for SALT. . . . As we went around the room, it became obvious that they had a very negative attitude toward the Soviet Union, as though it were the popular thing to do.
>
> I pointed out to them that we have negotiated this treaty for more than six years, and that the treaty on its own, without any linkage, was a benefit to ourselves and the Soviets. . . . We had to be fair, and recognize the terrible consequences of a Senate rejection of the treaty once it was negotiated. Détente would be destroyed, and our

*Western allies and the rest of the world would look on us
as warmongers. We would have no chance to control
nuclear proliferation, and our own people would lose faith
in the peace process and nuclear weapons control.*

                                    DIARY, JANUARY 24, 1979

Afterward, Senator Abe Ribicoff called me from his home to say
that he had been impressed by my arguments, and that if they
were presented forcefully to groups of senators, we might get
SALT II ratified. I had mixed emotions, but I was pleased that the
encounter with the senators had alleviated some of the anti-Soviet
and anti-SALT II feeling that had resulted from their visit to
Moscow.

When the Chinese military forces crossed the northern Vietnam
border in February 1979, the Soviet leaders immediately accused
us of complicity in the act—although this was, of course, untrue;
we had actually tried to dissuade the Chinese. The forces against
the success of the SALT negotiations seemed to be building up
both in the Senate and in Moscow, so I decided to reemphasize
their preeminent importance, even in a turbulent world. Late in
February, I went to Camp David to put the finishing touches on
such a foreign-policy address, which I delivered on February 20,
1979, at the Georgia Institute of Technology.

The question is not whether SALT can be divorced from this
complicated context [our many differences with the Soviets]. It
cannot. . . . It is in our national interest to pursue it, even as
we continue competition with the Soviet Union elsewhere in
the world. . . . To reject SALT II would mean that the inevitable competition in strategic nuclear arms would grow even
more dangerous. Each crisis, each confrontation, each point of
friction—as serious as it may be in its own right—would take
on an added measure of significance and an added dimension of
danger. It is precisely because we have fundamental differences
with the Soviet Union that we are determined to bring this
dangerous dimension of our military competition under control.

A week later I summoned Ambassador Dobrynin to the Oval
Office.

*I told him that I wanted to emphasize the fundamental
importance of our relationship with the Soviet Union.*

That I was concerned by the deterioration of the situation
in recent months. That both of us had to take [corrective]
steps.   DIARY, FEBRUARY 27, 1979

On March 2, President Brezhnev spoke out strongly in favor of
the SALT negotiations, and said he looked forward to signing the
treaty in the near future. In the following weeks the Soviet leaders accepted our proposal to prohibit encoding of missile-test
data, and also adopted our definition that more than a 5 per cent
modification of major characteristics would constitute a "new"
type of weapon. We were rapidly approaching the end of real
negotiations; very few SALT II issues remained to be resolved.

In the meantime, we had to deal with a related issue of great
importance. After the Iranian revolution, we had lost our two
monitoring stations that tracked the flights of Soviet missiles
launched from southern testing grounds. It was imperative that
we have adequate access to this data, to assure Soviet compliance
with the SALT II limits in the future. I promised Congress that we
would have this capability from satellites and from secret sites
in other countries before I would recommend implementation of
the new treaty.

This circumstance brought about an unpleasant encounter with
a member of Congress. Early in April, I helped Rosalynn write a
speech for her to deliver in Groton, Connecticut, at the keel laying
of the U.S.S. *Georgia*, a new nuclear submarine. Immediately
preceding her speech, the U.S.S. *Ohio* was being launched, and
Senator John Glenn, who claimed to be a supporter of SALT, was
to make remarks to the same audience. Rosalynn read an advance
copy of the Senator's speech and was appalled to discover that he
was going to denounce the SALT II treaty, which we were still
negotiating, and to demand that the Soviets not only give us
advance notice of all missile test firings, but also permit American planes to fly over Soviet test sites during the launchings.
Furthermore, he planned to say that there was no other way for
us to verify Soviet compliance with the prospective agreement. I
was furious. That evening I dictated some additions to Rosalynn's
speech, to refute what Glenn planned to say, and heeded her
urgent request not to call him while I was still so angry.

When I did call the next morning, April 7, I accused him of
trying to kill the nuclear arms limitation process while still claiming to be a strong supporter of SALT. In the most forceful possible
language, I told him that his planned comments were erroneous
and seriously damaging to our country; that he surely must know

that neither we nor the Soviets would permit observation airplanes of the other nation to fly over our own territory while we conducted missile tests; and that he was publicly questioning my word that I would only send a treaty to the Senate if Soviet compliance could be verified. I reminded him that he had a perfect right to work against the treaty when it was concluded, but that it was my duty, not his, to negotiate the original terms of the agreement.

At that moment I got an urgent call from Cy Vance, and so Glenn and I ended our conversation abruptly without reaching any agreement. Cy wanted to tell me that the Soviets had just accepted our SALT II proposals and had suggested an early summit meeting, at a time and place still to be determined. That afternoon at the shipyard, Glenn modified the remarks he had already distributed to the press, Rosalynn delivered her additional comments, and no serious harm was done.

This episode was of concern to me, because it indicated that I would have at least as difficult a time achieving ratification by the Senate as achieving a satisfactory treaty with the Soviets. I made sure that the military leaders were satisfied with all our negotiating positions, because I would be depending on their compelling testimony to convince some of the doubtful senators that ours was a beneficial agreement.

In preparation for the summit conference with President Brezhnev, I studied bilateral issues intensively, and also started to present the case for the treaty to the American public. This latter effort began with a speech to the American Newspaper Publishers' convention in New York on April 25, 1979. I put my heart into it.

> The possibility of mutual annihilation makes a strategy of peace the only rational choice for both sides. . . . We have a common interest in survival, and we share a common recognition that our survival depends, in a real sense, on each other. . . . This effort by two great nations to limit vital security forces is unique in human history; none has ever done this before. . . . SALT II is not a favor we are doing for the Soviet Union. It's an agreement carefully negotiated in the national security interests of the United States of America. . . . The issue is whether we will move ahead with strategic arms control or resume a relentless nuclear weapons competition. That is the choice we face—between an imperfect world with a SALT agreement, or an imperfect and more dangerous world without a SALT agreement.

I spelled out in some detail the important features of the prospective treaty. This speech provided the basis for literally hundreds of news conferences, speeches, and debates during the coming months, and for a constant series of briefings for members of the Senate and for other Democratic and Republican leaders. On May 9 I described for a Democratic congressional audience the importance of this treaty to me and to the nation.

> I've only got one life to live and one opportunity to serve in the highest elected office in our land. I will never have a chance so momentous to contribute to world peace as to negotiate and to see ratified this SALT treaty. And I don't believe that any member of the Senate will ever cast a more important vote than when a final judgment is made to confirm and ratify this negotiated treaty.

My advisers were very pessimistic about prospects for resolving any of our disputes with the Soviets at the Vienna summit meeting, June 15 to 18—an attitude that was vividly reflected in the briefing book prepared for me by teams from NSC and the State Department.

> *I was really peeved when I got the memorandum on the Vienna summit—the same degree of timidity that was apparent before we went to Camp David for the Mideast talks. . . . I told them to set maximum goals and work toward them; if we didn't reach those goals, at least we would have done our best—that I wasn't just interested in going to Vienna to the opera.*   DIARY, MAY 25, 1979

What we needed at the summit first of all was mutual understanding. I wanted the Soviets to know that the United States was driven by a desire for peace and an end to violence and aggression around the world. We would treat the Soviet leaders as equals, and not arouse their natural suspicion of others, which sometimes bordered on paranoia. It was important that the military leaders of both nations become acquainted, and that it be clear to everyone that neither country could hope to gain such a nuclear advantage that it could launch an attack without itself being destroyed. I also hoped to convince Brezhnev that we should begin immediate work on SALT III, which would encompass the limited-range weapons in Europe and provide for more drastic reductions in the intercontinental missiles capable of striking our own countries. I wanted the two of us to get to know each other better personally, and, with a SALT II agreement, demonstrate to the world that the two superpowers could work together for peace and nuclear arms control.

Before leaving for Vienna, there was one unpleasant issue I still had to study: how to make certain that our own land-based missiles were not vulnerable to a Soviet strike. The SALT II treaty authorized one new missile for each nation. Ours would be the MX, and we were trying to devise the most practical method of deploying it so that this land-based launcher could not be destroyed easily by a preemptive attack. All the proposals I had received would be complicated and expensive to implement. Of the choices, mobile launchers with several silos for each one seemed to be the best approach.

> *I discussed my disappointment with the weekly memorandum on MX mobile basing. It was a nauseating prospect to confront, with the gross waste of money going into nuclear weapons of all kinds.*   DIARY, JUNE 4, 1979

Before leaving for Vienna, I had a long talk with Governor Averell Harriman, who in his long diplomatic career had learned as much as anyone about the Soviet leaders. I took careful notes on his advice.

The Soviet leaders have a great respect for the U.S. President—more than for any other leader in the world. President Brezhnev looks on this meeting as one of the great events in his life, and has done everything possible to avoid failure. That is why he has repeatedly delayed it until he seemed reasonably sure that a SALT II treaty would be signed. His deepest commitment is to keep war away from his own people.

The system for acquiring and exchanging information within the Soviet Union is very poor, so Brezhnev will not be adequately briefed on some of the American attitudes and concerns. It is very important that you not surprise or embarrass him during the summit conference. He is old, human, and emotional, but much more vigorous than you might have been led to expect, and he will definitely be in charge of the Soviet delegation. [Alexei] Kosygin [who would not attend because of illness] is very sensible, and the entire Soviet leadership supports détente, as proven by many internal votes with which I am familiar.

242   J I M M Y   C A R T E R

They believe, along with us, that the nonproliferation policy must be implemented globally, and as strictly as possible. Brezhnev has been very disappointed at our Middle East policy of going alone and excluding the Soviets from the negotiating process. You will have to remember that the Soviet philosophy is to support liberation movements wherever they occur, and they believe in this just as deeply as Americans believe in human rights. They will not change this attitude. The Soviet leaders will want to emphasize the centrality of U.S.–Soviet relations, and to convince others that the enormous Soviet military machine is no threat to peace.

Be sure to let Brezhnev finish reading his notes, which will have been carefully prepared to express the collective position of the Soviet leaders. Then you will be able to have a more wide-ranging discussion with him and others in the Soviet delegation. Any concessions by them even on relatively unimportant items will probably come belatedly, and most likely from Brezhnev himself.   NOTES, JUNE 6, 1979

On the way to Vienna, I repeated to my colleagues the advice from Governor Harriman, and later we all agreed that his assessment had been very accurate. We worked the whole way over, dividing up responsibilities among our team and making sure that all of us understood the issues and would speak with a single voice. Cyrus Vance, Harold Brown, Zbigniew Brzezinski, General David Jones (the new Chairman of the Joint Chiefs of Staff) and retired General George Seigneious (who had now replaced Paul Warnke as head of our arms-control agency) spent several hours reviewing the best way for us to push hard for a strong start on SALT III. Jones agreed with me that even during the period covered by SALT II, we should propose an additional 5 per cent reduction in all categories of nuclear armaments each year through 1985, and be ready to put into effect immediately each element of SALT III as soon as it could be negotiated instead of waiting for a complete package, which might not be concluded for several years. We realized that Brezhnev was unlikely to make any snap judgments on these proposals, but we wanted the Soviets to leave Vienna with a clear picture of our plans for the future.

I have little trouble with changing time zones, and so I was up early the first morning in Vienna to jog a few miles and to put finishing touches on instructions to Secretary Vance for his preliminary meeting with Foreign Minister Gromyko.

Cy had had twelve points to discuss; when he came to see me after the meeting, he read off each item on his list and said "no" twelve times.

*Cy reported late in the afternoon that he had batted abso-
lutely zero, that Gromyko had been negative on every single item. Some of them are ridiculous positions for the
Soviets to maintain.*   DIARY, JUNE 15, 1979

We tried to keep in mind what Governor Harriman had said
about any Soviet concessions coming quite late and from the
President himself.

I met President Leonid Brezhnev for the first time at the palace
of Austrian President Rudolf Kirchschlaeger, where we were to
pay a formal call on him and Chancellor Bruno Kreisky. I had
carefully studied the latest intelligence reports about Brezhnev
and his supposedly failing health, and had also heard from the
French and German leaders that on his recent visits to their

countries he had been frail and not always alert. Eager to see him, I hoped that he would be vigorous and able to conduct the long discussions that lay ahead.

There was no need for me to worry. By arrangement, I arrived a few minutes ahead of Brezhnev. We greeted each other before an enormous contingent from the news media. He walked toward me slowly and carefully, but at a steady pace. Brezhnev seemed a little hesitant about approaching me, but I moved forward immediately and greeted him warmly. We stood with our heads close together and the Soviet interpreter between us, as hundreds of flash bulbs and television lights threatened to blind us both. Turning slightly away, we had a brief conversation, agreeing that our meeting had been long overdue and that such a delay should not occur again. As we turned back to face the cameras and lights, I told him we had more than two thousand reporters with us in Vienna. He responded that there were always too many, even in Moscow! The Soviet leader seemed to have some difficulty hearing the interpreter, but was otherwise forceful and alert. After the first few moments of small talk, we were adequately at ease with one another.

We walked together into President Kirchschlaeger's office and sat for a long time, until the silence became very uncomfortable. I gently reminded the Soviet leader that he was to speak first. He said in a loud voice that he had prepared a response to the Austrian President's speech. There was another long silence, and I finally smiled and said that all of us were very eager to hear the Austrian speech. The interpreters repeated each comment in the other languages—English, Russian, and German.

Eventually Kirchschlaeger made a very brief and fumbling statement; then Brezhnev pulled a prepared response from his pocket and read it, referring to a 1955 Soviet–Austrian treaty, friendship between the two countries, and an invitation to the Austrian leader to visit Moscow. Next I thanked the Austrians for their hospitality, commented on the importance of our meeting, and said I was confident that the peaceful environment of Vienna would be conducive to success. I described to Kirchschlaeger the demanding schedule requested by the Soviets and smiled as I expressed a hope that I could keep up with the energetic Soviet President. Brezhnev did not react.

This concluded the formal greetings, and Brezhnev and I then moved off by ourselves to chat for a few minutes as real people. I asked him if I would see him at the opera later in the evening, as had been arranged with the Soviet delegation. He seemed surprised and said he was tired, but that if I was there he would have to come. I told him it was not necessary and urged him to get some rest. After a few minutes of discussion with the interpreter, he said he would attend the performance but would leave after the first act.

He and I agreed that success was necessary for ourselves and for the rest of the world, and he startled me by placing his hand on my shoulder and saying, "If we do not succeed, God will not forgive us."

I felt close to him, and told the interpreter privately that it was not necessary for Brezhnev to come to the opera; rest was more important. But the interpreter said, "Oh, yes, it is already arranged for him to be there." As we walked down a few steps to leave the building, Brezhnev kept his hand on my arm or shoulder to steady himself. This simple and apparently natural gesture bridged the gap between us more effectively than any official talk.

That evening the top leaders of our two nations sat together at the opera—Mozart's *Abduction from the Seraglio*. The first and second acts were combined without an intermission, so it was quite late before Brezhnev and I were able to leave.

That night my advisers and I reviewed the day's events and plans for the upcoming negotiations. My ultimate goal was the total elimination of nuclear weapons, but I was also intrigued by the penultimate solution, which would be much more readily achievable: each side retaining small, exactly balanced, relatively invulnerable forces, confined either to submarines located in safe havens or to missiles in silos, which would be impossible to destroy except by the expenditure of the attacker's entire nuclear arsenal. These weapons could be used only to deter war, not to launch a preemptive attack. We also had a long talk about the need to stop production of all nuclear weapons, to seek some way to outlaw the use of such weapons in Europe, and to move on SALT III negotiations as soon as possible.

Cy, Harold, Zbig, David Jones, and I discussed the advisability of a mutual pledge of nonfirst use of nuclear forces. In Europe, the superiority of Soviet conventional forces now required the threat of our nuclear forces to deter aggression. I did not want to encourage an attack by promising the Soviets that a European war would be fought on their terms. I was convinced that if, as a result of Soviet aggression, a conventional war ever began in Europe, threatening the ultimate security or existence of our allies, it was likely to escalate into a nuclear war between the Warsaw Pact nations and Western Europe, despite any previous assurances to the contrary. Armed aggression would serve as the trip wire—the beginning of a war that might not be limited by any prior agreement on weapons. It was important to impress Brezhnev with this fact. A joint pledge with the Soviet leaders of nonfirst use of *any* military force in Europe would be acceptable for now. Later, success in balancing conventional military forces by mutual reductions, or a buildup in NATO forces to match Soviet nonnuclear capabilities, might make a pledge of nonfirst use of *nuclear* force advisable.

We decided that a total freeze in production and deployment of all nuclear weapons would be advantageous if it could be implemented without delay and if adequate verification procedures were devised. This would stop the Soviet deployment of SS-20's before we would be forced to match them with ground-launched cruise missiles or Pershing 2's.

I wanted immediate implementation of SALT II with its strict limits, an additional 5 per cent annual reduction in these limits for the five years of its duration, a commitment to lower SALT III limits by at least 50 per cent below those of SALT II, and the application of similar restraints on limited-range nuclear weapons in Europe.

All these agreements would require detailed negotiations. But much of the groundwork on definitions, procedures, and verification had already been completed in the SALT II negotiations.

At our first meeting in the American Embassy the following day, we Americans had a good opportunity to observe the Soviet leaders. There was never any doubt that Brezhnev was in charge, with Foreign Minister Gromyko always close by, speaking up frequently and forcefully whenever he seemed inclined to do so. He took a much harder line on almost every subject than anyone else. Dmitriy Ustinov, Minister of Defense, was highly respected by our military experts. Most of our immediate attention was focused on the other man of the Soviet team, Konstantin Chernenko, Politburo Member. We had what we believed to be good intelligence information that Chernenko might well be the heir-apparent, destined to lead the Soviet Union whenever the leadership had to change. Throughout our entire series of meetings in Vienna, he never made a noticeable comment.

Because I was acting as host, I requested that President Brezhnev make the opening statement. I took these notes of his remarks.

Some do not wish to see success between the United States and the Soviet Union in seeking peace, but most of the world wants success to come. The major result of the Vienna summit will be the conclusion of the SALT II agreement, but we can and will discuss other important problems.

It is best to start with the basics. There is a special responsibility on our two nations because we are so powerful and influential. Relationships can now be classified as good, since at least we have avoided war. We moved from being World War II allies into a state of sustained cold war, and it has not been easy to reverse the cold-war trend and arrive at the present state of cooperation. Some in the United States seem to think détente is a one-way street, but we know that peaceful coexistence is vital. There will inevitably be social and economic differences between our two nations, but this must never lead to war.

Then Brezhnev laughed, pointed at Cy Vance and said, "This man disagrees!" Everyone laughed, because Cy was considered to be the strongest dove among our group. He was quite discomfited. Brezhnev continued reading:

Improved relations can only come from a sense of equality between the two nations, a mutual sense of security, noninterference in the affairs of others, and peaceful coexistence as a major commitment. But first we must control nuclear weapons.

We have made good progress, but it is important to have continuity of policy in both nations. It is not wise to revise decisions once an agreement has been reached. Because of the system of government in the Soviet Union, our policies are naturally consistent. This has not always been the case with your government.

We all knew he was talking about our adoption of a much more aggressive position on SALT than had been spelled out by him and President Ford at Vladivostok in 1974.

We have broad global interests and so do our allies, and those interests must be protected. The Soviet Union is dedicated to support the struggle for emancipation and solidarity. Revolutions, which the Soviets do support, emerge only within other nations. The instigation for them never originates with us.

The Soviets have no hostile designs against the United States, and we expect the same treatment in return. Recently, relationships between our two countries have been uneven. The statements by President Carter have been good, but why the very large increase in military outlays?

Brezhnev then said we had doubled military outlays, but he

was interrupted by Ustinov, who said, "No, it is more accurate to say the military outlays have increased substantially."

President Brezhnev did not seem to mind the correction, and went on.

> Why speed up the arms race? Let us limit weapons, not increase them.
>
> The statements by President Carter and others that competition and cooperation must exist together provide a formula that rests on quicksand, and we are disturbed to have your leaders refer to us as "adversaries." The bad atmosphere in the United States cannot be attributed only to the press and the Congress. Sometimes the leaders of a nation contribute to bad relations.
>
> The major question is, shall we have good and stable relationships as equals? The Soviet adage is, "Don't carry stones inside your shirt."

I then replied, speaking from a few notes.

> There has been an excessive delay in this meeting, but now that we are finally together, we must make maximum progress. I was really impressed yesterday when President Brezhnev told me, "If we do not succeed, God will not forgive us!"

Brezhnev seemed somewhat embarrassed, and Gromyko said with an attempt at humor, "Yes, God above is looking down at us all."

I continued:

> The Soviet Union and the United States have never been military adversaries, and we must maintain this peaceful relationship in spite of serious differences. I agree that the SALT agreement is the most important item on our agenda, but because of the rarity of top-level meetings, we should make maximum use of this opportunity to resolve other problems. Many of our unnecessary differences result from a lack of understanding and consultation, and meetings between Vance and Gromyko have not always contributed to progress.

Everyone laughed.

> Our heads of state have met ten times since World War II, and some of these meetings have not been constructive. We

have found meetings with military leaders of other nations to be helpful, but such discussions between Soviets and Americans have never been held. The SALT II agreement will be a major achievement, with strict limits and some reductions in nuclear armaments being required, but we need to move immediately to SALT III, which we will discuss at a later meeting. We must remember that there is a serious competition between our countries for worldwide influence, some elements of which are potentially destabilizing. Neither country can dominate the other. Each nation is too powerful to permit this to happen. There is a great waste in the arms race, and in our necessary efforts to prevent regional hegemony caused by excessive ambition to expand influence.

A miscalculation or a misunderstanding could be catastrophic, and the excessive desire for secrecy by either nation can be counterproductive because this contributes to suspicion and leads to the taking of countermeasures.

I then pointed out that the Soviet Union had increased its military budget substantially each year for the last fifteen years, and until recently the United States had not matched this effort. However, we would do so in the future. Each of us would have to face the inevitability of military equivalency with the other. There would certainly not be any superiority or victory in a nuclear war. I emphasized that we should avoid confrontation by refraining from intrusions into troubled areas, either directly or indirectly through proxies. Neither country should impede the other's access to vital natural resources.

I expressed an interest in step-by-step expansion of all elements of arms control, including a comprehensive test ban with or without Great Britain, mutual and balanced force reductions in Europe, and SALT III. It was clear, I said, that any attempt by either of us to conceal our actions or to prevent adequate verification of compliance with agreements would nullify progress.

As the first morning session adjourned, all of us were impressed with the vigor of Brezhnev as compared with the reports we had heard, with his ability to make extemporaneous remarks, and his obvious though heavy-handed attempt at humor. He moves around with difficulty. At first his speech is slurred, but as he talks more and more and becomes animated, this speech defect seems to go away.   DIARY, JUNE 16, 1979

The afternoon session, also at the American Embassy, was to be devoted to SALT II. Again, Brezhnev spoke first.

> There is a tremendous significance to SALT II. Progress has not been easy and has often been delayed, not because of obstacles created by the Soviet Union. I realize, however, that the issues are both complex and delicate, and no blame should be alleged concerning bad faith on either side.
>
> SALT II does not end the arms race, and its final results are far from our liking, but it is mutually acceptable, adequately balanced, and equal. The documents are complete, and it is now time for us to exchange statements.

He and I read statements that had been negotiated as part of the overall agreement on cruise missiles and our Minuteman missiles. Then he made an evasive comment on the Soviet Back-fire bomber, saying only that he would not dispute our claim if we said their production rate was thirty per year. The advance agreement had been that he would give me a personal assurance that the Soviets were producing only thirty of the bombers each year, and that their production rate would not exceed this number as long as SALT II was in effect. I could not accept his comment now as an adequate commitment, although I had understood from Gromyko that this issue was very difficult for Brezhnev because he resented including any reference to the medium-range Soviet system when all of ours had been excluded from the SALT discussions. I made a note to pursue the matter.

Brezhnev then said the treaty would not be effective until it was ratified, and we argued this point at length, with Gromyko interrupting frequently each time Brezhnev seemed ready to yield. Their stance was a departure from international custom, and also from the convention of our two nations. The limited test-ban agreement, the Vladivostok limits, and the extension of the SALT I agreement were all being honored, although they had not been ratified.

Brezhnev expressed concern about any Soviet promise to maintain permanent equivalency of nuclear power with us which did not take into account additional French, British, and Chinese arsenals. He also said there was a definite limit on how much further they could go with arms control without counting all the medium-range and tactical weapons systems in Europe.

He emphasized very strongly that no unilateral amendments to SALT II by the Senate during the ratification process would be accepted, and then expressed his concern about the MX missile.

More than one silo for any missile would not be permissible under the agreement, he said. I pointed out to him that we had already covered this point, that the treaty was drafted so as to permit mobile MX missiles to be deployed, and that any system we devised would permit the Soviets to confirm our compliance with the agreed limits.

We exchanged statements that there would be no encoding of missile-test data for items covered by SALT II, and that no encoding of any kind would interfere with the other nation's verifying compliance with the agreements.

After the meeting Brezhnev, Gromyko, Chernenko, and Ustinov joined Vance, Brown, Brzezinski, and me at the American Embassy residence. We served them a drink, and Brezhnev immediately asked for supper. He was only half joking. Brezhnev and I discussed wine, grandchildren, the shortage of gasoline in both our countries, and the tremendous number of automobiles in the United States. The meal was served as soon as it was ready, because Brezhnev clearly wanted to retire early. During supper we offered several toasts, and he bottomed up his glass of vodka each time, teasing me when I failed to do the same. Some of the formality and restraint dissipated, but there was never an opportunity for free discussion of anything but nonsubstantive subjects. All in all, it was not a very successful evening.

The next day, Sunday, June 17, following church services and a beautiful performance by the Vienna Boys' Choir, we went to the Soviet Embassy for a session. I spoke first, and emphasized that we were ready to move beyond SALT II, with improved monitoring of nuclear arsenals from both sides; no encoding whatever of test data; prenotification of massive bomber flights and missile test launchings; improved monitoring stations; on-site inspection under certain circumstances; a reduction in the number of launchers, warheads, and total size of all warheads combined; and a moratorium on the construction of all new weapons. We would also be glad to consider a mutual reduction of 5 per cent annually in any of the weaponry categories I had mentioned, beginning while SALT II was in force. I said, too, that we were willing to agree to nonfirst use of *any* military force—both nuclear and conventional.

When I added that we needed to improve the invulnerability of remaining nuclear weapons, Ustinov interrupted to ask if such a development was not counterproductive. I told him no.

"What I have in mind is a much smaller number of nuclear weapons on each side, deployed so as to be relatively safe from destruction. One example of this would be safe havens for missile submarines, where they would be free of any antisubmarine warfare attempts by the other nation."

He seemed satisfied with this explanation, realizing that the most destabilizing threat was the ability of either nation first to destroy the retaliatory forces of the other and still have enough weapons remaining to launch a follow-up attack with relative impunity.

I also commented that, for a number of years, the nuclear arsenals of the United States and the Soviet Union would be so much greater than those of all other nations that the others could be ignored, but added that we should make every attempt to include them in future agreements to limit and reduce nuclear weapons. We seemed to agree on all aspects of our nonproliferation policies, both of us being determined to discourage the spread of nuclear explosives to other nations. I suggested that Brown and Ustinov might work together while in Vienna to overcome the long-standing impasse on conventional military force reductions in Europe.

Brezhnev agreed that we should halt production of nuclear weapons and reduce existing stockpiles, retaining the current ratios of weapons so that neither nation would gain an advantage. However, other countries must also be involved, he said. He was especially concerned about nuclear weapons in the Middle East and China, and the prospect for their development in Pakistan. Brezhnev then made a reference to the stalled Indian Ocean demilitarization talks. I reminded him that the Horn of Africa was in the northwestern part of the ocean, and that since we had begun the discussions, the Soviets had armed both Somalia and Ethiopia, war had broken out between the two countries, and thousands of Cuban troops had been sent into the Horn of Africa, along with many Soviet "advisers."

I told Brezhnev that his previous day's statement about the Soviet Backfire bomber was completely unacceptable, and that he must declare unequivocally that the production rate would not exceed thirty per year. We had had a long altercation about the history of our negotiations on this subject, and I made it clear that our acceptance of SALT II was dependent on this point. He finally interrupted me in midsentence to say loudly, "The Soviet Union will not produce more than thirty Backfires per year." I said that the United States reserved the right to produce an equivalent bomber, and we adjourned.

On the ride down the small elevator to lunch, Brezhnev and I were alone with the interpreters. At his request, I agreed to give him a written copy of my proposals concerning the next steps toward SALT III. Saying that this was the most important thing we could accomplish in Vienna, he suggested that we discuss the proposals further at our private meeting on Monday.

At the embassy, I printed out this note by hand and gave it to Brezhnev when we met again that afternoon:

June 17, 1979

MR. PRESIDENT:

STRONG AND IMMEDIATE PROGRESS ON SALT III IS IMPORTANT. I SUGGEST:

A) COMMITMENT TO DEEP CUTS IN WEAPONS—BELOW SALT II LIMITS

B) NO ENCRYPTION OF TELEMETRY [encoding], PLUS OTHER MOVES TOWARD EASIER VERIFIABILITY

C) STOP PRODUCTION OF NUCLEAR WARHEADS AND LAUNCHERS

D) PROVIDE SAFE OCEAN HAVEN AREAS FOR MISSILE SUBMARINES TO PREVENT DESTABILIZING ASW [antisubmarine warfare] DEVELOP-MENTS

E) NO TESTS OF DEPRESSED TRAJECTORY SUBMARINE MISSILE FIR-INGS [to prevent preparations for close-range attacks on either country from missile submarines]

F) CONCLUDE COMPREHENSIVE TEST BAN TREATY—WITH OR WITHOUT GREAT BRITAIN (HOPEFULLY WITH THEM)

G) PRE-NOTIFICATION OF MISSILE TESTS AND LARGE STRATEGIC BOMBER EXERCISES

H) NO TESTS OF ANTI-SATELLITE SYSTEMS OR ANTI-SATELLITE MISSILES

I) REGULAR CONSULTATIONS BETWEEN MILITARY LEADERS AND BE-TWEEN HEADS OF STATE, AND EXCHANGE VISITS

J) BEGIN TALKS TO LIMIT AND CONTROL NUCLEAR WEAPONS NOT COV-ERED UNDER SALT II [medium-range and other theater weapons]

K) IMPLEMENT AGREEMENTS AS THEY ARE CONCLUDED, WITHOUT NEC-ESSARILY WAITING FOR A FINAL AND COMPLETE SALT III AGREEMENT (FOR INSTANCE, SALT II LIMITS MIGHT BE LOWERED ANNUALLY BY 5%, AS MUTUALLY AGREED TO BE ADVANTAGEOUS)

L) NO NUCLEAR FUEL SALES TO COUNTRIES NOT UNDER NON-PROLIFER-ATION TREATY OR IAEA [International Atomic Energy Agency] SAFEGUARDS.

I concluded the note:

MR. PRESIDENT, THESE ARE SOME IMPORTANT AND PRACTICAL SUG-GESTIONS. WE WOULD LIKE TO HAVE YOUR CONCURRENCE AND OTHER SUGGESTIONS WHICH WE MIGHT CONSIDER. I WILL DISCUSS THIS WITH YOU TOMORROW.

Respectfully,
Jimmy Carter

It was now time for what I knew would be a difficult discussion of trouble spots around the world. I made the opening statement.

I would like détente to be extended from Europe to other places where differences exist. The United States has the will and the capability to defend its interests and the interests of its allies, and our maximum strength will be used if necessary.

We have certain areas of vital interest, and the Soviet Union must recognize these interests. One such area is in the Persian Gulf and the Arabian Peninsula. Restraint is essential on your part not to violate our national security interests.

When troubles develop, the American policy is to resolve them peacefully, but this has not been the Soviet policy. In the Horn of Africa, in Southern Africa, in the Middle East, and in Southeast Asia I have tried to achieve peace, but the Soviet leaders have done just the opposite. The military activities of Cuba are of deep concern to us. They now have more than 40,000 troops in Africa, constantly embroiled in every trouble spot, and now they are becoming more active in the Caribbean and in Central America. The Soviet Union has also encouraged and supported the Vietnamese in their invasion of Kampuchea.

We have worked in the Middle East to bring peace, after the Syrians refused to participate in a Geneva conference. Everything done at Camp David has been in accordance with the publicly expressed goals of the United Nations, the Soviet Union, and the United States. We need maximum cooperation from the Soviet leaders in establishing a peacekeeping force in the Sinai through the United Nations. If this is not forthcoming, the United States will move unilaterally to provide this service.

There are many problems in Iran and Afghanistan, but the United States has not interfered in the internal affairs of those nations. We expect the Soviet Union to do the same. Your propaganda attacks against us are endangering American lives in the two countries, and must be stopped.

I said, "My last subject is China." They all perked up, although both sides had already been listening intently to the interpreters' words.

After thirty years, normalization of relations between the United States and the People's Republic of China was long overdue. This new relationship can contribute to peace and stability, not only for our two countries, but also for the entire region and perhaps the world. Our goal is to move rapidly to build upon

our new agreements, but these improvements will never be at
the expense of Soviet–American relations.

Brezhnev took as hard a line as I had.

If we proceed on SALT III, other countries will have to be
involved, American forward-based [medium-range] systems must
be included, and SALT II must be implemented first. All strategic factors, some of which are very complicated, must be considered, and a simple 5 per cent annual reduction would not be
advisable.

Don't blame the Soviet Union for changes taking place in the
world. Contrary to allegations by some Americans, the Soviets
have not contributed to any instability in the so-called Arc of
Crisis extending from Northern Africa through the Persian Gulf.
We want to cooperate to preserve peace, but we have been
surprised and disturbed at the lackadaisical way the United
States refers to quite remote regions of the world as being of
vital interest to your country. [He was alluding to the Persian
Gulf.]

Speaking of legitimate national interests, European affairs
are extremely important to the Soviet Union because of proximity. The Soviet Union is part of Europe, and historically threats
to us and our achievements have been tied in with Europe.
World War II was a terrible experience for the Soviet people,
and this is still the paramount consideration when a Soviet
citizen considers international affairs. Europe is a heterogeneous
region, and the Soviets accept this fact and shape policies
accordingly.

Soviet leaders are very careful not to categorize the United
States as "adversary" or "foe," and we want the same treatment from you.

He added,

In the Middle East, Soviet–American statements and United
Nations actions have been violated, which has led to anti-Arab
action. It is already obvious that the Israeli–Egyptian treaty has
failed, and this has led to Israel's war against Lebanon. The
Soviet Union will counter any UN use of troops to bolster the
illegal accords between Israel and Egypt.

Brezhnev went on to say that China threatened to encroach on
the territory of its neighbors, and wanted to precipitate a world
war during which it would sit on the sidelines. The Soviet Union

had treaty obligations to Vietnam, and Chinese action could become too provocative. He claimed that in Kampuchea the citizens were thankful to the Vietnamese for overthrowing the abhorrent regime of Pol Pot, and that it was only natural for the Soviets to assist such an effort. In Africa, their policy was only to support the end of racialism and colonialism and not to seek any economic or strategic advantage. In Iran, the Soviet Union was following a standard of supporting peaceful settlement of struggles to transfer power. Brezhnev then asserted that the Soviets had first heard of the revolution in Afghanistan on the radio and did not instigate the change in government. He hoped that we would join the Soviets in discouraging attacks on the existing regime. (This was six months before the Soviet invasion of Afghanistan.)

Brezhnev continued,

We are strictly observing a 1962 agreement not to build up any forces in Cuba which might be considered a threat to the United States. You continue to complain about Cuban troops in Africa. We do not control these decisions, which are made by the Cuban leaders themselves. However, we do know that the troops are sent only in response to specific requests for assistance by the recognized governments in Angola and Ethiopia. The American leaders should remember that many foreign troops fought with George Washington during your own revolution.

He smiled.

Regarding the comments by President Carter about a Soviet presence in Vietnam, we have no bases there now, nor will we have any in the future. Soviet ships make routine business calls, and Soviet planes land in accordance with international custom. On the other hand, the United States bases are established at the doorstep of the Soviet Union in South Korea, Japan, and the Philippines.

With all the translations back and forth, it was quite late when we finished these long dissertations. I again asked Brezhnev to study very carefully my earlier comments. My concerns had not been alleviated by his words, because the fact was that when violence occurred in almost any place on earth, the Soviets or their proxies were most likely to be at the center of it. This kind of interventionism could precipitate a serious confrontation in the future if our own national interests should become involved.

Almost immediately we moved to the banquet room, still in the Soviet Embassy. The meal was greatly superior to the supper we had had the night before at our embassy. Our banquet had been adequate, but tonight's was exquisite. Brezhnev was particularly proud of the menu, which was printed in both Russian and English; he pointed out to everyone that he had not been able to read the one at our meal, which had been only in English. Despite this preliminary complaint, the Soviet leaders seemed determined that the evening be gay and enjoyable, and they succeeded. Several of them spoke English (which they never used in official meetings), Zbig and Harold spoke Russian, and even the interpreters were exceptionally spirited.

Again, Brezhnev offered frequent toasts. I arranged with the waiter for a tiny glass, shifted to a somewhat milder drink, and joined in the "bottoms up" ceremonies along with everyone else. There was a lot of jovial banter. Ustinov offered to make us a loan to buy Harold Brown a uniform to match his own. I replied that if Harold could resolve the European force reduction question with Ustinov, I would buy him a uniform, and added that since Ustinov had been so stubborn about it, he himself was keeping Harold from enjoying the prestige of fancy clothes.

I asked Gromyko if he was sincere about involving the other three countries—France, Great Britain, and China—in the future SALT III talks, and he gave a typically equivocal answer. When I offered to be responsible for France and Great Britain if he would be responsible for China, he threw up his hands in mock horror at the thought.

It was really a very pleasant evening, during which we addressed some of the serious issues in more relaxed language. There was a general realization that during the day's discussions we had outlined sharply differing approaches to the same events, and that a more careful study of the remarks made by me and Brezhnev could help us understand one another. Neither country was likely to change very much, but I was hoping the Soviets would take to heart our expressions of concern about their constant impulse to inject military aid into any trouble spot, and that they had listened carefully to my warning about the Persian Gulf region.

Late at night Amy and I jogged two miles, carrying flashlights around the paths of the embassy residence. I was already weary of speeches and conferences, and hated to think of all my responsibilities for the following day—my private discussions with Brezhnev, the last plenum meeting (with both delegations), the signing ceremonies with public statements, our departure from Austria, the flight across the Atlantic, and later that same evening my report to Congress!

The next morning, Brezhnev came to the American Embassy for our private meeting; only our two interpreters joined us. He asked if, as my guest, he should speak first. When I nodded, he read his prepared statement, beginning with routine assessments of the importance of SALT II and the mutual benefits of our frank discussions. Then he moved on to subjects he had not wanted to address in the plenum sessions.

> The most important single element is Soviet–American relations, and we must raise the level of understanding and confidence between our two countries. War will have to be totally ruled out. I would like to pursue the idea that in case of an attack on either of us from a third nation, the other will pledge to mount a joint rebuff. We need this kind of agreement, but although we have raised the subject with Secretary Vance, we have received no response.

I started to reply, but he requested that I permit him to complete his entire statement first. So I took careful notes and waited for him to continue. He seemed very eager to get to the next part, which turned out to comprise 90 per cent of the total. I summarized his comments in my notes.

> I want to speak about China. We have no objection to normal relations between your two countries, but it would be a serious mistake for anyone to use Peking's anti-Soviet attitudes to the detriment of the Soviet Union. We observed with great concern that China's first action following recognition by the United States was an attack on Vietnam. Their smiles and bows were certainly not compatible with this violation of stability in Asia. They seem to want the United States to cover their political rear. It is well known that China has territorial claims against Japan, Vietnam, India, and the Philippines, and they want Western elements to be used in these matters. Since the Chinese are not bound by any international agreements regarding nuclear weapons, this threat is of double concern.
>
> The Soviet Union favors normal relations with China, and we are now exploring opportunities for more talks. We want mutual respect, a pledge of nonuse of force, noninterference in the internal affairs of other countries, and an easing of tension. However, we would consider anything beyond the present line between China and the United States with grave concern, and

Soviet–American relations would suffer. Let me emphasize that there will be no anti-U.S. adventure by us under any circumstances.

Brezhnev talked about China at length and with great feeling. It was obviously the centerpiece of his presentation to me.

Then he spoke briefly about human rights, saying that the Soviet Union is not against discussing this subject on ideological grounds but that there is a problem in discussing it as a basis for nation-to-nation policy.

There can be no progress if trade is related to the question of human rights. We do not relate trade to the unemployment rate in the United States, nor to racial discrimination, nor to violations of the rights of women. I want to talk about peace, and how to improve Soviet–American relations, but human rights is a sensitive subject for us and is not a legitimate ground for discussion between you and me.

He closed by encouraging additional meetings, but without trying to establish a regular schedule. He was particularly eager for me to visit the Soviet Union. I asked him frankly if he was physically able to come to the United States, since it was the Soviets' turn on the alternating visiting schedule. He laughed, and said, "Yes! All I have to do is jump on a plane when the time comes, and I will be there without delay."

I told him we considered the new Sino–American relationship to be good for us, for the Soviet Union, and for the world. He shouted, pleasantly enough, "Certainly not good for the Soviet Union!"

I pursued the point, emphasizing that our influence would be used to preserve peaceful relations among nations, including those between the Soviets and the Chinese. We would not use our new friendship with China to the detriment of the Soviet Union, and would like the Soviet leaders to keep us informed about their own relations with China.

We then held an extensive discussion about encoding of missile-test data. I made it plain that we would have to monitor Soviet tests, and that we might wish to use flights over Turkey for this purpose.

He in turn read a prepared statement that sounded equivocal at first but turned out to be negative. Brezhnev referred to SALT III as the place to talk about monitoring from a third country, and linked my request for American flights over Turkey to his request for Soviet flights over Cuba. However, he did offer to investigate the matter further.

I told him there was another difficult subject I wanted to raise. He brightened up and said, "Only one?" When I referred to the United Nations emergency force in the Sinai, his interpreter pulled out a sheet on which a paragraph had been marked and handed it to him. Brezhnev said that any Soviet participation in such a force would imply approval of the treaty between Israel and Egypt; the Soviets could not agree to this. I informed him that a monitoring force would be provided with or without Soviet approval or help, but that we would prefer to cooperate with the Soviet Union whenever possible.

He kept looking at his watch and saying we were running overtime. We had built in some spare time into our last plenum session, so in spite of his impatience, I addressed one more subject.

President Brezhnev, the subject of human rights is very important to us in shaping our attitude toward your country. You voluntarily signed the Helsinki accords, which made this issue a proper item for state-to-state discussions. We have been gratified at the more liberal emigration policies you have established in recent months, and we were pleased to see Mr. Vins and others permitted to come to our country. Now you need to continue this policy and release Mr. Shcharansky and other dissidents.

Brezhnev then had a conversation with the Russian interpreter, who, I later learned from my own interpreter, told him that his previous statement about human rights was probably adequate. Brezhnev added extemporaneously, however, that Shcharansky had been tried and convicted in a Soviet court of law for espionage, and that as the leader of the nation, Brezhnev was bound to support the laws of his country. I reminded him again of the importance of this issue, and insisted that we would continue to press for progress.

By then it really was time to move on to the Soviet Embassy for final summaries of our earlier discussions. The only new idea put forward there was Brezhnev's special emphasis on the need for increased trade and the Soviets' absolute unwillingness to tie this subject to emigration policy or other human-rights issues.

The treaty-signing ceremony was impressive and dignified. After we finished signing the documents and handed them to one another, I shook hands with President Brezhnev, and to my surprise,

we found ourselves embracing each other warmly in the Soviet fashion. There is no doubt there were strong feelings of cooperation between us at the moment, and I was determined to pursue our search for peace and better understanding.

As we parted, I was somewhat disappointed at our inability to have made even more progress, but a new SALT treaty, clearer understanding of the many differences between us, and the sure knowledge that both of us wanted to avoid war with the other had all made the Soviet–American summit conference worthwhile. I saw no reason to change our basic policy of "cooperation when possible, competition when necessary."

After flying back to Washington, I spoke that night to a joint session of Congress, spelling out for the members and the television audience throughout the nation what three Presidents had accomplished in these negotiations over a period of more than six years.

> SALT II is the most detailed, far-reaching, comprehensive treaty in the history of arms control. . . . The SALT II treaty reduces the danger of nuclear war. For the first time, it places equal ceilings on the strategic arsenals of both sides, ending a previous numerical imbalance in favor of the Soviet Union. SALT II preserves our options to build the forces we need to maintain

that strategic balance. The treaty enhances our own ability to monitor what the Soviet Union is doing, and it leads directly to the next step in more effectively controlling nuclear weapons. Again, SALT II does not end the arms competition. But it does make that competition safer and more predictable, with clear rules and verifiable limits, where otherwise there would be no rules and there would be no limits.

SALT II is very important, but it's more than a single arms control agreement. It is part of a long, historical process of gradually reducing the danger of nuclear war—a process that we in this room must not undermine. . . . And, of course, SALT II is the absolutely indispensable precondition for moving on to much deeper and more significant cuts under SALT III.

The lobbying campaign we mounted throughout the nation during the next few months made the Panama Canal treaties effort pale into relative insignificance. Thousands of speeches, news interviews, and private briefings were held. The personal and political interests of each senator were analyzed as we assessed the prospects of the ultimate vote for SALT II. It was obvious that we faced formidable opposition, but we had a chance of success if we and the Soviets could demonstrate good faith, and if there were no obstacles to Senate confidence in the Soviet leaders.

Unfortunately, obstacles did develop. During the Labor Day holiday, American intelligence reports of the existence of a brigade of Soviet troops in Cuba were publicized. This confidential information had been conveyed to a number of government officials, including Senator Frank Church, Chairman of the Senate Foreign Relations Committee, who was at home in Idaho vacationing and campaigning for reelection. Church had previously been to Cuba and had come back to the United States with complimentary statements about Castro and his regime, but now he saw an opportunity to meet some of the conservative political attacks on his liberal voting record. He called a news conference and did everything possible to escalate the report into an earth-shaking event.

Church was a favorite of the Washington press, and an avowed supporter of SALT II. He had an almost perfect forum for expressing his views as chairman of a prestigious committee. We made a serious mistake in underestimating the impact of his inflammatory rhetoric. I soon came to realize that either Secretary Vance or I should have explained the situation to the American people immediately.

On Tuesday, the day after Labor Day, Senate Majority Leader

Robert Byrd came by to discuss the SALT treaty. He expressed concern about the Cuban situation, and we talked about it at some length.

> *I told him that there was no way to mandate that the Soviets withdraw those troops. In the early 60's they had 20,000 there—about 10 times what they have now—and chances are they'd had approximately this level of troops for the last 15 or 20 years. We'll have a PRC [Policy Review Committee] meeting on it today, and Cy will testify tomorrow.*
>
> *I think Byrd's on the verge of endorsing the SALT treaty, but the Cuban thing has got him concerned.*
> DIARY, SEPTEMBER 4, 1979

During the day, the news stories about Soviet troops swept across Washington and the nation like a fireball.

> *The major concern during the day was the Soviet troop presence in Cuba ... which is obviously not a threat to our country, not a violation of any Soviet commitment— but politically it's devastating to SALT. Cy was preparing for his noon meeting with the press and his afternoon meeting with the Senate Foreign Relations Committee. I talked to Frank Church, who promised to be moderate, but ... he was absolutely irresponsible in his statement that unless the Soviets totally withdrew the troops, SALT could not pass.*
> DIARY, SEPTEMBER 5, 1979

This was an example of a danger inherent in our democratic system: the tendency of politicians, even some of the best of them, to panic when faced with defeat and to act with uncharacteristic intemperance. Such tendencies are often encouraged and exacerbated by a press which thrives on sensationalism. Vance's assertions were not enough to calm the troubled waters, so on Friday, September 7, I went on television to reassure the nation. I also met with some of the key congressional leaders in a session that turned out very well. Senators Byrd and Goldwater made very responsible statements to the group, while Church sat mute during our long discussion.

A phrase in my public statement proved to be troublesome. I said, "we consider the presence of a Soviet combat brigade in Cuba to be a very serious matter and that this status quo is not acceptable." Further investigations confirmed that the presence of these troops was not a new development; the brigade was only a remnant of a much larger force that had been there since the early 1960's. It represented no offensive threat to the United States, and the Soviet Union promised that would remain the case. This assurance was accepted as satisfactory by my advisers and myself, but some had interpreted my earlier remark as a promise to remove the brigade. In any case, it was an embarrassment that the status quo was, in effect, accepted, and that for many years our government had not been aware of the brigade's existence.

Eventually, after some difficult weeks, we weathered the storm over the troops in Cuba. I began my laborious series of private meetings with individual senators to explain the advantages of SALT II, and continued to pick up votes as the Senate prepared to set aside the first few months of 1980 for the ratification debate.

I was particularly encouraged by growing support among the Senate leaders.

> *We then devoted the rest of our [congressional leadership] meeting to a discussion of SALT. Bob Byrd is obviously moving as a major proponent. He and Senator [Alan] Cranston have a constructive proposal on a compromise consisting of a 5-year defense commitment, and a provision that SALT III must make tangible progress for SALT II to continue in effect. Byrd outlined at length his belief that with an agreement to limit debate, public television coverage of the Senate debate would be constructive.*
>
> DIARY, OCTOBER 10, 1979

For several months I had been receiving reports of increasing Soviet pressure in Afghanistan and had approved several messages of warning to Brezhnev about any direct intervention there. Then, during the Christmas holidays, came the brutal Soviet invasion, which wiped out any chance for a two-thirds vote of approval. I discussed with Senator Robert Byrd and other supporters of SALT II how we might best preserve the effectiveness of the agreement. We decided that rather than have the treaty defeated or for me to withdraw it from consideration, it would be better to leave it in the Senate Foreign Relations Committee, postpone Senate action on it, and work with the Soviets for maximum observance of its terms by our two countries. By doing this, we would be able to keep its provisions intact. With the exception of achieving the requirement for unilateral Soviet dismantling of

250 of their missile launchers, both the United States and the Soviet Union continued to honor the agreement.

However, the nuclear arms control effort soon came under heavy attack. During the 1980 campaign, Governor Ronald Reagan called for a massive buildup in our nuclear arsenal, condemning the SALT II treaty and the negotiating techniques and principles followed by me and my Democratic and Republican predecessors in achieving this and earlier nuclear arms limitation agreements. He pledged to cast aside the SALT II treaty, calling it "fatally flawed." As the Republican presidential nominee, Reagan also rejected the nonproliferation effort, stating that it was none of our business if such countries as Iraq developed nuclear weapons. These statements of his caused deep concern among our allies, and among millions of Americans who were convinced that we should continue to strengthen our country's defense capability but at the same time do everything possible to reduce the threat of a nuclear holocaust.

> In the 34 years since Hiroshima, humanity has by no means been free of armed conflict, but at least we have avoided a world war.
> Yet this kind of twilight peace carries the ever-present danger of a catastrophic nuclear war, a war that in horror and destruction and massive death would dwarf all the combined wars of man's long and bloody history.
> We must prevent such a war. We absolutely must prevent such a war.   ADDRESS TO CONGRESS, JUNE 18, 1979

Our failure to ratify the SALT II treaty and to secure even more far-reaching agreements on nuclear arms control was the most profound disappointment of my Presidency. However, with the antagonism that Soviet action in Afghanistan had kindled in our country, ratification was, for the time being, an impossible task. We could only hope that an aroused public—in the United States and other countries—could convince the leaders of both superpowers that they must work to remove this nuclear shadow from over the earth.

NO MORE WAR

OCTOBER 6, 1981

Shortly after daybreak my telephone rang. I assumed the call was from my mother, who is also an early riser. However, it turned out to be a request from a television reporter, who wanted my comment about an attempted assassination of President Sadat. I was deeply concerned, and my immediate question was, "How is he?" Informed that he was all right, and that the would-be assassins had been captured, I responded to his original question by saying that Sadat was a great and good man, and that his most bitter and dangerous enemies were people who were obsessed with hatred for his peaceful goals.

DIARY, OCTOBER 6, 1981

Almost exactly eight years after the last major conflict in the Middle East, I was at home in Plains, studying my diary notes about the Camp David negotiations for these memoirs when the telephone call came. I quickly brought Amy's miniature television set into my study, and also placed a call to Egypt. I talked to Alfred Atherton, the United States Ambassador in Cairo, who reassured me that Sadat was only slightly wounded. He had received this information personally from Egypt's Minister of Defense, who had been with Sadat on the reviewing stand. For the first time since hearing the reporter's question, we were able to relax. Rosalynn suggested that we phone Prime Minister Begin, and he and I shared our gratitude that Sadat had escaped this attempt on his life.

I kept the television set at my side and monitored the news broadcasts all through the day. Slowly, the terrible truth became known. My wonderful friend, Anwar el-Sadat, was dead. Rosalynn and I sent word to his wife, Jihan, that we would come to Egypt, and we began to make plans for the trip on a commercial airline.

Later, both President Reagan and Vice President Bush decided that it would be too dangerous for them to go to Cairo, and I was asked to travel with former Presidents Nixon and Ford to represent the United States at the funeral. At first Rosalynn and I decided not to do so, because we wanted to go as personal friends and not in any official capacity; but the proposed arrangements had already been announced from the White House. After an argument with my staff, I agreed to accept the invitation for us to join the official delegation.

We three former Presidents were somewhat ill at ease when we first met at Andrews Air Force Base near Washington. I hardly knew Richard Nixon, and Jerry Ford and I had not seen each other since the highly partisan political campaign of 1980. Surprisingly, President Nixon was the one who eased the tension, by discussing with us his new home in New Jersey and the book he was writing. He complimented Rosalynn on her clothes and the color of her eyes, and President Ford and I listened as the two of them had a good conversation about Nixon's wife, Pat, the selection of furniture and carpets, and the Nixons' recent move from New York to Saddle River. By the time we were airborne, in the same plane we had all used as Air Force One, we were talking more freely with one another about the events in Sadat's life and how much he had meant to us personally and to the cause of peace.

During the flight to Egypt, Rosalynn and I sat across the table from Egyptian Ambassador Ashraf Ghorbal and his wife, Amal. We had long discussions about Egypt and what was likely to happen now that Sadat was gone. When Sadat had visited me in Plains during the past summer, he had told me about his plans to retire in April 1982, and turn over his duties to Vice President Hosni Mubarak. The Ghorbals were familiar with Sadat's desire to step down as Egypt's President, and understood that Sadat had been grooming the Vice President for the position.

Presidents Ford and Nixon sat across the aisle from Rosalynn and me at a table with former Secretary of State Henry Kissinger. We were all in the aftersection of the plane, normally used for the President's staff. Secretaries Alexander Haig and Caspar Weinberger were in the President's stateroom, and their staff members occupied the lounge usually reserved for dignitaries.

In Cairo, we found that security was extremely tight; the normally bustling streets of the huge city seemed almost deserted. We Americans shared the air of gloom and uncertainty that had settled over Egypt. Our delegation first called on Vice President Mubarak and the other government officials, who were quite certain that the assassination had been planned and perpetrated by a small group of religious extremists. The Egyptian leaders seemed confident that the country would remain calm in the future, and told us of their unanimous commitment to continue Sadat's policies.

To Rosalynn and me, the most memorable part of these sad hours was our visit with Jihan Sadat and the family.

When we arrived at their home, Sadat's son Gamal was on the front steps to greet us. Presidents Nixon and Ford, in the car ahead of ours, were welcomed first, but when the young man saw us approaching from the side, he left his post of duty, ran to embrace me, and began to weep on my shoulder. I felt as if he were my own son, and tried to console him in his grief. After a few moments we were ready to rejoin the others, who had paused for a while and then moved on into the house.

Jihan was superb. She was beautiful in her sorrow and in the strength and dignity with which she faced the large group that filled her sitting room. She expressed her gratitude that Sadat had died as he lived—erect, in uniform as a soldier of Egypt, surrounded by his friends, calmly facing attackers who were crazed by hatred, exhibiting quiet personal courage even in the final moments of his life.

> *Jihan made it clear to us that Sadat had given his life for the Middle East peace that he and Begin and I had consummated, and that she and Mubarak were ready to give their lives for the same goal. I pointed out to the group that Sadat was convinced before any of us that the Egyptian and Israeli people were ready for peace. He also was convinced that the Jordanians, Syrians, Lebanese, and other Arabs were ready for peace if it could be presented with the same degree of courage and boldness that Sadat had exhibited.* DIARY, OCTOBER 9, 1981

Earlier, Jihan had invited Rosalynn and me to come alone to see them or to remain behind with her after the others had left, which we did for a brief time. We decided it would be more appropriate for us to be with the other members of the American delegation, so we left after a few minutes to overtake them in the motorcade. Before leaving, Rosalynn promised to stay with Jihan the next day, during the funeral.

The funeral services seemed peculiar to us Westerners, lacking any sense of personal involvement or emotion. Several hundred world leaders, representing eighty nations, gathered first in a crowded pavilion. Except for the presidents of Somalia and Sudan, all the Arab leaders had refused to come to the funeral after Prime Minister Begin announced that he would attend. Their decision was indicative of the ill feeling that survived Sadat in the Middle East.

At the appointed time, we moved out of the large and ornate tent to the edge of the parade route and watched the passage of the horse-drawn caisson carrying Sadat's body. The men of the slain President's family followed, and then the Egyptian officials. Behind them walked the heads of state and other leaders. We had been asked to observe Moslem custom and have only men participate in the ceremony.

As I walked in the midst of kings and princes, presidents, chancellors, and prime ministers, I felt sure that they were all recalling in their own fashion what Anwar Sadat and his life had meant to them. We went slowly down the broad avenue toward the parade-ground reviewing stand where the assassination had occurred. The crowd of people was unstructured and slightly confused, moving ahead by fits and starts. Finally, when we reached the stand, we realized that arrival there signified the end of the funeral ceremony. One of the Egyptians pointed out to me the seat of honor in the front row, where Sadat had been sitting when the attack was launched against him, and we could see that many bullet holes were still evident in the ceiling and back wall, where they had been sprayed by the assassins' guns.

Jihan had been occupying the same seat as the funeral entourage approached. Rosalynn, Susan Mubarak, Mrs. Nimeiri (the First Lady of Sudan), and Empress Farah, the widow of the Shah of Iran, had been sitting with her. Now Vice President Mubarak, Jihan Sadat, and members of their families waited in a room just behind the stands to speak to the visiting statesmen, but there were so many people trying to go through the door that no one could move. I was near the back of the crowd, waiting until we could approach the entrance without being crushed, when one of the Egyptian soldiers guarding the door looked down and saw me. He nodded as he recognized me, and then he shouted, "Car-tair! Car-tair!" As if by magic, the parade guards opened an aisle so that I could reach the door, pushing the other dignitaries back out of the way. Somewhat embarrassed, I gathered the other Americans around me and we hastened forward. I embraced those who were in the receiving line, rejoined Rosalynn, and then we moved out the back door into the brilliant Egyptian sunshine. It was a disturbingly anticlimactic moment, and as Rosalynn and I were driven to the airport to leave the ancient city of Cairo, I was flooded with memories of my all-too-brief days with Anwar Sadat and our effort to find the peace for which he had now given his life.

ISRAELI SECURITY, LAND, AND PALESTINIAN RIGHTS

I've put in an awful lot of time studying the Middle East question.   DIARY, MARCH 7, 1977

We had quite an argument. . . . I think we should move much more aggressively on the Middle East than any of the others want to.   DIARY, FEBRUARY 3, 1978

Dobrynin wants Cy and Gromyko to resolve the remaining issues on SALT—"provided Vance can take time off from the Middle East."   DIARY, JANUARY 10, 1979

L ooking back, it is remarkable to see how constantly the work for peace in the Middle East was on my agenda, and on my mind.

My interest in the region had not begun when I moved into the White House. I had made an extensive visit through Israel in May 1973, while I was still Governor of Georgia, invited by Prime Minister Golda Meir to learn at first hand about her nation's geography and defense requirements. Scheduled at the end of an official trade mission to Europe, this semivacation also gave Rosalynn, Jody Powell, and me a chance to learn more about the land of the Bible, which we had studied since early childhood. We were furnished a Mercedes station wagon, a driver, and a young guide, and spent almost a week traveling around the surprisingly tiny country on a route which we had been permitted to choose ourselves. For three days, before dawn, I was in the streets of Old Jerusalem, and filled each day and night with exciting visits to holy places of ancient history and to sites where history was still being made.

We enjoyed a delightful luncheon with the Mayor of Nazareth, drove all around the Sea of Galilee, went to Cana, walked the hills around Capernaum, studied the excavations at Jericho, worshiped at Bethlehem, and swam in the Dead Sea. Rosalynn and I also walked along the escarpments of the Golan Heights, traveled slowly down the entire length of the Jordan River, rode the torpedo boats at Haifa, and viewed a parade at a military training center at Bethel, which had been used earlier for the same purpose by the Jordanians. I had a briefing by General Chaim Bar-Lev, the Israeli intelligence chief, on the military capabilities of Israel and its neighbors, and I took full advantage of every opportunity to discuss these matters with Prime Minister Meir and other Israeli leaders, including General Yitzhak Rabin, then hero of the Six Day War and soon to be Prime Minister.

This visit to Israel made a great impression on me. Later, in preparation for my presidential campaign, I continued my studies of the complicated history of the area. When I announced as a candidate, I singled out for special mention my support of the American commitment to the security of Israel.

In my affinity for Israel, I shared the sentiment of most other Southern Baptists that the holy places we revered should be preserved and made available for visits by Christians, and that members of other religious faiths should have the same guaranteed privileges concerning their sacred sites. I remembered that prior to the 1967 war there were no such assurances; under Jordanian rule, the areas were often closed, and some of the sacred burial sites and other holy places were vandalized.

The Judeo-Christian ethic and study of the Bible were bonds between Jews and Christians which had always been part of my life. I also believed very deeply that the Jews who had survived the Holocaust deserved their own nation, and that they had a right to live in peace among their neighbors. I considered this homeland for the Jews to be compatible with the teachings of the Bible, hence ordained by God. These moral and religious beliefs made my commitment to the security of Israel unshakable.

Another significant factor in my thinking was that both the United States and Israel are democracies. Israel's relatively small size and the number of her adversaries aroused in me a sense of responsibility to keep the Israelis able to defend themselves. Most Arabs had never accepted the 1947 vote of the UN General Assembly to partition the British Mandate of Palestine into a Jewish and an Arab state—but despite four wars the Israelis survived. I admired their courage, and was thankful for their success in establishing and sustaining their country.

These were thoughts I shared with many other Americans, but now I had been elected President and needed a broader perspective. For the well-being of my own country, I wanted the Middle East region stable and at peace; I did not want to see Soviet influence expanded in the area. In its ability to help accomplish these purposes, Israel was a strategic asset to the United States. I had no strong feelings about the Arab countries. I had never visited one and knew no Arab leaders.

It was obviously desirable to bring peace to the Middle East, but the issues involved were divisive and emotional. To confront them forthrightly meant bruising sensitive feelings on all sides. And if our efforts failed, we would create an image of fumbling incompetence. I remembered the frustrating attempts over the years to find a formula for peace, including a well-meaning effort known as the Rogers Plan, put forward by Secretary of State William Rogers while President Nixon was in office and Henry Kissinger was National Security Adviser. The plan described an Israeli withdrawal to prescribed boundaries between Israel, Egypt, and Jordan, along with security assurances to Israel and Jordan. It was easy to understand why it was not named the Nixon Plan, since it was rejected strongly by all the negotiating parties almost as soon as it was revealed. Presidents Eisenhower, Kennedy, Johnson, and Ford had apparently tried to avoid any active involvement in Middle Eastern disputes until a crisis actually erupted, and I was sure there was good reason for their restraint. I had my own ideas about what might be done, but decided to approach the subject with great caution.

There were some developments of significance that gave me both hope and concern. The most notable of these was Egypt's turning away from its alignment with the Soviet Union toward a posture of neutrality or even friendship with the United States. It was fairly obvious that the key to any future military threats against Israel was the Egyptians, who could provide the most formidable invading force and who had always been in the forefront of previous battles. They had also suffered most of the casualties in the recurring wars with the Israelis, and would be crucial to any future peace settlement.

President Sadat was facing a new set of circumstances. He had to confront increasing threats from his own African neighbors, but at the same time—now that the Sinai disengagement agreement had been reached following the 1973 war—he could feel more secure about Israel's intentions. Egypt was still legally at war with Israel, was participating in the total Arab boycott that prevented any trade or communication with Israel, and was keeping the Suez Canal closed to Israeli ships. Sadat had, however, made some slight moves toward moderation, which were already bringing on him severe condemnation from the PLO (Palestinian Liberation Organization) and other Arab militants.

There were hundreds of thousands of refugees from Palestine, many of whom had left when Israel was formed as a nation and others who had moved from their homes following the Six Day War in 1967. Large numbers also lived in and around refugee camps in the Gaza District, southwest of Jerusalem on the coast of the Mediterranean Sea. These people and the Palestinian Arabs who remained in their home villages and farms in the West Bank had all been living under Israeli military rule for almost ten years. For the Arab world the Palestinian issue was of transcendent importance. Depending upon their degree of militancy, the Arabs were either determined to forge an acceptable solution to this problem or resolved that Israel must be destroyed as a nation.

In order to achieve a comprehensive peace settlement serious obstacles had to be overcome. There had never been any direct communication between the governments in conflict except for rare clandestine meetings. None of the Arab states was willing officially to acknowledge Israel's status as a nation or even its right to exist. I knew from my briefings that there were moderate Arab leaders in Jordan, Saudi Arabia, and elsewhere who would privately admit their willingness to accept Israel's existence—but not publicly, since in their eyes, even the arrangements for talks with Israeli leaders could be interpreted as a form of diplomatic recognition, a future bargaining chip not to be given away freely.

The Israelis were ready to negotiate with leaders of the Arab nations, but they were just as determined, or even more so, not to talk to representatives of the PLO. Such a stance, too, might be interpreted as some form of recognition. The Israelis maintained that the Palestinians as individuals possessed rights which had to be recognized, but that they had no rights or status as a people or nation.

Most previous peace efforts, therefore, had been designed either to end one of the frequent military engagements or merely to devise some means by which negotiations could begin. The status quo sometimes seemed to suit the major protagonists, but I feared it could not be maintained for long.

The Palestinian issue was forcing the Israelis into an ever more isolated position in the world community. The Arab nations were unanimous in their determination to achieve worldwide recognition of the rights of the Palestinians, both those who lived under the Israeli occupation forces in the West Bank and Gaza and those who were refugees from their homeland and living in Jordan, Lebanon, and other nearby countries. The record of the Arab nations themselves toward the Palestinians left much to be desired. Before 1967, when Egypt occupied Gaza, and Jordan the West Bank, there had been no move on the part of either country to grant autonomy to the Palestinians. It was not generally remembered that these unfortunate people had been severely mistreated in some of their host countries, but there were constant and vivid reminders of the plight of those who lived under Israeli rule. Although the PLO was denounced by the Israelis as a band of terrorists, the majority of nations recognized the PLO as the representative of the Palestinian people. In international councils the PLO was making great progress, always at the expense of Israel.

Since I had made our nation's commitment to human rights a central tenet of our foreign policy, it was impossible for me to ignore the very serious problems on the West Bank. The continued deprivation of Palestinian rights was not only used as the primary lever against Israel, but was contrary to the basic moral and ethical principles of both our countries. In my opinion it was imperative that the United States work to obtain for these people the right to vote, the right to assemble and to debate issues that affected their lives, the right to own property without fear of its being confiscated, and the right to be free of military rule. To deny these rights was an indefensible position for a free and democratic society, and I had promised to do my best to seek resolution of problems like these, no matter where they might be found.

I recognized the legitimate needs of the Israelis to protect themselves against terrorism. But we needed to resolve the underlying problems rather than see continued violence, which threatened to spread beyond the Middle East and even to involve the superpowers.

⌣

I believe that the boycott of American businesses by the Arab countries because those businesses trade with Israel . . . is an absolute disgrace. This is the first time that I remember, in the history of our country, when we've let a foreign country circumvent or change our Bill of Rights. I'll do everything I can as President to stop the boycott. . . . It's not a matter of diplomacy or trade with me; it's a matter of morality.

SECOND PRESIDENTIAL DEBATE,
SAN FRANCISCO, OCTOBER 7, 1976

The Arab trade embargo against Israel also affected the United States directly, in that there was a secondary boycott which was being accepted by many American firms. This was obnoxious to me—to see business leaders in my own great country abjectly and greedily sign binding agreements not to do business with Israel as a prerequisite to making a deal in an Arab country. I was determined to end this embarrassment, and in the spring of 1977, after tortuous negotiation among the affected parties, my request for anti-boycott legislation from Congress was successfully met.

I had also said during the debates with President Ford that if any country should ever again declare an embargo on oil against our nation, I would consider that "an economic declaration of war, and would respond instantly and in kind. I would not ship that country anything. No weapons, no spare parts for weapons, no oil-drilling rigs, no oil pipe, no nothing."

We had domestic supplies of oil and other fuels, and could survive and even continue to prosper for a short while without imports. Other countries were not so fortunate; during the difficult days of the oil embargo in 1973 and 1974, they had learned the lesson all too well. The predictable and unfortunate result had already been the alienation of more and more nations from Israel. OPEC had considerably strengthened Arab clout in foreign capitals. Furthermore, in a future war of attrition, deliberately stretched out by Arab adversaries over a long period of time, the physical isolation of Israel could become much more complete, with its only dependable friend being the United States—also likely to be increasingly separated from other nations in such an extended engagement. In spite of every effort, it would be extremely difficult for us to keep Israel provided with arms and other supplies for many weeks or months under these circumstances. There was grave doubt, based on previous experience, that during such a war our cargo planes en route to Israel would even be given permission to fly over intimidated European or African countries, much less to land for necessary refueling. Furthermore, by the beginning of 1977, we ourselves had become increasingly dependent on foreign oil and therefore more vulnerable to future attempts at blackmail—with our own security directly threatened. We were deeply concerned, therefore, about the ultimate security of Israel and how it might affect the United States.

The basic instability of the region made another major war a constant threat. Lebanon, Israel's northern neighbor, was an international battleground as a result of continuing ethnic and religious struggles. This piteous area was torn apart by violence, as we knew from our own unhappy experiences. In June 1976, the

American ambassador to Lebanon had been kidnapped and murdered, and later his successor was forced to return to Washington. American nationals had to be evacuated from the country by sea.

Four Israeli–Arab wars in twenty-five years, embargoes and boycotts, frequent acts of terrorism, hundreds of thousands of refugees, internecine battles in Lebanon, a refusal by the disputing parties in the Middle East even to negotiate with one another to resolve differences—these were all chronic troubles. A sense of hopelessness prevailed, a general belief that nothing could be done to solve them. I was only thankful that there was no immediate Middle East crisis pressing on me during the first days of 1977.

During the campaign and after the election, I had long discussions with my security advisers about these and related issues and had to face many of them in public forums. Human rights, Israeli security, Soviet influence, Middle East peace, oil imports—these would be major concerns of our new administration. I struggled with the questions, and sought advice from all possible sources, only to be told by almost every adviser to stay out of the Middle East situation. It seemed that all the proposed solutions had already been tried and had failed. However, I could see growing threats to the United States in the Middle East, and was willing to make another try—perhaps overly confident that I could now find answers that had eluded so many others.

The official framework under which we had to work was the so-called Geneva Conference, a forum established under the auspices of the United Nations while President Nixon was in office. If ever convened, it was to be headed jointly by the United States and the Soviet Union, with participation by the Israelis and their Arab neighbors—and the Palestinians. This format itself was a big problem, which so far had defied solution.

In spite of their extreme complexity, the issues seemed to boil down to three primary ones: Israeli security; who owned the land; and Palestinian rights. Now I needed to talk to some of the Israeli and Arab leaders, to see if they shared my assessments and my ambitions.

Prime Minister Rabin came over from Israel. I've put in an awful lot of time studying the Middle East question and was hoping that Rabin would give me some outline of what Israel ultimately hopes to see achieved in a perma-

nent peace settlement. I found him very timid, very stub-
born, and also somewhat ill at ease. At the working supper
Speaker Tip O'Neill asked him, for instance, under what
circumstances he would permit the Palestinians to be
represented at the Geneva talks, and he was adamantly
opposed to any meeting if the PLO or other representatives
of the Palestinians were there. When he went upstairs
with me, just the two of us, I asked him to tell me what
Israel wanted me to do when I met with the Arab leaders
and if there were something specific, for instance, that I
could propose to Sadat. He didn't unbend at all, nor did
he respond. It seems to me that the Israelis, at least
Rabin, don't trust our government or any of their neigh-
bors. I guess there's some justification for this distrust.

I've never met any of the Arab leaders but am look-
ing forward to seeing if they are more flexible than
Rabin.   DIARY, MARCH 7, 1977

Aware of Rabin's great intelligence and personal courage, I
found this first meeting a particularly unpleasant surprise. I had
thought that among the Israeli leaders he would be the one most
committed to exploring new ideas and discussing the prospects
for progress with me. His strange reticence caused me to think
again about whether we should launch another major effort for
peace. However, I knew how weary the Israelis were of war and of
terrorism. There were few Israeli families who had not known the
loss of life from this constant violence. I was ready to move
forward, but now my experience with Prime Minister Rabin had
revealed a more difficult challenge than I had expected. I would
do anything within reason to help, but at least part of the initiative had to come from the disputing parties themselves.

Although Rabin's lack of interest in pursuing negotiations for
peace was disappointing, at least his visit had served to focus
American attention on the subject. It dominated my next news
conference, on March 9. The reporters came back to it again and
again. I had decided to plow some new ground, and proposed the
concept of two different borders for Israel—one marking the limits of national sovereignty and the other, farther out, forming a
defense perimeter, with Israeli or international forces in between
to guard Israel against attack. I also raised the possibility of an
interim period of two to eight years, during which the disputed
land between these two borders might be governed as a demilitarized area or a zone of peace. I advocated Israel's ultimate with-

drawal to the 1967 borders, with minor adjustments for security purposes; a termination of belligerence toward Israel by its neighbors; a recognition of its right to exist in peace; and free trade, tourist travel, and cultural exchange among the countries involved in the long-standing dispute. I announced to the reporters that I intended to meet with the leaders of Egypt, Jordan, Syria, and Saudi Arabia within the next two months.

I was trying to break down existing barriers by discussing some new approaches to the old questions, but it was difficult. In Israel, among the Arabs, and particularly among American Jews there were strong reactions against particular points they did not like. Secretary Vance met with a delegation of American Jewish leaders to explain our position, and within a few days the Arab ambassadors in Washington came to the State Department for a similar meeting. President Sadat requested that a scheduled United Nations debate on the Middle East be postponed until after his upcoming visit to Washington. At least the dialogue was picking up.

A week or so after Rabin's visit, I went to New York to address the United Nations, and did not help the situation much.

> *There was quite a flap about whether or not I would stand in the receiving line and meet the representative of the PLO, who are not recognized by us. When I got there I . . . went ahead and shook hands with everybody who came in, including the PLO representative, who was very embarrassed. It didn't hurt anybody.*   DIARY, MARCH 17, 1977

This action was sensitive because Kissinger had promised the Israelis at the time of the Sinai disengagement that the United States would not recognize or negotiate with the PLO until it acknowledged Israel's right to exist and accepted United Nations Resolution 242 as a basis for resolving the Middle East disputes. I had reconfirmed this commitment and I always honored it, knowing that the charter of the PLO still insisted that Israel be destroyed and that the PLO was responsible for many acts of terrorism in Israel.

The United Nations resolution was crucial because it emphasized the inadmissibility of the acquisition of territory by war, and called for a just and lasting peace in the area, withdrawal of Israeli armed forces from territories occupied in the Six Day War, guarantees of the territorial inviolability and political independence of every state in the area, and a just settlement of the refugee problem. The PLO leaders strongly objected to two points: any recognition of Israel as a permanent nation, and the absence of specific references to the Palestinians. The word "refugee" was not adequate for them.

Then, on April 4, 1977, a shining light burst on the Middle East scene for me. I had my first meetings with President Anwar Sadat of Egypt, a man who would change history and whom I would come to admire more than any other leader.

In preparation for his visit, I had been studying about him and his country for several weeks, reviewing the long record of our nation's involvement in Northern Africa and the Sinai region, learning about the level of economic aid to Egypt from the United States and other countries, trying to understand Sadat's relationship to his neighbors in Africa as well as to Israel, and the potential that existed for improving Egypt's lot in the future—if peace and security could be brought to that war-torn country.

At the beginning of Sadat's visit to Washington I thought he was a bit shy, or ill at ease, because he was sweating profusely as we exchanged our first words together. But he told me he had been unwell, with chills in Paris and a high fever since he'd arrived in our country. Sadat's complexion was much darker than I had expected, and I noticed immediately a callused spot at the center of his forehead, apparently caused by a lifetime of touching his head to the ground in prayer. He didn't smoke very much, but he always wanted his pipe nearby, and was irritated when his aide was slow in delivering it to him.

It soon became apparent that he was charming and frank, and also a very strong and courageous leader who would not shrink from making difficult political decisions. He was extraordinarily inclined toward boldness and seemed impatient with those who were more timid or cautious. I formed an immediate impression that if he should become a personal ally, our friendship could be very significant for both of us, and that the prospects for peace in his troubled region might not be dead.

At our first meeting, Sadat gave me new hope concerning the establishment of neutral or demilitarized zones within the Sinai, which could possibly lead Israel to withdraw from its occupation of this Egyptian land. He also somewhat improved his existing position on the possible nature of permanent peace, mentioning the possibility of an end to the Arab trade boycott against Israel. He believed that as time went by, Yasir Arafat, the PLO leader, would moderate his attitude toward Israel if the Palestinian issue was addressed, and promised to use his influence toward that end. I probed for the possible terms of a complete settlement, even including open borders and diplomatic recognition of Israel, but President Sadat would not respond to such a drastic proposal. The generations of hatred and the vivid memories of recent wars could not be overcome so easily.

That evening, after a working dinner, I invited Sadat upstairs so that I could clarify and confirm some of the hopeful comments he had made, and pressed him on the other key points.

When I asked him about Israel's withdrawal from occupied territories, he responded that "some minimal deviation from the 1967 borders might be acceptable." This was an important concession and, so far as I knew, unprecedented for an Arab leader. We had a long discussion about Jerusalem—the most sensitive issue of all—and he agreed that the city should never be divided again, as it was from 1948 to 1967. But he insisted that Arabs must have control over the area encompassing their own holy places, and that worshipers of all faiths needed free access to their shrines, without first having to obtain Israeli permission.

Sadat said he would have no objection to direct negotiations between Egyptians and Israelis, "provided the Palestinian issue is resolved." He and I both knew this to be a tall order as a prerequisite to other talks, but I presumed later that he would be willing for this point to be discussed simultaneously with other issues that were important to Israel.

He was cautious about promising any end to the Arab boycott against Israel, saying only that "with peace, it can be terminated." In his private talks with Secretary Vance, Prime Minister Rabin had suggested that open borders and trade between Israel and its neighbors would be the best evidence of a genuine willingness to resolve other differences. Sadat finally admitted, "This may be possible after some years, if good progress can be made."

It was getting late, and I decided to push my luck. I asked him again about the ultimate achievement—diplomatic recognition of Israel and exchange of ambassadors. I knew that the Israelis could not rest easy, even with other agreements, unless they were recognized as a neighbor with the full diplomatic status of other nations. Sadat shook his head emphatically and replied, "Not in my lifetime!" We parried back and forth on this, and I teased him by asking if he thought some of our successors might be more willing to achieve peace than we were.

We were in a good mood, and argued without restraint, even on the most delicate points. It was obvious that he was tired of war and saw Egypt's need to alleviate the simultaneous threats from Israel, Libya, and perhaps even Soviet-influenced Ethiopia through

Sudan. I pushed him hard on the open-borders and diplomatic-recognition points, reminding him again that he and I might not be in office long and could not leave this kind of progress to others. He reminded me of the great political pressures in the United States on me and Congress, and I tried to convince him that I was willing to face any necessary political risks to reach a peace settlement. He finally said, "It may be possible to have a clause at the end of an agreement saying that, if things go well, diplomatic recognition of Israel would come after five more years." All this was much more than I had hoped to get. After Sadat left, I told Rosalynn that this had been my best day as President.

I did not pursue these questions any further the next morning. We discussed his other regional concerns, and the possibilities for United States military and economic aid to Egypt. Even more than our late-night conversation, Sadat's final words convinced me that he was determined to make progress without delay. When we talked about military sales to Egypt, he said, "I would rather do without weapons that we need, like the F-5E fighter plane, in order not to endanger the possibilities of a Middle East settlement this year."

There was an easy and natural friendship between us from the first moment I knew Anwar Sadat. We trusted each other. Each of us began to learn about the other's family members, hometown, earlier life, and private plans and ambitions, as though we were tying ourselves together for a lifetime. Rosalynn and Sadat's wife, Jihan, sensed this special relationship and joined it easily. The news reporters often referred with some amusement to my claims of friendship with other people, but when I called President Anwar Sadat "my close, personal friend," both he and I—and perhaps even they—knew it to be true.

Within a few hours after Sadat's return to Egypt, Prime Minister Rabin announced his withdrawal as a candidate for reelection because of some allegations about his bank account in New York. We did not know it at the time, but this decision was to revolutionize the domestic political scene in Israel.

After a few weeks, Menachem Begin, then known to many Americans as a right-wing radical leader, was elected to head Israel's government. Israeli citizens, the American Jewish community, and I were shocked. None of us knew what to expect.

President Sadat was also concerned about this completely unexpected development, but he did not waste any time in accommodating himself to Begin's election. He soon met with President

Nicolae Ceauscescu of Romania, and asked him two questions about Israel's new leader: "Is he honest?" "Is he a strong man?" Both times, Sadat told me later, Ceauscescu had responded, "Yes." That was good enough for the Egyptian president.

Now I needed to meet with the other Arab leaders.

> *King Hussein of Jordan came. We all really liked him, enjoyed his visit, and believe he'll be a strong and staunch ally for us as we approach the time for a Mideast conference later on this year. . . . He said that for the first time in 25 or 30 years he felt hopeful that this year we could reach some agreements. I feel the same way. At this time my basic plan is to meet with the leaders of the nations involved, completing this round in May, then put together our own concept of what should be done in the Middle East, let Cy Vance make a trip around the area to consult with leaders, listening more than he talks, and then put as much pressure as we can bring to bear on the different parties to accept the solution that we think is fair.*
> DIARY, APRIL 25, 1977

Hussein accepted the principles of my public proposals for resolving the Middle East disputes, but emphasized that the basic rights of the Palestinians would have to be honored. He described the freedom of movement that was now routinely permitted between Jordan and the West Bank, but in deference to the Palestinians he did not seem to be pressing any claims of Jordanian sovereignty over the territory being occupied by Israel.

Late that night, Hussein, Rosalynn, and I sat on the Truman balcony, watching the planes land and take off from National Airport, and talked about both diplomatic affairs and personal matters. He was still emotionally drained by the recent death of his beautiful young wife in a helicopter accident. When he started telling Rosalynn how much he had appreciated my handwritten note, he began to weep, and our hearts went out to him. I asked him if he would like to visit the Georgia coast for a few days of rest, and he quickly accepted our invitation. We made arrangements with two of our young friends, Dr. Carlton Hicks and Jimmy Bishop, to be his hosts.

President Hafez Assad of Syria was next on my list. I made arrangements to see him in Switzerland immediately after the London economic summit conference. Before leaving London, I had a private breakfast with President Valéry Giscard d'Estaing of France. I had already become acquainted with him during the hours of economic discussions, but this was our first opportunity to meet alone. He was a brilliant and strong man, very confident of himself, somewhat autocratic in demeanor, but personable and cordial toward me. He did not waste words, and had a clear and analytical approach to the many issues we covered. We agreed on most of them, but I was troubled by his extremely antagonistic attitude toward Israel. He seemed quite convinced that the Israelis were international outlaws and that all the Arab positions were proper.

Soon afterward I flew to Geneva for the meeting with President Assad, which lasted three and a half hours.

It was a very interesting and enjoyable experience. There was a lot of good humor between us, and I found him to be very constructive in his attitude and somewhat flexible in dealing with some of the more crucial items involving peace, the Palestinians, the refugee problem, and borders. He said that a year or two ago it would have been suicidal in his country to talk about peace with the Israelis, but they've come a long way and were willing to cooperate. DIARY, MAY 9, 1977

This was the man who would soon sabotage the Geneva peace talks by refusing to attend under any reasonable circumstances, and who would, still later, do everything possible to prevent the Camp David accords from being fulfilled.

The more I dealt with Arab leaders, the more disparity I discovered between their private assurances and their public comments. They would privately put forward ideas for peace and encourage us in any reasonable approach. However, the peer pressure among them was tremendous. None of them—apart from Sadat—was willing to get out in front and publicly admit a willingness to deal with Israel. The threat of Palestinian terrorist attacks against some of their shaky regimes was one significant reason, but the concentration of oil wealth in the more radical countries, such as Libya and Iraq, was perhaps more important. Saudi Arabia was both rich and moderate—but again, supporting the peace process only in private!

There was also a private-public disparity, though of a different nature, among the leaders of the many organized groups in the American Jewish community. In our private conversations they were often supportive and, like the Arab leaders, urged us to explore every avenue that might lead to peace. They would deplore Israeli excesses, travel to Jerusalem to seek out moderate leaders who shared the same goals, and give generously of their time and money to any peaceful or benevolent cause. But in a public showdown on a controversial issue, they would almost always side with the Israeli leaders and condemn us for being "evenhanded" in our concern about both Palestinian rights and Israeli security. I presumed that with all the other condemnations of Israel in the United Nations and from many individual countries, American Jews, even feeling critical, did not want to make their criticisms public.

On May 24, I welcomed Crown Prince Fahd of Saudi Arabia to the White House. Although its territory did not border on Israel's, Saudi Arabia could play a powerful role in influencing the Syrians, the Jordanians, and the PLO to be cooperative, because the three groups were heavily dependent on Saudi financing. Furthermore, members of the royal family of Saudi Arabia were responsible for the protection of the holiest sites, destinations of religious pilgrimages throughout the world of Islam. This gave them special status in the eyes of other Moslems.

And yet, although the Saudis had great wealth, in some ways their country was relatively vulnerable. With a native population of only about five million and anything but a formidable military capability, they were therefore eager to achieve peace and stability in the Middle Eastern and Persian Gulf regions, but at the same time were very much concerned about potential terrorist attacks or popular dissatisfaction with the royal family.

My Cabinet officers and I had interesting and productive discussions with Crown Prince Fahd, Princes Saud and Mohammad, and other Saudi leaders during their visit to Washington. They were very frank and spoke freely about the intractable issues in the Middle East. Because the Saudis looked on atheism and communism with abhorrence, they despised and distrusted the Soviet Union. They considered the United States to be among their reliable friends. Above all, they were interested in the Palestinian question more than in any other.

After a working supper with about twenty members of Congress as guests, Fahd and I went upstairs for a half-hour talk about the Palestinians. I reminded him that we were bound by a commitment not to recognize the PLO nor to negotiate with its leaders unless they would accept United Nations Resolution 242 and acknowledge Israel's right to exist; only then would the PLO be able to participate in the ongoing peace process. Fahd agreed to help in every way he could with this problem.

After meeting with these key Arab leaders, I was convinced that all of them were ready for a strong move on our part to find solutions to the long-standing disputes and that with such solutions would come their recognition of Israel and the right of Israelis to live in peace. I agreed with their most important premise—that the Palestinian question would have to be addressed. But I was quite concerned that Israel, with its choice of a new prime minister, would not respond favorably to the peace effort I was contemplating.

> *I had them replay the "Issues and Answers" interview with Menachem Begin, Chairman of the Likud party and the prospective Prime Minister of Israel. It was frightening to watch his adamant position on issues that must be resolved if a Middle Eastern peace settlement is going to be realized.*   DIARY, MAY 23, 1977

In his first answer he stated that the entire West Bank was an integral part of Israel's sovereignty, that it had been "liberated" during the Six Day War, and that a Jewish majority and an Arab minority would be established there. This statement was a radical departure from past Israeli policy, and seemed to throw United Nations Resolution 242, for which Israel had voted, out the window. I could not believe what I was hearing. He went on to say that there were absolutely no circumstances under which any Israelis would consider participation by members of the PLO in a Geneva conference, even as members of the Jordanian delegation.

Other answers of this tenor made it clear that if he maintained these positions, there was no prospect of further progress in the Middle East. I still had some hope, though, because Begin was said to be an honest and courageous man.

During this time, I was increasingly concerned about criticisms of our peace initiatives from within the American Jewish community. My own political supporters were coming to see me, groups were meeting with Cy Vance, and stirrings within Congress were becoming more pronounced. They were already nervous about the Begin election and the replacement of the well-known leaders of the Israeli Labor Party, which had governed Israel for many years. Additionally, they were troubled about some of our proposals concerning the Palestinian issue and "dual borders," and my highly publicized and apparently friendly series of meetings with the Arab leaders.

It was necessary for someone outside my administration to give me public support. There was one man who was trusted by everyone as a friend of Israel, whom I knew to be wise and knowledgeable about the controversial issues in the Middle East. I invited Senator Hubert Humphrey to come to the Oval Office on June 9, outlined my plans for the region, and asked for his advice and help. He was very supportive, agreeing to make a public statement reflecting this attitude, and giving me a list of others who should be informed about what I was trying to accomplish. The following week I met with him again. This time he had other legislative leaders with him.

I tried to convince them that they must back me if I was to prevail in any peace initiative. It was particularly important now, as the time for my first meeting with Prime Minister Begin was approaching. I told them we would suggest a very broad definition of peace, involving direct negotiations between Israel and her neighbors, open borders and free trade, free passage of the Suez Canal and other waterways, and perhaps future diplomatic recognition. If we were successful, these would be unprecedented advances for Israel, guaranteed by Egypt—the Israelis' most formidable potential adversary in any future combat. We discussed the advisability of a Palestinian entity tied to Jordan, instead of a separate nation for the Palestinians on the West Bank, and agreed on the necessity of Israeli withdrawal from the occupied territories, with some minor border adjustments.

The meeting with the congressional leaders was constructive, and I was pleased with it. I set up more meetings with House and Senate leaders who had a special interest in Israel, and made good progress with all except Senator Javits, who informed me in the Oval Office that he would make a critical speech about my policy on the Middle East. At least he was kind enough to send me a copy of the text just before he issued it to the press.

Though many other issues claimed my attention, the Middle East question preyed on my mind. Convinced that some unforeseen prospects had developed, primarily because of Sadat's attitude, I continued to probe for every possible opening or new idea. Over the Fourth of July weekend, I had a chance to be alone for a couple of days and to think.

I caught up on back reading . . . and read an analysis of the Middle Eastern questions. Studied maps of Israel, Jerusalem, history of the Palestinian question, and the United Nations resolutions that are now the basis for future negotiations.   DIARY, JULY 4, 1977

Rosalynn and I came back to the White House for the Fourth of July celebrations. As we sat on the Truman balcony with the Mondales and our children and watched the skyrockets, aerial bombs, and other fireworks, the explosions were one more reminder of my responsibility to avoid war—to maintain the peace for my own country and to secure this same blessing for the Middle East.

I had to repair my damaged political base among Israel's American friends, and in the process build further support for our peace effort. Before Begin arrived, I held sessions with Jewish leaders from all around the nation, explaining my policies as I had to the congressional leaders. In most cases, their concerns seemed to be at least partially alleviated, giving me a little breathing room to prepare for the upcoming talks.

ⵗ

We welcomed Prime Minister and Mrs. Begin, having done a great deal of preparation for this visit. There have been dire predictions that he and I would not get along, but I found him to be quite congenial, dedicated, sincere, deeply religious. . . . I think Begin is a very good man and, although it will be difficult for him to change his position, the public-opinion polls that we have from Israel show that the people there are quite flexible . . . and genuinely want peace. My own guess is that if we give Begin support, he will prove to be a strong leader, quite different from Rabin.   DIARY, JULY 19, 1977

The opinion polls to which I referred showed that 63 per cent of the Israelis wanted peace with the Arabs, 51 per cent were willing to give up appreciable parts of the West Bank, 52 per cent thought the Palestinians deserved a homeland, 43 per cent thought this homeland should be on the West Bank of the Jordan River, and 45 per cent—exactly half of those who had an opinion—supported direct talks with the PLO if its leaders would recognize Israel's right to exist.

I outlined my proposed set of principles to Begin: first, that our goal was a truly comprehensive peace, one that would affect all Israel's neighbors; second, that it would be based on United Nations Resolution 242; third, that the definition of peace would be quite broad, including open borders and free trade; fourth, that it would involve Israel's withdrawal from occupied territory to secure borders; and fifth, that a Palestinian entity (not an independent nation) should be created. He said that he could agree with all of them except the Palestinian entity.

I then explained to the Prime Minister how serious an obstacle to peace were the Israeli settlements being established within the occupied territories. Israeli leaders continued to permit or encourage additional settlers to move into Arab neighborhoods, sending a signal of their apparent intentions to make the military occupation permanent. I reminded Begin that the position of the United States had always been that any settlements established on lands occupied by military force were in violation of international law. He listened very closely, but did not respond.

We then discussed affairs in Lebanon, Ethiopia, and Libya. I asked him about some recent Israeli airplane flights over Saudi Arabia, which he said he did not know about, but would stop. Begin gave me his views about the historical nature of Israel, which was interesting this time, although I was familiar with most of what he said from my studies of the Old Testament and more recent history. I had no idea then how many times in the future I would listen to the same discourse.

That evening, after our formal banquet, I continued with the Prime Minister what had become a very useful custom of mine. We went upstairs in the White House and had a long and frank discussion in complete privacy. He promised to keep an open mind on the controversial issues and stated that he was making tentative plans for direct meetings with Sadat.

Pleased with our discussions and inspired by his apparent eagerness to work with me, I sat up late that night after he left, writing down a summary of what was yet to be resolved. Having now met with the Arab leaders and with Begin, I could see some compromise positions that might be acceptable if we could ever work out the format for the planned Geneva talks.

The feelings of optimism had a short life. As soon as Begin returned to Israel, he recognized as permanent some of the settlements on the West Bank. Predictably, this act was the most important item of discussion at my next news conference. Shortly thereafter, when Secretary Vance traveled through the area, he sent generally favorable reports about the attitude of President Sadat and the other Arab leaders, but he was extremely discouraged after talking with the Prime Minister in Jerusalem. My colleagues and I decided to develop a reasonable proposal based on Cy's extensive talks, hoping that public opinion and the general desire for peace might be decisive.

On August 11, while Vance was still on his trip, Ambassador

Arthur Goldberg came by to offer me some advice. As a former Cabinet member and Supreme Court justice, and as head of our United Nations delegation when Resolution 242 was evolved, he had great experience in this area, and I listened closely. He urged me to proceed aggressively and suggested I bring together the Middle Eastern leaders at Geneva for long and extended negotiations, with Brezhnev and me presiding over the first sessions.

We still had two basic problems in setting up the Geneva meeting: the Arabs wanted maximum Palestinian participation, but the Israelis wanted none, and the Soviet Union was reluctant to alienate any of its Arab friends or to deal fairly with Israel. My administration continued to work on both problems, in spite of our heavy concentration on energy legislation and the Panama Canal treaties.

> *Assad in an interview in* The New York Times *proposed that the PLO not participate in the Geneva Conferences, but that the Arab League [a conglomerate group representing most of the Arab countries] might substitute for them. We'll pursue this idea!*   DIARY, AUGUST 29, 1977

For Syria, this was a very constructive proposal, but the issue was still the most sensitive one with both the Arabs and Israelis. Whenever the State Department even explored the question of how to involve the Palestinians, the Israelis objected very strongly. Yet somehow, the plight of these people had to be addressed if there was ever to be permanent peace.

When Israeli Foreign Minister Moshe Dayan came to Washington to discuss the peace process with me on September 19, I expected a difficult session. I had great personal respect for Dayan, because I knew he was striving to end the Israeli military occupation on the West Bank and at the same time retain adequate security for his country. However, I was then convinced that some of Israel's recent actions were the main obstacles to progress on the peace talks. I told him that I thought the gratuitous endorsement of a new group of settlements, the recent Israeli invasion of Lebanon, and the failure to make any reasonable proposals or counterproposals on the question of Palestinian representation were almost insuperable obstacles.

I asked Dayan to respond, and he said I was wrong. He promised that no more civilians would go into the settlements, but only people in uniform into the military sites. (This was a major concession, not to be honored later by Prime Minister Begin.) On

Lebanon, the six tanks sent in over the weekend would be the limit of Israeli involvement, he said. He even showed some flexibility on the Palestinians, proposing that there could be a joint Arab delegation for the opening session at Geneva; afterward PLO members could be part of the Jordanian delegation, provided they were not well-known leaders. When pressed, he said if these delegates ever informed the press that they were members of the PLO, it would not disrupt the talks. He insisted that Israel would negotiate over territory with only one nation at a time—with the Syrians for the Golan Heights, with the Jordanians for the West Bank, and with the Egyptians for the Sinai. He also suggested that a separate multinational group could be formed to discuss the refugee—or Palestinian—question. If Dayan was speaking accurately for Israel, the meeting had been surprisingly productive, possibly enough to let us bring the Arabs around.

Since the only forum the United States had to work on was the Geneva Conference under the aegis of the United Nations, we had to get the Soviet Union, as cochairman, to agree to the format we were so laboriously evolving. On September 23, during my meeting with Foreign Minister Gromyko, he told me, "If we can just establish a miniature state for the Palestinians as big as a pencil eraser, this will lead to a resolution of the PLO problem for the Geneva Conference." He smiled as I pointed out the difficulty of such a tiny state's being formed, and then agreed that peace would have to be more than just the end of war in the Middle East. The ultimate goal, he acknowledged, was normal relationships between the Arab and Israeli governments and people.

Those of us in my administration working on the problem were determined that none of my previous public statements or private commitments could be changed as we worked out with the Soviets the rules for commencing the peace talks. It was not easy to be firm in this resolve, but Secretary Vance was remarkably successful. Since some momentum was building up, the Soviets did not want to be excluded from the process.

The October 1 Joint Statement of the United States and the Soviet Union on the Geneva Conference set forth the principles which I had decided to pursue, but which neither the Israelis nor the Arabs were ready to accept. Both groups reacted negatively, as did members of the American Jewish community. I decided to meet with Dayan again, and with the Foreign Ministers of Lebanon, Syria, Jordan, and Egypt, while I was in New York to speak to the United Nations General Assembly.

My meeting with Egyptian Foreign Minister Ismail Fahmy was particularly significant.

[Fahmy] brought me a letter from Sadat ... urging that nothing be done to prevent Israel and Egypt from negotiating directly, with our serving as an intermediary either before or after the Geneva Conference is convened. Although Fahmy is a little more reluctant than Sadat, I found Egypt to be the most forthcoming and cooperative nation in the Middle East in working toward a peace settlement.   DIARY, OCTOBER 4, 1977

I felt particularly embattled at this time, and the news from Sadat was indeed welcome. (Shortly after this, Fahmy resigned in protest over Sadat's willingness to meet directly with the Israelis.)

The evening meeting with Dayan was long and difficult. Together, we moved toward an acceptable working arrangement for the Geneva Conference.

I think the meeting was very productive. He was obviously quite nervous and quite deeply concerned about the Soviet–American statement. I told him that our commitment to Israel still stood, that we were not trying to impose a settlement from outside on Israel.   DIARY, OCTOBER 4, 1977

I succeeded in convincing Dayan of the necessity of compromise, but he warned me that there would be strong opposition to our proposals in his government. I left Dayan at midnight; Secretary Vance and his aides spent two more hours with him finishing a draft statement.

Serious concerns still existed within the American Jewish community and Congress about the possible convening of the Geneva Conference. It was very difficult for people to realize that, if successful, our efforts would bring significant results. The mere commencement of peace talks between Israel and the Arab leaders would accomplish one major goal in itself: every Arab nation that agreed to attend would be recognizing Israel as a nation, with the right to exist in peace.

I later received reports of the argument within the Israeli cabinet meeting of October 11 when Dayan presented our proposals. Over strong opposition he prevailed, however, and as I believed the Egyptians and Jordanians were also amenable, only Syria remained a question mark.

This proved no small matter. Assad's earlier promises to me of cooperation seemed to be worth nothing. I was not going to rewrite our working paper, which contained significant concessions by the Israelis. After a few days, it appeared the whole process was breaking down. Then everyone would lose.

I worried about this situation for a week or so, and finally decided to play my only hole card—a direct appeal to President Sadat. On October 21, 1977, I sat down and wrote him a personal note, beginning:

> Dear President Sadat,
>   When we met privately in the White House, I was deeply impressed and grateful for your promise to me that, at a crucial moment, I could count on your support when obstacles arose in our common search for peace in the Middle East. We have reached such a moment, and I need your help.

I went on to urge his public endorsement of our proposals, emphasizing that it was "extremely important—perhaps vital" in bringing the disputing parties together. I had no idea what his response would be, but was confident that he would not let me down. I needed all the help I could get.

Senator Byrd called, concerned about the Middle East question being a partisan issue and not having enough

support for my position. He told me there was a lot of
quiet majority support, and I told him my problem was
that it was too quiet!   DIARY, NOVEMBER 2, 1977

The next day, he and two or three other Senate leaders made
strong statements endorsing our proposals for the peace talks.

On November 2, Sadat and I discussed by telephone his response
to my letter—the proposal of a summit conference to be held in
East Jerusalem, with the disputing parties and the leaders of the
permanent members of the United Nations Security Council attending. It was an innovative idea, but it would have aroused
enormous controversy and been doomed to failure. On top of all
our other problems, there was no way we could take on the
additional responsibility of adding the Chinese, British, and French
to the group. The potential negotiating table was already crowded
with the United States, the Soviets, the Arabs, the Israelis, and
the Palestinians. Because of Sadat's enthusiasm for his "bold
initiative," my negative response was a very difficult one for me
to deliver.

I did want the germ of the idea to stay alive, and so I continued
to encourage Sadat, who was probing in every direction to find a
means of convening a peace conference leading to Geneva. Sadat
had recently told Secretary Vance that he wanted to meet with
Begin, and Cy had already relayed this information to the Israeli
Prime Minister. On November 9, Sadat made the dramatic announcement to the Egyptian parliament that he would be willing
to go to Jerusalem. On November 15, Prime Minister Begin sent
his government's written reply to me to forward to the Egyptian
President. It was a fine invitation for Sadat to speak to the
Knesset (the Israeli parliament). Begin reminded me that for
twenty-nine years, six Israeli prime ministers had expressed their
readiness to go anywhere to meet with any Arab leader in the
search for peace.

That same day I had my first meeting with the Shah of Iran. I
urged him to support Sadat, which he did, but he warned me not
to expect the Saudi Arabians to favor the visit. I did what I could
to get foreign leaders to refrain from criticism until the results of
Sadat's visit could be assessed. However, it became apparent that
Sadat's announcement had made him very vulnerable. His greatest danger came from the accusation that he would seek only
bilateral Israeli–Egyptian agreement—that Sadat would betray
his Arab brothers and abandon the Palestinian cause merely to
get back the Egyptian territory in the Sinai. Vituperative attacks
on the Egyptian President continued to mount, in spite of re-

peated assurances from Egypt, Israel, and ourselves that a comprehensive peace was our goal.

> *I placed a call to Sadat, to give him my encourage-*
> *ment, my admiration. He was again overly effusive in*
> *his thanks to me. I haven't done anything . . . except to*
> *convince Sadat and Begin that each of them wanted*
> *peace.*   DIARY, NOVEMBER 18, 1977

When Begin and I talked, he was also very complimentary of me and extremely excited about Sadat's visit. I knew, however, that after their first exchange they would still have to face many of the same hard questions.

Meeting with Soviet Ambassador Dobrynin, I told him we needed an early response from the Soviets to Sadat's overture. I urged them to support the visit and to join us in minimizing criticism of Sadat, and made it clear that we would welcome cooperation, but that if they should adopt a negative attitude, we would take a unilateral lead toward a Middle East settlement.

President Sadat's visit to Jerusalem on November 19–21 and his speech to the Knesset were among the most dramatic events of modern history. At the First Baptist Church in Washington, we had a special early morning service during which I prayed pub-licly for peace, and then the congregation adjourned so we could return to our homes in time to watch the arrival ceremonies on television. Sadat made a great speech, spelling out in very blunt terms the Arab requirements for any peace settlement. The mean-ing of the words themselves was muted by the fact that he was standing there alone, before his ancient enemies, holding out an olive branch. The Israeli welcome to him was truly remarkable. The Israelis were also facing *their* ancient enemy.

Along with the people of Israel, Egypt, and most of the Western world, I was thrilled by this tremendous symbolic gesture—but in parts of the Middle East the reaction was just the opposite. Syria broke diplomatic relations with Egypt, and high officials in the Syrian, Libyan, and Iraqi governments called for Sadat's assassi-nation. As the days passed, without any other positive develop-ment, the prospects for a peace conference seemed ever more remote.

> *We've still not gotten any report from our ambassadors in*
> *either Egypt or Israel—from the President or the Prime*
> *Minister. There is general confusion in the Middle East about*

specifically what we should do next. The same confusion
exists in the White House.   DIARY, NOVEMBER 23, 1977

What next? There had been no time for advance consultations
or preparation for further discussions. In the euphoria of the
moment, it did not seem appropriate to go back to the timeworn
arguments about how a peace conference would be arranged or
who would attend. The unchanged presumption was that all of us
would eventually move toward a multinational Geneva type of
conference. President Ceauscescu of Romania and Prime Minister
Raymond Barre of France sent me word that they would help
encourage the more radical Arabs to cooperate. Sadat wanted to
shift the multinational peace conference bodily to Cairo, but when
it became obvious that no one would come, he finally proposed a
Cairo conference to prepare for the Geneva meeting.

The Soviets and all the other Arabs refused to come to Egypt.
Only the three of us—Begin, Sadat, and I—agreed to attend, and
it appeared that Sadat's grand gesture to bring all the parties
together might come to naught. I did not want to drive the Arab
leaders away from us and into the arms of the Soviets, so I asked
Secretary Vance to visit the key countries to assure them that the
goal of a comprehensive peace was not being abandoned.

Sadat's visit to Jerusalem had broken the Arab shell which had
been built to isolate Israel, and there were a few exploratory talks
between the Israelis and Egyptians. However, it was becoming
obvious that Sadat and Begin alone could not go very far in
resolving the basic problems that had not been touched—the
Palestinian issue, the withdrawal of Israeli forces from occupied
territory, Israeli security, or the definition of a real peace. I
continued to pray devoutly that they could do so, and was especially thankful for their new independence from us. But the process
was breaking down again, and both Sadat and other Arab leaders,
even including Assad, informed me that it remained necessary
for the United States to continue playing a leading role in
resolving the basic Middle East questions.

There are discussions going on between Hussein and Assad,
Hussein and Sadat, Assad and [King] Khalid [of Saudi
Arabia]. Maybe during another week we'll know what direc-
tion to take. . . . We want as much responsibility as possible
to be on Begin and Sadat.   DIARY, DECEMBER 6, 1977

In the Middle East, Cy found Hussein to be friendly, Assad cool.
We relayed an urgent message from Sadat to Begin, asking him to

make some statement about the Palestinians and the occupied territories. The Prime Minister responded with a request to come to Washington to present a new proposition, which, he said, could break the deadlock.

Meanwhile, I was under domestic pressure, this time from leaders of the American Arab community and its friends. They were quite critical of our support for Sadat.

They [the Arab-Americans] have given all the staff, Brzezinski, Warren Christopher, and others, a hard time.
DIARY, DECEMBER 15, 1977

When Begin arrived, we were impressed by his plan for the Sinai region, which was far more forthcoming than any previous proposal. In dealing with Egyptian territory, Begin had gone much further than any of his Labor party predecessors, expressing a willingness to return that portion of the Sinai from Sharm el-Sheyk up the coast to Eilat, and to withdraw Israeli forces if Sadat would demilitarize the Sinai east of the Gidi and Mitla passes. His proposal on the West Bank was not acceptable, however, although I considered it a step in the right direction.

Begin called it his "autonomy plan." He was willing to withhold Israeli claims of sovereignty over the West Bank for a limited period and grant to the residents of the occupied territories authority over domestic affairs. He emphasized that he wanted peace with all his neighbors, and that there would be no separate peace with Egypt.

We had a thorough discussion. I expressed my concern that his proposal was inadequate and that the inadequacy of it might cause the downfall of Sadat. I urged him not to make any public statement about it until after Sadat has a chance to assess it. He promised to do this.   DIARY, DECEMBER 16, 1977

Begin was favorably impressed the next day when I said that Sadat's initiative in coming to Jerusalem was like those of Begin's idol, Ze'ev Jabotinsky—a Zionist leader who had fought for the establishment of Israel as a nation—bold, and striving for a final conclusion without incremental negotiations. I was hoping, of course, that the Prime Minister would do the same, but all he would agree to say was that on the West Bank, "the Israeli military government would be abolished." He also agreed that whatever rights to settle in the West Bank area the Jews might claim, the Palestinian Arabs could claim the same rights to buy property and settle in Israel. Begin sounded much more flexible regarding the West Bank than I had expected, but I was to discover that his good words had multiple meanings, which my advisers and I did not understand at the time. He promised to be very cautious in his comments, so as not to embarrass Sadat.

> *I feel protective of Sadat, and in a strange way so does*
> *Begin.*   DIARY, DECEMBER 17, 1977

President Sadat would need all the protection we could offer. During the next few days, as Begin explained his plan to Prime Minister Callaghan in London and then to the Egyptians, it was attenuated substantially. He also sent me word that he would have to change his position on Arab property rights in Israel, claiming that his cabinet would not accept the promise he had given me.

Immediately after Christmas, Sadat and Begin met in Ismailia. Two diametrically conflicting reports emerged. Begin called the meeting a big success, saying that although they had issued separate statements on their positions, they were not as far apart as this might indicate. Sadat thought the meeting was a complete failure, a real setback for the peace initiative. In the absence of any further progress between Israel and Egypt, it was beginning to seem that the only permanent result of Sadat's visit to Israel might be the cancellation of the Geneva peace conference.

At the end of the year, I set out on a quick trip to Poland, Iran, India, and Saudi Arabia, and arranged for brief additional meetings toward the Middle East peace effort. Although I did not have time to go to Jordan, King Hussein joined the Shah of Iran and me in Tehran on New Year's Eve. The following morning, we discussed Sadat and his visit to Jerusalem.

> *All three of us agreed that we ought to give Sadat our*
> *support; that the basis for a Middle East peace settlement*
> *should be UN Resolutions 242 and 338; that there should*
> *be some minor modifications of the 1967 Israeli borders;*
> *that the people in the West Bank–Gaza area should have*
> *self-determination but not the right to claim indepen-*
> *dence.... Both the Shah and King Hussein said that*
> *they want to go after I do to Saudi Arabia and to Egypt to*
> *try to express support for Sadat.*   DIARY, JANUARY 1, 1978

They later made this effort, but soon all the Arab leaders decided not to issue any public statements endorsing Sadat's initiative. The safe thing for them to do was to sit back, let others do the tough negotiating, and see what happened. Again, they were privately supportive, publicly silent or critical.

At one point on the trip, Rosalynn, Cy, Zbig, and I discussed my first year in office and decided that, as far as foreign policy was concerned, 1977 had been the year of the Middle East. Some progress had been made toward bringing two of the former enemies together, but the prospects for further success were doubtful.

My next stop was Saudi Arabia, whose country and rulers interested me a great deal. I had heard that King Khalid was a quiet and reticent man who liked to avoid direct conversations with foreign visitors, but on the drive from the airport, I found him to be just the opposite. He was quite excited and extremely talkative, describing to me the interesting sights along the way and telling me about falcon hunting and about his method of governing. Each day he held open court, so that any citizen of his country could come in and visit with him. When he ate dinner and supper, his table was open for common people to dine; and in the evening, he set aside a public time when women could seek his help or advice, including those in the royal household. When the King traveled around the country into the desert regions, he carried along a complete portable hospital to serve the communities he visited, mounted on five or six Mercedes truck chassis. This treatment facility included operating rooms, x-ray machines, and intensive-care beds, and usually accommodated a hundred or more patients each day. During the same time, King Khalid himself ordinarily received visits from at least three hundred Bedouins. This behavior is a tradition of the el-Saud royal family. His Majesty said proudly, "This is a valued right of our people. Any leader who renounced this custom would be overthrown."

On January 3, we had some very rewarding discussions with the Saudis, led by Crown Prince Fahd. Although often the forceful spokesman for Saudi Arabia, he was quite deferential to the King, pausing to seek His Majesty's opinion about controversial subjects. I outlined our standard approach to the Middle East problems, and found the Saudis interested and constructive. They expressed their unequivocal support for Sadat, because they wanted peace and stability in the region, but merely smiled when I urged them to make this known through their public statements; they did not want to alienate the more militant Arabs. The Saudi leaders were knowledgeable, tough negotiators, surprisingly frank and good-humored. They made it obvious to me that they would accept some minor modifications in the 1967 Israeli borders, but they were adamant in their commitment to an independent Palestinian state.

They were the only Arab leaders I had met who maintained this strong position even in private. At a meeting in Rabat following the October War of 1973, the Arab leaders had agreed that the PLO would be the sole representative of the Palestinians and should have a nation-state on the West Bank. Now, with the prospect of peace, some of them thought it was time for the PLO to accept Israel's existence and work to settle the conflict under the general provisions of United Nations Resolution 242. Furthermore, almost all the Arabs could see that an independent nation in the heart of the Middle East might be a serious point of friction and a focus for radicalizing influence. A Palestinian homeland with ties to a sovereign Jordan would be more acceptable, some of them said privately. However, because of the powerful political influence of the PLO in international councils and the threat of terrorist attacks from some of its forces, few Arabs had the temerity to depart from their original position in a public statement.

We stayed in an opulent palace, the home of the late King Faisal. That evening we had a delightful official banquet, enjoying camel's milk and such staple Saudi foods as barley, chicken, and fruits. The King was especially interested in having me eat some of the desert truffles he himself had found on a recent hunting trip. These fungi, which grow under the ground when the deserts receive rain in November and December, are prized as a delicacy.

Since Saudi women are usually kept in relative seclusion, Rosalynn was a center of attraction when we traveled in public. There was some discussion about where she should walk among the American and Saudi dignitaries. When we decided to observe our own customs at least during those times, our hosts did not register any objection. Rosalynn had a delightful evening with the queens and princesses while we men were at the banquet.

I wanted to stay, but we had to cut short our visit in order to make a very brief stop in Aswan, Egypt, to see President Sadat. This was to be my most exciting visit of all because of intense worldwide interest in the Middle East. Although we had spoken on the telephone, this was the first time I had seen Sadat since he had gone to Jerusalem. I was eager to get a face-to-face report from him.

Our plane was on the ground in Aswan for only an hour and a half, but it was long enough for all the arrival and departure ceremonies, a photograph with Chancellor Helmut Schmidt, who was visiting, the general session including advisers, and my private conversation with Sadat. There were no differences between us, and we made brief comments to the press about the issues as we saw them.

It was obvious what Sadat had on his mind. "We are heading toward peace, real peace in the area—permanent peace." My own statement even included some carefully crafted phrases about the Palestinian question, which Sadat and I thought Israel might accept as one of the three parts of an ultimate agreement:

> First, true peace must be based on normal relations among the parties to the peace. Peace means more than just an end to belligerency.
>
> Second, there must be withdrawal by Israel from territories occupied in 1967 and agreement on secure and recognized borders for all parties in the context of normal and peaceful relations. . . .
>
> Third, there must be a resolution of the Palestinian problem in all its aspects. The solution must recognize the legitimate rights of the Palestinian people and enable the Palestinians to participate in the determination of their own future.

After taking off, we circled the Aswan Dam and followed the Nile River for a short distance. Rosalynn and I agreed that our first priority for a foreign vacation would be a return to Egypt. I immediately called Prime Minister Begin from the airplane and gave him a brief review of my visits with the leaders of Iran, Jordan, Saudi Arabia, and Egypt, promising him a more complete report by diplomatic cable.

Last, I visited Paris, where I had extensive discussions with President Valéry Giscard d'Estaing. The French gave us an extraordinary welcome—far beyond what normal protocol would have required. We laid a wreath at the Arc de Triomphe, and then, on the spur of the moment, Valéry and I walked down the Champs Elysées, waving and shaking hands with the crowds jammed along the way to greet us.

One of the emotional highlights of my life came the next day, with our helicopter trip to Normandy to visit the five beaches where Americans had landed during the final months of the Second World War. I had earlier complained to Valéry that we Americans had been hurt and annoyed by DeGaulle's arrogance and cold attitude toward the United States. He answered that De Gaulle considered it necessary at the end of the war to restore the spirit and self-esteem of France after the German occupation. Valéry seemed to respond to my comments in his gracious speeches. He pointed out at Normandy that we had liberated France, and even made his speech in English. Charles DeGaulle probably turned over in his grave. There were many tears as the bugler played taps over the American burial sites and I mentioned that the soldiers of the First World War had said, "Lafayette, we are here!" when they landed in France.

We drove slowly from the beaches into the nearby village of Bayeux, passing thousands of French citizens waving the flags of our two countries. A strong, cold wind was blowing, but the weather did not dampen any spirits. We all noticed one middle-aged woman standing in front of a picturesque farmer's cottage, holding an enormous and official-looking American flag and struggling to keep it erect in the gusting wind. She was wearing an old dress several sizes too small for her stout figure, hiked up well above her knees. The woman was smiling and weeping at the same time. We guessed that some American soldiers had given her their company's Stars and Stripes and that she may now have been wearing the same dress she wore to welcome them to France. To some driving by it may have been a ludicrous sight, but to me she looked absolutely beautiful.

Valéry and I had time for two or three hours of intensive discussions as we traveled back to Paris by train. I also had a chance to give our French friends a full report on my discussions with the Arab leaders. They were surprised by the extent of support for Sadat, which was certainly not apparent from any of the Arabs' public statements.

I returned to the United States on January 6, concerned about the deterioration in the Begin–Sadat relationship. What could be done to revive their progress toward peace? The Israelis were not honoring the commitment Dayan had given me about their settlement policy, but were building up those enclaves in the occupied territories as rapidly as possible. Whenever we seemed to be having some success with the Arabs, Begin would proclaim the establishment of another group of settlements, or make other provocative statements. This behavior was not only very irritating, but it seriously endangered the prospects for peace and Sadat's status both in Egypt and within the Arab world. The repeated Israeli invasions or bombings of Lebanon also precipitated crises;

a stream of fairly harsh messages was going back and forth between me in Washington and Begin in Jerusalem.

Secretary of State Vance spent a lot of time in the two countries trying to keep the negotiations going, but his was a difficult and thankless task. At a banquet in Israel attended by Cy and the Egyptian negotiating team, Prime Minister Begin's opening remarks offended the Egyptians. President Sadat ordered the withdrawal of all Egyptians from Israel and threatened to conclude the peace talks altogether. I called to urge him to leave his negotiators in Jerusalem, but he refused. Finally he decided to permit the Israeli military leaders to come to Egypt, because he had confidence in Israel's Defense Minister, Ezer Weizman.

> *Talked to Cy Vance, who's going to stay in Jerusalem and then go to see Sadat. He thinks that we can hold together the discussions, although they were on the verge of breaking down.*   DIARY, JANUARY 18, 1978

Two days later I had a long talk with Brzezinski about the entire Middle East situation. We were not making progress, and Sadat was letting us know that he was preparing to renounce the talks with Israel because of his growing embarrassment and frustration. We cast about for some action to be taken, and for the first time discussed the possibility of inviting both Begin and Sadat to Camp David to engage in extensive negotiations with me. I could not possibly spare the time until after we had completed some of my work with Congress, but it was obvious that something had to be done. That weekend, Cy came back to Washington with the dismal report that there was no prospect for the peace talks to succeed.

> *We decided to send Sadat an invitation to come over here and meet with me, maybe for a weekend at Camp David— and if the military and political talks break down, to have both Sadat and Begin over here together.*
>   DIARY, JANUARY 23, 1978

I asked Kissinger to come by for a private lunch with Rosalynn and me, so that I could tell him about the immediate plans. He agreed with my analysis and approach, but cautioned me against coming back from Camp David with any indication of substantial agreement between Sadat and me, because that would put the Israelis on the defensive. He recommended that I do everything possible to convince Sadat that we would not leave him standing alone, but would use our full influence to obtain a settlement. He did not think Begin had any intention of giving up the West Bank or moving Israeli settlers out of the Sinai, but he believed that the settlers would eventually leave voluntarily if placed under Egyptian protection. It was a helpful discussion as I prepared for Sadat's visit.

> *We had quite an argument at breakfast, with me on one side and Fritz, Cy, Zbig, and Ham on the other. I think we ought to move much more aggressively on the Middle East question than any of them seem to, by evolving a clear plan for private use among ourselves . . . discussing the various elements with Sadat, one by one, encouraging him to cooperate with us by preventing any surprises in the future, and by inducing him to understand Begin's position. The plan that we evolve has got to be one that can be accepted by Begin in a showdown if we have the full support of the American public. . . . I don't know how much support I have, but we'll go through with this effort.*   DIARY, FEBRUARY 3, 1978

The bone of contention was whether we should develop an "American plan" and try to sell it to Sadat and Begin. In effect, I decided on this course of action, but not to give our suggestions a name. I knew that any proposal would be doomed if it originated with us alone or bilaterally with either of the other two countries. Acceptable plans must always seem to come from joint negotiations. Of course, I also wanted Sadat and Begin to keep as much direct responsibility as possible for the success of the peace talks.

When Anwar and Jihan Sadat arrived, Rosalynn and I went to Camp David with them, a thirty-five minute flight by helicopter. The snow-covered landscape was lovely, and I thought they would like to walk the few hundred yards from the landing site to our cabin. This was a mistake. I wanted them to enjoy the stroll, but by the time we reached our fireplace, President Sadat was cold and extremely worried about his health. As we warmed ourselves, the Sadats said they were tired after their long trip from Cairo to Morocco and then to Washington. We had a quick supper, and they went to bed quite early.

The next morning, February 4, we held a long discussion, with Sadat doing most of the talking. First he reviewed recent events, beginning with our initial meeting the previous April, when he had told me that never in our lifetime would any Arab meet my definition of peace and establish normal trade and diplomatic relations with Israel. He recalled the handwritten note I had sent him the past autumn, urging him to take dramatic action to start some progress toward peace because we were bogged down in details. As he talked, I began to anticipate an ominous ending to his discourse, but decided not to interrupt. Uncharacteristically, Sadat was following a few entries on a small piece of paper. He and his staff had obviously prepared remarks in a more formal way than usual. I made some notes of that meeting.

> Sadat said that he, encouraged by Fahmy, had first proposed to me a meeting of the five big powers in Jerusalem, which I had rejected. He didn't want it anyhow. He listed the things that Israel really wanted: direct negotiations with Arab leaders, recognition as a permanent entity in the Middle East, to live in peace—true peace. . . . He said the Israelis never dreamed that Egypt would approve these points, but he decided that in one fell swoop he would accomplish all these Israeli desires. He thinks his initiative to go to Jerusalem took the Israelis by surprise, that they were not ready for peace, and possibly still are not. . . . At Ismailia he was completely disillusioned with Begin's "ridiculous" position. . . . When Begin proposed a political committee and a military committee, Sadat agreed before they even got to the conference room. When Begin raised the question of settlements in the Sinai, Sadat said he honestly thought it was just a joke. And then when Begin spelled out his self-rule proposal, which was quite different from the one he had outlined to me or to Prime Minister Callaghan, it was obvious that Egypt could not accept it. Begin was committed to his own proposal, and said to Sadat that they were leaving that afternoon. Sadat induced them to stay overnight. They made a joint statement to the press, which indicated that their positions were at odds.

Sadat was very bitter as he described Begin's attitude since that return visit to Egypt, saying that the Prime Minister had rejected advice from Dayan and from Weizman for a moderate position, and yielded to pressure from Agriculture Minister Ariel Sharon, who was calling for a massive program to settle hundreds of thousands of Jews in the West Bank. Sadat was convinced that Begin did not want peace.

Sadat then informed me that he is going to announce to the

National Press Club Monday that [the Egyptians] will discontinue their participation in the military or political talks, that they've given Israel everything they possibly could have dreamed of a year ago, that he had 100 million Arabs with him—90 per cent of the Arab world. . . . I pointed out, helped later by Vance and Brzezinski and Mondale, that this would be a very serious blow; would make Begin look good and Sadat look like an obstacle to peace.

I finally convinced him to put his statement in positive terms—that he would recommence the talks, provided Begin would accept United Nations Resolution 242 in its entirety, not insist on illegal settlements, and so forth. He and I spent a long time going through all the old issues, including the details of security requirements for Israel. I tried to persuade him to permit some of the Israelis to stay in the Sinai settlements under United Nations protection. He was quite flexible on all other points, but adamantly opposed to this one. He agreed to keep the major Egyptian military forces west of the mountain passes, in effect demilitarizing most of the Sinai region. Although he did not want a divided Jerusalem, he said there should be joint sovereignty over the area where the religious sites are located.

By the time we finished our conversations, I was reasonably confident that his upcoming speech to the press club would not be particularly damaging, and he did not disappoint me. Sadat was pleased when I told him I would be seeing Dayan soon and that we would invite Begin later in the spring. He promised to draft a counterproposal for Begin, but said it would not be as detailed as the Prime Minister's.

Dayan was scheduled to arrive in a few days, and in the meantime I squeezed in conferences with American leaders who were strong supporters of Israel to inform them about Sadat's visit. They agreed that Begin's settlements policy was a serious mistake, and were very surprised that after all these years, the Israelis now claimed that United Nations Resolution 242 did not apply to the occupied territories. At that time, our government's relations with Israel were not very good.

> *I watched Dayan's television program . . . when he insinuated that we were anti-Israel and no longer could be honest brokers—and . . . that Cy Vance in his opposition to the settlements was different in that position from my own.*   DIARY, FEBRUARY 12, 1978

None of this was true, and we could not understand why Dayan seemed nervous and confused on other issues. (From Dayan's later published explanation it is clear he was in a bad mood because he had received harsh criticism from the American Jews and had to defend a settlement policy he opposed.) After Cy had a long talk with him, Dayan had two questions for me: Would Sadat insist that Israel negotiate with Syria before a peace treaty could be signed? And would Sadat sign a treaty if the Sinai dispute could be completely resolved and principles agreed upon for the occupied territories and Palestinians, even though Hussein might refuse to join the subsequent talks? I told him the answer to the first question was no, but that Sadat had given conflicting signals on the second. When I sent the question to Sadat, there was no immediate answer, but several weeks later, in a long handwritten letter, President Sadat said the agreed principles would have to be specific and contribute to better understanding by everyone and not increase the confusion, and that he would need to have maximum participation by other Arabs.

I was in the midst of the Panama vote when, on March 10, Israeli Defense Minister Ezer Weizman came to see me for the first time. He made a good impression on all of us. Charming and level-headed, he had a very mature assessment of the attitude of the Egyptian leaders and what could be done to resolve the many differences still remaining between the two countries. Having worked closely with Begin for several years as a political associate and being the one Israeli leader who was trusted and liked by Sadat, Weizman assessed the issues with an air of confidence and a degree of objectivity that were rare among any of the Middle East leaders.

My discussion with Weizman was very useful, because Dayan, in his highly critical mood, had not helped much to prepare us for the upcoming Begin visit. Sadat had raised some very specific questions about Israel's attitude, several of which I could not answer. The meeting with Begin would be important, and I wanted it to be a pleasant and constructive session.

On the afternoon of March 11, I received word that PLO terrorists had launched an attack on the Israeli coast, killing thirty-five people. All but two of these victims were civilians. I immediately sent a message of condolence to Begin.

Three days later the Israelis retaliated with an invasion of Lebanon. In the fighting, more than a thousand noncombatants were killed and more than a hundred thousand left homeless. Israeli invasion forces remained in Lebanon. To me this seemed a terrible overreaction by the Israelis, and I instructed Cy to tell them that we would introduce a resolution in the United Nations

calling for their withdrawal from Lebanon and the establishment
of a United Nations peacekeeping force there; and that I was
particularly disturbed because American weapons, including extremely lethal cluster bombs, had been used in the operation,
contrary to our agreement when they were sold.

The Israelis were still in Lebanon when Prime Minister and
Mrs. Begin arrived on March 21. Rosalynn and I invited them to a
private supper, during which we learned a lot about them. They
told us about their early life together, the murder of his parents
and only brother in the Holocaust, and his imprisonments in
Poland and Lithuania for political activity. When the meal was
over, I understood some of his attitudes much better, but this new
understanding did not help much when we walked over to the
Oval Office to talk about official issues.

> *After supper he and I went over to my private office for an*
> *hour and a half of intense, sometimes emotional discus-*
> *sion about the Middle East. I reviewed the recent months,*
> *beginning with Sadat's visit [to Israel]. Gave Begin credit*
> *for what he had done in the way of response, and for a*
> *long time we talked back and forth, narrowing down the*
> *points to sharp issues for the first time in my relationship*
> *with Israel. He said that he was "wounded in the heart"*
> *when his December plan [offering to withdraw from the*
> *Sinai] had first received words of praise which had later*
> *faded away. That Sadat's visit to Jerusalem was only a*
> *grand gesture; that Egypt wanted an independent Palestin-*
> *ian state and total withdrawal. I told him this was abso-*
> *lutely not true. I knew for a fact. And if my presumption*
> *was correct, what would he be willing to do to achieve*
> *peace? The answer, in effect, was nothing beyond what he*
> *had already proposed.*   DIARY, MARCH 21, 1978

After the Prime Minister left, I called Secretary Vance and
found that he had gotten basically the same response from Foreign Minister Dayan, who had accompanied the Prime Minister
to Washington. We decided it was time to fish or cut bait, so
the next morning I got up much earlier than usual and jotted
down a few specific questions which would have to be answered.

> *In the meeting with Begin and Dayan I described the*
> *presumptions that Sadat and I had worked out for a*
> *possible peace settlement, namely: no complete withdrawal*
> *by Israel from the West Bank; no independent Palestinian*

nation; self-rule in the West Bank–Gaza Strip; withdrawal of Israeli forces to negotiated security outposts; some modification of the western boundaries of the West Bank; devolution of power to the local authorities from both Israel and Jordan; no claim of sovereignty [by either nation] for a five-year period; at the end of the five-year period the Palestinian Arabs who live in the occupied territory will have the right to vote either on affiliation with Israel or Jordan or continuation of the so-called "interim government" if they find it to be attractive; the ceasing of new or expanded settlements during time of active negotiation.

. . . I then read to Begin and his group my understanding of their position: not willing to withdraw politically or militarily from any part of the West Bank; not willing to stop the construction of new settlements or the expansion of existing settlements; not willing to withdraw the Israeli settlers from the Sinai, or even leave them there under UN or Egyptian protection; not willing to acknowledge that UN Resolution 242 applies to the West Bank–Gaza area; not willing to grant the Palestinian Arabs real authority, or a voice in the determination of their own future to the extent that they can choose between the alternatives outlined above. Although Begin said this was a negative way to express their position, he did not deny the accuracy of any of it. [These became known as "the six no's."]   DIARY, MARCH 22, 1978

Again, I was prepared to withdraw from the Middle East issue altogether. It would be a great relief to me, and I certainly had my hands full with other responsibilities. Dayan, perhaps stretching the bounds of his loyalty to the Prime Minister, tried to put the best face on the highly charged confrontation. He pointed out that the Israeli military camps were not located in populated cities, that the Israelis did not want any political control over the Arab population in the West Bank, that there was no objection to the Palestinians' exercising choice over their future, and that Israel recognized that something had to be done about the Arab refugees. I realized that Dayan was expressing his own deeply felt sentiments, but it was clear to everyone on both sides of the table that, unless he changed his positions, Begin was becoming an insurmountable obstacle to further progress.

This was a heartbreaking development, and I began to inform the congressional leaders who supported Israel about our failure, being careful to describe the positions of Sadat and Begin as accurately as I could, checking each point with my personal notes. Some of them met with Prime Minister Begin and confirmed "the six no's." They, too, were discouraged.

For the next month or so there was no change in the Middle East situation, except that the strains between us and Israel may have grown. There were two ongoing political struggles—over Israeli military forces in Lebanon and over our sale of F-15 fighter planes to Saudi Arabia. The first involved the United Nations, and the second would be decided in Congress, where tremendous pressure was being applied to block the sale.

On the first of May, Prime Minister Begin came over to join in the American commemoration of the thirtieth anniversary of the State of Israel, and I had a chance to meet with him for a private discussion.

> *I told him that peace in the Middle East was in his hands, that he had a unique opportunity to either bring it into being or kill it, and that he understood that the Arabs genuinely wanted peace, particularly Sadat. He had seen the expression on the faces of people in Cairo, Ismailia, and Jerusalem when they exchanged visits, and there was no doubt in his mind about it. . . . My guess is that he will not take the necessary steps to bring peace to Israel—an opportunity that may never come again.*   DIARY, MAY 1, 1978

We had arranged a White House reception after the meeting, inviting two hundred rabbis to celebrate Israel's anniversary. Twelve hundred people showed up at the gates. We asked all of them in, moving the entire affair out onto the South Lawn, and Begin and I made brief but somewhat emotional speeches. I promised our nation's permanent support for Israel, and offered to set up a commission to establish an American memorial for the victims of the Holocaust. Then Begin and I shook hands with every guest. It turned out to be a very positive and heartwarming experience, but had very little effect either in the Middle East or within our country. I still had serious political problems among American Jews, and a few days later we had to postpone two major Democratic fund-raising banquets in New York and Los Angeles because so many party members had canceled their reservations to attend.

The weeks dragged by. I had little time to devote to the Middle

East except to relay a few questions back and forth between Cairo and Jerusalem. There was no further direct communication between the two leaders, and at one time Sadat even spoke publicly of going to war.

Late in June, I called in a small group of Democratic "wise men"—senior leaders who were experienced in political affairs. Their advice was to "stay as aloof as possible from direct involvement in the Middle East negotiations; this is a losing proposition." At that time, I could not think of any reason to disagree with them, but there was just no way I could abandon such an important commitment unless the situation became absolutely hopeless.

A visit by Vice President Mondale to Israel and Egypt had already been planned. When he came back with a very discouraging report, we began to discuss how to deal with the failure of the peace initiative. We finally decided that Secretary Vance should meet with the foreign ministers of Israel and Egypt on neutral ground, in Leeds Castle in England, only to see if there was enough remaining desire for peace on which to build.

No positions were changed at Leeds, and Cy came back to Washington so that we could plan our overall strategy. Most of us were inclined to make one last major effort. At our regular Friday morning foreign-affairs breakfast, we spent much of our time talking about the Middle East. We tried to think of some way to induce Sadat and Begin to be more patient and less abusive in their public statements about each other. Sadat was very frustrated and angry, and seemed willing to precipitate some sort of crisis. When he announced that there would be no further negotiations, I did not understand what he was planning to do.

> Sadat has demanded that the Israeli military team leave Egypt. I think he's trying to set the stage for us to get involved more deeply in the Mideast dispute. That's our intention, but we want to approach it carefully.
> DIARY, JULY 27, 1978

> Sadat is meeting with the radical Arabs to try to repair his fences with them, which is not a good omen. My hope is that he still is depending on us and will accommodate what I propose.
> DIARY, JULY 28, 1978

I was really in a quandary. I knew how vital peace in the Middle East was to the United States, but many Democratic members of Congress and party officials were urging me to back out of the situation and to repair the damage they claimed I had already done to the Democratic party and to United States–Israeli relations. It seemed particularly ironic to be so accused, when I was trying to bolster our relations with Israel and strengthen its security.

I discussed the situation with Rosalynn, who was thoroughly familiar with the issues involved in the Middle East dispute and understood what was at stake. There was no prospect for success if Begin and Sadat stayed apart, and their infrequent meetings had now become fruitless because the two men were too personally incompatible to compromise on the many difficult issues facing them. I finally decided it would be best, win or lose, to go all out. There was only one thing to do, as dismal and unpleasant as the prospect seemed—I would try to bring Sadat and Begin together for an extensive negotiating session with me.

I asked Mondale, Vance, Brown, Brzezinski, and Jordan to come to Camp David for a special meeting on the Middle East. There I described what I had in mind. None of us thought we had much chance of success, but we could not think of a better alternative.

> *We decided to send Cy on to the Mideast in spite of Sadat's rejection of any further negotiations, and suggest that the two men come to Camp David for a meeting directly with me. We understand the political pitfalls involved, but the situation is getting into an extreme state, and I'm concerned that Sadat might precipitate a conflict in October, as he has hinted several times. The Arabs are really pushing Sadat and, [so as] not to stay vulnerable in the long run, I think he is wanting either to come back to them or to some resolution of the question.* DIARY, JULY 31, 1978

I wrote long, almost identical letters to Sadat and Begin, and Vance flew to the Middle East with the envelopes in his pocket. We were all sworn to secrecy until the two leaders could respond.

Both Begin and Sadat agreed enthusiastically to the Camp David invitation; Sadat asked only that we schedule the meeting immediately after the Moslem holy days, the first week in September. All three of us agreed to keep our plans confidential until we could make a simultaneous announcement on August 8.

On that morning, I briefed the congressional leaders, notified the two former Presidents, and gave the information to a few news leaders in advance of the public statement. With the exception of Senator Baker, who was cautious, and Senator Jackson, who was very critical, the response was positive and supportive. All of us wanted to minimize expectations, citing clarification of the issues as our objective. I had something much more substantive in mind, but had a lot of work to do before my ideas would be clear.

> *I told Cy to send messages to many of the world leaders, brief and noncontroversial, asking for their support. We'll ask the religious leaders to set aside a week of special prayer. . . . We will use every influence we have at Camp David to make it successful, and not put a time limit on how long we stay there. We will have no press contact except minimal, through one spokesman—that'll be Jody— and we'll hold down expectations of success between now and the meeting at Camp David. We will have to keep Sadat and Begin convinced before they get here that they must make concessions and negotiate freely. They both agreed not to have negative statements issued between now and the convening of the meeting.*
>
> DIARY, AUGUST 10, 1978

After our original decision to go to Camp David, I was deluged with warnings from my closest advisers and friends. It was only human to want to be "on the record" with an accurate prediction, particularly about such a highly publicized event as this summit meeting. No one, including me, could think of a specific route to success, but everyone could describe a dozen logical scenarios for failure—and all were eager to do so. I slowly became hardened against them, and as stubborn as at any other time I can remember.

Sadat and Begin found it difficult to comply with my request that they refrain completely from negative comments or those that portrayed a spirit of inflexibility. However, compared to past performances, they did very well.

I instructed both Vance and Brzezinski not to consult with each other but independently to devise briefing notebooks for me, envisioning an ultimate agreement. Neither of them would find this assignment easy.

My most difficult arguments were with Jody and Jerry Rafshoon, who were responsible for my relations with the press and for giving the American people an accurate report of my activities. They complained bitterly about my decision to exclude the press from Camp David during the negotiations, and came back repeatedly with a series of alternate plans for varying degrees of contact between the news media and members of the Egyptian, Israeli, and American delegations. I rejected them all, in what became an unpleasant confrontation. I felt that in going to Camp David we would be burning our bridges, that the meeting was an all-or-nothing gamble, and that what the press might report during the negotiating session was no longer important to me. It was imperative that there be a minimum of posturing by Egyptians or Israelis, and an absence of public statements, which would become frozen positions that could not subsequently be changed.

⤳

THIRTEEN DAYS

After four wars, despite vast human efforts, the Holy Land does not yet enjoy the blessings of peace.

Conscious of the grave issues which face us, we place our trust in the God of our fathers, from whom we seek wisdom and guidance.

As we meet here at Camp David we ask people of all faiths to pray with us that peace and justice may result from these deliberations.

JOINT STATEMENT ISSUED AT
CAMP DAVID, SEPTEMBER 6, 1978

It was an especially beautiful evening in one of the loveliest places on earth. We were staying for a few days of rest in the Brinkerhoff Lodge on the edge of Jackson Lake in Wyoming. The Grand Tetons rose into the clear sky across the water—some of our newest and most unweathered mountains, the sharp peaks a breathtaking spectacle. Earlier in the day, I had been fly fishing for cutthroat trout in the nearby Snake River. Then, late in the afternoon, Amy and I had picked wild huckleberries in a grove of quaking aspen near the cabin, and we all enjoyed a delicious berry pie for supper. Although it was not cold, Rosalynn and I built a small fire just to watch the flames in the open fireplace. All in all, August 29 had been one of those special days I would not forget.

But at its close my thoughts were not on the cutthroat trout, the delicious food, or the beauties of nature. It was late at night, and I was very tired. I was studying a thick volume, written especially for me, about two men—Menachem Begin and Anwar el-Sadat. In a few days, on September 5, I would welcome them to Camp David. I was already familiar with the issues we would be discussing, because we had debated them privately and through the news media for months—without success. Ours would be a new approach, perhaps unprecedented in history. Three leaders of nations would be isolated from the outside world. An intensely personal effort would be required of us. I had to understand these men!

I was poring over psychological analyses of two of the protagonists which had been prepared by a team of experts within our
intelligence community. This team could write definitive biogra-
phies of any important world leader, using information derived
from a detailed scrutiny of events, public statements, writings,
known medical histories, and interviews with personal acquaintances of the leaders under study. I wanted to know all about
Begin and Sadat. What had made them national leaders? What
was the root of their ambition? What were their most important
goals in life? What events during past years had helped to shape
their characters? What were their religious beliefs? Family relations? State of their health? Political beliefs and constraints?
Relations with other leaders? Likely reaction to intense pressure
in a time of crisis? Strengths and weaknesses? Commitments to
political constituencies? Attitudes toward me and the United
States? Whom did they *really* trust? What was their attitude
toward one another? I was certain they were preparing for our
summit conference in a similar manner.

From time to time I paused to consider the negotiating strategy
I would follow at Camp David; I made careful detailed notes.
These few quiet evenings away from Washington were an ideal
time for me to concentrate almost exclusively on a single major
challenge—peace in the Middle East. During the coming days at
Camp David, my studies at the foot of the Grand Tetons were to
pay rich dividends.

Now, Washington was calling me back home. The natural-gas
legislation and my entire effort for a coherent national energy
policy were in serious trouble. Both the Vice President and the
leaders of Congress thought we would lose this crucial legislative
fight unless I returned early to Washington. Fritz suggested that
the abbreviation of my vacation would demonstrate the importance we attached to the energy proposals. Deciding that we
could not risk a defeat, I returned to the White House.

To break the congressional deadlock over the natural-gas bill, I
decided to contact every member, as we had on the Panama
Canal treaties. Soon we began to make some progress. Except for
energy, I shifted as many of my responsibilities as possible to the
Vice President and other members of my administration, so that
during the remaining few days I could concentrate on my preparations for the Middle East summit meeting.

To be sure I was apprised of the latest developments and to
have the personal advice of our most knowledgeable people, I
recalled to Washington our Ambassadors from Egypt and Israel.

Hermann Eilts, who came in from Cairo, was an expert on the affairs of the entire Middle East. He understood the Arab countries, leaders, and people, and he knew the history of Israel at first hand, having been stationed in the region for more than thirty years—since the nation of Israel was born. Sam Lewis, who headed our team in Israel, had already demonstrated to me that he both understood and was trusted by the Israeli officials. On more than one occasion, I had even become angry with him because I thought he was representing the views of Israel too strongly when they differed from my own.

I invited Eilts and Lewis to a private lunch in the Roosevelt Room, adjacent to the Oval Office, so that they could brief me thoroughly on what to expect at Camp David from the two negotiating teams. It was important for me to meet with them together, so they could listen to one another and more accurately assess the prospects for success. Both ambassadors confirmed Begin's and Sadat's enthusiasm for the idea of the summit meeting.

Their on-the-spot reports made me even more critical of the strategy briefing books prepared for me by the State Department and the National Security staff, whose expressed goals for Camp David had been very modest. Their only hope was that we could derive a declaration of principles as a basis for future negotiations. Often, under such circumstances, the tendency of a group of advisers was to arrive at the lowest common denominator of goals, to be very cautious in predicting or expecting a significant victory, and to make thorough plans for explaining or rationalizing prospective failure. Sometimes this approach was sound, but in this particular case, we had already risked the possibility of total failure and great embarrassment. We could not lose much more by aiming for success.

I directed our negotiating group to assume as our immediate ambition a written agreement for peace between Egypt and Israel, with an agenda for implementation of its terms during the succeeding months. I was convinced that if we three leaders could not resolve the very difficult issues, some of which had never before been addressed forthrightly, then no group of foreign ministers or diplomats could succeed. Both President Sadat and Prime Minister Begin were courageous men, well-liked and trusted in their own countries, who could make tough decisions with relative political impunity. If the *overall* settlement proved to be popular, then some of the unpopular details would be acceptable.

I had no idea whether we would succeed. I only knew that we were at a turning point and that the stakes were very high. We were prepared to stay as long as necessary to explore all the potential agreements. Our plans called for three days, but we were willing to stay as long as a week if we were making good progress and success seemed attainable. We never dreamed we would be there through thirteen intense and discouraging days, with success in prospect only during the final hours.

Over the weekend I tried to wrap up as many issues as possible. My telephone calls to key senators on the natural-gas legislation were encouraging, and I was impressed with Robert Byrd's determination to win this legislative struggle.

It was important for me to be alone for a while at Camp David before my guests arrived, because until the last minute I had been deluged in Washington with suggestions, requests, information, and advice. One important meeting had been with Ed Sanders, a White House adviser, who had given me a summary of the attitude of the American Jewish community leaders. They were said to be more restrained than we had expected, and this encouraged me greatly in my later arguments with Begin.

I instructed the Vice President to take charge of things in Washington, and on Monday, September 4, I went to Camp David with all my maps, briefing books, notes, summaries of past negotiations, and my annotated Bible, which I predicted—accurately, as it turned out—would be needed in my discussions with Prime Minister Begin. Before it was all over, I would also have mastered major portions of a good dictionary and thesaurus, and would have become an amateur semanticist as well.

I wanted Rosalynn with me during the coming days for personal support and advice, and to help me with routine duties between negotiating sessions. Chip was also with us, to run errands and to keep me relatively free from interruptions as I studied and made my plans.

Despite my efforts to the contrary, expectations had built up to a fever pitch. My only hope was that, in the quiet and peaceful atmosphere of our temporary home, both Begin and Sadat would come to know and understand each other better, and that they would trust me to be honest and fair in my role as mediator and active negotiator. It was soon to be obvious that Sadat seemed to trust me too much, and Begin not enough.

It is not easy now to describe my own feelings as the time approached for my meeting with the two leaders at Camp David. Without being melodramatic, perhaps I can draw a parallel to the attitude of many servicemen who go into battle or the feeling of some of my shipmates and me while we served in the submarine force. There was a curious fatalism about the process.

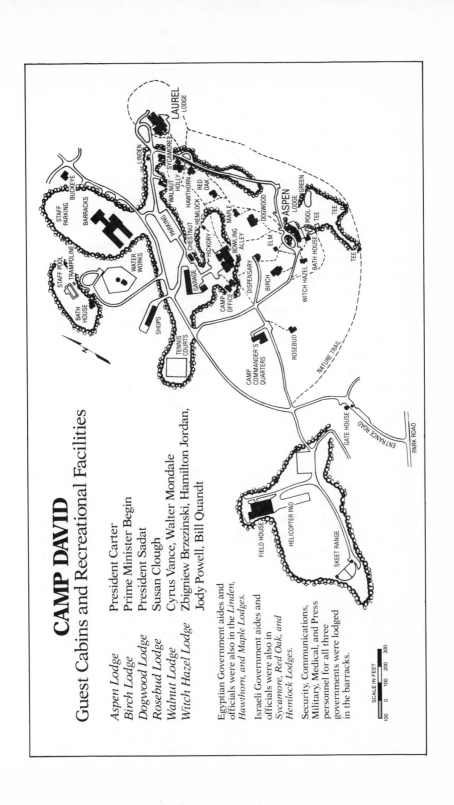

CAMP DAVID
Guest Cabins and Recreational Facilities

Aspen Lodge	President Carter
Birch Lodge	Prime Minister Begin
Dogwood Lodge	President Sadat
Rosebud Lodge	Susan Clough
Walnut Lodge	Cyrus Vance, Walter Mondale
Witch Hazel Lodge	Zbigniew Brzezinski, Hamilton Jordan, Jody Powell, Bill Quandt

Egyptian Government aides and officials were also in the *Linden, Hawthorn, and Maple Lodges.*

Israeli Government aides and officials were also in *Sycamore, Red Oak, and Hemlock Lodges.*

Security, Communications, Military, Medical, and Press personnel for all three governments were lodged in the barracks.

SCALE IN FEET
100   0   100   200   300

Much of the pain and trepidation comes when the original commitment is made and one has to accept the prospect of serious danger or failure. Subsequently, each passing day can be enjoyed with a sense of relief or thanksgiving that one is spared. We had already made the irrevocable decision to go to Camp David and to accept the risks and dangers; now we were ready to accept each day, hoping for the best.

All the physical arrangements had been made, and they taxed the capacity of the small mountain camp. It had not been designed to accommodate so many people, especially when they came from three different nations and represented three distinct cultures. Each of us had his own secretarial staff, communication facilities for managing the affairs of his respective government, personal physicians, cooks trained in the preparation of American, Egyptian, or kosher food, and major advisers who were expert in the subjects we were to discuss. Sadat, Begin, and I had private cabins within a stone's throw of each other. None of the other cottages was more than a few hundred yards from us, and all of them were packed to the limit with people. These constraints were a blessing in disguise, because hundreds of other bureaucrats and would-be advisers from all three countries were struggling to find an excuse to join the historic deliberations. We were remarkably successful in keeping them out and in minimizing visits to and from our private place.

Camp David is truly beautiful, with the cottages (all named after trees) and paths snuggled on top and down one side of a small mountain and sheltered by a thick growth of stately oak, poplar, ash, locust, hickory, and maple trees. A security fence encompasses about 125 acres of rocky terrain, and the close proximity of the living quarters engenders an atmosphere of both isolation and intimacy, conducive to easing tension and encouraging informality. A few golf carts and bicycles were available, but most of the time people walked among the cottages and meeting places.

Almost everyone in the camp spoke English, so we did not need interpreters. For those not actually at work, motion-picture projectors would run continuously—almost twenty-four hours a day. The principal negotiators would have little time for them, but others would view several movies each day before the meetings ended. Because of the space restrictions, each of us had to limit our aides to a minimum number. President Sadat had on his team Mohamed Ibrahim Kamel, Minister of Foreign Affairs; Boutros Ghali, Minister of State for Foreign Affairs; and Osama el-Baz,

Under Secretary of Foreign Affairs. Prime Minister Begin's key assistants were Foreign Minister Moshe Dayan, Defense Minister Ezer Weizman, and Attorney General Aharon Barak. Secretary of State Vance stayed with me most of the time, and National Security Adviser Brzezinski and Assistant Secretary of State Harold Saunders worked closely with us.

When they could leave Washington after normal working hours and particularly during the final days of the conference, Vice President Mondale and Secretary of Defense Brown participated in the negotiations. The ambassadors of the three nations were actively involved, and each of the top negotiators had one or two aides.

During the days ahead, the members of the negotiating teams were to become much more involved in the outcome of our deliberations than I had originally anticipated. Two of them whom I had never met, Barak and el-Baz, would be spending many hours in private sessions with me, going over the detailed language of the various proposals and searching for compromises that might be acceptable to Begin and Sadat, who would not be participating in these discussions.

Before the negotiations could begin, however, all of us tried to understand the issues involved and to search out some acceptable solutions to the questions. My own list included these items as having already been decided:

Jerusalem will be an undivided city, with free access to holy places.
Egypt will end its economic boycott against Israel.
Israeli access to the Suez Canal and other international waterways will be guaranteed.
Israel must have security, including some presence on the West Bank.
There will be an end to the state of war and a declaration of peace.
Egypt will have undisputed sovereignty over the Sinai.
Jordan and the Palestinians will be given a major negotiating role.
There will be phased implementation of any agreements (implementation in sequential steps).
Future negotiations are to be continuous and in good faith.

Though there was partial agreement on such issues as the following, the minor differences could be very significant.

REPRESENTING EGYPT:

Anwar el-Sadat, President
Mohamed Ibrahim Kamel, Minister of Foreign Affairs
Boutros Ghali, Minister of State for Foreign Affairs
Osama el-Baz, Under Secretary of Foreign Affairs
Ashraf Ghorbal, Ambassador to the United States
Ahmed Maher, Director of the Foreign Minister's Cabinet
Abdul Rauf el-Reedy, Director of Policy Planning,
    Foreign Ministry
Nabil el-Araby, Legal Director of Foreign Ministry
Ahmed Abou el-Gheite, Office of the Foreign Minister

REPRESENTING ISRAEL:

Menachem Begin, Prime Minister
Moshe Dayan, Foreign Minister
Ezer Weizman, Defense Minister
Aharon Barak, Attorney General and Member-designate
    of Supreme Court
Avraham Tamir, Major General, Director of Army
    Planning Branch
Simcha Dinitz, Ambassador to the United States
Meir Rosenne, Legal Adviser to the Foreign Minister
Elyakim Rubenstein, Assistant Director, Ministry
    of Foreign Affairs
Dan Pattir, Public Affairs Adviser to the Prime Minister

REPRESENTING THE UNITED STATES:

Jimmy Carter, President
Walter Mondale, Vice President
Cyrus Vance, Secretary of State
Zbigniew Brzezinski, National Security Adviser
    to the President
Hamilton Jordan, Staff of the President
Jody Powell, Press Secretary of the President
Harold Saunders, Assistant Secretary of State for
    Near East Affairs
Alfred Atherton, Ambassador at Large
Hermann Eilts, Ambassador to Egypt
Samuel Lewis, Ambassador to Israel
William Quandt, Staff of National Security Council

UN Resolution 242 would be the basis for any peace agreement. (Begin did not accept some of the terms as applicable to the West Bank.)

There should be normal relations between the two countries. (Sadat was not at all ready for full diplomatic recognition of Israel.)

None of us preferred an independent Palestinian state. (But Sadat wanted Palestinian self-determination, while Begin supported a limited form of autonomy.)

Israelis should terminate their military rule in the West Bank–Gaza. (No one was sure what Begin meant by his promise to do so.)

I also listed some of the certain problems, such as:

Dismantling of all Israeli settlements on Egyptian soil.

No new settlements to be built in any occupied territory.

All parts of Resolution 242 to apply to the West Bank.

Free participation of Palestinians in all future negotiations.

What the permanent status of the West Bank would be.

Israel's perceived threat from Egyptian military forces in the Sinai.

Arab role in Jerusalem.

Nature of any final agreement.

Because of the historic importance of the negotiations and the unique personal interrelationships at play within Camp David, I kept meticulous notes, recording verbatim some of the more significant statements made in my presence. After each session, I immediately dictated a complete record of the discussion from my written notes, which my secretary transcribed. Cy, Zbig, Fritz, Ham, or Jody read the one original copy that was made; then it was returned to me.

Here is my account, based on what I recorded during the thirteen days, in much more detail than other days or events of my administration.

TUESDAY, DAY ONE *(September 5, 1978)*

Rosalynn had come to Camp David in time to help me greet President Sadat in the early afternoon. His wife, Jihan, had to remain in Paris to be with one of their grandchildren, who was ill. I had particularly wanted the three wives to be with us, so they could ease some of the tension and create a more congenial atmosphere. There was no compatibility at all between Begin and Sadat on which to base any progress. This warmer relationship would have to be created from scratch.

Waiting for Sadat to arrive, I discussed the prospects with Rosalynn. Sadat would be much more willing to strive for a comprehensive agreement, while Begin would probably want to limit what might be achieved, because he was more satisfied with the status quo and was very leery about giving up any control over the West Bank or the Israeli settlement area in the Sinai.

Sadat was strong and bold, very much aware of world public opinion and of his role as the most important leader among the Arabs. I always had the impression that he looked on himself as inheriting the mantle of authority from the great pharaohs and was convinced that he was a man of destiny. Deeply religious, he had asked that a special place be found for him to worship. We set aside the room in Hickory cottage where we always had church services when our family was at Camp David.

Sadat was, perhaps, excessively impatient with the weakness of others and frequently derided some of his fellow leaders in the Middle East, but at least he respected Begin's strength and courage. With Sadat, that was a good place to start.

Nevertheless, Sadat also seemed somewhat impatient with Begin, distrustful of him. Determined to succeed, he was therefore inclined to form a partnership with me in opposition to Begin. His first preference was obviously a settlement; his second, an agreement with me which would be so good for Israel that Begin would be condemned if he rejected it.

About 2:30 P.M., Rosalynn and I received word that Sadat would soon be arriving. We walked up to the helicopter landing pad to welcome him. He and I were very glad to see each other again, and I suggested that we might have a brief talk before he walked the few more steps to his cabin for a rest. He would be housed in the same cottage he had used before, when he and Jihan had visited us during February. Sadat was the only foreign leader who had been to Camp David with me.

When he and I sat behind my cabin—Aspen—on the terrace, he did not waste any time expressing his thoughts and plans. He emphasized that he was eager to conclude a total settlement of the issues, and not merely establish procedures for future negotiations. He was convinced that Begin did not want an agreement and would try to delay progress as much as possible. Sadat stated that he would back me in all things, and that he had a comprehensive settlement plan "here in my pocket." He let me know that he was prepared to be flexible on all issues except two: land and sovereignty.

For instance, he concurred with me that if Begin would negotiate in good faith, the agreement should include the establishment of diplomatic relations and the end of the economic boycott against Israel. He predicted that it would be very difficult to hold Prime Minister Begin to the main issues. Sadat told me that as far back as 1971, he had offered to conclude a comprehensive settlement with Israel and had discussed this offer with Secretary of State William Rogers, but without success. He said that all Israelis must leave Egyptian territory and that any agreement had to provide for the Palestinians, for the West Bank, and for future agreements between Israel and her other neighbors. The details could be worked out by me.

Then he stood up to leave. President Sadat had suffered a mild heart attack a few years earlier and was always very careful about his own health. He wanted to go to bed and to meet with me again tomorrow morning. I informed him that I would delay suggesting any of my own proposals until after he and Begin had had a chance to explore all their differences. Sadat replied, "I will try to protect you by putting forward good proposals and make it unnecessary for any United States proposals to be offered."

I reminded Sadat that it was absolutely necessary that he and I understand Begin's problems and his attitudes. Tomorrow I intended to outline for him my impressions of the Israeli leader and the political circumstances which constrained his possible courses of action. He listened without comment, and went to his own cottage, less than half an hour after he had landed at Camp David.

About two hours later, Prime Minister Begin landed on the mountaintop, and we went down to Aspen for a brief conversation. I was pleased that his wife, Aliza, was scheduled to arrive in a few hours. The Begins always seemed very close, and I was sure Aliza would be as helpful to him during the coming days as Rosalynn would be to me.

Our greetings were friendly, but we were both somewhat ill at ease. I had wanted to generate an atmosphere of informality from the beginning, but in his attitude and words, Begin approached the initiation of talks in a very thorough and methodical way. His questions were not about substance; he was concerned about the daily schedule, the procedures to be followed, the time and place of meetings, how a record of the proceedings would be kept, how many aides would be permitted on each side, and so forth. This approach was one of his characteristics with which we were familiar, and I was not surprised. He and I were both very methodical about such matters, and I would have wanted answers to the same questions. I responded that my preference was to meet privately and separately with him and Sadat first, and then the three of us could decide how best to proceed. He seemed reluctant about this kind of session with principals only, and was eager to have us meet with at least two advisers each, referring to this as a "three-three-three" meeting.

Begin, too, seemed to look on himself as a man of destiny, cast in a biblical role as one charged with the future of God's chosen people. A student of the Bible, he preferred to use biblical names for places, and referred frequently to God's messages to Moses and to other leaders of the Jews. A man of deep beliefs, he had during his entire adult life demonstrated his dedication to the establishment and preservation of his country, and I knew that he deserved the respect he received from his associates. However, I also knew that his preoccupation with language, names, and terms could severely impede free-flowing talk.

I explained to the Prime Minister that President Sadat did not wish to work that evening but preferred to rest, and asked if he also wished to wait until the following morning for our discussion of the issues. He was eager to begin that evening, however, and we arranged for him to come back to my cabin after supper, for me to meet with Sadat in the morning, and then for the three of us to get together during the first afternoon—all without any aides in attendance. By then, we could decide on the format of our more detailed negotiations.

He pointed out to me that there had not been an agreement between a Jewish nation and Egypt for more than two thousand years, and that our meeting was historically unprecedented. However, unlike Sadat, Begin was clearly planning for an agreement at Camp David only on general principles, which might then serve as a basis for future meetings, when the specifics and remaining differences could be resolved by the Ministers of Foreign Affairs and Defense. I objected strongly to this plan, and told the Prime Minister that we three principals could not expect others to settle major issues later if we could not do so now, and that all the controversial questions should be addressed among us directly.

As he was preparing to leave after our stilted and somewhat superficial discussion, I told him that Sadat had expressed a concern about Begin's preoccupation with details at the expense of the major issues. Begin looked up quickly and said, "I can handle both." I believed him, and hoped he would be inclined to prove it.

After the Prime Minister departed, Rosalynn and I discussed a proposal that she had been pursuing with some of the interfaith religious groups around Washington—that all three leaders issue a call for the world to join us in prayer for the success of our efforts at Camp David. We approached the other two leaders. Sadat agreed immediately. Begin liked the idea, but first he wanted to see the text. This characteristic response was a prelude to our relationship at Camp David. After the Prime Minister had been over the prayer request word by word, it was issued as our first and last joint statement until after our discussions were concluded almost two weeks later.

Rosalynn and I went out late in the afternoon for a bicycle ride, and along the paths we had a chance to meet with the Egyptian and Israeli leaders and staff members who were staying in Camp David. They were keeping aloof from one another, clustered in small groups and talking only to fellow countrymen and to us Americans. After all, during the last twenty-five years their families had suffered and died at the hands of one another, and some of the military and political leaders responsible for those deaths were present.

Through their leaders, we urged everyone not to relay to the outside world any information about negotiating positions or successes and failures as the talks progressed. On the few occasions when an indiscreet statement was made to someone outside, it became known instantly through the resulting news stories. As we all came to believe that the same restrictions were being observed by everyone, it was easier to enforce the necessary discipline. There is no doubt in my mind that success would have been impossible if we had explained our own opinions or goals to the press each day. It would have been difficult to be flexible, with every necessary change in position being interpreted as a defeat for one or more of the negotiating parties.

I discovered later that there had been an additional restraint on unauthorized conversations: both the Egyptians and the Israelis had naturally assumed that we were tapping their telephones. However, this was not the case.

From the beginning, our differences were obvious, even in personal habits. Prime Minister Begin was the soul of propriety. He preferred to wear a tie and coat and strictly observed protocol, always reminding President Sadat and me that he was not a head of state and therefore did not rank as an equal with us. When I wanted to see him, he insisted that he come to my cottage and not the other way around. He stayed up late hours, worked very hard, kept close to his aides and advisers, and walked to the dining area at Laurel Lodge to eat with all the other Israelis and with most of the Egyptians and Americans.

President Sadat wore immaculate sports clothes—usually without a tie. He stayed in his cabin more than the rest of us, observed the greatest possible self-discipline on exercise, rest, and diet, and took a four-kilometer walk at the same time early each morning. He never ate at Laurel with the others, but preferred to dine in privacy. When I wanted to talk to him on the spur of the moment, I would call first and then go to his cottage.

We Americans looked upon ourselves as a bridge between the other two camps, and tried to ease tensions and make everyone feel at home. I dressed informally, and whenever possible I ran, swam, rode bicycles, or played tennis to get some much-needed exercise. Between meetings, I spent a lot of time keeping notes of negotiations already held, or preparing for the next session. Most of the time I met sequentially with the leaders of the other two nations, so I really didn't have much time off. In addition, later on, when we reached a stalemate that could be resolved only by many hours of detailed drafting, all three of us found it profitable for me to work directly with Begin's and Sadat's subordinates instead of with the leaders themselves.

The United States group was a smooth-running and well-organized team. There was no way to distinguish between the staff members who worked under me directly and those who worked for Dr. Brzezinski or Secretary Vance. Even in times of fatigue, stress, or disappointment, I do not recall a single unpleasant difference among us. Our goals and our negotiating positions were clear, and we were able to adjust quickly to changing circumstances.

After supper that first night, Begin and I met alone in my cabin. When there, we always used a tiny private office down the hall from the main living room. It hardly seemed suitable for such important talks, but its relative seclusion, easy access from the nearby cottages occupied by Begin and Sadat, and good view looking south down the mountainside made it seem right.

Begin was always ready to work early or late. My first goal that evening was to put him at ease and assure him there would be no surprises. I described my understanding of Israel's special problems and positions, and emphasized again the importance of our meeting. I told him we had plenty of time. We were isolated at Camp David and could remain so as long as necessary to reach agreement. We should not depend on referring problems to our subordinates to solve at a later time. I assured him that we would have no bilateral secrets, and that I would not give to Sadat nor to him any official United States proposals without discussing the unofficial drafts first with both sides.

Where we could not reach a final agreement on an issue at Camp David, I said, we should carefully define what differences remained, so that we would not later have to start at the beginning of the debate. I reserved the right, and had the duty, to put forward compromise proposals, and might on occasion merely adopt either the Egyptian or the Israeli position if I believed it to be best. I would not be timid, but would not deal in surprises, I assured him again. Begin insisted repeatedly that the Israelis see any American proposal before it was presented to Sadat, and claimed that he had an official commitment from President Ford that this procedure would be followed. I assumed that my approach would not violate that commitment.

I spelled out to Begin the advantages of a good rapport between him and Sadat during the days ahead. I believed that as they got to know each other, it would be easier for them to exchange ideas without rancor or distrust. Yet in fact, for the last ten days of negotiation leading up to our final agreement, the two men never spoke to one another, although their cottages were only about a hundred yards apart.

This first evening I was determined to accentuate the positive. I emphasized our awareness that Israel's security was paramount and that Begin's team could not be satisfied with hazy guarantees on this crucial issue. I also told him that his self-government proposal for the Palestinians was bold and gratifying in its basic concept, and that his willingness to recognize Egyptian sovereignty over the entire Sinai was a constructive development which had not been adequately acknowledged. From my notes I started to list all the areas of agreement as I understood them.

Begin interjected that on the security issue, which Israel considered vital, the Egyptians had taken just the opposite view. This was the most crucial point for the Israelis. If they were to withdraw from the West Bank or allow the Arabs there to have enhanced political status, they wanted to be certain that no successful military attack could be launched against them. With total withdrawal from the West Bank, their security problems would be very serious. I described the Egyptian position, admitting that there were some differences, with the reminder that it was the differences that had brought us together at Camp David.

Begin then outlined without modification his previous position on the Sinai, emphasizing his most disturbing point—that the Israeli settlements on Egyptian soil were a necessary buffer between Gaza and Egypt. He said he wanted a complete agreement with Egypt, but first would need an agreement with the United States. He had tabulated that the total time of negotiation between their two countries had been only thirty-two hours, and that this was obviously inadequate. We would all need patience, he said, and could not hope to reach an early settlement. He was talking not about years, but about a matter of a few months to work out the remaining differences. He knew that Sadat suspected the Israelis of deliberate delay, but he added that this was not true.

He then addressed the issue of a separate agreement with Egypt, to the exclusion of the Palestinians, Jordanians, and Syrians. Begin believed that an agreement on the Sinai might come first, with a later accord on "Judea and Samaria." (Begin always referred to the West Bank by the two biblical names—I presume to engender the notion that this was the promised land which God Himself had given to the Jews.) But he was not asking for such a procedure now, he said, because he knew it might be embarrassing to Egypt if its leader did not appear to represent the interests of other Arabs who were not present. He realized how strongly Sadat would object to any agreement implying that Egypt had acted only for its own benefit. It was encouraging to me that Begin acknowledged the Egyptian concerns.

The Prime Minister believed the Sinai region should be demilitarized, but that the three airfields the Israelis had built there should be kept by them for three to five years. Afterward, one or perhaps two could be for civilian purposes, with Egypt in control but Israel retaining the right to use them. As far as he was concerned, turning one airfield into a United States airbase would be perfectly all right.

We had anticipated this proposal, and I responded that we did not desire any military bases in the heart of the Middle East, but that if it was necessary for peace and both Israel and Egypt insisted, we would consider such an idea. Later, Begin was to raise this issue several times. It seemed important to him, either to generate a permanent American military presence in the area or to better justify his demand that the Israeli settlements in the Sinai be perpetuated. If Sadat made one exception on sovereignty— by allowing an American base on his territory—then he could reasonably be expected to make another.

Begin proposed that the question of sovereignty over the West Bank–Gaza area be left open, and reiterated that some Israeli military forces would have to be kept there. He was convinced that if Israel pulled out completely, the PLO terrorists would take over within twenty-four hours. But he stated emphatically that he was willing for the West Bank Palestinians to have autonomy— Begin always said, *"full* autonomy." (We were destined to spend several hours one evening seeking a common understanding of what "autonomy" meant—unsuccessfully.)

I then reviewed with Begin the consequences of failure, and the fact that the present influence in the Middle East of both Israel and the United States would be seriously eroded if we demonstrated to the world that we could not find peace. I described the potential vulnerability of Iran, Saudi Arabia, Jordan, and Egypt in case of a general war. All of them were needed to provide a stabilizing effect on the region in the face of building radical pressures. (The Shah was having serious problems within his country; Saudi Arabia was vulnerable to a serious attack because of its small population and lack of a well-developed military force; Jordan's King Hussein had to be very careful to assuage his more formidable neighbors and his large Palestinian population; and Egypt had now become vulnerable to extreme political and economic pressures because Sadat's peace offensive was so unpopular with the Arab "revisionists.") We both knew how eager the Soviets had been to inject themselves back into the region after Sadat had expelled them from Egypt, but their handicap was that no one trusted them, and they had very little to offer other than weapons for sale.

Begin was concerned about the permanence of any peace accord, even if he and Sadat could come to a complete understanding. I reminded him that any agreement would last as long as it appeared to be advantageous to the people as well as the leaders involved. In this case, I was convinced that the benefits of peace would be so obvious that the commitments would be honored. The direct interest and influence of the United States would help ensure it, no matter who might lead our nations in future years. I pointed out that our three nations and we three leaders were strong enough to prevail, even if other more radical leaders disagreed with certain aspects of our settlement and tried to disrupt what we had done.

I then addressed the desirability of a formal signed treaty or treaties, incorporating any results of our discussions at Camp David. Briefly, I outlined the widely varying formats and terms of the treaties involving my own nation with which I was familiar— with the other nations in the North Atlantic Treaty Organization (NATO), with Australia and New Zealand (ANZUS), with South Korea, and with Japan. We would have enough flexibility to encapsulate almost any potential settlement within the frame-

work of an international treaty. I had no objection to an Egyptian–
Israeli peace treaty signed in the absence of other Arab nations,
so long as the overall agreement included the crucial elements of
Palestinian rights, resolved the questions concerning the West
Bank, and provided a procedure for future treaties between Israel
and its other neighbors.

We then addressed the really tough issues. I told the Prime
Minister that Sadat would never yield on the question of leaving
Israeli settlements anywhere in the Sinai region. For him, complete sovereignty over the Sinai meant a total absence of Israeli
dwellers. Begin did not respond, but it was my impression that he
thought I was mistaken about this, and that with proper induce-
ments through other Israeli concessions, Sadat might change his
mind.

Another potentially serious difference was the phrase from United
Nations Resolution 242, "inadmissibility of acquisition of territory by war." The Arabs would all insist that Israel acknowledge
the applicability of this principle in any treaties signed, because
it would recognize that lands occupied by Israel after the Six Day
War had not legally changed hands. Begin understood this well,
and said that the principle was good, but he would agree only if
the word "belligerent" was inserted before the word "war." He
said Israel had been attacked by its Arab neighbors, and the war
was a defensive act by his country; therefore, Israel had a right to
occupy the lands taken in its own defense. This interpretation of
242 was to become a very difficult problem, on which the discussions almost foundered.

We then discussed the equally serious problem of the Palestinians—how they should govern themselves after the Israeli military government was terminated, how many now living in
surrounding countries would be permitted to return to their homeland, and the status of Israeli settlements in the West Bank and
Gaza. There were sharp differences of opinion on these points,
which were really the most important of all as far as the Arabs
were concerned. Israeli security and Palestinian rights—these were
the two crucial demands which would be so hard to reconcile.

Begin and I got into a brief argument about "symmetry," or the
equal treatment of Arabs within Israel and Israelis within the
West Bank concerning the right to own property. Begin admitted
that his position on this issue had changed after he had met with
me in Washington, but he repeated that he had been overruled by
his own cabinet after he had returned to Israel in December. His
new position was that the Arabs could not buy land in Israel

unless they were Israeli citizens, although Israelis would have the right to acquire land in the West Bank.

Begin was not willing to admit that all the provisions of United Nations Resolution 242 applied to the West Bank and Gaza, nor that the questions of the Sinai settlements and air strips would have to be resolved before a peace treaty could be signed. I demurred, but did not spend much time arguing these issues this first night.

We discussed Jordan's future participation in peace negotiations, and were concerned about King Hussein's timidity and his predictable reluctance to arouse the anger of other Arab leaders. This was important because Jordan itself is in many ways the natural homeland for the Palestinians, and the question of sovereignty over the West Bank territory naturally involved Jordan. In order to give the Palestinians autonomy officially, someone had to grant authority to them. Begin was not about to admit that Jordan now had this authority, with the exclusive right to give it away. Instead, he said this issue could be resolved later, with authority remaining in the hands of the Israeli military government in the meantime.

Begin had repeatedly promised full autonomy for the West Bank Palestinians, and I pushed him on how much freedom they would have. He replied that the only powers they would not be able to exercise would be those relating to immigration of Palestinian refugees and the security of Israel. This sounded like good news, but later the Israelis would seek a veto power over almost anything of substance the Palestinians could decide, even claiming that such matters as road construction and water supplies affect the security of Israel.

In general, the conversation was discouraging. I had hoped that Begin would bring some new proposals to Camp David, but the Prime Minister simply repeated almost verbatim the old Israeli negotiating positions. There were few indications of flexibility, but at least I made it clear that we wanted final decisions at Camp David and that we were going to put forward our positions forcefully. He agreed with this—without apparent enthusiasm. We said good night at about 11:00 P.M., about two and a half hours after he had come to my cabin.

With Begin's permission, I had taken very careful notes, to ensure accurate transmission of his views to President Sadat the next day. Now, after dictating a summary of our discussions, I had a brief meeting with Cy Vance and Zbig to go over my notes with them. They were already thoroughly familiar with Begin's boilerplate positions, which he had not discernibly modified. I jotted down some ideas for my next day's meeting with President Sadat, walked a few steps down the hall, and went to bed well after midnight. It had been a long day.

WEDNESDAY, DAY TWO *(September 6, 1978)*

I got up at my usual early hour, and went over my dictation. Then Rosalynn and I played tennis for about an hour, ate breakfast, and discussed my talk with Prime Minister Begin and my plans for the day. We had all this spare time because President Sadat preferred not to begin his official day before 10:00 A.M., after he had completed his exercise regimen.

Sadat was always punctual, calm, and self-assured; he was brief and to the point in all his discussions. He tried not to tell others anything he thought they already knew. Rarely dwelling on details or semantics, he spelled out his positions in broad terms with emphasis on the strategic implications of decisions, and was very interested in other countries in the Middle East area and the impact of our deliberations on them.

When he arrived at my cottage, Aspen, we went to the same room, which we would use throughout the entire time at Camp David. Only when larger groups were involved did I move to another building, where the senior staff conducted its sessions. I first gave him a brief report of my meeting with Prime Minister Begin. I told him that it had been basically nonproductive and that Israel's previously known positions had been reiterated, but that this in itself was necessary as a first step for progress among us. It was very important, we agreed, not to put Begin on the defensive at this early stage of the discussions, but to let him spell out Israel's position for the record.

I emphasized to Sadat that unless the proposals were patently fair to Israel, Begin's government and the Israeli people would not support them. I also reminded Sadat of the importance of public opinion in the United States and the intense interest that the American Congress and public would have in the terms of an agreement as it related to the security of Israel.

Sadat responded that the Prime Minister was a very formal man, difficult to approach or to understand. He believed Begin was bitter, inclined to look back into ancient history rather than to deal with the present and the future. He promised to go to extremes in being flexible, in order to uncover the full meaning of Begin's positions, and stated that if our efforts at Camp David should be unsuccessful, then when the equitable Egyptian proposals were made known, they would bring the condemnation of the world on the Israeli leader.

I pointed out that Begin was a man of integrity and honor, with very deep and long-held opinions. It was difficult for him to change. He had spent a lifetime in public affairs developing his ideas, expounding them, and defending them, even at great personal danger. When he was elected to his present office, his campaign statements were quite clear on some of the issues we would be negotiating, and any change in his position made necessary through compromises would be the object of criticism in the open, aggressive, and free political environment existing in Israel. I did not want anyone to be embarrassed by either success or failure at Camp David, but a positive attitude during our discussions was essential, to build up mutual confidence and to improve our chances for success.

I sat at my desk, taking notes as I had the night before. Now it was Sadat's time to spell out Egypt's position. He sat erect and spoke calmly, referring to a few notes he had brought with him. Sadat said there were two points on which he could not be flexible. One was land, and the other was sovereignty. These were closely related, but I needed to know exactly what he meant. He explained that Egypt must have every inch of her land returned, with unequivocal sovereignty over it, and that other Arab nations must be treated the same. I interrupted to ask how he assessed the difference between sovereignty on the Golan Heights and in the Sinai versus the West Bank and Gaza. He said there was a great difference. There were recognized international boundaries for Sinai, all of which belonged to Egypt, and for the Golan, all of which belonged to Syria. I asked him where he ascribed sovereignty in the West Bank and Gaza, and he replied, "Sovereignty rests among the people who live there—not in either Jordan or Israel." He would not yield any of the occupied land to Israel, at least in this early session. All of it should go back to Egypt, Syria, or the Palestinians, he said.

Unlike Begin, Sadat wanted a firm framework for a permanent peace, and was eager to deal with all the specific issues while we were together in this place. He agreed with my suggestion that, once a "framework for peace" was signed, aides could draft a peace treaty over a period of not more than three months, incorporating the agreement into legal and diplomatic terms.

During one of their earliest discussions after Sadat had visited Jerusalem, he had told the Prime Minister that no major Egyptian *attack* forces would move further east toward Israel than the mountain passes in the Western Sinai, presently monitored by

American technicians as a result of the demilitarization agreement following the most recent war in 1973. Sadat was extremely angry because Begin still insisted that he had said *any* forces, even after Sadat corrected him several times. Sadat brought this point up as an indication of Begin's intransigence and his inability or unwillingness to communicate rationally.

Sadat was also convinced that what Begin really wanted was to keep the West Bank. He had been told of an alleged incident when the Prime Minister was asked by some Jewish leaders from France, "What do you want?" and Begin placed his hand on a map of the West Bank and replied, "I want this."

It was clear that we had a long way to go before a mutual feeling of trust and respect could be established between the two men. Over the next eleven days, I was to spend much of my time defending each of the leaders to the other. Part of this effort was devoted simply to an explanation of both systems of government—the imperatives of political life for Begin in a democracy, and the sensitive role Sadat was having to play in representing, without their expressed approval, the interests of other Arabs. Our Ambassadors to Israel and Egypt and other experts on Middle Eastern affairs found me to be an eager student during these days.

Sadat next handed me the plan he had mentioned when he first arrived, spelling out the opening proposal of the Egyptians. As I read it my heart sank; it was extremely harsh and filled with all the unacceptable Arab rhetoric. It blamed all previous wars on Israel, and demanded that Israelis offer indemnities for their use of the occupied land, pay for all the oil they had pumped out of Egyptian wells, permit the refugees free entry to the West Bank, withdraw all their forces entirely to the original pre-1967 boundaries, allow the Palestinians to form their own nation, and relinquish control over East Jerusalem. Sadat let me read it through without comment, and when I had finished, he said he would like to offer me some modifications which could later be adopted as acceptable to him. He cautioned me not to reveal these to anyone, because it would destroy his negotiating strength if his final positions were to be placed on the table at this early time. He had carefully studied the points I had been making during the past few months, he said, and he found them reasonable. He recalled the first time we had met, and his conviction then that some of my dreams would never be realized in his lifetime. Now he was prepared to make those dreams come true, because he was convinced that the people of the two countries and most of the world wanted peace.

As President Sadat delineated for me what he would accept in a final agreement, I saw for the first time that we might possibly achieve substantial success. With a few notable exceptions, his positions had a good chance of being satisfactory to the Israelis. It would certainly not be an easy task to convince both parties, but a basis for peace now existed. Under certain circumstances, Sadat might even agree to my frequent request to him that full diplomatic relations be established between Egypt and Israel, including open borders and an exchange of ambassadors. With the cooperation of the United States and others, routine postal service, communications, transportation, and trade could be instituted and maintained. Sadat sketched a tentative outline of how we might handle the questions of Palestinian refugees, representation of Arabs within the governing authority of the West Bank and Gaza, peacekeeping forces for the Sinai region, and possible minor modifications in the West Bank borders. He even went so far as to say bluntly that Jerusalem should not be divided. He was adamant that the military "points," or outposts, of the Israelis in the West Bank could only be maintained during the interim period prior to the determination of sovereignty for that region, but that this period might possibly be extended somewhat if, at the time, he could trust the Israeli leaders. His condition for that extension was a commitment by the Israelis to withdraw their military forces and terminate the military government under certain circumstances and at a specific time to be determined.

Concerning Hussein and Jordanian participation in the negotiations and implementation of an agreement in the future, Sadat said he would be prepared to continue with the negotiations and implementation of agreements until Hussein was ready to do his duty.

I was pleased so far, but I told him there would have to be additional flexibility. He said, "On a short-term interim agreement I can be flexible, but any final agreement will have to include much more completely the Arab provisions that I have described."

Typically, Sadat drew the conversation to a close by making a strategic analysis of the situation in Saudi Arabia, Iran, Afghanistan, Sudan, and South and North Yemen. He seemed especially worried about the vulnerability of Saudi Arabia, adding that if a real threat ever developed there, he would be willing to help. He had told Crown Prince Fahd, "Your borders are my borders." In spite of the Saudis' public criticism of his peace initiative, he was still willing to uphold this commitment.

We agreed to schedule the first meeting among all three of us for three o'clock that afternoon. But when I proposed that we meet with the advisers and aides in the evening after supper, Sadat objected. He wanted his position to be assessed thoroughly by Begin before any aides were brought into the discussions.

Sadat's objection highlighted the contrasting attitudes of the two leaders. While at Camp David, Sadat wanted to make Egypt's decisions himself, did not like to have aides present when he was with me, and seemed somewhat uncomfortable when they were around him. His closest advisers, the Vice President and Prime Minister, were in Cairo managing the affairs of Egypt. Throughout our stay at Camp David, Sadat spent little time with his staff. In contrast, Begin relied very heavily on his aides and advisers. I was soon to be thankful that each of these men had developed his own style, because in Sadat's case, the leader was much more forthcoming than his chief advisers, and in Begin's case, the advisers were more inclined to work out difficult problems than was their leader.

Sadat's plan was to present his written proposals to me and Begin at the afternoon meeting. I knew they were certain to be rejected—with feeling—and my assessment was that he thought Begin would not agree to any settlement. Sadat wanted a strong initial proposal on the record, to appease his fellow Egyptians and the Arab world, but during the negotiations he would be willing to make major concessions (within carefully prescribed limits), so that his final proposal would prove to everyone the reasonableness of his approach. The first part of this strategy was a waste of time, but the latter part suited me perfectly, because if the Egyptian proposals were indeed reasonable, there was at least a fighting chance that the Israelis would accept them.

I told Sadat that the afternoon meeting was likely to be nonproductive and perhaps even unpleasant, and that it might be better to invite Dayan and Weizman. He finally agreed, with some reluctance, to include advisers the following morning.

After Sadat left, I went over my notes carefully with Fritz, Cy, and Zbig over lunch. We were all concerned about Sadat's harsh opening proposal and Begin's inflexibility on all the issues. However, we were not overly discouraged, because Cy and Zbig reported a much more forthcoming attitude among the other Israelis, and I was counting on Sadat's promised concessions.

Begin came first to the afternoon meeting. I told him quickly that Sadat would present a very aggressive proposal and cautioned him not to overreact. Also, that President Sadat was not yet ready for a three-three-three meeting, but that we would try to schedule one for the next morning. On procedural matters,

Begin was uncharacteristically compliant, perhaps in deference to his sense of protocol that we were heads of state, while he was only a prime minister. However, he never let this attitude spill over into the substantive negotiations.

Sadat soon arrived, saying that he had just enjoyed a good meeting with Ezer Weizman. Begin seemed to have no objection to such meetings. Among the Israeli delegation, Ezer was a special favorite of Sadat, and on occasion all of us would be willing to use this relationship as an additional avenue of communication between the two delegations.

I decided to play a minimal role during these first sessions, so that the other two leaders could become better acquainted and have a more fruitful exchange. I knew what they had to say—I could have recited some of the more pertinent passages in my sleep. I asked Sadat to begin, but he used his higher rank and requested that Begin do so. Begin said that many differences between the two nations were not yet resolved, and that the basic disagreements were so broad as to require a few months of negotiation by technicians working full time five days a week. He then asked about our observance of Sabbath days. Sadat worshiped five times each day, with special prayers on Friday; we had Christian services on Sunday; and the Jews observed the Sabbath on Saturday. We decided that each of us would attend our own religious services, but refrain from working together on the peace settlement only for one full day—Saturday.

As it turned out, the United States team did most of the draft-ing of the texts on Saturday. (In all, the American team prepared twenty-three versions of the Framework for Peace. I wrote the original Sinai agreement personally, and I think there were eight different texts before we finished.)

Begin seemed grateful that we would refrain from negotiating on his Sabbath. He said with some emotion that we needed to start a new page and forget past disagreements. Sadat said, "Yes, yes."

I then asked Sadat to respond to Begin's remarks. He said there was already a fundamental difference of opinion, even in these preliminary comments, about what we were to accomplish at Camp David. He stated that his peace initiative to Jerusalem had brought forth a new era. The era of war was coming to an end, he said. Sadat reiterated what he and I had agreed, that we our-selves must produce a comprehensive framework for peace, not avoiding any of the controversial issues, and then give the techni-cians three months of drafting time merely to put our agreement into final form. This version would then comprise the permanent treaty of peace.

I noted that Sadat was strangely ill at ease, uncharacteristi-cally fumbling for words and repeating himself several times. Begin waited very patiently until he got through, then made a comment that when the Catholics choose a new pope, they say "Habemus Papam" (We have a pope). He wanted us to be able to announce, "Habemus Pacem" (We have peace).

This was the last time I remember the Prime Minister waiting patiently for someone else to finish speaking. He was a very aggressive debater, and later, when I visited the Israeli Knesset and tried to speak above the hubbub, I realized where he had derived his training and his negotiating habits. With this one exception of interrupting other speakers, Begin was the epitome of propriety and good manners. Both he and Sadat were some-what nervous, but on their best behavior at this first meeting.

Sadat said that he looked on the Camp David meeting as a climax, and he hoped that the spirit of *King* David, the great leader of Israel, would prevail at *Camp* David. He said quietly but firmly that there could be no partial agreement, and certainly no separate agreement. Begin replied that he had never put forward any proposal for a separate agreement, but that if there should be sequential agreements, with other countries later coming forward to join the peace effort, then we should be ready and willing to accommodate them. This jockeying back and forth was signifi-cant. Begin wanted to deal with the Sinai, keep the West Bank, and avoid the Palestinian issue. Sadat was determined to address all three.

On this question, I sided with Sadat, of course, and stated that the principals must address all the controversial issues directly. The United States would reserve the right to put forward its own ideas on an equal basis with the other two, because there might be times when either one of them might accept, albeit reluctantly, a proposal originating with me which they would be unwilling to accept from one another. Begin said these concepts were all right with him.

It was time for the discussion of specific issues; I nodded to Begin to start. He said that he had made a proposal in December concerning self-rule in the West Bank–Gaza areas, had not received an adequate response, and was looking forward to hearing Sadat's counterproposal.

I asked Sadat specifically, "Are you willing to act in the administration of the West Bank and to conclude an Arab–Israeli treaty if Jordan is not willing to participate?" He replied, "Yes, we are." I then asked if he was willing to negotiate a Sinai agreement at the same time that a West Bank–Palestinian treaty was being concluded, and he replied affirmatively but added, "I will not sign a Sinai agreement before an agreement is also reached on the West Bank." Sadat was to prove adamant on this point.

He then began to read his extremely tough and unacceptable proposal, after requesting that Begin not respond to it until he had discussed it with his aides. When Begin agreed, they both seemed relieved.

During the reading of the paper, Begin sat without changing his expression, but I could feel the tension building. When it was over, no one spoke for a while, and I tried to break the tension by telling Begin that if he would sign the document as written, it would save all of us a lot of time.

I was surprised when everyone broke into gales of genuine laughter. After a few moments Begin asked, "Would you advise me to do so?" I said no, we had better consult with our aides. All of a sudden both men seemed happy, friendly. Begin made a very nice statement about how glad he was to get the document, how hard he knew the Egyptians had worked on it, and how much he appreciated the thoroughness of their preparation. Listening to it had been very interesting to him, he said, but reading it would be much more informative.

We agreed to meet again the following day, and I invited them to go for a walk with Rosalynn and me. Sadat declined, saying that he had already had his exercise for the day, but the Prime

Minister decided to go find his wife and join us. We parted in good spirits, everyone patting each other on the back. It was the high point in feeling until the final hours, many days later.

Later I came to believe that Begin had been relieved because the Sadat paper was so ridiculously harsh. It incorporated all the timeworn Arab demands and charges against the Israelis and must have been written by a real hard-liner. Begin clung to this document, and during the days ahead he would repeatedly use Sadat's demands as proof of the unreasonable attitude of the Egyptians. I think Sadat was relieved because Begin had not become angry and stormed out of the room. At that time in my cottage, though, I could not understand the reason for the strange hilarity and good will.

Half an hour later, when we were walking through the woods, Prime Minister Begin became very excited about Sadat's proposals being so drastic and unacceptable. After reading the document over, he was convinced that it was either an opening gambit or would be an obvious impediment to progress. I tried to convince him it was the former.

Rosalynn and I always enjoyed seeing Menachem and Aliza Begin together. They have been through a lot, they understand and support one another, and they share in the telling of interesting stories about their family background. She is obviously a strong woman with great influence on her husband. Rosalynn was a partner in my thinking throughout the Camp David negotiations, and I presumed that Begin discussed all the issues freely with his wife. Although they took time out to have coffee with each other a time or two, and went shopping together at a nearby mountain folk festival, the two wives were, in effect, an integral part of their own national delegations.

After supper, I brought the entire American group together in my cottage to discuss the apparent damage Sadat's proposal had done. Begin was treating it as an insurmountable obstacle, and the other members of the Israeli delegation were also deeply troubled. We knew that Sadat was ready to make immediate modifications, but it seemed advisable for me to meet with all the Israelis before Begin and Sadat met again with each other, so that I could ease their concern. I asked Cy to arrange such a session. Then we watched the movie *Shane* before going to bed.

THURSDAY, DAY THREE *(September 7, 1978)*

Beginning at 8:30 A.M, I met for two hours with Begin, Dayan, and Weizman. Vance and Brzezinski were with me. We all sat around a table in Camp David's original conference center, a small cottage known as Holly. Everyone had read the Egyptian document, and it was naturally the first subject of our discussion.

Prime Minister Begin was now even more excited and irate about the tone and substance of the document than he had been during our walk the previous evening. He said, "This smacks of a victorious state dictating peace to the defeated!" Begin reviewed the text in detail, and finally concluded, "This document is not a proper basis for negotiations."

I tried to calm the group without denigrating Sadat's effort. I wanted to file Sadat's paper and go on to more realistic options for our discussions, but it soon became obvious that such a course would not be possible. Begin insisted that we analyze the Egyptian proposals in detail.

The discussions were of benefit to me, however, because in the presence of Dayan and Weizman, the Prime Minister outlined much more clearly than before the basic Israeli attitude toward the more controversial issues. He focused on words and their meaning.

Sadat used the word "Palestinian" to mean the Arab dwellers throughout what had been Palestine under the British Mandate, many of whom were now refugees or living under the Israeli occupation forces. Begin exclaimed, "Palestinians! This is an unacceptable reference. Jews are also Palestinians. He must mean 'Palestinian Arabs.'" This was to develop into a difficult issue later on, which could be resolved only by special footnote entries in the signed agreement.

"Conquered territory! Gaza was also conquered by Egypt," Begin continued. I pointed out that Egypt was not claiming sovereignty over Gaza.

"Sinai settlements! There is a national consensus in Israel that the settlements *must* stay!" This claim was to become the most serious problem of all. Sadat was absolutely insistent that all Israelis must move out of his territory, and Begin was equally insistent that no Israeli settlements in the Sinai would *ever* be "dismantled."

We had a heated discussion about borders. How much the 1967 borders would be modified was a constant argument. The official Arab position was that the borders should be restored to their exact locations as they had been prior to the Six Day War. The Israelis wanted maximum flexibility in the final borders, with some leaders, though not Begin, calling for partition of the disputed West Bank territory. I told the Israeli delegation that the key question was: "Are you willing to withdraw from the occupied territories and honor Palestinian rights, in exchange for adequate assurances for your security, including an internationally recognized treaty of peace? If not," I said, "Egypt will eventually turn away from the peace process, and the full power of the Arabs, and perhaps world opinion, will be marshaled against you."

The expanding settlements under Begin's government were creating doubt that the Israelis were bargaining in good faith concerning any reduction in Israeli influence on the West Bank. This was the root of Sadat's distrust of Begin's motives, and I must admit that I shared the belief that the Israeli leader would do almost anything concerning the Sinai and other issues in order to protect Israel's presence in "Judea and Samaria." I expressed this concern as forcefully as possible. Begin's response was evasive. He said that the subject of "minor" or "major" modifications of pre-1967 borders would come up only if there was no peace plan—only if a border was needed between the Jordan River and the sea. His proposal was that everyone simply live together, with the question of sovereignty to be decided later.

We were discussing a crucial issue, and the arguments became sharper and more heated.

I replied that an Israeli commitment to withdraw was imperative, but that I was not trying to specify how much. I insisted that the interim proposal to let the Palestinians have full autonomy be as forthcoming as possible, with maximum authority for the people who lived on the West Bank and in Gaza. A continuing military occupation and deprivation of basic citizenship rights among the Arabs was unacceptable to the world, and contrary to the principles which had always been such an integral part of Jewish teachings and religious beliefs about freedom from persecution of others and personal liberty for all human beings.

Dayan asked, "What does withdrawal mean? Troops, settlements? Will I be a foreigner on the West Bank? Will I have to get a visa to go to Jericho? With autonomy, can the Arabs there create a Palestinian state? Can they resettle the refugees from Lebanon to the West Bank? Who will protect us from Jordan? Who will be responsible for controlling terrorists?"

I asked for Israel's answers to Dayan's questions, but Begin shifted back to Sadat's proposal and began to analyze it again in minute detail. It was obvious that we were wasting time.

I became angry, and almost shouted, "What do you actually want for Israel if peace is signed? How many refugees and what kind can come back? I need to know whether you need to monitor the border, what military outposts are necessary to guard your security. What else do you want? If I know the facts, then I can take them to Sadat and try to satisfy both you and him. My problem is with the issues that do not really relate to Israel's security. I must have your frank assessment. My greatest strength here is your confidence—but I don't feel that I have your trust. What do you really need for your defense? It is ridiculous to speak of Jordan overrunning Israel! I believe I can get from Sadat what you *really* need, but I just do not have your confidence."

Weizman replied, "We wouldn't be here if we didn't have confidence in you."

I repeated my point. "You are as evasive with me as with the Arabs. The time has come to throw away reticence. Tell us what you really need. My belief is that Sadat is strong enough to make an agreement here—and impose it on other nations. I believe I can get Sadat to agree to your home-rule proposal if you convince him and me that you are not planning to keep large parts of the West Bank under your permanent control."

I accused Begin of wanting to hold onto the West Bank, and said that his home-rule or autonomy proposal was a subterfuge. He resented this word very much and brought it up many times in our subsequent discussions.

While Begin and I cooled off, Weizman outlined some of the changes that had taken place during the last eleven years— differences on the West Bank, in Jerusalem, with the Egyptians, and new possibilities such as a joint police force to control terrorism. He stated flatly that a complete withdrawal of Israeli settlers was not possible but that real home rule was.

I stressed again Sadat's courage and his personal sacrifice in making the peace initiative. A demilitarized Sinai and Egypt's signed agreement with Israel would serve to protect Israel's security in the world community, and even within the Arab world, after Sadat and we were gone as leaders. I emphasized that, in Begin, the Israelis had a prime minister with a demonstrated willingness to give his life for Israel's security. Thus, if we wasted this opportunity we would never have it again.

Begin was unmoved. He turned again to the Sadat paper, saying that it would force the Jews to become a minority in their own country, that it smacked of the Versailles Treaty, and that in general Sadat wanted peace with an Israel that would be not only vulnerable, but doomed. He would demand that Sadat withdraw the written proposal.

I said, "Sadat will never withdraw his proposal. Any of us should have the right to put forward anything we desire. This paper may also represent a Saudi perspective, which Sadat has to accommodate. You can be equally effective in rejecting the paper by saying it is unacceptable."

Then, with our approval, the Israelis conducted a long discussion in Hebrew. This came to be a very convenient way for them to speak in confidence without having to disrupt the meeting by withdrawing from the room. On rare occasions, it resulted in Begin's changing his mind. This was one of those times.

Begin said, "All right. We will not ask for withdrawal. We will simply say it is unacceptable."

It was now time for Begin and me to go to our 10:30 A.M. meeting with Sadat, and I asked the four who would remain to continue their discussion of the specific issues that had been raised. This had been an unpleasant and heated argument, but it was necessary and understandable because of the one-sided nature of Sadat's proposals.

Begin and I walked together from Holly to Aspen, arriving at the front door of my cottage just in time to greet President Sadat. I led the way down the hall to the study and sat behind the desk. They took the other two chairs, facing each other across the desk, as before. At the very beginning, I decided to withdraw from the discussion between Begin and Sadat. I wanted them to address each other directly. While they talked, I took notes without looking up, and they soon refrained from talking to me or attempting to seek my opinion.

Begin was well prepared, and he did not waste any time. He was brutally frank as he discussed each issue in Sadat's paper.

Sadat remained silent and impassive until Begin derided the idea of Israel's paying reparations for the use of the occupied lands. Then he interrupted, and a hot argument took place. Sadat was incensed because Begin rejected the idea that his nation should pay for the Egyptian oil which was being pumped at that moment to Israel. They began arguing about who had conquered whom, and I had to intercede to convince them that neither was claiming that the other represented a defeated nation. They calmed down a little, but the subject of land was central for both and could not be avoided. They continued their discussion of territory, with Sadat accusing Begin of being interested primarily in the retention of occupied land. Begin retorted that 24,000 square miles of territory were involved, that he was offering to return more than 90 per cent of it to Egypt now, and merely postponing the sovereignty question on the other 2,340 square miles—a figure which, I assumed at the time, was the area of the West Bank and Gaza.

It was a telling point, and Sadat decided to shift ground. He said we needed to discuss basic principles, and not get bogged down in precise numbers of square meters or other details. One of the principles which could not be ignored was the phrase, "inadmissibility of acquisition of territory by war." He said this was the essence of the question. He leaned forward in his chair, pointed his finger at Begin, and exclaimed, "Premier Begin, you want land!" Sadat reminded us that the disputed phrase was extracted directly from United Nations Resolution 242, which all of us agreed to be the foundation of our peace efforts. He was fervent in condemning "the Israeli settlements on my land."

All restraint was now gone. Their faces were flushed, and the niceties of diplomatic language and protocol were stripped away. They had almost forgotten that I was there, and there was nothing to distract me from recording this fascinating debate.

Begin repeated that no Israeli leader could possibly advocate the dismantling of the Sinai settlements, and he added that four other conditions would have to be met before the Sinai could be returned to Egypt.

Begin had touched a raw nerve, and I thought Sadat would explode. He pounded the table, shouting that land was not negotiable, especially land in the Sinai and Golan Heights. Those borders were internationally recognized. He pointed out that for thirty years the Israelis had desired full recognition, no Arab boycott, and guaranteed security. He was giving them all of that. He wanted them to be secure. "Security, yes! Land, no!" he shouted. There was no need for United Nations forces in the area, he declared; Israel and Egypt could defend themselves. He promised that in the Suez, there would be no restrictions on navigation, nor in the Straits of Tiran. A permanent end to belligerency— all this, and more. But, he said, he must terminate the discussions if Begin continued to prove that he wanted land.

Begin was calmer than Sadat. He responded that he had already demonstrated his good will by changing a long-standing policy of his government concerning the Sinai land between Eilat and Sharm el-Sheyk. His predecessors had been determined to keep this land, and he was offering it back to Egypt, which was very difficult for him. He added that the continued presence in the Sinai of a few homes of Israeli settlers was not an infringement on Egyptian sovereignty.

Sadat claimed that the Israeli Knesset, under Prime Minister

David Ben Gurion, had annexed the Sinai. Begin denied this, and there was a heated argument, with each offering to produce the minutes of the Israeli parliament to prove his point. Begin attempted to conclude this fruitless discussion by conceding that Egypt was not claiming sovereignty over Gaza, and added that he was not now preparing to pursue his own claims of sovereignty over the occupied territories in the West Bank and Gaza. He acknowledged that Jordan's Hussein also claimed the same land.

This concession did not satisfy Sadat. He maintained that neither Israel nor Jordan could claim sovereignty over the West Bank; self-determination by the residents of the land was the only measure of sovereignty, and would lead ultimately to a Palestinian state. In his opinion, such a state should not be independent nor have military forces, but should be linked to either Israel or Jordan. His preference was Jordan. He knew that King Hussein wanted the West Bank, but he emphasized again that the area belonged neither to Israel nor to Jordan.

The two leaders then got sidetracked on a long discussion of Lebanon, Sadat saying that only the influence of Israel was causing the disturbance; that Syria was in Lebanon because of Israeli intervention on behalf of the Christians; that King Khalid of Saudi Arabia could force Syrian withdrawal in twenty-four hours if the Arabs were convinced that the Lebanese would be left alone; and that in his opinion, Assad should withdraw his forces. Sadat said there was a sect of the Maronite Christians under a Major Haddad who were utterly disreputable, supported and financed and armed by the Israelis, and that this was the crux of the whole problem. Under Begin's orders, the Lebanese government could not even send its troops into its own southern territory.

Begin replied that he had tried to get Major Haddad to permit the Lebanese troops to come into the southern part of their country, but Haddad had refused.

The two leaders had a long and hot argument, repeating themselves several times. My attempts to change the subject were futile, but eventually the discussion ran its course, and I was finally able to remind them that only our success at Camp David would let us join Assad, Khalid, and others in working out the difficult problems of Lebanon.

Just then I received a report that Congress had voted to uphold my veto of a major bill, and we discussed democracy for a while. It was a welcome break. Both Begin and Sadat agreed enthusiastically that democracy was the best form of government, and Sadat said he was very proud to be shifting his own country toward democracy.

This peaceful interlude was interrupted almost immediately, when Sadat said that the warm feelings he had developed during his visit to Jerusalem had been destroyed because "minimum confidence does not exist anymore since Premier Begin has acted in bad faith."

I replied that this mutual feeling of bad faith was something I would like to correct, that they were both honorable, decent, and courageous men, and that I knew both of them well. Respect was warranted on both sides, but misunderstandings had to be cleared away. I used as an illustration the most irritating example, Sadat's statement in Jerusalem, "My forces will not exceed the Mitla and Gidi passes." Begin had misinterpreted what he meant, and had subsequently inferred that Sadat was not a man of his word. Sadat then felt that Begin did not trust him, and resented it deeply. We discussed this point for fifteen confusing minutes.

I then insisted that Prime Minister Begin not interrupt, and asked President Sadat what he had said and what he had meant. He repeated the exact words Begin had quoted; there was no question about what he had actually said in Jerusalem. But he went on to say that he obviously did not mean that minimal police and security forces could not go into the Sinai to maintain order in their own territory. He meant that no Egyptian strike forces would go into the Sinai, which might be a military threat against Israel.

I asked him, "What do you mean by this?" He said, "I mean no tanks, no artillery, no missiles."

I then remarked that had I been in Jerusalem, that is the way I would have understood the remark, as the only logical interpretation. Begin listened carefully and did not comment further on this point, but soon the discussions on other issues became very bitter again.

I acted as a referee and put them back on track, and on occasion explained what was meant when there was an obvious misinterpretation. Strangely enough, every so often laughter broke out. Once, for instance, one of them referred to kissing Barbara Walters, the television journalist, and wondered if the cameras were on and what his wife might think. Another outburst of laughter came during an argument about which one of them was responsible for the hashish trade through the Sinai between Israel and Egypt.

We had light refreshments during our discussions, but no other interruptions. About 1:30 P.M., after three solid hours of argument, we decided to adjourn for a few hours to eat, rest, and consult with our advisers.

Before we parted, I insisted on recapitulating the questions and problems still remaining—some of which we had already discussed, some not; some of which were minor, some major.

The Sinai—demilitarization, and how to define the word. This subject had hardly been touched, and would comprise the major terms of any Egyptian–Israeli treaty.

Israeli settlements in the West Bank, Gaza, and Sinai region. Begin was violently opposed to the dismantling of *any* Israeli settlements; Sadat felt just as strongly that there could not be one Israeli settler left in the Sinai, and that the West Bank and Golan Heights settlements should also be removed.

An independent Palestinian state. This was what Begin seemed to fear most; Sadat believed it was inevitable, but preferred limits on its independence.

The maintenance of Israeli defense forces at certain points in the West Bank and in Gaza. Israeli security was vital, and we had to determine how the military government would be withdrawn from the West Bank, the Palestinians given full autonomy, and Israel granted the right to retain some forces in specified military outposts.

Termination of Israeli military rule in the West Bank and Gaza, and the devolution of power. Begin claimed that Israel had authority over the land and therefore the sole right to grant this authority to the Palestinians; Sadat rejected this claim, and insisted that only the Palestinians themselves had any legitimate claim on the occupied territories.

The nature of "full autonomy" for the Palestinians promised by Israel. Begin claimed his country would be very generous here, but all the evidence was to the contrary.

Conflicting sovereignty claims over the West Bank. This involved the vital question of whether Israel's acquisition of territory by war was justified. Begin claimed that Israel had not initiated the 1967 war, and that if a war was defensive, then occupied territory could be kept by the victor.

Jerusalem—whether it should be divided, and how it should be administered. Sadat spoke up to say he had no thoughts of a divided Jerusalem. Begin retorted that Sadat wanted coequal, different sovereignties over parts of the city—a contradiction in terms.

The final definition of peace—an end to the embargo against Israel, enhancement of trade, open borders and waterways, diplomatic recognition, and the exchange of ambassadors. Sadat interrupted to say that he had previously offered unilaterally to guarantee open borders and full diplomatic exchange, but because of Begin's bad attitude, he was reconsidering the commitment.

Refugees—how many could return; what kind; who was to monitor. The Israelis wanted a minimum number of Arabs moving back into the West Bank, and insisted that they had the right to veto any such decisions; the Egyptians wanted maximum immigration, reunification of divided families, with full rights of the Palestinians to make decisions about the West Bank.

The Sinai airfields. The Israelis wanted to continue using them and to have the United States take over their operation; Sadat wanted all of them removed completely.

The participation by Jordan and other Arabs in future negotiations concerning the administration of territories. Sadat was confident that if a good agreement could be worked out concerning the West Bank and Palestinian rights, then Jordan and the Palestinians would participate in future negotiations; Begin couldn't have cared less about discussing the issue right now, but he was willing to provide for this eventuality later on *if* it was absolutely necessary.

Mutual defense treaties, which might some day involve the United States. Begin wanted them; Sadat encouraged the idea; I was convinced it would be a serious mistake if we were to continue being influential in resolving differences between Israel and her other neighbors. For us to be a formal ally of Israel would make it impossible to mediate between Israel and the Arab nations.

Recitation of this list was very depressing to me. All of us agreed it was reasonably complete and that we had a long way to go. At least we had been making progress in defining issues, even though we had not yet resolved any of them.

We adjourned under considerable strain. Begin expressed his complete confidence in Sadat, and it was quite conspicuous that Sadat did not make a similar statement in response.

I did not know where to go from there. We had accomplished little so far except to name the difficult issues. There was no compatibility between the two men, and almost every discussion of any subject deteriorated into an unproductive argument, reopening the old wounds of past political or military battles. Under intense pressure, the Egyptian leader moved away from details and words and into the realm of general principles and broad strategic concepts. When he was feeling pressed, the Israeli leader invariably shifted to a discussion of minutiae or semantics, with a recurrent inclination to recapitulate ancient history or to resurrect an old argument. Sadat had immediately outlined to me the two or three points on which he would not yield and had, in effect, given me a free hand to negotiate with great flexibility on almost all the other issues—full diplomatic recognition of Israel being one exception. The Israeli delegation was very reluctant to trust us with any revelation of its real ultimate desires or areas of possible compromise.

These differences shaped the negotiating technique I developed in the days ahead, and eventually opened up the road to an agreement. I would draft a proposal I considered reasonable, take it to Sadat for quick approval or slight modification, and then spend hours or days working on the same point with the Israeli delegation. Sometimes, in the end, the change of a word or phrase would satisfy Begin, and I would merely inform Sadat. I was never far from a good dictionary and thesaurus, and on occasion the American and Israeli delegations would all be clustered around one of these books, eagerly searching for acceptable synonyms. Would the Israelis withdraw "out of" certain areas or "into" military encampments? What was meant by "autonomy," "self-rule," "devolution," "Palestinian people," "authority," "minor modifications," "refugees," "insure, ensure, or guarantee," and so forth? The Egyptians were never involved in these kinds of discussions with me.

On any controversial issue, I never consulted Sadat's aides, but always went directly to their leader. It soon became obvious to all of us, however, that Dayan, Weizman, or Attorney General Barak could be convinced on an issue more quickly than the Prime Minister, and they were certainly more effective in changing Begin's mind than I ever was. The contrasting attitudes of the two leaders in dealing with details dovetailed very well, allowing me to plan our approach with increasing effectiveness whenever we reached one of the frequent crises. Had both men been preoccupied with semantics or details, my job would have been much more difficult.

More important was the bottom line: all three of us wanted peace; the people of Israel and Egypt wanted peace. Our efforts at Camp David were now prominent in the eyes of the world, and we did not want to fail—both leaders looked on themselves as men of destiny, holding the future of their nations in their hands.

When we agreed to meet again in the afternoon, none of us had any idea it would be our last meeting together for the duration of the negotiations. Paradoxically, it was the profound differences between them that allowed us to find a way to save the day. But these very differences would make things much worse before they could improve.

At the beginning, the afternoon meeting reflected the strain of the earlier arguments. Begin immediately went back to his original desire to avoid the difficult problems at Camp David. He said that regarding the Sinai issues, including settlements and airfields, we should turn the problem over to the military leaders, who could then meet for a few weeks, resolve the differences, and report back to the heads of state for approval. He did not care where these negotiations might be held.

Sadat quickly replied that this would be a complete waste of time. Without specific direction from the top, there would be no way that his Defense Minister could negotiate for Egypt. He added that under no circumstances would he yield on the Israeli settlements, and there would never be any military presence in the Sinai airfields. He did agree, with a flick of his fingers, that the place of a meeting was of no importance.

Begin said that Sadat would get the Sinai back, but we had to remember that Israel had suffered repeatedly when King Farouk, President Nasser, and President Sadat had all sent Egyptian forces to attack Israel from that area. He reminded Sadat of the transient nature of our own leadership but the permanent nature of the consequences of our decisions. He tried to convince Sadat that we had to be very careful not to make a mistake through undue haste. (Also, I felt sure he was trying to postpone the decision on removing Israeli settlers and airfields.) He said he would serve only two and one-half more years, and that Sadat had previously announced that he would not seek reelection. Sadat nodded. Begin added that the American President was limited to a maximum of six more years. Therefore, our terms in office were finite, but our agreement would be lasting. The differences between them over phased implementation involved only a matter of three to five years, Begin said, and if Sadat had a counterproposal concerning the time of implementation of a Sinai agreement, he would consider it. He went on to outline why Israel wanted to keep the airfields for a few years under military control and then maintain at least one for permanent civilian use.

Sadat stated that absolutely no military control would be permitted over Egyptian territory by Israel, the United States, or any other nation, and that Egypt had no use at all for the airstrips the Israelis had built. He would prefer that they be plowed up when the Israelis withdrew.

The Prime Minister then asked about navigation in the Straits of Tiran; whether Sadat would keep his commitment that they would be an open international waterway. Sadat replied, "Of course. I said so before and I will keep my promise."

Sadat launched into a long and eloquent presentation about the Egyptian people—how well they had responded to his peace initiative, and how they were not interested in hard bargaining with Israel. He added, "They will never accept an encroachment on their land or sovereignty. When Premier Begin says he will keep the Israeli settlements in the Sinai and defend them with force, it is an absolute insult to Egypt. I have tried to provide a model of friendship and coexistence for the rest of the Arab world leaders to emulate. Instead, I have become the object of extreme insult from Israel, and scorn and condemnation from the other Arab leaders. The Israeli attitude has worked against other Arabs' being willing to attempt peace with Israel. My initiative has come not out of weakness, but out of strength and self-confidence. With success at Camp David, I still dream of a meeting on Mount Sinai of us three leaders, representing three nations and three religious beliefs. This is still my prayer to God!"

This statement made quite an impression on both Begin and me. It obviously came from Sadat's heart.

The Prime Minister responded well, agreeing with the proposal for us to meet on Mount Sinai. He then reminded us that it had also taken courage to invite Sadat and to receive him in Jerusalem—the commanding officer of the nation that had launched a sneak attack on Israel only five years earlier in the October War, killing thousands of young Israeli troops. The hospitality with which Sadat had been received by the people of Israel was a true indication of the depth of their desire for peace, Begin said.

He then made a good debating point, which greatly annoyed Sadat—that the people of Egypt could be easily manipulated by Sadat, and their beliefs and attitudes could be shaped by their leader. There was a time when Sadat had convinced the Egyptian people that the Soviet Union was their best friend. Subsequently, because of Sadat's changed opinion, the Soviets were not their friends, and 19,000 technicians and advisers were sent back to Russia—a development received enthusiastically by the Egyptians. In 1967, Sadat convinced his people that the Israelis were their greatest enemy and that Egypt was threatened from the east. The same thing happened in 1973, and two wars were the result. Then, just four years later, in 1977, Sadat was received by his people as a hero with his initiative for peace, when he said that the Israelis were now Egypt's friends. It was obvious that under strong leadership, the opinion of the Egyptians could be changed.

Now, Begin went on, it was important that the few Israeli settlers in the Sinai be accepted by the Egyptian people as no threat to them and as no encroachment on their sovereignty. There were little more than two thousand Israelis in the thirteen Sinai settlements. The removal of these settlements would not be acceptable to Israel. Sadat could, if he wished, convince his people to accept them as permanent residents.

There seemed an absolute deadlock on the Sinai settlements. Within a few minutes Sadat announced angrily that a stalemate had been reached. He saw no reason for the discussions to continue. As far as he was concerned, they were over. Sadat then ignored Begin, stood up, and looked at me.

I was desperate, and quickly outlined the areas of agreement and the adverse consequences to both men if the peace effort foundered at this point because of the differences we had just discussed. I emphasized the United States' role in the Middle East, and reminded them that a new war in this troubled region under present conditions could easily escalate into another world war. I asked them to give me at least one more day to understand as best I could the positions of the two delegations, to devise my own compromise proposals, and to present my views to both of them. I pointed out to Prime Minister Begin that if the only cause for his rejection of the peace effort was the Sinai settlers, I did not believe the people of his nation or the Knesset would agree with him. It was my belief that he could sell this action to his people if he would let the settlers leave Egyptian territory.

He disputed this, saying that there was *no way* he could sell a dismantling of the Israeli settlements to his government or to his people. (He always said "dismantling," although we pointed out to him that the buildings need not be destroyed but could continue in use, after the Israelis left, if that was his preference.) To move the settlers would mean the downfall of his government— an outcome he was willing to accept if he believed in the cause. But he did *not* believe in it.

They were moving toward the door, but I got in front of them to partially block the way. I urged them not to break off their talks, to give me another chance to use my influence and analysis, to have confidence in me. Begin agreed readily. I looked straight at Sadat; finally, he nodded his head. They left without speaking to each other.

Had I known then that the two leaders would both stay at Camp David, I would have enjoyed the "silent drill" of the U.S. Marine Corps much more that evening. We had set up bleachers on the helicopter landing field and arranged for the Marines to

entertain our visitors with a marvelous display of military preci-
sion. The highly trained troops marched in close-order drill, fixed
bayonets on their rifles. Without audible commands or music,
they performed intricate maneuvers, sometimes twirling the heavy
firearms and sharp blades within a hair's breadth of one another.
Then came the music, including medleys of patriotic tunes from
all three nations. It should have been a night of excitement and
pleasure, but everyone was discouraged and unhappy. Most of the
spectators sat in strained silence. The word had spread like wild-
fire through Camp David that the talks had broken down.

During a brief reception for the Marine leaders and other visitors, I asked Sadat to let me meet that evening with the Egyptian
delegation. Mondale and Brown joined me, Vance, and Brzezinski;
and Egypt was represented by President Sadat, Deputy Prime
Minister el-Touhamy, Minister Kamel, and Minister Boutros Ghali.
We met at 10:30 P.M. and worked for two hours.

I opened the discussion. "I know you are all very discouraged
right now. The issue we addressed today was the Israeli settlements in the Sinai, which may be the most difficult one of all.
Our position is that they are illegal and should be removed. On
this, your views and ours are the same. President Sadat and
Prime Minister Begin both have very deep and adamant feelings
about this matter, and I do not yet know how it can be resolved.
All of us will explore every possibility with the Israeli delegation,
in hopes that we might uncover some route to progress. I ask that
you give me some more time before you leave."

Sadat replied, "My good friend Jimmy, we have already had
three long sessions. You know that on two issues I cannot
compromise—land and sovereignty. I cannot yield conquered
land to Israel, and if sovereignty is to mean anything to Egyptians,
all the Israelis must leave our territory. That man Begin is not
saying anything today that he might not have said prior to my
Jerusalem initiative. I am willing to have open borders, work on
other issues, and bring in other Arabs. The man is obsessed, and
keeps citing old European precedents. Begin haggles over every
word, and is making his withdrawal conditional on keeping land.
Begin is not ready for peace."

I said, "Mr. President, Begin is a tough and honest man. In the
past he has been quite hawkish. He sees his proposals as a start-
ing point, and he has been quite forthcoming, compared to other
leaders of Israel who preceded him. His present control over the
Sinai was derived from wars which Israel did not start. That is
Begin's perspective. Thus he feels that he has been very coopera-

tive with his proposals. On the settlements, Begin sincerely wants them to continue. One of his goals is to isolate Gaza from the Sinai, with the settlements as a buffer. Since you have now promised not to let major military forces go beyond the passes to threaten Israel, there is no longer a legitimate reason for him to maintain the settlements. We do not agree with him and he knows it, but so far he persists. It is extremely painful for him to change his position on these settlements. On the airfields, the Israelis want some arrangement for transitional control, and I believe this should be worked out. I myself will try to devise an acceptable formula for the West Bank."

Sadat said, "I have had two earlier discussions about these settlements, with Dayan and with Weizman. I told Dayan in Jerusalem that one of the main reasons for the October War was the settlement at Yamit in the Sinai. Dayan then said he was ready to abandon it for peace. Weizman has said that keeping the Sinai settlements is important only as a precedent for Golan and the West Bank. As for the airports, Weizman has agreed with Defense Minister Gamasi that they are not necessary. The Israelis have urged us to exclude you Americans from any discussions. They want the West Bank, and are willing to give back the Sinai to me in exchange for the West Bank. They have ignored completely my great gesture."

Then Mondale spoke. "One of the most powerful arguments is that the Sinai is yours, and the world and Israel acknowledge that it is yours. There should be no Israeli settlements on it. But what about the other issues—can they be resolved?"

Sadat said, "I must have also a resolution of the West Bank and Gaza. I cannot do the Sinai alone. I am ready to be flexible, but not on the Sinai."

I replied, "Sovereignty issues are different in the Sinai and Golan Heights from the West Bank. Begin cannot now accept foreign sovereignty over the West Bank, and I agree with him. For the time being, we must permit the Jews and Arabs to live together. We should be able to work out something on self-rule. Also, the Israelis want some assurance that the United Nations forces cannot be withdrawn from Sharm el-Sheyk and other key points in the Sinai after Israeli troops leave. And I would like to make one final comment about Prime Minister Begin. He is an honorable man, although tenacious. Even if he does not want United States participation in the talks, the other members of the Israeli delegation want us here."

Sadat said, "I am willing to give them two years to phase out the Sinai settlements."

I replied, "You must be more flexible on the exact time—two or three years."

Sadat: "Okay."

Brzezinski discussed the West Bank problems for a few moments, and then he focused on the Sinai, mentioning Israel's desire that there be a United States airbase near Yamit.

Sadat objected to this idea. "This would be bad for you and for us. It will make you look as though you are looking for a military base on my land."

I suggested to Sadat that he let me develop a paper based on some of his own positions with which I agreed, Begin's proposal on home rule for the West Bank and Gaza, plus my own proposals which might be acceptable compromises. I would have to count on him for maximum flexibility to accommodate the Israeli position.

Kamel said, "The whole Arab world expects from the United States something that is in keeping with your known positions. Otherwise moderate Arab governments who cooperate with you will be quite vulnerable. Withdrawal from the Sinai and Golan Heights must be to international borders. All Israeli settlements are illegal, but on the West Bank they can have time. The dismantling need not be rushed; for the time being a freeze will do. On the Palestinian question, we need in the agreement what you and President Sadat said at Aswan: that the Palestinians must have a voice in the determination of their own future, and their problem must be solved in all its aspects. We are glad to be rid of the Soviets, and we do not want them back. That is why we want your proposals to be consistent with your stated positions. We value our good relationship with the United States and want to maintain it."

I replied, "You cannot now negotiate and resolve all the specific issues concerning the West Bank and the Palestinian problem without the Jordanians. Neither can we. We cannot convince the Israelis to withdraw from the Golan Heights if the Syrians refuse to discuss the matter with Israel. We have no intention of negotiating on behalf of Syria or Jordan. They can come in later, when they see the benefits of our own agreement. There will have to be some general language evolved now at Camp David, particularly concerning the West Bank and Israel's problems with its other neighbors. On the Sinai, it can be much more specific, because you and Israel, the principal parties, can now negotiate directly with one another. Begin's proposal for home rule on the West Bank does provide a basis for resolution of problems during a transition period. If King Hussein does not come in, I hope President Sadat will substitute for him for a while. The Israeli proposal does not deserve to be rejected out of hand."

I had been worrying about how to handle some remaining differences between Egypt and Israel, and now thought of a precedent which might be applied. "On a few unresolved issues there can also be different Egyptian and Israeli interpretations. This is what was done in the Shanghai communiqué between my country and China. We both agreed that there was one China, but we did not destroy the agreement by trying to define 'one China' too specifically." The wording had been precise, but the meaning deliberately obscure, permitting each nation to interpret it as desired.

Kamel said, "The Palestinians would prefer their affairs to be administered by other Arabs rather than by so-called 'home rule.' Otherwise they will be chewed up by Israeli settlements."

Vance asked, "Suppose the authority for home rule was granted to the Palestinians from all three nations—Israel, Jordan, and Egypt?"

Sadat said, "I can agree to that—combining our ideas with Begin's plan through such a formula. The Israeli withdrawal from the West Bank area would then be to agreed security points, and the Palestinians could govern themselves without interference from the Israelis within the previously occupied territory."

As we prepared to adjourn, I said, "Stalemate here would just provide an opportunity for the most radical elements to take over in the Middle East. A trial period for the West Bank can work, if we agree on it. If we don't, then Moscow and the radicals will rejoice. All of you must understand our special commitment to Israel, and the fact that the Israelis do indeed want peace. They have not yet responded adequately to the Sadat peace initiative—but they have offered to leave the Sinai and to give autonomy or self-government to the West Bank Arabs; and our hope is that they will stop building settlements in the West Bank and remove them from the Sinai. All of this should be acknowledged. We simply must find a formula that both Egypt and Israel can accept. If you give me a chance, I don't intend to fail."

We adjourned after midnight, and all of us—Americans and Egyptians—felt much better than we had during the Marine drill. This had been a busy day, and we were exhausted as we left.

Although I have described in detail only those meetings in which I participated and took notes personally, during each day our people were hard at work assessing the attitudes of the Egyptian and Israeli delegations, probing for possible agreement, drafting proposals derived from my own meetings or theirs, and trying to engender a more cooperative attitude within the camp. While I had met with Begin and Sadat that morning, for instance, Fritz, Cy, and Zbig were with Dayan, Weizman, and Barak. During the afternoon, this group was joined by Harold Brown as the discussions continued with some of the Egyptian delegation to probe for the intentions behind the Egyptian paper. Then the American group met again with the Israelis to talk about how refugees could be returned to the West Bank, what specific locations and troop strengths were considered necessary for security, how to handle the settlements issue, and what authority might be given an interim regime. After each such session, members of the American team would give me a written report, just as I let a few of them read my dictated notes.

The delegation members who were not themselves involved in the negotiations held long strategy sessions, reviewed documents, drafted papers, and conducted the routine business of the three nations with those left behind in Washington, Cairo, and Jerusalem. For others, the motion-picture projectors ground away, and there were bikes to ride, books to read, and quiet trails for walking. It was gratifying to see a few more conversations between Egyptians and Israelis, but these seemed to wax and wane as harmony among the leaders improved and deteriorated.

Although we had been at Camp David only three days, the affairs of the rest of the world seemed to fade rapidly from our minds. My world became the negotiating rooms, the study where I pored over my notes and maps of the Middle East, and the swimming pool, tennis court, bike and jogging paths, and quiet and secluded trails through the thick woods where nobody roamed except me. During the brief times between discussions, I craved intense exercise and lonely places where I could think, and sometimes pray.

FRIDAY, DAY FOUR *(September 8, 1978)*

I was up early again this morning to work by myself on formulations which might possibly break the deadlock, or at least provide enough incentive to keep both negotiating teams in the camp. A sense of gloom and foreboding still prevailed, and my personal notes indicate how anxious I was. Our team spent two hours with the Israelis during the morning to follow up on our midnight discussions with the Egyptians. Sadat's aides had told Brzezinski they were seriously considering leaving, convinced that Begin would never yield on the settlements issue.

I arranged to see Begin at 2:30 P.M. and Sadat two hours later. When the Israeli leader arrived, there was very little I could say. My only option was to outline again the areas of agreement and request flexibility on his part. He complained that the United States negotiators were all agreeing with the Egyptian demand that the Sinai settlements be removed, and that this was no way for a mediating team to act. Then he pulled from his pocket the dog-eared copy of Sadat's demands and began once again to delineate its unacceptable portions. I tried to convince him that this was not the final Egyptian position, and that the Egyptians were willing to be accommodating within the limits previously explained to him. I had been assured of this by Sadat, but said that I now needed to explore all the issues with Begin, to understand the equivalent degree of Israel's flexibility.

Begin said he did not see how honorable men could put forward one thing publicly and a different thing privately.

I explained that there were some things the Egyptians could not propose as their own preference, but might be willing to accept if they knew it was my desire and if in the general negotiation the totality of an agreement was considered to be in Egypt's interest. There were different degrees of intensity in Sadat's beliefs; he had told all of us that he would not yield on sovereignty or land, but would try to compromise on other issues. I said that this attitude toward the negotiations was the reason Sadat strongly desired the United States to be a full partner in the talks—to probe for acceptable modifications in the original proposals of both nations.

Prime Minister Begin ignored this comment completely, and listed in detail the elements of the original Sadat demands, even though many of them had never been pursued by the Egyptians and others had almost immediately been abandoned.

He then gave another half-hour explanation of why it was imperative that the Sinai settlements be retained, pointing out that there were 400,000 people in Gaza who were highly susceptible to subversion and might prove a threat to Israel.

He stated emphatically, "I will never personally recommend that the settlements in the Sinai be dismantled!" He added, "Please, Mr. President, do not make this a United States demand."

I noted with great interest, but without comment, the change in his words and was heartened by it. "Never personally recommend" did not mean that he would never permit the settlements to be removed. The change was subtle but extremely significant. If others in Israel could be made to assume the onus for the decision, then finally there was at least a possibility for resolving this vital issue.

I reiterated that Sadat was flexible, and that the Egyptians' written position was not their final one. (Once Sadat made up his mind on an issue, he was immutable. The challenge was to avoid a final decision by him until after I had a chance to give him all my arguments, and to let him know how strongly I was going to pursue the particular point.) I also stated to Begin that I absolutely disagreed with him about the settlements, now that Sadat had agreed there would be no attack forces in the Sinai. Instead, there would be 130 kilometers of demilitarized desert between Egypt and Israel, with buffer zones and monitoring stations to insure that this commitment would be honored. I emphasized that there were no reasons for the settlements to exist after a peace agreement, and that they would be a source more of aggravation and dissension than of peace and security.

Once more Begin implored, "Mr. President, do not put this in a proposal to us."

I responded, "Mr. Prime Minister, we cannot avoid addressing the most contentious issues, and this is the one on which the entire Camp David talks have foundered so far. I cannot let Sadat tell me not to discuss Israeli security on the West Bank. I cannot let you tell me not to discuss the Israeli presence on Egyptian territory."

He pointed out that there had to be two agreements at Camp David; the most important was between the United States and Israel, and the other, of secondary importance but obviously also crucial, was between Israel and Egypt. The most important one would have to come first. He wanted the world to know that there were no serious differences between Israel and the United States.

It was true that the relationship between our two nations was vital to Israel, but I also knew it was a good negotiating tactic by either Sadat or Begin first to reach agreement with me and then to have the two of us confront the third. Sadat had understood this strategy before he arrived at Camp David. Begin was just now beginning to realize the disadvantage of being odd man out. I must admit that I capitalized on this situation with both delegations in order to get an agreement; it greatly magnified my own influence.

The Prime Minister then discussed the West Bank settlements in some detail, and asked me again not to include a discussion of any Israeli settlements in conversations between our Cabinet members and other negotiators, nor to mention them in any United States plan.

I replied that I could not agree that I would produce a plan which excluded the settlements, and asked him bluntly if he objected to our producing a United States proposal at all.

He answered that he did indeed object, that he had always thought it was a bad idea. This was a belated admission of an attitude that had become apparent to us all. Begin went on to say that any United States plan would become the focal point of dissension and disagreement after we adjourned from Camp David, and that there was no likelihood of its being accepted by either the Israelis or the Arabs. Those who would disagree with individual parts of the proposal would take out their displeasure on the United States, which might turn the entire Arab world against us.

I told him I was prepared to face such an eventuality, because the alternative was a deterioration in the present situation, which might lead to war that involved the security of my own country. Political considerations—even the loss of some friendships—were not my paramount concern.

I reminded him that for months Sadat had urged me to play an active role, to be a full partner, and that I saw no possibility of progress if the United States should withdraw and simply leave the negotiations to the Egyptians and Israelis, who honestly did not trust each other and often admitted an absence of even mutual respect. I noted that when Sadat had arrived at Camp David, the first analysis he had made was that Begin did not want a peace agreement and only wanted land.

Begin replied, "Both of those claims are false."

I said, "I realize that, but that is the way the Egyptians feel. This atmosphere between the two of you is not conducive to any agreement. We are going to present a comprehensive proposal for peace. It will not surprise either you or Sadat. When it is finished tomorrow, I will present it to you first, and then to the Egyptians. I can see no other possibility for progress."

It was almost four o'clock, and we had to end the discussion. There was really not much more to say. As he left, Begin asked me if it was possible for Weizman to meet with Sadat regarding the four items concerning the Sinai. I told him that all *five* items, *including* the settlements, should be discussed between them, that I was on my way to Sadat's cabin and would arrange for the meeting he had suggested. He then asked if Rosalynn and I would join the Israelis for the Friday evening meal, and we arranged for him and Mrs. Begin to stop for us on the way to supper. I asked if Sadat was also invited, so that I might encourage him to come, but the Prime Minister replied, "No, not this time."

When I arrived at Sadat's cabin, he welcomed me warmly. He had prepared some heavily flavored mint tea, which I always enjoyed. I told him that we faced some serious problems and asked him to be patient. It would be very embarrassing to me if both nations were to reject the proposals on which I had been working. My impression after meeting with Prime Minister Begin this afternoon was that the Israelis were sure to reject them.

Sadat promised that he would be totally patient and would under no circumstances put me in a difficult position. He wanted to know my plans for the coming days at Camp David.

I told him that Begin did not want me to present an official United States proposal, but that I had already informed him the paper would be completed tomorrow and presented first to the Israelis and then to Sadat. I would spend the Jewish Sabbath concluding my work on the draft, preparing a summary of the agreements and differences, and having the texts typed for distribution. After study, each group should present its views to me, and I would relay them to the other. The time for the three of us to meet together was over. I would continue to meet individually with the two leaders, back and forth, until the best possible compromise had been evolved, at which point the three of us, along with our key advisers, would all meet.

He asked, "This would be a final meeting?"

I replied that it might have to consist of more than one session, but it would be the time for final arrangements. In fact, we never reached a point where an agreement was imminent enough to bring them both together, so such a meeting never took place.

Sadat promised that if my plan did not violate land and sovereignty issues over the Golan Heights and Sinai, he would support any reasonable proposal I might put forward. He insisted that the United States and Egypt must agree.

I told him I would honor his confidence, that I would be sure to protect the rights of the Palestinians and other Arabs, and that I would certainly not put him in an embarrassing position.

He said, "I will be flexible, and will stay here as long as there is hope for a success."

This conversation had taken about fifteen minutes. We then held an extensive discussion about Lebanon—how important it was that we all work to bring peace to that country. Sadat asked if I had devoted much time to this problem. I had to admit that since direct American interest was aroused primarily in moments of crisis, we had not mounted a concerted effort to find a permanent solution to the continuing Lebanese tragedy. He urged me to work with France and Saudi Arabia in order to remove the Maronite Christians' dependence on Israel. Cooperating with Lebanese President Elias Sarkis, he said, the Arab and Western nations could meet the needs of the Lebanese people.

In answer to my next question—if he would be willing to meet with Ezer Weizman—he smiled broadly and responded that he would look forward with pleasure to the appointment.

We ended our meeting with a mutual pledge of friendship and fair settlement of the Middle East peace talks. Sadat said that he had no animosity toward Begin or the Israelis, did not wish to put them in an awkward position, and wanted mutual success rather than a victory over anyone.

That evening Rosalynn and I had a delightful time with the entire Israeli delegation, enjoying a delicious kosher meal and trying to join in the robust singing. The Israelis seemed carefree and lighthearted, in a completely different mood from their attitude during our discouraging negotiations. Although no concessions had been made and there was no tangible basis for any optimism, I was much more encouraged as we returned to our cabin.

SATURDAY, DAY FIVE *(September 9, 1978)*

On this day and all others, I had to conduct the affairs of our nation between meetings and study of the Middle East issues. Fritz Mondale handled everything possible for me in Washington, and took a helicopter up to Camp David whenever he could get away at night or on weekends. When my Cabinet members or others needed to talk to me personally or have me sign some official document, they also made quick trips, although they never stayed long. Realizing how busy I was with the peace effort, everyone tried to relieve me of most of the routine administrative duties of the Presidency.

I spent almost the entire day working on the comprehensive proposal to be presented to the two delegations, consulting very closely with the other members of the American team. There were more than fifty distinct issues to be resolved, some of them separable but most of them closely intertwined. None of them was new. We tried to put them into perspective, and to spell out the sequence of events we might expect after we concluded our work at Camp David.

I was not getting much sleep, and fatigue was taking its toll. At times, I had difficulty remembering all the intricacies of international law, the history of past negotiations, the composition of military forces, the geography of the area, the nuances of what Begin or Sadat had said, the reports from meetings my advisers had held with the other delegations, and the arguing points that I had to use on the spur of the moment to keep the talks going. Now we were having to look to the future and devise an agreement that might resolve the apparent deadlock between Begin and Sadat. I knew that Sadat and I could come up with a reasonable agreement which a majority of Israelis would gladly accept. My major task was to convince Prime Minister Begin. In a way, I understood his dilemma. He was the one who was being pressured to change the private and public commitments of a lifetime. Although he had my sympathy, I was not reluctant to do all I could to persuade him.

The only thing that would succeed was a proposal that was patently fair, that did not violate Sadat's broad principles, and that—hopefully—we could sell to the other members of the Israeli delegation. From daybreak and throughout Saturday, the entire American delegation bent to this task, and shortly after midnight the document was ready to be put into final form.

Our proposal incorporated all the attractive items. Among these were: an end to war; permanent peace; free transit by Israel through all international waterways; secure and recognized borders; a full range of normal relations between nations; phased withdrawal by Israel from the Sinai; demilitarization of that area; monitoring stations to insure compliance with this agreement; termination of blockades and boycotts; a procedure for settling future disputes; the extension of the principles to future agreements between Israel and its other neighbors; rapid granting of full autonomy to the Palestinians, followed by a five-year transition period for determining the permanent status of the West Bank and Gaza; withdrawal of Israeli armed forces from the West Bank into specified security locations; a prompt settlement of the refugee problem; and a three-month period to complete a peace treaty between Egypt and Israel.

It also included American judgments on the most controversial issues: inclusion of the phrase "inadmissibility of acquisition of territory by war"; the possibility of full diplomatic recognition of Israel by Egypt; the participation by Jordan and the Palestinians as equal partners with Israel and Egypt in all future negotiations concerning the West Bank, including control of returning refugees; recognition of the legitimate rights of the Palestinian people and their participation in determining their own future; linking of the West Bank and Gaza to Jordan; authority in these areas to be devolved jointly from Egypt, Israel, and Jordan; a strong local police force with Jordanian participation; and the application of United Nations Resolution 242 in determining the permanent status of the West Bank. In addition, there was a paragraph defining the status of Jerusalem. We had decided to call for the removal of all Israeli settlements from the Sinai, and a freeze on settlements in other occupied territory until all negotiations were complete, but we would not include this request in the first draft. Otherwise, Prime Minister Begin would have concentrated on it almost to the exclusion of the other issues.

SUNDAY, DAY SIX *(September 10, 1978)*

We planned to present our proposals to the Israelis and Egyptians late on Sunday afternoon and evening, but first we needed a change of scenery—to do something to break the tension and relieve the monotony of looking at nothing but the Camp David trees and meeting rooms. A few months earlier, Jody Powell and I had invited Shelby Foote, the historian, to Camp David. He had given us a special briefing on battles fought in the area during the War Between the States, and then we had visited some of these sites together. One was Gettysburg, which is just inside Pennsylvania, a few miles from Camp David. Now it seemed a good place for an outing after our church services and lunch.

We adopted an important ground rule: no discussion of the peace talks with each other or with the press while we were on the trip. Sadat and Begin rode in my limousine—I sat between them—and we had a pleasant talk about the countryside and about Abraham Lincoln and the War. I had made a special study of Gettysburg for the previous visit, and I soon discovered that all the military leaders from both Israel and Egypt were quite familiar with the terrain, the tactics followed during the fighting, and the strategic circumstances prevailing at that time. They had studied the classic Battle of Gettysburg in military schools. During our tour, they were given a sober reminder that the people of our country had suffered horribly when brothers fought each other. As we examined the field pieces and noted the casualty figures, all of us agreed that the weapons of the time had been developed to an extraordinary degree compared to medical science and the ability to treat wounds. Prime Minister Begin showed relatively little interest in the battle history, but he was excited and intrigued to be at the site of Lincoln's famous address. He seemed to know it by heart, and considered it one of the best and simplest speeches ever made.

Late in the afternoon, after returning from Gettysburg, we had our meeting with the Israelis. Mondale, Vance, Brzezinski, Dayan, Weizman, and Barak joined Begin and me. I knew this would be a crucial session, in which I would have to secure the Israelis' confidence and give them a positive preview of the kind of peace settlement I thought would be acceptable in Israel when its terms were revealed.

I began by stressing that the meeting was the culmination of months of work and years of planning in the hope of bringing peace; the consequences of failure were clear. I tried to assure them that the document was a balanced one, but had to acknowledge that the final decisions would not be easy for either side.

"There are phrases in it which both you and Sadat will find difficult to accept—not because they would hurt your countries, but because they are different from positions you have taken and statements you have made in the past. My task will now be hopeless if either of you rejects the language of United Nations Resolution 242.

"Sadat is willing to continue negotiations toward a final peace treaty even if King Hussein is not, but Sadat received a message today from Hussein saying he would be willing to join the agreement if it is acceptable to him. In any case, it is important to remember that an agreement between Israel and Egypt would preclude any successful attack against your country by other Arab countries. Without Egypt, they could not successfully challenge you. This in itself would be a major source of security, but of course, it should be seen only as a first step on the way to agreement with the other Arab states.

"This document which I am about to hand you will be given tonight to Sadat. I hope you will be flexible and minimize any proposed changes.

"We are holding back on three issues: sovereignty of the West Bank and Gaza—not to be resolved here at Camp David; Israeli settlements—they will need to be treated separately; and specific agreements on the Sinai withdrawal. I would like to resolve the last two issues during our negotiations here."

After everybody had read the document, Begin said, "Sadat's original proposal and this one may decide the future of the people of Israel. Therefore, I would propose we adjourn so that we can reflect on it. There are positive elements in it; there are also some that could cause grave peril to our people. After study, we could then give you our reaction in all candor. We would also ask that you defer giving this to President Sadat. According to a presidential letter of December 1975, the United States promised to coordinate with Israel any proposal it puts forward for a peace settlement. Furthermore, since there are now an Egyptian document and one from the United States, there should also be an Israeli document for publication. I have already told Sadat that his is unacceptable. Therefore we will produce our own, because all three should be published. I will leave this room deeply worried, so please adjourn this meeting until, for example, 10:00 P.M."

I replied, "If you insist, I will, of course, have to defer to your request for adjournment, but my own preference is to explain now some of the substantial differences between this plan and the Egyptian demands." I pressed forward hurriedly. "I did not draft this proposal with the idea that either side would alter it substantially. I have tried to keep in mind what Israel wants and needs. Most essential is your permanent good relationship with Egypt, which would assure adequate security for Israel. This document avoids the difficult issue of total withdrawal from the West Bank, it gives you guaranteed access to the Straits of Tiran and through the Suez, freedom of movement of people across the borders, an undivided Jerusalem, an end to the boycott on trade and commerce, and a guarantee against the deployment of any Egyptian attack forces in the Sinai beyond the Mitla and Gidi passes.

"This document is not meant for publication. Only the final version will be published after Israel and Egypt have both accepted it. There are some more things I want for Israel, and may be able to get, including full diplomatic recognition and the exchange of ambassadors between you and Egypt. On the settlements, anything acceptable to both you and Sadat is all right with me. My commitment is to continue to try to represent your interests and to negotiate for you with Sadat, and I will help in any way possible, including withdrawing from direct involvement, if that is necessary. I believe that Sadat will be willing to accept this basic document."

We then had a heated discussion about the language in United Nations Resolution 242—"inadmissibility of acquisition of territory by war." Begin insisted again that this formulation was unacceptable. Brzezinski pointed out that our proposal for the West Bank called for permanent boundaries to be drawn, as determined by negotiation.

The Prime Minister responded, "This language applies only to wars of aggression; therefore we cannot base our negotiations on it. The war of 1967 [Six Day War] gives Israel the right to change frontiers."

He was angry, and so was I.

I replied, "Do you reject United Nations Resolution 242? Your definition of its meaning is biased. To delete this phrase would mean that we have no basis for negotiation now or in the future. What you say convinces me that Sadat was right—what you want is land! We are not precluding any future negotiations with your neighbors."

Begin retorted, "The problem of security also involves territory. We are willing to return Sinai. For the time being we are conceding, as Dr. Brzezinski admits, our legitimate claims of sovereignty over Judea, Samaria, and Gaza."

The discussion was getting nowhere. We had simply begun to rehash old arguments. I hoped that Dayan, Weizman, and Barak could do more with Begin than I. We adjourned until 9:30 that evening.

I reported these developments to Sadat, and he agreed to my request that we postpone my scheduled meeting with him until the next day.

The same American and Israeli participants met again in the evening. I never dreamed when we sat down at 9:35 P.M. that we would still be arguing at 3:00 in the morning.

Begin began. "Parts of the document are deeply appreciated and positive—a beautiful number [paragraph] on Jerusalem. We appreciate your efforts, but we have a proposal for some changes. Tomorrow we will have a response to the Egyptian document. Tonight we have responses to your proposal, number by number."

Attorney General Aharon Barak began, one by one. The first series of proposals were to delete all references to United Nations Resolution 242. I had intended to let the Israelis go through all their proposed changes before responding to any of them, but I could not restrain myself.

I interrupted. "This is not the time to beat around the bush. If you had openly disavowed United Nations Resolution 242, I would not have invited you to Camp David nor called this meeting."

Begin replied, "We do not consider the resolution to be self-implementing—that includes the preamble—and this has been our position for eleven years."

To me, this claim was gobbledygook for rejecting the only document on which all Middle East peace efforts had been based. Israel and almost all other UN members had accepted it in its entirety. I said, "Maybe that is why you haven't had peace for eleven years. So far tonight, all your suggestions have been to delete parts of the United Nations Resolution. Israel has repeatedly endorsed 242, but now you are not willing to respect the language. If you don't espouse 242, it is a terrible blow to peace."

Begin countered, "I am willing to respect it, but not as a basis for what follows in your proposal."

I retorted, "The entire United Nations Resolution consists of only one sentence; you cannot cut it up. There are a few words important to President Sadat, and one such phrase is the inadmissibility of territorial change by war."

Dayan suggested, "Our proposals regarding the Sinai and the West Bank don't involve territorial change, but knowing the Arab interpretation of the disputed phrase, we don't want it. Resolution 242 doesn't commit us to go back [to 1967 borders] everywhere."

I said, "Our document makes clear that borders have to be negotiated. If Sadat agrees with our paper, then that becomes his position as well. Sadat genuinely wants an agreement with you, and in some ways he is representing the Arab world. He is not trying to undercut your negotiating positions with Syria and

Jordan on the permanent status of the Golan Heights and the West Bank. He does want to resolve the Sinai issue here—some years from now, the others can be resolved. You can then work out either a self-government or partition for the West Bank. That is why the wording here is flexible, and you should take advantage of it. But this cannot be merely an Israeli–Egyptian treaty."

Begin spoke again. "We don't object to your praise for Sadat, but he wants us to go back every inch. Sadat wants an agreement with Israel on his terms, and these are a danger to Israel. We speak here of the very existence of our nation."

Weizman urged, "Let's move on."

This kind of exchange took place for hours as we laboriously analyzed every sentence in the American proposal. We argued about how to word the guarantee by Sadat that the waterways would be kept open for Israeli shipping, with Begin claiming that the Egyptians had no right to close the Suez Canal to Israeli shipping in the first place and that therefore Sadat's willingness to open it now could not be considered a concession. Begin seemed completely unconcerned with the Palestinian problem. He objected to almost every reference to the Palestinian issue, including the phrases, "resolve the Palestinian problem in all its aspects" and "legitimate rights," stating that the latter was a tautology and there was no telling where it might lead. Begin also insisted that we change the words "Palestinian people" to "Palestinian Arabs."

A serious problem developed when we got to the part about autonomy for the Palestinians (or "full autonomy," to use Begin's frequently repeated phrase). As the Israelis proposed alternate language, it became clear that they did not want to give the residents of the West Bank and Gaza any appreciable control over their own affairs. Although they had already agreed to withdraw their military government, to confine their forces to prescribed security points, and to cut their military presence by more than half, they now wanted to plant Israelis throughout the region, in order to maintain "public order." Additionally, they wanted a veto right over decisions made by the local citizens on any subject.

I declared, "What you want to do is make the West Bank part of Israel."

Vance added, "The whole idea is to let the people govern themselves. You are retaining a veto!"

Begin responded, "We want to keep the right to do so—but we don't intend to do so."

I said, "No self-respecting Arab would accept this. It looks like a subterfuge. We are talking about full autonomy—self-control. You are not giving them autonomy if you have to approve their laws, exercise a veto over their decisions, and maintain a military governor."

Begin insisted, "Autonomy doesn't mean sovereignty."

Weizman replied, "We want to have a time factor, to give the idea a test."

I said, "Sadat will not negotiate on the details you have proposed. He doesn't give a damn whether there are eleven or fifteen departments in a West Bank government. What is important is whether these people have an irrevocable right to self-government. If I were an Arab, I would prefer the present Israeli occupation to this proposal of yours."

We then spent a lot of time with dictionaries, looking up the meaning of "autonomy," "sovereignty," and "rights."

Dayan finally said, "We shall reconsider our objections—we will look into it. If we accept your language, it is because we understand that Sadat cannot negotiate such details. We are not after political control. If it seems that way to you, we will look at it again."

I wanted to allay their fears. "I will try hard to make sure that only the permanent residents of the West Bank and Gaza will participate in the negotiations—not all Palestinians. Sadat is looking for formulas which will not isolate him, but I will try to get him to agree. If you delay implementation of the West Bank agreement for three years, however, Sadat will also delay the signing of any peace treaty."

In their discussions with Vance and Brown, the Israelis had previously said they would withdraw their military forces and redeploy them in prescribed security locations. Now they wanted to delete this commitment from the document. I pointed out that it would be better to keep our language, sign the agreement with Sadat, and later work with Hussein to determine the exact location and composition of security outposts in the West Bank area. We finally agreed that I would submit the language to Sadat, indicating where the Israelis disputed it.

The arguments continued. Begin proposed inserting "Jerusalem, the capital of Israel," but then dropped the suggestion when Dayan ridiculed the idea of getting Sadat to sign such wording. I also added that the United States does not recognize this claim. We continued to argue about almost every point in our document, including the issues on which the Israelis had previously agreed. It became obvious that Begin had devised a hard-line position, analogous to the one Sadat had presented the first day. The difference was that Begin was debating every point tenaciously, while Sadat had made it clear to us from the beginning that his document included extreme Egyptian positions on which he would not insist. It was very aggravating and discouraging at this late hour, but with the help of Dayan, Weizman, and Barak, we made some slow progress.

We finally adjourned, and I asked Dayan to walk back with me to my cottage. He was a competent and level-headed man. I felt that if either he or Weizman were heading the delegation, we would already have reached agreement (although it was Begin's proposal on the Sinai that had helped to bring us to Camp David). I needed Dayan's special assistance at this time, but recognized the necessity of his loyalty to the Prime Minister. Although we were both exhausted after a long day, it was time for a serious talk.

I told Dayan that I considered Begin to be unreasonable and an obstacle to progress, and was beginning to have doubts about his genuine commitment to an agreement and to a subsequent peace treaty. I outlined the moves Sadat had made to be forthcoming, and his private assurances to me concerning additional flexibility—provided a few crucial points were honored. I asked Dayan to help me within the Israeli delegation with these few issues.

Dayan understood my problem but was convinced that Begin did want an agreement. He said that the issue of the settlements was the most difficult for Begin, especially as it concerned those in the Sinai. He asked me to try to induce Sadat to let the title to the settlements be transferred to Egypt but allow the Israelis to continue to live there for a limited time, just as they would be permitted to live in Cairo or Alexandria. This request seemed reasonable to him, and might satisfy both Begin and Sadat, he said.

I promised to bring this matter up with Sadat, but did not think there was any chance for success, because he would consider it a violation of Egyptian sovereignty. The subject had been almost exhausted as far as I was concerned. Since arriving at Camp David, more than half my time with Begin, whether or not Sadat was present, had been spent in discussing the Sinai settlements.

Dayan hoped that the airfield near Sharm el-Sheyk could be turned over to the United Nations peacekeeping forces, the one near El Arish to the Americans, and the one near Etzion retained by the Israelis for a time. I was not yet familiar with the geography of the Sinai, but promised to talk to Weizman and later to

Sadat. Soon I was to be involved in this question up to my eyeballs.

We talked quietly about the other issues during these early morning hours, alone except for Dayan's aide, who remained on the road ready to drive Dayan to his cabin in a golf cart. Daybreak was approaching, but it was still dark as Dayan turned to leave. He had difficulty seeing the trees between him and the path, and when he walked into one of them, I was reminded of how seriously his eyesight was impaired. My heart went out to him; I considered him a friend and a proper ally. Because Prime Minister Begin trusted his Foreign Minister and relied on him for advice, this discussion was to be an important and fruitful one. I was bone tired, but I could now approach the few remaining hours I had to prepare for my meeting with President Sadat with more enthusiasm—and more hope that we might be successful.

MONDAY, DAY SEVEN *(September 11, 1978)*

Although I got up early to incorporate into our proposal the Israeli changes with which we agreed, a final typed version was not ready when Sadat arrived at Aspen. He came alone, and we discussed the prospective Sinai negotiations while we waited.

Though I was not well prepared, I outlined the kind of agreement I had in mind, including Dayan's proposals. Sadat was not willing to let any of the airfields remain on his land, and he immediately rejected the idea of Egyptian title to the Sinai settlements while Israelis continued to live in them.

When I asked him if he would permit Jews from any nation, including Israel, to live in Cairo or in Aswan, he replied, "Of course." I pointed out to him that in that case it was not logical to exclude them from the Sinai settlements.

Sadat said, "Some things in the Middle East are not logical or reasonable. For Egypt, this is one of them."

He was firm—they would have to leave.

I asked whether he would insist on the destruction of the facilities. Sadat replied, "The Israelis can remove whatever portable facilities are there. If they wish, they can remove the buildings. But I need places for my people to live, and we will be glad to use whatever is left. I will accommodate the preference of the Israelis, and will put this in writing if necessary. Also, I will be responsible for finding a homesite elsewhere in Egypt for any settlers who wish to live in my country."

He wanted the withdrawal of all Israelis from the Sinai to be completed within two years. I preferred three years, to accommodate Israeli needs, and he agreed.

The documents arrived, and Sadat read the entire proposal aloud, pausing occasionally to comment or to suggest a change. The first difficulty came as a surprise; he made a new demand that Egyptian and Jordanian armed forces be allowed in the West Bank–Gaza areas. I objected strongly, but he replied that otherwise he would be agreeing to exclusive Israeli military occupation in those territories.

I asked him to include in the document new language which would provide for diplomatic recognition, the exchange of ambassadors, joint cultural programs, and expanded trade between Egypt and Israel. He responded that with different Israeli leadership, he would do so, but that Begin's attitude precluded his being so forthcoming at this time. I persisted (and was to do so for several days), because this would be seen as a generous gesture, would set a tone of real peace and harmony, and would be good for both countries. The Israelis were not involved in this discussion, and Sadat knew it. It was just between him and me. For now, I did not win the argument.

Then we discussed Jerusalem, which everyone at Camp David recognized as *the* no-win issue. It was charged with emotion. Begin knew he represented Jews all over the world, and Sadat knew that in a way he was speaking for more than five hundred million Muslims. I tried to convince Sadat that he would be better off not trying to solve this problem at Camp David. No matter what kind of compromise might emerge, he would be severely criticized by radicals of all persuasions; he should let King Hussein and others share the responsibility for any agreement concerning the Holy City. He listened carefully, but did not comment.

Sadat said that he and his legal advisers would go over the paper in detail, and after supper tonight we could get together for another session.

I was pleased. With the exception of the very serious question of Arab armed forces in the occupied territories, the changes he had suggested were quite modest. However, we were certain that his advisers would have many technical proposals. Secretary Vance told me that they had a reputation of being the most contentious of all Arabs in international negotiations.

While Sadat and his team were going over our proposals, we had almost twenty-four hours free to meet with the Israelis and for me to prepare for the upcoming new negotiations concerning the parallel agreement on the Sinai itself.

Late in the afternoon I met at my cabin with Weizman and Israeli General Avraham Tamir. I wanted a better understanding of their previous negotiations with General Gamasi and other Egyptians on the Sinai, and Ezer gave me a full report. Again, I took careful notes and studied the maps in detail. They had prepared a special copy of their battle charts for me, on which the Hebrew names had been changed to English.

Apparently Weizman and Gamasi had done a good job and had made a lot of progress on the delineation of military zones and on agreed limitations on armaments in those zones. Serious problems remained concerning three major airfields and several small ones scattered through the area; these questions could be resolved only by the heads of state. Some had been built by the Egyptians and captured by the Israelis; others were built by the Israelis after they had seized the land. Some were close to the international border between the two countries; others were deep in the Sinai, nearer to the Suez Canal. Israel is such a small country that Weizman and Tamir felt they needed space just to maneuver their planes in the air, but Sadat was willing to let them use his territory only until the withdrawals of forces were completed. With a smile, Weizman said that he was already having a hard time finding a place to park all the military equipment the Israelis were getting from the United States.

When I discussed Sadat's new demand for the presence of Jordanian and Egyptian armed forces in the West Bank–Gaza areas, the Israelis immediately responded that it would be out of the question. Then Tamir, who had the reputation of being an extreme hawk, suggested that joint Israeli–Jordanian patrols might be very beneficial along the Jordan River and even south of the Dead Sea, all the way to Eilat. He added that this innovation would be very difficult for any Israeli politician to propose to the nation. (In the final Camp David accords, it was accepted by both nations.)

Cy called me during this meeting to report that the Egyptians wanted an additional twelve hours, so that Sadat and his advisers could study my proposals more thoroughly—a bad sign.

I found Weizman preoccupied with a fallback position for Israel, because he obviously did not think it likely we would get a document signed here. His major question was, "What are we going to do to prevent rapid loss of contact between Egypt and Israel when and if we fail at Camp David?"

Meanwhile, Secretary Vance and Ambassador Eilts had a very difficult meeting with their counterparts from Egypt. Preliminary comments from the Egyptians on the revised United States framework proposal indicated that they viewed it as a substantial retreat from our previous positions. But Sadat had not yet spoken.

Later that evening, I met for about two hours with Dayan and Barak. During this meeting I noticed that all of us were quite drowsy, because we had had practically no sleep during the past thirty-six hours. But strangely enough, I found Dayan more hopeful, more determined to succeed even than Weizman, who was ordinarily the optimist. He seemed willing to accept failure, however, rather than consider the removal of all Israeli settlers from the Sinai. I wished that Dayan knew Sadat better. They were hardly acquainted, and had had very little chance to talk out the important issues together.

Attorney General Aharon Barak was outstanding, and later became a real hero in the Camp David discussions. He knew the law, understood Begin well, and was trusted by him. He had already been selected to serve on the Israeli Supreme Court, but had postponed taking this position so that he could work with us at Camp David. This evening he said quite clearly that the settlements were extremely important, and typically explained the reason. He said that if Sadat, or later his successor, should violate the Egyptian commitment and move strike forces beyond the passes as a threat to Israel, it should be justifiable and inevitable to move Israeli forces into the Sinai west of Gaza, ostensibly to protect the settlers, but actually to protect the nation of Israel. He added that the removal of settlers from the Sinai would also set an unfortunate precedent for Israeli settlements on the West Bank and the Golan Heights. I suspected that the latter was the more important issue. His frankness was encouraging because it indicated that he trusted me enough to tell me about the Israelis' real concerns. I felt close to both Dayan and Weizman, but neither had been as forthcoming on this issue.

I asked Dayan and Barak to help me with Sadat's demand about Jordanian forces in the West Bank area, and Barak suggested that this item be included as one of the matters to be resolved within five years in future negotiations with Jordan and the Palestinians.

Then they gave me some good news—Begin was not going to reject my paper out of hand. He would have several levels of action. One was complete acquiescence on an issue; another was approval by him, with a referral to the Israeli cabinet or Knesset for confirmation of his decision; the last was disapproval and a recommendation against acceptance, but again with referral to his government for final action. Both of them thought this last reaction was likely to be the case on the Sinai settlements, but they told me they were only guessing.

I then offered to drop the Sinai discussions altogether and concentrate my efforts on the more comprehensive framework document. But Dayan suggested that I proceed with a proposal of my own which Sadat might possibly accept. At least it would define and clarify the issues. I agreed to draft a Sinai document and present it to both delegations.

When I next expressed my disappointment in the Israeli reaction to my earlier proposal, Dayan showed genuine surprise, and asked that we review the changes they had proposed. Later, after doing so, I realized that they were not as serious as I had thought, although there were still major items of contention. I suppose the fatigue and the tedious arguments with Begin had painted the whole picture gloomier than it actually was.

After this meeting at Holly, I returned to Aspen, dictated my notes of the night's discussions, and finally got to bed a little after midnight. I had never been more tired in my life.

TUESDAY, DAY EIGHT *(September 12, 1978)*

While I was at Camp David, we had unusual success in dealing with Congress. Hamilton Jordan and Jody Powell, who were with me, kept me posted about events in Washington. Throughout each day, I also received frequent staff reports and often talked to key members of the House and Senate. There seemed to be a new mood of support on Capitol Hill, perhaps because the members knew we were working hard to achieve peace.

Early that morning, I went for a long bicycle ride, and as I returned to my cottage, I observed a heated discussion between the Egyptian President and his principal advisers on his own front porch. This was most unusual, and worried me. Sadat arrived for our visit five minutes late. He seemed very troubled and was somewhat evasive in his greetings. I made a few innocuous remarks, but he did not appear to be listening. He held a paper in his hand, to which he never referred. It was not a copy of our proposal; I never found out what was in it. I immediately felt that he had come to tell me the Camp David negotiations were over, and I decided to delay any such announcement by discussing for a while the strategic implication of a peace agreement on regional and global issues.

To emphasize the shift in tone of our discussions, I suggested that instead of going to my study, we sit by the pool in a new location. I told him I was becoming increasingly concerned about the entire Middle East and Persian Gulf regions, with the threat of the Soviet Union in South Yemen, Afghanistan, Ethiopia, Libya, Iraq, Syria, and possibly Sudan. It was imperative that he and I begin to shift our influence toward resolving those more serious border issues rather than continuing to be almost exclusively focused on the Israeli–Egyptian dispute. A successful resolution at Camp David was necessary for this purpose—to release a large portion of the Egyptian armed forces now marshaled along the Suez looking toward Israel, and to give a new impetus to a general search for peace. I pointed out that Sadat had five divisions lined up facing Israel; a peace treaty would let his friends in Sudan and Saudi Arabia, as well as his potential enemies in Libya and Ethiopia, know of this new Egyptian capability to act militarily, if necessary.

Sadat was impressed with my argument, but turned quickly to his original purpose in coming to see me. It was apparent, he said, that Israel was not going to negotiate in good faith and had no intention of signing an agreement. As we of the United States struggled to deal with Israeli demands, in quest of the elusive peace settlement, we were putting forward proposals which would alienate the Arab world. Such an outcome would also drive a wedge between Egypt and the United States, in spite of his and my best efforts.

I asked him for an example, and he mentioned the problem with the language concerning Jerusalem. I knew this was now becoming an equally serious concern of Begin's. Sadat was also worried about the text as it referred to the Palestinians. I reminded him that the exact wording in our document had been drafted personally by me and him at Aswan, and that in Vienna he and the Israeli opposition leader Shimon Peres had also used language similar to ours concerning borders. He acknowledged all this, but still seemed inclined to back away from the wording.

I spoke slowly and somewhat sadly. "This will leave me in a very difficult position, because our word of honor is at stake. After reaching agreement with you on this critical wording, I have let the Israelis know that we would stand by these very words, and for you to ask me to reverse myself is unacceptable."

He replied, "The document must be something on which both of us agree and which Arabs in other countries can later accept, even with a predictable degree of reluctance."

He seemed especially worried about the Saudi reaction, and I promised to invite Crown Prince Fahd to Washington at an early date to go over our agreement with him. This assurance only partially alleviated his concern. I reminded him that he had already crossed the bridge of Arab condemnation when he had gone to Jerusalem. I said that this had been one of the bravest acts of a political leader in my lifetime. The Arabs were already familiar with the Aswan and Vienna words, and their displeasure would not be exacerbated by repetition of those same phrases here at Camp David, particularly if they were made to realize that it would free him and me to turn to more acute problems of the moderate Arabs throughout the Middle East.

My comments seemed effective, and Sadat soon departed, still very troubled but without having delivered to me the fatal message of failure and departure.

Vance and Brzezinski came to report that, like Sadat, the other Egyptians were extremely anxious about our draft proposal and about possible adverse reaction throughout the Arab world if it should become public. However, the Israelis had been surprisingly cooperative during the morning meetings, with Barak and Dayan coming forward with some beneficial and generous suggestions for improving the draft text. I decided to work that afternoon on the terms for an Egyptian–Israeli treaty, and spread the Sinai maps out on the dining table to begin this task, writing the proposed agreement on a yellow scratch pad.

Within three hours I had finished, and walked over to Sadat's cottage to go over the draft with him. I began to read it aloud, but he reached out for the pad, read it carefully, made two changes which would make it more pleasing to Israel, and handed it back to me. "It's all right," he said. I promised to bring him a typed copy before going over it with the Israelis. Our meeting had lasted less than twenty minutes.

I ate supper with the Israeli delegation in the dining hall, and during the meal Begin said he wanted to see me as soon as possible for the most serious talk we had ever had.

He came to my cottage at about 8:00 P.M., and said again, "This is the most serious talk I have ever had in my life, except once when I discussed the future of Israel with Jabotinsky." (Ze'ev Jabotinsky had been Begin's political mentor in Israel's struggle for independence.) Then he went into an impassioned speech about the use of United Nations Resolution 242 language in the text of our Camp David agreement.

He acknowledged that his government had approved the Resolution and had repeatedly reconfirmed it as applicable, but he was unwilling to use it in the Framework for Peace. He showed me several old newspaper clippings from different nations which included United Nations Resolution 242, where the preamble, with the words "inadmissibility of acquisition of territory by war," had been omitted. I was certain the omission had been inadvertent or was done simply for condensation, but to him it was an adequate justification for us to omit the crucial words now. He concluded this part of his comments by saying, "Israel cannot agree under any circumstances to a document which includes this phrase, and I will not sign it."

As he spent another hour talking about the settlements in the Sinai, he became very emotional. Once he mentioned Jerusalem, and quoted to me the Bible verse from Psalms, "If I forget thee, O Jerusalem, let my right hand forget her cunning." After that, he repeatedly said, "Better my right hand should lose its cunning than I should sign such a document!"

Near the end, he pulled from his pocket a brief typed statement and read it to me. It stated that we had met at Camp David, and that Israel and Egypt appreciated the invitation they had received from the United States. As an alternative to this statement, he said, we could list the items on which there was agreement and the others on which we could not agree, and issue these lists as proof of the progress we had made. He claimed that he sincerely wished he could sign my proposal, but the will of the Israeli people must be represented by him as their Prime Minister.

I pointed out that I had seen public-opinion polls every two or three weeks in which a substantial majority of the Israeli people were willing to accept a peace treaty with an end to the settlements, the removal of Israeli settlers from the Sinai, and the yielding of substantial portions of the territory in the West Bank now under Israeli military government. I was distressed by his attitude and, perhaps ill-advisedly, said that my position represented the Israeli people better than his.

He brought up my previous reference to his West Bank self-government plan as a "subterfuge," and quoted Brzezinski as saying that the Egyptians and other Arabs looked on the Israelis as a colonialist power because of their military rule over the Palestinians.

It was a heated discussion, unpleasant and repetitive. I stood up for him to leave, and accused him of being willing to give up peace with his only formidable enemy, free trade and diplomatic recognition from Egypt, unimpeded access to international waterways, Arab acceptance of an undivided Jerusalem, permanent security for Israel, and the approbation of the world—all this, just to keep a few illegal settlers on Egyptian land.

As he left he said, interestingly, that Israel did not want any territory in the Sinai, and none in the West Bank *for the first five years.*

WEDNESDAY, DAY NINE *(September 13, 1978)*

After this meeting with Begin, I decided to concentrate on a new Framework draft, and to work directly with Aharon Barak and Osama el-Baz. Barak seemed to have Begin's trust, and el-Baz, the most militant of the Egyptians, could speak accurately for the Arab position. If el-Baz agreed to something, the other Egyptian aides would go along, and I could always override him, if necessary, by going directly to Sadat. At the same time, I could depend on Barak to influence Begin. Both these men were brilliant draftsmen, fluent in English, and they understood the nuances of the difficult phrases with which we had to work. Cy Vance stayed with me during these long sessions, and the four of us made painstaking but steady progress on the main document, while Zbig and the other members of our team worked with the foreign ministers and top men in the other delegations. They could build on what we produced, and feed us ideas for resolving differences.

We sat around the desk in my study for hours, trading back and forth. For instance, we had to resolve the deadlock on the phrase "inadmissibility of acquisition of territory by war," and I proposed that we delete it from the main text, append the entire resolution to the agreement, and note that both parties agreed to "United Nations Resolution 242 in all its parts." Barak agreed, but el-Baz was doubtful. I offered to let him delete any phrase in this part of the text he did not like, and he chose, "They have both also stated that there shall be no more war between them." His position was that if Israel did not withdraw from the Sinai, a war might be necessary. Barak did not object, and we closed the deal.

Again our problems were manifested in the use of different phrases. To us and the Egyptians, it was "West Bank"; to Begin, it was "Judea and Samaria." To us, it was "Palestinians" or "Palestinian people"; to Begin, it was "Palestinian Arabs." We finally decided to use our language in the Egyptian and English texts and to use his words in the Hebrew text, and that I would either write Begin a public letter or add a footnote to explain the difference.

Many of the suggestions Vance and I had expected to be opposed were accepted immediately by Barak and el-Baz, and few of these were ever again questioned by their superiors.

We did a lot of work on the Jerusalem paragraph. It referred to Jerusalem as the city of peace, holy to Judaism, Christianity, and Islam, and stated that all persons would have free access to it, free exercise of worship, and the right to visit and travel to the holy places without distinction or discrimination. We agreed that Jerusalem would never again be a divided city, that the holy places of each faith should be under the administration and full authority of their representatives, that a municipal council drawn from the inhabitants should supervise essential functions in the city, and so forth. We were delighted when both Begin and Sadat approved the text.

Some differences could not be resolved. Barak refused to discuss the Israeli settlements at all, saying that it was a subject only Begin could address. El-Baz, backed by Sadat, refused to include a commitment to open borders and full diplomatic recognition.

This day the four of us stayed together for almost eleven hours and were pleased with our work, but toward the end of our sessions came a disturbing incident. El-Baz startled me by insisting that it was Egypt's position that Israel could not be a party to decisions concerning refugees coming into the West Bank area. When I asked incredulously if Sadat had reversed himself on this point, Osama finally admitted that he had not even discussed the matter with Sadat—that the idea was his own, but that he thought Sadat would agree. I grew angry, and accused him of misleading me and being disloyal to Sadat in the process. I started to terminate the meeting, but Cy convinced me to stay a few more minutes while we concluded the session.

I asked el-Baz to go and tell Sadat I wanted to see him immediately. But in a few minutes the Egyptians sent back word that the President had retired for the night and asked that he not be disturbed.

I walked down to Holly to thank Begin for the Israelis' constructive attitude during the day. I outlined the general terms of the Sinai agreement, and told him that Vance and Brzezinski were presenting a copy of it to Dayan and Weizman. Predictably, he said that he could not accept any language that called for Israel to remove its settlements, and also predictably, I said we could not have any agreement without this formula. We parted with a friendly handshake.

I went to bed late, tired but pleased. Sadat was staying, the Israelis were being more helpful, and we had a good new plan for a Sinai agreement leading to a peace treaty.

For some reason, though, I could not sleep. This is a rare problem for me; even during times of deep worry or crisis, I have little trouble sleeping well. I was worrying about President Sadat, and whether he was safe. We were dealing with some extremely emotional subjects for the Arabs, and it was obvious that some of his more militant advisers were deeply committed to the goals of the Palestinian Liberation Organization and other radical groups. Sadat had been and was making decisions with which they strongly disagreed. I could not forget the heated discussion I had observed on Sadat's porch. I remembered that earlier tonight Sadat's views had been directly misrepresented by one of his key advisers, who professed to speak for Egypt but had not even discussed the issue in question with his President, and I recalled that tonight when I had wanted to see Sadat, his aides told me that he had uncharacteristically retired early and could not be disturbed. In the middle of the night, about 4:00 A.M., I got up, talked to the Secret Service agents and to Brzezinski, and directed that security around Sadat's cottage be strengthened and kept alert. Later, my concerns seemed groundless, but at the same time I was greatly relieved to see President Sadat in good shape the next day.

THURSDAY, DAY TEN (September 14, 1978)

I was waiting for Sadat when he emerged from his cabin, and I joined him for about an hour during his regular morning walk. I did not mention my nighttime concerns to him.

As was his morning custom, we walked at a rapid military pace for four kilometers (and a little extra this morning). There was a comfortable feeling between us, and I decided to make a gratuitous proposal that we provide for a major highway to connect Jordan with the Sinai near Eilat. He was interested in the idea. He volunteered that he would be willing to let the Etzion airbase be used to serve Eilat, so long as it was operated exclusively by the Egyptians. Sadat said he could accept the entire Jerusalem proposal if there was a provision for the flag of Islam to fly over Islamic holy places, but acknowledged that Begin would be reluctant to agree to this because of its symbolism of sovereignty.

Sadat made one interesting observation. Since our visit to Gettysburg he had been thinking that I, as a Southerner, could understand what it meant to be involved in a terrible war, and also knew how difficult it was to rebuild both material things and the spirit of a people after a recognized defeat. He had observed how long it had taken the wounds of our war in Vietnam to be finally healed with my election, and his hope was to encourage all people in the Middle East to heal their hurt and hatred and to move confidently toward an era of peace.

When I returned from the walk, Barak was waiting for me. He was still encouraged about the positive attitude prevailing among Begin and the other Israelis. He suggested that I discuss the Sinai questions with Dayan, who was more knowledgeable than he about the subject. Dayan and Weizman came to see me, and soon it all boiled down to—the settlements. In desperation, I promised to draft language allowing this issue to be left open for future resolution, without preconditions, for at least three months. Thus, the question might be finessed with Sadat.

No luck. When I showed my new draft to Sadat, he immediately stated that there *were* preconditions—one being the airfields, and the other being the settlements, and that he would negotiate on *when* they would be withdrawn, not *if* they would be withdrawn.

I asked, "What procedure do you suggest if the Israelis will not agree to move the settlements?"

He replied, "I will sign the American document anyway, because it will describe my position."

This impasse would be the end of our effort for peace. I could not think of any way to resolve this fundamental difference between the Israelis and the Egyptians. On the Sinai settlements, Begin did not stand alone among his delegation. So far as I could tell, the Israelis were united in their belief that the settlers could not be moved. All during the day I consulted with Fritz, Cy, Zbig, and the other members of our team, and I also talked to Barak several times. Apparently there was no answer that would satisfy both sides.

We began to make plans to terminate the negotiations, and I instructed the Vice President to cancel all his appointments for the weekend. We were in serious trouble, and I needed him to come help me minimize the damage.

I went to ask Dayan how we could best end the deadlocked talks, and he said he preferred a paper that would list each paragraph, with the differences delineated side by side. At least our ten days of work would not have been totally in vain, and the world would know that we had tried.

That evening I began to list the differences between the two nations, and was heartbroken to see how relatively insignificant they really were, compared to the great advantages of peace. I sat on the back terrace late into the night, but could think of no way to make further progress. My only decision was that all of us should work together to leave Camp David in as positive a mood as possible, taking credit for what we had done and resolved to continue our common search for an elusive accord.

FRIDAY, DAY ELEVEN *(September 15, 1978)*

I awoke to the realization that we could go no further. I called the American delegation to Aspen, and we discussed how to deal with our failure. I would spend the day getting proposals from Sadat and Begin, so that I could summarize the differences and prepare the final document on Saturday. On Sunday we would adjourn, issue a joint communiqué, and put an embargo on further public statements from all three delegations until noon on Monday. I wrote out this proposal by hand, and Fritz delivered it to President Sadat and to Prime Minister Begin. Both accepted it.

I instructed staff members to begin drafting an outline of a speech for me to make to Congress, explaining what we had attempted during the two weeks at Camp David and why we had not been successful. They also took the private notes I had compiled the previous evening to put them into more formal words, listing the unresolved differences between Egypt and Israel and enumerating the benefits that would accrue to both nations if a peace agreement could be reached in the future.

The pressures from Washington were building up. Attorney General Griffin Bell and FBI Director William Webster had come to Camp David the previous day with urgent business, and Harold Brown needed to see me today about matters relating to our nation's armed forces. These kinds of visits were becoming more frequent and time-consuming.

As I was getting ready to meet with Vance and Brown, Dayan reported that he and Sadat had just concluded an unsatisfactory meeting. It had been arranged by Weizman in hopes that the two men might find some basis for continuing the talks. Then Vance told me that Sadat had just sent for him.

After Harold and I had been at work for about twenty minutes, Vance burst into the room. His face was white, and he announced, "Sadat is leaving. He and his aides are already packed. He asked me to order him a helicopter!"

It was a terrible moment. Now, even my hopes for a harmonious departure were gone. I sat quietly and assessed the significance of this development—a rupture between Sadat and me, and its consequences for my country and for the Middle East power balance. I envisioned the ultimate alliance of most of the Arab nations to the Soviet Union, perhaps joined by Egypt after a few months had passed. I told Vance that the best thing for us to do now, to salvage what we could, would be to refuse to sign any document with either country—just to terminate the talks and announce that we had all done our best and failed.

Then I asked Brown and Vance to leave me. When they were gone, I remained alone in the little study where most of the negotiations had taken place. I moved over to the window and looked out to the Catoctin Mountains and prayed fervently for a few minutes that somehow we could find peace.

Then, for some reason, I changed into more formal clothes before going to see Sadat. He was on his porch with five or six of his ministers, and Vance and Brown were there to tell them all good-bye.

I nodded to them, and walked into the cabin. Sadat followed me. I explained to him the extremely serious consequences of his unilaterally breaking off the negotiations: that his action would harm the relationship between Egypt and the United States, he would be violating his personal promise to me, and the onus for failure would be on him. I described the possible future progress of Egypt's friendships and alliances—from us to the moderate and then radical Arabs, thence to the Soviet Union. I told him it would damage one of my most precious possessions—his friendship and our mutual trust.

He was adamant, but I was dead serious, and he knew it. I had never been more serious in my life. I repeated some of the more telling arguments I had previously used at our meeting by the swimming pool. He would be publicly repudiating some of his own commitments, damaging his reputation as the world's foremost peacemaker, and admitting the fruitlessness of his celebrated visit to Jerusalem. His worst enemies in the Arab world would be proven right in their claims that he had made a foolish mistake.

I told Sadat that he simply had to stick with me for another day or two—after which, if circumstances did not improve, all of us simultaneously would take the action he was now planning.

He explained the reason for his decision to leave: Dayan had told him the Israelis would not sign any agreements. This made Sadat furious. He had accused Dayan of wasting our time by coming to Camp David in the first place. His own advisers had pointed out the danger in his signing an agreement with the

United States alone. Later, if direct discussions were ever resumed with the Israelis, they could say, "The Egyptians have already agreed to all these points. Now we will use what they have signed as the original basis for all future negotiations." It was a telling argument. I thought very rapidly and told him that we would have a complete understanding that if any nation rejected *any* part of the agreements, *none* of the proposals would stay in effect.

Sadat stood silently for a long time. Then he looked at me and said, "If you give me this statement, I will stick with you to the end." (He kept his promise, but it never proved necessary to give him any such statement.)

Those were sweet words to hear. I went back to Aspen and told Rosalynn, Fritz, Cy, Harold, and Zbig that everything was all right. I described my conversation with Sadat, and we pledged ourselves to silence and went back to work. It had been a bad time.

Our staffs continued with the "failure plans," based on our leaving Camp David on Sunday. But I did not want to give up. That afternoon and evening I went over the proposals—the Framework and the Sinai document—with Vance and Mondale. Then Fritz and I went over to Sadat's cottage for a social visit. We had decided merely to be friendly, to let him know how much we appreciated his decision not to leave, and later to watch the world's heavyweight boxing match between Muhammad Ali and Leon Spinks. However, Sadat wanted to talk about the negotiations, and I recapitulated the situation in Fritz's presence, to make sure that all of us had the same understanding of the terms under which we would work for the last few crucial hours.

I said, "Sadat has been the linchpin in the negotiations. Provided the rights of the Palestinians are protected, I have maximum flexibility on the West Bank and Gaza. In Sinai, we must preserve the integrity of sovereignty and land. We are determined to put together a document that we can both sign, and we're still hopeful that Prime Minister Begin will be willing to sign it too. If not, then my hope is that the only remaining issue will be the Israeli settlements on Egyptian territory."

Sadat agreed, which reconfirmed his promise to me earlier that day.

We then watched the Ali–Spinks fight together. Sadat was an admirer of Muhammad Ali, and after his victory, we placed a call to congratulate him. I didn't get Ali on the phone until 1:30 A.M., long after Sadat had gone to bed. I invited Ali's young daughter to come to visit Amy, and Ali told me he was going to keep the title for six months and then retire. He was very pleased and excited that Sadat, Fritz, and I had watched the bout.

During the evening, Cy and Zbig had been negotiating with the Israelis, but without making any progress on the settlements. After getting a report from Cy, I went to bed.

SATURDAY, DAY TWELVE *(September 16, 1978)*

I got up earlier than usual and wrote down all the items in the Sinai document with which the Israelis could possibly disagree. I simply listed them, and then went for another long walk with President Sadat. When I asked if there was anything I could do for him personally or for his people if we should ever be able to achieve peace, he replied, "I want you and your wife Rosalynn to come to Egypt for a visit." I promised we would.

I then probed very hard for some opening on the Sinai settlements issue, but without success. Sadat was willing to agree not to dismantle the buildings, to allow United Nations forces to be stationed in the area, and to wait three years after the peace treaty was signed for the people to leave. But they had to leave— that was it.

Later I walked over to Holly, where the Americans and Israelis were talking, and discussed the same issue with Dayan. The best I could get out of him was his personal willingness to have the settlers leave after twenty years. He said that Begin would not agree even to such an extended time period if there had to be an ultimate commitment for them to leave. On the West Bank, Dayan was willing to agree to no *new* settlements—to be specified in an exchange of letters between me and the Prime Minister. He added that Begin was feeling somewhat excluded from the negotiating process, since I had not seen him lately, and suggested that I meet with only him and Barak that evening, because Weizman had met with Sadat that morning.

I then went to see Weizman, to find out about his meeting with Sadat. As he walked to Aspen with me, he reported that Sadat would be willing to say in the Sinai document that future negotiations would settle the issue of the Israeli settlements. I was startled, because this was not at all what Sadat had just told me. I knew that in general Ezer was an optimist, and that at Camp David, unfortunately, this attitude had rarely been justified. Weizman said he had also predicted to Sadat that the Knesset would vote to remove the settlements; Dayan had told me the opposite.

At this point, as far as the settlements were concerned, we had conflicting reports from the Egyptian President and three levels of opposition in the Israeli delegation: Begin wanted no commitment to withdrawal; Dayan was willing to promise withdrawal after an extended period of time; and Weizman believed that the settlers should leave if the Knesset would agree.

When Sadat and el-Baz came to meet with me and Cy in the afternoon, I reported Weizman's impression and asked Sadat to clarify his position on the settlements issue. He responded that Ezer's report was completely erroneous; he had described his attitude accurately to me during our walk that morning.

I listed all the advantages that might come to Egypt with a peace agreement.

We then reviewed the more specific Sinai proposal, and found no significant disagreement except over the Israeli settlements— and no disagreement at all between myself and Sadat.

On the more comprehensive Framework, we were also very close. In referring to the Palestinians' authority on the West Bank, I agreed to find a synonym for "self-government." (Sadat thought the word sounded too much like Begin's "self-rule.") With great pressure I induced him to accept the language we had evolved on Jerusalem, provided there would be an exchange of letters reconfirming the historic United States position that East Jerusalem was part of the West Bank. Sadat agreed that the Wailing Wall should always be retained exclusively by the Jews.

I told him that there was no alternative to my handling the question of the settlements directly and personally with Prime Minister Begin, who would be arriving in just a few minutes. Sadat left, having been in an exceptionally sober but nevertheless constructive mood.

Cy and I were very pleased with this meeting, and although we had missed another meal, we considered it well worthwhile.

Begin came with Dayan and Barak, for which we were thankful. If anyone at Camp David had influence on Begin, it was these two men.

Cy and I ate some crackers and cheese as I listed the benefits of the proposed agreement to Israel. Immediately Begin began talking about the blessed settlements, but I insisted that we go through both documents in an orderly fashion, paragraph by paragraph. I wanted the Israelis to realize how few differences remained. In an hour we were finished with the Sinai document, and it was obvious to me that Sadat would be willing to accept almost all the Israeli demands for change. The few others were not very important to Begin, and I felt sure that he would not insist on them.

We then moved to the settlements again, and Begin insisted that he would negotiate with Sadat on all other items for three months in search of a final peace treaty and the resolution of all remaining differences. If this effort was completely successful, he would submit the settlement withdrawal question to the Knesset. I told him again and again that this proposal was totally unacceptable to Sadat, who insisted on a commitment to remove all Israeli settlers from his territory *before* any other negotiations could be conducted.

I thought the discussion would never end. It was obviously very painful for Prime Minister Begin, who was shouting words like "ultimatum," "excessive demands," and "political suicide." However, he finally promised to submit to the Knesset within two weeks the question: "If agreement is reached on all other Sinai issues, will the settlers be withdrawn?"

I believed this concession would be enough for Sadat. Breakthrough!

I asked Begin if he would maintain a neutral position as the Knesset debated the issue, but he would not promise. He did agree, however, to remove the requirements of party loyalty and let each member of the Knesset vote as an individual. He assured me that the same would apply to cabinet members. I questioned Dayan, but he would not give me a firm commitment of support.

We all agreed that what we had just decided represented a great step forward.

We then had a surprisingly amicable discussion about the Framework for Peace. Barak was a tremendous help as we went over the entire proposed text. Dayan was quite forthcoming on the Palestinian question, and said with some enthusiasm, "We'll let the Palestinians join the Jordanians during the negotiation of the peace treaty with Israel." To accommodate Sadat's request, we searched for a synonym for "self-government for the Palestinians," and came up with "how the Palestinians shall govern themselves." There was no apparent difference, so no harm was done. By this time I had become a master at making insignificant editorial changes to overcome significant objections.

I had a lot of latitude in dealing with the West Bank–Gaza questions. Fortunately, Sadat was not particularly interested in the detailed language of the Framework for Peace, and with the exception of the settlements, Begin was not very interested in the details of the Sinai agreement.

On Jerusalem, I told the Israeli leaders that Sadat had accepted the paragraph as drafted for the Framework text, but he wanted a separate exchange of letters, so that each nation could make public its own different ideas as part of the official record. Israelis would not have to participate in the exchange, but could let their views be known if they preferred to do so.

On the West Bank settlements, we finally worked out language that was satisfactory: that no new Israeli settlements would be established after the signing of this Framework for Peace, and that the issue of additional settlements would be resolved by the parties during the negotiations. This would be stated in a letter, to be made public, from Begin to me. (Begin later denied that he had agreed to this, and claimed that he had promised to stop building settlements only for a three-month period. My notes are clear—that the settlement freeze would continue until all negotiations were completed—and Cy Vance confirms my interpretation of what we decided. This was the only serious post-Camp David disagreement about our decisions, so our batting average was good.)

After the Israelis left, Vance and I agreed that we had a settlement, at least for Camp David. There was no doubt that Sadat would accept my recommendations on the issues we had just discussed with Begin. What the Knesset might decide was uncertain, but I was convinced that the people of Israel would be in favor of the overall agreement, including the withdrawal of the settlers from the Sinai. Weizman would be a big help. I intended to try in every way possible to shape world opinion and to get the American Jewish community to support this effort.

SUNDAY, DAY THIRTEEN *(September 17, 1978)*

I was eager to meet with President Sadat, and he and I quickly went over the proposals for the final language. The few predictable changes that he advocated would, I was sure, be acceptable to the Israelis. The only serious problem was his desire to delete the entire paragraph on Jerusalem. I knew that the Israelis wanted the same thing, but I confess that I did not tell Sadat. I reserved this concession just in case I needed some bargaining points later on. We discussed the potential problem with the United Nations peacekeeping force now in the Western Sinai, whose mandate might expire if a new agreement was signed between Egypt and

Israel. With a peace treaty, we assumed there would be no justification for United Nations forces to remain. We made plans for handling this problem if it should later arise.

I redrafted all the language in both documents to incorporate what I thought would be acceptable to the two delegations, and then walked down to Holly, where Vance and our team were meeting with Dayan and the other Israelis. I called Dayan out, went over my suggested compromise language, and asked him to help me during these final hours and with the Knesset when the time came for a vote. Dayan said that he was absolutely certain the parliament would never vote for a withdrawal of settlers prior to negotiation of an Egyptian–Israeli peace treaty.

I left him and walked to Weizman's cottage. He saw me and came running out, but I was already at his door. We laughed because the cabin was in such a mess and he was embarrassed to have me see it. I understood, however, that the Israelis were packing to leave Camp David and that every cottage was jammed full of people. He walked to Aspen with me, and promised to make an all-out fight in the Knesset to get a favorable vote.

In the meantime, a serious problem had erupted with the Israelis. Vance had just shown them a copy of our draft letter that would go to Sadat, restating the United States position on Jerusalem, which had been spelled out officially in United Nations debates over the years. There was an absolute furor, and Begin announced that Israel would not sign *any* document if we wrote *any* letter to Egypt about Jerusalem.

Hamilton Jordan called to tell me that the Israeli objections to a Jerusalem letter were extremely serious; the Israelis were determined to sign no agreement at all. Vance confirmed Ham's report, and explained that none of the Israelis had understood that we were going to write a letter "criticizing Israel for occupying eastern Jerusalem," even after we had explained the letter exchange last night.

Back at Holly, I had a very unpleasant session there, with Dayan, Weizman, Barak, Mondale, Vance, and Brzezinski. I asked for a text of our United Nations ambassadors' statements in the debates concerning Jerusalem. Ambassadors Charles Yost, Arthur Goldberg, and William Scranton had spoken on the subject, but I had never read all of what they actually said.

I then asked Barak to walk with me to Aspen to go over the text of our proposed letter, in order to find language which might be acceptable. He was just as adamant as the other Israelis, insisting that the situation was hopeless. However, I proposed that we strike out of our letter all the actual quotations from the United Nations speeches and simply say that the United States position was as it had been expressed by the three ambassadors. Dayan and Barak both agreed to go over this changed text with Begin. It was another tense moment.

Earlier, my secretary, Susan Clough, had brought me some photographs of Begin, Sadat, and me. They had already been signed by President Sadat, and Prime Minister Begin had requested that I autograph them for his grandchildren. Knowing the trouble we were in with the Israelis, Susan suggested that she go and get the actual names of the grandchildren, so that I could personalize each picture. I did this, and walked over to Begin's cabin with them. He was sitting on the front porch, very distraught and nervous because the talks had finally broken down at the last minute.

I handed him the photographs. He took them and thanked me. Then he happened to look down and saw that his granddaughter's name was on the top one. He spoke it aloud, and then looked at each photograph individually, repeating the name of the grandchild I had written on it. His lips trembled, and tears welled up in his eyes. He told me a little about each child, and especially about the one who seemed to be his favorite. We were both emotional as we talked quietly for a few minutes about grandchildren and about war.

Then he asked me to step into his cabin, requesting that everyone else in the room leave. He was quiet, sober, surprisingly friendly. There were no histrionics. He said that the Jerusalem matter was fatal, that he was very sorry but he could not accept our letter to Egypt. I told him I had drafted a new version and submitted it to Dayan and Barak. He had not yet seen it. I suggested he read it over and let me know his decision, but that there was no way that I could go back on my commitment to Sadat to exchange letters. The success of any future peace talks might depend on his and Sadat's assessment of my integrity, and I could not violate a promise once it was made.

I walked back to Aspen, very dejected. Sadat was there with el-Baz, both dressed to go back to Washington. I asked everyone else to leave and told Sadat what was happening. We realized that all of us had done our best, but that prospects were dim indeed.

Then Begin called. He said, "I will accept the letter you have drafted on Jerusalem." I breathed a sigh of relief, because it now seemed that the last obstacle had been removed.

We frantically worked on a final draft of the agreements, clearing the texts with el-Baz and Barak as we went along. We were making plans to return to Washington, in spite of a thunderstorm that was sweeping across the top of the mountain. I prepared a schedule and gave it to Fritz to carry to both leaders for their approval.

I looked up to see Hamilton and Jody out on the terrace, anxiously peering into my window. When I gave them a thumbs-up sign, they beamed with relief. The tension was broken, and although I was exhausted, it was a pleasure to make decisions about the texts, transportation to Washington, television appearances for the three of us, a signing ceremony at the White House, packing to leave Camp David, and how to keep Begin and Sadat apart until after everything had been put into final form and officially confirmed.

Then Barak came in with Begin's draft of the language about the West Bank settlements and on the Knesset vote. Both were unsatisfactory and contrary to what we had earlier agreed. I read to Barak from my detailed notes what we had mutually decided, and told him to take the letters back to the Prime Minister. Barak confirmed that my language was accurate.

In a few minutes, Begin called to say that he could not accept my language on the Knesset vote, because he interpreted it as a threat to the independence of the parliament. This point was difficult to understand, but it was essential. Sadat's willingness to negotiate was contingent on the Knesset's approval of Israeli withdrawal of the settlers. Begin wanted it stated that the peace negotiations *would* commence after the Knesset voted, but I insisted that it say that the peace negotiations would *not* commence until *after* the Knesset had voted. After some argument, Barak finally agreed to my formulation. I wrote it out on a sheet of tablet paper, and gave it to the Vice President to take to both leaders for approval. In a few minutes I went into my front room and was surprised to see Fritz there. He said that the two leaders were together in Sadat's cottage, and he had been reluctant to interrupt them. I decided to go myself, because I thought it was crucial for me to intercede if they were arguing.

I ran toward Sadat's cabin, and saw that Begin was just leaving in a golf cart with Barak. He was quite happy as he told me that they had had a love feast and that Sadat had agreed to Begin's language on the Knesset vote. I knew this could not be true, and I asked Barak to tell me exactly what Sadat had said. Each time he tried to answer, Begin would have something else to say. I finally asked the Prime Minister point-blank to let Barak answer my question.

Barak described the conversation to me. What Begin had asked was, "Do you think the Knesset should be under pressure when it votes?" Predictably, Sadat had replied, "No, the Knesset should not be under pressure." That was all. Begin had interpreted this to mean that he could draft any language he preferred to insure that the Knesset would be free of any implied adverse consequences if its decision should be negative.

I asked Barak to come with me. Begin excused him, and we went to my cabin just a few steps away. I checked the Israeli language most carefully. It was a *very* confusing point, and all of us were dead tired. Momentarily, my mind seemed to clear and I thought of a way to phrase all three final letters that would be satisfactory to both Begin and Sadat. Susan typed them, and I sent a copy to each leader and to all our own delegation with the instructions, "This is the exact language to be used. Do not use any other language on or off the record."

Only then did I fully realize we had succeeded. I called Rosalynn first. For several days she had been filling speaking engagements for me and taking care of White House social affairs, coming to Camp David when she could. This afternoon, accompanied by Aliza Begin and the wives of the two ambassadors, she was attending a cello concert by Mstislav Rostropovich in the East Room, one of a series of performances that had been scheduled for nationwide telecast. Then I called the Democratic and Republican congressional leaders to give them a brief report. In the meantime, Sadat was paying a courtesy call on Begin, and later they met me in front of Aspen. We embraced enthusiastically, went to the helicopter, and flew to the White House together.

On the way, we talked about the need for action to bring peace to Lebanon, and Begin promised to help us by giving his full support to the Sarkis government in Beirut and doing everything possible to minimize bloodshed. I placed a call to President Ford, and all three of us spoke with him.

Then we landed at the White House for a signing ceremony and a press conference. It was the first time I could remember that I had been glad to leave Camp David and come back to Washington.

Because the new fall television programs were heavily advertised at this time, we had an extraordinarily large viewing audience. Senator Kennedy was among those who called to offer congratulations. It was widely suspected that he was going to run against me for President, and he later joked that he'd had to cancel his speech to the Democratic convention in New Hampshire (where the first primary election is held).

As I look back on the thirteen days, I can evoke the emotions I felt then as the negotiations surged ahead or faltered. It seems extraordinary how many intense hours I spent cooped up in the small study at the end of the back hall at Aspen. Some of the most unpleasant experiences of my life occurred during these days—and, of course, one of the most gratifying achievements came at the end of it.

In addition to those I have mentioned often in this report, I must commend the superb work done by the other members of our delegation, especially Harold Saunders, Bill Quandt (NSC Middle East specialist), and Ambassadors Sam Lewis, Hermann Eilts, and Alfred Atherton. Hamilton Jordan helped me carry out my routine presidential duties, and gave us good advice in dealing with the members of the other two delegations. Jody Powell had one of the most difficult jobs—to represent all three nations every day in briefing the crowds of news reporters who surrounded Camp David. After the first day or so, the media stories based on Jody's general briefing became quite accurate and responsible, even though the reporters never received any account of the specific negotiations. Susan Clough had to do the work of several people in typing minutes of meetings, my personal notes, and new drafts of texts, and in distributing all these among our delegation while maintaining absolute security.

Those of us who were at Camp David really got to know each other—that is, everyone except Begin and Sadat. It was to be much later, after the final peace treaty was signed, that a modicum of friendship and respect developed between the two men. The tension and the intense personal relationships during the negotiations stripped away the facades with which people in public life often surround themselves for self-protection. We had no need, while working in the privacy of Camp David, to convince the public that we were wise, forceful, consistent, or superior in our negotiating techniques.

As far as the United States was concerned, while at Camp David I made only two specific promises to Sadat and Begin: to visit Egypt, and to consult with Israel on how we might help with moving the Sinai airfields.

We arrived back at the White House at about 10:15 P.M., and went directly to the East Room, where our signing of the documents and some brief remarks preempted the new prime-time television shows scheduled for that Sunday evening. Immediately thereafter, Sadat and Begin left the White House. All of us needed a good night's sleep—and we certainly deserved one.

The Framework for Peace in the Middle East and the Framework for the Conclusion of a Peace Treaty Between Egypt and Israel were two major steps forward. For a few hours, all three of us were flushed with pride and good will toward one another because of our unexpected success. We had no idea at that time how far we still had to go.

AFTER CAMP DAVID

The most emotional time of all was after the agreement was reached. I read in the news that Israeli teachers who were out on strike, having heard about the Camp David agreement, voted unanimously to go back to work.   DIARY, SEPTEMBER 18, 1978

In spite of the general euphoria in many places, there were still some immediate problems. I realized, of course, how important it was to involve the other Arab leaders as soon as possible, particularly King Hussein and the Saudi rulers. While at Camp David, President Sadat had told me that Hussein was willing to help us implement the agreement, and that he and Hussein had made arrangements to meet in Morocco when Sadat was on the way home to Egypt. Now, I learned that the King had interrupted his vacation in Majorca, cancelling the visit with Sadat, and was returning to Amman. When I reached him by telephone, I discovered that he was under pressure from some of the other Arabs to reject any role in the forthcoming negotiations to implement the terms of our agreement. I explained the advantages to him and to the Palestinians of the accords we had signed, and he promised, somewhat reluctantly, not to make any public comment or decision until we had informed him thoroughly about the documents.

I then asked Secretary Vance to go to Jordan and Saudi Arabia as soon as possible to brief the leaders there. When I contacted Crown Prince Fahd, he told me that he would welcome the visit, and suggested that Vance stop in Syria to give President Assad the same information. Surprisingly, Assad also seemed eager for the briefing.

I spent most of Monday afternoon working on my address to Congress about the Camp David negotiations. Begin was out making speeches, but I had Fritz go over to ask Sadat if he had any suggestions for statements or phrases that might help us with the Palestinians or other Arabs. Sadat's only advice was, "Just do not aggravate the Israelis, some of whom are quite excitable and unpredictable people."

That same afternoon, we heard reports that Prime Minister Begin was making negative statements to Jewish audiences concerning the arrangements for Jerusalem, withdrawal from the West Bank, new settlements in the occupied territories, Palestinian refugees, and future relationships with Israel's other neighbors. When we were together at the Capitol for my report to Congress, I discussed with Sadat and Begin what a serious problem this was. Begin's statements were certain to alienate the moderate Arabs and the Palestinian leaders, and to impede any further progress on the Palestinian and West Bank issues. It seemed that suspicions at Camp David were proving well founded. Begin wanted to keep two things: the peace with Egypt—and the West Bank.

When my report to Congress was delivered, President Sadat and Prime Minister Begin were in the balcony of the House Chamber. It was a warm and enthusiastic session, even emotional at times. I had had to prepare the speech hurriedly, and in the car on the way to the Capitol, I had decided to add a Bible verse from the Sermon on the Mount: "Blessed are the peacemakers: for—?" I could not remember whether "they shall be called the children of God" or "theirs is the kingdom of heaven." Luckily, I guessed right, and made them God's children. That quote got most of the headlines.

⌐

Had a meeting of key Jewish leaders, along with Fritz and others. We reminisced about the extreme strain between them and me and the rest of the Jews in the United States. I pointed out in a nice way that the controversies that I had put on the table that caused the strain had been the source of ultimate success, and hoped that they would not only work to repair the political damage, but to restrain Begin, who is acting in a completely irresponsible way.   DIARY, SEPTEMBER 19, 1978

This meeting was delightful, full of fun and good cheer, and we welcomed it because it was so rare. All of us were happy about the Camp David accords. But the respite was to be quite brief, because Begin continued to disavow the basic principles of the accords relating to Israel's withdrawal of its armed forces and military government from the West Bank, negotiations on an equal basis with the Palestinians and other Arabs, and the granting of full autonomy to the residents of the occupied areas. His statements, which were in sharp contrast to those of the American and Egyptian delegations, soon created understandable confusion among those who were intensely interested in the Middle East.

When Prime Minister Begin came by my office before leaving Washington, I gave him a sign reading, "Shalom, Y'all," which had been sent up by some of my Georgia friends. After everyone else left, I talked to him privately about the good prospects for cooperation from some of the other Arab leaders, and warned that his remarks were making it almost impossible for them to join in any future discussions. His reply was evasive and non-committal, and I had a feeling that he really did not want any early talks involving the Palestinians and other Arabs. The next day in New York, Begin continued his disruptive comments. We considered sending the Vice President to talk to him again, but decided that the damage had already been done. We would just have to salvage what we could.

Despite Begin's provocations, Camp David was viewed as a tremendous success by the American public. I was flooded with requests to take different groups to Camp David to resolve long-standing disputes involving civil rights, inflation, labor and management, environmental quality, and consumer affairs. I even heard from a group of Latin American leaders who wanted me to settle boundary disputes in Central America. I told them all that in the future my preference would be to go to Camp David with Rosalynn and Amy—and not with George Meany, Ralph Nader, or President Anastasio Somoza.

I ordered a set of large and detailed maps of the Sinai region, spread them on the floor of my White House study, and began to go over the exact geographical lines to be followed in concluding the Israeli–Egyptian peace treaty. We needed to move rapidly. Private messages to us made it clear that the Saudis were supportive of the peace process; and Assad was cautious but leaving the door open, not wanting to be cast alone to the Soviets. In conversations with Vance and in his messages to me, King Hussein seemed to be interested and constructive. We agreed to his request that he submit some questions about the Camp David accords and then distribute the American answers to other Arab leaders.

The Soviets' reaction to the Camp David agreement was predictable. On September 20, Gromyko told me that the Israelis had won everything and Sadat and the Arabs had gained nothing. I tried to convince him in person, as well as the other Soviet leaders, to cooperate and to urge the Syrians and Palestinians to join in the future talks, but was not surprised at their negative reaction. President Brezhnev wrote to urge me to abandon the Camp David process and return to the Geneva Conference format.

However, I did get important encouragement the next week.

The news came through that the Knesset had voted to approve the Camp David agreement and remove the Israeli settlers from the Sinai. This was a remarkable demonstration of courage, political courage, on the part of Prime Minister Begin, who had to go against his own previous commitments over a lifetime [and] against his own closest friends and allies who sustained and protected him during his revolutionary days.   DIARY, SEPTEMBER 27, 1978

In October I had my hands full with the last days of the congressional session, the SALT negotiations with the Soviets, and my attempts to wrap up normalization with China. I was also preparing answers to the list of questions sent to me by King Hussein on behalf of the Arab leaders. I wanted my comments to be constructive and absolutely true to the letter and spirit of the Camp David accords.

We invited the foreign and defense ministers of Egypt and Israel to Washington to work out the details of the peace treaty— the exact language outlining the new relationship between Israel and Egypt and the schedule for Israel's withdrawal from the Sinai. Everyone agreed to negotiate without press statements and without my being personally involved; Secretary Vance and his staff would provide liaison and make sure the talks stayed on track.

A *framework* had been signed, but not the treaty itself. Now a treaty draft had been prepared, but the negotiators immediately ran into trouble. There was an argument about how to make clear that the old Egyptian–Arab mutual-defense agreements did not prevail over the new treaty, and some dispute about how soon the Israelis would make their first withdrawal and whether Sadat would then be willing to exchange ambassadors. Begin was giving Dayan and Weizman little authority to negotiate; concessions they made here were often reversed from Jerusalem. The underlying question was whether there would be no more than a separate treaty with Egypt, without follow-up action on the West Bank and on Palestinian rights.

Vance had to go to South Africa to work on the Namibia problem, and then on to Moscow. Zbig was on his way to Rome as one of the excited leaders of our delegation to the investiture ceremonies for the new Pope, who, like Brzezinski, was Polish. So I met personally with the negotiating teams. The Israelis were forthcoming on the Sinai withdrawals, agreeing to leave the El Arish area quite early, but the Egyptians were not ready to accept immediate diplomatic ties with Israel. I assumed that Sadat would agree to do so, if other differences could be resolved. After meeting with the delegations separately, we drafted a text that seemed to decide the remaining questions.

> *I think we've put together the Israeli–Egyptian peace treaty text. I called Dayan early this morning to encourage him to work out any final details before he went back to Israel. It's probably a serious mistake for him to go back now, because I don't know how we can handle another redrafting job done by the Israeli cabinet.* DIARY, OCTOBER 21, 1978

As the delegations departed, I sent a personal message to Sadat and Begin, urging them to accept the text we had devised. My worries about their response were offset by some good news from Saudi Arabia, delivered by King Khalid in person, and accompanied by a strong supportive message from Crown Prince Fahd, indicating that the Saudis would support the Camp David negotiations on the West Bank–Gaza, and would try to hold the Arab nations together in a positive attitude toward us and Egypt during a forthcoming meeting of Arab leaders in Iraq early in November.

Although I asked Begin and Sadat for cooperation, Begin announced plans to expand the West Bank settlements and revealed that he was thinking of moving his office to East Jerusalem. In response to my letter urging him not to create further impediments to the peace process, he informed me that his actions on the West Bank settlements were designed to assuage the feelings of some of his political allies, who had now turned against him.

Cy Vance was supervising the negotiations, but not much could be accomplished under the circumstances. The Israelis were upset about the American answers to Hussein's questions concerning the meaning of the Camp David language. I had approved the answers, after carefully checking their accuracy, and had sent a copy of both questions and answers to the Israelis and the Egyptians. Begin's reaction was to accuse Assistant Secretary of State Harold Saunders of acting on his own initiative rather than with official authority when he went to Jordan with our responses. I received a typically equivocal message from Hussein, leaving open the possibility that either the Jordanians or the Palestinians might negotiate as agreed at Camp David, but making no commitment.

Cy continued to work on the Middle East with discouraging results. It was difficult to negotiate with the Israelis, because they continuously tossed the ball from Dayan and Weizman to the cabinet to Begin and back. Dayan told us that he could not speak for Israel anymore, because each point had to be specifically cleared in Jerusalem. I understood that within his own party Begin was suffering politically at the hands of some opponents to the Camp David accords. Sadat was also causing problems, because he was under intense pressure from the other Arabs to avoid a separate peace agreement with Israel.

> *It is obvious that the negotiations are going backwards. . . .*
> *I told Cy to withdraw from the negotiations at the end of*
> *this week, to let the technicians take over, and let the*
> *leadership in Israel and Egypt know that we are through*
> *devoting full time to this nonproductive effort. It's obvi-*
> *ous that the Israelis want a separate treaty with Egypt;*
> *they want to keep the West Bank and Gaza permanent-*
> *ly. . . . And they use the settlements [on the West Bank]*
> *and East Jerusalem issues to prevent the involvement of*
> *the Jordanians and the Palestinians.*
>
> DIARY, NOVEMBER 8, 1978

In spite of our frustration, I was determined to keep alive the Middle East peace effort. I decided to focus again on my central point: the differences between the two nations were minuscule compared to the enormous advantages to each of a treaty of peace. I constantly reminded the two leaders of this, and called both of them on the phone to get them to renew their support of the dying effort.

Sadat offered to delay Israeli withdrawal from Egyptian territory in the Sinai in exchange for assurance of free elections of Palestinian representatives in the occupied territories; he urged me not to abandon our common effort. But Begin was in no mood to be flexible, and denied our claims that Israel had changed its position, saying that Weizman was not authorized to speak for his country. I reminded him that Dayan was the head of his team and that Dayan, Weizman, and Barak had all agreed among themselves before they took a position with us and the Egyptians. I could not understand why he singled out Weizman for special criticism. When I persisted in asking the Prime Minister about his own views, he responded each time that he was merely a member of the cabinet and had only one vote.

Meanwhile, King Hassan came over from Morocco, very optimistic about the Iranian and Middle East matters, saying that the Shah could keep his enemies at bay simply by holding popular elections. He also said that my concerns over Middle East peace were groundless, because what we had done at Camp David was irreversible. He was well-meaning and quite knowledgeable and helpful on other matters, but I thought he was wrong on both these counts.

The King was a great admirer of Abraham Lincoln, and after the state banquet that evening I took him by to see Lincoln's bedroom. We met my mother, who was spending the night upstairs.

> *She had recently been to Morocco. She said she smelled all the 21 types of perfume in the palace dressing room where she stayed. He offered to give her some perfume, and she said, "No." Mother laughed and said, "You damn foreigners are all alike." He laughed also and put his arms around her and gave her a kiss. I doubt that the King's been called a "damn foreigner" before, and I don't know anyone else who could get away with it.* DIARY, NOVEMBER 14, 1978

When the Arabs met in Baghdad, the Saudis joined the "rejectionists" in their condemnation of the Camp David agreements. They maintained to us, perhaps accurately, that the conference action would have been much more drastic without their moderating influence. I was disturbed that the Saudis had not fulfilled their earlier commitment to me; and all of us were angered when Hussein subsequently became a spokesman for the most radical Arabs.

Both Begin and Sadat continued to be under heavy pressure. In Jerusalem, the Prime Minister even came under physical attack from some right-wing extremists. On the way to a party conference, his automobile was splattered with eggs and tomatoes, and one of the militants climbed on it and broke the windshield. I sympathized with Begin, because he had to face the strong opposition forces that are an inherent part of a democracy. When I called Sadat, I found him in good spirits—jovial, friendly, and confident. He had been communicating directly with the Saudis and was obviously encouraged by what they had told him, despite the publicized reports from the Baghdad conference.

Vice President Hosni Mubarak came to the United States on November 16 to tell me what the Egyptians were offering: a peace treaty, immediate use of the Suez Canal for Israel, West Bank–Gaza negotiations to commence a month later, Israeli interim withdrawal from the Sinai when success was attained at least on Gaza, ambassadors exchanged after another month, and complete Sinai withdrawal after two or three years. Mubarak made a good impression. At ease, he spoke forcefully and directly, was more tenacious than Sadat in pursuing an Egyptian request for assistance, and seemed well informed about international affairs in general. Sadat had sent me word that his vice president enjoyed his full confidence—just as Mondale enjoyed mine.

Mubarak noted that we had resolved 90 per cent of the problems at Camp David, and that, of the remaining questions, only one-fourth had still not been answered. However, these few were serious. He said the Egyptians wanted to be as flexible as possible, but could not have a separate treaty without assurance of future progress on the West Bank. Therefore, the timetable for action on the West Bank was very important to them.

On November 21, Begin called to tell me that the Israeli cabinet had agreed to accept the month-old treaty draft, but had ruled out any timetable for discussions of agreement on the West Bank. Sadat, too, had hardened his position. To break the deadlock, I sent Vance to the Middle East again. From Egypt he reported success in selling a compromise proposal we had drafted, but he was disappointed in Israel. On December 13, I told him to come home. We had just concluded the China normalization agreement with Deng Xiaoping—much more quickly than anticipated—and I needed Cy in Washington to help me with it.

As 1978 came to an end, I was pleased with the congressional achievements and with our new relationship with China. We were almost at the end of our SALT discussions with the Soviets, and had an excellent agreement in prospect. However, events in Iran were increasingly troublesome, and our hard-won accords in the Middle East were coming apart. I invited Secretary and Mrs. Vance to spend the night with Rosalynn and me at Camp David, where we took several hours to discuss the agenda we would face during 1979. The Middle East dispute was the heaviest political burden, even above SALT and China–Taiwan. It was very time-consuming, and it would have been a relief to all of us to be rid of the responsibility for such frustrating and thankless negotiations.

> *We reviewed the Mideast question in minute detail, and decided that we would continue to move aggressively on it and not postpone the difficult discussions, even though they were costly to us in domestic politics.*
>
> DIARY, DECEMBER 29, 1978

We continued trying to get other Arabs to back the Camp David peace process, but now there was very little for them to support. With Israel and Egypt at odds even on the peace treaty, which was generally considered to be the easiest part, it was not possible to get Hussein or Fahd to come forward in favor of the more difficult process of working out an agreement on the West Bank.

By joining the negotiations, the Palestinians could make a great stride toward realizing many of their goals. We had a report that Yasir Arafat, the PLO leader, had sent an agent to the Saudis to request that Hussein be a spokesman for the Palestinians in carrying out the Camp David process. But none of the Arabs was willing to move on this unless Arafat would take the responsibility himself—and he chose not to. Instead, Arab leaders and the PLO kept the Palestinian-rights issue at the fore in such international forums as the United Nations, successfully arousing worldwide support for their position.

These constant United Nations votes were irritating to us, and having to deal with these diversions made our negotiations more difficult. The most sensitive issues—such as settlements, Jerusalem, and sovereignty rights—needed to be discussed in private among the parties directly involved, and not in a demagogic fashion among 150 nations.

During the first few weeks of 1979, we were almost totally preoccupied with the new Congress, China normalization, and the downfall of the Shah of Iran. Instability in the Persian Gulf area should have been an additional incentive to the Saudis, Jordanians, and other Middle East states to seek peace and stability among themselves, but there was no evidence that they understood this.

> *We had an assessment of the apparent dead end on the Mideast negotiations, with Israel and Egypt both intransigent and quibbling over details. I directed State and NSC to back off and take another look. . . . Harold [Brown] will be go-*

ing to Saudi Arabia, Egypt, Israel, and perhaps Jordan the first part of February, and . . . we'll issue specific instructions to him, because he'll have both military and diplomatic duties to perform.   DIARY, JANUARY 26, 1979

Secretary of Defense Brown came back without being able to report any progress, but with a renewed conviction that Sadat and the Israelis wanted to try again. We invited the chief negotiators over to Camp David, where Cy joined them. Egyptian Prime Minister Mustafa Khalil was authorized to conclude an agreement, but Foreign Minister Dayan was directed only to explore possibilities for progress and report back to Begin and his cabinet. After a few days, they all suggested that Begin come over, so that real negotiations would be possible. When invited, he accepted, but later said that he would have to check with the cabinet, then that he would wait until Dayan came back to Jerusalem with a report, and finally that it would not be appropriate for him to meet with merely the Prime Minister of Egypt. I was in a quandary about Israel, so I asked both Begin and Sadat to come to see me, with Begin to make the first trip.

Begin reluctantly decided to come, wanting to wait until next week. I pressured him into arriving here Thursday evening. He later sent word that he did not want to go to Camp David, and was not even bringing his Foreign Minister or other cabinet members with him—and even said he would not discuss substantive issues. Sadat was . . . willing for Egypt to negotiate at any time, and on any issue, but insisted on the comprehensive nature of the Camp David agreement being preserved.   DIARY, FEBRUARY, 27, 1979

Israeli public-opinion polls indicated strong support for the peace process, but the Prime Minister seemed to be swayed by his cherished political beliefs and by the influence of his close associates, and was not pursuing a final settlement aggressively. Our only option was to keep the effort alive and work for an agreement, or, if we failed, to let the differences be publicized and to disengage ourselves with minimum damage.

Now, at best, we could have a bilateral peace treaty followed by extended negotiations on the West Bank and on Palestinian rights. At worst, the Egyptians and Israelis would break off relations, Egypt would rejoin the other Arabs as enemies of Israel, and the Palestinians on the West Bank and in Israel itself would increasingly demonstrate for full citizenship rights, causing a bloody confrontation which might arouse the entire world against Israel.

When Begin arrived on March 1, his first public statement at the airport was that he would refuse to sign any worthless document that would be a step away from peace. In the Oval Office he seemed unusually nervous; Cy, Zbig, and I did what we could to put him at ease. He wanted to speak first, and I let him do so.

Begin made a long, rambling statement about the power of Israel's land forces and their readiness to join Egypt in an attack on Libya or to defend Saudi Arabia. He described how, in 1970, Israel had used its army to stop Syria's move into Jordan. He asked for more airplanes and tanks, and suggested that we needed to have a mutual defense agreement. He then said that he had suffered terribly in Israel from the Camp David concessions he had already made, and enumerated them all: to withdraw from the Sinai, to remove the settlers, to grant autonomy on the West Bank, and so on. He was ready to go ahead with the agreement, he told me, but Egypt's demands for a time schedule on West Bank progress were irresponsible and contrary to the Camp David accords.

The Prime Minister never mentioned any American involvement in moving the airfields out of the Sinai nor the withdrawal of Israeli forces. He did not seem especially interested in the terms of the peace talks. His purpose seemed to be to convince us that Israel should be the dominant military power in the area, and that it was our only reliable ally in the Middle East.

I acknowledged the mutual interests of our two countries in maintaining peace, but pointed out that we had strong and valuable friendships with such other nations as Saudi Arabia, Jordan, and Egypt—and that these good relations must continue. I reminded him that these nations were a powerful restraining force on terrorists and on the more militant Arabs, and that there was a limit to how long Sadat could stay apart from other Arab leaders while the peace talks foundered. I reviewed the adverse consequences of failure, and the ultimate threat to Israel if Begin should permit his country to become isolated in the world because of intransigence and belligerent acts or statements. Emphasizing the danger to Israel of having the United States as its only constant friend, I said I hoped that in five years Israel's relations with France and other European countries would be as good as those with the United States. We then moved from the Oval Office to the Cabinet Room to join a larger group of advisers.

Begin ... was very strong, negative, apparently confi-

dent. . . . Begin said that Sadat still wants to destroy Israel, and that Israel will not accept any interpretive notes. Then he went down a list of eight things and condemned them, even though some were Israel's own original proposals. Throughout the entire discussion I emphasized over and over that this was a very difficult problem, requiring flexibility on both sides; that Begin had made no proposals at all to resolve the differences. Therefore there had been no progress, and the prospects at this point were dismal. That Sadat had heavy pressures on him to withdraw from the negotiations altogether—had given Israel everything that they had originally wanted, but that Israel had continually raised its demands. I recognized that Israel has made major concessions also. . . . We have gone as far as we can in putting forward suggested compromise language, with practically no constructive response from Israel.

DIARY, MARCH 2, 1979

That Friday evening, we joined the Israelis for supper. There was a lot of singing, but Begin and I were preoccupied with other matters. I was convinced the peace effort was at an end. In spite of my disappointment, it would be a relief to escape this political thicket.

When we returned to the White House, Rosalynn had a fever and went to bed. I put on a heavy coat and sat on the Truman balcony alone, wondering what in the world we could do next. Sadat was adamant in his positions; I had not been able to penetrate past Begin to his cabinet, the Knesset, or the Israeli people; and the American public was getting weary of our continuing obsession with an apparently futile effort.

I decided to pursue with my top advisers the possibility of my going to Egypt and then to Israel—getting together with Sadat and making my strongest appeal to the Israelis. My main purpose would be to remind them what they would be giving up if the peace treaty were lost.

Saturday, Cy, Harold, Zbig, and Jody worked on this proposal. With, I think, the exception of Zbig, they're all concerned about it. Jody is generally the most timid in the whole group on almost every issue. During the 24-hour period, Hamilton came back from Georgia, Fritz from California. Hamilton was strongly in favor of my going to Egypt. Fritz was very concerned about the negative

impact of going to Israel if the whole thing was doomed
to failure.   DIARY, MARCH 3, 1979

My proposal was an act of desperation. There were no alternatives that would work with any certainty, and a nonproductive
trip by the President of the United States to the Middle East
would greatly dramatize the failure. As usual, Zbig was somewhat unorthodox and daring, whereas Jody was concerned about
the damage to public relations if Sadat or Begin rejected our final
proposals. He also knew very well how low we had already sunk
in public opinion, partially because of the never-ending negotiations that had followed the euphoria of the Camp David accords. I
was inclined to go to Cairo and Jerusalem, but had not yet made
a final decision.

That night, Menachem and Aliza Begin had supper with us, and
he and I had a long private talk. I tried to orient his thoughts
to the situation in Israel five or ten years in the future, asking him
to consider the regional and worldwide implications of failure to
complete the Camp David process. But this was not his way of
dealing with issues. We made no progress at all.

The next day, I got a message from Sadat saying he wanted to
come to Washington to blast Begin as the cause of our failure, to
present Egypt's case to Congress and the American people, and to
take the whole Middle East issue to the United Nations for further action. I sent him a message to stay cool for forty-eight hours
and let the pressure build up on Begin. What I did not tell Sadat
was that I needed a little more time to decide what to do.

We worked out some treaty texts that were barely acceptable to
the Israelis but did not quite comply with the key points on
which Sadat was insisting. We had made a proposal on the Sinai
that was fairly well balanced but would require some flexibility from Sadat for Egyptian approval. Begin submitted the text
to his cabinet, and informed me that it had been accepted. I
called Sadat, and without giving him any details, told him the
Israelis had accepted a preliminary draft of the treaty. I also let
him know I was considering a trip to Egypt and Israel. He was
overjoyed, and I definitely decided to go. I then asked Begin to
come from Blair House to the Oval Office, where I told him I was
going to Egypt and was ready to accept his repeated invitations
to visit Israel. He guaranteed that I would have a good reception,
and seemed pleased about my plans. Begin said that after our
Saturday night talk he hadn't been able to sleep at all, worrying
about the consequences of failure.

Understandably, Sadat began to insist on seeing the treaty

texts the Israelis had adopted. I decided to send Brzezinski with them personally, to explain some of the more difficult parts and to review the strategic considerations which might help to ease Sadat's anticipated objections to the wording itself. Once more, I wanted Begin to have his way with particular phrases and depended on Sadat to be flexible on language and to take the long view concerning the effect of the agreement.

> *I informed Sadat that Zbig was coming. He replied, "Great! Your trip will be a wonderful event, and a complete success." He repeated, "I can assure you, Mr. President, complete success."*   DIARY, MARCH 5, 1979

From then on, I felt that I had a guarantee from President Sadat that my mission would not fail—or at least, that a failure would not be caused by differences between him and me. I told Zbig not to reveal this conversation to anyone, and gave him a handwritten letter to deliver to Sadat, designed to encourage his generosity on some of the treaty language. The note said, in part, "The language may not be exactly what you want, but the target date issue and the 'priority of obligations' issue are such that you can accept them and legitimately claim a victory. You may or may not completely agree with me on the nuances of the exact words but, in any case, the differences are minimal when compared to the overall strategic considerations which you and I must address together."

In order for me to leave the country, we had to cancel Fritz's plans to attend the inauguration ceremonies in Venezuela and Brazil so that he could be at home to deal with the many issues we were facing: Iran, the struggle for control of Yemen, the multilateral trade negotiations, Taiwan legislation, final stages of the SALT discussions, Panama Canal treaties implementation legislation, the protection of wilderness areas in Alaska, and hospital cost containment. Before I left, we made progress on some of these issues, and I also approved our administration's policy on the decontrol of oil prices.

When Rosalynn and I arrived in Cairo, we felt a glow of welcome, warmth, and friendship which remained throughout the visit. Over the opposition of some of his close advisers, Sadat accepted the troublesome texts, and within an hour he and I resolved all the questions which still had not been decided after all these months. I was concerned about his isolation in the Arab world and the threats that had been leveled at him after the announcement of my trip. He said, as usual, "My friend, you take care of the Israelis, and I will take care of the Arabs."

> *In my private visits with Sadat he emphasized again and again that his main concern was about me, and that he wanted my trip to be a "smashing success." But he directed me to negotiate fairly, in the best interests of Egypt and Israel. It was imperative to him that the United States and Egypt stand together, no matter what might be the outcome of the negotiations. He reviewed briefly the result of his trip to Jerusalem and our Camp David talks, and the fact that the agreements we reached there comprised the first progress for Palestinians in thirty years. There was a sharp difference between the Israelis and the Arab world about what "autonomy" meant. [Sadat felt that the] "full autonomy" so freely expressed but so narrowly defined by Begin might ultimately be a trap for him, because the world would take the side of people seeking democracy and autonomy—this being an easier issue to understand than the extreme complexities of the peace treaty we were trying to negotiate.*
>
> *I reminded Sadat that Begin . . . had gone much further than the other Israeli government leaders who had preceded him; that in Begin's mind he went too far at Camp David. Sadat understands that Begin may wish to back out if he gets a chance, or wait until after 1980 when there is a President in the White House who may not be so equally balanced between the Israeli and Arab interests. Sadat understands that it's important to conclude the negotiations now.*   DIARY, MARCH 8, 1979

The Egyptian President repeated his inclination to go along with the ambassadorial exchange in return for territory, saying he would either sell us all the oil produced in the Sinai so we could deliver it to Israel, or else he would let Israel have it on a strictly competitive basis. I did not pursue the point then, but was convinced that he would later be willing to guarantee Israel's right to purchase the oil directly.

The personal friendship and trust between Sadat and Mubarak was obvious. The two men came from the same province, and Mubarak was totally loyal to his President.

The remainder of our visit was delightful, designed to let the Egyptians and the rest of the world know the closeness between

us, the ties between our nations, and the overwhelming support
of the Egyptian people for the peace process. We particularly
enjoyed a trip from Cairo to Alexandria, moving slowly through
the beautiful farming regions of the Nile delta on a fine old train
built in 1870. Our car was completely open on both sides, and we
felt that we were right in the midst of the hundreds of thousands
of people along the way. There were no apparent worries about
security. In Alexandria we were welcomed by the largest and
most enthusiastic crowds I have ever seen. As I told Sadat, describing my reception would be one time a politician would not
have to exaggerate.

Before leaving Egypt I spoke to the parliament and visited the
pyramids at Giza. Begin's and Sadat's distrust of one another and
their personal incompatibility had become one of my concerns, so
on the way to the airport, I asked Sadat if he were willing either
to go to Jerusalem or to have Begin come to Cairo. He said,

"Both." I then asked if it would be best to have the Prime Minister just visit the airport, and Sadat replied, "No, I want him to come to the center of Cairo to let the world know with our great welcome how much the Egyptian people believe in the peace treaty if it is signed."

Bob Lipshutz had been in Israel for a day or two, and sent me word from Ezer Weizman that if the Egyptians agreed to the same language the cabinet had approved, everything could be worked out. Weizman cautioned me about the first reactions there, saying, "What the Israelis fear most of all is peace itself." He explained how difficult it was for the Israelis to have confidence in their trust of ancient enemies; to be beleaguered was the more familiar feeling. Since Sadat had now approved the disputed language, I felt confident of success as we approached the Tel Aviv airport.

I rode to Jerusalem with Begin and President Yitzhak Navon. Navon was a delightful companion—level-headed, intelligent, and friendly. He pointed out the remarkable number of different racial and ethnic groups that had come to Israel, and how they were living together in harmony. Begin and Navon wanted me to stop at the outskirts of the city for a ceremonial breaking of bread with Mayor Teddy Kollek and the Chief Rabbi. However, the security men reported angry demonstrators at the site, and said that we would probably be pelted with eggs. The demonstrators were there and some of them were angry, but they saved the eggs. Most of the signs were in Hebrew. The most prominent one, in English, said, "WELCOME, BILLY'S BROTHER!" All this made me aware that we were in a true democracy.

We went directly to the Prime Minister's home, and we and our wives enjoyed a very good supper. For the first time since we three leaders had left Camp David, I felt confident that we would finally have a peace treaty. Sadat's position was very generous, and seemed reasonably compatible with what the Israelis wanted.

> Then I asked Begin if he wanted to go into the study, because I was prepared to give him a report on my meetings with Sadat, review the outstanding issues, and hopefully expedite his acceptance of the treaty terms, arrange for the signing ceremonies, and have a conclusion of my trip to the Mideast without any further interruptions.
>
> He seemed to show little interest in my conversations with Sadat. We arrived at the point that Sadat wanted him to come to downtown Cairo and for Sadat to come to Jerusalem for the signing ceremonies. Begin told me then

for the first time that he could not sign or initial any agreement; that I would have to conclude my talks with him, let him submit the proposals to the cabinet, let the Knesset have an extended debate, going into all the issues concerning the definition of autonomy, East Jerusalem, and so forth, and then only after all that would he sign the documents.

I couldn't believe it. I stood up and asked him if it was necessary for me to stay any longer. We then spent about 45 minutes on our feet in his study. I asked him if he actually wanted a peace treaty, because my impression was that everything he could do to obstruct it, he did with apparent relish. He came right up and looked into my eyes about a foot away and said that it was obvious from the expression on his face that he wanted peace as much as anything else in the world. It was almost midnight when I left. We had an extremely unsatisfactory meeting, equivalent to what we'd had the previous Saturday night at the White House. DIARY, MARCH 10, 1979

I sent word ahead for Cy and the others to meet me in my room at the King David Hotel. I described what had happened, and told them that Begin did not seem at all interested in what either we or Sadat had to say about the peace negotiations. We decided that our only hope was to present the facts to the Israeli cabinet the next day. Rarely have I been so frustrated as I was that evening. I was convinced that Begin would do everything possible to block a treaty and to avoid having to face the problem of the full autonomy he had promised to the Palestinians on the West Bank. He was obsessed with keeping all the occupied territory except the Sinai, and seemed to care little for the plight of the Arabs who were having to live without basic rights under Israeli rule.

The next morning I paid a courtesy call on President Navon, and outlined to him what had occurred the night before. He had never heard of any such commitment by any prime minister to a cabinet, and pointed out that Begin was perfectly at liberty to negotiate on behalf of Israel, as all his predecessors had been.

The Prime Minister then picked me up for an impressive service at Yad Vashem, the memorial to the Holocaust victims. Moving slowly through this shrine, I was filled with extraordinary emotion. It was much easier for me to understand Begin's extreme caution concerning the security of Israel. The historic persecution of the Jewish people had always been known to me—but now it was a more vivid reality. Afterward, in a somber mood, we drove for a brief visit to the graves of Theodor Herzl, the founder of modern Zionism, and Ze'ev Jabotinsky.

I then left Begin and went to a Baptist church service. While the pastor spoke, I got my thoughts in order, planning how best to emphasize to the Israeli cabinet the broad advantages of peace and the consequences of failure.

Begin asked me to preside over the cabinet meeting, and in spite of many interruptions I finally completed my remarks. All those present then found themselves devoting their energies to the question of how to say in the final agreement that none of Egypt's previous agreements with other Arabs could possibly conflict with the new treaty with Israel. We spent hours talking about the difference between "derogate," "is not inconsistent with," and "contravene." The only thing we accomplished during the entire afternoon was to agree on "contravene"! I did the best I could to appeal directly to the individual members of the cabinet, which was a very impressive group. Several of them expressed to me privately their hope that we could work out an agreement before I returned to Washington.

We arrived late at the state banquet, but there was time for toasts from Navon, Begin, and me. I made my pitch again to this distinguished group of leaders. After the banquet I stood at the doorway and shook hands with everyone, and the cabinet members left for an all-night session.

On Monday morning we met two hours later than planned with the full membership of the Israeli cabinet—sixteen men plus Begin. They were quite concerned about oil supplies to Israel after the return of the Egyptian wells, and were reluctant to agree that the Egyptians should have free access to the Gaza district. We had to end our meeting before making any apparent progress, in order for me to visit the Knesset.

> *I laid a wreath on the war dead memorial outside, went in with the Speaker of the Knesset, was introduced, and gave my speech. There was quite a buzz among them when I said that the people were ready for peace, but that the leaders had not yet shown that they had the courage to take a chance on peace. Begin apparently resented this comment, but it was accurate and needed to be said.*
>
> *When Begin got up to try to speak, he was interrupted constantly by shouts and rudeness. He seemed to take delight in it, beaming with pleasure every time it occurred. One of the women members of the Knesset, Mrs. Cohen, was expelled.* DIARY, MARCH 12, 1979

Strangely, in the rough and tumble of the Knesset debate, I learned a lot about Prime Minister Begin, and felt friendlier toward him. Although some of the other leaders were very embarrassed at occasional comments and the complete absence of order, he seemed to relish the parliamentary combat, and in his asides to me was very proud of this display of democracy at work.

During the speeches by Begin and Shimon Peres, I wrote a note to Vance, telling him to meet with the cabinet during the afternoon and concentrate on only two issues: an adequate supply of oil for Israel and assured access for Egypt to Gaza. During that same time, I met with the twenty-five members of the Knesset's Foreign Relations Committee, and listened while the leaders of the various political factions expressed their hopes and concerns to me. This session was an excellent, constructive exchange of views. I had a good chance to give the participants a review of the remaining differences and to answer their questions. Then I went back to my hotel, thoroughly exhausted.

Cy and Zbig came in late that afternoon to report another fruitless meeting with the Israeli cabinet, saying that no progress had been made. There was no need for us to stay in Israel any longer, and we made plans to leave the following day.

I then decided that I would call Begin, ask him by for breakfast tomorrow morning. That I would then call Sadat and ask him to meet me at the Cairo airport for a report on the lack of progress in Israel. DIARY, MARCH 12, 1979

We were then astonished to hear that Begin had told the press we had made substantial progress and only a few issues of substance remained to be resolved. Dayan called Cy to say that he, Weizman, and several other cabinet members had gotten together to see how to salvage the talks, which were otherwise doomed to fail. I suggested to Cy that he invite Dayan over to discuss some possible resolution of the issues. They met while Rosalynn and I accompanied the archaeologist, Professor Yigael Yadin, to see the remarkable Dead Sea scrolls that he and his father had devoted their lives to preparing. He said one of the frustrated dreams of his life had been to visit the antiquities in Egypt. I asked him if it would be all right for me to arrange such a visit with Sadat, and he said, "Yes, if you can do it secretly." I promised to do so, whether or not we had a peace treaty.

Quite early the next morning, I met with my advisers to go over the final talking points on the disputed issues. They reported comments from several of the cabinet members to the effect that a strong majority of them was satisfied with our proposals, but that Begin was still unconvinced.

For some reason, Prime Minister Begin insisted on his wife's accompanying him to breakfast. When they arrived, I suggested that the wives might enjoy being together while he and I ate alone. We stood at the window and looked out over Old Jerusalem for a few minutes before sitting down. I told him that we wanted a settlement before I left the Middle East, and I reviewed again the proposals which were necessary for Egypt and seemed to me advantageous for Israel. He finally admitted that of his seven concerns, four had been alleviated, but that at best he could submit any agreement to the cabinet on a Thursday, let them consider it on Sunday, and allow two or three days for minimal debate.

I could easily see a clear resolution of the remaining issues. I told him again that the Sinai oil would come to Israel, and that if delivery were interrupted, we would guarantee his country an adequate supply at prevailing world prices. Sadat would agree to exchange ambassadors as soon as Israel kept its promise of early withdrawal from the Western Sinai. The only other issues were the granting of an additional element of freedom to the Palestinian Arabs and Egyptian access to Gaza.

I pressed him hard, and Begin finally agreed that the Palestinians would be permitted peaceful political activity, and that he would lift some of the restraints on movement of inhabitants within the West Bank and Gaza areas. He also said that families could be reunited within the West Bank and Gaza but only if it did not involve immigration of Palestinians from Lebanon, Jordan, or other countries. As for Arab political prisoners being held by the Israelis without trial, he stated that at present they were holding only a few Arabs—he thought thirty-two—who had not been given the right to a trial. This detention was authorized under an old British law; its repeal was under consideration.

I pushed for an answer concerning the entire Egyptian–American proposal.

> *I asked if he wouldn't give me his opinion on what he would do. He said no, he would not even express an opinion to me because this would imply a cabinet commitment, which he was not willing to give. I called Cy and asked him and Dayan to join us.*   DIARY, MARCH 13, 1979

Dayan responded strongly and favorably to our proposals, while Begin listened without comment. After hearing Dayan, I decided to delete all references to Gaza in order to give Begin a chance to claim some kind of victory on the language. After they left, Weizman came by to say that he would support the proposed resolution of the remaining issues.

In the lobby, as we were preparing to leave, I asked Begin if he would accept our proposals provided the Gaza language was deleted. When he said he would, I believed I could get Sadat to accept the entire proposal. We had a good chance for an agreement! I outlined to him what I intended to say in Cairo after meeting with Sadat.

On the way to Tel Aviv airport, Navon and I had an interesting discussion about the ancient texts of the Bible, the Talmud, and the Midrashim, and how scholars were still working on interpreting them. Begin had little to say, but at the airport he made a surprisingly upbeat public statement—apparently having forgotten about his strange "commitment" to the cabinet.

The flight from Tel Aviv to Cairo is very short, and I spent the time briefing the other Americans on the last-minute developments in Israel. When I stepped on the ground and embraced Sadat, I told him, "You will be pleased." He responded, "My people in Egypt are furious at how the Israelis have treated our friend Jimmy Carter." I answered, "It wasn't bad."

We met with Sadat, Mubarak, Khalil, and my old negotiating friend from Camp David, Osama el-Baz. I outlined what had been decided in Israel, and urged them to accept the entire package without further delay. The changes in our original proposals were insignificant. There was some equivocation among his advisers, but after a few minutes Sadat interrupted to say, "This is satisfactory with me."

When we were alone, I asked him to exchange ambassadors early, to offer a pipeline from the oil wells to Israel, to strive to reduce the anti-Begin comments in the Cairo press, and to invite Yadin to visit Egypt. He agreed to all these requests. As I left the room, Hamilton suggested to me that I call Begin, which I did as my departure statement was being typed.

I had received a short note from my secretary: "It's from the 'peanut gallery' . . . but a good number of your staff and others, though we have no way to express it, feel strongly much respect, admiration, and love for the truly great man President Sadat is, and the great man you are." Leaving out the reference to myself, I read the note to the Egyptians, who listened with evident emotion. We were all quiet for a moment, and then our ebullient spirits returned as I answered their question about the definition of a "peanut gallery."

The breakthrough had come so late and so swiftly that no one

at home knew about it. As soon as we were airborne, I called a
despondent Vice President to give him the good news, and then
talked to the congressional leaders. Bob Byrd had begun orches-
trating complimentary statements from a bipartisan group of
senators, because they were convinced that my trip would be very
embarrassing. By the time I got Tip O'Neill on the phone, he had
already heard about the agreement. He said, "Mr. President, you're
not just a deacon anymore, but a pope!"

> We arrived at Andrews [Air Force Base], and had hun-
> dreds of Cabinet members, Congress members, their fami-
> lies, and others to meet us. It was a very thrilling sight at
> 1:30 in the morning to see them all there. Got back to the
> White House. Amy was waiting for us. It was good to be
> home. We consider the trip to be very successful.
>   I resolved to do everything possible to get out of the
> negotiating business!   DIARY, MARCH 14, 1979

It disgusted me to find that the American press was very negative,
particularly CBS News. The reporters accused Jody Powell of
misleading them with pessimistic statements during the last few
hours in Jerusalem (when we all thought we had failed), alleged
that the treaties were "bought" at a price of $10 to $20 billion
(completely untrue), and claimed that we had agreed to a mutual defense treaty with Israel (which was never even discussed
on the trip).

Henry Kissinger telephoned to congratulate me, saying that I
was working him out of his career of criticizing the government
by not leaving him much to criticize.

Most foreign leaders were supportive, calling the peace treaty a
significant step forward, but some of the Arab nations announced
sharp economic and political sanctions against Egypt.

Ironically my standing in the public-opinion polls went down,
probably because of the negative press treatment, and because
after the one great upsurge of joy following Camp David, the
ensuing delay had been such a disappointment. Most of the people were as tired of it as I was.

Fritz and I decided that Bob Strauss, who had served as Special
Trade Representative in my Cabinet, would be a good negotiator
to carry out the remaining provisions of the Camp David accords.
He had done an outstanding job on some important international
trade negotiations after they had almost been given up for lost,
and we hoped he might have equal success with the items on the
West Bank and Palestinian rights. When I called him in, he had

no idea what I wanted. Informed, he was overwhelmed, and for once was at a complete loss for words. Finally, he stammered out, "I've never even read the Bible—and I'm a Jew!" I said, "It's not too late to start reading, and Kissinger is also a Jew." He was very pleased and excited. We agreed not to let anyone know about this decision until I could work out his exact role with the State Department and with the Egyptian and Israeli leaders.

Despite some adverse reaction at home and abroad, nothing could diminish the importance of peace. No matter what might happen in the future, it was much more likely that American interests in the Middle East would be enhanced by this new relationship between our two friends, and the people in Egypt and Israel could reap great economic and political benefits if their leaders could capitalize wisely on this opportunity for progress and stability.

Sadat and Begin came to Washington for the signing of the treaties. After a characteristic flurry of last-minute disputes about language, we had a very satisfactory ceremony on March 26. In a huge tent on the south lawn for the evening banquet, it was thrilling to see enemies welcome each other and share memories of the wars. Ezer Weizman's son, Sha'ul, had been severely injured in 1970 near the Suez Canal by an Egyptian bullet that penetrated his skull. He came over to our table, and we watched as he was embraced by President Sadat and his son. That evening Sadat told me he had decided not to go to Jerusalem again, but he repeated his invitation to Begin to come to Egypt immediately.

A few days later, Begin visited Cairo. He was ecstatic when he called me, practically shouting into the telephone. "I had a wonderful visit to Cairo! The people of Egypt opened their hearts to me. In the morning, tens of thousands lined the streets on both sides, and cheered and waved, and took me to their hearts. I am very moved. I left my car for a while, to the disturbance of the Egyptian secret service, and went into the crowd, which was crying, 'We like you, we love you!' It was absolutely wonderful. Yesterday's reception was at the Qubba Palace. The evening was a 'thousand nights into one.' "

Sadat also called, very pleased with the progress they had made for implementing the early phases of the treaty terms. He and Begin were trying to outdo each other in maintaining the momentum toward peace. Sadat said they could finally take the burden of negotiating from my shoulders. I replied, "If you do, my fervent prayers will have been answered!"

For several months, the peace process continued without interruption, but only by skirting the other issues. With the exception of removing the settlements, the Sinai withdrawal did not seem to present a serious political problem for Begin at home, but the Arab world and its many allies in international organizations continually raised the questions of settlements in the occupied territories, the status of Jerusalem and the West Bank, altercations in Lebanon, and Palestinian rights. One after another, resolutions on these subjects—all condemning Israel—were introduced in the United Nations and other meetings, where they almost always passed overwhelmingly. Only the threat of a United States veto in the United Nations Security Council prevented the adoption of more serious proposals involving political and economic sanctions by the international community against Israel.

I was still convinced that an effort to carry out all the provisions of the Camp David accords in good faith would lead to the realization of the legitimate goals of Israel, its neighbors, and the Palestinians. But this was not yet to be. Some Arab militants still harbored bitter hopes that Israel could ultimately be destroyed; direct negotiation or recognition of Israel by any Arab nation would be counter to that goal. With the exception of Sadat, moderate Arab leaders were not strong enough to buck this tide of emotion-filled prejudice. Some Israelis refused to give up their undying prayer that they could cling to the occupied Arab territories, ignore the Palestinian right to self-determination, and still obtain acceptance among Israel's neighbors and in the world community as a permanent and peace-loving nation. There were not enough strong Israeli leaders to prevail against this shortsighted and counterproductive sentiment. We did the best we could to bridge this wide gap and won a partial victory.

Looking back on the four years of my Presidency, I realize that I spent more of my time working for possible solutions to the riddle of Middle East peace than on any other international problem. At the beginning, I never dreamed of the many hours of exhilaration and despair that lay ahead. As was the case with the Panama Canal treaties, I have asked myself many times if it was worth the tremendous investment of my time and energy. Here again, the answer has not always been the same. It will depend on the wisdom and dedication of the leaders of the future. Two of the men who worked so hard for peace are dead. Anwar Sadat was bold and generous, and Moshe Dayan understood the Arabs and their needs better than any other Israeli I have known. Both were able to envision a future of peace, and both had the courage to risk the displeasure of their peers to seek it.

My hope has been that the peace treaty can convince other Arab leaders of the advantages of negotiations in good faith, and that the courage of President Sadat will inspire them and the Israeli leaders to make similar bold moves for peace. Only history will reveal if my hopes and prayers are to be answered—or if another round of bloody confrontations will ultimately lead to an international tragedy.

IRAN AND THE
LAST YEAR

IRAN

We have no intention, neither ability nor desire, to inter-fere in the internal affairs of Iran.

NEWS CONFERENCE, JANUARY 17, 1979

On the south lawn of the White House, I stood and wept. Tears were streaming down the faces of more than two hundred members of the press. It was a memorable moment. In the distance we could hear the faint but unmistakable sounds of a mob, shouting at the mounted police who had just released canisters of tear gas to disperse them. Unfortunately, an ill wind seemed to have been blowing directly toward us as we greeted the leader of Iran, and the gas fumes had engulfed us all.

With the television cameras focused on me as I welcomed the Shah to our country, I tried to pretend that nothing was wrong. So, with difficulty, I refrained from rubbing my eyes and avoided the extreme irritation that afflicted most of the others.

The Shah and his wife, Farah, were deeply embarrassed, and apologized several times to Rosalynn and me for having been the object of the Iranian student demonstrations. We reassured them, pointing out that the situation seemed to be under control and no harm had been done.

That day—November 15, 1977—was an augury. The tear gas had created the semblance of grief. Almost two years later, and for fourteen months afterward, there would be real grief in our country because of Iran.

The Iranian ruler, Mohammed Reza Shah Pahlevi, tolerated little political opposition at home, but allegations were increasingly heard in the United States that his secret police, SAVAK, was brutalizing Iranian citizens. Public demonstrations had taken place here against the Shah. As his arrival date approached, extraordinary precautions had been taken to protect him against violence or embarrassment. Every person who entered the White House grounds had been checked carefully, and the District of Columbia and U.S. Park Service mounted police were directed to keep the chanting demonstrators at a safe distance from the welcoming crowd.

After a brief ceremony, the Shah and I moved into the White House for a presentation of Iran's Bicentennial gift to the United States—a remarkable tapestry portrait of George Washington. Then we walked to the Cabinet Room to begin our official discussions.

The Shah was a likable man—erect without being pompous, seemingly calm and self-assured in spite of the tear-gas incident, and surprisingly modest in demeanor. The air of reticence in his first conversations with me could not have been caused by his unfamiliarity with American Presidents. Since he had met with President Franklin Roosevelt in Tehran in 1943, he had been a frequent visitor to the White House. I was the eighth American President he had known!

A much warmer atmosphere now prevailed than when we had first communicated a few months earlier.

> The Shah of Iran sent an angry message to me ... that because of the one-month delay in presenting the AWACS proposal to Congress, he was thinking about withdrawing his letter of intent to purchase these planes from the United States. I don't care whether he buys them from us or not.   DIARY, JULY 31, 1977

So read my first diary entry about Iran and the Shah. I was attempting to reduce the sale of offensive weapons throughout the world, but it was not possible to make excessively abrupt changes in current practices, because of contracts already in existence. The Shah had previously ordered a system of ground-based fixed radar stations, to be located around the land borders of Iran for detecting enemy planes and for directing Iran's air defense forces. I felt that it would be less expensive and more effective to replace them with AWACS (aircraft warning and control systems), which could be obtained either from us or from European suppliers.

I had submitted the proposed sale to Congress on July 7, 1977, but the House International Relations Committee had rejected it on the grounds that the security of advanced electronic devices could not be assured in Iran. I then had to withdraw the proposal to prevent its final rejection by Congress. The Shah considered this delay an insult to Iran, and it precipitated his irate message. As he habitually bought military equipment from many sources, it would have been all right with me if he decided to buy similar equipment elsewhere. His temper soon cooled, however, and the proposal was resubmitted to Congress in September. This time the members of my administration did their homework on Capitol Hill, and the sale was not disapproved.

I continued, as other Presidents had before me, to consider the Shah a strong ally. I appreciated his ability to maintain good relations with Egypt and Saudi Arabia, and his willingness to provide Israel with oil in spite of the Arab boycott. At the time of his visit to Washington in November 1977, I was especially eager to secure his influence in support of Sadat's dramatic visit to Jerusalem, which had just been announced.

My intelligence briefings revealed that despite increases in the Iranian standard of living from the distribution of oil revenues, the Shah's single-minded pursuit of his own goals had engendered opposition from the intelligentsia and others who desired more participation in the political processes of Iran. SAVAK was notorious for its ruthless suppression of any dissent and I was informed that there were 2500 (the Shah said "below 2500") political prisoners in the Iranian jails. The Shah was convinced that immediate suppression was the best response to opposition, and he was somewhat scornful of Western leaders (including me) who did not emulate his tactics.

When asked on November 4 by international correspondent Arnaud de Borchgrave what kind of "scenarios" he feared most in the years to come, the Shah had replied, "Growing terrorism, permissive societies, democracy collapsing through lack of law and order. If things continue on their present track, the disintegration of Western societies will occur much sooner than you think under the hammer blows of fascism and communism. Freedom is not something that does not have a breaking point, and your enemies would like you to reach that point." It was clear that he did not believe the warning applied to Iran.

Now, in the Cabinet Room with Vice President Mondale, Secretary of State Vance, and National Security Adviser Brzezinski, I listened closely as the Shah gave an excellent analysis of the troubled situation around the Persian Gulf area. Also, quietly and proudly, he dwelled on the changes which were taking place in the lives of his own people. He quoted improving statistics on employment, education, housing, transportation, and health care, obviously pleased with the fruits of his leadership.

Iran's growing middle class, well-educated students, and strong religious community seemed a foundation for stability and further progress. But I knew from American intelligence reports that these three groups carried the seeds of dissension within Iran, and I felt it advisable to speak to the Shah alone about the potential problems he faced.

After we left our second general meeting, he joined me in my small private room near the Oval Office. I asked if I might speak frankly, and he agreed. I had rehearsed my brief statement, to be sure I could deliver my entire message without unduly embarrassing or insulting my guest.

"I am familiar with the great improvements which have been made in your country," I told him, "but I also know about some of the problems. You have heard of my statements about human rights. A growing number of your own citizens are claiming that these rights are not always honored in Iran. I understand that most of the disturbances have arisen among the mullahs and other religious leaders, the new middle class searching for more political influence, and students in Iran and overseas. Iran's reputation in the world is being damaged by their complaints. Is there anything that can be done to alleviate this problem by closer consultation with the dissident groups and by easing off on some of the strict police policies?"

The Shah listened carefully and paused for a few moments before he replied somewhat sadly, "No, there is nothing I can do. I must enforce the Iranian laws, which are designed to combat communism. This is a very real and dangerous problem for Iran—and, indeed, for the other countries in my area and in the Western world. It may be that when this serious menace is removed, the laws can be changed, but that will not be soon. In any case, the complaints and recent disturbances originate among the very troublemakers against whom the laws have been designed to protect our country. They are really just a tiny minority, and have no support among the vast majority of Iranian people."

We discussed the subject for a few minutes more, but it soon became obvious that my expression of concern would not change the policies of the Shah in meeting a threat which, I am sure, seemed very real to him. He was aware of Iran's poor image, but considered it quite a progressive move merely to allow civilian attorneys for defendants who were accused of being communists. It was a sensitive subject between us, because some news sources had attributed the disturbances in Iran to my frequent statements in support of human rights throughout the world. Still, we ended our first meeting in good spirits. The discussion about human rights had not been embarrassing. On the contrary, it had been private and personal, making it easier afterward for us to talk to one another about human rights and other delicate issues.

After Congress adjourned in December, I made a nine-day trip to several nations, including Iran. On the last day of 1977, in his public toast in my honor, the Shah emphasized the close relations that had evolved between our two countries over several generations. He also mentioned the "high ideals of right and justice, moral beliefs in human values" as characteristics of American society.

In my response, I acknowledged the value of the good relationship between our nations, and referred to Iran as "an island of stability in one of the more troubled areas of the world." I went on to quote an ancient Persian poet recommended to me by Empress Farah:

Human beings are like parts of a body, created from the same essence. When one part is hurt and in pain, others cannot remain in peace and quiet. If the misery of others leaves you indifferent and with no feeling of sorrow, then you cannot be called a human being.

Stability and human rights—I would recall these phrases often during the months ahead. In my brief overnight visit, I saw no visible evidence of the currents of dissatisfaction which, though underestimated by the Shah, I knew to be there.

> *CIA gave me a definitive analysis of the economic and political problems of Iran. The Shah has asked our Ambassador and the one from Great Britain to give him advice on how to handle the trend toward democracy and a more liberalized society. The Shah has moved very rapidly and has alienated a lot of powerful groups, particularly the right-wing religious leaders who don't want any changes made in the old ways of doing things.*
>
> DIARY, OCTOBER 25, 1978

During 1978, the Shah attempted to respond to demands from his people for a greater voice in public affairs, but instead of restoring order and harmony, his faltering efforts only aroused further dissatisfaction—expressed through public clashes, mostly by religious groups, with Iranian police. American intelligence reports during the summer, however, indicated no cause for serious concern. According to a CIA assessment, issued in August, Iran "is not in a revolutionary or even a prerevolutionary situation." The report went on to say that the military was loyal to the monarchy and that those who were in opposition, both the violent and the nonviolent, did not have the capacity to be more than troublesome in any transition to a new regime.

The increasingly frequent disturbances continued to be of concern to me, and our intelligence services kept me abreast of changing circumstances. On September 8, the Shah declared martial law throughout Iran, following which there was a bloody confrontation between the police and a large crowd of demonstrating Moslems. Several hundred people were killed by bursts of machine-gun fire. After this incident, the strength of the demonstrators grew, as they demanded the Shah's abdication and he attempted to control the disorders with ever more stringent military discipline.

At times, the Shah tried to pacify the dissidents. He granted amnesty to hundreds of opposition leaders—including Moslem leader Ayatollah Ruhollah Khomeini, who had recently moved from Iraq to Paris. Under pressure from the Moslem leaders, the Shah also began to terminate some of his relations with Israel, although the oil supply was maintained. Yet his problems mounted. Serious strikes in the oil fields caused production to plummet from six million to less than two million barrels a day.

I received frequent reports from our embassy in Iran, indicating the gravity of the Shah's troubles. Still, Ambassador William Sullivan joined all my other advisers and me in believing that the Shah was our best hope for maintaining stability in Iran. On October 28, 1978, Sullivan sent a cable to Washington stating that "the Shah is the unique element which can, on the one hand, restrain the military and, on the other hand, lead a controlled transition. . . . I would strongly oppose any overture to Khomeini. . . ."

The Shah, under growing pressure, was considering early and more far-reaching changes in the structure of the Iranian government and a drastic transformation of his own role.

The Shah expressed deep concern about his own future, trying to decide whether to set up an interim government, set up a military government, or perhaps even to abdicate. We encouraged him to hang firm and to count on our backing. DIARY, NOVEMBER 2, 1978

It was becoming increasingly evident that the Shah was no longer functioning as a strong leader, but was growing despondent and unsure of himself. He was doing his best to conceal the extent of his domestic turmoil from the outside world, but I knew he needed all the support the United States could properly give him, short of direct intervention in the internal affairs of his country.

The Shah still had a mind of his own, and had no desire for anyone in our country to give him directives. He asked for advice on occasion—from me and from other foreign leaders. Sometimes he took it, and sometimes he did not. During his time of crisis, my advisers and I always worked toward the most desirable outcome acceptable to him, while making plans to deal with a number of other eventualities which were less desirable but beyond our power to prevent.

I sent him a message stating that whatever action he took, including setting up a military government, I would support him. We did not want him to abdicate. Concerned about any potential challengers to his throne, the Shah had always resisted building up a strong political organization around him, which might have included some of the more responsible opposition leaders. He had even kept the leaders of each branch of the military separate from the others, requiring them to report individually and directly to him.

Until this time, those opposing the Shah had been fragmented, as a succession of dissident leaders struggled for ascendancy. Now an identifiable leader was emerging. Perhaps because of his remoteness and air of martyrdom enhanced by fifteen years of exile, his constant and unswerving opposition to the Shah, his religious beliefs bordering on fanaticism, and his militant attitude in demanding action and violence, the Ayatollah Khomeini had gained increasing influence over the anti-Shah forces. Although he was still in Paris, Khomeini was sending taped messages into Iran, calling for general strikes, the overthrow of the Shah, and the establishment of an Iranian republic.

We continued our support for the Shah's various proposals to change Iran's government. At this point he seemed to be moving quickly toward a coalition government which would include representatives of some of the dissident groups. He was trying to devolve power from himself onto his hand-picked successors in accordance with the provisions of Iran's constitution—which, of course, had been written under his own direction.

Still, there was no question in my mind that he deserved our unequivocal support. Not only had the Shah been a staunch and dependable ally of the United States for many years, but he remained the leader around whom we hoped to see a stable and reformed government organized and maintained in Iran. We knew little about the forces contending against him, but their anti-American slogans and statements were enough in themselves to strengthen our resolve to support the Shah as he struggled for survival.

By early November, Ambassador Sullivan had become convinced that opposition leaders would have to be given a much stronger voice in Iran's affairs than the Shah was willing to consider. I could not disagree with this, but my basic choice was whether to give the Shah our complete backing in his crisis or to predicate support, as Sullivan increasingly seemed to prefer, on the Shah's acquiescence to suggestions from the American Embassy.

The Shah is on very shaky ground. I told Cy to be sure that the State Department officials below him supported my position—that the Shah should know that we are with him. DIARY, NOVEMBER 10, 1978

Meanwhile, through their propaganda machine, the Soviets were doing everything possible to aggravate the situation. Aware of the 1500-mile border shared by Iran and the Soviet Union, I was concerned that the Soviet leaders might be tempted to move in, a repetition of what they had already done three times in this century. Already the Soviet propagandists were accusing the United

States of controlling political forces in the troubled country. President Brezhnev and I exchanged private and public warnings about interference in the internal affairs of Iran. I let him know that we would not intervene, but that we would honor our commitments to Iran and that we fully supported the Shah.

The key to stability was the monarch himself, supported by the military. To learn how he was responding to the enormous pressures on him, I invited the Iranian Ambassador, Ardeshir Zahedi, to come to the Oval Office. He reviewed the situation for Brzezinski and me.

> *The essence of it was that the Shah had strengthened himself somewhat recently—politically, militarily, and also psychologically. . . . The Ambassador told me frankly that there was no clear concept in the mind of Iranians what the Shah had given to the Iranian people or what he could accomplish with his leadership, that he had no public-relations program under way or in progress, that he had no advisers around him who could prepare such an effort, and that there was no political structure within Iran to succeed if and when elections were held.*
>
> *We expressed our concern about this. Zahedi claimed several times that the Shah was eager for him to be a court minister or prime minister, but we have some intelligence information that Zahedi has offered to fill these posts and the Shah has not been enthusiastic about it.*
>
> DIARY, NOVEMBER 21, 1978

A general strike began in Iran. Several hundred thousand demonstrators took to the streets to demand that the Shah be ousted. Zbig asked former Under Secretary of State George Ball to come in as a consultant to the National Security Council in assessing what the United States could do about the troubles. We were particularly worried about the approaching holy days, when Iranians were expected to fill the streets and work themselves into a frenzy. Khomeini was calling for bloodshed, but on this occasion the massive throngs ignored the Ayatollah's call for violence. Yet the disturbances continued.

> *The strike has been getting worse again in Iran. It is increasingly obvious that the Shah must share substantial governmental authority with civilians, including the opposition, in order to prevent having to abdicate.*
>
> *I went over with George Ball his recommendations that*

*we force the Shah to broaden the base of political author-
ity in his government. My first inclination is to see what
the Shah intends to do and get his personal assessment,
and then decide how much to push him to bring in the
opposition leaders. The Shah desperately wants to keep
control of the military, which may or may not be possible.*
                                          DIARY, DECEMBER 14, 1978

*We sent a list of questions to the Shah, and he responded
well to them. The summary of his comments to us is that
he wants to retain his position as Commander in Chief of
the Armed Forces, let the civilian government share defense budget responsibilities with him, and let one of the
leaders put together a coalition cabinet without his interference. He feels better than he had felt in weeks gone by.
With a threat of being fired or not paid, some of the oil
workers had gone back to work, just about doubling production in recent days. But of course the issue in Iran is
still in doubt.*   DIARY, DECEMBER 18, 1978

Over the Iranian holidays the situation grew much worse, with
numerous strikes wreaking economic havoc. Personally and through
the State Department I continued to express my support for the
Shah, but at the same time we were pressing him to act forcefully
on his own to resolve with his political opponents as many of the
disputes as possible. His basic plan of asking one leader to assemble a coalition government seemed sound, but he was having
a hard time convincing anyone of stature to serve in a top position. Because the growing strength of the anti-Shah forces resulted in constant turmoil, and because the Shah seemed unwilling
to grant anyone else enough real authority to govern, several of
his appointees resigned and others refused to serve. It seemed
that every time the Shah finally decided to make a conciliatory
move, it was a few days too late to satisfy anyone, even his closest
advisers and supporters.

At the end of the year, the Shah had settled upon Shahpour
Bakhtiar, a Western-educated moderate, who accepted the position of Prime Minister. The newly chosen leader demonstrated
surprising strength and independence, immediately calling for
the Shah to leave Iran, for the secret police to be disbanded, for
those responsible for shooting demonstrators to be tried, and for
civilians to be in charge of Iran's foreign affairs.

Despite his previously declared willingness to do so, the Shah
now announced that he was not ready to leave Iran. He was

prepared to leave at a later time, he told his advisers, but wanted to do so in a dignified fashion in accordance with the Iranian constitution—after the new leaders were firmly established in office and the parliament had endorsed his actions.

It was obvious even to his own supporters that the Shah would have to leave the country before order could be restored. The reports I was receiving from the CIA, the State Department, and from diplomats of other countries, led me also to feel the Shah would have to leave. However, I agreed with him that he should do so with dignity, in accordance with his own schedule, and only after a stable successor government had been established. The *majlis* (parliament) approved Bakhtiar as Prime Minister, but Khomeini announced from Paris that no one who was loyal to the Shah would be acceptable to him as the permanent leader of Iran.

During the early days of January 1979, it seemed possible for Bakhtiar to succeed in establishing a cabinet under the existing provisions of the Iranian constitution. Although Bakhtiar was never supported by Khomeini, I thought there was a chance for their relationship to improve. Bakhtiar had demonstrated a degree of independence and forcefulness, and apparently had the confidence of some of the dissident groups in Iran.

Ambassador Sullivan, however, was recommending that we oppose the plans of the Shah, insist on his immediate departure, and try to form some kind of friendship or alliance with Khomeini. I rejected this recommendation because the Shah, Bakhtiar, and the Iranian military leaders needed consistent American support. Reports in the Washington press, however, indicated deviations within the State Department from my policy of backing the Shah while he struggled to establish a successor government.

Because Sullivan seemed unable to provide us with adequate reports from the military, which was a crucial source of information and advice, Secretary Brown and I concluded that we needed a strong and competent American representative in Tehran to keep me informed about the military's needs. One of his responsibilities would be to strengthen the resolve of the military leaders and encourage them to remain in Iran in order to maintain stability even if the Shah should decide to leave. I ordered General Robert Huyser, Deputy Commander of United States forces in Europe, to carry out this assignment in Iran.

At the request of Ambassador Zahedi, we also made arrangements for the Shah and his immediate family to use the Walter Annenberg estate in California if he later decided to "take a vacation in a foreign country."

At the Guadeloupe meeting:
(l-r) Schmidt, Carter, Giscard, Callaghan

On January 4, 1979, I went to Guadeloupe to meet with the leaders of France, Great Britain, and Germany, but I had to spend a great deal of my time working on the Iranian crisis. Secretary of State Vance stayed in Washington with the Vice President to monitor the situation in Tehran. My instructions had been to do everything possible to strengthen the Shah, but during these days I became increasingly troubled by the attitude of Ambassador Sullivan, who seemed obsessed with the need for the Shah to abdicate without further delay. He was getting quite nervous, and sometimes reported that the Shah would not see him. I was still relying on some of his reports, which I later realized were not accurate or balanced. Sullivan insisted that we should give support to Khomeini, even if it meant weakening Bakhtiar and the coalition government he was trying to form. The Iranian military leaders still supported the Shah and had no inclination to strengthen Khomeini's influence in any way. Sullivan's reports about the military's attitude were often at variance with those of General Huyser. Realizing that the situation in Iran was terribly confused and that all the military leaders were not speaking with the same voice, I wanted more than one opinion. Over time, however, I came to trust Huyser's judgment.

> *Some of the top military leaders had been to Sullivan to tell him, "We will not permit the Shah to leave Iran. We will at least place him on an [Iranian] island. We plan a coup to take over the government, to clean up Iran and to*

*eliminate violence. Bakhtiar may form a token govern-
ment and we will give him token support." Sullivan's
opinion was that the Shah was involved in this arrangement, was knowledgeable about it, and that his unavail-
ability was deliberate.*

*Cy wanted strongly to stop any such move as this [coup],
even though Fritz said the Shah was probably supporting
this particular plan. I insisted and instructed Cy eventually to take action to retain our relationships with the
Shah and with the military—our only two ties to future
sound relationships with Iran, since we didn't know the
form of government it might take if the military was
eliminated as a major factor.*　　DIARY, JANUARY 4, 1979

We instructed Sullivan to see the Shah as soon as possible in
order to ascertain his attitude toward these military plans. Cy
wanted us to stay away from both the military and the Shah, in
favor of Bakhtiar. My own belief was that the Shah, the military
leaders, and Bakhtiar were all acting in concert. At that time I
thought the Shah and the military would prevail.

The next morning the Shah told Sullivan that he had complete
control over the military leaders and that they would make no
move to restrain him in any way. He said he planned to leave
Iran in order to strengthen Bakhtiar, and that those who had
considered a military coup would instead support Bakhtiar's government but would stand by to take over if he should fail. General
Huyser met with the military leaders and reported that they
indeed supported Bakhtiar. They wanted to stay as aloof as possible from any public relationship with the United States, in
order to strengthen their support among the Iranian factions.

In long discussions about world affairs at the Guadeloupe meeting, I found little support for the Shah among the other three
leaders. They all thought civilian government would have to be
established, and were unanimous in saying that the Shah ought
to leave as soon as possible. They agreed with me, however, that
the military should be kept strong and united, and there was no
support among them for Khomeini or the revolutionaries. Giscard
reported that he had decided earlier to expel Khomeini from
France so that his country would not be the source of dissension
and revolutionary efforts, but that the Shah had thought it would
be better to keep Khomeini there, instead of letting him go to
Iraq or Libya or some other place where he might orchestrate
even more trouble.

After I returned to Washington, Sullivan continued to insist that we go directly to Khomeini in Paris to evolve some working arrangement with him. I considered this recommendation carefully, but rejected it because our forming any relationship with Khomeini would indicate a lack of support for the struggling new government in Iran, which the Ayatollah had sworn to destroy. Instead, I asked Giscard to find out if there was any possibility that Khomeini might support Bakhtiar. In response, Khomeini only repeated his previous statement—that Bakhtiar was unacceptable to him.

Sullivan apparently lost control of himself, and on January 10 sent Vance a cable bordering on insolence, condemning our asking the French President to contact Khomeini instead of doing it ourselves. He used such phrases as "gross and perhaps irretrievable mistake," "plea for sanity," and "incomprehensible." He seemed unable to present an objective analysis of the complicated situation in Iran. I was well aware that he had been carrying out some of my directives halfheartedly, if at all. Now, since he had changed his mind in recent weeks about supporting the Shah, his activities and statements cost him much of the confidence he had previously enjoyed from the Shah and his associates—and from me. I told the Secretary of State to get Sullivan out of Iran, but Cy insisted that it would be a mistake to put a new man in the country in the midst of the succession of crises we probably faced. I reluctantly agreed, but from then on I relied primarily on General Huyser, who remained cool and competent. He sought to maintain as wide a range of contacts as possible around Tehran during these last days of the Shah's reign, and as far as I could tell, he always sent back balanced views.

Bakhtiar announced that the Shah would be leaving Iran on January 16. I expected him to come to the United States after a brief stop to visit Sadat, who had extended an open invitation for the Shah to stay in Egypt. Khomeini made known his intention to return to Iran some time after the Shah's departure. It had been my hope that he would stay in France and give the new government a chance to restore order and end the crippling strikes, but on January 12 Khomeini announced that he would definitely go back to Iran. I was convinced that this move could cause the downfall of Bakhtiar, leaving a military coup the only alternative to a radical regime or complete anarchy.

I called Giscard d'Estaing quite early in the morning, asking him to contact Khomeini and to do everything he

could to delay Khomeini's departure from France. Giscard
was willing to cooperate. Said ... he had no way to
prevent Khomeini's leaving France, but could delay it
somewhat. His government's only policy was to support
the Bakhtiar government. Valéry said he has no relation-
ship with the Iranian military, and that he believes the
visit by the Shah to the United States would be a mistake.
It would be much better if he would go to a more neutral
country for a while before winding up here in our country.
Later in the day he called back. Giscard reported that
Khomeini has no plans to leave Paris for the moment. He
didn't know what "for the moment" means, but that
Khomeini is afraid he might lose his life if he goes to Iran.
Khomeini's final aim is to overthrow the Bakhtiar gov-
ernment. DIARY, JANUARY 14, 1979

The Ayatollah's tape-recorded speeches sent into Iran were condemning the United States equally with the Shah for alleged
crimes. Through Huyser, we continued our efforts to reinforce the
Iranian military's ties with Bakhtiar, and asked the Saudis, Egyptians, Moroccans, Jordanians, and several other Moslem countries
to give their support to the new government and encourage
Khomeini to stay out of Iran. After a few days, however, more
than a million marchers in Iran rallied to back Khomeini. He
announced from France that he was forming a provisional government, ending his fifteen years of exile, and returning to Iran
without further delay. Bakhtiar then offered to resign and let the
Iranian people choose their form of government, provided Khomeini
would remain in Paris.

The departure of the Shah from Iran to Egypt and then to
Morocco was curiously anticlimactic, because we had been anticipating his move and because the Shah and his retinue wanted it
seen as a temporary absence rather than a historic event. Nevertheless, this marked the end of his thirty-eight-year reign.

During the evening, Zahedi told Brzezinski that after con-
sulting with Sadat and Hassan [of Morocco], the Shah
had decided not to come to the United States, but to stay
and to move his family to Morocco. This suits me fine,
although Brzezinski was somewhat disturbed. I think the
Shah's presence in a Moslem country is better for Bakhtiar,
and the influence of King Hassan among other Moslems

is good to keep Khomeini under control. And I believe the
taint of the Shah being in our country is not good for
either us or him.   DIARY, JANUARY 20, 1979

Zbig felt that it was better for us if the Shah would come to the
United States, so that we could demonstrate to the world our
continuing support for an old ally. The Shah knew that he could
come; we had made final arrangements for his journey to the
Annenberg estate. I surmised, however, that the royal family
contemplated an early return to Tehran and wanted to remain
in a nearby Moslem country instead of severing almost all ties
with their region by coming to the United States.

The Shah left behind him a shaky government, uncertain and
disorganized military commanders, and an aroused people calling for the Ayatollah to come home as its spiritual and political
leader. Bakhtiar let us know that he was considering arresting
Khomeini if he flew into Iran, but then he decided that to do so
would precipitate widespread violence in his country. He was
struggling to avoid further bloodshed. The officials of the Iranian
coalition government closed all airports to prevent Khomeini's
return, and Bakhtiar announced that he would fly to Paris instead. When Khomeini's aides approved this visit, Bakhtiar said
he would permit the Ayatollah's return to Iran, still hoping that
somehow this might help restore order.

Typically, Khomeini reversed himself at the last moment and
refused to see Bakhtiar in Paris. He then flew into Tehran on
February 1, to be welcomed by hundreds of thousands of supporters. I considered bringing Huyser out of Iran for his own safety,
but as there was no excessive disorder, I decided to keep him
there. The Iranian military leaders wanted him, and his influence
and reports were very valuable to us in Washington.

During all this time, we were busy evacuating the many Americans who wanted to leave Iran. Since the beginning of the disturbances, we had brought out more than 25,000, but almost 10,000
were still there. Sullivan now said that all American citizens
except diplomatic personnel could no longer be protected and
should leave the country. We worked constantly to get our people
out, but we did not want any publicity about it. Millions of
Iranians were in the streets, and thousands had already been
killed in the struggles between the government officials and the
Khomeini forces. Almost miraculously, no American had been
attacked, in spite of the Ayatollah's picturing us to his supporters
as foreign devils.

Khomeini then announced that Mehdi Bazargan would be his choice for Prime Minister, but Bakhtiar clung to power. The military leaders promised to remain neutral during what was practically a civil war. On February 14, some Marxist guerrillas besieged the United States Embassy for two hours before being dispersed by Khomeini supporters.

At this point I decided to bring General Huyser home to give me a personal report. He told me there had been a remarkable difference in interpretation of American policy between himself and Ambassador Sullivan. I replied that this had been evident from the beginning of the year, but that I thought we had made our instructions clear. He pointed out that both he and Sullivan had read the same dispatches from the White House and the State Department; but Sullivan thought we should not oppose Khomeini's take-over because his rule would lead to democracy, whereas Huyser thought it would lead only to catastrophe. Sullivan thought the military should stand aloof rather than participate in the political processes of Iran; Huyser thought the military should clearly support the existing government until a new constitution could be written and put into effect. Huyser believed the military had made adequate plans to protect its equipment and installations, and that it would stay off the streets. He had dissuaded some of its leaders from attempting a coup, and from moving out of other parts of Iran into the more stable southern part.

As I compared what he told me with what our Ambassador in Iran had done and said, I became even more disturbed at the apparent reluctance in the State Department to carry out my directives fully and with enthusiasm. Its proper role was to advise me freely when a decision was being made, but then to carry it out and give me complete support once I had issued a directive. Cy sent one of his deputies to Iran to straighten out Sullivan or remove him, and I asked the Iranian desk officers and a few others to come to the White House.

I laid down the law to them as strongly as I knew how. I pointed out how difficult the Iranian questions had become, and described my procedure for making decisions. Sullivan had not been the only one who had caused me trouble. There had been a stream of news stories in Washington, seeming to originate with those who opposed my judgment that we should give our support to the Shah, to the military leaders, and later to Bakhtiar. I told them that if they could not support what I decided, their only alternative was to resign—and that if there was another outbreak of misinformation, distortions, or self-serving news leaks, I would

direct the Secretary of State to discharge the officials responsible
for that particular desk, even if some innocent people might be
punished. I simply could not live with this situation any longer,
and repeated that they would have to be loyal to me or resign.
And then I got up and left the room.

There had not been any differences between my position and
that of the National Security Council staff or the Defense Department, but in order to balance the slate, I met with Zbig's
people too. Since there was no problem with them concerning
Iran, I merely cautioned them about the contention and excessive
competition that sometimes existed between the White House
and the State Department, and directed that they take the
initiative at every level to form closer working relations with
their equivalents at State.

> *Zbig is a little too competitive and incisive. Cy is too easy
> on his subordinates. And the news media constantly ag-
> gravate the inevitable differences and competition between
> the two groups. I hardly know the desk officers and others
> in State, but work very closely with NSC people. When we
> have consulted closely, like in the Mideast area, at Camp
> David, and otherwise, we've never had any problems be-
> tween the groups.* DIARY, FEBRUARY 7, 1979

After a few days, the Iranian military simply disintegrated, and
on February 11, Bakhtiar and the members of the *majlis* resigned.
Bazargan then became Prime Minister, and with the support of
Khomeini, began to consolidate his authority. He and his predom-
inantly Western-educated cabinet members cooperated with us.
They protected our embassy, provided safe travel for General
Philip C. Gast, who had replaced Huyser, and sent us a series of
friendly messages. Bazargan announced publicly his eagerness to
have good relations with the United States, and said that Iran
would soon resume normal oil shipments to all its customers. But
as the weeks passed, he ran into more and more trouble from
Khomeini's revolutionaries, who formed armed bands all over
Iran and arrested hundreds of people, trying them on the spot
and executing them. It was difficult to know who had the backing
of the Ayatollah, and Bazargan soon threatened to resign if
Khomeini's aides did not refrain from interfering with his government. Khomeini gave this promise, but frequently reneged.

I had hopes that the Ayatollah would stay in the holy city of
Qum, seventy-five miles south of Tehran, permitting Bazargan to

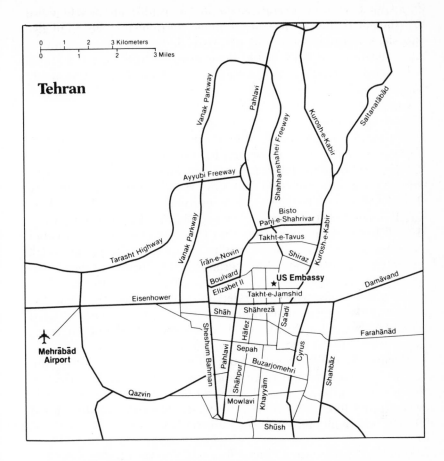

Tehran

0 1 2 3 Kilometers
0 1 2 3 Miles

Vanak Parkway

Pahlavi

Shahhanshahei Freeway

Kurosh-e-Kabir

Saltanatābād

Ayyubi Freeway

Vanak Parkway

Bisto
Panj-e-Shahrivar

Takht-e-Tavus

Tarasht Highway

Īrān-e-Novin

Shiraz

Kurosh-e-Kabir

Boulvard
Elizabet II

★ US Embassy

Damāvand

Eisenhower

Takht-e-Jamshid

Shāh Shāhrezā

Sa'adi

Farahānād

Mehrābād
Airport

Sheshum Bahman

Pahlavi

Hāfez

Sepah

Cyrus

Shahbāz

Shāhpur

Buzarjomehri

Qazvin

Khayyām

Mowlavi

Shūsh

govern the people peacefully with the backing of the major political and religious factions. It became obvious, however, that no
government officials were to be in control of the country.

Then we got word that our military observation sites in northeastern Iran were under siege and that we could no longer operate our equipment, which was designed to monitor Soviet test
missile launchings across the border.

The most disturbing incidents were the capture of American
personnel. First, there was the short-lived seizure of our embassy.
Then, twenty Air Force employees were taken by Iranians at one
of our intelligence monitoring sites and released after a frightening interval of several days. The street mobs sometimes whipped
up anti-American feelings to a fever pitch. As quietly as possible,
we continued to urge the several thousand Americans remaining
in Iran to leave and struggled to provide transportation for them.

At the same time, there were some favorable signals. Khomeini sent his personal representative to see Secretary Vance, to pledge increased friendship and cooperation, and to seek our assurance that we were supporting the new Prime Minister and a stable government. Despite the turmoil within Iran, I was reasonably pleased with the attitude of the Iranian government under Bazargan.

Before and immediately after the Shah's departure from Iran, we had left open our invitation for him to come to the United States, but he had decided to stay in Morocco. Now, after two months, we began to hear that King Hassan wanted the Shah to leave. On March 15, the night I returned from the Middle East after concluding the peace treaty negotiations between Egypt and Israel, King Hassan requested that we accept the Shah. I was not worried about providing him with adequate security, although there were militant anti-Shah groups in the United States. However, primarily because of the intense hatred now built up in Iran among the mobs who controlled the country and the resulting vulnerability of the many Americans still there, I decided that it would be better for the Shah to live elsewhere. I asked Cy to scout around to help him find a place to stay.

Eventually the Shah settled upon the Bahamas, but later complained about the high prices and moved on to Mexico. Despite his great wealth, he seemed obsessed with the belief that people were trying to cheat him. He still wanted to come to the United States, where he had some enthusiastic advocates.

> *Kissinger called to ask me to let the Shah come to the United States.*   DIARY, APRIL 8, 1979

> *David Rockefeller, . . . came in to spend some time with me. . . . The main purpose of this visit, apparently, is to try to induce me to let the Shah come into our country. Rockefeller, Kissinger, and Brzezinski seem to be adopting this as a joint project.*   DIARY, APRIL 9, 1979

A vocal group of the Shah's friends continued to urge us to invite the Shah. They approached Vance and Brzezinski repeatedly and on occasion appealed directly to me. They had an ally in Zbig, but could not convince me or Cy. Each time, we explained the potential danger to those Americans still in Iran, emphasizing that the Shah had been living comfortably in Morocco, the Bahamas, and now Mexico. Each time, they went away partially mollified, only to return again. Some were merely representing the Shah's interests, while others, like Zbig, thought we must show our strength and loyalty to an old friend even if it meant personal danger to a group of very vulnerable Americans. The arguments raged on, and the question was brought to me at least weekly from some source, but I adamantly resisted all entreaties. Circumstances had changed since I had offered the Shah a haven. Now many Americans would be threatened, and there was no urgent need for the Shah to come here.

> *We finally decided to let Cy contact the embassy in Iran to get their estimate on the possible consequences of letting the Shah come in. I don't have any feelings that the Shah or we would be better off with him playing tennis several hours a day in California instead of in Acapulco.*
> DIARY, JULY 27, 1979

Predictably, our embassy people in Iran recommended against our inviting the Shah to the United States. We had already reduced our Tehran diplomatic staff to less than 75 people, compared to about 1100 before the revolution began. We had also completely revamped the embassy's security features, and were convinced that with the support of the host government, our people would be safe. However, the staff's recommendation confirmed my own decision to continue moving Americans out of Iran and to let the Shah stay in Mexico. (Earlier, during the spring, Chargé d'Affaires Bruce Laingen had replaced Sullivan as head of our embassy in Tehran.)

In some ways, the situation in Iran had improved during the spring and summer of 1979. On May 5, Iranian Foreign Minister Ibrahim Yazdi had made a major speech, outlining the basis for his country's foreign policy: complete commitment to the Palestinian cause, improvement of relations with the United States, and a noncommittal attitude toward the Soviet Union. After the first flurry of arguments between Prime Minister Bazargan and Khomeini, they had apparently decided to avoid one another and, to a surprising degree, go their separate ways.

Bazargan, Yazdi, and a few other government officials were permitted to run the government, and they performed their duties responsibly. But Khomeini had ultimate authority. His statements and actions were irrational, and he and some of his fanatical followers kept Iran in constant turmoil. Because of the continuing bloodbath, some of his close advisers were leaving him; others were being assassinated. As his own problems mounted, he lashed out more and more at the United States. While the government was seeking in many ways to restore normal relations with us, Khomeini was identifying us to his followers in the streets as the source of all their troubles.

Finally, chanting mobs began to demonstrate against Khomeini, and in some of the provinces there were rebellions and demands for autonomy. Khomeini cracked down on the press, and even outlawed the playing of music on all Iranian radio and television programs, stating that music was "no different from opium" and was corrupting the young people of the country. Doubting his ability to deal with the economic and social problems of the nation under Khomeini's leadership, Bazargan asked to be relieved of his duties. When Khomeini urged him to continue as Prime Minister and promised him more support, Bazargan reshuffled his cabinet and decided to stay in office; I was glad to have him there.

On the first day of October 1979, I heard about the Shah's illness. In his evening report, Vance noted that David Rockefeller had sent his personal physician to Mexico, and that if the Shah's ailments were serious, we might be asked to admit him for treatment. Cy added, "Our Chargé d'Affaires [Bruce Laingen] in Tehran says local hostility toward the Shah continues, and that the augmented influence of the clerics might mean an even worse reaction than would have been the case a few months ago, if we were to admit the Shah—even for humanitarian purposes."

On October 17, Cy received another report from Rockefeller telling us the Shah was quite ill with a disease difficult to diagnose and to treat. It had been thought to be infectious hepatitis, but a significant deterioration in his condition now led some of the doctors to suspect cancer. The physicians wanted to bring the Shah to the Cornell University Medical Center in New York for a complete examination. An eminent Columbia Medical School professor was to see the Shah on October 18, and then consult with the State Department Medical Director before making a joint recommendation to Vance about what treatment the Shah required.

Cy explained all this to me in his October 18 evening report, and added, "If we decide to permit the Shah to come to the United States for treatment, we would want to inform the Iranians that we were doing so for humanitarian purposes and to leave open any question of future residence." In the margin I wrote "OK," and returned a copy of the document to Vance.

The following morning, a Friday, we had our regular foreign-affairs breakfast. Cy made it obvious that he was prepared to admit the Shah for medical reasons. I was now the lone holdout. I asked my advisers what course they would recommend to me if the Americans in Iran were seized or killed. Cy suggested that we get another assessment of the question from Tehran.

It happened that Henry Precht, the State Department's Director for Iranian Affairs, was in Iran with Laingen at the time. They were instructed to inform Bazargan and Yazdi of the Shah's condition, tell them of our possible plans to provide treatment for him, and seek their assistance. The next day, I received a message from Laingen. He had given a complete report to the two top Iranian officials, told them that neither the Shah nor his wife would be involved in political activities while in the United States, and asked for a guarantee of protection for American citizens in Iran. They had responded that there undoubtedly would be a sharp reaction in the country, but that they could guarantee the protection. We turned down their request to permit Iranian doctors to examine the patient, but the State Department agreed that their doctors could consult with the Shah's American physicians when the examination was completed. (Later, a New York newspaper questioned the American physicians about the proposed arrangement, and they indicated an unwillingness to participate in any such consultation.)

On Saturday, October 20, I flew to Boston to speak at the dedication of the new Kennedy Library, and then went to Camp David. There I received a "super sensitive" memorandum from Warren Christopher, who was acting as Secretary of State while Vance was in Bolivia. He reported, "We have now learned the Shah's illness is malignant lymphoma compounded by a possible internal blockage which has resulted in severe jaundice. The lymphoma responded satisfactorily when chemotherapy was started several months ago, but recently the chemotherapy has been less effective. The Shah has not had essential diagnostic tests which are necessary to establish proper diagnosis and further chemotherapeutic approaches. Dr. Kean of the Cornell Medical School, who last saw the Shah yesterday, has advised us that these diagnostic studies cannot be carried out in any of the medical facilities in Mexico, and he recommends that the examination take place in the United States. David Rockefeller has asked that we admit the Shah to Sloan Kettering Hospital in New York City for diagnosis and treatment. The State Department's Medical Director supports Dr. Kean's recommendation."

Christopher went on to recommend that we notify Bazargan of

the circumstances. Unless his reaction was strongly negative (in which case we would consult further), we would notify the Shah he could come to New York for diagnosis and treatment. He added, "Mexican President López Portillo informed the Shah on October 19 that he could return to Mexico following medical treatment here." Christopher added that Vance had endorsed this approach prior to his departure for La Paz. Brzezinski's forwarding memorandum concurred in the recommendation but objected to giving Bazargan a voice in the decision.

> *I told Brzezinski to permit the Shah to go to New York for medical treatment, and just inform our embassy in Tehran that this would occur.*   DIARY, OCTOBER 20, 1979

My instructions to the State Department were to notify the Iranian officials, not to seek their permission or approval. Cy reported to me on October 22: "The Iranian Government reacted with moderation when informed by us that the Shah will visit the United States for medical reasons. We have told them that neither the Shah nor the Shahbanou [Empress Farah], who will arrive in New York tonight, will engage in political activity."

On Monday the Shah arrived in New York, and for the next week or so there were objections in Iran but no reason for alarm about the safety of the Americans there. Nevertheless, we monitored the situation carefully. Through the State Department I received a series of reports about the Shah and about the situation in Iran:

> Iranian public reaction to the Shah's hospitalization in New York has been restrained. Tehran press reports have been straightforward and low-key, without any editorial comment. The PGOI's [provisional government of Iran] announcement that the Shah was "terminally ill" may have been an attempt to defuse emotions. Embassy Tehran reports that the past two days have been calm. In response to our request, the security forces guarding our compound have been augmented. A demonstration from Tehran University is scheduled to pass by the Embassy on Friday.   OCTOBER 24, 1979

Rockefeller's staff has told us that the Shah's lymphoma is a Class III malignancy which may be too advanced to irradiate and that chemotherapy treatment will require a minimum of eight months. His doctor tells us this condition gives him a 50/50 chance to survive the next 18 months; if he does so, he could then live for several more years. Meanwhile, the Shah's recuperation from his operation will require another two or three weeks' hospitalization.   OCTOBER 26, 1979

Tehran police expect up to one million people to take part in a demonstration at the American Embassy tomorrow, a religious holiday, to protest the presence of the Shah in the United States. [This report went on to describe the security precautions taken by us and the Iranian officials.]   OCTOBER 31, 1979

Today's anti-Shah demonstrations in Tehran passed without major incident. A crowd of 3,500 demonstrators gathered in front of our Embassy to chant slogans and place banners on the outside walls. A much larger crowd heeded the instructions of the demonstration's organizers and did not advance beyond a square located about three miles from the Embassy. The crowd in front of the Embassy was peaceful and controlled, and none of the demonstrators entered the compound. The Iranian Government cooperated fully by augmenting the police elements which normally protect the Embassy compound. Our Chargé is aware of no plans for further protests in the immediate future.
NOVEMBER 1, 1979

Sunday, November 4, 1979, is a date I will never forget. Early in the morning I received a call from Brzezinski, who reported that our embassy in Tehran had been overrun by about 3,000 militants, and that 50 or 60 of our American staff had been captured. Immediately afterward, I talked to Secretary Vance, who reviewed with me again the precautionary measures that had been taken and the assurances of protection we had received from the Iranian officials. We were deeply disturbed, but reasonably confident that the Iranians would soon remove the attackers from the embassy compound and release our people. We and other nations had faced this kind of attack many times in the past, but never, so far as we knew, had a host government failed to attempt to protect threatened diplomats. We had a firm pledge from both the Iranian Prime Minister and the Foreign Minister to give our staff and property this protection. During the past week or two, even Khomeini's forces had helped to dispel crowds of demonstrators near the American Embassy.

Prime Minister Bazargan did his best to keep his word and to remove the militants, but after a few hours passed without forceful action we grew increasingly concerned. We began to contact any officials we knew in Iran, both in the Bazargan Cabinet and within the so-called Revolutionary Council, where government and religious leaders made the basic decisions about the nation's policies. All our efforts were fruitless. The militants had become overnight heroes in Iran. Khomeini praised their action, and no public official was willing to confront them. Bazargan and Yazdi resigned in disgust, but this did not help set the Americans free.

It was not at all clear what the militants wanted. My impression was that originally they had not intended to remain in the embassy or to hold the Americans captive beyond a few hours. However, when they received the adulation of many of their fellow revolutionaries and the support of Khomeini and other leaders, they prolonged their illegal act. As kidnappers, they seemed to have no clear ideas about ransom, except to repeat the cry we had been hearing ever since January 16 of the previous year— return the Shah and his money to Iran.

> *I spent most of the day, every spare moment, trying to decide what to do. . . . We began to assess punitive action that might be taken against Iran. We still have 570 Americans there. I directed that the companies who employ these people be informed to get them out of the country. We also asked the Algerians, Syrians, Turks, Pakistanis, Libyans, PLO, and others to intercede on behalf of the release of our hostages. It's almost impossible to deal with a crazy man, except that he does have religious beliefs, and the world of Islam will be damaged if a fanatic like him should commit murder in the name of religion against 60 innocent people. I believe that's our ultimate hope for a successful resolution of this problem. We will not release the Shah, of course, as they demand.*
>
> DIARY, NOVEMBER 6, 1979

As soon as the embassy was seized, an Iran working group was formed in the State Department, headed by Henry Precht, Director for Iranian Affairs. Twenty-four hours a day, the work of this group never ceased; they were to continue their efforts until the crisis was over. None of us dreamed that we would wait more than fourteen months before our prayers were answered and our people were finally home.

A HARD WINTER

These last few days have been among the worst I've ever spent in the White House. . . .

DIARY, FEBRUARY 7, 1980

The first week of November 1979 marked the beginning of the most difficult period of my life. The safety and well-being of the American hostages became a constant concern for me, no matter what other duties I was performing as President. I would walk in the White House gardens early in the morning and lie awake at night, trying to think of additional steps I could take to gain their freedom without sacrificing the honor and security of our nation. I listened to every proposal, no matter how preposterous, all the way from delivering the Shah for trial as the revolutionaries demanded to dropping an atomic bomb on Tehran.

Although Khomeini was acting insanely, we always behaved as if we were dealing with a rational person, publicizing our efforts as little as possible. I asked Pope John Paul II to contact Khomeini directly, which he agreed to do. (Later, the Ayatollah made an insulting speech about the Pope.) I urged the people in my administration and the members of Congress not to use abusive language about Khomeini or the kidnappers which might provoke violence against the hostages. To prepare for possible military action, I had satellite photographs taken to determine where Iran's airplanes and other armed forces were located. I wanted to avoid such action if possible, to prevent the spilling of blood on both sides, but it would be inevitable if the hostages were harmed. I was restrained from a preemptive military strike by the realization that the Iranian fanatics would almost certainly kill the hostages in response.

On November 6, two days after the American Embassy was taken, we commenced plans for a possible rescue operation. One by one, various proposals were discarded as impractical or unlikely to succeed without considerable loss of life on both sides. The greatest problem, which seemed at first insurmountable, was the inaccessibility of the American Embassy compound—located more than 600 miles from the nearest operating aircraft carriers and deep within the heavily populated urban center of Tehran. Although we had regular surveillance of the embassy grounds, there was also no way to know precisely where the hostages were being held, and our reports indicated that the guards were determined and quite alert.

Meanwhile, I began action to expel the Iranian students (many of whom had not been in school for years) who were in our country illegally. I also forbade any Iranian demonstrations on federal property, and became quite irritated when my legal advisers and some staff leaders came back repeatedly to argue that this order might infringe on the constitutional right of free speech. I was certain I was right. American anger and frustration had risen as the days passed and the prisoners were not released. With our hostages in captivity, American citizens—including the President—were in no mood to watch Iranian "students" denouncing our country in front of the White House. I was convinced that the demonstrators might precipitate a riot, in which they would be killed or cause the deaths of others. Such an event would have been bad enough in itself, but violence of this kind would very likely have been highly publicized in Iran, and might have caused Americans to be killed or injured in retaliation. After listening to the legal arguments two or three times, I finally directed that no one discuss it with me anymore, and that my orders be carried out without exception and without further delay. Afterward, we had to go through a legal battle about it, but the federal courts upheld my decision as a proper and constitutional exercise of presidential authority.

On November 9, I went to the State Department to meet with the hostages' families. Although the building was only a few hundred yards from the White House, the trip seemed long to me. There was no way for me to know how the families would react, but when we finally met, it was obvious that they and I shared the same feelings of grief and alarm. Secretary Vance and I briefed them on what had occurred, and explained some of the steps we were taking to insure the safety of their loved ones in Iran. The conversation was emotional for all of us, and afterward I was pleased when the families issued a statement of support for me and called on the nation to remain calm. This meeting was the beginning of a close relationship between us, which never faltered during the succeeding months.

In the days that followed I continued to take short-term action, while planning for contingencies I hoped to avoid.

Meeting with families of the hostages

The Syrians, Swiss, Algerians, and French diplomatic persons were permitted to see the hostages during the day, and they seemed to be in good condition. I told Cy to get all [other] Americans out of Iran. The Fluor Company has refused so far to cooperate, since their employees carry a special pass from Khomeini. I told Cy to tell them either to get out or we were revoking their passports.

I asked Cy for his opinion on punitive action to be launched against Iran. His recommendations were exactly what I had already decided tentatively with our military people. We want it to be quick, incisive, surgical, no loss of American lives, not involve any other country, minimal suffering of the Iranian people themselves, to increase their reliance on imports, sure of success, and unpredictable. No one will know what I've decided . . . except Fritz, Zbig, Harold, David [Jones, Chairman, Joint Chiefs of Staff], and Cy.   DIARY, NOVEMBER 10, 1979

That same day Rosalynn returned from visiting the Cambodian refugee camps in Thailand, and I described to her what we had been doing about Iran. She felt strongly that we should stop buying Iranian oil and announce this decision as soon as possible. "People around the country might think you are under pressure from the Iranians," she said, "and that you are refraining from military and other drastic action because we might lose some of our oil supplies." I discussed this suggestion during the day with several members of the Cabinet, all of whom responded positively.

Two days later, I ordered that the United States discontinue oil purchases from Iran. My proclamation described the action as a move against the criminal officials who were condoning kidnapping, and not as a means to encourage conservation in our country. At the same time, I instructed Secretary of Energy Charles Duncan to do everything possible to cut back on all American oil imports and total consumption. We urged other nations to do the same. The worldwide oil shortage was already driving prices sky high.

I began to consider freezing all of Iran's assets—primarily consisting of gold and cash deposits—held in American banks both in our country and abroad. I hesitated only because such action was likely to reflect adversely on us as a reliable trading partner and might frighten other major depositors and investors into a massive transfer of their funds to other countries. Also, it had to be legal, to avoid a federal court injunction that would embarrass our nation. I directed Treasury Secretary Bill Miller and my other advisers to research the law to see how much authority I had, and then prepare legal documents so that, if necessary, the decision could be put into effect without delay. Cy Vance and I also assessed the advisability of breaking diplomatic relations with Iran, but decided against it; we had to keep open every possible avenue of communication, and the diplomatic status of the hostages was one characteristic that provided them some possible immunity from additional harm.

There were so many conflicting questions and ideas during this time that we took extra steps to insure maximum harmony among the many agencies involved. At least once each day my top advisers—the Vice President, Secretaries of State, Defense, and Treasury, Attorney General, National Security Adviser, members of the Joint Chiefs of Staff, my Press Secretary, Legal Counsel, Director of the Central Intelligence Agency, and others as necessary—met in the Situation Room at the White House to discuss Iran. When I did not meet with them, they prepared written minutes almost immediately after they adjourned. Any question of policy was referred to me, either during the meeting or in a series of questions within the written report. I would answer the questions and give additional instructions, and then could feel reasonably confident that everyone would work by the same rules. In times of emergency or when there was an especially difficult decision, we met in the Oval Office or the Cabinet Room, so that I could participate in the full discussion. Throughout the long months of this ordeal, we maintained a remarkable degree of harmony and confidentiality among the disparate groups, with practically no damaging leaks.

During the early weeks of the Iranian crisis, it was necessary for me to watch the situation very closely, to assess a wide range of options—including military action if the hostages were injured— and to be able to react instantly to any opportunity to secure their release. I had many other responsibilities that could not be overlooked, but I did decide to cancel unnecessary trips away from Washington. On November 8, I postponed a state visit to Canada, and a few days later canceled scheduled trips to Pennsylvania and Florida and a vacation visit to Sapelo Island, Georgia. Staying close to Washington quickly became standard policy. Once the custom of eliminating unnecessary travel had been adopted, to renounce it was to indicate reduced interest in the hostages or a loss of hope that they would survive.

My decision to remain near Washington would become controversial, particularly because it coincided with the official beginning of the 1980 Democratic presidential campaign. The same week the hostages were taken, Governor Jerry Brown and Senator Edward Kennedy announced as candidates for President. I decided that until the hostages were freed I would not make political appearances, even if it interfered with my own announcement on December 4.

⌒

I had always intended to seek reelection. A year earlier, in November 1978, Vice President Mondale and I had reached an agreement to run once again as a team. When Senator Kennedy had come to the White House for a visit in March 1979 and I told him of this decision, he reaffirmed his support for me. I do not know what his real intentions were then; later that spring, his constant public criticism of my policies was a strong indication that he was planning to run himself.

I met with Ham, Jody, Jerry, Tim, Fritz, Rosalynn, Stu, Frank, and Dick Moe [the Vice President's aide] to talk about the political situation. To summarize, I told them that they should screen their entire staffs, to tell everybody that we were faced with difficulty now, and that it was very likely to get worse in the future. If they couldn't take the pressure, to get out. I felt personally confident that we

were doing a good job for the country, that we would
prevail again in this Congress as we have in the previous
Congresses, that I would win in 1980 no matter who ran
against me, and that I was going to fight to the last
vote.   DIARY, JUNE 12, 1979

Based on the public-opinion polls, the general presumption
around Washington was that if Kennedy decided to run, I would
have no chance of being renominated and would probably not
even try. At an evening meeting I held in June with House members to explain the Panama Canal treaties implementation legislation, a small group asked me privately if I dared face Kennedy in
a primary election. I replied affirmatively, and added a few words
to describe my confidence in spite of the dismal poll results they
had seen. The next day, to my surprise, my somewhat brusque
remark was reported in the news.

I had lunch with Fritz. He thought that my comment
concerning "whipping Kennedy's ass" was ill-advised. His
is kind of a lonely voice. Some of my staff members say it
was the best thing for morale around the White House
since the Willie Nelson concert.   DIARY, JUNE 20, 1979

After the American hostages were seized, I did not ignore the
Democratic primary contests, but depended on Fritz, Rosalynn,
and others to do the campaigning while I concentrated on the Iran
crisis and my other duties.

At 5:45 this morning Bill Miller called to say that Iran
had ordered the withdrawal of their funds. I told him to
implement the standby plan we had already developed to
impound all the Iranian property in this country until we
could ascertain the degree of debt Iran owes us in every
possible form. I had breakfast with the Republican con-
gressional leaders, and also signed the funds-freeze order
just before we ate.   DIARY, NOVEMBER 14, 1979

There had been near unanimous support around the world
for our termination of oil purchases from Iran, but some dissenting voices were heard when we froze the Iranian funds. I had no
doubts about it. It was imperative that we apply maximum political and economic pressure on the Iranian leaders to bring them

to their senses. I thought that depriving them of about twelve billion dollars in ready assets was a good way to get their attention.

On November 17, Khomeini announced that the Iranians would release the women and blacks "who were not American spies." We had sent strong warnings that the trial or punishment of any hostage would bring serious consequences, involving military action, so we viewed this release of thirteen of the hostages with mixed emotions. It would be good to have them back, but Khomeini was treading on thin ice with his comment that those who still remained in prison were spies who were subject to trial. Typically, he spoke in obscurities, so that no one could discern his true intention.

> *There was some confusion about what Khomeini actually said—"if the Shah is not returned, the hostages could be tried" or "will be tried." We tried to get the Farsi or Persian-language version, to translate it ourselves for more accuracy. Later it turned out that he said different things to different interviewers.*   DIARY, NOVEMBER 18, 1979

The entire Persian Gulf region was feeling the effect of the revolution in Iran. A spasm of political terrorism in Saudi Arabia precipitated another emergency for us. A group of radicals invaded the holy mosque in Mecca, a profoundly sacrilegious act. A radio broadcast from India erroneously reported that Americans were involved in the attack on the holy site, and a mob in Islamabad, Pakistan, quickly formed, burning our embassy; an American sergeant lost his life in the attack. President Mohammad Zia immediately dispatched Pakistani troops to protect our personnel and property, called to extend his personal apologies to me and to the American people, and insisted that his government would pay for all the damages.

The violence in Saudi Arabia and Pakistan, on the heels of Khomeini's statements about trials and punishment for our hostages, were grave threats to world peace, and I called again for assistance from our allies. Prime Minister Margaret Thatcher was strong and wholly supportive. She endorsed all our actions and promised her full backing. President Giscard d'Estaing was polite, saying his cabinet would condemn Iran at its next meeting. Chancellor Schmidt, coolest of the three, told me he would merely reissue a supportive statement. Sadat offered every possible help, including military assistance if we should decide to punish Iran with our armed forces. The Saudis promised to keep as many Arab nations as possible arrayed against Iran in the United Nations and other international forums. Prime Minister Ohira of Japan asked for our suggestions on how his country could give more help.

Over a long period of time some of these offers evaporated, but we took what we could get and were thankful for it. It soon became apparent, however, that even our closest allies in Europe were not going to expose themselves to potential oil boycotts or endanger their diplomatic arrangements for the sake of American hostages, and would be very cautious in their public statements and actions. Only the direct threat of further moves by the United States would have any real effect on some of our friends and on the Iranians.

The day after Thanksgiving, November 23, I gathered my key advisers—Mondale, Brown, Vance, Brzezinski, Jones, Turner, Jordan, and Powell—to meet with me at Camp David, so that we could have an extensive and uninterrupted discussion of the hostage crisis and draft a public statement to convince the world that serious consequences would ensue if the American prisoners were harmed. First, we decided that should a public trial of the hostages occur, we would interrupt all commerce with Iran as soon as the first trial began. We studied the detailed maps and charts of the coastal waters. My own judgment was that the best and surest way to stop all ship traffic would be to mine the entrances to all Iranian seaports. We were capable of doing it immediately and without delay or serious threat to our own forces. Effective minesweeping operations by Iran or its potential supporters would be almost impossible. A naval blockade by our surface ships might have been equally effective, but it would have involved repeated confrontations between us and ships of many other nations, some of which might be damaged or sunk if they tried to run the blockade.

We also had to meet the more serious possibility of physical punishment or execution of the hostages. In this case, I was prepared to make a direct military attack on Iran. We pored over aerial photographs of oil refineries and many other targets of strategic importance there, and planned how best to carry out our threat to the Iranian leaders of quick punitive action. I wanted our message to Khomeini to go to our major trading partners as well, so that they would be more eager to discourage Iran from Khomeini's oft-repeated threat to punish our people. I knew that other countries did not want to see the international waterway leading into the Persian Gulf sealed off. Because we did not have direct communication with Iranian officials, we asked several of our friends to deliver our stern warning. That way, our message was understood by many world leaders. We were not bluffing, and they knew it.

The Iranian militants were now demanding that the Shah be turned over to them for trial, which would almost certainly be followed by execution; that the United States apologize to the world for alleged "crimes against the Iranian people"; and that financial damages and the Shah's assets be paid over to Iran. I never gave serious consideration to *any* of these demands from the kidnappers. It would have besmirched our nation's honor to do so.

However, during that first month, Secretary Vance and I decided on a few principles for an ultimate resolution of the disputes with Iran, and discussed these with UN Secretary General Kurt Waldheim. If the hostages were released unharmed, we would permit an international commission to investigate any allegations by either side; the Iranians would have access to United States courts to pursue any claims against the Shah's family or others; existing legal contracts would be honored; and diplomatic affairs would be handled in accordance with international law and custom. We asked Waldheim to pursue these points with the Iranians, but not to deviate from any of them without express permission from me.

We also took our case to the United Nations Security Council, and later to the World Court. It was important to demonstrate maximum support among other nations for our condemnation of Iran and to lay a firm legal base for future settlement of financial claims. We considered the remote possibility that the unpredictable Iranians might even come forward to use one of these international bodies as a means to resolve the issue. I also went over an assessment of the embassy documents that had fallen into the hands of the militants, and found that they were not damaging.

The governmental turmoil continued in Iran. Because the Iranian Foreign Minister had been consulting with United Nations officials on resolving the hostage crisis, he was replaced.

> We were notified that the Foreign Minister of Iran was
> dismissed and a guy named [Sadegh] Ghotbsadeh was
> made Foreign Minister. Every time one of the Iranian
> government officials shows any sign of rationality, he is
> immediately incompatible with Khomeini and is replaced.
> DIARY, NOVEMBER 28, 1979

On November 15, David Rockefeller had called to tell me that the Shah recognized the problems he had caused us in coming here, and thought he would be able to leave the United States in a few days. He had responded well to radium treatments, was able to sit up a little, and wanted to see either Cy Vance or Lloyd Cutler. I did not like this suggestion, and told Rockefeller that the last thing I wanted was to have anything at all to do with the Shah's decision to leave; it might be interpreted as our yielding to pressure from Iran. He understood, but said he would also like to escape his responsibilities for the Shah's movements.

The Shah was preparing to go back to Mexico. Although we had been careful not to force his departure, we nevertheless hoped that his move might trigger action by the Iranians to resolve the hostage issue and let their troubled country return to normal.

> *About 6:30 Cy called with the unbelievable news that the Mexicans had reversed themselves during the day and now would not be willing to accept the Shah in their country. López Portillo [the Mexican President] is not a man of his word. I asked Zbig and Fritz what to do, in their opinion. They were taken aback, as I was, with the Mexican action.*
>
> DIARY, NOVEMBER 29, 1979

I was outraged. The Mexicans had no diplomatic personnel in Iran, had moved all their people out of the country, and did not need Iranian oil. We'd had every assurance from them that the Shah would be welcome. They had given us no warning of their reversal; apparently the President of Mexico had simply changed his mind at the last minute. It was a serious blow.

Sadat immediately reissued his invitation for the Shah to return to Egypt. Given that Sadat was already in trouble in the Arab world and with some of his own people because of his peace initiatives toward Israel, this was a selfless and courageous gesture. He wanted to help the Shah and his family and was also eager to give the United States all possible assistance, but we were reluctant to have him burdened with this responsibility. I called Egyptian Ambassador Ghorbal, who said that all of Sadat's top advisers were worried about the consequences of the Shah's arrival there.

> *I called Fritz, and told him that our two basic options were to help the Shah go to Egypt for a limited period of time or be moved to one of our own military bases until*

he recuperated and we could find a permanent place for him. Fritz said that between these options, he preferred that the Shah go to Egypt. I told Harold Brown to let me know the best place in the United States to send the Shah, and for him to call me back shortly.

Ghorbal, in the meantime, talked to [Egyptian Vice President] Mubarak. They are quite concerned about the circumstances and the timing of the Shah's coming to Egypt, but they say that Sadat is firm in his offer. The situation is that I want him to go to Egypt but don't want to hurt Sadat. Sadat wants him to stay in the United States but doesn't want to hurt me. It is a decision for me to make. Harold called back to say that either Fort Sam Houston or Lackland Air Force Base—both near San Antonio—would be the best place for the Shah to go if we have to keep him here. . . . Cy reported that they [State Department officials] were belatedly [approaching] Argentina, South Africa, and Austria, but there was little prospect of any of them taking the Shah any time soon. I told Cy not to talk to me any more about it, but to prepare to move the Shah to a U.S. military base as early as possible on Sunday, tomorrow.   DIARY, DECEMBER 1, 1979

The next morning the Shah was at Lackland. A few days later, Cy reported that leaders in Costa Rica, Paraguay, Guatemala, Iceland, Tonga, the Bahamas, South Africa, and Panama had all indicated their willingness to let the Shah come to their countries. But some of these offers were quite shaky, and soon the only two real options were South Africa and Panama.

The Panamanians sincerely wanted to help, reiterating their invitation for the Shah to stay in an island villa off their coast. To look into this, I sent Hamilton Jordan, who had become a friend of General Torrijos' during the Panama treaty discussions. He soon called to tell me that Torrijos was firmly committed to receiving the Shah. When Ham and Lloyd Cutler met the next day in San Antonio to discuss it with the Shah, they found that both he and his wife were willing to go to Panama. The Shah's main concern was that there be an adequate communication system, because he wanted the ability to be able to respond to the charges against him from Khomeini and other Iranians.

During this difficult time, we needed all the support at home that we could get. Most of the major political leaders—at least those who were not running for President—were helpful in their public statements. One of my concerns was former Secretary of State Henry Kissinger. There is no way to keep anything secret in Washington; a stream of his criticisms to foreign diplomats and others in the United States and in Europe had reached our ears. His remarks had particularly infuriated Secretary Vance, so I asked Kissinger to come by for a talk, to work out our differences and to give him a report about Hamilton's trip to Panama.

Kissinger promised to help us with the SALT II treaty and said that some of his published criticisms concerning Iran had been taken from interviews given prior to the hostage seizure, that he would avoid similar comments during the crisis, and that he was satisfied with the arrangements for the Shah's stay in Panama. After this conversation, things were better for a few days—and then reverted to their former state.

Even before the Shah was settled in his new home, Iranian Foreign Minister Ghotbsadeh was trying to arrange for a trip to Panama to seek legal extradition of the Shah to Iran. I received Torrijos' assurance that the Shah would be kept safe.

By now it was nearly Christmas. The hostages had been imprisoned for almost six weeks.

The lighting of the great Christmas tree south of the White House had always been a very festive occasion. Several thousand people would assemble in the biting cold to wait patiently for me to say a few words about joy, peace, and goodwill, and then illuminate the beautifully decorated tree. Earlier, a family friend of Secretary Vance had suggested that we leave the tree dark, to signify our sorrow about the hostages' loss of freedom—and light the tree only on their return.

The dark tree was symbolic of that holiday season. In spite of the uplifting religious theme, it was a sad time. I was worrying about the hostages, working to get enough United Nations Security Council votes to implement worldwide sanctions against Iran, trying to think about the developing political campaign, resolving last-minute disputes about the 1981 budget, and refraining from a normal social and political life.

> We made a few phone calls to my mother and others. It's relatively lonely at Camp David, just Rosalynn, Amy, and I being here. This is the first time in twenty-six years that we haven't been with our folks at Christmas—since the year my daddy died. . . . Amy wanted to get up at 5:30, which we did. We had a very fine exchange of gifts.
>
> DIARY, DECEMBER 25, 1979

Two days after Christmas there was another shock to a world which yearned for peace. Since May 1979, we had been observing closely the increased Soviet presence in Afghanistan, and admonishing the Soviets about their obvious moves toward intervention in the political affairs of the small neighboring country. By September, a few thousand Soviet military "advisers" were stationed around the capital city of Kabul, while the Russian leaders claimed to us and to other countries that they were merely responding to the requests of the Afghan leaders for help in maintaining order. Now, during the holidays, the Soviets embarked on a massive airlift into Afghanistan. I returned from Camp David to the White House immediately because of this ominous event.

> *The Soviets have begun to move their forces in to over-throw the existing government. . . . 215 flights in the last 24 hours or so. They've moved in a couple of regiments and now have maybe a total of 8,000 or 10,000 people in Afghanistan—both advisers and military. We consider this to be an extremely serious development.*
>
> DIARY, DECEMBER 27, 1979

The Soviets still claimed their action was in response to an appeal by the Afghan government leaders to strengthen their security forces, but there were obviously other purposes for such a large-scale operation. In the past, Soviet leaders had not hesitated to use their own troops to maintain domination over the Warsaw Pact countries or surrogate troops from Cuba and Vietnam to accomplish their ends elsewhere. However, this was the first time they had used their troops to expand their sphere of influence since they had overthrown the government of Czechoslovakia in February 1948 and established a Soviet puppet government there.

The invasion of Afghanistan was direct aggression by the Soviet armed forces against a freedom-loving people, whose leaders had been struggling to retain a modicum of independence from their huge neighbor. President Hafizullah Amin of Afghanistan—who, the Soviet leaders claimed, had invited them in—was immediately assassinated, and in his place the invaders installed an Afghan leader of their own persuasion, who had been hiding in the Soviet Union.

The brutality of the act was bad enough, but the threat of this Soviet invasion to the rest of the region was very clear—and had grim consequences. A successful take-over of Afghanistan would give the Soviets a deep penetration between Iran and Pakistan, and pose a threat to the rich oil fields of the Persian Gulf area and to the crucial waterways through which so much of the world's energy supplies had to pass.

I sent Brezhnev on the hot line the sharpest message of my Presidency, telling him that the invasion of Afghanistan was "a clear threat to the peace" and "could mark a fundamental and long-lasting turning point in our relations." I added, "Unless you draw back from your present course of action, this will inevitably jeopardize the course of United States–Soviet relations throughout the world. I urge you to take prompt constructive action to withdraw your forces and cease interference in Afghanistan's internal affairs."

Brezhnev came back with a devious message, repeating his false claim that the Soviets had gone in at the request of Afghan leaders because of "armed incursions from without into Afghanistan territory"—which, in fact, were nonexistent. He repeated an earlier promise: "As soon as the reasons which prompted the Afghan request to the Soviet Union disappear, we fully intend to withdraw the Soviet military contingents from Afghan territory."

Despite this promise, the Soviets poured more forces across the border, until there were about eighty thousand Soviet troops in Afghanistan. Armed mostly with small and outmoded weapons, the freedom fighters put up surprisingly fierce and effective resistance. If the Afghans could continue their courageous struggle, the Soviet leaders would have to settle for a long, drawn-out, and costly war. They were condemned overwhelmingly as aggressors by the world community, even by some of their closest allies and friends.

The Soviet Union, like Iran, had acted outrageously, and at the same time had made a tragic miscalculation. I was determined to lead the rest of the world in making it as costly as possible. There was a balancing act to perform—America being the leader, but at the same time consulting and working closely with the other nations. To be effective, punitive action had to be broadly supported and clearly defined.

The members of the National Security Council had almost continuous meetings about Afghanistan and Iran, and I worked with congressional leaders and briefed key members of the press to be sure that the American people understood the strategic ramifications of the Soviet invasion. I also consulted closely with our European allies, President Tito of Yugoslavia, President Ceauscescu of Romania, the leaders among the Moslem nations, and particularly President Mohammad Zia of Pakistan, to plan our most effective response to this aggression.

This is the most serious international development that has occurred since I have been President, and unless the Soviets recognize that it has been counterproductive for them, we will face additional serious problems with invasions or subversion in the future.

DIARY, JANUARY 3, 1980

There were three areas within which we could move: military, economic, and political. Direct military action on our part was not advisable, but within my National Security Council we inventoried every conceivable alternative. Worldwide condemnation, continuing publicity about the Soviet crime, economic sanctions that would hit the Soviets where they were most vulnerable, and indirect military assistance to the Afghan freedom fighters were all available options.

Some of these moves would require substantial sacrifice and would be very difficult to implement, but we did not flinch from any of them. The interruption of normal trade and a possible withdrawal from the Moscow Olympics were the kinds of actions which would directly affect the lives of many American citizens. An overwhelming vote of condemnation in the United Nations would require a lot of work with other countries.

The worst disappointment to me personally was the immediate and automatic loss of any chance for early ratification of the SALT II treaty. Furthermore, the situation created a threat to both Iran and Pakistan which had not existed previously. If the Soviets could consolidate their hold on Afghanistan, the balance of power in the entire region would be drastically modified in their favor, and they might be tempted toward further aggression. We were resolved to do everything feasible to prevent such a turn of events.

The invasion also affected the way I would proceed with my political campaign. Within the White House, there had been a running argument about whether I would participate in a national television debate in Des Moines, Iowa, with other Democratic candidates. Iowa would soon hold its party caucuses—the first political test in the nation—and the result of these caucus votes would be very significant in my struggle with Kennedy and Brown. Earlier, I had accepted the invitation, but now I felt that with the simultaneous crises in Iran and Afghanistan it would be a mistake for me to begin campaigning actively. As a result of recent events, I had many additional duties. Further, my postponing political activities would let the world know how seriously we continued to view these disturbing circumstances. Rosalynn agreed, but most of my staff members and campaign leaders were on the other side of the argument. As I told them, "I would go to the Iowa debate as a President and leave there as a political candidate."

The day after the take-over of Afghanistan, I decided not to go to Iowa and called our supporters there to give them my reasons. A few thought it would hurt us politically, but all agreed I had made the right decision.

My next decision would have an even more significant impact on the people of Iowa—whether or not to impose a grain embargo on the Soviet Union. Other economic steps would have some effect, but an analysis of possible sanctions revealed that this was the only one which would significantly affect the Soviet economy. The Soviets were very short of grain, and supplies were available in only a few other countries, such as Canada, Australia, and Argentina. For an embargo to be effective, we would need cooperation from both American farmers and these foreign grain producers.

Such a step would be drastic, and especially difficult for me. During the early 1970's, President Nixon had repeatedly imposed grain embargoes in an attempt to stabilize domestic market prices, and in the 1976 campaign I had promised not to do so unless our nation's security was at stake. I knew that some farmers had interpreted my statements as a pledge not to interfere with the free marketing of grain under any circumstances. Furthermore, as a farmer myself, I understood that the American farm community could be seriously damaged if such enormous sales were canceled without compensatory action by our government. Reserves would pile up, and prices might drop precipitously. If a grain embargo were imposed, we would have to find a way to prevent such consequences.

Grain sales to the Soviet Union was only one of the sensitive questions I had to resolve.

> We had a long discussion about the 1980 Olympics. We will make a statement saying that this issue is in doubt, but not make a decision yet about whether to participate. This one would cause me the most trouble, and also would be the most severe blow to the Soviet Union. Only if many nations act in concert would I consider it to be a good idea.   DIARY, JANUARY 2, 1980

For the Soviet Union, the Moscow Olympics was much more

than a sporting event. They saw it as a triumph for communism and a vivid demonstration to other nations of the world that the Soviets represented the true spirit of the ancient Olympics. For several years, the state propaganda machine had been promulgating this theme, and the government had made an enormous investment in facilities for the quadrennial games. In more than a hundred nations, including our own, thousands of athletes and many businesses and communications firms had already committed themselves to participate. To interrupt all this preparation would be a serious step indeed.

It would be much easier for me to take other steps—to reinforce our military forces in the Indian Ocean and Persian Gulf region, cancel planned visits and meetings with the Soviets, bar their fishing fleet from United States waters, deny them international credits, tighten up on any transfer of high-technology equipment, and strengthen our ties with other countries who were naturally fearful of Soviet aggression, including China. We were considering all these moves. We pushed hard for a vote of condemnation in the United Nations, ultimately with success. This was the first time such action had ever been taken against one of the leading nations of the world. In a highly secret move, we also assessed the feasibility of arranging for Soviet-made weapons (which would appear to have come from the Afghan military forces) to be delivered to the freedom fighters in Afghanistan and of giving them what encouragement we could to resist subjugation by the Soviet invaders.

There were some things I did *not* want to do; one of the most important of these was scuttling the SALT II treaty. It was patently of advantage to the United States and vital to the maintenance of world peace. On January 3, I sent a letter to Senator Robert Byrd, asking him not to bring it to the floor for a vote, but to leave it on the calendar for future action. Because of American disgust with the Soviet invasion, the treaty would have been defeated overwhelmingly, and to withdraw it from the Senate might have made it almost impossible to resubmit in the future or for most of its terms to continue to be observed. This action was the best I could do at the time to keep it alive.

> *We discussed how far we wanted to go with economic measures against the Soviet Union. I want to go the maximum degree—interrupting grain sales, high technology, cancelling fishing rights, reexamining our commerce guidelines, establishing a difference in COCOM [an international committee which set rules for trade with com-*

munist nations] between the Soviet Union and China,
cancelling visits to the Soviet Union, restricting any sort of
negotiations on culture, trade, and so forth. . . . possibly
withdrawing from the Olympics. We're asking Australia
and Canada not to replace the grain we might withhold.
Argentina doesn't have any on hand in addition to what
they've already sold. We'll give Pakistan aid, both eco-
nomic and military, working hopefully through a consor-
tium of nations. . . . I agreed to let India have nuclear
fuel for their Tarrapur plants.   DIARY, JANUARY 4, 1980

During the afternoon of January 4, I informed my staff and
Cabinet, Vice President Mondale, Tom Watson (our ambassador
to the Soviet Union, whom I had recalled to Washington), and the
congressional leaders of my plans, and that evening I described
them to the nation. Fritz objected strenuously to the grain embargo, concerned about possible injury to American farmers. I
assured him that we would do whatever was necessary to maintain grain prices and to compensate the farmers for any loss,
letting all American taxpayers share the cost equitably. In effect,
we could substitute our own government for the Soviets in the
purchase of the grain, and protect the farmers, elevator operators,
and grain dealers from loss. Then we would sell as much of the
grain as possible on other international markets. We would not
interfere in the sale of the eight million tons that were committed
to the Soviet Union by a long-standing international contract, but
another seventeen million tons, which they had recently bought,
would not be delivered. The Vice President was not convinced by
my explanation, but when I could not be dissuaded, he was loyal
in backing my decision. As he traveled through the Midwestern
states on the campaign trail, he defended my action to anxious
farmers.

It was interesting that on these punitive measures, the State
Department advocated stronger action than the National Security Council staff, a reversal of their usual attitudes. Brzezinski
was remarkably sober, concerned about future relationships
with the Soviet Union. I was sobered, too, by my conversation
with Fritz and by our strained relations with the Soviets, but I
was determined to make them pay for their unwarranted aggression without yielding to political pressures here at home.

In the midst of all the international crises, the intrusion of the
political campaign seemed almost unreal, but there was no way
to avoid it. Although I was not actively campaigning, I did agree

to an interview with John Chancellor of NBC News, who was asking all the presidential candidates similar questions. The first questions were about Iran and Afghanistan, which seemed perfectly normal to me. Then came the unexpected ones—unexpected by me because I had such life-and-death issues on my mind. "What do you think about school busing?" "What is your position on homosexual rights?" "Do you think that marijuana should be legalized?" I was startled, and fumbled as I tried to focus my attention on those questions I had answered so many times during the campaign four years earlier.

That same weekend, Rosalynn and I watched on television the debate of the Republican candidates in Iowa. As is almost always the case, the news reporters and the public were impressed by the general demeanor of the candidates and their appearance of forcefulness and ease before the camera, and not so much by their stands on the issues, however conflicting.

> *I thought Baker came out worst, Crane and Anderson came out best, Connally bombed out. Dole looked and acted like a hatchet man. I thought the winner was Ronald Reagan, who didn't show up.*   DIARY, JANUARY 5, 1980

It was interesting to observe my future potential opponents and to see them wrestle with some of the difficult questions I was having to answer every day. One of these was in the news and had strong political overtones: the Soviet grain embargo. With the exception of John Anderson, they all opposed it.

Although we had to work hard to maintain the embargo among other nations, for the remainder of the year it was very effective. Both Canada and Australia agreed not to replace American grain in sales to the Soviet Union, and at first Argentina did the same. Our relations with the Argentine leaders were very poor because of our protests over their abominable human-rights record, but for a time, world opinion about the Soviet invasion induced them to refrain from doing business with the Soviets. When their new harvest began, however, they soon changed their minds, to take advantage of the high prices offered them—but in any case, they had little extra grain to sell. Some of the European countries had some surplus grain, but they cooperated fully with the embargo. For instance, President Giscard d'Estaing stated, "The Soviets have broken the principles of détente. The actions of the United States as a superpower are justified. France will not substitute embargoed items, and will make no grain sales." On the other

hand, he cautioned against initiating another cold war, noted
that the ball was now in the Russian court, and suggested that
the withdrawal of Soviet troops would be the test of their
intentions.

We had made careful plans for supporting grain prices as we
imposed the embargo against the Soviet Union, and had closed
the grain markets for two days so that grain could not be traded
until we could explain our program. Nevertheless, when the markets reopened, prices dropped the limit for the day. I was already
very concerned about many troubling issues, and this news struck
me like a hammer blow. But we continued our explanations to
the public, and soon had some good tidings on the ticker tape.

> *The grain prices were very good. This is quite a relief to
> me. I don't know why the early news from the grain
> markets on Wednesday was so depressing, but it was one
> of the low points of my administration. Corn was up 34¢,
> wheat up 13¢, soybeans up 8¢. Unbelievable!*
>
> DIARY, JANUARY 11, 1980

After a few days of hard campaigning in Iowa, Rosalynn returned home to report that displeasure among the farmers had
been substantially alleviated by the improving prices of grain.

In addition to keeping the prices as stable as possible, we
wanted to minimize the quantity of grain that would have to be
purchased by the federal government. Secretary Bob Bergland
and other administration officials marshaled a worldwide effort
to sell American corn and wheat, concentrating on such countries
as Mexico and China, which imported large quantities but had
not been good customers of ours in the past. We were to be very
successful, breaking all-time world records in grain sales during
1980, in spite of the restraints on Soviet trade.

On Sunday, January 6, I met with Secretary General Kurt
Waldheim, who had just returned from his diplomatic mission to
Iran. He had tried to explain to the Iranians the principles that
Vance and I had presented to him, but found complete chaos in
Tehran. He spent the first hour with me in a very emotional and
excited recitation of his horrible experiences there, at times with
tears in his eyes. Waldheim believed his life had been in danger
on three different occasions and that he was lucky to be alive. He
was convinced the Iranians had no government at all; the terrorists were making all the decisions. He did not think sanctions
against Iran would ever bring about the release of the hostages.

The Iranians wanted to set up an international tribunal, to try the Shah and the United States, and to get restitution of their funds (with other countries acting as intermediaries) before they would consider letting the Americans go free—all of which I had made clear we would never accept.

After a great deal of lobbying, we got an excellent vote in the United Nations Security Council on sanctions against Iran. The Soviets voted "no," and I publicly branded them outlaws, who did not favor even the enforcement of international law. It was then I decided to devote my upcoming State of the Union address primarily to United States–Soviet relations and the threat to peace.

I was not always successful in encouraging other nations to condemn Soviet aggression. When Indira Gandhi was reelected as Prime Minister of India, I called to congratulate her and to ask for her cooperation regarding our hostages and the Soviet presence in Afghanistan. She was polite but cool. It was obvious that she did not wish to discuss anything of substance. Within a few days, I learned why. The Indian representative's speech in the United Nations was as strongly supportive of the Soviet invasion as were those of Czechoslovakia and Vietnam. Even Cuba was more reticent in its praise than India.

In fact, one surprising development was Cuba's adverse reaction to the Soviet invasion. Fidel Castro had been trying to get his country elected to a seat on the United Nations Security Council, and seemed likely to prevail even against firm United States opposition. After he first refused to criticize the Soviet action, he lost support and had to withdraw from contention. It happened that during this time, Cuba was scheduled to host a meeting of the NAM (Non-Aligned Movement) countries. This organization had first been created by the responsible leaders of India, Yugoslavia, and Egypt, and some of them still remembered the original concept of true nonalignment. Cuba, a Soviet puppet, had not remembered. Most of the others became irate because of Cuba's reluctance to condemn the Soviet invasion, and Castro was apparently feeling the heat. He sent me word that he wanted to discuss Iran and Afghanistan, and I asked Robert Pastor, Latin American specialist on the National Security Council staff, and Peter Tarnoff, Executive Secretary of the State Department, to go to Cuba for a secret meeting with him.

Our emissaries to Cuba reported a startling frankness in an 11-hour discussion with Castro. He described without any equivocation his problems with the Soviet Union; his

loss of leadership position in NAM because of his subser-
vience to the Soviet Union; his desire to pull out of Ethiopia
now, and Angola later; his involvement in the revolution-
ary movements in Central America but his aversion to
sending weapons or military capability to the Caribbean
countries; and so forth. He is very deeply hurt by our
embargo. Wants to move toward better relationships with
us, but can't abandon his friends, the Soviets, who have
supported his revolution unequivocally.

DIARY, JANUARY 18, 1980

The reasons for this long discourse were unclear to us, but it was at least obvious that Cuba was embarrassed to be aligned with the Soviet Union in the public debates. This attitude was certainly indicative of the great diplomatic losses suffered by the Soviets among the less developed countries of the world. Decades of propaganda effort to project themselves as the peace-loving defender of small countries had gone down the drain. We did not doubt for a moment that their close ties with Cuba would continue—at a cost to them of more than $8 million each day—but we wanted to be certain that other nations did not forget the Soviet crime.

Throughout the crisis over Afghanistan, the meetings between me and my advisers about the hostages had continued without slackening. In spite of many other responsibilities, the hostages were always in my mind.

I got a letter from one of the hostages which remarkably was mailed in Iran and had not been censored. It was written the day after Christmas. He pointed out that they were denied basic human rights; confined in a semi-darkened room without sunshine or fresh air; were given no news of any kind; hands kept tied day and night; bright lights burning in the room all night long; constant noise so they are unable to sleep properly; not permitted to speak to another American, even those in the same room. He slept on a hard floor for 33 out of the 53 nights. Has been given only three brief periods of exercise outdoors in the 53 days. His personal mail is being withheld. He points out that he's not been visited by any representative of the U.S. government, apparently not understanding that we have not been able to visit him. That he's seen no friendly diplomatic representative of any other country.

That when the clergymen came in on Christmas eve, none of the prisoners was permitted to worship privately. It was obviously a propaganda charade put on by the Iranian kidnappers.

I discussed it with Cy and Jody. The letter is authentic, and Cy will call [the hostage's] family to give them the basic information. We will not disclose the identity of the person, but in a day or two will make public the circumstances under which our prisoners are being held.

DIARY, JANUARY 16, 1980

Later, it was revealed that this letter was from Robert Ode, a very mature and responsible State Department employee. I was sickened and additionally alarmed to hear about the bestiality of the Iranian captors. How could any decent human beings, and particularly leaders of a nation, treat innocent people like this—week after week?

On January 14, the Iranians had decided that all foreign reporters were to be kicked out of Iran. This was good news. The change would reduce the demonstration of hatred against the United States presented almost every day before the television cameras outside our embassy, and this in itself would have a calming influence on people in both countries. However, I was concerned that the Iranians might be contemplating action which they wanted further to conceal.

Perhaps the most highly publicized issue of all at this time was how to deal with the 1980 Olympic Games in Moscow. Before making a decision, I held many meetings with my advisers and consulted closely with other heads of state and with sports leaders in our country. I did not want to damage the Olympic movement, but at the same time it seemed unconscionable to be guests of the Soviets while they were involved in a bloody suppression of the people of Afghanistan—an act condemned by an overwhelming majority of the nations of the world. It was not an easy decision; we had been hoping our dilemma could be resolved by a firm commitment from the Soviet leaders to withdraw their military forces. However, Ambassador Dobrynin had not brought back any messages from Moscow other than repetitions of the same specious arguments.

I announced our decision about the Moscow Olympics on a "Meet the Press" interview show on January 20. We would send a message to the International Olympic Committee, with copies to other government leaders in the world, stating that unless the

Soviets withdrew their troops from Afghanistan within a month, there should be no participation in the Moscow games. We would help to find another site and participate in the financing and arrangements for the change. In response to a follow-up question, I made it clear that, even if we had to stand alone among nations, American athletes should not go to Moscow while Soviet troops were still trying to crush the Afghan people. I knew the decision was controversial, but I had no idea at the time how difficult it would be for me to implement it or to convince other nations to join us.

The next day, January 21, the 1980 election process officially began with the Iowa caucuses. The domestic political situation had changed dramatically since November 4, when the American Embassy had been seized in Tehran. At that time Senator Kennedy had been an overwhelming favorite, but he had injured himself that same night in a disastrous CBS interview with Roger Mudd, when he had seemed to be incompetent and confused. Later, his ill-advised comments condemning the Shah, his opposition to punitive actions against the Soviets, and the memories of his Chappaquiddick accident had accelerated the decline in his popularity. American patriotism was high, and the nation had rallied around me as I faced the joint difficulties in Iran and Afghanistan. Fritz and Rosalynn were representing me well on the campaign trail, and other members of my political family were also doing a good job of explaining the complicated issues.

When the results came in, I had won an overwhelming victory over Kennedy—by a margin of 2 to 1—carrying all but one of the 99 counties in the state. Kennedy's extremely liberal stance on economic issues was not popular in Iowa. In addition, a lot of people there thought it improper for him to condemn some of my decisions of recent weeks concerning Iran and the Soviet Union.

The last of the controversial decisions had yet to be taken. Two other actions were needed to demonstrate our resolve, enhance our readiness, and remind the rest of the world how vital our stakes were in the Persian Gulf region.

We did not need to draft young people to serve in the armed forces, but it was necessary to register them, so that we could mobilize more rapidly if the need should arise. The key Cabinet officers and most of my staff members agreed with my plans, but I had a near-rebellion on my hands when it came to Fritz Mondale and Stu Eizenstat. They thought I was overreacting to the Soviet invasion, and that registration would be politically damaging to our campaign for reelection. They had strongly opposed the grain embargo, but this disagreement was much worse. I listened to all the arguments they marshaled against the idea, but decided to proceed.

The other decision was to include in my State of the Union speech on January 23 a warning to the Soviets concerning any further threat by them against the Persian Gulf.

> Let our position be absolutely clear: An attempt by any outside force to gain control of the Persian Gulf region will be regarded as an assault on the vital interests of the United States of America, and such an assault will be repelled by any means necessary, including military force.

This statement was not lightly made, and I was resolved to use the full power of the United States to back it up. I had already discussed my concerns about the Persian Gulf area with the Soviet leaders during the Vienna summit conference in June 1979, but their subsequent invasion of Afghanistan made it necessary to repeat the warning in clearer terms. Some news reporters dubbed my decision the Carter Doctrine and called it an idle threat, because, they said, we could not successfully invade Iran if it were to be attacked by Soviet troops.

The fact was that mine was a carefully considered statement, which would have been backed by concerted action, not necessarily confined to any small invaded area or to tactics or terrain of the Soviets' choosing. We simply could not afford to let them extend their domination to adjacent areas around the Persian Gulf which were so important to us and to other nations of the world.

We had been successful in keeping secret the presence of six American diplomats who had found refuge in the Canadian Embassy at the time our embassy was taken. (Some news organizations knew about these diplomats, but at my request did not reveal the information.) Now, with minimum news coverage and the resulting quiet on the streets of Tehran, it was time for our attempt to bring them back to the United States. This was a real cloak-and-dagger story, with American secret agents being sent into Iran to rehearse with the Canadians and Americans the plans for their safe departure. The agents and those being rescued would have to be furnished with disguises and false documents that appeared authentic, and they needed enough instruction and training to convince the Iranian officials that they were normal travelers and business visitors from other countries, including Canada. There were several delays and many adventures as our plans were put into effect.

One agent was sent in as a German—with a forged passport, of course. He adopted a false name, with the middle initial "H." When he reached the customs desk, the officials stopped him to comment that it was very strange for a German passport to use an initial rather than the entire name; he had never seen one like this before. He began to interrogate our man more closely, and the quick-witted messenger said, "Well, my parents named me 'Hitler' as a baby. Ever since the War, I've been permitted to conceal my full name." The customs official winked and nodded knowingly, and waved him on through the gates.

On January 25, everything was in place. Three days later I received word that the six Americans were free. (On the same day—January 28—Abolhassan Bani-Sadr was declared the newly elected President of Iran.) Until some of the Canadians and our intelligence agents were also out of Iran, we could not reveal that our first rescue mission had been successful, but when the news was finally released on January 31, Ambassador Kenneth Taylor and the other courageous Canadians became instant heroes. They well deserved the outpouring of gratitude from millions of Americans, who were especially thankful for this rare good news from Iran.

This was not the only occasion when we used secret agents to help us. Most of our communication with the Iranian leaders was conducted through the Swiss Embassy in Tehran. However, we also opened up an avenue through an Argentine businessman, Hector Villalon, and a French lawyer, Christian Bourguet, who, because of their business and legal dealings with Iranian officials, were frequent visitors to the country. The Panamanians made the first contact with them in December, and it proved to be of great benefit to us.

Both the Iranians and the Panamanians preferred to deal with Hamilton Jordan, because he was close to me, was not in the State Department (which the Iranians claimed was controlled by David Rockefeller), and because Ham had been instrumental in moving the Shah to Panama without his efforts being publicized at the time. Between their frequent trips to Iran, Bourguet and Villalon met with Hamilton and Assistant Secretary of State Saunders several times in Europe and in the United States. The negotiations were so confidential that when Ham called in to make a report to me in the White House, he used a code name. On one occasion Bourguet came to the White House to give me a personal report. He was a calm, slightly built, heavily bearded man, apparently in his late thirties, who would have looked at home in the audience of a Bob Dylan concert—or in a courtroom working without fee on a civil-rights case. Villalon, whom I did not meet until 1981, was an urbane international businessman, with the reputation of being like a high-class South American riverboat gambler. All I know is that these two men repeatedly risked their lives to help us, and I and the people of our country will always be indebted to them.

In Tehran, the two adventurers were able to meet regularly and without any apparent problem with Foreign Minister Ghotbsadeh, President Bani-Sadr, and other members of the Revolutionary Council. Using simple word codes they had developed, they would call Hamilton directly from Tehran to report progress or ask questions about our policy. I had been highly dubious about their authenticity, until Villalon and Bourguet were given a letter signed by Bani-Sadr and Ghotbsadeh, designating the two men to represent Iran in finding a way to release the hostages. Throughout the early months of 1980, we began to rely more and more on our secret emissaries. Through them we finally seemed to be making some progress.

> *Cy met with me and David [Aaron, Deputy National Security Adviser] and Hamilton to get an update on the Iranian response. Apparently Bani-Sadr is sending word to us directly that he wants to proceed with a resolution of the hostage question. His inclination is to wait until after the 26th of February, when he can put his government together. (He also said he wanted to get rid of Ghotbsadeh.) He [Bani-Sadr] does not want us to identify him as a friend of the United States or as a moderate. He wants to be known as a revolutionary, protecting the interests of Iran against both superpowers' threats. We decided to maintain our multiple approaches to Iran.*
>
> DIARY, FEBRUARY 4, 1980

This was the most encouraging development since our embassy had been seized. Khomeini had forbidden any Iranian official to even talk to an American, yet now the President of Iran was planning with me how to get our hostages home. Although Bani-Sadr was apparently keeping his plans secret from some other members of the Revolutionary Council, Ghotbsadeh was deeply involved. Although at odds personally, these two men were our best hope, and so we wanted to see them consolidate their political strength. I was pleased at some of the reports we were getting.

> *Ham got a call from his people in Iran. They've been meeting regularly with Ghotbsadeh since they got over there—I think four times. They met twice with Bani-Sadr, and say that everything seems to be pretty well on track. There are some minor differences, which may become major differences when they are revealed to us. They claim they haven't been to bed in 3 or 4 days, and they're asleep now while the Revolutionary Council meets. At the end of the Revolutionary Council meeting it was announced that Bani-Sadr has become the new chairman of it.*
>
> DIARY, FEBRUARY 5, 1980

Bani-Sadr began to make speeches in Iran designed to isolate the militants from the general public and to remove the aura of heroism from the kidnappers. We read his words with great interest, hoping they signified Iranian preparation for release of the hostages. There was no way for the American people to know about our efforts, which had to be kept secret in order to succeed, and they were becoming increasingly frustrated by the long delays and absence of progress. I understood their anger, but at least I had glimpses of progress and moments of hope, although they could be shared with only a very few others.

Our allies, too, were impatient. I had a serious problem in keeping them and others with us in sustained opposition to the illegal actions in Iran and Afghanistan. Some—such as Great Britain, Canada, Australia, Egypt, and Panama—were staunch and always helpful; others were a constant source of trouble. Helmut Schmidt was now criticizing the British for supporting our position, and opposed any kind of sanctions against either the Soviet Union or Iran. The French position was a shifting one. We tried unsuccessfully to have a meeting of the foreign ministers who usually attended the economic summit conferences, so that we could discuss common action.

> *I worked all day Saturday. Up early, discussing the international situation with Vance—the serious problems the French have caused by withdrawing from the conference in Bonn, and the rapidly changing French foreign policy position on the Soviet invasion. They've had at least five*

*different public positions: first saying that this was no
threat to Western Europe; then a ... public statement by
Valéry condemning the Soviets and saying this was a
threat to détente; then Giscard's visit to India, where he
issued a noncommittal statement with Mrs. Gandhi; then
his meeting with Helmut and a very strong [and support-
ive] communiqué they issued; and then more recently
saying that they could not attend any meeting that did not
contribute to friendship between us and the Soviet Union.
I don't know what's going on in France.*

DIARY, FEBRUARY 9, 1980

We had to move ahead on our own, beginning to build on the
groundwork laid by Bourguet and Villalon. I needed some way to
formalize the arrangements we had been working out with President Bani-Sadr, and decided that Vance would go to New York
for a meeting with Kurt Waldheim to make plans for another
United Nations delegation to visit Iran. The preparations for this
visit would be made in Tehran by our two French emissaries. I
wanted a precise, written document of understanding between
the Iranians and me, so that there would be no last-minute
misunderstandings to abort a potentially successful effort.

According to the joint arrangement that was being evolved
through the United Nations by the Iranian officials and ourselves,
a five-person commission would visit Iran. Both Iranian President
Bani-Sadr and I would have to approve some well-known third
world leaders, who would comprise the delegation. It was understood that the United Nations representatives would not embarrass
any of the hostages or interrogate them about their past actions. The
hostages would all be moved permanently to a hospital, so that we
could be sure they were receiving good care. A report would be
issued by the commission to the United Nations, the hostages would
be released, the report would be published, and finally Bani-Sadr
and I would make statements, worded as agreed ahead of time.

I was very pleased with how much the Iranians had been
willing to change their originally announced positions. They had
first called for the Shah's return, the confiscation of his estate,
individual trials of our hostages as spies, and condemnation of
the United States in an international forum. None of these demands was part of the current terms.

I considered our own change of position insignificant: we were
now prepared to let an investigation be conducted *before* the
hostages were released, provided the results were not published
until afterward.

The Iranians were ready to move, and so were we. They had agreed that the international commission members could visit all the hostages, and Bani-Sadr had said the hostages could be released within forty-eight hours if he and I could reach agreement. More significantly, he stated that Khomeini had also approved the general provisions of the plan. I was inclined to be flexible on some of the details, provided the hostages would be taken away from the militants. But there was still some confusion about the step in the proceedings when the hostages would be permitted to leave Iran. One of the top Iranian officials wanted to meet with us in Paris to continue work on the agreement, and I approved another trip for Hamilton and Hal Saunders. Through Bourguet, the official insisted on permanent anonymity and on meeting alone with Hamilton. After some discussion, I agreed to both requests, hoping that the Iranians would be more forthcoming if the State Department was bypassed. Ham went to the meeting in Paris, and afterward I missed Amy's first solo violin recital in order to welcome him home.

> *Ham came in about 7:30, and gave us a written report on his visit with [the Iranian official] in Paris. In general, Ham reported that he was pleased. [Official] criticized [another Iranian leader] very severely, and was equivocal about any sort of time schedule for releasing the hostages. Seemed to be very honored that Ham would come. Pleased to get a copy of the letter I wrote Ham saying that we would expedite the entire process and carry out our part of the bargain if Iran is willing to release the hostages early. [Official] seems to be very antagonistic toward the Soviet Union. Asked Ham if we would assassinate the Shah. Claims to be the preeminent confidant of Khomeini, and said he has been catching hell all over Europe because they are holding the hostages.*   DIARY, FEBRUARY 17, 1980

This report was hazy on some points, but not particularly discouraging. It was better than most reports I was receiving during this troublesome winter.

I was having a series of campaign victories, but Congress was stalling on our vital energy legislation and would not move on the Alaska lands bill. Some members were creating repeated obstacles to draft registration; many others were trying to circumvent the grain embargo. Almost a hundred thousand Soviet military men were now stationed in Afghanistan, unsuccessfully trying to subdue the fiercely resisting freedom fighters. Their predicament was becoming reminiscent of the American involvement in Vietnam. The public was more supportive of me than it had been a few months ago, but becoming more restive with each passing week because of our seeming impotence in dealing with international crises. World oil prices had doubled since the Iranian revolution began, and inflationary pressures were an ever-present problem. The familiar ups and downs were mostly downs.

And then came the Winter Olympics and the ice-hockey game between the all-powerful Soviet Union team and the unknown and unsung Americans. It was one of the high spots of my year when the young Americans won—a very emotional moment.

> *I immediately called the coach, Herb Brooks, congratulated them, and invited him and the team to the White House Monday. He responded that he strongly supported our not attending the Moscow Olympics in the summer. Said they had one more game to go against Finland Sunday morning, and they wanted the gold medal now.*
>
> DIARY, FEBRUARY 22, 1980

I was hoping this victory and the gold medal were an omen of better days ahead. But that was not to be.

ALMOST FREE

Sadat said the political maneuvers in the Arab world were just shouting; that his major concern was restraining the adverse reaction among Egyptians toward their Arab brothers. . . . He said in the Arab world that we need only deal with Saudi Arabia. The Arab condemnations would never be able to change history; that history had already been written by me, him, and Begin. And then he said, "That man [Begin] has 'chang-ed' for the better."

DIARY, APRIL 24, 1979

The confrontations with the Iranians over the hostages and with the Soviets concerning Afghanistan were not my only responsibilities in that part of the world. I was also trying to preserve the benefits of the Camp David accords and the Egyptian–Israeli peace treaty, and to protect these two agreements against attacks from outside and from within the two countries. A period of euphoria had followed the signing of the treaty in March 1979; for the first time Sadat and Begin were able to communicate in a constructive and harmonious way. In our regular telephone conversations, Sadat seemed quite certain that he could work out any further difficulties with the Israelis. He felt there was no reason to be concerned about Arab threats to disrupt the peace process.

Nevertheless, the drumfire of criticism continued—against Sadat from other Arab nations and against Begin within Israel. A stream of condemnatory resolutions designed to obstruct the Camp David process emanated from the United Nations, most of them aimed at Israel. Sometimes we had our hands full trying to deal with these attacks on Israel and at the same time to uphold the parts of the agreement that called for the protection of Palestinian rights. In spite of my differences with Begin over the terms of the negotiations, I wanted to see him stay in office and use his strength to implement the more difficult aspects of the Israeli commitments: to Egypt, concerning withdrawal from the Sinai; and to the inhabitants of the West Bank, concerning self rule. I had decided to appoint Robert Strauss as special negotiator for the

Middle East, to relieve me and Cy Vance of the day-to-day work and also of some of the political burdens of dealing with such a sensitive and often controversial subject. At first Vance disagreed strongly, but eventually he accepted the idea.

> *There's a general feeling that Begin's government is going to go under in the next 60 days because of dissatisfaction in Israel concerning economics, and also because of Begin's health. We don't think this will be good for the peace prospects. Had a long discussion about the Palestinian– UN resolution, and how we could move forward toward peace without committing political suicide. My own preference is that Strauss take charge of dealing with the Israelis, American Jews, and Arabs. Cy said he'd just as soon resign if he was going to be a figurehead, but I think later on he cooled off a little. It's obvious to me that there's no advantage for me or Vance to be in the forefront of this difficult issue. We can set the policy, and Strauss can carry it out and deal with these diverse groups with more political impunity than I can.*
>
> DIARY, AUGUST 3, 1979

All this was easier said than done. As had been the case since I first became President, there seemed to be no way I could stay out of Middle East affairs. Only ten days after I wrote the above entry, our Ambassador to the United Nations, Andy Young, as President of the Security Council, met in his apartment with the representative of the Palestine Liberation Organization. He notified Israel's United Nations Ambassador about the meeting, and the information immediately became public. State Department officials felt that Andy should have informed them more frankly about his actions. American Jewish leaders felt that we were attempting to recognize or negotiate with the PLO, and black leaders believed that Ambassador Young had been unjustly condemned for merely doing his duty as leader of the Security Council. During the furor following this incident, Andy resigned and I appointed his deputy, Donald McHenry, to take his place. Andy had *not* violated the United States agreement with Israel concerning the PLO, but he should have informed the Secretary of State more fully about the controversial meeting. A mountain was made of a molehill—another indication of the politically charged character of the Middle East dispute.

At the end of October 1979, the time had come to organize my reelection campaign. I would face strong opposition in my own Democratic party and also from the Republicans, and felt that the right man to coordinate the effort was Bob Strauss. He had been doing a good job in the Middle East, but we agreed that his skills could best be used in this political campaign position. After consultation with Mondale, Vance, and others I decided to ask Sol Linowitz to assume full-time responsibility for the Middle East talks. He had demonstrated his ability in negotiating the Panama Canal treaties, and I hoped he could bring the same skills to the lagging peace talks.

On the first day of the new year, I called Sadat and Begin to express my good wishes, and to encourage them as they prepared for another meeting in Aswan. But in spite of our best efforts, the Aswan meeting and subsequent discussions accomplished little toward resolving the vital issues of Palestinian rights, voting privileges for Arabs in East Jerusalem, and the ultimate status of the West Bank. There were repeated complaints in the United Nations and other international forums about Israel's building more and more settlements in the West Bank and about its incursions into Lebanon in response to terrorist attacks. Late in February, we made a costly mistake about the most sensitive of all issues—Jerusalem.

The long-standing position of the United States was that we were opposed to the establishment of any Israeli settlements in the occupied territories; we considered them to be illegal and an obstacle to peace. On this, the American stand was compatible with that of most other nations. However, at Camp David I had agreed that the status of Jerusalem would be determined through negotiations, and that we would not modify our existing stand on this issue as it had been expressed over a period of many years in various United Nations resolutions. We would either abstain from voting or veto any new resolutions on the subject. Now we were faced with another in a series of resolutions drafted to include both settlements and Jerusalem.

> *I approved our abstaining from voting on a UN resolution concerning Israeli settlements, because they also included the paragraph on Jerusalem.*
>
> DIARY, FEBRUARY 29, 1980

This was a routine decision I made at our regular Friday morning foreign-affairs breakfast, based on a recommendation I had received from the Secretary of State. Unfortunately, that was not the end of the matter.

Cy called me during the morning, first of all concerned about his budget cuts. . . . Later he called me back and said that they had deleted references to Jerusalem from the UN resolution and had adopted our proposed amendments. Under those circumstances he wanted to vote "aye" on the settlements resolution. I told him to go ahead.
                                              DIARY, MARCH 1, 1980

Again, this procedure was normal for me concerning the numerous United Nations resolutions on which we had to vote. It was not my custom to read their exact texts, because most often they were amended and redrafted repeatedly up until the time for the actual votes. After this particular vote, however, there were screams of anguish from many sources.

Fritz and Ham told me that the Israelis and the American Jews were extremely upset about the UN vote on the settlements and Jerusalem. I told them that the Jerusalem references had been deleted. They showed me a copy of the resolution as it was passed, with "Jerusalem" being mentioned six times. I couldn't believe it. I called Warren Christopher. He said he thought "Jerusalem" had been deleted. I called Cy in Chicago. He said he thought "Jerusalem" had been deleted. After some flailing around all afternoon, and after a conference with Eppie [Israeli Ambassador Ephraim Evron], we finally issued a statement saying that the vote at the UN was cast through error because of a breakdown in communications with the UN delegation. The problem was in the State Department. I don't think McHenry got proper instructions. . . .

My understanding with Begin was that we would let the issue of Jerusalem and the issue of dismantling existing settlements be resolved in the peace negotiations. That's why the error was serious. But I'm convinced that even though it's embarrassing to admit a mistake, we resolved it okay.   DIARY, MARCH 3, 1980

My optimism was not justified. With my explanation to Begin I had perhaps restored some of my credibility as a mediator of the Middle East disputes, but this snafu was a serious political blow to me—both the original vote and the accurate image of confusion among Ambassador McHenry, the Secretary of State, and me. The equivocation after the United States vote had served to emphasize the dramatic nature of the error. Later, this episode was a direct cause of my primary losses in New York and Connecticut, and it proved highly damaging to me among American Jews throughout the country for the remainder of the election year.

Partially because of the effect of this event on the Camp David process, I decided to send Sol Linowitz to Egypt and Israel, and then to ask both Begin and Sadat to come to Washington to discuss the full range of Middle East issues with me. Not much progress was being made concerning autonomy for the West Bank Arabs, and I wanted to understand the prospects for resolving some of the remaining differences.

> *I gave Sol Linowitz his instructions before he goes to Israel and Egypt tomorrow. Again, we reached the same tactical approach as we had at Camp David—that is, to try to devise a package of proposals that would be acceptable to me, Sadat, and to the Israeli people . . . hopefully forcing him [Begin] to join in with us. . . . Sol understands and agrees with this approach. He will meet with 10 or 12 other Israeli leaders while he's in the country this weekend, to try to hammer out language that would accomplish the goal I've just described.*
>
> DIARY, MARCH 20, 1980

The key question now was how to induce Prime Minister Begin to implement the portion of the accords which called for full autonomy for the Palestinians residing in the West Bank and Gaza. He had successfully withstood political pressure at home on many of the Camp David terms, but on this particular issue he seemed as reluctant as anyone to make concessions in order to carry out the agreement he had already signed. When Dayan came to see me, he said that there would be no more progress as long as Begin was heading the government, because he was firmly committed to retaining maximum control over the West Bank in spite of the Camp David commitments. This opinion was confirmed by other Israeli leaders who came to Washington. Dayan believed that the avenue to success would be unpublicized withdrawal of Israeli military forces from the occupied territories, steadily turning over more and more authority to the West Bank residents. He also made an interesting suggestion on the sensitive subject of Israeli settlements, saying that if the Israelis wanted to maintain twenty or thirty settlements with four or five thousand dwellers, then the Palestinians should be assured that fifty thousand or perhaps a hundred thousand of their people could come back from the neighboring countries to settle in the West Bank area. He said he had already proposed this in the Knesset, and thought it would have real possibilities in the future. Since I had first known him, Dayan had been trying to end the Israeli military occupation, believing it contrary to the very character of the Jewish people and the main stumbling block to undisputed international acceptance of Israel. Although his comments were somewhat encouraging, I knew that by this time he had fallen into disfavor with the Begin government, and retained little influence with those in power.

When Sadat arrived in Washington on April 8, we had a harmonious and constructive conversation. He was willing to ignore the original May deadline which he and Begin had set for concluding the peace talks, and extend it into the future as long as I thought might be productive. To him, the only date of any importance was the general election date in the United States; his one hope, he said, was that I would be returned to office for another four years. The attitude of the Arab "rejectionists" did not concern him, although he did promise to do everything possible to strengthen his ties with the Saudis. Sadat then offered to provide irrigation water to Israel's Negev Desert if it was needed, and assured me that a committee of elected mayors from the West Bank–Gaza areas would be satisfactory as a temporary governing body for the Arabs if the early election of a new self-governing authority proved impossible. He was willing to say publicly that there should be no separate Palestinian state, certain that this was also the true preference of the Saudis and other moderate Arabs, although they were unwilling to say so.

When Begin came over to see me a week later, we had a pleasant meeting, but made little progress on the key issues. However, it did become clear that for both of us the Camp David accords had now become almost like the Bible, with the words and phrases taking on a special importance. When we got into an argument, we would flip the pages of the accords, searching for a way to authenticate our own opinions. The problem was that the actual words—such as "autonomy," "security," "Palestinian rights," and even "West Bank"—had different meanings for each of us and those we represented. Without success, I tried to convince Begin that he should limit or declare a moratorium on additional settlements in the occupied territories. As we discussed a broad range of issues, I grew disturbed over his lack of concern about adverse public opinion in the United States or other countries as a result of his statements and actions concerning peace, Palestinians, settlements, and Lebanon.

At the end of my meetings with the two leaders, certain things were obvious. Both were committed to carrying out the provisions of the peace treaty and considered the agreement binding on them and their nations. Both were still paying lip service to the exact words of the other provisions of the Camp David accords, but there was a great difference between Egypt and Israel about what the words meant. Sadat wanted maximum autonomy for the Palestinians on the West Bank, while Begin wanted just the opposite. The American position was unchanged—without full autonomy as described in the Camp David document, there was no prospect for real peace.

Now Linowitz was to pursue every possible avenue to further progress, but my guess was that at best, both sides would mark time until after the American election was over. One thought occurred to all my staff: compared to our dealings with the Iranians so far, the Israeli and Arab negotiations had been like a wedding feast.

As important as the Middle East problems were, my most pressing duty still was to secure the release of the hostages and reduce the growing tensions in the Persian Gulf area. Through our two intermediaries, Bourguet and Villalon, we had worked out a scenario with President Bani-Sadr for getting us out of our predicament. Based on the principles already articulated by the United States, it was a fairly complicated plan, with a description of what each of us—the United Nations commission, the Iranians, and we—would do and say at every step of the carefully orchestrated process. Briefly, the plan called for these steps:

1. Following a public request from Iran's Revolutionary Council, a five-member United Nations commission would be formed, its members to be approved by Bani-Sadr and me.
2. The commission would be a fact-finding body and not conduct any kind of trial. Its members would listen in private sessions to grievances from both sides, and would visit Iran to obtain evidence.
3. The members would visit the hostages, but only to determine their condition and not to interrogate them in any way.
4. The hostages would then be transferred to a hospital, thus being removed from control of the militants and coming under the custody of the Iranian government.
5. The commission would make its report to Secretary General

Waldheim, and the hostages would be allowed to leave Iran simultaneously.

6. Subsequently, other disputes between the United States and Iran would be discussed by a joint commission formed by the two governments.

This plan of action was an enormous step forward, because in addition to the Shah's return being deleted from the Iranians' demands, there were now two identifiable Iranian leaders with whom we could work. Both President Bani-Sadr and Foreign Minister Ghotbsadeh were committed to an early resolution of our differences.

Nevertheless, although our two friends Villalon and Bourguet were in Tehran doing everything possible to keep the plans on track, they faced some serious handicaps: the weakness of Bani-Sadr; the personal incompatibility of Bani-Sadr and Ghotbsadeh, who would not speak to each other; the strong opposition to any action by the fundamentalist religious leaders; and the unpredictability of the reclusive Ayatollah Khomeini. The presumption was that the Revolutionary Council, in which the fundamentalists were a minority, would assure the completion of the plan.

The United Nations delegation assembled in Geneva and then proceeded to Tehran, arriving on February 23. Its members had high hopes of success. The Iranian officials had endorsed the mission, and all details of the scenario were apparently resolved. But at the time of their arrival, there were ominous developments in Iran. Khomeini announced that the Iranian parliament would have to make the ultimate decision on setting our people free. Since the new government could not be elected and constituted before the middle of April, this statement signified a serious delay if the volatile leader did not change his mind. Furthermore, the militants were defying orders of Bani-Sadr and the Revolutionary Council that the international delegation could visit all the hostages. They would listen only to the Ayatollah, who was secluded in Qum and refusing to accept any responsibility. On many previous occasions he had privately encouraged other revolutionary leaders, then betrayed them and condemned them publicly if a decision proved unpopular. This time, the President and other members of the Council were threatening to resign if Khomeini did not back up their orders to the kidnappers.

Under this pressure, Ahmad Khomeini, the Ayatollah's son, finally announced that the hostages should be visited; and Ghotbsadeh said he had received word that Khomeini wanted custody of the hostages transferred to the government.

*Ghotbsadeh reported, through our intermediaries, that he
was excited and gratified at these developments.*

*During the afternoon, the prospect developed that the
hostages would be turned over to the Revolutionary Council this evening, and that the committee would go in to see
them this weekend. . . . The hostages would then be examined by physicians, and perhaps moved to a hospital. And
the hope has been held out that their ultimate release
might be expedited.*   DIARY, MARCH 6, 1980

*We're getting into a phase now of changing from "student
kidnappers" to "government kidnappers." Hamilton called
in the late afternoon to say that the hostages would be
transferred to the Revolutionary Council tomorrow morning at 8:30 United States time.*   DIARY, MARCH 7, 1980

At the suggestion of the United Nations delegation, I dictated a
taped message to the hostages, letting them know the depth of our
nation's concern about them and encouraging them not to give up
hope. By the next day, my own hopes were dashed. Khomeini
announced that he did not support transfer of the hostages, and
Bani-Sadr and Ghotbsadeh were unable to get the Council to
reconvene.

*Khomeini instructed the Revolutionary Council not to let
the UN commission visit the American hostages unless
the commission first condemned the United States and
the Shah for illegal acts. He will permit them to visit the
"American spies"—a few of the hostages—ahead of time.
This is obviously unacceptable. It shows that the UN
commission must return. And it also shows that there is
no government in Iran other than the fanatics.*

*. . . We'll hold off breaking diplomatic relationships.
We'll impose economic sanctions as soon as the commission is clear of Iran. We'll investigate the possibility of
confiscating Iranian assets in addition to just impound-
ing them. We should not attack Bani-Sadr and Ghotbsadeh,
because they have indeed been the ones who have tried
hardest to get the hostages out.*

*. . . Vance called during lunch to say that the UN
commission had been asked by Bani-Sadr to stay over
until tomorrow night to meet with the Revolutionary Council to receive a proposal for a simultaneous statement on
American and Shah abuse and an announcement that the*

*hostages could all be visited by the commission. I told Cy,
"Absolutely not!" This was unacceptable to me. There's
no way to trust the Iranian government officials, because
they can't speak with any authority.*

DIARY, MARCH 10, 1980

The scenario had been worked out in careful detail, with the
full knowledge and support of the Iranian officials. Only on this
basis had we approved the sending of the United Nations commission to Iran. We remained convinced that the elected leaders
wanted the hostages out, and an end to the stalemate that was
wreaking havoc with their country's economy and political structure. However, Khomeini, apparently deranged, had overridden
the government and aborted the resolution of the crisis. This
failure of our best efforts was a bitter disappointment. It seemed
that we had now lost our last chance to set the Americans
free.

I met with congressional leaders and explained what had happened in Iran, pledging them to secrecy about the exact procedures and the Iranian leaders who were involved. We did not
want these officials executed by the fanatics. The unanimous
recommendation of the American legislators was for me to be
patient, not to cause any uproar that might endanger the hostages, to have confidence in the United Nations commission's
approach, and not to take any military action. Interestingly, it
was the Republicans who spoke up most strongly with this advice.

Cy Vance then went to New York to meet with the members of
the delegation. This group of distinguished world citizens brought
back conflicting views of the situation there. They were all inclined to return to Iran after the hostages were transferred from
the militants to the government, but some thought Bani-Sadr was
acting for Khomeini and was a strong man, while others believed
he had hidden during the past two weeks to avoid responsibility
and was very weak. They all reported a growing disenchantment
with the militants throughout Iran.

My own belief was that Bani-Sadr was weak, and in a showdown had thrust upon Ghotbsadeh the leading role in seeking
freedom for the hostages. Khomeini had also tried to avoid any
responsibility one way or the other, but the militants had forced
it on him. He had betrayed his own Islamic republic by siding
with the terrorists against the official decision of the elected
government representatives—an act that would perpetuate disorder and chaos in Iran during the months ahead.

In Europe and elsewhere there were sharp debates about how much the United States should be supported on the crises in Iran and Afghanistan. Germany was being difficult. An election was approaching, and the leftists were opposed to any further criticism of the Soviet Union's occupation of Afghanistan. When Helmut Schmidt came to Washington for a visit, I was sharply critical because he had yielded to this pressure.

A long meeting with the Chancellor. He was primarily on the defensive because I persisted in asking what more the Federal Republic would do to help us with Afghanistan, and what actually they had done that provides pressure on the Soviet Union. The answer to both those questions apparently is "Nothing," except that Schmidt recommitted himself firmly and personally . . . that he and Giscard d'Estaing would join us in the Olympic boycott. 75% of the German people, according to a poll I've seen, favor the boycott if the other European countries and the United States participate.   DIARY, MARCH 5, 1980

Within a few days, I had another visitor from Germany. We had quite a different conversation.

Franz Josef Strauss came by to see me. He will be the nominee of the opposition party running against Helmut Schmidt. He was extremely strong, powerful, impressive, somewhat disturbing in the fervent exposition of his ideas. His military commitment, his belief that the Western alliance should stand together, his support of all our actions against the Soviets, his contempt for the French equivocation, all put him in perfect harmony with our own attitudes and beliefs. He said that Helmut had lied to him by claiming that we still would not provide neutron weapons even though Germany was willing to accept them. I told him that from the beginning the Germans had not been willing to accept neutron weapons unless one of the other Continental nations would also join in the deployment.

. . . He said when he met with the French to talk about the Soviet invasion of Afghanistan, that the French officials told him the Soviet invasion was an expression of weakness, not strength. And Strauss's reply was, "How many expressions of weakness will be necessary before Soviet troops are in Paris?"

I liked him, but I can understand why in the election

campaign he prefers to let [Helmut] Kohl, the president of their party, be the public spokesman while he takes a more moderate posture as a candidate. He could frighten people.
                                        DIARY, MARCH 13, 1980

On March 22, after all our efforts to negotiate with Iranian officials had proved fruitless, Mondale, Vance, and I had a full briefing from our military leaders about the latest plans for a rescue mission, which were much more feasible than those presented at the outset of the ordeal. They still needed more work and I was not yet convinced that we should proceed, but I wanted to investigate all options.

One of the possible staging areas for our rescue team was in an isolated desert region about two hundred miles south of Tehran, which seemed from aerial photographs to be smooth enough for night landings by the transport planes needed for the mission. I authorized the flight of a small airplane to the site for a close visual examination of the desert sand—to see how smooth and firm it was. This exploratory flight had to be made when the weather and moonlight would be conducive to success. We all understood that I was not making a final commitment to proceed further with a rescue attempt; at the same time, I wanted the long-standing training operations and planning to continue.

That weekend, on March 24, the Shah flew from Panama to Egypt. The Panamanian and American presses blamed the trip on Kissinger and Rockefeller. Regardless of who might have been responsible, I had strongly opposed the move because of its potentially adverse effect on Sadat, but this consideration did not seem to concern the Shah, who claimed falsely that he was in danger in Panama.

Predictably, the Iranians held us responsible for moving him nearer to Iran and away from the possibility (never more than an Iranian dream) that the Shah might be extradited from Panama. They threatened again to hold trials and punish the hostages, and the Revolutionary Council voted to postpone indefinitely the run-off elections for the *majlis*. In effect, this further delayed any possible consideration of the transfer or release of the hostages.

I decided it was now time to put more pressure on Iran. We redoubled our efforts among our friends to use their strongest possible influence in Tehran and to let Bani-Sadr know that the United States was planning to impose much more stringent sanctions and possibly close the Iranian seaports if the hostages were not released by the first of April. I talked personally to the leaders of Great Britain, France, and Germany, and sent messages to the others, stressing that our patience had run out; only if Iran were induced to release the hostages could another even more serious confrontation between the two countries be avoided.

These efforts paid off. For the first time, I felt that all our allies were really helping us to the maximum extent of their ability. As my April 1 deadline approached, I received a positive report from Iran.

> *About 1:45, Cy reported that Ghotbsadeh had sent word to us that Bani-Sadr will make a statement tomorrow at noon Tehran time [4:30 A.M. in Washington], saying that the Revolutionary Council with Khomeini's approval had decided to transfer the hostages away from the students to the government on Tuesday. This story was already leaking from the Revolutionary Council. They asked the United States to acknowledge this move as being constructive, and also to point out that the Iranians had said the* majlis *would make a decision on the full release of the hostages and call on them to expedite this process. If this develops to be a true report, it would be the most encouraging thing we've had lately out of Iran.*   DIARY, MARCH 30, 1980

If things went as Ghotbsadeh had said they would, it would be necessary for me to respond publicly to Bani-Sadr's 4:30 A.M. (EST) statement. My response was to be made through the news media, and I wanted to be sure that Iran got the message loud and clear. Without knowing what was going on, the American press would obviously be confused and might have negative headlines or report my early-morning response in a distorted fashion, alienating the already suspicious Iranians.

> *I decided late in the afternoon to have in a few key newsmen—Ben Bradlee, Murray Gart, Jack Nelson, and the Chicago* Tribune *and* New York Times *chief reporters—and I just told them frankly what was going on and urged them to be responsible in their reporting. A severe renunciation of the so-called Khomeini message or a condemnation of Ghotbsadeh might very well undo the apparent move by the Revolutionary Council toward transferring the hostages.*   DIARY, MARCH 30, 1980

Ghotbsadeh had already contributed to the confusion. In order to generate a more positive attitude toward the United States in Iran, he had fabricated a message from me to Khomeini. Although he admitted this deception on "Issues and Answers," some of the American reporters were still uncertain what was true.

On Monday morning, the time for Bani-Sadr's statement went by without our hearing anything, but Ghotbsadeh sent word that it had only been delayed. We monitored the Iranian news broadcasts all day, very disappointed not to hear any report of his speech, which was supposed to contain a specific paragraph prearranged with us. But encouragement came from a CBS News report that the Revolutionary Council had indeed voted to transfer the hostages, and Cy was notified by the Swiss and other sources that Bani-Sadr's announcement would be forthcoming.

I called a full National Security Council meeting to discuss the imminent prospect of transferring the hostages from the militants to the government, the promise of Iranian parliamentary action to release the hostages as soon as the election process was completed, and additional actions we would take against Iran if my April 1 deadline was not met. Bani-Sadr was now supposed to speak before noon in Tehran, on Tuesday, April 1. I asked my key advisers to meet in the Oval Office at 5 A.M., the earliest we could hope to get an English version of his remarks.

Right on schedule, we received a quick translation of his speech, and noted with pleasure that it included the key statement. The Iranians would transfer the hostages, provided we made it clear that we understood Bani-Sadr's statement and therefore would not impose any additional sanctions. I made the prearranged response—in fact, I repeated the statement at least three times to the assembled reporters in the Oval Office. From the State Department, we also acknowledged that the Iranians planned for the *majlis* to resolve the hostage issue as soon as the new parliament could be formed.

> *I called the press in about 7:15 and outlined what was going on ... saying that if Bani-Sadr carried out his commitment, we saw no need to impose additional sanctions above those which have already been imposed and which will be continued.*
>
> *... Late in the day, Bani-Sadr announced that we had not met conditions he had laid down for the transfer of the hostages. I decided to go ahead and call an NSC meeting ... to impose all the sanctions, expel all their diplomats, collect all the claims against Iran, maybe prohibit any more people coming into this country from Iran—and to act without further delay.*
>
> DIARY, APRIL 1, 1980

Within a few hours, we received a different message out of Iran, probably from Ghotbsadeh, saying that the United States had met the Iranian demands because we had decided not to take action on the sanctions. We decided to let the situation stew for a day or two until we could get a direct report from the Swiss or from Villalon, who was in Tehran. Later, Bani-Sadr stated that our response was adequate. As President, he seemed very uncertain and weak in a showdown. Foreign Minister Ghotbsadeh was really gutsy, and took a lot of personal risks in seeking a resolution to the crisis.

To my dismay and bewilderment, some news stories accused me of arranging a phony exchange of messages with the Iranian leaders so as to affect the outcome of the Wisconsin primary, which was held on this same day. These false reports grew into a refrain that was sung over and over during the months ahead, and eventually became accepted as the truth by many political commentators.

On the next day, April 2, I received a report that our small plane had flown hundreds of miles into Iran at very low altitude, landed in the desert, examined the possible rescue staging site, and returned without detection. The pilot reported that it was an ideal place—a smooth and firm surface, adequately isolated, with only a seldom-used country road nearby. My advisers and I decided to complete our tentative plans for a rescue mission, to assemble the necessary equipment, and to prepare the team that might be sent into Iran. Because of the prospective transfer of the hostages away from the militants, I still believed the rescue mission would not have to be launched.

On April 3, after meeting with the militants, two members of the Revolutionary Council announced that the hostages would be turned over to the government on Saturday, April 5; the militants said they would accede to the request of the government. Bani-Sadr announced once more that the hostages would be transferred, but added that the Council would take no action without Khomeini's approval. In an interview with ABC he said, "Don't worry, the transfer will be carried out." But experience dictated caution and doubt. We mixed in a little hope and prayer.

Friday, April 4, brought nothing but bad news.

All during the day we communicated with the Iranians, either directly through Bourguet and Villalon or through Swiss Ambassador [Erik] Lang. They were joined in the *effort by Archbishop [Hilarion] Capucci, who is a hero in the Revolutionary Council because he was convicted in Israel for smuggling weapons to the Palestinians. He tried to convince the terrorists to turn over the hostages to the `government because holding them was damaging the revolutionary government structure in Iran.*

Bani-Sadr and Ghotbsadeh were apparently convinced from the beginning. The Revolutionary Council varied between voting unanimously to move ahead with the transfer, or at times with 2 votes against it and 3 abstentions [out of a total of 25]. It was a comedy of errors, and eventually, because the Council was not unanimous, Bani-Sadr took the case to Khomeini, who decided against the transfer.

. . . Bourguet, Villalon, and Lang all recommended against any sort of further explanation of the U.S. position, or any further assurances to them [the Iranians]. So we held firm consistently. The only struggle going on was within the Revolutionary Council itself, where Bani-Sadr again failed to show any leadership capability and let just a couple of people stand between him and a resolution of the issue. DIARY, APRIL 4, 1980

It was obvious to me that the Revolutionary Council would never act and that, in spite of all our work and the efforts of the elected leaders of Iran, the hostages were not going to be released. I decided to move ahead on additional economic sanctions, an embargo against the shipment of any goods to Iran except food and medicines, breaking off diplomatic relations and the expulsion of all Iranian diplomats, and a census of all financial claims against Iran. We again asked all our allies and other countries to join us in these actions, and to consider breaking diplomatic relations with Iran at an early date if the hostages continued to be held. Cy Vance met with more than twenty ambassadors in Washington to explain our decision and to seek the support of their countries. I also discussed various possible military operations with my most senior advisers.

The next day, Henry Precht called in the Iranian Ambassador to tell him that all their diplomats would have to leave the country immediately. The Ambassador was angry, and told Henry that the hostages were well cared for and were under complete control of the Iranian government. Precht had been in charge of our special hostage group since our people were first kidnapped, and he knew the facts. He looked straight at the Ambassador and said, "Bullshit!" The Iranian Ambassador stalked out of the building and complained to the American press about mistreatment and abusive language.

> *I wrote Henry a note, saying that one of the elements of good diplomatic language was to be concise and accurate and clear, and his reply to the Iranians proved that he was a master of this technique.* DIARY, APRIL 8, 1980

During the afternoon of April 9, President Giscard d'Estaing called to say that a group of European foreign ministers would meet in Lisbon to prepare a demand to the Iranians that the hostages be released, and that if they should get an equivocal or negative answer, they were going to take further joint action. I told him not to permit a delay, because equivocation was a typical Iranian tactic. He promised the Europeans would not wait. I reminded him that only a short time remained before we had to take more forceful steps, including military action, and that their combined influence on Iran could make the difference between a successful and unsuccessful resolution of the crisis.

My hope had been that the Iranian leaders would behave courageously. Now I realized this was not to be. Another serious development was that Iraq was threatening to invade Iran. We had no previous knowledge of nor influence over this move, but Iran was blaming us for it nevertheless.

> *The Iranian terrorists are making all kinds of crazy threats to kill the American hostages if they are invaded by Iraq—whom they identify as an American puppet.*
> DIARY, APRIL 10, 1980

We could no longer afford to depend on diplomacy. I decided to act. On April 11, I called together my top advisers, and we went over the rescue plans again. Because the militants in the compound had threatened to "destroy all the hostages immediately" if any additional moves against them should be launched, we had to plan any action with the utmost care. In the Cabinet Room with me were Vice President Mondale, Secretary Brown, Dr. Brzezinski, Deputy Secretary of State Christopher, Central Intelligence Director Stansfield Turner, General David Jones, Hamilton, and Jody. (Secretary Vance was on a brief and much needed vacation.) Earlier, I had developed a long list of questions for the military leaders. Their answers had become much more satisfactory as the training and preparations for the rescue operation had progressed. David Jones said that the earliest date everything could be ready was April 24. I told everyone that it was time for us to bring our hostages home; their safety and our national honor were at stake. When the meeting adjourned, everyone understood that our plans had to be kept a carefully guarded secret. Not wanting anything written in my diary that might somehow be revealing, I made this cryptic entry:

> At the NSC meeting we discussed all the options available to us on Iran. There are a few more economic measures we can take before we move to the military options. These involve such things as interruptions of air travel to and from Tehran and the interruption of telecommunications, including news broadcasts. At this meeting we made the basic decisions about the order of priority of our options.
>
> DIARY, APRIL 11, 1980

When Vance returned, he objected to my decision to rescue the hostages and wanted to present his own views to the NSC group. His primary argument was that we should be patient and not do anything which might endanger their safety. I held the meeting on April 15, but no one changed his mind.

We took every possible step to conceal our preliminary moves in preparation for the hostage rescue mission, encouraging the few people who had to know about airplane and helicopter movements to believe they might be related to the possible laying of mines. On the evening of April 16, we met in the Situation Room for a thorough review of every aspect of the operation. This session lasted two and a half hours, and I was particularly impressed with mission commanders Generals James B. Vaught and Philip C. Gast, and Colonel Charles Beckwith. These were the leaders who, working with the Joint Chiefs of Staff and the Secretary of Defense, would direct the mission after I authorized it to begin.

In their meticulous description of every facet of the operation, I received satisfactory answers to all my many questions. I informed the military leaders that they had my complete confidence and support, and I made it clear that there would be no interference from the White House while the mission was under way. However, I wanted to be kept constantly informed. Beginning that night, we were a team, realizing that all of us were responsible for the lives and safety of the captive Americans—and for the reputation of our military forces and nation.

Although I felt the weight of the responsibility and was prop-

erly concerned about what the future might hold, I had no doubt
that the time was ripe. Because I was so clear in my resolve, I
looked forward to the mission. The plans and training had been
completed. The necessary helicopters and transport planes on
American aircraft carriers had been stationed south of Iran or
nearby, in such friendly countries as Oman and Egypt. We did
not notify the leaders of these countries about the purpose of our
visits, letting chance observers surmise that they involved aid to
Afghan freedom fighters or preliminary steps leading toward some
kind of mining operation along the coast of Iran.

The Delta Team met the helicopters at Desert One, for
transportation by air to Desert Two, a mountain hideout
southeast of Tehran. From Desert Two, trucks were prepared
to drive the Delta Team into the city.

We had blueprints of our embassy buildings in Tehran, of course, and we had talked to the black and female hostages who had been released before Christmas, although they were unable to tell us much about the others. Much more important, we received information from someone (who cannot be identified) who was thoroughly familiar with the compound, knew where every American hostage was located, how many and what kind of guards were there at different times during the night, and the daily schedule of the hostages and their captors. This was the first time we knew the precise location of the Americans.

Our agents, who moved freely in and out of Tehran under the guise of business or media missions, had studied closely the degree of vigilance of the captors. They had grown lax, and security around the compound was no longer a serious obstacle to a surprise entry by force. Our satellite photographs of the embassy compound and the surrounding area kept us abreast of any changes in the general habits and overall composition of the terrorists' guard details. We could, for instance, identify individual cars and trucks that went inside the compound each day.

Life for the guards around the embassy grounds seemed to have settled into a relaxed and humdrum existence, perfectly designed for a lightning strike by a highly trained and well-equipped force which, with night-vision devices, could easily distinguish in the dark between our people and the Iranian captors. We would need six large helicopters to fly into the center of Tehran, pick up the three Americans in the foreign-ministry building and the other hostages in the embassy, and carry them and the rescue team to safety.

The biggest problem was how to travel the enormous distance from the sea or from other countries to extract the hostages from the center of Tehran. Our solution was to fly in seven helicopters (later changed to eight to provide two rather than one backup) from our aircraft carriers in the Gulf of Oman to the remote area—now known as Desert One—that had been surveyed earlier. The only drawback of this site was a seldom-used dirt country road going by it, but the team was prepared to hold any passersby, hide their vehicles, and release them only when it was too late for the operation to be disrupted. Everyone was under strict orders from me not to harm any innocent bystanders and to avoid bloodshed whenever possible.

The helicopters were scheduled to take off on Thursday, April 24 at dusk (10:00 A.M. Washington time) and arrive about three hours later, at approximately 10:30 P.M. Iran time. This six-hundred-mile flight from the Gulf of Oman would push to the limit the capabilities of these aircraft. They would be joined at Desert One by six C-130's carrying the ninety members of the rescue team, plus fuel and supplies. After the team was transferred from the C-130's to the helicopters, the airplanes would leave Iran, and the helicopters with the rescue team would fly a short distance northward into the nearby mountains, where they would arrive at about 4:00 A.M. and be hidden from view during the following daylight hours. This place was remote and uninhabited, and detection would be highly unlikely. Communication between the Pentagon and the rescue team, using satellites and other relay facilities, would be instantaneous. I would receive telephone reports from David Jones and Harold Brown.

The next night, provided everything went well and I decided the rescue mission should proceed, the trucks our agents had purchased would be removed from a warehouse on the outskirts of Tehran, driven to a point near the mountain hiding place, and used to carry the rescue team into the city. At a prearranged time, the rescue team would simultaneously enter the foreign-ministry building and the compound, overpower the guards, and free the American hostages. Guided by radio communications and prearranged schedules, the helicopters would land at the sites, picking up our people and carrying them to an abandoned airstrip near the city. From there, two C-141's would fly all the Americans to safety across the desert area of Saudi Arabia. The helicopters would be left in Iran. I planned to notify the Saudis only after the rescue mission was completed.

We were all agreed on the need for the mission, except Secretary Vance, who was concerned about whether we should make the rescue effort at all. I could understand his worry about the risk to the hostages, but I was convinced that our people would be far safer in the hands of the American rescue team. Cy had threatened to resign on several earlier occasions. It was obvious that he was now deeply disturbed about the proposed rescue mission, although he and I had agreed previously that if I decided to act with force, a rescue mission would be preferable to a possible mining operation. I still needed Cy, valued his opinion, and relied heavily on his services as a dedicated and competent public servant.

The day after our detailed briefing from the mission commanders, I made this diary entry:

> *Vance has been extremely despondent lately, and I called*
> *Warren Christopher in this morning to talk to him about*

what should be done. He advised me to meet with Cy late in the afternoon to add some personal concern to help resolve the problem.

. . . Called Cy in for an extended discussion. For the third or fourth time, he indicated that he might resign . . . but after he goes through a phase of uncertainty and disapproval, then he joins in with adequate support for me. He said he would stay on, but afterward would reserve the right to say that he disagreed with some of the policies on Iran.   DIARY, APRIL 17, 1980

On April 18, I had quite a discussion with my closest advisers about how to deal with the congressional leadership on the Iran decisions. Fritz led the argument for minimum advance notice and maximum secrecy. Cy took the opposite tack, maintaining that we should advise the Democratic and Republican leaders in the House and Senate. I agreed with Fritz, intent on keeping to an absolute minimum the number of people who knew about the mission. One or two key members of Congress might be consulted when our final plans were under way, but I would notify a larger group of the leadership of the House and Senate only after the rescue operation had reached the point of no return. We also planned the procedure (after the mission was completed) for notifying Oman, Saudi Arabia, and Egypt, whose territories would be used or crossed during the mission. It was absolutely imperative that there be no leaks. Any suspicion by the militants of a rescue attempt would doom the effort to failure, at the same time endangering the lives of all the hostages and of our rescue team. Success depended upon total surprise.

Even at this last moment, I continued to monitor the attitude of the Iranians, in the hope that there might still be some possibility of an early release of the hostages. If not, I wanted to prevent their having any suspicion of our plans. To accomplish both these purposes, I decided that Hamilton should keep his second appointment with the top Iranian official. This rendezvous took place before dawn in a private apartment somewhere in Europe. The official had traveled from Iran just to send me his assessment and advice about the situation in Tehran. He gave Hamilton a very discouraging report, saying that there was no chance of our people being released under any circumstances before the new parliament could be elected and organized. He estimated that the elections would be held on May 16, and that it would then take at least four or five weeks more to form the official body. In the meantime, he hoped that we would be patient and do nothing of a punitive nature that might drive Iran into the arms of the Soviets.

Hamilton left him with the clear impression that our patience had run out but that we were willing to keep talking as long as I was convinced that the Iranian parliament would resolve the issue quickly as soon as it was constituted. After returning to Washington, Ham summarized his report to me by categorizing the meeting as "a final attempt to peacefully resolve the crisis." He concluded, "Based on the analysis I obtained from [the Iranian official], there is absolutely no chance the hostages will be released for two and a half to three months, and an even greater chance that it will drag on five or six months. This only supports the tentative decision that you have already made."

Periodically, we were still receiving messages from Chargé d'Affaires Bruce Laingen, mostly through the Swiss Ambassador in Tehran. Now, on April 19 (the same day as Hamilton's report to me), the State Department received through this channel a message from Laingen recommending that we take strong action against Iran. He and two of his staff members were still in the foreign-ministry building a few blocks from the American compound, where they were kept imprisoned.

These two reports from Iran—one from a spokesman within the government and the other from the head of the American diplomatic team—confirmed my resolve to proceed with the rescue. My persistent anxiety was to maintain secrecy. However, I was soon forced to share the news with one other head of state, when I received information about disturbing stories originating with a former British officer in Oman, who was employed by the Sultan.

He had reported to British officials in London that we had planes in Oman (which was true) and that they were loaded with ammunition and supplies for the Afghan freedom fighters. The British and Omanis were getting nervous, and I had to send Warren Christopher to London to brief Prime Minister Margaret Thatcher and Foreign Minister Peter Carrington about the true purpose of the planes. Christopher was careful not to ask them for any comment, but simply informed them about our plans for the rescue.

We listened carefully to all news reports, but heard only one other indication of a leak. In monitoring radio broadcasts all over Iran, we heard a story from up near the Iraqi border of an attempted rescue mission. It turned out to be a repeat of a conjectural story which had run earlier in the Washington *Star*—no damage was done.

On Monday, before the rescue mission was to be launched, Secretary Vance, in effect, resigned.

> *Our Iranian plans are going on as scheduled. I had Cy, Zbig, and Harold come by to talk about the question of consulting with Congress, and also how to handle the postoperative time.*
>
> *The Methodists at General Conference in Indianapolis passed an embarrassing resolution [about Iran], mentioning Western imperialism, and so forth. It went to Khomeini, Bani-Sadr, and others. Bishop [William R.] Cannon, D. W. Brooks, and three others want to come in and see me sometime this week, to encourage us not to take military action. I told Cy I wanted him to meet with them. He said he could not do it.*
>
> *I stood up, and the three men left.*
>
> DIARY, APRIL 21, 1980

Not another word was said. Although simply stated in my diary, this was a very serious moment—the first time I, as President, had ever had anyone directly refuse to obey an official order of mine. My heart went out to Cy Vance, who was deeply troubled and heavily burdened. He was alone in his opposition to the rescue mission among all my advisers, and he knew it.

Cy came back to see me late in the afternoon and submitted his letter of resignation, since he could no longer support my policy toward Iran. I took his letter and said I would keep it. We discussed the fact that my general views and political philosophy were very close to his, and that there was no serious difference between us on major issues of American foreign policy. We agreed that I would speak with him later about whether he should leave, but I said I would not try to talk him out of it. We both knew he had made an irrevocable decision—the only decision possible.

On Wednesday, April 23, I received a last-minute intelligence briefing about Iran, encapsulating information received from all available sources. The substance was that there was little prospect of the hostages' release within the next five or six months, and that everything was favorable for the rescue mission. Our agents in and around Tehran were very optimistic.

That evening, I met with Senator Robert Byrd to discuss the Iranian question, primarily to receive his opinion about necessary notifications to Congress on any possible military action in Iran.

I told him that before we took any of the military acts that had been prominently mentioned in the press—mining, blockade, and so forth—I would indeed consult with Congress. And that at this time I had no plans to initiate this kind of action.

He drew a sharp distinction between the need to consult on a military plan, and the need to inform Congress at the last minute on any kind of covert operation.

DIARY, APRIL 23, 1980

Byrd and I went over a short list of senior senators of both parties who should be notified of any secret operation of this type. I had planned to let him know about the impending rescue mission at the end of this conversation, but now I decided to brief him and the others during the following night, after our team was actually in place and ready to enter Tehran. I therefore told him that such an operation was imminent, but not when it would be launched. Senator Byrd was completely trustworthy, but it was my impression that he would prefer to be informed at the same time as other top congressional leaders. After he left the White House I wondered if it would have been better to involve him more directly in our exact plans for the mission. His advice would have been valuable to me then—and also twenty-four hours later.

The next day was one of the worst of my life. I wanted to spend every moment monitoring the progress of the rescue mission, but had to stick to my regular schedule and act as though nothing of the kind was going on. I asked Zbig to keep notes for me, while I tried to keep my mind on such routine duties as meeting with representatives about legislation, a private session with Israeli Labor party leader Shimon Peres, and a briefing for Hispanic leaders about our anti-inflation program.

Here are some of Brzezinski's notes, using Washington time, with my own clarifying comments in brackets added later.

10:35 A.M. President briefed by ZB on latest intelligence and on the initial stage of the operation. Take-off as planned.
12:00 P.M. Lunch, President, Vice President, Vance, Brown, Brzezinski, Jordan, Powell. First indication that two helicopters may be down short of landing site. [Although the weather forecast had been good, the helicopters ran into severe localized dust storms. One returned to the carrier, and another was left in the southern desert. We never knew until the final personnel count when it was all over that this helicopter crew

had been picked up. It was a major worry for me right through the mission.] Iranian post noted two aircraft flying low, without lights. [Our intelligence services were monitoring radio broadcasts throughout Iran.]

3:15 P.M. Two helicopters down; naval task force thinks rest have landed and picked up crews, and thus six are on the way. Should know about Desert One in about half an hour. No upgrading of gendarmerie alert. [The Iranians had small police stations scattered around in the villages and towns. We successfully avoided them. There were no alerts until after our entire rescue team was completely out of Iran.]

All C-130's have landed. Initial problem: three [Iranian motor] vehicles observed. One got away. One of the above, a bus with some 40 [44] people, presumably detained. Brown/ Brzezinski consult and agree that no basis for abortion [of mission]; will consult further as information comes in, and Brzezinski will brief the President and obtain his guidance. [This was unexpected bad luck. We had observed this site for several weeks, and vehicular traffic near it was rare. Almost immediately after our landing, though, there was a busload of people, and then a fuel truck followed closely by a pickup truck. The two latter appeared to be driven by smugglers of gasoline, who took off across the desert in the pickup. It was highly unlikely that they would go to the police. In fact, Colonel Beckwith believed they thought our team was Iranian police. But the bus passengers would have to be prevented from sounding an alarm. I approved the removal of all of them to Egypt by C-130 until the rescue itself was concluded, when they would be returned to Iran. We were very careful to avoid any casualties.]

4:21 P.M. General Jones has heard from General Vaught [who was in Egypt and in overall charge of the operation] that everything is under control at Desert One. No one hurt or eliminated. Escaped vehicle proceeded southwest to town 15 miles away, which has gendarmerie post, unmanned at night. Four helicopters refueled at 4:00 P.M. EST; two being refueled. [One had been forced down temporarily in the sand storm, then pressed forward to join the others. This put us somewhat behind schedule, but in itself was no problem.] One that went down has gone back to the carrier. Vaught expects everything to be over in 40 minutes. Has report that everything "green" at drop off, and transport is ready.

4:45 P.M. Brown to Brzezinski: "I think we have an abort situation. One helicopter at Desert One has hydraulic problem. We thus have less than the minimum six to go." C-130's to be used to extract. Request decision on mission termination from the President literally within minutes [because of the importance of completing the operation during nighttime].

4:50 P.M. The President, after obtaining a full report from Brzezinski, requests full information from Brown and Jones and specifically the recommendation from the ground commander. [Ground commander Beckwith, and Vaught in Egypt, both recommended termination, complying with the previous plan which required a minimum of six helicopters.]

4:57 P.M. The President to Brown: "Let's go with his recommendation," and the mission is aborted.

At this point, the Vice President, Christopher, Powell, and Jordan joined me and Zbig in my small study, later followed by Vance, and then Brown. Although despondent about the failure of the mission, we felt we had the situation well under control. Careful plans had been made to abort the operation at any time there might be unforeseen problems or a chance of detection. I was grievously disappointed, but thanked God that there had been no casualties.

5:18 P.M. Brown informs the President that we don't know whereabouts of one helicopter and don't know the crew loss.

5:32 P.M. President calls Jones on secure phone and learns all crews not accounted for. President instructs that needless military action be avoided; air cover if needed for extraction, but an engagement should be avoided. Show of force first before shooting down any Iranian planes. [All of this referred to the helicopter crew we believed to be on the ground in southern Iran. If necessary, I was ready to send in military forces from the aircraft carriers to protect the crew. At one point, intelligence sources reported a beeper signal from the downed helicopter.]

Discussion of what communication to make to the Iranians and of the needed report to the American people. [After our rescue team departed, I needed to calm the Iranians, who would find our abandoned helicopters. I planned to tell them the truth, and hoped they would believe it.]

5:58 P.M. President on secure phone informed by Jones that helicopter smashed into C-130; some casualties; may be very serious; team transferring into another C-130. [I was sickened with concern about our men. Brief delays seemed like hours as I waited to obtain accurate reports about casualties. All of us sat quietly, very tense. I prayed.]

6:21 P.M. President informed by Jones that a number dead in

the crash—helicopter crew, pilot of C-130, and some passengers [members of the rescue team]. The rest are being extricated by C-130. [In taking off to move away from the loaded transport planes, the helicopters had kicked up clouds of dust with their swirling blades. In the poor visibility, one of the helicopters had flown into the nose of the airplane, which itself was preparing to take off. The two aircraft were engulfed in flames, and it was impossible to extract the bodies of the dead Americans. All others were loaded in the other five C-130's and left Desert One, en route to Masirah, a small island off the coast of Oman. Our men had been on the ground for about three hours.]

7:05 P.M. President informed by Jones that at least six probably dead; the team will be back on the ground [in Masirah] around 10:00 P.M.

7:45 P.M. The group without the President convenes in the Cabinet Room to work on necessary notifications and statements. [I sat alone in my small office, listing everything I needed to do to prevent any harm to our hostages, to protect our agents in Tehran, to notify leaders of other nations in the area, and to inform some American leaders and later the general public. First, we had to get our rescue team out of Iran, undetected if possible.]

8:05 P.M. The President joins group in Cabinet Room. [I sent for CIA Director Stan Turner to determine how much time our agents deployed in Tehran for the rescue mission would need to leave the country or to protect themselves from discovery.]

9:05 P.M. Turner joins the group. Discussion of the situation in Iran and implications for public statement. [We had a long discussion about the timing of a public announcement. It was necessary to delay any acknowledgment of our presence in Iran until all our team was out of the country. As soon as it was safe to do so, we wanted to anticipate the Iranians with our announcement of the operation, so as to prevent their exaggeration of the rescue mission into an all-out invasion—a version that might cause them to harm the hostages. We had a number of people stationed in Tehran with trucks, radio equipment, and other compromising materials, who had to be notified and given a chance to protect themselves.]

11:05 P.M. Brown provides fuller debrief on the situation: all helicopter crews accounted for; eight dead, and three burned. [I directed that once the dead men's identities were known, Harold Brown and Fritz Mondale would be responsible for notifying their families.]

11:55 P.M. The President decides public announcement at 2:00

A.M.—changes that to 1:00 A.M., with congressional calls to begin immediately. [We had picked up a few gendarmerie radio broadcasts, although no official alarm had been raised in Iran even three hours after our planes had cleared Iranian airspace.]

The next morning, I dictated a final diary entry.

> *The cancellation of our mission was caused by a strange series of mishaps—almost completely unpredictable. The operation itself was well planned. The men were well trained. We had every possibility of success, because no Iranian alarm was raised until two or three hours after our people had all left Iran.*
>
> *I was exhausted when I finally got to bed, after calling Rosalynn in Texas to tell her to cancel her campaigning for tomorrow and to come on home. She was most disturbed, because she didn't have any way to know what had happened. She knew from my guarded comments that we had had serious problems, but I did not want to give her any reports on the telephone.*
>
> *I had planned on calling in a few members of the House and Senate early Friday morning, before the rescue team began its move into Tehran, in accordance with Bob Byrd's suggestion and Lloyd Cutler's advice. But I never got around to that.*   DIARY, APRIL 24–25, 1980

I am still haunted by memories of that day—our high hopes for success, the incredible series of mishaps, the bravery of our rescue team, the embarrassment of failure, and above all, the tragic deaths in the lonely desert. I actually slept a couple of hours, and then got up early to prepare my television broadcast, which would explain to the American people what had occurred.

In my brief statement, I took full responsibility for the mission, outlined what had happened, and gave my reasons for the effort. I reminded the world of the continuing Iranian crime and praised the courageous volunteers who had given their lives for the freedom of others.

I will always remember the people who gave me their support that day. The first one who called after my early-morning announcement was Henry Kissinger, full of praise and approval of our attempt and offering to help me in any possible way. I asked him to call the networks and wire services and make a statement. He did so right away. Sadat also offered his immediate help, as did Prime Minister Ohira and most of our European allies. Among the American people, we had overwhelming support, for which I was particularly grateful.

As soon as they returned home, I wanted to meet the members of the rescue team (known as "Delta"). Without any notice to the news media, I flew to see the team on Sunday, April 27. Their identities and location were confidential. When I stepped off the helicopter, Colonel Beckwith was waiting. He was really a tough guy, a former University of Georgia football player who had grown up a few miles from my hometown of Plains and had dedicated his life to self-sacrifice for our country in the most dangerous and personal kind of combat service. His chin was quivering and tears were running down his cheeks. I opened my arms, and we embraced and wept together. He said, "Mr. President, I'm sorry we let you down!" For a few moments he couldn't talk, while I expressed with all my heart my appreciation for what his men had done. Then he said, "Will you let us go back?" I told him we were in the struggle together, and that I would do everything possible to find freedom for our fellow Americans. I meant to bring them out, and I would certainly rely on the Delta team, as we had before, if I decided it was necessary. Although I did not say it at the time, I knew that the Iranians would be vigilant about detecting another intrusion into their country; the hostages were being dispersed to various locations then unknown to us. Furthermore, we had not been able to devise a significantly different rescue scheme that was feasible—and to repeat the first one might be suicidal.

Beckwith told me that after the last helicopter had failed in the desert, he had made an instant decision to recommend withdrawal, and that he had no doubt it was right. I asked why they had not destroyed the remaining helicopters before they left Iran, and he explained that the helicopters were loaded with ammunition; any fires or explosions would have endangered the C-130's on which their lives depended.

I also met with five Iranians who had helped us with the mission. They, too, were eager to return and assist us. Then I went around and talked to every one of the men individually, expressing to them again and again our nation's gratitude for their heroism. They were superb. I would not hesitate to put my own life into their hands.

Now that the mission was over, I had to choose a new Secretary of State. When I returned to Washington, I met with my staff members and other advisers to tell them that Cy had resigned and to get their ideas. I said that Zbig had immediately told me he did not want to be considered and that my own choice was Senator Edmund Muskie, with Warren Christopher as my next choice if Ed was not available. They were unanimous in their belief that either Muskie or Christopher would be an excellent choice.

The next day, Senator Muskie discussed the matter with his wife, his staff, and the governor of Maine, and decided without hesitation to take the job. Warren Christopher was pleased with this decision. The members of Congress were astonished that Muskie would be leaving the Senate, but happy that Ed would be Secretary of State. So was I.

We then had to respond to a rash of false news reports about the rescue operation. Among them were charges that I had slashed back on the Defense Department plans and made them inoperable and that Colonel Beckwith and his men had wanted to go forward with the mission, but I had terminated it over their objections. Secretary Brown wanted to let Beckwith answer some questions from the press, but Charlie had been trained to conceal his identity and was reluctant to do it. He insisted on coming by to explain to me why he was going public.

With Colonel Charles Beckwith

While he was in the Oval Office, he paid me a compliment that may never be exceeded. With some embarrassment, he said, "My men and I have decided that our boss, the President of the United States, is as tough as woodpecker lips." Before he left, we agreed that he and I would walk together behind a bird dog around the fields of our native south Georgia—some day when both of us had more time.

The first Saturday in May, I invited Muskie, Brown, Christopher, Brzezinski, Aaron, and several of their top assistants to Camp David for an extensive discussion about foreign affairs and the relationship between the White House and the State Department.

> *After our discussion, my strong opinion is that Ed should be a senior statesman and a spokesman for our country on foreign policy, and minimize his detailed work within the Department, his negotiating time, and also his role in protocol affairs. These were the three things that Cy had spent much of his time doing, and was very reluctant to be a strong spokesman—I think because of natural modesty.*   DIARY, MAY 3, 1980

Ed Muskie assumed some of the State Department concerns about White House "competition," but the issue was relatively unimportant to him. He enjoyed the role of public spokesman, and had an easier relationship than Vance with Zbig and the staff around the Oval Office. Not as knowledgeable as Cy about the details of diplomacy, Ed nevertheless brought to the Secretary's office a broad and mature understanding of our nation itself and its international role, derived from his years as governor and senator, his leadership in the Democratic party, and his campaigns for top national office. Even more than Cy had, he depended on Deputy Secretary of State Warren Christopher. In fact, all of us depended on Christopher, whom I have described openly (without any dissenting comments) as the best public servant I ever knew.

One of the most difficult duties I had to face as President was the memorial service held on May 9 at Arlington National Cemetery for the eight servicemen killed in Iran. I had already visited the three injured men in a Texas hospital. Now we would honor the dead. All the families were to be there, and I was painfully aware of their sorrow. I wanted to express my condolences and thanks to them, but feared that some of them might rebuff me because I was the one who had ordered the rescue mission to be launched. As Rosalynn and I entered the small waiting room, I saw the wives, children, and parents of the men whose bravery we had come to recognize. They were watching me as we approached. One of the young wives came forward and held her hands out to me, and she was soon in my arms. The little children also reached out in an attitude of friendship, some of the smallest ones clasping me around my legs. I spoke to each of them. They were very proud that their loved ones had been courageous enough to endanger their lives for their country, for their fellow citizens, and for the cause of liberty. They all seemed more concerned about my feelings than their own sorrow. I was overwhelmed with gratitude toward the brave men who had been lost, and to their families who gathered around me. Their quiet courage and sensitivity exemplified in a special way the voluntary sacrifice and nobility of the men and women who served in the military forces, dedicated to preserving the freedom of us all.

Memorial Service, May 9, 1980

BELEAGUERED

I have a lot of problems on my shoulders but, strangely enough, I feel better as they pile up. My main concern is propping up the people around me who tend to panic (and who might possibly have a better picture of the situation than I do!).   DIARY, JULY 31, 1980

T he reaction of the Iranians to the rescue mission was mixed. At first, they were confused and frightened about the nature of the American military presence in their country. Then the officials claimed that, in some way, they had repulsed our forces. But soon they had to admit that no alarm had been sounded anywhere in Iran until we had announced that the operation was over. This realization caused the different leaders in Iran to blame each other for the failure to detect so large a military force. The final and prevailing reaction of the Iranians was to claim a great victory over the United States; the embarrassing photographs of our damaged aircraft were vivid evidence to back their claim.

I certainly took no pleasure or amusement in this, although I hoped that their emphasis on our failure would help prevent any further harm to the hostages. Later I learned from some of them that the raid had frightened their guards into treating them better— one consolation. After the captive Americans were dispersed to several secret locations, they were kept under heavy guard and also moved from place to place in order to keep them concealed from us. Even with a maximum intelligence effort, there was no way to tell exactly where all of them were.

Now the Iranians were in the throes of choosing their public officials and trying to form a government. With little previous experience in democratic processes, they went through a series of elections, including multiple runoffs for the members of parliament, subsequent elections for a speaker, and then the nomination and ultimate election of a prime minister. Both Khomeini and Bani-Sadr had announced that the *majlis* would make the final decision on what to do with the imprisoned Americans, and

524

I waited from week to week, observing their political comedy of errors with impatience and chagrin.

For a while, Bani-Sadr and I had the same goal—to avoid any further direct confrontation between our two countries. I did not wish the nervous Iranians to kill the hostages, and we both wanted an end to Iran's tedious election process.

During a White House briefing for community leaders on April 30, a visitor asked a pertinent question: "Mr. President . . . in view of the most recent developments in Iran, is there a chance that the people can see you, that you can be with them and you can get out in the countryside, you can get out in the States and be with us?"

It was time for me to give the answer which my aides and I had been discussing for a long time. I replied, "Yes," and explained that although extraordinary circumstances had demanded my presence in the White House and still required most of my time, many of my responsibilities had been alleviated. I would always keep before the American people the plight of the hostages, but a rescue attempt, although unsuccessful, had been completed; our allies were giving us better support with Iran; the sanctions against the Soviet invaders had been defined; our anti-inflation proposals were being favorably considered by Congress; and I believed we would soon have a comprehensive energy policy for our country. I added, "None of these challenges are completely overcome, but I believe they are manageable enough for me to leave the White House for a limited travel schedule."

From this remark, some news reporters claimed that I now thought the hostage situation was manageable. If anyone knew how difficult it was to manage, I did.

Although I actually traveled very little, it was a relief to know that I was no longer constrained to stay so close to Washington. I had worked out with my security advisers the procedures and placement of forces to meet any foreseeable development in Iran. But I hoped that my announcing a more normal schedule would help to relieve tension and might contribute to an expeditious decision by the Iranian parliament to release the Americans. Also, as the question indicated, I needed to have more direct contact with the American people. I could answer their questions, better receive their suggestions, and, I hoped, let them demonstrate their support for my policies.

Even with a substantial lowering of rhetoric in Iran and in the United States, I continued to keep the economic and political pressure on Iran. I maintained our military forces in the seas near the Iranian coast, continued the trade embargo, and sent their leaders reminders of my long-standing threats—to interrupt all their commerce if the hostages were placed on trial, and to inflict severe military punishment if any were harmed.

I was also pursuing measures against the Soviet Union, whose troops were still in Afghanistan. Throughout the spring, Congress and I had been trying to induce the United States Olympic Committee and the committees in as many other nations as possible not to attend the Olympic Games scheduled in Moscow. This was a difficult task, coordinated by Presidential Counsel Lloyd Cutler. We had to struggle all the way; the outcome was always in doubt. Most Olympic committees were wholly independent bodies, whose members deeply resented any government involvement in their decisions. Nevertheless, in television interviews, speeches, and through direct appeals during their official meetings, I and many other national leaders pointed out that it would be a violation of Olympic principles of good sportsmanship and fair play to be guests of the Soviet Union under existing circumstances.

After a heated debate, the United States Committee, on April 22, decided by an overwhelming vote not to send a team to Moscow; eventually fifty-five nations made the same decision. A few others merely sent token groups or allowed individuals to go to Moscow on their own.

During the early months of 1980 the most serious domestic problem was inflation. The runaway price of oil triggered by the Iranian revolution had brought rapid increases in the inflation rate throughout the world. In the first quarter of the year, the wholesale price index had increased more than 25 per cent in Italy, Great Britain, and Japan, and more than 13 per cent in West Germany, where for decades the control of inflation had been a prime consideration. Our rate of increase, at 20 per cent, was slightly better than most. Still, that we shared the problem with others did not help us; we had to do something about inflation in the United States.

In March, to meet the problem, I called upon Congress to make major revisions in the federal budget I had presented in January. I had already worked for three years to impose budgetary discipline on the federal government, with some success. After inheriting a 1976 budget deficit of $66 billion, amounting to about 4 per cent of the GNP (Gross National Product) of our country, I now had a 1981 budget before Congress with a projected deficit of only .5 per cent of the GNP. My new goal was to reduce the deficit to zero. This would be a great achievement in itself, and would tell the American public and the business and financial communities that Congress and I had the ability to take strong action against inflation and budget deficits, even in an election year.

The Republicans were cautiously supportive, committed in principle to reducing the deficit, but obviously reluctant to be ahead of the Democrats in proposing difficult budget cuts that might be politically unpopular. The congressional leaders and I went ahead with our plans. We worked more closely on devising a balanced budget than we had on any previous issue. The budget committees gave this effort top priority and worked steadily with my Office of Management and Budget, the White House staff, and Cabinet officers. As frequently as possible, I joined the discussions, and also coordinated our total effort with the Chairman of the Federal Reserve System. We were all determined to succeed, and finally agreed on enough specific budget reductions and other actions to reach our goal—provided that our commitments would indeed be carried out and that the economic projections of OMB and the Congressional Budget Office were accurate.

> *In the evening I met for an hour or so with the key Senate and House Democrats who had worked on the anti-inflation package. It was an inspirational meeting. The members of Congress were so proud of themselves.... [They] have been] willing to cooperate.... The outcome of it, I think, will be a good anti-inflation proposal.*
> DIARY, MARCH 13, 1980

To demonstrate their resolve at the time, the congressional leaders had even called on me to exercise my authority to impose an oil-import fee, in order to reduce imports and raise additional revenue, which would insure that we would not develop a budget deficit. I welcomed the suggestion, although the impact of the import fee would be felt in gasoline price increases of about ten cents a gallon. I made clear to the congressional leadership my willingness to take full responsibility for this action. They promised to stand firm in face of the inevitable pressures from lobbyists for the oil companies and others.

On March 14, I announced the result of our work to the public, and we began drafting the revised budget document. I was proud of what had been evolved, because it required a lot of courage among the members during an election year to support a $13 billion cut in budget expenditures, imposition of a hiring freeze and reductions in federal personnel, selective restraints on credit, which I requested from the Federal Reserve, and the conservation fee on imported oil. Revenue from the oil fee was not needed to balance the budget, but would be used as a reserve fund if our economic projections proved to be disappointing.

With the approval of most congressional leaders, at the end of March I was able to sign and send to them a balanced budget for Fiscal Year 1982. We congratulated each other on this rare achievement, although we all realized that it was much easier to devise a program than to get enough votes to pass every part of it.

> This balance in the budget has been brought about not by increasing revenues or taxes, but by reductions in expenditures. This will be the first balanced budget that our nation has had in 12 years, and only the second balanced budget in the last 20 years. . . . We have a real fight ahead. It is not going to be an automatic thing that we succeed, but I'm absolutely determined that we shall succeed. . . . I'll exercise my authority as President to veto bills that I consider to be a threat to a balanced budget.
> REMARKS AT SIGNING CEREMONY, MARCH 31, 1980

Financial-market reaction and a reduction in consumer spending indicated almost immediately that there was a lot of confidence on the part of the financial community and the public in the unprecedented bipartisan commitment by the administration, the members of Congress, and the Federal Reserve Board. Interest rates began to drop about 1 per cent per week. My economic advisers were predicting that the inflation rate would be no more than 6 per cent by late summer and fall.

Consumer spending was also reduced drastically—too drastically. Although only slight restraints were imposed on credit-card use, many card holders began to believe that it was almost unpatriotic to buy items on credit. Because of this and other reasons, our country went into a very brief but steep recession. Soon officials of the Treasury Department and the Federal Reserve had to tell consumers that it was all right for them to resume more normal buying habits.

The downward trend in inflation and interest rates boded well for home-building and other industries—but these same favorable results, along with the indications of recession, seemed to lessen public pressure on Congress to hold the line on the budget deficit.

Unfortunately, Congress was also under strong pressure from both ends of the political spectrum. From the right, with Governor Ronald Reagan as its chief spokesman, came demands for unprecedented tax cuts and defense expenditures. From the left, Senator Kennedy orchestrated the cry for an expensive new round of government programs for jobs, housing, health, welfare, and the like.

Caught in the middle, the centrist members of Congress were finding it very difficult to act on their part of the program to hold down spending and maintain taxes. Some of them were now trying to take away from me the authority I already had to impose an oil-import fee. We had agreed to cut federal spending by more than $13 billion and to increase revenue through more efficient collection of taxes, but no action was being taken on these items by Congress. This was to be a running battle between us during the remainder of the year, contributing to the divisions within the Democratic party and to the image that we could not act together to control deficit spending and inflation.

> *I had a disappointing meeting with the Democratic congressional leadership. There is no discipline, and growing fragmentation in Congress. The Senate voted yesterday, for instance, for a budget that would be balanced only if part of the oil-import fee was to be used, and at the same time voted with only 19 dissents to put a restraint on the imposition of the import fee. The Congress disgustingly refrains from passing the other two energy bills, and on occasion can't even get the conference committees to meet. Jim McIntyre feels that they may not even get . . . appropriations bills in final form until after the election in November. They are running out of time, and I am running out of patience. This is a new low in performance for the Congress since I've been in office.*
>
> DIARY, MAY 13, 1980

The import fee was a test case. After I announced in March, with congressional support, that the fee would be imposed, the oil industry and other lobbyists had gone to work on Capitol Hill. In this particular case, the oil companies were able to marshal public support against increased gasoline prices, and the congressional leaders simply abandoned their commitment and capitulated. On June 4, a resolution killing the fee was passed in the Senate (by 73 to 16) and the House (by 376 to 30).

Now I had to make a very difficult decision. In order to sustain my veto, I would have to get at least one-third of the votes in either the Senate or the House, but indications were that the votes were not there. I hated to have a veto overridden by a

Congress dominated by my own party. This had not happened to a Democratic President since Harry Truman's time—in 1952. However, it was crucial to our country that the anti-inflation program remain intact. I also considered it a matter of principle to do everything possible to carry out the announced commitments of our party's leaders, even if they had backed off. On June 5, the day after Congress voted, I vetoed the bill that included a provision to take away my authority to control oil imports, and asked the Democratic leadership to back me on this issue and help me get the votes to sustain my veto.

Because of the strong sentiments expressed in their vote on the measure, our efforts in the House of Representatives were hopeless, but I still had a chance in the Senate. We had been making some progress, depending on the Democratic congressional leaders to hold together the support of at least thirty-four senators. However, at the last minute, primarily because of the unpopularity of the proposed increase in the gasoline tax, the Senate effort collapsed. On June 6, my veto was overridden.

This outcome drove another deep crack into our common effort to control inflation and keep the budget balanced. Politically, the vote was a public confirmation of the schism that had developed in our party—a problem that would prove to be much more intractable than we suspected at the time.

The divisions in our party continued to widen during the election campaign. Jerry Brown had withdrawn from the race in early April, but many Democrats, genuinely concerned about my relatively conservative policies on tax and budget matters, rallied to the Kennedy banner. Others saw me as excessively embattled and politically vulnerable.

Although I was challenged strongly in some of the states, from the earliest days I was confident of gaining the nomination because of the overall favorable results of the many caucuses and primary elections. It was clear from our polling data that the American people did not want Edward Kennedy to lead the nation. He showed up fairly well as a candidate within the Democratic party, but much of his voter approval melted away even among his own supporters when they faced the prospect of his actually serving in the White House.

We had to face one recurring problem: whenever it seemed obvious that the ultimate contest with Kennedy would be decided in my favor, the people tended to use the primaries simply as a protest—a means to express their displeasure about the hostages, the economy, or any other aggravating issue. This kind of reaction resulted in uneven election results and delayed our final, inevitable victory. Furthermore, some titillated voters simply did not want to see the contest ended, and would vote for the underdog just to keep it going. (I remembered with mixed emotions the good old days when I had profited from these votes at the expense of the more likely winners.) Paradoxically, some of our worst election results came when I seemed most certain to win the Democratic nomination.

Fritz and I needed several months to pull together our badly divided party, to prepare for the general election, and to have some uninterrupted time during which the stigma of politics would not impede my efforts to deal with domestic and foreign issues as a President rather than as a candidate. But my hopes that I could rise above the fray were soon dashed, and I came to realize again how attractive a political goal the Oval Office is. When it became obvious that I would win far more delegates than were necessary for the nomination, Kennedy and his supporters tried a new tack.

During the last week in May they began calling for an "open convention." Since I was sure to win a substantial majority of the delegates in the caucuses and primary elections, the only remaining chance to defeat me was to induce some of my delegates to vote differently at the convention from the way their people had instructed them at home. It was only natural that the other hopefuls, the news media, and those who wanted to continue the exciting contest would grab this banner of an open convention and run with it. Although the proposal sounded democratic, in an open convention the delegates could ignore the results of the state elections, violate their promise to represent the expressed preference of voters, and be free to negotiate on their own. It really amounted to a call for a "brokered" convention, where the final decisions would be made by secret trading for delegate votes in the private rooms of the convention hall.

I was very angry about this effort to make last-minute changes in our party rules. His overwhelming defeat in the primaries having disproved Kennedy's major premise for running—that he could win and I could not—there was no logical reason for him to persist in the debilitating campaign which so weakened his party's chances for success in November. The result of his protracted effort was that Fritz and I were required to spend an enormous amount of our time and resources after the convention in winning Democratic voters back to our side. Many of them were alienated permanently by Kennedy's repeated claims that old people had to eat pet food because I did not care for them, or that I had betrayed the principles of our party and was no different in political philosophy from Ronald Reagan.

In an attempt to heal our differences, immediately after the primary elections and before the convention, I invited Senator Kennedy to the White House for the sole purpose of persuading him to support the Democratic ticket in the general election. After some delay, he finally came to see me.

> *It took him about an hour to fumble around and say we still had issues dividing us, and we needed to have a personal debate in front of the TV cameras in order to resolve those differences. However, he would not agree to support me and Fritz even if we had such a debate.*
>
> *... I told him that we would treat his people fairly at the convention, that I intended to get a majority of the delegates, and the best way to resolve any differences between us on issues was through the platform process, including an open floor debate, before the delegates' vote. He discounted this process completely, and seems to be obsessed with the idea of a personal debate.*
>
> DIARY, JUNE 5, 1980

Under any circumstance, he would have a major role to play at the convention—a chance to speak and enunciate his views through the platform proposals to be put forward by his supporters. Apparently this was not enough.

In addition to a splintered political party, I had many other problems to face as President and as the prospective Democratic nominee for reelection. Although at first there had been strong support for my effort to rescue the hostages, disillusionment grew rapidly after my failure to gain their freedom. During the next three months, my standing in the public-opinion polls fell; one survey showing that only about 20 percent of those interviewed approved of my handling of the Presidency. I could certainly understand their feelings, because I shared their anger and frustration about the hostages. There were no encouraging signs from Iran, the situation in the Middle East was not improving, more and more Soviet troops were being sent into Afghanistan—and our allies were divided about ways of dealing with all these problems.

At home, Congress was in disarray and, unknown to me then,

my brother Billy's relations with Libya were about to become a political cause célèbre in the press.

I was not dejected by all these circumstances, but simply took one day at a time and worked even harder than usual to try to overcome as many of the difficulties as possible. All of us in the White House and on the campaign trail were doing our best, and I felt confident that eventually the American people would come to realize that there were no better alternatives than the ones I had chosen. Rosalynn and I had a kind of blind faith that we would be successful in overcoming great political odds, as we had done so many times before.

As the hostage problem continued to be a fact of daily life, it seemed that one crisis followed another—or, rather, was added to the one that never went away. In the spring and summer I had to deal with a stream of illegal Cuban refugees who began coming to our country. We welcomed the first ones to freedom, but when the stream became a torrent, I explored every legal means to control the badly deteriorating situation. Even so, it was impossible to stop all of them, just as we had never been able to intercept the hundreds of thousands of Mexicans who pour across our common border each year.

Because of problems within Castro's regime, at least 10 per cent of the total population of Cuba was trying to escape, and looking for any possible means to come to the United States. At the same time, in Miami and throughout our country, there were tens of thousands of Cuban–American families eager to bring their relatives out of Cuba to join them here. In many cases these people were influential, with the financial resources to pay for their relatives' travel either openly or by a clandestine route.

Under pressure at home, Castro began actively encouraging many Cubans to emigrate. Although most of the emigrants were good citizens, we were soon to discover that some were mental patients and criminals. Other countries in the Caribbean region did not want any of the Cubans. Even when we were successful in diverting boatloads to Costa Rica or Colombia, many of the refugees eventually succeeded in realizing their fondest desire—to reach the shores of Florida.

I sympathized with the plight of the refugees, but they were coming in illegally, and I was sworn to uphold the laws of our land. Yet, in this area, my enforcement power was relatively limited. Historically, our country has had a policy of accepting immigrants (including the parents and ancestors of most of us)—and our laws had been designed accordingly. I could only keep the number to a minimum, and struggle to process the refugees in accordance with the laws of the United States. We treated the new immigrants properly and humanely, but it was costly in political popularity.

On May 19, a natural tragedy had occurred which was very costly in lives and property. The eruption of Mount St. Helens, about seventy-five miles south of Seattle, was the most formidable natural disaster with which I had to deal as President. There were dozens of casualties, silt deposits covered a broad area hundreds of miles to the north and west, and clogged river channels isolated many cargo ships upstream. We faced a multistate job of cleaning up the mess, which required the closest cooperation among all levels of government and would eventually cost about one billion dollars in federal disaster-relief funds alone. This mountain area had been monitored closely by the volcanologists, and the eruption was not unexpected, but the intensity of the explosion had been greatly underestimated. A few scientists had perished, many visitors to the beautiful wilderness area were missing, and some of the permanent residents who had ignored repeated warnings were buried under volcanic ash.

> *I flew out to the area three days after the eruption to see what could be done about the damage and to receive an assessment of the threat of further volcanic activity. . . . We left early the next morning by helicopter for an almost unbelievable inspection tour. . . .*
>
> *The volcano had erupted with an explosive force which the scientists estimated to be equal to 10,000,000 tons of TNT, and the damage was frightening. Trees in the line of sight of the blast had been burned instantaneously fifteen miles away, and then the pressure wave which followed had leveled every tree in an area of 150 square miles. One cubic mile off the north side of the mountain had been pulverized, most of it into ash the consistency of face powder, and this ash had flowed like water down the mountain, carrying large chunks of ice from the snow and mountain glaciers, plus white-hot molten lava which bubbled up out of the earth in mighty streams.*
>
> DIARY, MAY 22, 1980

The horrible destruction, the total devastation of the landscape as we knew it, was a reminder of my responsibility to reduce the threat of a much greater catastrophe that was under our control—

nuclear war. I wanted to keep the SALT process alive and lay the groundwork for controlling the tactical weapons being focused on Europe. In June 1979, after rejecting my proposal for a freeze on nuclear weapon production and deployment, the Soviets had rushed to complete the installation of their SS-20 missiles.

Because of the rapidly developing imbalance in intermediate-range missiles in Europe, other NATO leaders and I decided in December 1979 to meet this threat with a limited number of Pershing 2 missiles and ground-launched cruise missiles, to be deployed in Europe beginning in 1983. We had been working to correct the disparity ever since I began in office, but it had proved extremely difficult to get agreement among all our European allies to deploy the retaliatory weapons. Now the Dutch and Belgian leaders equivocated to some degree on the joint effort, but the other nations made a firm commitment to proceed.

It was not always easy to do so. Some people in the Western countries were ready for us to yield nuclear dominance to the Soviets in Europe, and to depend on the benevolent spirit of the Soviet leaders instead of on our own strength and will to defend ourselves and to keep the peace. This misguided attitude would remove any incentive for the Soviets to negotiate on arms control, and make it impossible to restrain intermediate-range nuclear weapons through mutual agreement between East and West.

As we approached the June 22 economic summit conference in Venice, a serious problem developed between Chancellor Schmidt and me. In his campaign speeches in April, he had first made a statement that some kind of three-year moratorium might be advisable on the deployment of any more nuclear weapons in the European theater. The English translation of his remarks read: "It would serve the cause of peace if during the next three years both sides were to desist from any further deployments and begin negotiations on mutual limitations soon."

This statement was widely interpreted by the press and some of our more doubtful allies as a reversal of Germany's position and an abandonment of the December 1979 agreement for NATO to deploy additional missiles. I knew that this interpretation had been of concern to Helmut himself, because he had called me immediately after his speeches to say that the European press was distorting his comments. He told me he was not in favor of a freeze on NATO's deployment of new weapons, but was merely suggesting that we might begin negotiations with the Soviets during the time it would take us to install our missiles. This was a possible interpretation of his remarks, but the emphasis of his explanation to me was completely different from what he was saying to the German public. We both wanted to minimize any damage that might have been caused to allied unity by his statement. He told me that in order to calm some of the furor in Europe, he planned to contact the political and military leaders in the Netherlands, Belgium, Italy, and other countries and tell them what he had actually meant.

Schmidt's remarks had alarmed me, but his public statement that he stood firmly behind the NATO agreement to modernize our forces, and my understanding that he was calling the other European leaders, partially alleviated my concern.

For a while I forgot about the incident, but then news stories and diplomatic reports made me realize that Schmidt was repeating a version of his original comment in the politically charged forums of Germany. Again, his finely tuned suggestions were being interpreted as a proposal for a moratorium, and some of our allied leaders were calling Washington to express their dismay.

Muskie, Brown, and Brzezinski drafted a message expressing our concern about the confusion generated by Schmidt's statements. After I approved the text, it was sent to Bonn. At first there was no adverse reaction to the message, but later, when the general substance of the dispatch became known to the public, the Chancellor began to feel that he had been embarrassed by our criticism. After he complained about it, I reexamined its wording closely to see if we had inadvertently been offensive in some way, but the message seemed appropriate as drafted, and we could not understand the reason for his displeasure. We had been very careful to refer to "conflicting press reports," which "incorrectly have claimed that you have proposed an East-West freeze on TNF [theater nuclear force] deployments," and I had added to the closing paragraph the sentence: "When questioned by the press this week, I have stated that you were one of the originators of the common commitment to meet the formidable SS-20 threat with allied action on TNF, and that your position has not changed."

Before we could get to the annual economic summit conference, I heard that Helmut had become quite angry over the message. Since it was important for us to resolve any misunderstanding between us as soon as possible, I arranged to meet with him immediately after we both got to Venice. Muskie, Brzezinski, and Foreign Minister Hans-Dietrich Genscher were also present in the small hotel room.

Shortly after arriving I had an unbelievable meeting with

Helmut Schmidt ... ranting and raving about a letter that I had written him, which was a well-advised message. He claimed that he was insulted, that he had never reneged on any of his pledges. I told him that I knew he had not reneged, that the letter was not insulting. [In a long and rambling tirade, Helmut objected to parts of SALT II, complained about our inadequate aid to Pakistan, accused me of not being sincere in negotiating for nuclear arms control, remarked that Germany was not our 51st state, claimed that Vance had failed to carry out a promise to amend UN Resolution 242, said that Christopher and Brzezinski had misled him on the Olympics question, and so forth. Repeatedly, I tried to calm the Chancellor, to correct his errors, and to explain to him the position of the United States on the various charges he was making. Eventually, he relaxed enough to listen to what we were saying.]

Schmidt was quite emotional. When Zbig responded in a heated fashion, I tried to cool Zbig off. Ed Muskie then joined me in explaining to Schmidt why we all needed to support the theater nuclear force, and not create confusion about it. Schmidt then pointed out that he would carry an accurate, firm message to the Soviet Union leaders in Moscow, and asked me if I would make a statement to the press that I did have confidence in him, and that we agreed on the theater nuclear force. I told him that I would be glad to. We then went out and I made a statement to the press as we had agreed. He said he confirmed everything that I said. And then he departed. ... Later, when I saw Genscher, he said he was thankful that I handled the difficult situation as I did.

DIARY, JUNE 21, 1980

Helmut Schmidt seemed to be torn between the conflicting political forces in his country. In private conversations he was very tough in dealing with the Soviet threat, often the leader among Europeans in proposing strong action. But in German political debates, he emphasized the opposite facet of the same question and seemed reluctant to do anything which might be interpreted as anti-Soviet. At times this conflict made it difficult for Americans to understand him and was the reason for some of our problems. There were many reports from news reporters and others in Europe and in the United States concerning his critical comments about me, Secretaries Vance and Muskie, Dr. Brzezinski, and other officials in our government. These persistent criticisms, often highly publicized, helped to legitimize anti-American sentiments in Germany. Perhaps to compensate for these reports, Schmidt would publicly deplore any negative comments from others in Germany about the United States or its leaders.

During my four years in office, I had many fierce arguments with Prime Minister Begin and a few other national leaders about matters involving principle or policy, but this discussion in Venice was the most unpleasant personal exchange I ever had with a foreign leader. However, it was soon a thing of the past. The next morning, when we had a private breakfast for the seven heads of state, Helmut was very friendly, as though nothing had happened.

Since this was an economic summit, our primary discussions involved energy, inflation, unemployment, trade, investment, productivity, and how we could address these common themes individually and in concert. We also made sure that we had time to discuss diplomatic and political matters. I had three major goals: a mutual pledge of our best efforts to reduce the amount of energy consumed for a given level of productivity; continued support by the other nations in our fervent efforts to free the American hostages in Iran; and unanimous condemnation of the Soviet Union, with a strong demand that the Soviets withdraw their troops from Afghanistan.

The Japanese and British were standing very firmly with us on all these issues. The Canadians and Italians had little to say about the struggle with the Soviets, but were generally supportive. Pierre Trudeau reconfirmed his commitment that Canada would not exceed its normal wheat shipments to the Soviet Union. It was the French and Germans who concerned us most. Schmidt worked hard and kept his promise about the Olympic boycott, but the French Olympic Committee, with only half-hearted opposition from the government, had decided to send a team to Moscow. Further, Giscard had secretly arranged an apparently friendly meeting with Brezhnev in Poland after the invasion of Afghanistan, an act which proved to be as unpopular in France as it was in the United States. Both Giscard and Schmidt were under heavy pressure from leftist political groups to minimize their criticism of the Soviets.

There is a strong inclination at the summit meetings to evolve a unanimous report, either by compromises or by using more general language in order to avoid unresolved specific issues. Also, with an opportunity to discuss complicated matters personally, in private, rather than to depend on subordinates or diplomatic messages—or the news media—it is easier to resolve many differences. Finally, it is not as politically dangerous to approve a controversial point if six other leaders do the same.

This time the final communiqué was substantive. We committed ourselves to reduce the amount of energy used for a given level of economic growth by making our conservation efforts even more stringent. We adopted an ambitious agenda for trying in every possible way to break the OPEC stranglehold on the world economy, and we also completed an agreement on political matters—including strong and unanimous condemnation of the Soviet Union for threatening world peace by its thrust into Afghanistan.

On June 26, we returned to Washington. The 1980 Democratic Convention was less than two months away, and I really had a lot of political work to do. There were a number of prerequisites for a successful campaign year. We needed a united Democratic party, the precluding of a viable third-party challenge, a demonstration by me and Congress of an effective team effort in stabilizing the economy and controlling inflation, and, above all, the safe return of the American hostages from Iran. I was quietly confident, but as I assessed the political handicaps we faced, there was certainly no room for excessive optimism.

Shortly before going to Venice, I had met with leaders of the key financial institutions on Wall Street and found them very supportive of our economic policies. They had liked the budget and had not recommended any income tax reductions for 1980. They had expressed a preference for a moderate tax cut in 1981, of $20 or $30 billion at most—provided our anti-inflation program continued to work.

Now I returned from my European trip to face growing pressure in Congress for a relatively large tax cut in 1980—which, after the vote against the oil-import fee, would be the second major departure from our concerted anti-inflation program. If Congress was successful in legislating the tax reduction, the policy shift would be very damaging to our party's chances. Even talk about it was destroying confidence in the Democrats' ability to maintain a consistent economic policy during this election year.

Governor Reagan, who had become the apparent Republican nominee, was still calling for large additional increases in defense spending and for massive tax reductions—far beyond anything the country had ever seen. His program (known as Kemp–Roth) was based on the beguiling supposition that enormous tax cuts, primarily for corporations and very rich people, would give them more money to create jobs and would actually result in increased federal tax revenues, which could then be used for more weapons, and so forth. This ridiculous theory had been rejected with some scorn by both Democrats and Republicans when put forward by a few congressional candidates in 1978, but Reagan was a more persuasive salesman than those who had previously failed. He claimed that even with greatly increased spending as well as much less revenue from taxes, he could nevertheless balance the budget more quickly than we—and on a permanent basis! This combination of proposals defied economic logic, but public-opinion polls indicated that a substantial portion of the American people believed these promises. Their conviction did not concern me so much at the time; the big problem was that congressional leaders began to feel the political heat.

These leaders had been courageous back in March in their commitments to work with me and the Federal Reserve Bank to balance the federal budget. In those days, we had discussed at length the temptations that lay ahead as candidates entered the intense competition of trying to please the voters. The promise of low gasoline prices, new federal social programs, financial aid for local and state governments, big increases in the defense budget, and attractive tax reductions would inevitably be offered to a waiting public by some members of Congress before the election year was over. Fritz Mondale and I were determined to be resolute, trusting that a more responsible policy would stand the test of time and eventually (I hoped before election day) prove to be the best politics, after all.

In many congressional districts, opponents perennially vie to outdo one another in calling for a bigger military establishment—a contest that became a problem for us as Congress made its budget decisions. Although our original January budget proposal had included a real growth in military spending of about 5 per cent above and beyond the inflation rate, Congress was wanting to increase the defense budget an additional $7 billion, and even to include such wasteful items as the recommissioning of old aircraft carriers and battleships. But the most damaging blow to fiscal integrity had come while I was in Venice, when Senator Robert Byrd and some of the other Democratic leaders had announced their support for a tax reduction that would at least partially match Reagan's offer. Public confidence in our commitment to maintain discipline and fiscal restraint began to fade away, and we could feel new signs of increasing inflation and higher interest rates as those previously ebbing tides began to reverse.

For now, we had to decide how to handle this split in the ranks of the Democratic leadership.

We discussed among Miller, Schultze, Eizenstat, and Jody what our approach should be concerning the tax situation, since Miller's going to be on "Issues and Answers" tomorrow. We decided not to advocate a tax reduction for 1980, not to encourage the passage of a law even this year to be effective in '81, but to insist that the fiscal restraints on the budget and the anti-inflationary nature of any tax increase be included. We'll continue to wrap the Kemp–Roth proposal around Reagan's neck as best we can.

DIARY, JUNE 28, 1980

We kept working on the economy, monitoring various proposals that were surfacing from political leaders in both parties. Even my own economic advisers were not immune to the same temptations, as they attempted to act on my behalf.

We then had an economic meeting. The team [Mondale, Miller, Schultze, Eizenstat, Strauss, McIntyre, and others] came down, unanimous in asking me to approve a tax reduction and a moderate spending program to assuage Kennedy and to stimulate the economy. I was adamantly against it and, after considerable discussion, prevailed. I think everyone left convinced we had made the right decision: to hold firm; to oppose any tax reduction in 1980; to permit [a 1981 tax reduction] to be discussed, probably not voted on later this year; and not to deviate from our strict commitment to a restrained budget.   DIARY, JULY 13, 1980

A few days later, Federal Reserve Board Chairman Paul Volcker came by to let me know that he would give testimony to Congress, and that his position, as well as that of key economists, was compatible with mine. Former Chairman Arthur Burns also came to tell me that he would resist any tax cut this year, oppose any indexing of income tax, and that he planned to state his opinions openly and publicly. This kind of support was very helpful to me.

I had several meetings with the Democrats in Congress who were searching for a way out of the tax-reduction dilemma. There was great diversity of opinion among the leadership.

Byrd followed up on a conversation I had with Lloyd Bentsen last night, and put out the possibility of a joint resolution by Congress and signed by me that would commit the Democrats at least to a tax cut and other action in

1981, [and thereby] finesse the argument that presently exists between me and the Senate. That way, they'll have a tax "bill" this year. [Representative] Jim Wright [from Texas] thought there should be no tax cut; this is the best politics.

Russell Long took a typical attitude by saying, "Let the Senate pass a Christmas tree, but let the House pass a responsible bill. Work out the differences in Congress. If it is still irresponsible, Mr. President, you can always veto it." (I presume ten days before the election!) Dick Bolling, Al Ullman both took strong exception to this, as did Bill Miller and myself.   DIARY, JULY 22, 1980

When they saw that Kennedy had no chance to win, many of the liberals demanded that I adopt his positions on taxation and government spending, and began threatening to support Representative John Anderson, the Illinois Republican, who had decided to run as an independent candidate after all his efforts had failed in the Republican primaries. I considered Anderson a political chameleon, who would adopt any position in order to get a few votes or a newspaper headline. He was most successful with the media—almost always being treated favorably, and projected as a major candidate although he had no party, had been chosen by no convention, and had never won either a state primary election or a caucus victory. The political support his candidacy attracted was one of Governor Reagan's greatest assets, and one of my biggest liabilities.

The Republican Convention came and went with no surprises, except for the extraordinary, serious consideration by Reagan of letting former President Gerald Ford share the responsibilities of governing with him as an almost co-equal Vice President. This would have been a startling and unprecedented arrangement, but it was finally abandoned as representatives of the two men discovered the difficulty of dividing the Presidency into two parts.

I had not watched the television coverage of the convention, but I was pleased that Governor Reagan was the nominee. With him as my opponent, the issues would be clearly drawn. At the time, all my political team believed that he was the weakest candidate the Republicans could have chosen. My campaign analysts had been carefully studying what he had been saying during the Republican primary elections, and it seemed inconceivable that he would be acceptable as President when his positions were exposed clearly to the public. An enormous tax cut for the rich, slashes in social security and programs for the poor and aged, federal aid to private schools, an unprecedented increase in defense spending, a rejection of SALT, indifference to the proliferation of nuclear weapons, a preference of Taiwan over China, some evasive statements concerning civil rights and human rights, and a virtual rejection of the Camp David accords as a basis for peace in the Middle East were the kinds of expressed intentions that we thought would make him quite vulnerable. I did not realize then that the press and public would not believe that Reagan actually meant what he was saying—although we tried to emphasize the radical nature of his departure from the policies of my administration and from those of my predecessors in the White House.

I wanted to pursue these differences in a series of debates, beginning as soon as possible after the Democratic Convention.

> *In the morning, about 9:00 o'clock, I called Reagan and congratulated him on his victory. Told him that I would welcome a chance for several debates in different regions of the country. He responded favorably, and Fritz arranged to challenge George Bush to a debate also.*
>   DIARY, JULY 17, 1980

My political team wanted to schedule a long series of two-man debates, in order to overcome the natural advantage Reagan, as a professional performer, would have in a first debate. We were convinced that over a more extended period of time, he and I would have to get down to specific issues, where my knowledge of foreign and domestic affairs would give me an edge. Furthermore, all the public and private polls indicated that votes for John Anderson were much more likely to come at my expense, and so to concentrate all public attention on the two major-party candidates would help minimize this adverse factor.

The problem with our assessment was that the Republicans saw it the same way, and therefore insisted on just the opposite: to include the independent candidate, Anderson, as an equal in the televised debates or, as an alternative, to severely limit the number of head-to-head debates between me and Reagan, scheduling any such events as late as possible.

As the Democratic Convention approached, I continued to suffer an erosion of popular support. Too many of my current efforts, though necessary, were politically damaging. The grain embargo; the boycott of the Olympics; the oil-import fee; restraints on consumer spending; strict limits on federal expenditures for both domestic and defense items; energy conservation measures; patience in dealing with the hostages; arguments against a quick tax cut; attempts to resolve the Middle East dispute about Jerusalem, the West Bank, and the Golan Heights; the Democratic party debate about an "open" convention—all these made me vulnerable to criticism by my political opponents. I was convinced that my decisions had been the right ones. My hope was that the public would eventually agree with me, and that, in the meantime, there would be some good news on the economy or about the imprisoned Americans in Iran.

For now the news was mostly about my brother Billy and his relationship with Libya. It was the main story as I went to Camp David on July 25. Rosalynn stayed in Washington, preparing to go to Peru to represent me at the inauguration of the newly elected president there. She called me twice early in the morning, distressed at the wild news stories about Billy, Libya, me, and my administration, saying she needed to be calmed down before leaving for South America. I told her to reread the words of Jesus from our previous night's Bible chapter, which happened to be John 14 ("Let not your heart be troubled: ye believe in God, believe also in me").

～

For me, Rosalynn, our children, and my mother, the four years I spent as President were for the most part an exciting and rewarding time. The only one of our family who really suffered because of the experience was my brother Billy. Thirteen years younger than I, Billy was only five years old when I left home for a career in the Navy. I hardly knew him eleven years later, when Rosalynn and I returned to Plains after my father's death. As soon as he finished high school, Billy married his only sweetheart, Sybil Spires, and then joined the Marines. A few years after he had completed his four-year tour, I asked him to join me and Mother as a minority partner at Carter's Warehouse. He and I worked together until I moved to Atlanta as governor of Georgia. Then, Billy ran the warehouse business with only minimal direction from me.

When the hordes of news reporters descended on Plains during the final months of the 1976 presidential campaign, they found Billy to be hard-working, intelligent, well-read, witty, popular with the farmers in the area, and something of a country philosopher. Over the months he became caricatured, not unkindly, as an entertaining red-neck country bumpkin, always ready with a

lively quip about government, politics, the press, or any other subject of current interest. Billy liked to take the other side of any argument, and could hold his own in defending an unpopular and sometimes bizarre position. He enjoyed the attention and the growing popularity. He also took advantage of the chance to present the other side of the Carter family—not so serious, full of fun and laughter. Perhaps his most famous quote was, "My mother joined the Peace Corps when she was 70, my sister Gloria is a motorcycle racer, my other sister, Ruth, is a Holy Roller preacher, and my brother thinks he is going to be President of the United States! I'm really the only normal one in the family."

Billy became a natural for talk shows and television comedy, and was in great demand for highly paid appearances at public events. He was always certain to draw a big crowd and to give full value in entertainment. Eventually, these activities took their toll on him. He was making a lot of money, but he spent more and more time away from the warehouse and his family, and began to depend too much on alcohol to keep him going. A certain bitterness seemed to creep into his humor, both on the stage and in private gatherings, and we began to worry about him and about his health.

> *Talked to Billy about the warehouse, and how it was going. He still says he's going to leave the first of September, take some kind of public-relations job. . . . I hate to see Billy hurt himself. I'm afraid that he might take something that's very attractive while he's the center of media attention, but then in a year or so it would be gone and he won't have any stability in his life.* DIARY, JULY 28, 1977

In 1978, Billy made a highly publicized trip to Libya with a group of Georgia legislators and businessmen. Early the next year, when a Libyan delegation traveled around our country to decide where to locate a permanent trade mission, I learned from the news reports that Billy was serving as one of its hosts at a reception in Atlanta. This was of some concern to me, but it was not an earthshaking event. We had full diplomatic relations, Libya supplied us with more than 10 per cent of our imported oil, and there were many American investments in the country. Furthermore, the Governor, the President of Georgia Tech, and other officials were joining in the welcome to the visitors.

Billy quickly became the focal point for attacks from opposite sides. At first he was criticized among some friends and neighbors because some of the Libyan visitors were black. Then Billy's spur-of-the-moment answers to some probing questions from reporters caused more serious problems. When asked if he did not realize that his association with the Libyans would be criticized by American Jews, he replied, "There are a lot more Arabs than there are Jews." This statement was widely interpreted as being anti-Semitic. Billy denied these allegations, of course, but the damage was done.

All this was very disturbing to us in the White House. Both Jody and I were deluged with questions from news reporters. Billy explained to us exactly what he had said and assured us that none of it was intended as any kind of slur. However, almost all his public-appearance contracts were canceled overnight, and the news stories began to concentrate almost exclusively on his excessive drinking and "peculiar" acts and statements. What had been funny and attractive about him now became just the opposite. He was still the same person, but for the public his character had changed completely.

Matters went from bad to worse. Billy was deeply hurt and

confused; he soon admitted that he had become an alcoholic. He decided to face the problem squarely and try to overcome it, and became a patient at the alcoholism treatment center in Long Beach, California. He did extremely well. All of us who love him were pleased with his rapid progress and this proof of his personal courage.

To this date, Billy has never taken another drink—in spite of some terrible financial burdens and the highly publicized investigations of his relations with Libya.

Following the visit of the Libyan delegation to the United States, Billy's income dropped to nearly zero. He was having difficulty paying the debts he had accumulated during his halcyon days as a popular entertainer. Many of his friends left him, and the Libyans offered to help. Through intermediaries, they made arrangements for him to represent them in the sale of their high-quality oil, and agreed to lend him some money as an advance on future earnings. Before he was able to embark on this business venture, there was a lot of publicity about it, and a flood of accusations swamped him and his family—based primarily on his failure to register at the outset as an agent of a foreign country. This was a legal requirement, which Billy and his attorneys had been discussing with the federal agencies for several months.

Now, however, the Department of Justice, the Internal Revenue Service, and various congressional committee investigators descended on him. Billy was forced to spend his full time with accountants and lawyers, trying to answer subpoenas, produce old financial records, and counter the almost bewildering avalanche of charges made against him.

He was the President's brother, and therefore fair game. Each day, wild and exaggerated accusations would be made by or reported in the press, and each time the burden would be on Billy to prove his innocence. Any comment about him was sure to make instant headlines. My heart went out to Billy and his family, but his attorneys and mine recommended against our communicating directly with each other or exchanging any information or ideas that might be questioned later. Eventually, Billy was given a chance to testify at length before a Senate committee, and he placed all the facts on record. The worst that could be said in the end was that he made some errors in judgment, for which he paid dearly. In laborious detail he answered all the charges against him to the federal agencies, to Congress, and to the American public through the news media.

Many of the allegations involved me and others in my administration. There were public claims that Billy had improperly used his influence with our government concerning airplane sales to Libya, that I had interfered in the Justice Department investigation of Billy and given him confidential information about the case, and that Libyan money had been given to me or transferred to Carter's Warehouse in Plains. There was no truth in any of these trumped-up charges or others like them but it took us several weeks to compile a report to Congress certifying that *no one* in the entire government had done *anything* that was illegal or improper.

As the convention approached, I needed to work to heal the wounds in the Democratic party and to hold Congress together on our legislative program. Instead, I was bogged down answering a multitude of charges about myself and my administration that were absolutely baseless. The Libyan mess, which was dominating the news, was wreaking havoc with our efforts to deal with anything else on the political scene or in Congress, and I wanted to resolve it as soon as possible. Some of my staff members were getting desperate.

> *Their recommendation to me again was that we should make a preemptive offer to testify on the Hill. I questioned whether or not the committee working under Bob Byrd with Bob Dole, Senator [Charles] Mathias [of Maryland], and others in a highly charged atmosphere would be willing to arrange for my testimony to be given first, whether they would be organized, whether they would demagogue the question, and whether they had any intention of holding substantive hearings before the Democratic Convention.*
>
> DIARY, JULY 28, 1980

My arguments against going to testify before the congressional committee were effective; the next day I had everyone except Jody convinced it would be a serious mistake. Billy was already scheduled to testify, and I had a lot of confidence in him. People were inclined to underestimate his intelligence and his ability to communicate effectively. He was sober now and himself again, preparing for his upcoming sessions with the Senate investigators.

I met a second time with the congressional leaders and told them that I had prepared a complete report for the public and Congress; that there was nothing of which we needed to be ashamed—absolutely no secrets that would be embarrassing; and that I had instructed everyone in my government to reveal all the facts.

But the press continued to have a field day with the Billy–Libya issue. There was nothing we could do about it. Charges were flying right and left about me and others in our government. It was almost impossible for us to prove the innocence of an entire administration. A new charge that erupted just before the convention was that I had given Billy secret cables involving Libya, to help him in his dealings with the Libyans and perhaps in some way profit myself. The fact was that I had sent my brother a copy of an unclassified message from our Ambassador in Tripoli following Billy's visit there in 1978. The cable simply reported that Billy had behaved himself very well and that the Ambassador thought the visit was a positive event for our country. Soon afterward, the message had been issued to the press at the request of one of the national columnists. Now there were several days of lurid headlines before we could go through all the diplomatic messages dealing with Libya to be certain that none of them had improperly fallen into Billy's hands. It was inevitable that, again, the publicity about the explanation was minuscule compared to the original accusations.

After I completed the basic work on my convention speech and—almost simultaneously—my preparation for refuting all the allegations about Billy and Libya, I felt much better. I was confident that within a few days this crisis would be over, and that after the Democratic Convention I would have a chance to present my views to the public, let them be contrasted with Reagan's, and prevail in the election.

> *In preparing my own acceptance speech notes, it's become more and more obvious that Reagan and I have perhaps the sharpest divisions between us of any two presidential candidates in my lifetime—and also that his policies are a radical departure from those pursued by Ford and Nixon. I also am convinced that on the major issues—concerning the farmers, women, minorities, labor, educators, the elderly, and other groups—we're on the right side, and if we can present our case clearly to the American people, we will win overwhelmingly in November.*
>
> DIARY, JULY 31, 1980

My one-hour televised news conference August 4 was devoted almost entirely to the question of Billy's relationship with Libya and any possible ties among Billy, Libya, and my administration. There was nothing for me to hide. The news stories still had

to run their course, but we had successfully refuted all the allegations and broken the backs of those who had been threatening
daily to make some embarrassing revelation. The relief was tremendous. It was hard to believe how much time and effort it had
taken me and those who worked with me to present the facts to
the people, and how the press had ignored such crucial political
issues to concentrate so heavily on my brother.

Unfortunately, my political troubles with other Democrats were
not over.

For instance, a serious problem for me in New York was Mayor
Ed Koch, who claimed to be my supporter but overlooked few
opportunities to attack me and my administration. I had worked
closely with his selfless predecessor, Abe Beame, and with Governor Hugh Carey when New York City was facing bankruptcy.
With a good cooperative effort, involving Koch after his election,
we were successful in getting congressional approval for legislation which had worked well to ease the city's severe financial
problems. At that time, the new mayor had been effusive in his
thanks and his promises of undying friendship. Now, he seemed
determined to damage our campaign as much as possible. Fritz
and several others tried unsuccessfully to convince him that because the Democratic Convention was going to be held in New
York City (a decision that had been made many months before),
he should exhibit some degree of loyalty to the party, to me, and
to other Democratic candidates. I finally had a chance to talk
to him face to face.

> *I went to New York to speak to the Urban League....
> Koch rode in the car with me, and I gave him hell for his
> daily stabbing me in the back. He pulled out a list of
> things that he said could be done with only a stroke of the
> pen. They involved changing the basic general revenue-
> sharing laws that had been in effect since Nixon's admin-
> istration! I told him that with friends like him, I didn't
> need any enemies—and with supporters like him, I didn't
> need any Republican opponents.*   DIARY, AUGUST 6, 1980

The convention was to begin on Monday, August 11, and I was
not scheduled to arrive in New York until the third day, after the
voting on the party rules and most of the platform planks. Rosalynn
and I went to Camp David before the opening session, taking with
us long lists of delegates to be called about the upcoming rules

vote on the question of an open convention versus delegate loyalty. A vote against delegate loyalty would be interpreted as a vote against me and Fritz for the nomination. Working from 5 × 8 cards covered with biographical data, including the latest information about each person's allegiance, Rosalynn and I spent hour after hour on our two telephones, sharing notes and responsibilities as we talked to the people who were pledged to us by state law and by party rules. We reminded them, one by one, of old friendships and of the adverse consequences should they betray the trust of their people back home, who had already voted and who expected the delegates to cast their convention vote accordingly. Literally thousands of calls had already been made to this same group of Democrats by my supporters and by the Kennedy forces. Rosalynn and I concentrated on the most difficult ones or the ones who were influential enough to sway a few other votes. We had excellent results from our barrage of calls; our concerns soon faded away—in spite of the news reports that the issue was still very much in doubt.

I worked with my political team at the convention on how we might minimize the damage to Fritz and me from the more radical proposals that were being put forward in the platform debates. I was also writing my speech, pleased with the developing drafts. Without being negative in tone, my words were designed to show that the nation would be making a momentous decision between two basic philosophies of government.

The speech would lay the groundwork for the general election campaign. My immediate problem was to meet the challenge within my own party. The key question—equivalent to the nomination vote—came Monday night on the open-convention issue. We had done our homework, and our support was firm. When the vote finally came, we did even better than we had expected.

In the evening about 9:00 we got a good solid vote, with a 550 margin to hold our position on the rule—which in effect meant that the Kennedy campaign was over. He called shortly afterward to tell me that he was going to withdraw his name from contention. I asked him if he was going to endorse and be on the platform with me Thursday. He said that would depend on how we worked out the details of the platform planks. I pointed out to him that there had to be a lot of differences between us because that was the basis on which he ran against me and that we couldn't expect any substantial compatibility above

and beyond what we already hammered out. He agreed, and
seemed to be in a good mood.   DIARY, AUGUST 11, 1980

The next night during the platform debates, Senator Kennedy
made a very stirring and emotional speech, after which we
had the voice votes on a number of issues. The result was that
some planks in the platform were much more liberal than either
the general public or I wanted.

The following day Rosalynn and I went to New York for the
nomination vote. Since my family was in the convention hall, I
asked Bob Strauss, Charles Kirbo, Mayor Tom Bradley of Los
Angeles, and Esther Peterson to be with me at the hotel during the
vote. Although it was now certain we would win, we were surprisingly excited when the final decision came; it had been quite a
battle.

Early Thursday morning I jogged in Central Park, met with
various delegations during the day, and issued my own public
assessment of the platform, giving the reasons for my inability to
support some of the items. That night I went to Madison Square
Garden to accept the Democratic presidential nomination for the
second time. As I listened to Fritz Mondale give his fiery acceptance speech, I thought about all that had happened since the

first time, four years ago. Now I felt much older, more experienced, and more heavily burdened.

Reporting on Senator Kennedy's appearance with me on the platform after my speech, the news stories emphasized his lack of enthusiasm as an indication that the split in our ranks had not been healed. This accurate impression was quite damaging to our campaign, and was to linger for a long time.

THE ELECTION
OF 1980

Reagan is different from me in almost every basic element of commitment and experience and promise to the American people, and the Republican party now is sharply different from what the Democratic party is. And I might add parenthetically that the Republican party is sharply different under Reagan from what it was under Gerald Ford and Presidents all the way back to Eisenhower.

TOWN HALL MEETING, TRUMAN HIGH SCHOOL,
INDEPENDENCE, MO., SEPTEMBER 2, 1980

The convention marked the end of my downward spiral in the polls. On August 18, Rosalynn's birthday, we learned that Reagan's lead of 25 percentage points had been cut to 7—a remarkable turnaround. This seemed a good present for Rosalynn from the people of the country. My own gift to her was a beautiful little picture frame, within which I had written Ecclesiastes 9:9 in Spanish, translated from The Living Bible: "Live happily with the woman you love through the fleeting days of life, for the wife God gives you is your best reward down here for all your earthly toil." She and I agreed that we were now facing more earthly toil, which we hoped would end in a tangible reward on November 4.

Although I had never seriously considered refusing to run for reelection, it was now much easier for me to understand why President Lyndon Johnson had made such a decision in 1968. I could have done a better job in the Oval Office if I had been a President without being a candidate—not only because there would have been fewer demands on my time, but also because many of my official actions would not have been under such unceasing scrutiny for possible political motivations.

Late on Sunday afternoon, August 24, my political advisers and I had our first postconvention political meeting, to assess the latest poll results and to discuss our approach to the general election campaign season.

554

*Pat [Caddell] has finished a nationwide analysis among
likely voters. . . . With Anderson in the race, we're about 6
points down. All of the criteria for measuring candidates
have improved in my direction; [those] . . . against Reagan
(such as "likely to get us in a war") at this early stage
have very little significance in the voters' minds, but Pat
is sure that later, as the people actually face their choice,
these negative factors will become increasingly important. . . .*

*All of us except Fritz thought that my campaign ap-
pearances should be substantive in nature—in an automobile plant, . . . a steel plant, in a synthetic fuel plant,
solar power, coal mines, transportation, an improved port
facility . . . and so forth. Fritz thought the American
people wanted to see me [more as a candidate, not as a
President] actually campaigning and asking for votes. I'll
do some of that because we need to raise money, but I
think Fritz is wrong on the primary thrust of the campaign effort.*   DIARY, AUGUST 24, 1980

For the next two months, the most politically advantageous
approach, we decided, would be to have as many debates as
possible with Governor Reagan. I accepted an invitation from the
National Press Club for such an event, but Reagan quickly rejected the challenge.

We had good news and bad news on the political front. Hamilton Jordan reported that we were making progress with some of
the labor unions that had defected to Kennedy, but many of the
more liberal Democrats were announcing their support of Anderson. I tried to repair damaged relations with other Democratic
leaders. We worked out a modest program to create some new
jobs and to reject any commitment for a tax cut in 1980. I hoped
these stances might enable Kennedy and some of his supporters
to accept my candidacy with more enthusiasm. I also wanted to
reassure my own supporters that we were striving for maximum
cooperation within the party.

*After lunch I met with Bob Byrd. We had a remarkably good
meeting, ironing out our political and personal differences.
Also, the suggestions that he made to me on the economic
package were exactly compatible with what I had already
planned to do—which may not be an accident on his part.
Afterward he reported exuberance about our meeting and
its success.*

I followed this with a meeting with Tip, Jim Wright

*[Majority Leader], Al Ullman [Chairman, Ways and Means
Committee], Bob Giaimo [Chairman, Budget Committee].
It was also good. Later I met with Senator Kennedy. . . .
We talked about our families, about Amy and Patrick, about
our mothers, about the difficulties of the campaign, the
need to be friends in the future. . . . Afterward he had a very
positive press conference.*   DIARY, AUGUST 25, 1980

We decided that the best place to kick off our fall campaign was
in Tuscumbia, Alabama, on September 1. In 1976, the key to my
victory had been strong loyalty from my fellow Southerners. To
prevail against Reagan, it would be necessary for me to keep this
support. The Tuscumbia region, which included parts of Tennessee
and Mississippi, was a conservative area of blue-collar workers
and farmers who might be inclined toward my opponent's
end of the political spectrum. I wanted to show that we could
meet any challenge, remind people of my Southern roots, and
make a progressive speech sharply distinct from my opponent's
promises and the Republican platform.

On the way in from the airport to the political rally there were
groups of Klansmen, wearing their white sheets and waving
"Reagan for President" signs. Within the huge crowd of more
than fifty thousand people, a few—perhaps a dozen—were demonstrating against me. This was my first direct confrontation
with the Ku Klux Klan since it had paraded around the State
Capitol in Atlanta as I dedicated a portrait of Dr. Martin Luther
King, Jr. It was important to remind the world that these racist
cowards did not represent the South. Jody and I discussed what I
might say in response to the demonstrators. I was pleasantly
surprised when I got the biggest applause with my condemnation
of the Klan.

Our region, the Southland, has been through a lot of pain and a
lot of change, but we came out all right in the end because of
our determination to move ahead and to face our problems
together. There are still a few in the South, indeed around the
country—some I heard from today—who practice cowardice
and who counsel fear and hatred. They marched around the
State Capitol in Atlanta when I was Governor. They said we
ought to be afraid of each other, that whites ought to hate and
be afraid of blacks, and that blacks ought to hate and be afraid
of whites. And they would persecute those who worship in a
different way from most of us. As a Southerner, it makes me feel
angry when I see them with a Confederate battle flag, because I

remember Judah P. Benjamin, who was Secretary of State of the Confederacy; he was a Jew. And I remember General Pat Cleburne of Arkansas, who died in battle not very far from this very spot, and General Beauregard of Louisiana—brave men. Both were Catholics, and so were many others who served under that flag. And sometimes I see the raising of a cross, and I remember that the One who was crucified taught us to have faith, to hope, and not to hate but to love one another.

As the first man from the Deep South in almost 140 years to be President of this nation, I say that these people in white sheets do not understand our region and what it's been through, they do not understand what our country stands for, they do not understand that the South and all of America must move forward.

I looked forward to the campaign, knowing that it was well organized, at least partially financed by public funds, and conducted by an experienced team who knew me and Fritz well and who understood how to help us best present our case to the American public. We had a well-devised strategy, and all of us were ready to work as hard as humanly possible. I knew this, but I also understood that these assets could fade into relative insignificance if the people of our country did not believe I could successfully resolve the problems that confronted us.

The most gripping and politically important was still the holding of American hostages in Iran. Earlier in the year, I had not considered the hostage crisis politically damaging to me. In many ways, it had helped rally the public to my side. Now, however, the grief I felt over the hostages' continued incarceration was mixed with the realization that the election might also be riding on their freedom.

After several months of inaction, the Iranians had now decided to respond to our persistent efforts to resolve the issue. One factor might have been the death of the Shah on July 27. In a strange way typical of the entire episode in Iran, I learned that our diplomatic efforts, trade embargo, and worldwide pressure on the Iranians might be having their desired effect. An emissary from the Ayatollah Khomeini to Germany sent us word through German Foreign Minister Genscher that he wanted to talk to a high American official to work out terms for the hostages' release. Although we had no way to substantiate his credentials, I realized that this was a significant development. Until now, no Iranian had been authorized by Khomeini to talk to any of our officials. We had long known that some of the revolutionary leaders had been educated in Germany and had close ties there, but this particular news from Bonn came without warning. In my diary, I referred to it cautiously and in somewhat cryptic language.

> *Ed Muskie called, and said he must see me immediately and alone. I told him to come over. He brought Chris [Warren Christopher], and I called in Zbig. We had a message through Genscher from Iran, to which I responded affirmatively. This is part of a series of responses we've had. This one may have more substance than some of the others, at least.*   DIARY, SEPTEMBER 10, 1980.

The Iranian's name was Sadegh Tabatabai, and he relayed to us a tentative proposal that omitted most of the unacceptable elements we had already rejected many times. Tabatabai claimed that his credentials would be established by a public statement to be made by the Ayatollah, describing the exact proposal he had come to Germany to present.

> *We continue to get favorable messages out of Iran. With prior arrangement or notification to us, Khomeini made a speech confirming the earlier proposal that had been made to us through the Germans. The militants later corroborated what Khomeini said, limiting the demands to return of Iranian assets, return of the Shah's assets, and agreement not to interfere in Iranian affairs. At the foreign-affairs breakfast we did not discuss this because of the high secrecy involved, but we later prepared for Christopher to go to Europe to follow up on the proposals.*   DIARY, SEPTEMBER 12, 1980

Our hopes had been shattered so many times that I approached this new development with some skepticism. Still, we could not help expecting that this might be the major development we had long awaited. The new Iranian proposals were generally acceptable—and apparently designed to be accepted. We were ready to return those Iranian assets which were not needed to pay outstanding claims; the Shah's family had long ago moved his own estate holdings to other countries; and the last thing I wanted was to become involved in Iran's internal affairs. We prepared negotiating instructions for Warren Christopher very carefully, making our proposals as forthcoming as possible without violating any of the principles we had followed since the crisis began.

At this time, there was a Soviet military buildup along the

Iranian border, and we needed to acquaint our European allies with the information we had. Christopher went to Europe, as far as other officials in the Pentagon and State Department knew, for the sole purpose of sharing this evidence with the heads of state of Great Britain, France, and Germany, and consulting with them on how best to coordinate our warnings to the Soviet leaders to stay out of Iran. Only a very few of us knew that, while in Bonn, Chris would also be meeting with Tabatabai.

Their exploratory conversations were quite encouraging, with the Iranian emissary acknowledging that our proposals were reasonable. Claiming that he was transmitting them with a favorable recommendation to Khomeini and other government leaders in Tehran, he took careful notes, and prepared to return to Iran to make a personal report.

As fate would have it, the Iraqis chose the day of his scheduled arrival in Iran, September 22, to invade Iran and to bomb the Tehran airport. Typically, the Iranians accused me of planning and supporting the invasion. By the time Tabatabai finally arrived in Iran a week or so later, the revolutionary leaders had shifted their attention from releasing the hostages to defending their own country against the invaders.

I preferred a cease-fire between Iran and Iraq, concerned about the safety of the hostages under combat conditions. Also, if the fighting was halted but the threat remained, the belabored Iranians might possibly decide it would be in their best interest to release the prisoners in order to restore some of their standing in the international community, bring an end to our economic boycott, and gain the use of their confiscated billions of dollars. Although Iran had formidable armed forces if they could ever be marshaled, many of the top military leaders had been killed, and the entire country was completely disorganized. On their first thrusts across the border, the Iraqis had been able to penetrate thirty or forty miles.

The Iranians, suspecting that all their Arab neighbors were plotting against them, threatened to attack Saudi Arabia and Oman across the Persian Gulf. We discouraged these nations from permitting the Iraqis to launch attacks from their lands, hoping to keep the battle area from spreading through the already troubled Persian Gulf region. At the same time, I consulted with the Saudis about the specific threat against them, and decided to deploy some of our AWACS (Aircraft Warning and Control System) planes to the peninsula to help with defense. I was also prepared to send United States F-15 fighter planes if they should be needed for protection against the Iranian F-4's.

A limited war continued, but soon Tabatabai was back in Bonn, and the members of the *majlis*—the Iranian parliament—were discussing again the terms for releasing our people. We maintained maximum pressure, keeping before the Iranians our most reasonable proposals.

> *While I was in Winston-Salem at the fair, Christopher called to give me an encouraging message from Tabatabai, saying that "the American proposal has fallen on fertile ground." We're trying to push for some sort of understanding, no later than early next week.*
>
> DIARY, OCTOBER 9, 1980

Again, we were working through the Germans. We received word that all the hostages were back in the embassy compound, in good condition, and that there seemed to be a consensus among the top Iranian officials that it was time to free the American prisoners. Now they were making sensible inquiries concerning issues which would be addressed after our differences were resolved, such as a request for an inventory of military materiel and spare parts that had been ordered from the United States prior to the revolution. They also made some suggestions we rejected immediately, such as a phased release of the hostages in four groups, provided we acquiesced sequentially to some of their demands. This would have been a vivid demonstration of progress, but would also have expressed our willingness to let them single out certain hostages as being more worthy of release than others. Our consistent reply was, "We want them all."

When Iranian Prime Minister Mohammed Ali Rajai came to New York in October to plead his country's case against Iraq in the United Nations, we suggested that he meet either with Secretary Muskie or with Christopher while he was there, to follow up on the Tabatabai talks. He refused, but the American position was adequately driven home by the United Nations representatives of dozens of other nations. They simply would not consider seriously any of Rajai's complaints as long as Iran continued to hold the Americans. The Prime Minister took a clear message back home to Tehran: Iran would continue to suffer and be isolated in the world community unless the hostages were set free.

At home, the political campaign seemed almost equally stagnant. In late September, there was a lot of campaigning going on, but the American people seemed to be waiting to make a decision. As the underdog, I was having a lot of trouble raising the campaign funds the law authorized above the basic federal allotment. We were not gaining or losing any ground, and barring some breakthrough on the hostages or major improvement in the economy, we simply had to hammer away at the sharp differences between myself and Governor Reagan and trust that the voters would eventually make the right choice.

We analyzed Reagan's statements thoroughly, appalled at his positions on many crucial issues. The news reporters generally seemed to ignore the consequences of his policies, or else assumed that he really did not mean what he was saying. This placed on us the unpleasant responsibility of doing the commentary. We asked various Democratic leaders to warn the people about the consequences of Reagan's avowed purposes, but their voices were ignored by the press and public.

I finally decided that Fritz Mondale and I would have to do it ourselves. We assumed that speaking out on these matters was a legitimate element in a hard-fought campaign, but I learned the hard way that I had to be extremely careful about what I said. On several occasions the press took a few critical words out of my extemporaneous comments on issues and interpreted them as a personal attack on Reagan. That was the last thing I intended—not because I particularly wished to protect my opponent from a harsh phrase, but because the political damage was afflicting me as much as it was him.

With a lead in the polls, Governor Reagan was still coasting in early October, staying almost isolated from the press or from any sort of interrogation. He was also refusing to debate me unless Anderson were included. During this time, less than a month before the election, the press continued to ignore the substantive issues in the campaign and to concentrate almost exclusively on who might debate whom, Reagan's "blunders," and my "meanness" to my opponent.

Another serious problem we could not overcome was the bitter attacks on me from the conservative religious and political groups. They accused me of being "soft on Communism," betraying America by "giving away the Panama Canal," subverting the teaching of children by organizing a new Department of Education, encouraging abortion and homosexuality, trying to destroy families by supporting the Equal Rights Amendment, and lowering America's guard against the Soviet threat by negotiating the SALT treaty. I had had some problems with these groups in 1976, and as soon as it became clear that I would be renominated, they came back in full cry. The Reverend Jerry Falwell, the leader of Moral Majority, was one of the worst, in that he had a large audience and was quite careless with the truth.

> *Falwell has lied in Alaska [and repeated the story to other audiences] by claiming that he met with me in the Oval Office, and that I told him I had to have homosexuals on my staff because there were homosexuals in the United States who needed representation in my inner circle. I have never had a private meeting with him. He has never been in the Oval Office. I have never had any such conversation.*   DIARY, AUGUST 7, 1980

The only time I remembered seeing Falwell was at a meeting with twelve or fifteen other religious leaders. Bob Maddox, one of my White House assistants, listened to a tape recording of the meeting which had been made for the participants, and could find no such comment by me or anyone else in the group. When confronted with this evidence Falwell admitted that he had fabricated the tale. Nevertheless, one of the "religious" television spots aired during the general election campaign depicted a concerned mother telling her child that I was a bad man because I encouraged homosexuality.

Although the charges of some of the right-wing television preachers and other conservative spokesmen seemed ludicrous, they had a cumulative effect. Either through tax-exempt religious broadcasts or well-financed Political Action Committees, the messages were drummed into the consciousness of American voters day and night. Total expenditures for the campaign were limited by law in order to insure equity, but none of this right-wing special-interest programming was charged against the Republican total.

Even with all our efforts, Governor Reagan was picking up strength among Jewish voters as well. His promises to espouse Israel's arguments in the peace negotiations, the charges about Billy and Libya, errors committed by our United Nations delegation on issues sensitive to Israel, and perhaps most important, the pressures on Israel to carry out the agreements concerning Palestinian rights and withdrawal from the Sinai, all contributed to this trend.

In spite of inevitable political difficulties such as those I have described, on a broad national basis I had picked up support. With about three weeks to go before the election, my own polls showed that I had almost drawn even with Reagan. Pat Caddell told me he was very pleased with what he called the "internals," which indicated that in their more basic attitudes, the American people were feeling steadily more compatible with me and more concerned about my opponent. Some of Reagan's recent statements about nuclear weapons and their possible use had again caused serious problems for him; he had to make a hurried television address to assure the country that he was not going to get us into war.

At the same time I was receiving some good news on the international front, for a change. After more than three years of hard work, I was finally able to announce agreement between Greece and Turkey on terms for Greek reentry into NATO. At home, even the economic news was better, with sure signs that the recession was over. Although there was still widespread concern about high rates of inflation and interest, the inflation rate had now held steady at 7 per cent for the past three months. As I campaigned around the country, it was obvious that the tone of my reception had improved considerably. All of us were confident as we approached the final stretch.

I had begun to enjoy the campaign, even though it had been a remarkably serious one. My team and I even joked about another *Playboy* interview, just to liven things up and relieve the tense and rather solemn atmosphere. Laughs were few and far between, so we cherished a small one when it came along.

> *I went to Grand Rapids, Michigan, and found out later that I had called it "Cedar Rapids." When Gerald Ford went out castigating me for it, he shouted to the TV cameras that apparently I didn't even know that Michigan was one of the 48 states.*   DIARY, OCTOBER 25, 1980

President Ford, famous for his confusion about places, then had to spend a day or two convincing the news reporters that he really did know there were fifty states.

The most constant concern of mine, both as President and as a candidate, was bringing our hostages home. I was increasingly encouraged. As the Iranian parliament planned a major debate during the last week in October, word came from Tabatabai and other sources that Khomeini and the militant captors were ready to end the stalemate and resolve the issue. My security advisers and I made all the final plans for success.

> *We'll probably not have much notice. Everybody agreed with me that Cy Vance would be a good one to head up our effort in making this a nonpartisan event, and we*

agreed that Vance might want to go over to Europe to meet with the hostages, since they will probably be there around five days before coming home—for medical examinations, debriefings, and so forth.

DIARY, OCTOBER 24, 1980

In the *majlis*, the votes were running about 100 to 80 in favor of our position, but the hard-liners were still trying to prevent the release of the hostages. In violation of Khomeini's expressed wishes, they were simply staying away from the sessions to prevent the presence of the two-thirds of the membership required to make a final decision. In all our statements, we were playing down prospects for success in order to lower expectations and avoid the great surge of revulsion among Americans which we knew would come with another disappointment. However, in spite of our caution, the hostage question was dominating the news; it was not possible for us to control rising hopes throughout the country.

The campaign was in the final stretch. At last we had gotten agreement from the Republicans for a two-man debate. Because all of us were concerned about Reagan's ability as a "great communicator," we concentrated on understanding the different constituencies that would be most affected by a Republican victory, and planned my debating points accordingly.

The Republicans had worked their strategy well in preventing a series of direct debates between the two nominees, and in postponing the only scheduled debate until the last minute. It was to be held in Cleveland just a week before election day, with little time left afterward to change basic voter attitudes. I was relaxed, confident that I could hold my own.

I talked to Amy on the phone about the upcoming debate. I won't see her again for about a week. She said that the atomic bomb was the most important issue, and we had a discussion about what a kiloton was, what a megaton was. She discusses international issues, including the hostage crisis, almost like an adult.   DIARY, OCTOBER 26, 1980

My comment during the debate about Amy's concern over nuclear weapons made her the most famous antinuclear advocate in America because of the ridicule it aroused from Governor Reagan and the news reporters. This was an unpleasant episode, and my political team later reproved me for the damage. It was obvious that I had not expressed myself well, but at the time I thought that if a twelve-year-old girl worried most about the atomic bomb, it indicated how deeply the dangers of nuclear weapons had permeated everyone's consciousness.

The night after the debate, six days before the election, I dictated a few notes:

> *In the debate itself it was hard to judge the general demeanor that was projected to the viewers. Reagan was, "Aw, shucks, this and that. I'm a grandfather, and . . . I love peace," etc. He has his memorized lines, and he pushes a button and they come out. Apparently made a better impression on the TV audience than I did. But I had a list of things [to say], which we believe . . . will become preeminent in the public's mind as they approach the point a week from now of actually going to the polls to decide on a leader for the nation for the next four years. Both sides felt good after the debate.*
>
> *. . . But anyway, he accomplished his purpose; we accomplished ours. We'll see whose basic strategy is best when the returns come in next Tuesday.*
>
> DIARY, OCTOBER 28, 1980

Governor Reagan gained some strength as a result of the debate, but Pat Caddell's polls showed that we got most of it back during the remainder of the week. By the weekend I was informed by Pat that we were about even, although other polls indicated that we were still somewhat behind. In those last few days, I moved as rapidly as possible to all the key places I could reach, coordinating my appearances with those of Rosalynn, Fritz, and others. The excitement rose, and there was a certain fervor among the crowds that was heartening to me.

> *A lot of electricity. Excitement. My hands are getting pretty well scratched up on the back, because the crowd gets emotional. And a lot of people weep. It's kind of a high-pitched shrill sound that comes out of crowds now. I'm sure that as the election approaches, the same thing happens to other candidates, but there's a lot more intensity of interest than there has been in weeks gone by.*
>
> DIARY, OCTOBER 31, 1980

Early on Sunday morning, just two days before election day, the *majlis* finally got a quorum, debated for three or four hours, and voted. I was in Chicago when Warren Christopher called me at 3:45 A.M. to report that the parliament had chosen to approve the four points which were compatible with what Khomeini had announced and which Warren had already discussed with Tabatabai in Bonn. There were also a few unacceptable elements in the text of the resolution, concerning the claims procedure and confiscation of the Shah's property, but overall it was very encouraging.

I decided to cancel my day's schedule and fly back to Washington. I told Rosalynn and Fritz the news, and asked Ed Muskie to notify the congressional leaders as well as Reagan and Anderson. Just before we left Chicago, I was informed that the *majlis* had authorized Prime Minister Rajai and President Bani-Sadr to implement the agreement with us.

I will never forget the flight back to Washington, heading eastward into the rising sun. I was in the cockpit of Air Force One talking to the flight crew, and through the towering clouds we watched one of the most beautiful sunrises I have ever seen. My prayer was that the Iranian nightmare would soon be over, and that my judgment and my decisions might be wise ones. In a strange way, I felt relieved. It was out of my hands. Now my political future might well be determined by irrational people on the other side of the world over whom I had no control. If the hostages were released, I was convinced my reelection would be assured; if the expectations of the American people were dashed again, there was little chance that I could win.

Back at the White House, I read the Iranian document through rapidly and realized that the differences between our two positions were still quite significant. We did not want to reject the proposal outright, but drafted a response designed to keep the discussions going. It was transmitted to the West German Embassy in Tehran, and Ambassador Dr. Gerhard Ritzel reported that he would try to get an immediate appointment with Prime Minister Rajai.

I issued a public statement saying that the proposal by the *majlis* was a good and constructive move, that it could lead to positive results, and that my actions on behalf of the United States would not be affected by the calendar or the impending election. I repeated that I wanted the hostages released, but only if it was done in such a way that the honor and integrity of our nation would be maintained. I added that the leaders of Congress and the other presidential candidates were being kept informed.

The next morning I was up early to receive a report from Iran.

Ritzel had presented our response to Rajai. Khomeini had told the militants that he wanted the hostages turned over to the government so that all the students holding them could help on the war front, and the government had announced that the Algerians would be "responsible" for the hostages. We did not know what this last statement meant. We did know that two large buses, which had not been there before, were now being kept parked just outside the compound. However, as the hours passed, no other news came out of Iran.

Before leaving for my last thirty-six-hour campaign swing around the country, I believed I had pulled almost even with Reagan over the weekend. In order to win, I would have to gain additional support, but the time for most Americans to listen to candidates had passed. The news media were saturated with reports about the hostages. Election day would be the anniversary of the hostages' kidnapping, and all during Monday and Tuesday there was a stream of stories recapitulating the sad events of the past fifty-two weeks. The television programs were especially persistent and vivid. When the public began to realize that the latest events in Iran would not lead to the hostages' freedom, a wave of disillusionment swept the country. We were making thousands of telephone calls daily, which served as an instant opinion poll, and from them we detected a precipitous drop in support. It was a bad time for incumbents, as the voters expressed their disgust with our nation's apparent impotence in the face of several disturbing problems—Iran foremost. All of us continued our futile effort to overcome it by campaigning as hard as we could.

I reminded traditional Democratic voters of the effect on their lives of a potential Republican victory. In my speeches I continued to pound away at the same theme: our party had always represented the middle-class and working people of America, and had initiated such beneficial programs as social security, minimum wage, TVA, Medicaid and Medicare, and the more recent laws guaranteeing basic civil rights—all over the opposition of Republicans. At the same time, we had a better record on controlling inflation, providing jobs, keeping a strong defense, and maintaining lower federal deficits. I continued this tradition. Every four years, Republican candidates tried to make the voters forget the record of history, and often they succeeded. As a minority party, they could win only when Democrats voted for them. I called on our people to give me their support. This last night in particular, the response to my words was heartwarming, but I realized that the odds were against me. It was not easy for me to face defeat, and I rejected the idea as long as I could.

Pat was getting some very disturbing public-opinion poll results, showing a massive slippage as people realized that the hostages were not coming home. The anniversary date of their having been captured absolutely filled the news media. Time, Newsweek, U.S. News—*all had cover stories on the hostages. And by Monday only a tiny portion (I think Pat said 19 per cent) thought that the hostages were going to be coming home any time soon. This apparently opened up a flood of related concerns among the people that we were impotent, and reminded them of all the negative results of OPEC price increases, over which we had no control—and the hostages being seized, over which we had no control—and the Soviets' invasion of Afghanistan, the Cuban refugee situation, the high interest rates, attributable at least in part to the huge OPEC oil price increase.*

Almost all the undecideds moved to Reagan. Strangely enough, my favorable rating improved—the way I handled the Iran situation went up, and the percentage that thought it was used for political purposes dropped down. . . . But there was a general sense of rejection of incumbents. By late Monday, when we were in Oregon and Washington, we knew that the prospects had faded away for us to win.

On the way back to Plains, where I was going to meet Rosalynn and vote, Stu [Eizenstat] came up to my cabin to try to say something about it, and burst into tears. I put my arms around him to comfort him. It was hard for us to believe the dimensions of what Pat was telling us, but it later proved to be accurate.

DIARY, NOVEMBER 3, 1980

When I got home, Rosalynn and I discussed the Caddell figures. She did not seem very surprised. In spite of the bad news, we were remarkably at ease. We talked about how my necessarily more conservative economic policies had created a still unhealed breach in the Democratic party, and how ironic it was that the issues on which we had expended the most effort were the very ones that had lost us so much political support. We enumerated some of the times when she had urged me to avoid an issue or postpone an act or statement that might be politically costly. Unlike some of the previous discussions, this was not an argument between us, but a mutual analysis. Even as we faced defeat, I was still convinced that my decisions were justified.

Most of the things we did that were difficult and contro-versial cost us votes in the long run. Camp David accords, opening up Africa, dealing with the Cuban refugees, Pan-ama Canal treaties, the normalization with China, energy legislation, plus the hostages and the Soviet invasion of Afghanistan—particularly the hostages. Also, the Kennedy attacks for eight months hurt a lot. I spent a major por-tion of my time trying to recruit back the Democratic constituency that should have been naturally supportive— Jews, Hispanics, blacks, the poor, labor, and so forth.

After we voted, I made a speech on the depot platform, went over to see Mother, flew back to Washington. . . . Rosalynn and I went in and took a nap during the after-noon. Talked to Pat about 2:30. He said the early returns [from exit polls, interviews with voters as they left the polling places] showed that we were not doing well, but were fragmented.

Warren Christopher reported no progress on the hostages.

DIARY, NOVEMBER 4, 1980

The political team, awaiting the results:
(l-r) Powell, Moore, Wise, Kraft (with telephone),
Strauss, Jordan, Rafshoon, Lipshutz

Beginning at 7:30 P.M., the networks called the election for Reagan. It was obvious to everyone that I had lost—an overwhelming defeat. At about 9:30, I went over to the Sheraton-Washington Hotel and made a brief concession speech. My decision to concede so early was later criticized because the polls had not closed on the West Coast, so that it may have hurt some of the Democratic candidates there. Perhaps it was a mistake, but at the time I did not want to appear a bad loser, waiting until late at night to confirm what everyone already knew.

Rosalynn, Kirbo, the children, and I talked quietly for a while before we went to bed. We had all done our best, and had no feelings of bitterness or recrimination toward anyone.

It is painful even now to recall those last two days of the campaign, and the dismal results that I had to face on election night. After the Iranian *majlis* had voted on Sunday and it became clear that the hostages would not be freed, Rosalynn and I knew my support had sharply fallen. But it was no time to dwell on potential defeat; we had to keep working until the last possible moment. Furthermore, I could not afford to show my concerns to the American public or even to those closest around me in the campaign. All of us had to retain a shred of hope to strengthen us for a few more hours.

After all the campaigning was over on the night before the election, I was not surprised or shaken when Jody gave me the bad news from Caddell. It hurt me deeply, but I had already accommodated the disappointment that was to come officially the following day. Even so, we did not anticipate the magnitude of our defeat. To lose all but six states and to have our party rejected and the Republicans gain a majority in the Senate were additional embarrassments for me.

I had to find a silver lining in the cloud of defeat. At least it was a relief that the political campaign was over. A lot of work remained to be done during the next two and a half months, and I could perform these duties as a President, and not as a candidate. I was thankful for this small blessing.

TRANSITION

I will work hard to make sure that the transition from myself to the next President is a good one, that the American people are served well. And I will continue as I have the last 14 months to work hard and to pray for the lives and the well-being of the American hostages held in Iran. I cannot predict yet what will happen, but I hope you will join me in my constant prayer for their freedom.

FAREWELL ADDRESS TO THE AMERICAN PEOPLE,
JANUARY 14, 1981

T he morning after the election, I woke with a full realization of what had occurred. During the early hours I thought about some of the decisions I would have to make about my life. I had to face the reality of personal and official challenges. As had been my custom for many years at such moments, I turned to Charles Kirbo and Rosalynn for advice. We sat around the breakfast table in the White House while Kirbo explained to me in general terms our family's financial status. During the four years since my election, our warehouse business had gotten heavily in debt, and the interest payments on our numerous loans had lately been exceeding the total income of the business. Kirbo had done the best he could as my trustee, but Billy's departure, large accounting and legal fees during the many investigations, and the tight restrictions I had imposed on Kirbo to prevent any conflicts of interest had proved very costly. It certainly did not boost my spirits to hear his report. Rosalynn and I decided it would be best to sell Carter's Warehouse as soon as possible. Our hope was that the proceeds might get us out of debt.

Then Muskie, Brzezinski, and Warren Christopher joined me in the Oval Office so that we could assess the hostage situation. Since I had been the embodiment of so much of the Iranian hatred, we hoped that my defeat might now give the Iranian leaders a face-saving excuse to resolve the crisis. I remembered hearing about Khomeini's statement, back in May, that the hostages would not be released until after the American election. As we could not count on this, we analyzed again the confusing statements that had come out of Tehran during the most recent debates in parliament. It was now apparent that Algeria would be acting as a mediator between the United States and Iran, so we went over the final terms on which we would be willing to settle our differences. I instructed Ed and Chris to set these down on paper and submit them for my approval.

I met for half an hour, 45 minutes, with the press. Just a kind of going-away session to let them know that we were in good shape and had no hard feelings or bitterness; that I was going to have a good transition period; that I would be supportive of Reagan if he seemed to make progress on matters important to me like inflation, unemployment, SALT, and so forth. Reminded the nation that I was still the President until January 20th.

DIARY, NOVEMBER 5, 1980

In the afternoon, Rosalynn and I went to Camp David to unwind for a few days and to continue making plans. We had never discussed what we would do in case of defeat, so the future was wide open. At first—for just a few hours—we considered living in Atlanta, but soon agreed that we should go to our own home in

Plains, try to pay our debts, and spend a while getting our financial affairs back in shape. Both of us thought it might then be
possible to write about our experiences in public life. Later, as
private citizens, we would continue to work for the causes that
were still important to us. In spite of inevitable temptations to
the contrary, we decided to remain relatively quiet during the
early months of the new President's term, so that he would have
adequate opportunities to put his programs into effect without
my creating an additional handicap for him. Also, it was my hope
that he would more quickly change some of his ill-advised campaign promises if I were not demanding from the sidelines that he
do so.

Amy was heartbroken about having to leave her Washington
friends, but Rosalynn and I were in a fairly good mood. To
keep up our spirits, we joked about some of the heavy burdens that would soon be borne by Republican shoulders. We had
been apart most of the time during recent months, as Rosalynn
had campaigned separately from me. It was hard for us even to
remember the last time we had been together and able to relax
completely, and we really enjoyed each other's company. We took
a lot of exercise, went fishing in Pennsylvania and in nearby
streams, and I had time for some woodworking in the Camp
David carpenter's shop. During this time Rosalynn and I also
made dozens of telephone calls around the country, thanking
people for their help and support and reassuring them about
the future.

I spent several hours each day performing my presidential
duties. By the end of the week, I had caught up on accumulated
paper work, spelled out an ambitious legislative agenda for the
upcoming lame-duck session of Congress, and approved all the
documents Christopher would carry to Algeria, where he would
be seeking the release of the hostages. This was one task that I
particularly wanted to complete before I left office—in time, I
hoped, to bring our people home for Christmas.

Early on Monday evening we returned to the White House. For
the first time since the election, Rosalynn seemed seriously depressed. I tried to cheer her up by talking about our home in
Plains, what we could do with the house and yards, how we
would be working together if we both decided to write books, and
what it would mean to be free from campaigning or serving in
public office for the first time in almost twenty years.

I also reminded her that I would have other semiofficial duties to keep me busy and, as always, I would be counting on her help. Under federal law, more than twenty-five million documents, letters, files, and mementos of the administration belonged to me, and I was responsible for their proper storage during the coming years. It would be an important task to raise enough money to build a library to house these records for historians and scholars, and also to present for visitors a record of my life and years in the White House. I decided to deed the memorabilia to the federal government after they were properly inventoried, so that archivists could prepare them for permanent filing by the time the buildings could be completed.

As one of the youngest of former Presidents, I expected to have many useful years ahead of me. Neither Rosalynn nor I wanted to become involved again in commerce or business, unless we found later that our family income needed to be supplemented in this way. We decided that it would be better to continue using my influence, perhaps with greater freedom now, to promote the same ideals I had espoused during my Presidency. It might prove possible in some way to be involved in the effort to reduce nuclear arsenals, not only those of the United States and the Soviet Union but of the other nuclear nations. The proposals that I had made to Brezhnev had been somewhat attractive to him, I still believed—and logical to any thinking person. Without attempting to represent the government of my own country as a former President, there was, perhaps, a worldwide forum I might address which could influence the actions of political leaders. I had the same kind of thoughts about alleviating tension in the troubled areas of the world, promoting human rights, enhancing environmental quality, and pursuing other goals which were important to me. These were hazy ideas at best, but they gave us something to anticipate which could be exciting and challenging during the years ahead.

It was interesting to make such plans, but there was no way I could forget I was still President. There was a lot I wanted to do before leaving office.

Prime Minister Begin came to Washington on November 13, and I had a chance to discuss some of the remaining Middle East issues with him. At first he was quite ill at ease with me, apparently uncomfortable about my defeat, but after I assured him that I had accepted the results of the election with equanimity, we joined our advisers and began our talks.

This meeting with Begin was my first indication of what would be ever clearer during the coming weeks—my power as a defeated President was not equal to that of one who is expected to remain in office. In spite of my best efforts, there would be little substance to my discussions with the Prime Minister. The Israelis preferred to await the new administration in order to continue any top-level negotiations. Before the election, Sadat had also expressed his preference to wait until the new year, and so it now seemed best to encourage Reagan to assume this responsibility after his inauguration.

The next day, Vice President Mondale came back from a brief vacation in Puerto Rico. We had a long discussion about current events, prospects for an orderly transition, and the remaining legislative agenda. Fritz seemed to have the same feelings I had about the election—disappointment with the results, a conviction that we had done our best, and confidence about a pleasant and productive life in the future. He was obviously interested in running for President in 1984, but it was too soon to be making any firm plans. For now, we had our official duties to perform.

We set the same kind of ambitious legislative goals as we would have if we had been reelected. I particularly wanted to pass permanent legislation to protect the Alaska lands, to complete the few remaining elements of our total energy package, to provide for the safe disposal of toxic wastes, and to finish our efforts to deregulate major industries. After meeting with the Vice President and my other advisers, I decided to prepare a budget for the coming year with the same care and personal attention as if I were continuing in office. We would take a sound approach, involving continued steady increases in defense spending, cautious tax reductions, tight constraints on federal spending, and holding the freeze on hiring personnel. In this way, we hoped, some of the Republican campaign promises might be forgotten.

However, many of the postelection comments were causing us concern.

Charlie Schultze came by to outline the dangers of the renewed Reagan commitments on massive tax cuts, large increases in defense spending, plus some of the other domestic items which are very costly . . . tuition tax credits, and so forth. There is apparently a struggle going on between the conventional and conservative advisers on the one hand and the Kemp–Roth radical advisers on the other. So far Reagan seems to be going with the radical advisers, but he probably will have to change.

DIARY, NOVEMBER 17, 1980

I then invited President-elect Reagan to come by to see me in the Oval Office. I considered this visit very important, and had carefully prepared a list of the most significant issues that needed to be discussed—issues which only a President could ultimately resolve.

Reagan listened without comment while I covered each point. Some of them were very sensitive, involving such matters as the management of our nuclear forces in time of attack on our nation. I urged him to take plenty of time to learn about these arrangements before Inauguration Day, so that he could be thoroughly instructed on the procedures to be followed in an emergency. I described some top-secret agreements we had with a few other nations. Again, he did not comment or ask any questions. Some of the information was quite complex, and I did not see how he could possibly retain all of it merely by listening. I asked him if he wanted a pad so that he could take some notes, but he responded that he could remember what I was saying.

I continued to go from item to item, and when I paused again, he asked if he could have a copy of my notes. They were extremely brief reminders—just a few words on one 3 × 5 card—to prevent my overlooking any of the fifteen or twenty subjects, but I quickly had my secretary make a copy for him.

Since I was particularly worried about some of his campaign comments (though I did not mention them, of course), I then talked to him about China, describing the careful balance that had been worked out by Presidents Nixon and Ford and myself and emphasizing the sensitivity of the Chinese to the Taiwan issue. I reviewed such defense considerations as the interrelationship among cruise missiles, the "stealth" aircraft, and the B-1 bomber. Then I listed some of the advantages to our country of honoring the terms of SALT II, pending its ratification, and of maintaining a strong nonproliferation policy. He sat quietly through a brief review of the latest developments in Afghanistan and the hostage situation.

I told him how difficult it was for any President to get Congress to approve adequate foreign-aid legislation, recalling that almost exactly four years earlier, President Ford had told me that this was one of the biggest headaches. I outlined my plans for completing a solid budget, and reminded him about my long-standing freeze on the hiring of federal employees.

Finally, I covered some special presidential problems with regard to the Germans and a few other European countries concerning defense matters; Poland; Nicaragua; the proposed F-15 sales to Saudi Arabia; and the need for aggressive action by our leaders in the Middle East peace process. This list comprised some of the essential items that needed to be discussed personally by the two of us. He waited patiently until I had finished, and then the President-elect asked me to conduct all foreign and defense business with his adviser, Richard Allen, pending his choice of a Secretary of State, a Secretary of Defense, and other members of his Cabinet.

We talked about what was being done to save opposition leader Kim Dae Jung's life in South Korea, and I thanked him for sending a message to President Chun Doo Hwan urging that Kim's life be spared. At that point, Governor Reagan made his first real comment. He expressed with some enthusiasm his envy of the authority that Korean President Park Chung Hee had exercised during a time of campus unrest, when he had closed the universities and drafted the demonstrators.

He had been with me almost an hour and it had been a pleasant visit, but I was not sure how much we had accomplished.

Later, I instructed Muskie, Brown, and Brzezinski to delay any immediate action on the pending arms sale to Saudi Arabia, because Governor Reagan had sent word to me after our meeting that he wanted to participate in this decision. We submitted the Saudi requests to Richard Allen and waited for the incoming team's opinion. Any decision had to have the approval of the new President, because the law required a waiting period of twenty working days for congressional assessment before an arms sale of this kind could be consummated, and the legislative schedule made it impossible to complete the process before Inauguration Day. Five items were at stake in the decision: the lease or sale of AWACS, improved racks on F-15's for ejecting bombs, airborne tankers to refuel the fighter planes, an air-to-air missile, and larger fuel tanks to extend the range of the F-15's.

> *All of us decided that we should not go forward with the multiple-ejection racks nor with the refueling airplane at this time. We all agreed that we should let them [the Saudis] have the missiles and also keep the AWACS on station in Saudi Arabia, manning them with American crews. Over a period of 3 or 4 years in the future we might decide to sell the planes to Saudi Arabia. The question is on the fuel tanks. My own inclination is to approve them, but it's necessary to get Reagan to agree before we either notify the Saudis of our nation's position or start consulting with the members of Congress. . . . [Muskie] called*

back later to say that Richard Allen had presented to Reagan a written document requiring an answer on the F-15's and other sales to the Saudi Arabians. We'll see what comes of it.   DIARY, NOVEMBER 24, 1980

This entire issue was a political hot potato because any additional sales to the Saudis would be strongly opposed by Israel and by many members of Congress. I was willing either to take full responsibility or to share a decision with the new administration leaders. Since final action could not be taken in any case until 1981, I wanted to accommodate the President-elect. Having promised the Saudis an answer, we felt honor-bound to give them one without further delay.

More than anything else, it was still Iran and our hostages that gnawed away at me. I went to Camp David with my family for the Thanksgiving weekend, expecting a visit any day from an Algerian delegation that had just been in Iran. I had spent many hours studying the domestic and international laws and customs concerning claims settlements and other issues, and, while at Camp David, I had something of an argument with my legal advisers about a "hold harmless" clause they had drafted to be included in our next response to Iran. It was a guarantee that after the hostages were released, no American citizen could legally seek damages from the Iranian government. I was strongly opposed to this, and eventually prevailed. I decided to let the Iranians choose the World Court, the claims-settlement mechanism available through the International Chamber of Commerce, or perhaps some bilateral arrangement, with the Algerians to mediate. Although the Algerians were working on the overall settlement problem with real determination and courage, my advisers and I were not overly optimistic.

We have to remember that [Iran's] Prime Minister Rajai is strongly anti-American, very primitive in his outlook, highly suspicious, and not eager to see the hostages released. We still don't have any sure word, by the way, as to who is in charge of the hostages at this moment. The militants continue to claim that they've turned them over to the government, but the government refuses to acknowledge that this has been done. . . . There's no way to tell what the facts might be.

DIARY, NOVEMBER 29, 1980

IRAN AND THE LAST YEAR 581

It had become obvious that whichever officials might ultimately make the final decision to release the hostages, their political opponents in Iran would condemn them severely. Although Iran was suffering terribly from the economic, political, and social chaos that had resulted in large measure from the kidnapping of our people, there were still powerful political leaders there who insisted that the hostages be kept in captivity. President Bani-Sadr was away at the battlefront; formerly helpful, he was now making negative statements about the current negotiations. The decision by many members of the parliament to disobey Khomeini and prevent the formation of a quorum late in October had been a vivid indication of the currents of opposition that still permeated the newly formed Iranian government.

By the time we returned to the White House on Monday, Christopher had gone over our proposal with the Algerian team. They thought it was reasonable, and we decided to let the Iranians know that this was our last proposal, and that if they rejected it, they would have to start all over again with the new administration sometime next year. I decided to send Chris to Algeria to meet with Foreign Minister Mohammad Benyahia and others who were acting as intermediaries. It was imperative that they understand the finality of our position, which had not really changed in any material way since we had made our first proposal to them almost a year ago.

⸺

The lame-duck legislative session was remarkably productive. The Democrats had no further reason for political backbiting, and the Republicans were quite eager to pass some of the more controversial bills before this Congress ended, so that they and the new administration would not have to repeat two years of work when the new Congress convened. Action was completed on all but one of the energy bills, on a landmark act establishing a "Superfund" to help ameliorate the blight of toxic-waste sites, and—finally—on the Alaska lands bill for which I had waited so long.

The Superfund legislation set up a system of insurance premiums collected from the chemical industry to clean up toxic wastes. This new program may prove to be as far-reaching and important as any accomplishment of my administration. The reduction of the threat to America's health and safety from thousands of toxic-waste sites will continue to be an urgent but bitterly fought issue—another example of the conflict between the public welfare and the profits of a few private despoilers of our nation's environment.

The bill to protect more than a hundred and fifty million acres of land in Alaska was among the most gratifying achievements of my term. Over almost insuperable odds, we had fought for four years to reach agreement. The final version of the bill was very close to what we had originally proposed. In the meantime, by executive order and complicated parliamentary maneuvers, Interior Secretary Cecil Andrus and I had worked with such key congressional supporters as Representative Mo Udall to protect the land pending congressional action, and prevent unwarranted exploitation of its precious natural resources.

The Alaska lands legislation was extremely intricate, involving not only great areas of land but also the most complex delineations of varying kinds of use, including such issues as hunting and fishing with and without professional guides, harvesting of mature timber, building of different kinds of access trails and roads, exploratory drilling for geological surveys, special privileges for native Indians and Eskimos, navigation of streams, and the interrelationship of federal and state governments in enforcing the laws. I had studied the maps for many hours, trying to make sound judgments that were fair and would stand the test of time. (There were four maps with which I became thoroughly familiar while I was President: Alaska, the Sinai peninsula between Israel and the Suez Canal, the Panama Canal Zone, and that portion of Iran including Tehran and a desert area lying about 200 miles to the south.)

There have been few more pleasant occasions in my life than when I signed the Alaska National Interest Lands Conservation Act. The document was almost six inches thick, and I tried to describe its significance in a few words at the bill-signing ceremony on December 2, 1980.

> We are setting aside for conservation an area of land larger than the State of California. By designating more than ninety-seven million acres for new parks and refuges, we are doubling the size of our National Park and Wildlife Refuge System. By protecting twenty-five free-flowing Alaskan rivers in their natural state, we are almost doubling the size of our Wild and Scenic Rivers System. By classifying fifty-six million acres of some of the most magnificent land in our Federal estate as wilderness, we are tripling the size of our Wilderness System.

... I've been fortunate. I have seen firsthand some of the splendors of Alaska. But many Americans have not. Now, whenever they or their children or their grandchildren choose to visit Alaska, they will have the opportunity to see much of its splendid beauty undiminished and its majesty untarnished.

This act of Congress reaffirms our commitment to the environment. It strikes a balance between protecting areas of great beauty and value and allowing development of Alaska's vital oil and gas and mineral and timber resources. 100 per cent of the offshore areas and 95 per cent of the potentially productive oil and mineral areas will be available for exploration or for drilling. With this bill we are acknowledging that Alaska's wilderness areas are truly this country's crown jewels and that Alaska's resources are treasures of another sort. How to tap these resources is a challenge that we can now face in the decades ahead.

〜

For the first time, the Democratic leaders were beginning to see some advantages in being the minority party.

Had our final congressional-leadership breakfast. There was a different tone today—one of a degree of relief that the Democrats will not be responsible for all the problems in the future. One example was the debt-limit extension, where Tip came in very tense because in January we had to extend the debt limit, which would run out late in February. Bob Byrd informed Tip that the Democrats in the Senate had decided to let the Republicans worry about it—let them scrape up the votes for a change. Tip was instantly astonished, then relieved just to think about such a situation.   DIARY, DECEMBER 2, 1980

Even if I had wanted to do so, there was no way for me to begin shifting responsibility to others. The Soviet military was maneuvering around the borders of Poland, the fate of the hostages was uncertain, my staff was having serious problems in trying to identify or cooperate with the Republican transition teams, and I was genuinely concerned about some of the radical proposals being considered by my successor in both domestic and foreign policy.

In spite of all these worries, I was satisfied with what we had accomplished in Washington. Most of us were now looking forward to the freedom of our new life. I was especially proud of my Cabinet and my White House staff. They had served our country well. On December 3, in our last official Cabinet meeting, the individual members enumerated briefly the accomplishments of the past four years. It was not difficult, for this group at least, to agree that we would have won the reelection battle in a sweep if we had been able to convince the American people of the accuracy of this same report!

Early in December, not quite a year after Soviet troops had invaded Afghanistan, we became convinced that their military forces were preparing to move into Poland. The Polish trade unions had formed the political front "Solidarity," and with broad backing among the people and with support from the church, they were building strength and wresting concessions from the government leaders. There seemed no way that the Polish officials could control this movement toward freedom, which appeared completely incompatible with their regimented system of government. Something had to give. The Soviet leaders were between a rock and a hard place, already being condemned for their aggression in Afghanistan and suffering from the grain embargo and other trade restraints we had initiated. In spite of our efforts to the contrary, some of the European countries had not been at all emphatic or persistent in opposing Soviet actions, but we were hoping they would be more forceful in joining us to prevent another similar act—this time in Poland. We were monitoring Soviet military preparations very closely. Fifteen or twenty divisions were ready to move; for the first time, Czech and Soviet forces were conducting night exercises together. The Soviets were surveying invasion routes, had set up an elaborate communications system throughout Poland, were conducting intensive photo reconnaissance flights out of Czechoslovakia and East Germany, and were holding their military forces in a high state of readiness.

We decided to share our information with other leaders who might have some influence in preventing another Soviet violation of world peace. I sent Brezhnev a direct message warning of the serious consequences of a Soviet move into Poland, and let him know more indirectly that we would move to transfer advanced weaponry to China. I asked Prime Minister Gandhi to pressure Brezhnev (who was about to visit New Delhi), and warned the opposition leaders in Poland so that they would not be taken by surprise. I and other administration officials also made public statements about the growing threat to European stability.

> *We're continuing our worldwide effort to arouse informa-*
> *tion and interest in the Soviet moves toward Poland. . . .*
> *The Soviets have not denied our public statement, and*
> *Brezhnev has not answered my hot-line message. This is the*
> *first time that has occurred.*   DIARY, DECEMBER 8, 1980

I was convinced that the Soviets would already have moved into Poland if they had not been bogged down in Afghanistan and condemned by most nations of the world for it.

In addition to the threat to peace in Europe, trouble was brewing in Central America. We were trying to maintain our ties with Nicaragua, to keep it from turning to Cuba and the Soviet Union, and at the same time to help the people of El Salvador. I was insisting that the Salvadoran leaders protect the rights of their own people. The situation there was terrible: the murder of four American nuns, we believed by Salvadoran soldiers, was another incredible act the country's officials were trying to ignore. I sent envoys to assess the situation, and they came to the White House to give me a personal report.

> *They had been to the site where the American nuns were*
> *killed. They have been talking very closely with [José*
> *Napoléon] Duarte (who is likely to be the new president to*
> *replace the five-person junta), and also to [Jaime Abdul]*
> *Gutierrez, who is going to take over as commander in*
> *chief of all the military forces, having been elected by the*
> *Army Corps. This may bring some stability into El Salva-*
> *dor, but they are going through a bloodbath down there,*
> *having killed perhaps 9,000 people and buried them pe-*
> *remptorily. My emissaries said they could hear hand gre-*
> *nades and automatic rifles going off all during each night*
> *as people were killed. They don't have anybody in the jails;*
> *they're all dead. It's their accepted way of enforcing the*
> *so-called law.*   DIARY, DECEMBER 11, 1980

I was determined that the murderers of the nuns be brought to justice, that elections be scheduled, that some equitable system of justice be established and that promised land reforms be carried out. We had to convince the Salvadorans that brutal persecution of their own people was the major obstacle to their economic and political stability. Their top priority was to obtain more military weapons, but we held firm to our policy.

As the days passed, we worked with the Algerians and Iranians, trying to educate them about our laws and to persuade them of the truth concerning the Shah's assets and the limits we had reached in our proposals to them. The Algerians were very knowledgeable, reasonable, and patient; they understood that some of the Iranians were ignorant about Western law and custom.

We don't have the slightest idea how much the Shah's family assets amount to. I would guess approximately one-thousandth as much as the Iranians claim the value to be—maybe $20 to $60 million maximum (probably none of it in the United States), compared to $20 to $60 billion that the Iranians have claimed. Their claim is $56.4 billion, for instance, as filed in some lawsuit in New York.   DIARY, DECEMBER 12, 1980

As we prepared to leave the White House, all of us worked hard to thank those who had been so helpful to us during the past four years. Different interest groups asked for appointments with me, to discuss our accomplishments and the work that still needed to be done, and to ask advice about how to deal with the incoming administration. Some of them had been staunchly loyal and supportive; others, including many of the liberal activists, had defected to Kennedy and then Anderson and had been antagonistic toward me because I had not met all their demands without modification. I could not help thinking that some of them were the same Democrats who had cost Hubert Humphrey the election in 1968.

I met with the Advisory Committee on Women.... I've enjoyed getting to know these women leaders, some of whom were almost emotional in their approval of what we have tried to do and have actually done. If they and the blacks and the Hispanics and the consumers and the environmentalists and others had been as friendly toward

me a year ago as they are now that I'm going out of office,
I would not have had any trouble getting reelected.
DIARY, DECEMBER 16, 1980

Rosalynn and I also had a flood of personal visitors, who were taking us up on old invitations to come see us. Many of them were friends or relatives who wanted to be in the White House just once in their lives and saw this as their last chance.

The White House is absolutely jam-packed full of visitors.
I dread going over there for a meal, and I guess it's even
worse on Rosalynn. It's like a hotel. Each one of the people
is nice and welcome, but collectively there are just too many.
DIARY, DECEMBER 16, 1980

I really had a lot of work to do, with the duties of the Presidency unabated and with the many extra chores caused by our leaving. Instead of going to the mansion to work at night, I would welcome our stream of guests and then return to spend longer hours in the Oval Office.

One of the things my staff and I wanted to do was leave on record as a benchmark for the next administration our own assessment of policies on defense and foreign affairs, with suggestions about how these policies might be improved in the future. Here are a few unclassified thoughts extracted from my notes after one of the National Security Council sessions on this subject.

The Persian Gulf is crucial to the security of the United States and our allies. Although we would not be able to meet a direct Soviet intrusion into Iran with conventional ground forces, we have to make it clear to them and to the world that such an invasion would precipitate a worldwide confrontation between us and the Soviet Union, which would not be limited to the Persian Gulf area. No one could guarantee that in such a broad conflict both sides would remain restricted to the use of conventional forces. These points have been spelled out in my State of the Union speech earlier in the year, and it is imperative that everyone know that we mean what we say.

We should also make it clear to the European allies that they will have to do more to defend themselves. The trend toward neutrality, particularly in Germany, is very serious and threatening to the Western alliance. If the Persian Gulf is attacked or seriously threatened, we would have to shift our emphasis away from Europe toward that region, and the Europeans ought to know this and be prepared for it. If present trends should continue, the American public will become increasingly dubious about the value of the European alliance, and our primary commitments will be shifted elsewhere in the world. This would not be good for us or them. We have serious doubts among us that some of the European governments will keep their present commitments on defense budgets and other politically sensitive decisions, much less make additional commitments for improved cooperation and defense capability. In order to induce these governments and people to stand firm with us, we will have to consult with them closely and be constantly and clearly in the forefront of moves for peace, human rights, and nuclear arms control.

I have pointed out to the other members of the Council that the demands for defense expenditures comprise a bottomless pit which we can never fill. One of the most serious problems we have, as I have said many times to this group, is the inclination on the part of our military leaders—the Joint Chiefs of Staff and the civilian leaders as well—to seek more money by savaging ourselves, constantly denigrating America's formidable military capability. This hurts our own country and our allies' confidence in us, and might lead the Soviet leaders to make a suicidal misjudgment based on the chorus of lamentations from the Pentagon and defense contractors that we are weak and impotent.

We all agree that a major continuing commitment to arms control will be imperative—not only for us and our reputation as a peaceful nation, but for our relations with the Soviets as well. The nation's total budget will be increasingly limited in the years ahead, no matter who might be serving as President.

One of our most serious concerns is Governor Reagan's failure to realize the enormous value to us of friendship with China. All of us are resolved to work with his advisers, from the Vice President-elect on down, to convince them to change his often expressed desire to shift our emphasis back toward Taiwan.

We are convinced that if we can buy at least five or six years' time in getting along with the Soviets, even on the basis of a shaky détente, the trends will be in our favor, provided our nation's long-standing policies are continued by the next administration. Our emphasis on friendship with the third world, on human rights, peace, and arms control will provide us the advantages in a peaceful competition, and the Soviets could not gain against us on that basis. We also need to have a well-conceived strategy for economic warfare against the Soviet Union if it should become necessary in order to restrain its aggressive tendencies—some expanded form of punitive action, like the grain embargo, which could be effective but one major step short of war. A maximum effort should be made to include our allies in this planning, so that they will be firmly committed to take joint action, and the Soviet leaders will understand clearly in advance the serious economic consequences to them of additional aggression.

We need to have some tangible buildup of our Caribbean military forces, as a clear but quiet signal to everyone that we will protect our interests in that region. It will be very important to remain a champion of human rights in order to convince those who are throwing off oppression that they need not turn to Havana or Moscow to find an understanding friend.

Finally, we presume that the Reagan Administration will continue to play an aggressive role in carrying out the Camp David peace commitments, realizing that without our strong leadership, it is highly unlikely that Sadat and Begin can make any appreciable progress.

We put these and other items of a more sensitive nature in the official records as information and perhaps guidance for the new administration. It was a fairly brief summary of what we would have done had we stayed in office.

Even after the election was over, there still seemed to be a lot of campaign rhetoric coming from the Republicans, particularly concerning the economy. This was, we presumed, a prelude to a major thrust in Congress during 1981 for a dramatic new approach to taxation, to the role of government in social programs, and to defense spending.

> Reagan and the press are playing up the so-called economic emergency. As a matter of fact, with the exception of interest rates, everything is going surprisingly well. Unemployment, inflation, retail sales, gross national product, value of the dollar, trade balance—all these things, even housing starts—are [performing] very nicely. I'll have to get Charlie and Bill and Jody to speak out more clearly. All of us admit that the very high interest rates do not bode well for future employment and economic growth.
>
> DIARY, DECEMBER 17, 1980

The prime interest rates were still high but dropping slowly. We were especially pleased that the hard-fought energy battles were paying off. Even with reasonable economic growth, oil imports had fallen rapidly; and although foreign oil purchases were still excessive, we expected the best annual trade-balance figures in more than five years and the second-best quarterly report in history.

We labored over the budget, using our own economic policies as the presumptions for future activity. The new leaders would have an opportunity to change our recommendations before the fiscal year began in October 1981, but our figures were realistic, and we treated our successors fairly in preparing budget data and proposals. I had promised Governor Reagan the use of our budget personnel when our work was done, and his team was already preparing its own proposals.

Shortly before Christmas, we received the overdue response from the Iranians. In spite of the good efforts of the Algerians, it proved to be ridiculous and unacceptable. They demanded that we turn over to the Algerians $25 billion as a guarantee against the settlement of future claims and counterclaims—more than twice the total amount of Iranian assets we had been holding. Now that we only had a month to go, the situation looked hopeless. The leaders of Iran would have to reverse themselves completely and publicly before we could even approach each other's positions on the very important issues of returning money, handling the Shah's assets, and the settlement of claims.

The only good news from Iran was that the Algerians had visited the hostages and let us know that they were all alive and accounted for.

> *The Algerian delegation came up with Chris and Lloyd and Ed to give me a report on their visit with our hostages. Abdelkrim Ghraieb, the Algerian Ambassador to Iran, saw all 52 of them, and he believes that 49 are located within 10 or 20 minutes of the American Embassy in two separate locations—in a hotel or apartment building type of place. They are in good shape. They talked to all of them. Some refused to have their pictures taken; all but 10 wrote letters to their folks back home. The Iranians were quite accommodating and agreed to let the Algerians deliver mail back and forth to the American families. The Algerians are quite eager to help us successfully negotiate the release of the hostages.*   DIARY, DECEMBER 28, 1980

The Algerians now wanted to be very careful, so that they would not be responsible if the negotiations were a total failure or if we or the Iranians later defaulted on a commitment. We reviewed our plans for any eventuality and consulted with the Reagan appointees, to be certain that they would honor the agreements we might make with Tehran through Algiers.

> *I also instructed my people this weekend to prepare for a breakdown in negotiations and possible hostage trials. I will declare a state of belligerency or ask Congress to declare war against Iran. We will freeze the Iranian assets permanently, go directly to the United Nations Security Council, and call for complete sanctions against Iran. I hope these actions won't be necessary, but they are the ones we have had to consider for the last 14 months. Military action like a blockade or mining will probably come after these things are done on a diplomatic and trade scale.*
>
> *[Alexander] Haig and Allen have refused to be briefed on the Iranian situation. A guy named Fred Ikle is the only one that's been designated for a briefing. We've had no contact with the Reagan people in Defense. Cap Weinberger has not even been to the Pentagon at all, and he has not designated any deputy. Although Haig has been appointed [Secretary of State] and has visited for some superficial discussions with Ed and Chris, he has not designated a deputy either. . . . We've still not been able to get any word back from Haig or Reagan on the F-15 sales to Saudi Arabia. They're supposed to meet on Tuesday, and after they do and report back to the State Department, I'll decide how to notify the Saudis about the current situation.*   DIARY, JANUARY 2, 1981

We presumed that the new administration leaders were consulting among themselves and were avoiding top-level briefings on some of the very sensitive issues in order to keep the full responsibility on the incumbents. If this was the reason, it was fine with me; I was content to continue business as usual. The formation of the government and the selection and appointment of top officials were far behind schedule, and I realized that Governor Reagan had his hands full with these responsibilities.

However, we felt that with thorough briefings there would be a much smoother and more effective transition of authority to the Republican leaders. Some of their statements during the confirmation hearings made our own jobs more difficult. For instance, Caspar Weinberger testified publicly that our policy forbidding Soviet intrusion in the Persian Gulf was something of a blunder, and said he would certainly not be bound by any agreements with our NATO allies concerning a fixed percentage increase in defense expenditures. This testimony weakened the thrust of our determination to keep the Soviets out of the Persian Gulf region, and let the NATO allies more easily off the hook concerning our common goal of a 3 per cent annual budget increase for a stronger defense. Chancellor Schmidt had already proposed an increase of only 1 per cent, but he had privately promised us that the figure would later be revised upward.

The Republicans finally told us that they preferred to wait until after Inauguration Day to make a decision on the F-15 enhancement and other requests of the Saudis. Harold Brown drafted a letter to this effect for my approval, and then let Alexander Haig go over it before it was sent to Saudi Arabia.

After the Algerians delivered our rejection of the latest Iranian demands, we watched Iranian statements and actions very closely. I received information from various sources that a hot debate was raging among their officials about what should be done. The Iranians moved Bruce Laingen and his two fellow diplomats from the foreign-ministry building to another location, presumably so that they could be with the other forty-nine. This move concerned me very much, because the three had never before been considered prisoners—merely diplomats in residence.

Two days later, I received some rare good news.

> *The afternoon was devoted to the Iranian response to our latest proposal. It comes very close to an acceptance. There will still be the problem of setting up an adequate claims arrangement. . . . In the evening I approved a response to go to the Algerians to be presented to the Iranians.*   DIARY, JANUARY 6, 1981

Our position was firm; we had long ago taken the most forthcoming stance we could in keeping with our laws and national interests. When Benyahia expressed disappointment in our reply, I sent Christopher to Algiers to explain the limits we were facing. We would not see him again until after I had left office.

The Iranian leaders asked the *majlis* to meet in order to authorize negotiations with us through the Algerians to resolve the hostage issue. We had been through too many disappointments to anticipate success, but I labored to understand all the extremely complicated financial and diplomatic issues so that I would be ready to make instant decisions if events should later begin to move at a more rapid pace. Furthermore, we prepared the many legal documents that would be necessary for the massive transfers of a portion of the seized Iranian funds.

Lloyd Cutler reports that they're still having trouble with the twelve [U.S.] banks and the Iranian National Bank in clearing up questions concerning the transfer of the $4.8 billion. Also, there would be some delay in transferring the gold to Algeria. So the time is running out, and it would probably take 3 or 4 days after the Iranians agreed on all the issues before we could actually deliver the assets and get the hostages free.　　　DIARY, JANUARY 13, 1981

We were now in our final week. We held the last White House banquet for some of the trade-union leaders and others who had worked closely with us during our four years in Washington. After supper, John Raitt performed, singing some of his favorite selections from *Carousel*, *Oklahoma!*, *The Pajama Game*, *Shenandoah*, and *Man of La Mancha*. It was a warm and friendly evening, relatively informal, without any prepared speeches to detract from the delightful atmosphere. Privately, several of our guests paid us compliments about some of the accomplishments of our administration, but the most memorable of all was offered in heavily accented English by one of our honored guests—a courageous man and a renowned cellist who had recently come to our country looking for freedom and a new life. He was a special friend of ours, who had given a solo recital at the White House on the afternoon Sadat, Begin, and I had come back from Camp David to sign the peace accord.

Slava Rostropovich gave an excellent little speech at our table, pointing out that the masses of people were often wrong—that what was significant was the personal relationship that developed between leaders or performers or artists and others. He said that we had meant more than anyone in the United States to him and his family when they came here from the Soviet Union. He pointed out that the masses made a mistake on November the 4th, as they had when they rejected Beethoven's Ninth Symphony, rejected La Traviata, *and in the first performance of* Tosca *the audience reacted against it so violently that they couldn't even raise the curtain for the third act. He*

*said history was going to treat my administration the
same way they did Verdi, Puccini, and Beethoven. It was
beautiful.*   DIARY, JANUARY 13, 1981

Now that is the kind of speech a defeated candidate likes to
hear!

The next day I signed about a hundred letters to foreign leaders—
some substantive, others simply courteous messages expressing my
appreciation for their cooperation with us and wishing them well
in the years ahead. Rosalynn and I expressed our personal thanks
to more than fifty thousand people in our country. We enjoyed
remembering the pleasant and productive friendships we had
formed with so many Americans. I devoted many hours to my
farewell speech to the nation. I wanted it to cover a few of the
issues of historical significance on which we had concentrated—
peace, human rights, arms control, and environmental quality—
and not be critical of Reagan, even though he would differ
strongly with me on almost every subject I discussed.

The release of the American hostages had almost become an
obsession with me. Of course, their lives, safety, and freedom were
the paramount considerations, but there was more to it. I wanted
to have my decisions vindicated. It was very likely that I had
been defeated and would soon leave office as President because I
had kept these hostages and their fate at the forefront of the
world's attention, and had clung to a cautious and prudent policy
in order to protect their lives during the preceding fourteen months.
Before God and my fellow citizens, I wanted to exert every ounce
of my strength and ability during these last few days to achieve
their liberation. I knew that if we failed, it might take many
months to reweave the fabric of complex agreements that had
been so laboriously created.

I talked to Chris in Algeria several times. Saturday night, January 17, he said it was possible to have an agreement by Sunday
noon. Teams were working through the night in Algiers and in
Tehran. All the arrangements for medical examinations and transportation for the hostages had been completed, but we still had a
lot of loose ends concerning the financial arrangements. For instance, Sunday morning the Iranians were insisting that we pay
them the value of gold as it was when we had seized it, claiming
that it was our fault that its price had dropped. We would
agree to return to them only the same number of ounces we had
taken.

By noon on Sunday, all the agreements were ready for my

signature. My family and I were now at Camp David for the last time. While waiting for the documents, I took some photographs of places there that had become important to us—the cottage where we had stayed, the small study where I had negotiated for so many hours with the Egyptians and Israelis, the little table on which Cy, Zbig, and I had drafted the China normalization proposal, the room where we had held chapel services and Sadat had worshiped, and a few scenes in the woods and along the paths, where we had spent so many enjoyable hours.

After signing the documents, we bade farewell to Camp David and returned to the White House. The final countdown had begun. Praying for the freedom of our people, I went to the Oval Office, where I would remain during most of the last forty-eight hours of my Presidency.

⁓

My first official visitor to the Oval Office four years earlier had been Max Cleland, whom I had called in to request that he serve as Administrator of Veterans Affairs. A Vietnam veteran and triple amputee, he had represented American veterans with distinction for four years. Now he was my last official visitor.

> *Max Cleland came to tell me good-bye. He brought me a plaque with a quote from Thomas Jefferson:*
>
> I HAVE THE CONSOLATION TO REFLECT
> THAT DURING THE PERIOD OF MY
> ADMINISTRATION NOT A DROP
> OF THE BLOOD OF A SINGLE CITIZEN
> WAS SHED BY THE SWORD OF WAR.
>
> *This is something I shall always cherish.*
> DIARY, JANUARY 20, 1981

⁓

Acknowledgments

I am grateful to many people for their contributions to this book:

Ray Jenkins, Hamilton Jordan, Zbigniew Brzezinski, Stuart Eizenstat, Jerry Rafshoon, Jody Powell, Gene Patterson, and Rosalynn Carter;

the official White House photographers of my administration—Billie Shaddix, Karl Schumacher, Jack Kightlinger, Mary Anne Fackelman, and William Fitz-Patrick;

all those at Bantam Books who have worked so hard, especially Lou Wolfe, F.X. Flinn, and Barbara Cohen, as well as the copyeditor, Ruth Hein;

the members of the Carter Presidential Materials Project—Don Schewe, Martin Elzy, Dave Alsobrook, Roslyn Wright, and Bob Bohanan;

my staff at Plains—Faye Dill, Lori Fossum, and Susan Clough.

Thank you, and thanks also to the many others who helped but are not mentioned by name.

Index

619